TURNER & THE SEA

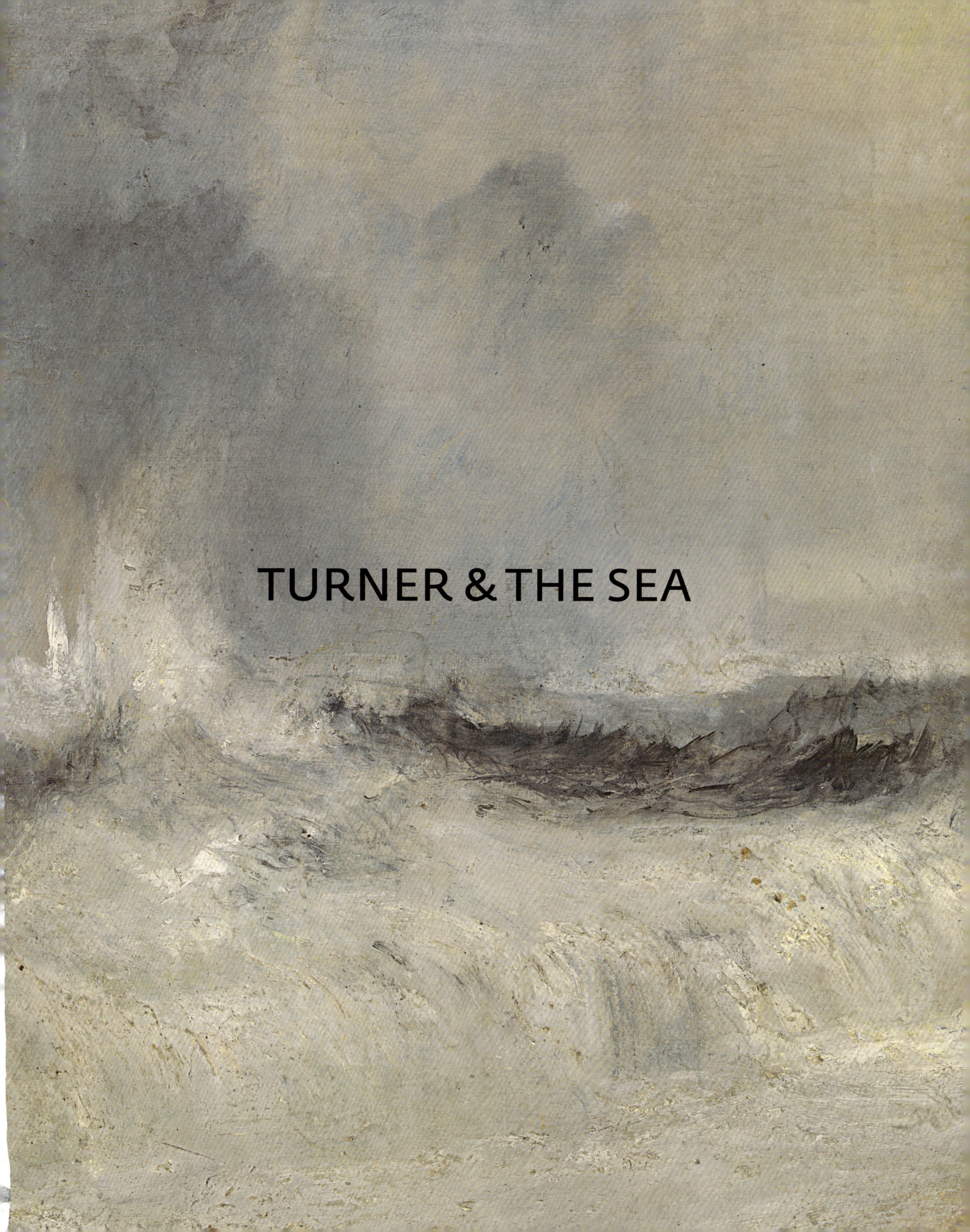

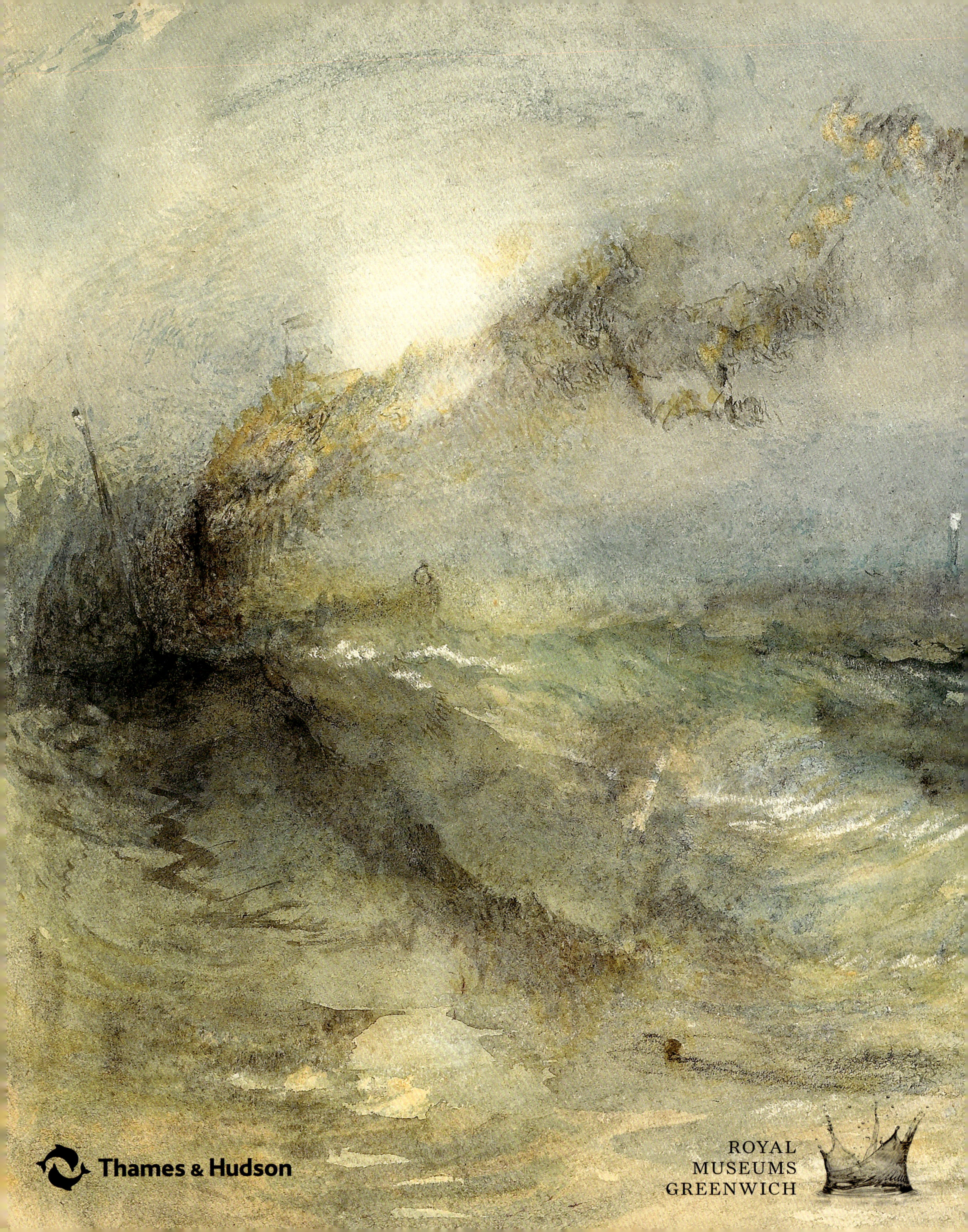

Thames & Hudson

ROYAL
MUSEUMS
GREENWICH

NATIONAL MARITIME MUSEUM

TURNER & THE SEA

Christine Riding and Richard Johns

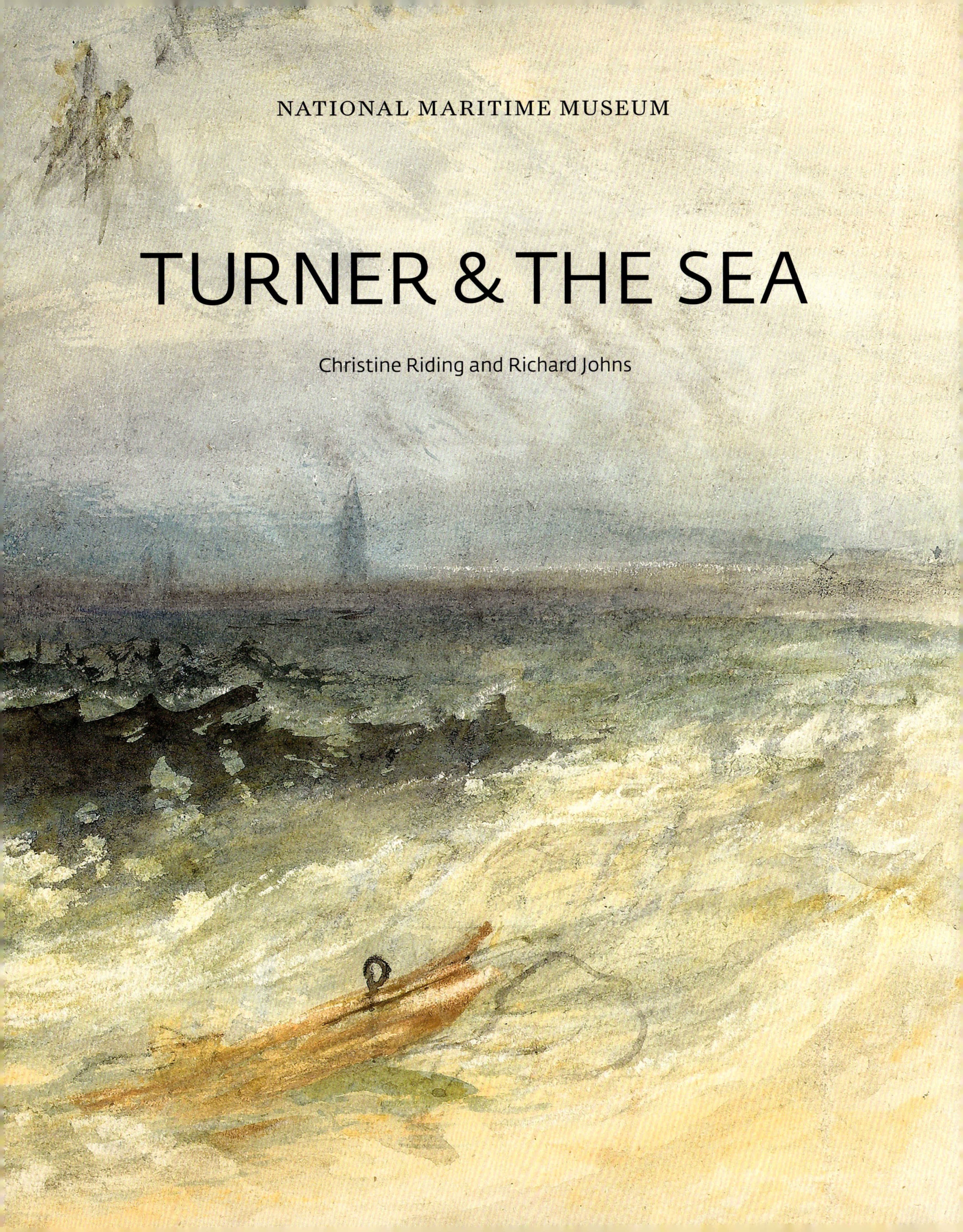

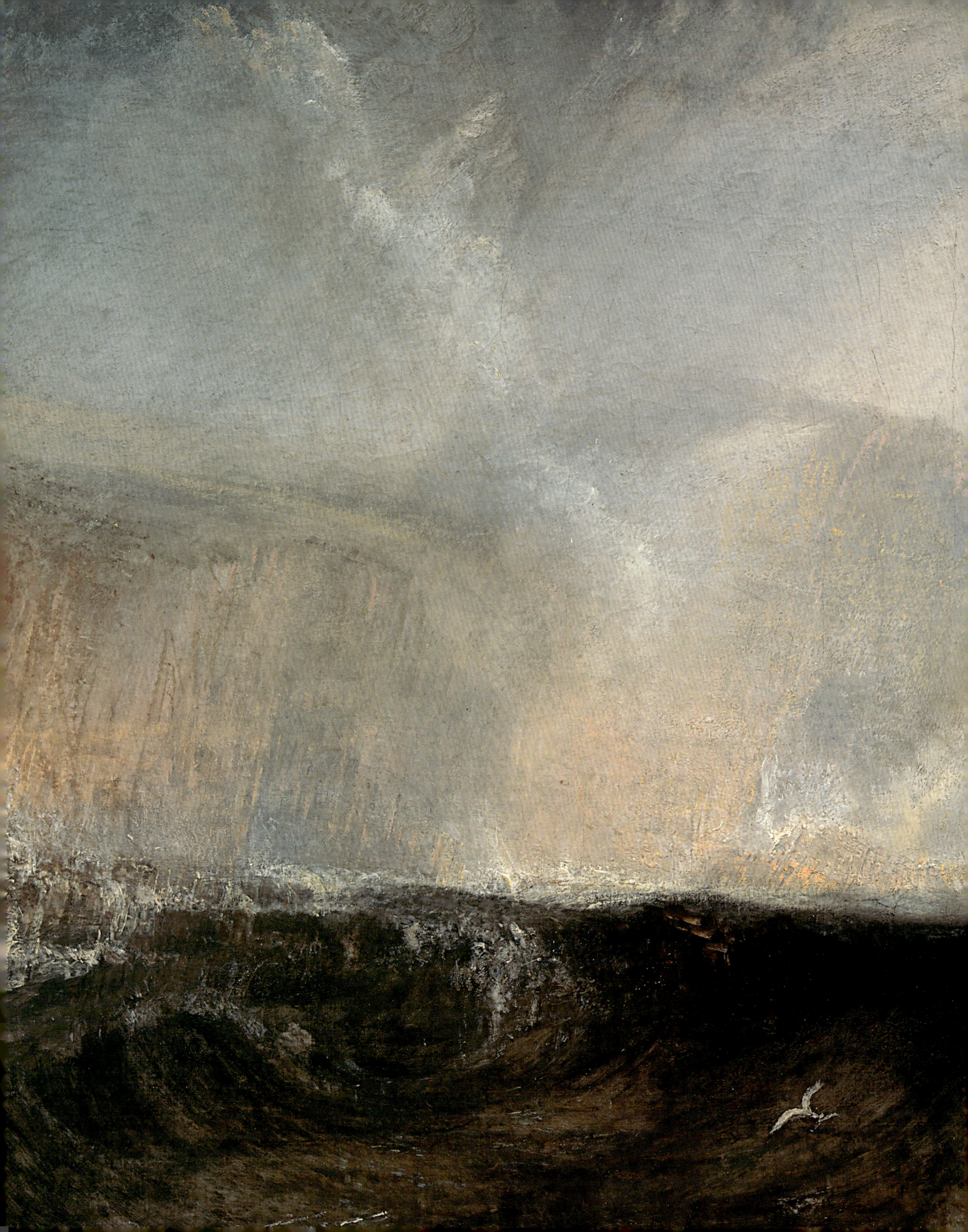

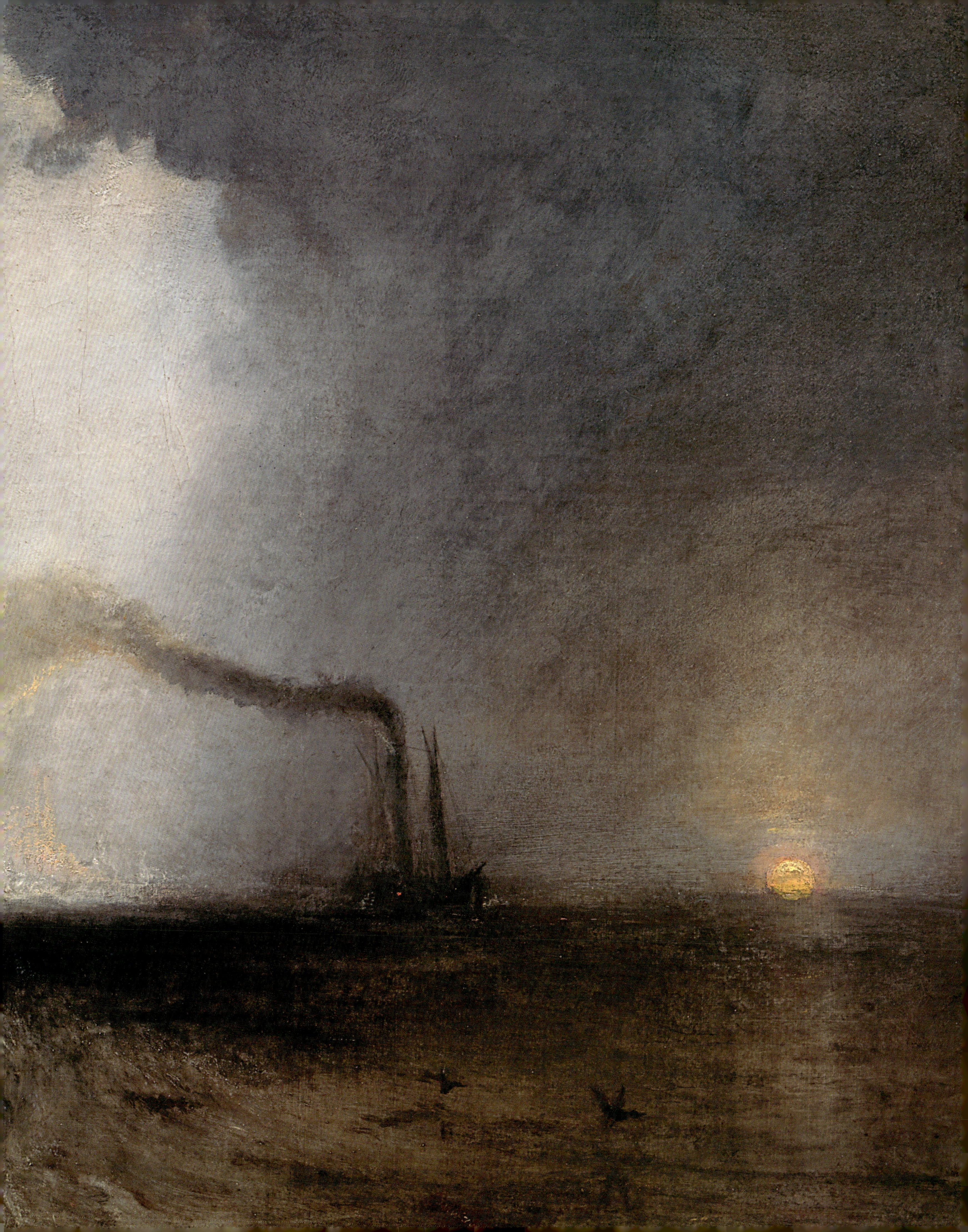

Published to accompany the exhibition *Turner and the Sea*

National Maritime Museum, Greenwich, London
21 November 2013–21 April 2014

Peabody Essex Museum, Salem, Massachusetts
31 May–1 September 2014

First published in the United Kingdom in 2013 by
Thames & Hudson Ltd, 181A High Holborn, London WC1V 7QX
in association with Royal Museums Greenwich, the group name for the National Maritime Museum, Royal Observatory Greenwich, Queen's House and *Cutty Sark*

www.rmg.co.uk

Reprinted 2014

Designed by Sarah Praill

British Library Cataloguing-in-Publication Data
A catalogue record for this book is available from the British Library

ISBN 978-0-500-23905-6

Printed and bound in China by C&C Offset Printing Co. Ltd

Page 1
J.M.W. Turner
Waves Breaking against the Wind c.1840 (detail of [124])

Pages 2–3
J.M.W. Turner
A Steamer off Ostend c.1840 (detail of [117])

Pages 4–5
J.M.W. Turner
Staffa, Fingal's Cave 1832 (detail of [128])

Page 9
J.M.W. Turner
London from Greenwich Park 1809
Oil on canvas 90.2 x 120 (35½ x 47¼)
Tate. Turner Bequest 1856

Note
Dimensions of works are given in centimetres and inches, height before width. Figure numbers refer to contextual images. All catalogue entries are written by the author of the main essay for each related chapter, except for [72–82] by Richard Johns and [83–88] by Christine Riding.

Contents

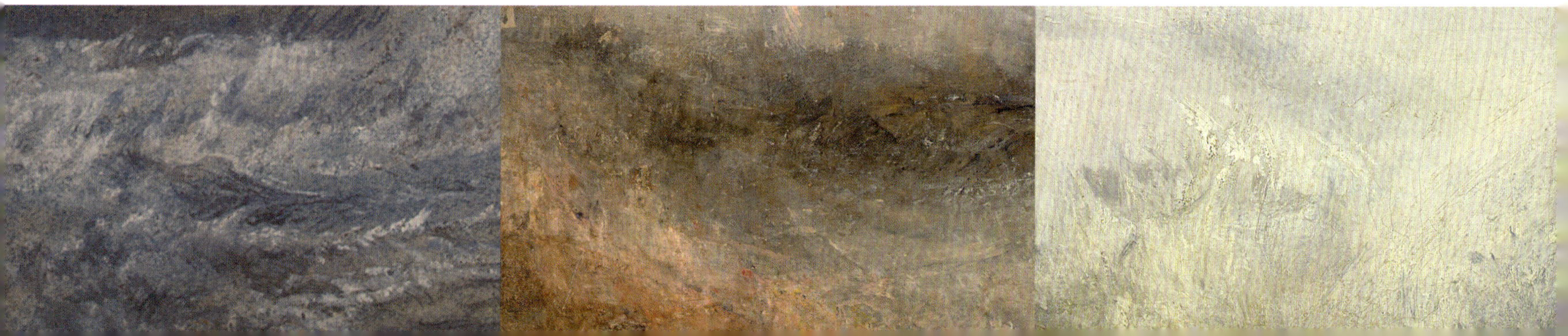

Foreword

J.M.W. Turner is one of the most influential painters in the history of British art. He was also the nineteenth century's greatest and most prolific marine artist, and one for whom naval and maritime Greenwich provided a rich source of inspiration. His atmospheric prospect of London from One Tree Hill in Greenwich Park (opposite), painted in 1809, celebrates the rich architectural and cultural heritage of the site, prominently featuring Inigo Jones's Queen's House and Christopher Wren's Royal Hospital for Seamen. At the centre of the painting, he includes the colonnades and pavilions of the school for the children of naval seamen, still under construction, which over a century later would become the National Maritime Museum.

On subsequent visits, Turner would have seen his own magnificent painting of the Battle of Trafalgar here, in the Naval Gallery which occupied the Hospital's Painted Hall from 1824 to 1936. That already celebrated survivor of the battle, the 'Fighting *Temeraire*', passed this exact spot on 6 September 1838, on its way up-river to Rotherhithe for breaking up, the subject of one of Turner's most famous works. So it is especially appropriate that the Museum should be the venue for the first major exhibition to examine the artist's lifelong engagement with the art of the sea.

Many works in the exhibition have not been seen in the UK for some years, and we are greatly indebted to the generosity of all our lenders, both private collectors and public galleries, for making such an exciting and important project possible. We are particularly grateful to Her Majesty The Queen for lending a major painting from the Royal Collection, and to our colleagues at Tate for their generous support for the project and for allowing our exhibition curators to delve deep into the Turner Bequest. Sincere thanks are also due to the Patrons of Royal Museums Greenwich, whose commitment and generosity have helped to bring *Turner and the Sea* to the public eye. Finally, I would like to pay tribute to colleagues at the Museum who have contributed to both the exhibition and this accompanying catalogue, in particular the lead curator Christine Riding and co-curator Dr Richard Johns.

Dr Kevin Fewster AM FRSA
Director, Royal Museums Greenwich

List of Lenders

Her Majesty Queen Elizabeth II
The Barber Institute of Fine Arts, University of Birmingham
Bristol Museums and Art Gallery
The British Museum
Calouste Gulbenkian Foundation, Lisbon
Hastings Museum and Art Gallery
Indianapolis Museum of Art
Manchester City Galleries
Metropolitan Museum of Art, New York
Musée national de la Marine, Paris
The National Gallery, London
National Gallery of Art, Washington
National Museums Liverpool
National Trust
The Nelson-Atkins Museum of Art, Kansas
Portsmouth City Council
Private lenders, UK
Royal Albert Memorial Museum and Art Gallery, Exeter
Sir John Soane's Museum, London
Somerleyton Hall, Suffolk
Southampton City Art Gallery
Sterling and Francine Clark Art Institute, Massachusetts
Tate
The Victoria Gallery and Museum, University of Liverpool
Yale Center for British Art, New Haven

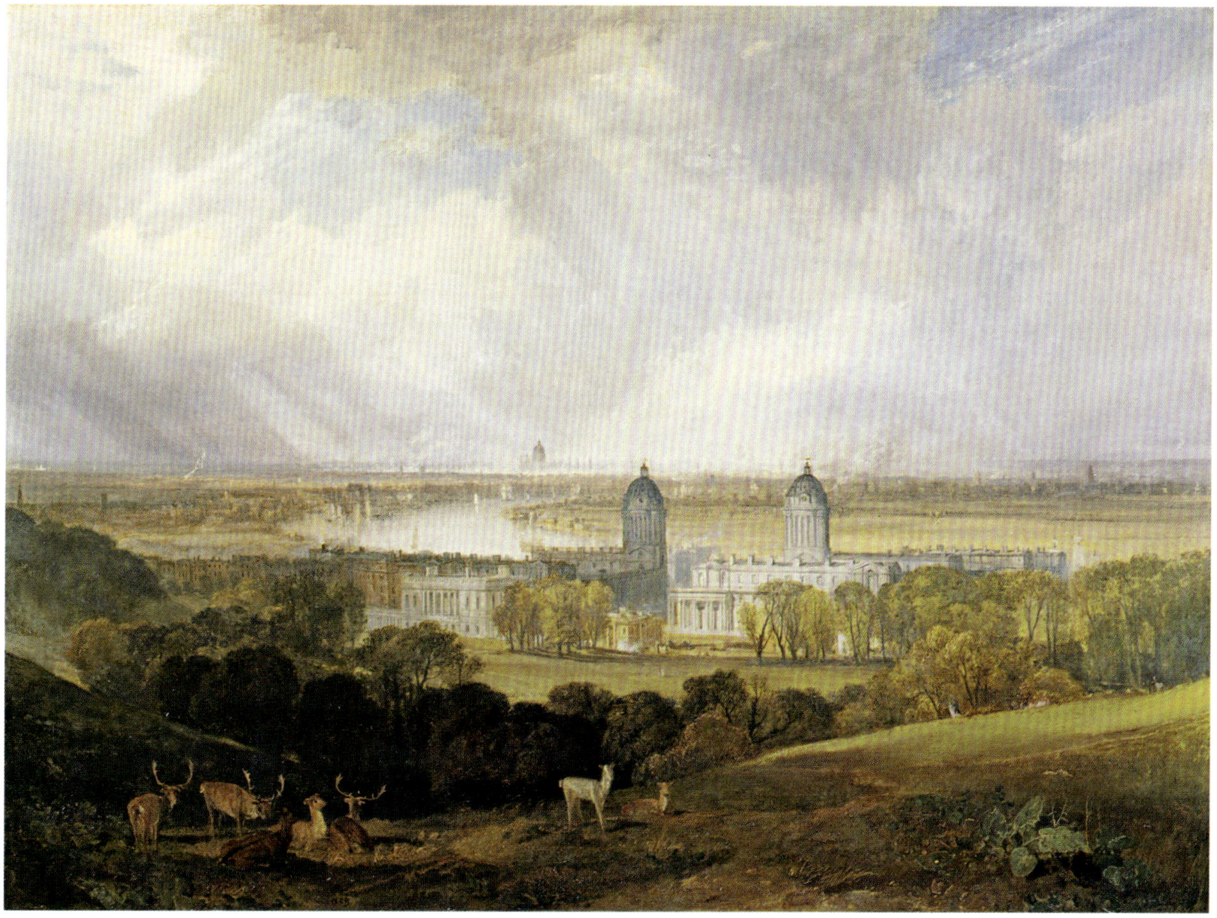

Introduction

Christine Riding

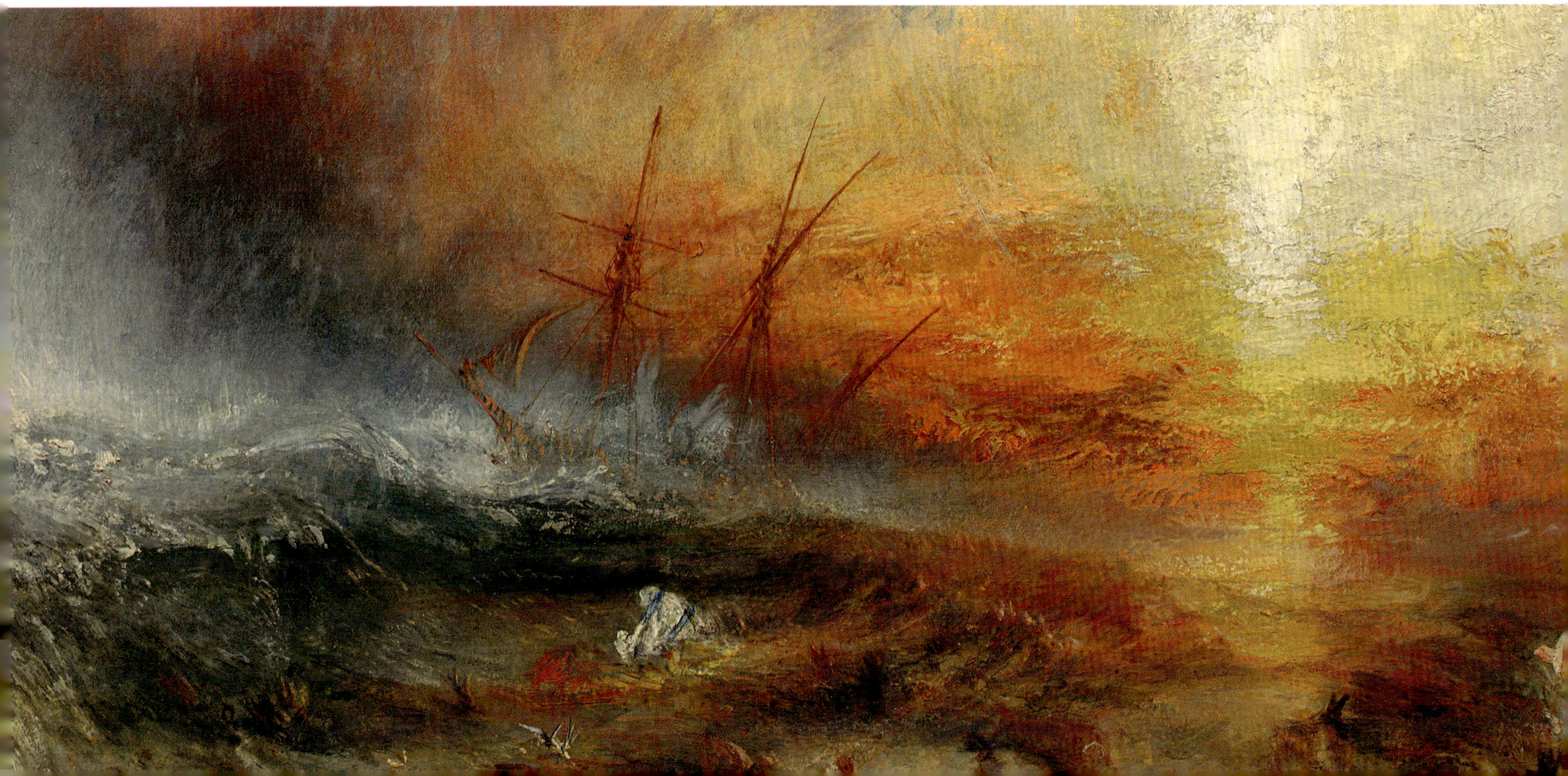

In 1884, Robert Leslie, son of the artist C.R. Leslie, recalled his first encounter with J.M.W. Turner in the early 1830s, during a visit to the Sussex seat of the Earl of Egremont:

> The sun had set beyond the trees at the end of the little lake in Petworth Park; at the other end of this lake was a solitary man, pacing to and fro, watching five or six [fishing] lines or trimmers, that floated outside the water lilies near the bank. 'There,' said my father, 'is Mr. Turner, the great *sea* painter.'[1]

Turner, of course, engaged with landscape art in its broadest sense. Even so, it is true to say that he painted the sea more often than any other subject: from the earliest paintings upon which his reputation was founded to his later most experimental and contentious work, the sea remained at the centre of the artist's vision, just as it loomed large elsewhere in the nation's cultural and political life. However, it is today rare to find Turner described primarily as a '*sea* painter'. But that in itself is suggestive of his success in bringing the art of the sea from the margins to the very centre of the British art world.

In an early attempt to summarize Turner's contribution to marine painting, the art critic John Ruskin contrasted *The Wreck of a Transport Ship* [76], a scene of storm at sea, with the 'peculiar calmness' of *Dort, or Dordrecht, the Dort Packet-Boat from Rotterdam Becalmed* [fig. 1] – both of which declare the artist's commitment to a rich Continental legacy – as representative of the great variety of his work. The two paintings, Ruskin concluded, 'may be considered as the principal symbols ... of Turner's two strengths in Terror and Repose'.[2] The juxtaposition of 'storm' and 'calm' had a long tradition in marine painting. During a career spanning some five decades, Turner produced images of the sea that far exceeded such established conventions and rules, and in the process defined an entirely new maritime aesthetic. That the sea should have been a site of such endless pictorial possibilities for Turner is, in a sense, intrinsic to the subject itself, given its supreme changeability and elusiveness. This may go some way to explaining the comments of one critic in 1834, who, while reviewing Turner's seascapes on display at the Royal Academy, noted that 'there is perhaps no branch of art which presents a wider field for exaggeration than that of marine-painting'.[3]

It is the unprecedented diversity of the artist's creative engagement with the sea that provides the subject of this book, placed within the wider social context into which Turner was born, and to which he made such a significant contribution: that is, Britain's distinctly 'maritime character' during the first half of the nineteenth century.[4]

OUR NAUTICAL EXISTENCE

The integral relationship between Turner's artistic practice and this broader maritime culture can be usefully demonstrated by a contextual reading of another early scene of maritime disaster, *The Shipwreck* [fig. 2 and 75]. Around the turn of the nineteenth century, the depiction of storm and shipwreck was associated with artists as diverse as the Dutch painter Willem van de Velde the Younger, and the French artists Claude-Joseph Vernet and Philip James de Loutherbourg, each of whom was an important artistic model for Turner. While past and present masters would always inform his art, Turner put a premium on personal experience and disciplined observation of the natural world. Among his many surviving sketchbooks there are preliminary designs relating to the painting's composition or subject in the Calais Pier Sketchbook [100] and in two Shipwreck sketchbooks [94 and 95]. A number of these draw directly on the artist's experience of a rough passage to France in 1802.

Turner's predilection for seafaring and his close engagement with the dynamics of water, so amply demonstrated in his prolific output, featured prominently in subsequent commentaries. In a biographical sketch published in 1852, just a few months after Turner's death, the journalist Cyrus Redding recalled a short sea voyage they had shared, noting that '[the] coast scenery

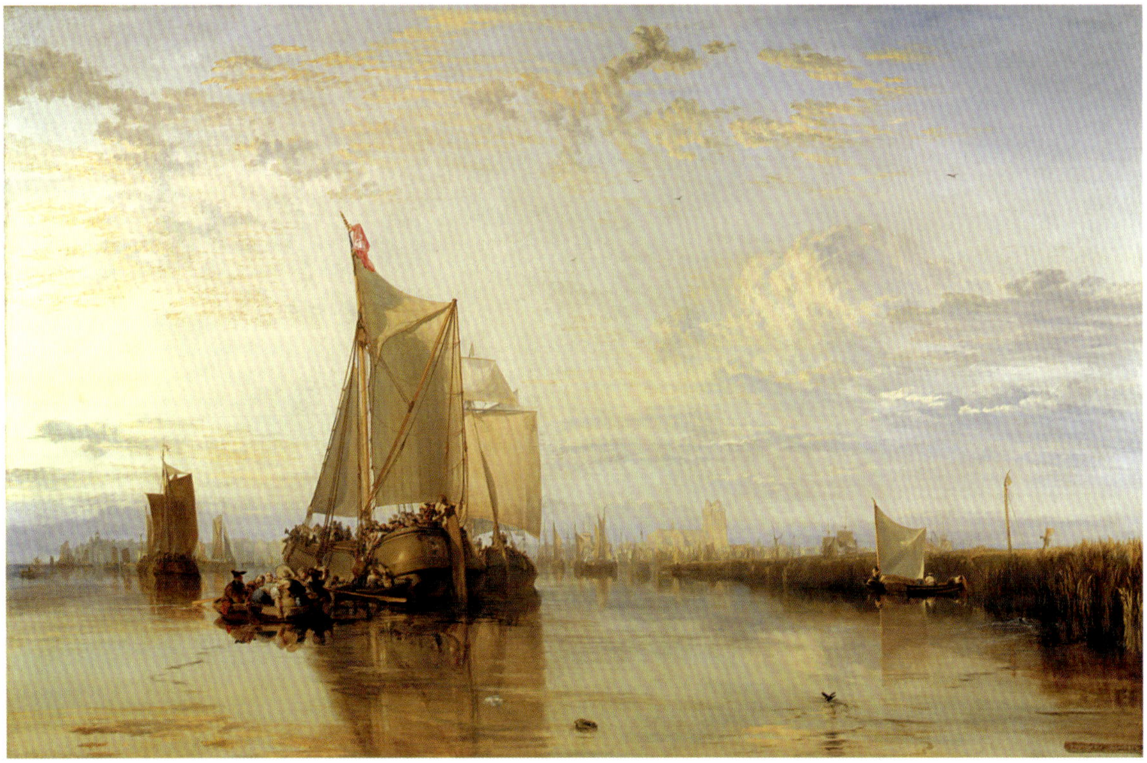

Fig. 1

J.M.W. Turner
Dort, or Dordrecht, the Dort Packet-Boat from Rotterdam Becalmed 1818
Oil on canvas 157.5 x 233 (62 x 92)
Yale Center for British Art

Fig. 2

J.M.W. Turner
The Shipwreck 1805
Oil on canvas 170.5 x 241.5 (67⅛ x 95⅛)
Tate. Turner Bequest 1856

was just to his taste; he was an excellent sailor'. He continued by describing the painter's behaviour during the journey: 'Turner looked on with the most artistic watchfulness. When we were on the crest of a wave, he now and then articulated to myself – for we were sitting side by side – "That's fine! – fine!"' And even during stormy weather, while fellow passengers (including a soldier) succumbed to seasickness, 'Turner sat watching the waves and the headlands ... like Atlas, unmoved.'[5] Of course, Turner's keen powers of observation and memory did not result in literal translations of the sea, ships or coastline. Many years later the American artist Edward Moran discussed Turner's manipulation of topographical details for artistic effect in a treatise on marine painting, much of which is concerned with the English painter. 'It is not to be supposed,' Moran noted in 1888, 'that Turner's sketches of particular localities are strictly correct.' He continues:

> I once took a lot of Turner's engravings of views on the English coast, and went with them, as nearly as I could judge, to the exact spots from which they must have been taken – at Hastings, Dover and other south-eastern points – going out in a boat and rowing about until I found the right place. Well, the result settled all doubts as to his accuracy. He is very inaccurate – wilfully so ... his knowledge of the forms of land

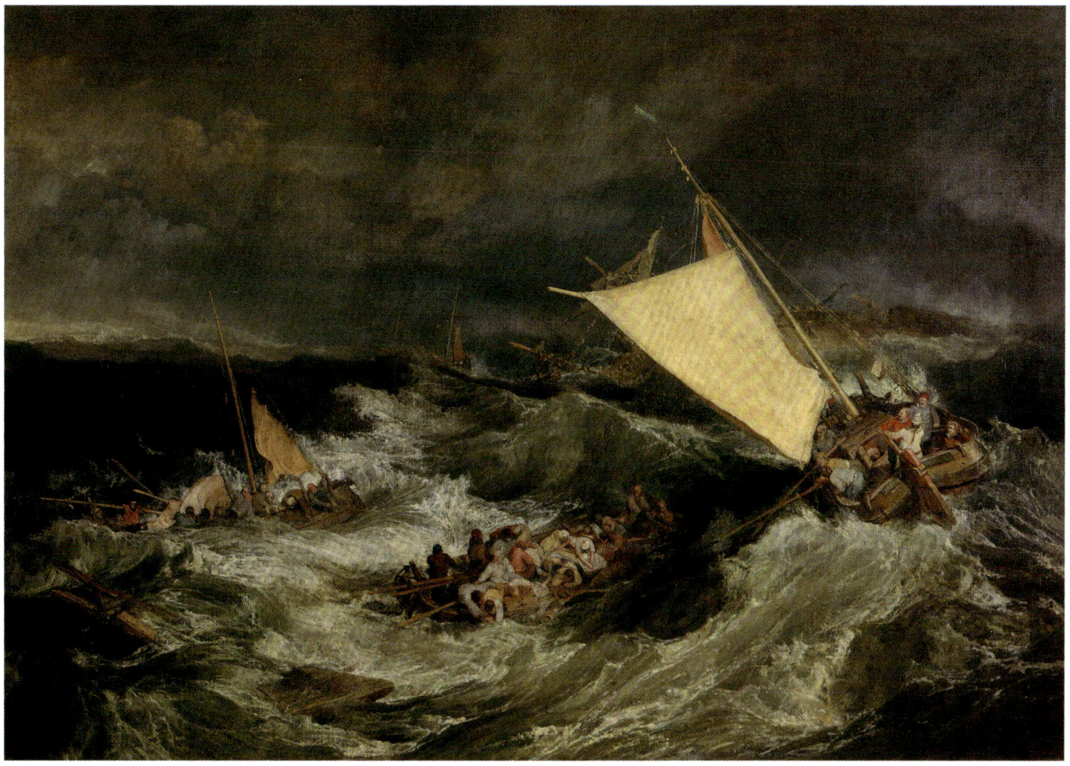

> and sea and cloud was so thorough that he could do pretty much as he pleased with them, and yet keep within the bounds of naturalness.'[6]

In the case of *The Shipwreck*, the immediacy and apparent 'accuracy' of the representation, even when divorced from the topographical demands of a coastline, have prompted some scholars to identify Turner's painting directly with the wreck of the 'Earl of Abergavenny', an East Indiaman bound for Bengal and China, which sank off Portland Bill in Dorset in February 1805 with the loss of 260 lives.[7] The 'Abergavenny' remains one of the worst disasters in British waters, and whether it influenced Turner's choice of subject or not, the recent news of such a terrible event cannot have failed to resonate with the painting's early audience.[8] As a maritime and island nation, there was a broad-based fascination in Britain with the ever-present risks and challenges of seafaring. The lure of the sea is confirmed by the popularity of voyage narratives – some two thousand were published in Britain during the eighteenth century – and shipwreck narratives, which during Turner's lifetime became a distinct literary sub-genre.[9] The 'Abergavenny' spawned a number of such publications, including *An Authentic Narrative of the Loss of the Earl of Abergavenny* by William Dalmeida (1805), which rapidly ran through several editions.[10]

This wreck was made even more noteworthy because the captain of the 'Abergavenny' was John Wordsworth, the brother of William, the poet. Given these personal connections to the sea, it is pertinent here that Turner's *Shipwreck* was bought by Sir John Leicester in January 1806 but exchanged for another painting the following year, according to Turner's biographer Walter Thornbury, on account of 'Lady Leicester having lost a favourite nephew at sea, and being unable to bear the associations the scene called up.'[11] William Wordsworth's direct response to his brother's death was to author a number of poems in his memory, including *Elegiac Stanzas Suggested by a Picture of Peele Castle in a Storm*, composed in April 1806. The picture of a ship foundering in a violent sea alluded to in the poem's title was by Turner's nemesis at the time, the connoisseur and amateur artist Sir George Beaumont, who was a friend and patron of both Wordsworth and Samuel Taylor Coleridge.[12] Albeit provoked by a family tragedy, Wordsworth's poem nonetheless neatly demonstrates two major concerns of Turner's career: first, the powerful synergy between painting and poetry; second, the broader perception, promoted within Britain's cultural elite, 'that the ocean [was] at once their nation's proper domain, the central geographical theatre of their age, and the main natural force shaping their world'.[13] Indeed, Byron's oft-quoted line from the so-called 'shipwreck canto' of *Don Juan* (1819), 'We enter on our nautical existence', describes the moment when the traveller departs from his native shores to face the long voyage ahead.[14]

Unsurprisingly, given the vogue for such subjects, Turner's *The Shipwreck* was the first of his paintings to be engraved and published in January 1807. However, his dramatic representation arguably went beyond then standard ideas of the pictorial 'sublime' – a spectacle for the consumption of an art-interested elite – to embrace both the commercial potential of the subject and the mundane yet tragic reality of a maritime nation. The painting has also been linked to the highly successful republication in 1804 of William Falconer's celebrated poem *The Shipwreck* (1762), complete with a biographical memoir of the author by James Stanier Clarke, then a naval chaplain, and illustrations engraved after designs by the marine artist Nicholas Pocock. While the 1804 publication may well have acted as an added stimulus, Turner in fact already knew and admired Falconer's poem and may even have owned a version as early as 1795, published within volume ten of Robert Anderson's *The Works of British Poets*.[15] Falconer's reputation as a sailor-poet is important here for a number of reasons. In Anderson's biographical sketch of 1795 he was described as being 'bred to the sea', and the 'dangers which he really experienced', including surviving a shipwreck in about 1750, 'he feelingly described' in his poem as follows:

> Again she plunges! hark! a second shock
> Tears her strong bottom on the marble rock!
> Down on the vale of death, with dismal cries,
> The fated victims shuddering roll their eyes,
> In wild despair; while yet another stroke,
> With deep convulsion, rends the solid oak.[16]

The authenticity of Falconer's eventful narrative was reinforced by his copious notes, explaining weather conditions and other technical details to the reader. The relevance of these details to the contemporary reception of Turner's seascapes was underlined by the reviewer for *The Times*, writing in 1797: in response to one of the painter's earliest exhibited works, *Fishermen Coming Ashore at Sun Set, previous to a Gale* (see p. 25), the critic judged that it represented 'the sickly appearance of the setting sun at sea, preparatory to a storm, as it is described in Falconer's poem'.[17]

Turner's lifelong interest in the creative association of painting and poetry as a means of elevating landscape art to the level of history painting, then widely regarded as the most intellectually and formally challenging of artistic genres, has been explored largely through the excerpts he appended to his exhibited works. These included, at different times, quotes from British poetry such as John Milton's *Paradise Lost*, James Thomson's *The Seasons* and Byron's *Childe Harold's Pilgrimage*, and, from 1812, his own manuscript poem *Fallacies of Hope*.[18] But Falconer's life and work suggested a more personal parallel with Turner's own experiences and ambitions. Anderson's biographical sketch of Falconer, for example, noted that his 'true genius' had surmounted 'every obstacle' (the poet was not only a low-ranking seaman but, like Turner, the son of a barber) and furthermore that:

> [the] situation of a *sailor* may be thought unfavourable to the *poet*; but the two characters are not incompatible; for none but an able sailor could give so didactic an account, and so accurate a description of the voyage and catastrophe related in this performance; and none but a genuine poet could have embellished both with equal harmony of numbers and strength of imagery.[19]

J.S. Clarke came to the same conclusion, noting in the introduction to his new edition of *The Shipwreck* in 1804 that 'even to the pedant ... the distance between Virgil and Falconer is not so great as he may have imagined'.[20] This latter comment is especially pertinent given that Falconer's poem recounts the final voyage of the merchant ship 'Britannia', elevating the autobiographical, national and moral significance of its contemporary subject with multiple references to classical literature. Virgil's *Aeneid* is often read as a foundational epic of ancient Rome, which follows and is modelled on Homer's *Iliad* and *Odyssey*. In Falconer's poem, the 'Britannia' is wrecked on the coast of Greece, the site of a once great civilization, and thus portends the fall of the British Empire. Turner similarly invited comparisons between past and present imperial powers – Carthage, Rome, Venice and Britain – throughout his work. Indeed, *Ulysses Deriding Polyphemus – Homer's Odyssey* [fig. 3], a rare example among Turner's paintings of a classical seascape, has been recently described with its near contemporary *Slavers Throwing overboard the Dead and Dying* [fig. 46] as 'dramatising respectively, the heyday and the decline of British imperial ambitions'.[21]

Turner's own poetic efforts frequently made nautical allusions that were common to the period. In the so-called Salisbury Sketchbook of 1799, for example, he jotted the following awkward but evocative lines concerning the vicissitudes of sexual relationships:

> Love is like the raging Ocean
> [Wind?] that sway, its troubled motion
> Woman's temper ever bubbling
> Man the early bark which sailing
> In the unblest treacherous Sea.[22]

And while gathering material for *Picturesque Views on the Southern Coast of England* during a sketching trip in 1811, he penned a substantial sequence of verses, intended to complement the published images, that find parallels with the language employed by Falconer, thus asserting his own familiarity with nautical matters:

> Whoever lucklessly are driven
> From Portland seeks an eastern haven
> Must luff against the South west gail
> And strike for Poole alone the tortured Sail
> For Wight again their safe return denys
> The needles brave the force of Southern skies.[23]

In the event, Turner's couplets seem to have been rejected by the engraver-publisher, William Bernard Cooke, for being (in his estimation) clumsy, bordering on unintelligible.[24] Yet these verses remain of interest, not least in demonstrating Turner's responsiveness to the poetic potential of the sea and seafaring and for the deep concern they reveal for the plight of Britain's coastal and maritime communities. Turner's respectful interest in the views of sailors is underlined by the recollection of Robert Leslie, in a letter to John Ruskin dated 1884, of a visit to the artist's home in Queen Anne Street: 'I particularly remember one visit, in company with my father and a Yankee sea captain, to whom Turner was very polite, evidently looking up to the sailor capacity, and making little apologies for the want of ropes and other details about certain vessels in a picture.' He continues:

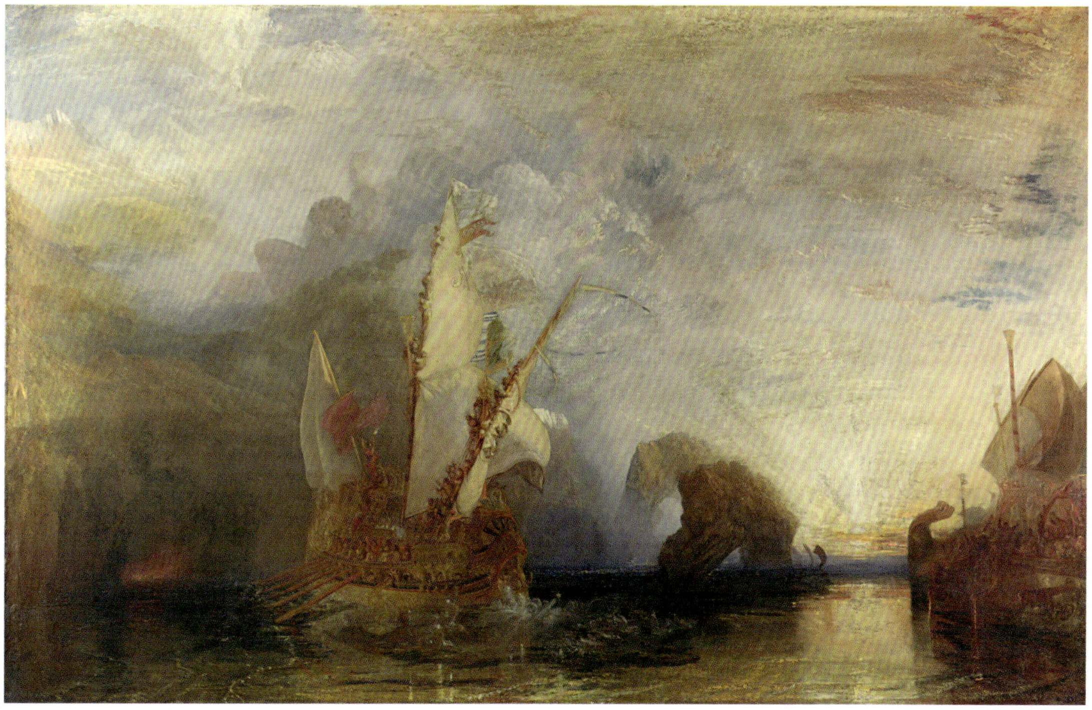

Fig. 3

J.M.W. Turner
Ulysses Deriding Polyphemus – Homer's Odyssey 1829
Oil on canvas 132.5 x 203 (52½ x 80)
National Gallery. Turner Bequest 1856

> No one knew or felt, I think, better than Turner the want of these mechanical details, and while the sea captain was there he paid no attention to any one [*sic*] else, but followed him about the gallery, bent upon hearing all he said. As it turned out, this captain and he became good friends, for the Yankee skipper's eyes were sharp enough to see through all the fog and mystery of Turner, how much of real sea feeling there was in him and his work.[25]

The 'Yankee skipper' in question was Captain Morgan, who was subsequently responsible for carrying Turner's *Staffa, Fingal's Cave* [128] to New York in 1845 on behalf of the artist's first American patron, Colonel James Lenox.

While *Staffa* expressed an overtly contemporary (and, by the standards of the day, unconventional) idea of marine art, Turner continued to explore the historical origins of the genre. In 1833, he exhibited a painting entitled *Van Goyen, Looking out for a Subject* (The Frick Collection). For the reviewer in the *Athenaeum*, Turner was making allusions to the seventeenth-century Dutch artist Jan van Goyen's practice, which was based first and foremost on personal observation, no matter what dangers might be incurred. Thus van Goyen 'manned a yacht, stood out to sea, and often in a still sea, and sometimes on the edge of battle, sketched the warships of his country – hence the truth and beauty of his delineations'.[26] What eluded the reviewer was that Turner was at the same time making comparable claims for himself. Hence, as Barry Venning has observed, the painting is 'nothing less than a portrait of the artist as a sea-going man ... something of a manifesto picture'.[27]

In this context it is perhaps equally poignant that Turner was at this time exhibiting a sequence of paintings on the subject of a historical figure, Admiral Maarten Harpertszoon Tromp (1598–1653). As Tromp had been instrumental in establishing the Dutch nation as a leading maritime power, these works are usually understood as commentaries on contemporary political events between Britain and the Kingdom of the Netherlands (see [84]). However, they could just as easily relate to Turner and his position as the leading artistic figure in the national school of art. The potential for Tromp to act as a kind of alter ego is underlined by the title that accompanied the final painting in the series, exhibited in 1844: *Van Tromp, Going About to Please his Masters, Ships a Sea, Getting a Good Wetting* (J. Paul Getty Museum). Tromp had been dismissed from the Dutch navy, having pursued his own tactics. He was later reinstated after having 'swallowed his pride and come to terms with authority'.[28] Turner shows the chastened admiral negotiating a particularly difficult nautical manoeuvre. Given the critical battering latterly experienced by Turner himself, not least in response to his highly experimental seascapes, including another 'manifesto' painting, *Snow Storm – Steam-Boat off a Harbour's Mouth* [131], it is difficult not to read the 'good wetting' in Turner's title as a wry reference to his own critically exposed situation.

In keeping with his reputation as an experienced traveller, Turner's contemporaries sometimes remarked upon his distinctly seaman-like figure. To give just one example, in his affectionate tribute to his friend, Cyrus Redding noted that in his personal appearance Turner 'somewhat resembled the master of a merchantman'.[29] The artist may even have encouraged such comparisons when, in the last years of his life and in the interests of anonymity, he adopted the persona of a retired naval officer.[30] His companion of many years, Sophia Charlotte Booth, had been married to a mariner (prior to Mr Booth, her second husband) and had hosted Turner at her guesthouse overlooking the harbour at Margate. Thus the name 'Admiral Booth' may simply have emerged as a good-humoured pseudonym for his unorthodox domestic circumstances. In the absence of a knighthood (unlike his contemporary Augustus Wall Callcott), or the ultimate mark of professional artistic success – the presidency of the Royal Academy – we might also see in the self-appointed rank of admiral a recognition of sorts for his lifelong service to the art of the sea.

A NARRATIVE OF ADMIRAL BOOTH

Joseph Mallord William Turner came from the kind of respectable but modest circumstances that produced many professional artists during the eighteenth and nineteenth centuries. He was born in 1775 in Maiden Lane, Covent Garden.[31] His father, William, was a barber and wig-maker and his mother, Mary (née Marshall), the daughter of an Islington salesman.[32] From an early age Turner showed considerable artistic prowess. Tradition has it that his talents were encouraged by his father, who boasted to the artist Thomas Stothard: 'My son, sir, is going to be a painter.'[33]

Turner's early professional career was as an architectural and antiquarian draughtsman. In 1789 he was admitted as a student of the Royal Academy Schools by a panel of artists that included its founding president and guiding force, Sir Joshua Reynolds. The following year, Turner exhibited his first work at the Academy's annual exhibition, a small watercolour view of Lambeth Palace. In 1791, he made the first of many sketching tours in search of topographical material, taking in Bath, Bristol and other West Country sights. In the years that followed, he joined a circle of young artists, including Thomas Girtin, who met at the house of the physician and art collector Dr Thomas Monro to copy and colour drawings from his collection. Girtin became Turner's friend and rival before his untimely death at the age of twenty-seven.[34] Having exhibited watercolours for seven years, to some critical acclaim, Turner showed his first oil painting, *Fishermen at Sea*, in 1796 [14]. This painting, a view off the southern coast of England near the Isle of Wight, underlined the young artist's ability to assimilate established styles associated with seventeenth- and eighteenth-century British and Continental landscape and marine painting (see 'Charted Waters'). At the same time, it announced the contemporary sea, its human concerns and narratives, as a major preoccupation of Turner's artistic enterprise. He went on to explore many different branches of marine painting, including battle pictures, scenes of storm and shipwreck, and a succession of coastal and Thames estuary subjects. A series of ambitious watercolours on the scale of oil paintings also included coastal scenes; for example, *Pembroke Castle: Thunder-Storm Approaching* (current location unknown), exhibited at the Royal Academy in 1801, and its sequel, with the storm clearing, in 1806 [77].

By the turn of the nineteenth century, Turner had achieved prominence as a painter in both oil and watercolour, and had begun to attract commissions from some of the most notable patrons of the day. His first commission for a seascape came from the Duke of Bridgewater in 1800, for a companion to van de Velde's *A Rising Gale* (Toledo Museum of Art). The resulting painting secured the artist's reputation when it was exhibited to critical acclaim at the Academy in 1801 [fig. 6]. Within a few years, by 1805, *Ships Bearing up for Anchorage* [72] had been bought by the Earl of Egremont. Besides the immediate advantages of selling his work, this kind of patronage gave Turner privileged access to some of the most important private art collections in Britain.

An early indication of Turner's success and developing ambitions was his move in 1799 to Marylebone, a fashionable area of London. At 64 Harley Street, on the corner of Queen Anne Street, he shared studio accommodation with John Thomas Serres, a marine artist and author of the *Liber Nauticus* [18]. It was also around this time that Turner began his relationship with Sarah Danby, with whom he had two daughters, Evelina and Georgiana. In November that year Turner was elected an Associate of the Royal Academy, and three years later, aged twenty-six, he was the youngest artist to become a full Academician – an occasion he marked by extending his signature from 'W. Turner' to 'J.M.W. Turner RA'. While undoubtedly ambitious and increasingly confident in his own talents, Turner's participation in the affairs of the Academy was also emblematic of his wider aspirations for a national school of art, in which landscape (including marine painting) would play a central role.

In the summer of 1802, Turner took advantage of the temporary Peace of Amiens between Britain and France to conduct his first Continental tour, sponsored by Lord Yarborough, whose son Charles Anderson-Pelham subsequently acquired *The Wreck of a Transport Ship* [76], and possibly the politician and landowner Walter Ramsden Fawkes.[35] On the return journey, after taking in Switzerland and northern Italy, he visited the Louvre (called the Musée Napoléon from 1803) in Paris, where he sketched and made notes on the work of several canonical European painters, including Titian, Nicolas Poussin and Jacob van Ruisdael [fig. 8]. Widely acknowledged to be the most innovative landscape artist of his generation, he was by now also beginning to attract negative criticism for his ever more challenging work. This came, in particular, from Sir George Beaumont and other conservative critics (including some Academicians), primarily for the apparent lack of finish in his exhibited seascapes.[36] Seeking an alternative to the exhibition rooms of the Royal Academy, he built a picture gallery at the back of his Harley Street house and began to display his own work there from 1804. In 1811, Turner had a new gallery entrance created on Queen Anne Street.

For most of Turner's adult life up to the age of forty, Britain was embroiled in war against Revolutionary and Napoleonic France. The impact of the conflict on the life of the nation, on land and sea, was a major theme in his work (see 'Trafalgar Squared'). In December 1805, he travelled downriver to the Medway to sketch the 'Victory', Vice-Admiral Horatio Nelson's flagship, which was anchored off Sheerness following its return from the Battle of Trafalgar. The next year he showed *The Battle of Trafalgar* [fig. 16] at his gallery alongside other pictures, possibly including *The 'Victory' Returning from Trafalgar* [fig. 20]. In the same year he also exhibited for the first time at the newly opened British Institution, a private society for showing the work of past and present artists. The Institution was formed and controlled by wealthy collectors, including Beaumont, Egremont and John Julius Angerstein, to rival the artist-governed Royal Academy. During the summer of 1806, Turner stayed with the artist William Frederick Wells at Knockholt, Kent, where the two friends discussed the concept that would become the *Liber Studiorum*. This ambitious print project, conceived in emulation of Claude's *Liber Veritatis*, functioned as a manifesto for British landscape art and promoted Turner's extraordinary creative range in the genre (see ''M' for Marine'). Later that year he was appointed Professor of Perspective at the Royal Academy, and in 1811 he delivered his first series of six lectures that reached far beyond the subject of perspective.[37]

From July to September 1811, Turner toured the South West making drawings for *Picturesque Views on the Southern Coast of England* (see [39 and 40]). This was his first major series of topographical engravings, and the first of a number of collaborations with W.B. Cooke. In addition to his growing involvement with print culture, from 1819 Turner's work reached a wider audience through a succession of private and commercial exhibitions in London. In March, eight of his paintings were shown along with works by other British artists in the gallery of Sir John Leicester's London home on Hill Street. Later that year, more than sixty of his watercolours were displayed at Fawkes's London residence in Grosvenor Place (Fawkes had purchased *Dort* the previous year).[38] During the 1820s and early 1830s, Turner gave his permission for a number of exhibitions in commercial galleries in London. From February to August 1822, Cooke staged one at his gallery in Soho Square, which included more than twenty of Turner's watercolours, and this was followed by two further exhibitions there in 1823 and 1824. Also, by the end of 1822 Turner had received a commission from George IV to paint his second treatment of *The Battle of Trafalgar* [58], the largest work he ever completed, which was installed at St James's Palace in 1824. Five years later, the King presented it to the National Gallery of Naval Art at Greenwich Hospital for Seamen.

Following the initial success of the *Southern Coast*, Turner journeyed to East Anglia in 1824 to gather material for a series focusing on the east coast of England [50]. The following year, he began work on the even more ambitious *Picturesque Views in England and Wales* (see [51 and 52]), his largest topographical print project, which occupied much of his time for the next sixteen years.[39] During the Academy exhibition of 1827, Turner showed *'Now for the Painter'* [59] and *Port Ruysdael* [63] – his first open seascapes for eight years. The former was reputedly titled in friendly (but pointed) rivalry with the young Clarkson Stanfield, who in the 1830s was regarded by many as the leading marine artist of his generation (see 'Contested Waters'). In October 1844, Stanfield was appointed the first Honorary Curator of Paintings at Greenwich Hospital, and shortly afterwards oversaw the complete redisplay of its Naval Gallery with Turner's *Trafalgar* as a centrepiece of the main hall. Turner may have seen the new display during a subsequent visit to Greenwich.

Such important cultural developments as the Naval Gallery and the National Gallery (both founded in 1824) may have prompted Turner to focus increasingly on the role of national collections in nurturing and promoting contemporary British art, and his own artistic legacy (see 'Making Waves'). The death of his father in 1829 had a profound effect – their close personal relationship apart, William Turner senior had for many years assisted his son in his studio, stretching and varnishing canvases. The day after his father's funeral, Turner drew up his first will, which included the provision for the donation of two paintings to hang alongside two canvases by Claude in the National Gallery. Turner subsequently made revisions to his will, culminating in 1848 with a new codicil that referred to his bequest to the nation and display of all 'finished pictures' still in his possession (see 'Imagining the Sea').

Turner always divided critics, never more so than in his late career. One of the notable exceptions to this trend was the universal praise for his final 'Trafalgar' painting, *The Fighting 'Temeraire'* [87], exhibited in 1839. Overall, however, his late seascapes suffered from a barrage of abuse, in particular *Slavers*, which one reviewer in 1840 thought was 'impossible to look at without mingled feelings of pity and contempt', and *Snow Storm – Steam-Boat off a Harbour's Mouth*, exhibited in 1842, which was dismissed as incomprehensible.[40] To the young art critic John Ruskin, however, Turner's work of this period underlined his liberation from the stifling conventions of past masters and embodied the highest principles of landscape art by its uncompromising 'truth to nature'.[41] Having read the reviews of the Royal Academy exhibition of 1842, he decided to write a response that would 'blow the critics out of the water'.[42] This became the seminal work *Modern Painters* (1843–60). At Turner's death in 1851, Ruskin owned two of his oils, including *Slavers*, and around thirty watercolours. His single-minded admiration for Turner, so powerfully expounded in his published works, encouraged a new audience for the artist's paintings, many of which had remained unsold. The wealthy businessman Elhanan Bicknell, for example, who financed Joseph Hogarth's print of *The Fighting 'Temeraire'* in 1844, in the same year bought eight earlier paintings by Turner, six on one day.[43]

Since 1833, Turner had stayed regularly in Margate with Mrs Booth, his landlady and companion. As his health began to fail, in 1846, he moved to live with her in Chelsea, at 6 Davis Place on Cremorne New Road – then an unfashionable riverfront location. He sent his final seascape to the Royal Academy in 1849. This, *The Wreck Buoy* [88], ranks among his most enigmatic works – a painting that he had begun and 'finished' as a young man, but which he then reworked in old age, transforming the image in the process as if to declare that his life's work was, and would remain, forever 'in progress'. Turner died in his Chelsea home on 19 December 1851, aged seventy-six and very wealthy. In accordance with his wishes, he was buried in the crypt of St Paul's Cathedral alongside Reynolds, Thomas Lawrence and other celebrated Academicians – 'my Brothers in Art' as he described them – and also near to his hero, Lord Nelson.[44]

1

CHARTED WATERS

Richard Johns

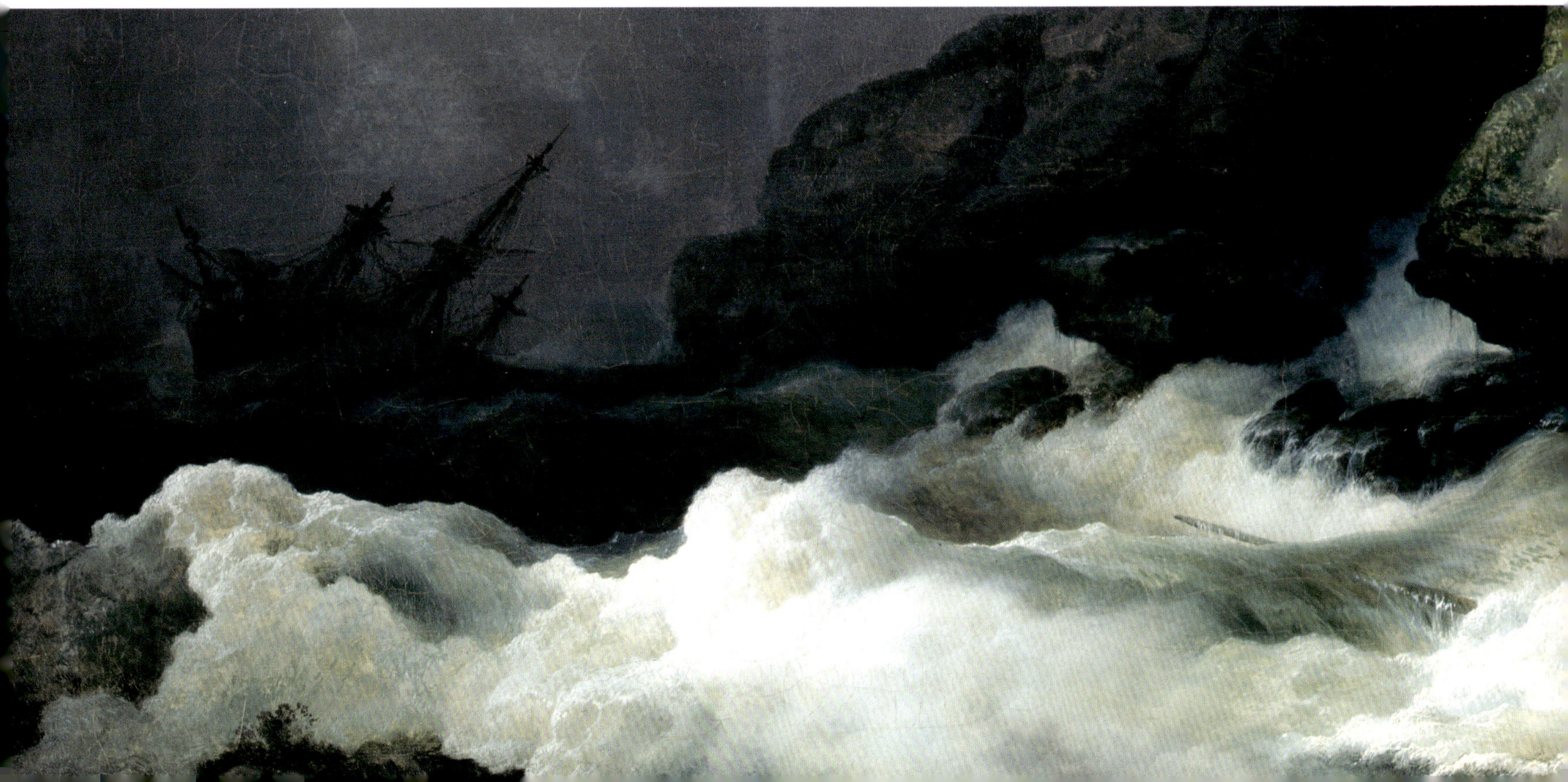

Reviewers of the Royal Academy's annual exhibition in 1797 were struck by the performance and promise of an unknown young painter. '[We] have no knowledge of Mr. Turner,' wrote one seasoned critic, '[but] the present Picture is an undeniable proof of the possession of genius and judgement, and what is uncommon in this age is that it partakes but very little in the manner of any other master.'[1] Another visitor agreed: 'I am entirely unacquainted with the artist, but if he proceeds as he has begun, he cannot fail to become the first in his department.'[2] The work that had captured the critics' attention was *Fishermen Coming Ashore at Sun Set, previous to a Gale*, and the 'department' in which the artist promised to excel was marine painting – a branch of art that had featured prominently in the Royal Academy's shows, though barely at all in its teaching, since its establishment thirty years earlier. Known today only in engraved form, as one of nine marine subjects included in the artist's *Liber Studiorum* [27], *Fishermen Coming Ashore* was one of three evening or moonlit fishing scenes that Turner submitted to the Academy in the late 1790s. The other two were his earliest known work in oil, *Fishermen at Sea* [14], admired for its buoyant boats and undulating waves when it was exhibited in 1796, and *Fishermen Becalmed previous to a Storm, Twilight* from 1799.[3] As a group, these three coastal views were judged by one of the artist's earliest biographers to possess 'many of those fine qualities of conception and execution which critics recognise with delight in the best works of his best time'.[4]

What made Turner's first seascapes stand out on the Academy's crowded walls? They were not especially large paintings, nor is there any suggestion that they were displayed to great advantage. Rather than competing with the works of other artists for size and eye-catching effect (a tactic for which Turner later became renowned), these temporal coastal scenes demanded a closer kind of viewing. With an understated drama and subtle variation of light and colour, they were designed to seduce the Academy audience by offering respite from the visual cacophony all round them of portraits, grand-manner history paintings, expansive landscapes and, most strikingly, explosive renderings of naval battles. It was with these dramatic naval scenes in mind, painted by older, more established marine painters such as Nicholas Pocock and Robert Cleveley, that Turner's most enthusiastic reviewer praised the 'singularity of perception' which distinguished the young artist's work from those who 'too servilely followed the steps of each other'.[5] Tellingly, when Turner exhibited *The Battle of the Nile* in 1799, competing with works on the same subject by Pocock and Cleveley, it elicited none of the praise heaped on his coastal scenes. Depicting the explosion of the French flagship 'L'Orient' at the climax of the battle, Turner's work was accompanied by an apocalyptic extract from Milton's *Paradise*

Lost, which elevated the war against Revolutionary France to the level of biblical epic. Despite Turner's evident ambition for his first battle piece, however, the painting (now untraced) was damned for its mistaken palette and for failing to produce 'the grand effect' demanded by the event, and otherwise ignored.[6]

A NATURALIZED ART

The response to Turner's first sea pieces indicates the premium that the critics were inclined to place on a painter who appeared to operate against the grain. What those critics played down, however, is the significant extent to which the artist's early seascapes relate, deliberately and necessarily, to a long and rich international culture of maritime art. The most celebrated exponent of marine painting in Britain through the eighteenth century was the Dutch artist Willem van de Velde the Younger [4 and 5], one of several land- and seascape painters who travelled to Britain from the Low Countries during the second half of the seventeenth century. Born into a family of mariners and artists, van de Velde established a reputation as one of the foremost marine painters in Amsterdam before moving to London in 1672/3 with his father, Willem the Elder, at the behest of Charles II.[7] As the official purveyor of 'Sea Fights' for the Restoration court, and the first choice of naval officers and others with a personal or professional investment in Britain's global maritime affairs, the van de Velde studio (initially working for nearly twenty years from the Queen's House at Greenwich) introduced into British art a Netherlandish tradition of marine painting that would, in every sense, become naturalized. The close observation of nature and attention to detail, for which Dutch painting was later both admired and criticized, were employed by the van de Veldes to develop a specialized technical style that traded on first-hand knowledge of ships, maritime lore and the conventions of naval warfare. It proved enormously popular and, on his death in London in 1707, van de Velde the Younger bequeathed a thriving studio as well as a model, and a market, for maritime art that reached far beyond the court-centred culture from which it had sprung. To the sea painters who followed, van de Velde was the figurehead of a nascent British school of marine painting.

Peter Monamy was among the first and most prolific of several British-born artists to continue in the Dutch painter's manner during the first half of the eighteenth century. In his wake, Samuel Scott [fig. 4], Charles Brooking and Francis Swaine emerged as the most prominent marine artists of their generation, producing battle paintings, ceremonial scenes and bespoke ship portraits for a predominantly naval clientele, for whom the patronage of maritime art extended notions of good seamanship, success in battle and command of the seas.[8] Although each painter developed his own distinctive style and specialism, the underlying authority of van de Velde remained paramount. This was most evident in the high value placed by artists and patrons on the close observation and accurate delineation of the working sea: the 'forms and buildings of shipping with all the tackles ropes & sails', in the words of the artist and writer on art George Vertue, which, coupled with a 'neatness and clean pencilling of sky and water', formed the basis of a shared maritime aesthetic.[9]

The increasingly conspicuous role of the navy in the cultural and political life of the nation ensured a continued interest in marine painting, as new ways of consuming art brought the genre to a broader public: through high-end prints [17], the richly decorated supper boxes at Vauxhall Pleasure Gardens from 1742 and, in the later 1740s, as part of the ostensibly more refined display of contemporary painting within the new buildings of the Foundling Hospital. The visibility and quality of marine painting in mid-century London prompted the Swiss miniaturist Jean André Rouquet, an unusually sympathetic foreign correspondent on the condition of the arts in England, to report in 1755 that 'Marine painting in Vandervelt's taste is a branch of the art in which one need not be afraid to affirm that the English excel.'[10] By the time the Royal Academy was established in 1768, the genre arguably enjoyed a prominence in British art that was second only to portraiture.

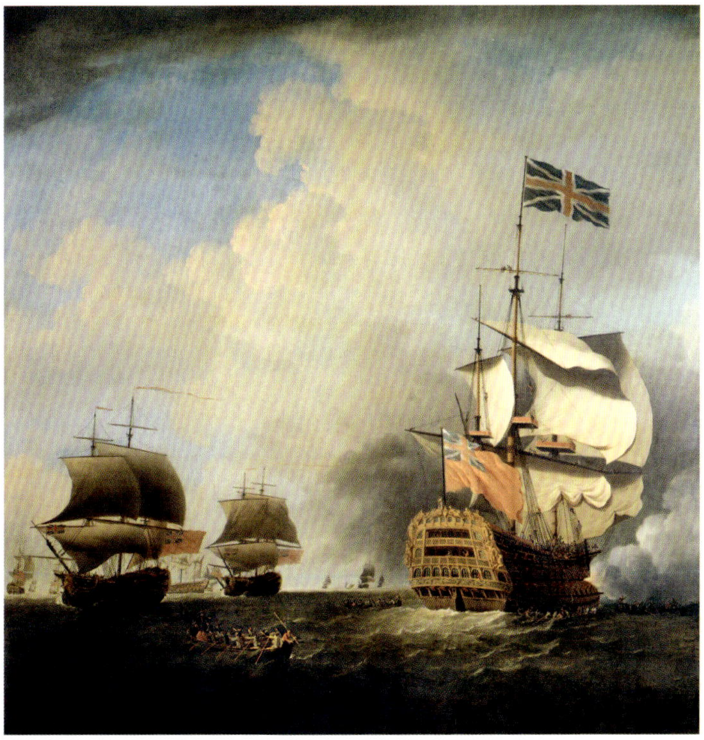

Fig. 4

Samuel Scott
A First-Rate Shortening Sail c.1736
Oil on canvas 228.6 x 219.7 (90 x 86½)
National Maritime Museum

Yet only one of the thirty-four founding Academicians, Dominic Serres, was a dedicated marine painter, and he was not British. Born in Gascony, south-west France, Serres began his working life at sea, eventually becoming master of a merchant ship trading in the Caribbean.[11] He was taken prisoner by a British frigate off Havana and brought to England in the mid-1750s. Encouraged by Brooking, Serres soon established a successful career in his adopted country, initially producing images of newsworthy naval battles for the London print market and becoming the preferred artist of a growing number of senior naval officers. Serres was an active participant in London's early exhibiting societies, and as an Academician had exhibited more than a hundred seascapes by the time of his death in 1793. His career coincided with a period of near-continuous naval activity, which provided a constant source of military subjects, from the Seven Years' War to the American War of Independence and beyond. The austere geometry and formal repetition of his later work, perhaps most striking in the diagrammatic representation of *The Battle of Negapatam* [11], marked the culmination of the technical, documentary style of battle painting that had been introduced a century earlier by van de Velde. In some respects, Serres's identification with the Dutch painter could hardly have been closer, and he continued to produce paintings that he described as 'in the style of Vanderveld' throughout his career. His embellishment of several drawings by van de Velde is highly suggestive of how he regarded his own enterprise as a direct continuation of – even an improvement on – the work of his celebrated predecessor.[12]

In 1780, the height of Serres's career was marked by his appointment as official marine painter to George III – the first position of its kind since the van de Veldes had each been granted an annual salary of £100 by Charles II. In the same year, Joshua Reynolds, President of the Royal Academy, encouraged another emerging marine painter, Nicholas Pocock, to look to the well-established example of van de Velde for harmony of colour when representing the elements, and to 'paint from nature' as the celebrated French marine painter Claude-Joseph Vernet had done in Rome.[13] Reynolds's thoughts on the subject were undoubtedly informed by Serres, his fellow Academician, whose early artistic career had also drawn on the dramatic coastal scenes of Vernet, with whom he corresponded for several years, eventually meeting him in Paris in 1785. Reynolds (who had known Vernet in Rome in the 1750s) had little else to say about 'ship-painting', but his few words of advice identified the two principal, Continental markers against which maritime art in Britain was charted during the second half of the eighteenth century. Indeed, the work of these two very different artists from different ends of the Continent encapsulated the breadth of achievement across two centuries of marine painting.

During a long and highly successful career, Vernet became one of the most widely admired painters in eighteenth-century Europe. For twenty years he was a major artistic force in Rome, before returning to Paris where he was fêted by the philosopher and art critic Denis Diderot as one of France's greatest and most versatile living painters.[14] His coastal landscapes, typically conceived in pairs or groups of four to represent different weather conditions and times of day, were a particular favourite among British Grand Tourists, who accounted for around half of his patrons in Rome [6 and 7]. By the time of Reynolds's advice to Pocock, Vernet's stormy coastal scenes and moonlit calms had become emblematic of British aristocratic taste in the genre. Above all, his reputation rested on the sophistication with which he fused aspects of the work of the seventeenth-century old masters who appealed most to his eighteenth-century patrons. Whether in a single painting or across a series, Vernet combined the Arcadian beauty of Claude's glowing harbour scenes and the rugged, untamed landscapes of Salvator Rosa: in effect, uniting the contrasting aesthetic appeal of the beautiful and the sublime (two guiding categories of eighteenth-century art theory) within a coherent pictorial series. Moreover, the rich personal mythology that bolstered Vernet's reputation, including his legendary willingness to expose himself to the dangers of a storm at sea, established a lasting example of maritime artistic achievement. Diderot encapsulated the reasons for Vernet's international appeal most succinctly upon seeing the artist's substantial contribution to the Paris Salon of 1765: 'What beautiful skies! What water! What compositional intelligence! What prodigious variety in these scenes!'[15]

Vernet's considerable impact on the visual culture of the sea and coast in Britain was most apparent in the work of another French artist, the painter, polymath and showman Philip James de Loutherbourg. Born in Strasbourg in 1740, de Loutherbourg trained in Paris before moving to London in 1771 at the invitation of the actor-manager David Garrick, to become his scenic director at the Theatre Royal, Drury Lane. His parallel range of gallery subjects included pastoral landscapes, apocalyptic history paintings and equally dramatic battle pictures [53]. Stormy coastal scenes, often featuring a shipwreck or smugglers [10], formed part of a wider exploration of the sublime possibilities of landscape that also included fiery images of the dawning Industrial Revolution. At the same time, other painters, including Thomas Gainsborough and George Morland, explored the picturesque (and picaresque) potential of the coast in different ways as an extension of their usual practice as landscape painters [8].

Meanwhile, Pocock and Cleveley continued to focus on the lucrative field of specialist marine painting, seeking to match the level of technical and topographical knowledge that had long been recognized and valued in the work of van de Velde. They exhibited regularly alongside de Loutherbourg, Gainsborough and others with some critical and commercial success, and their paintings were especially praised for their high degree of accuracy. However, despite its popularity (or, perhaps, because of it), their work remained resolutely untheorized within the Academy, which aspired to intellectually more demanding forms of picture making. One rare attempt to define and promote contemporary maritime art in the broadest sense appeared in the *Naval Chronicle*, the monthly journal founded in 1799 by the naval chaplain James Stanier Clarke and John McArthur, secretary to Admiral Lord Hood, with the principal aim of publishing memoirs and accounts of naval actions, alongside all manner of essays, illustrations and correspondence on the subject of Britain's maritime affairs. Compiling an inventory of the various 'Marine Designs' exhibited at the Academy in 1799 (including Turner's *Fishermen Becalmed* and *The Battle of the Nile*), the editors of the *Chronicle* situated marine painting within a wider naval culture and conversation, warning those gentlemen 'who are unacquainted with the intricate anatomy of ships' that they were ill-qualified to appreciate (and thus, it is implied, to criticize) the labours of marine painters.[16]

Turning their attention to the Royal Academy (which at the time occupied part of Somerset House, the same building as the Navy Board), the journal's editors apportioned neither praise nor blame to individual works in the exhibition. However, they prefaced their account with a lucid apology for the genre as a whole. Contemporary artists in the field were beholden to what the *Chronicle* described as the 'cramped' grammar of the particular: their ambition 'confined to portraits of particular ships, or correct representations of particular actions, which forbid the artist from indulging in the fine rolling phrenzy of imagination'.[17] These comments were inadvertently reinforced by the scientific naval context in which they appeared, which promoted a similar set of 'particular' values. The inventory of Academy marines was preceded by a series of 'philosophical papers' on various nautical themes – a disquisition on the stability of ships, a letter recommending a new type of compass – and was followed by a chart of the Bay of Aboukir prepared by Pocock, the journal's resident illustrator, 'from the drawing of a French officer', complete with a diagram of Nelson's fleet destroying the French line at the Battle of the Nile.

While the *Chronicle* insisted that marine painters moved 'in a space of peculiar Grandeur, and Sublimity', the context in which the claim was made revealed the degree to which the work of living marine painters had become disconnected from the aesthetic and intellectual priorities of the British art establishment. Broadly put, the issue lay in the visible disparity between the traditional values of marine painting, which placed a premium on the representation of technical and topographical knowledge, and the stated ambitions of the Academy, which privileged the general, abstract principles of history painting above all else. As marine painting became more deeply engaged with the immediate concerns of Britain's imperial struggle for global supremacy, its alienation from the Academic ideal became more conspicuous. Thus Turner first came to notice not as a battle painter to rival Pocock and Cleveley, but as a painter of coastal scenes that, while they continued to address themes of immediate national concern, drew on the cosmopolitan example of Vernet as well as on new ideas about what made van de Velde an artist worthy of emulation. The *Chronicle*'s ultimate defence that marine painting in Britain was 'in its infancy' at the close of the eighteenth century, can be understood as a response to the Academy's infantilization of the genre during the previous thirty years. But the journal's editors did not get it quite right: marine painting was not so much newborn in Britain as it was being reinvented, and Turner played the leading role in that process.

WHOSE VAN DE VELDE?

Almost a hundred years after his death, Willem van de Velde's standing in Britain was as high as it had ever been. The extraordinary international success of Vernet notwithstanding, few within the British art world would have disagreed with the claim, made in 1793, that van de Velde was 'the most eminent Sea-Painter that did, or perhaps ever will, exist'.[18] However, as the century drew to a close, the terms on which the Dutch painter's legacy was judged, especially as it related to the history of painting in Britain, was undergoing a significant change. The anonymous author of *The Beauties of the Dutch School* continued:

> His Pictures cannot be too much admired ... Whether the transparency and brilliancy of his colouring, the elegant disposition of his vessels, the free and animated touch of his figures, the beautiful gradation of his distances, or the great effect of the smoke in his Battle-Pieces ... be considered, he in every respect stands unrivalled.[19]

This was a powerful claim, intended to maximize the commercial value of the artist's work at a time of growing interest in seventeenth-century Dutch painting among collectors in Britain. The author's emphasis on the 'brilliancy'

celebrated instances of creative audacity in the history of British art. But the work was not only a pivotal moment in Turner's career. In the event, Turner's competitive response to the Duke of Bridgewater's van de Velde may have done as much for the Dutch artist's posthumous reputation as it did for his own. The staged encounter between the 'unrivalled' master of the seventeenth-century seascape and the most exciting young talent of the present confirmed the status of both artists, demonstrating that marine painting as a genre could command attention alongside the most revered proponents of Italianate landscape, Claude Lorrain and Gaspard Dughet, within one of the finest collections in Britain.[25]

Throughout the eighteenth century aspiring marine painters had regularly produced copies or variations of well-known works by van de Velde as a way of advertising their own credentials. For example, when the marine artist Peter Monamy was promoted to the livery of the Painter-Stainers' Company in 1726, he presented his fellow liverymen with a large painting closely modelled on a celebrated work by van de Velde the Younger: a portrait of the 'Royal Sovereign' in a calm [fig. 7]. Under very different circumstances, after a century during which the London art world had changed beyond recognition, Turner's public response to van de Velde amounted to a powerful restatement, or renegotiation, of the historical connection between British marine painting and the Dutch tradition from which it had grown. However, the difference between these two public artistic moments is important. Whereas Monamy had chosen to mark his arrival by responding to an English calm, painted by van de Velde in

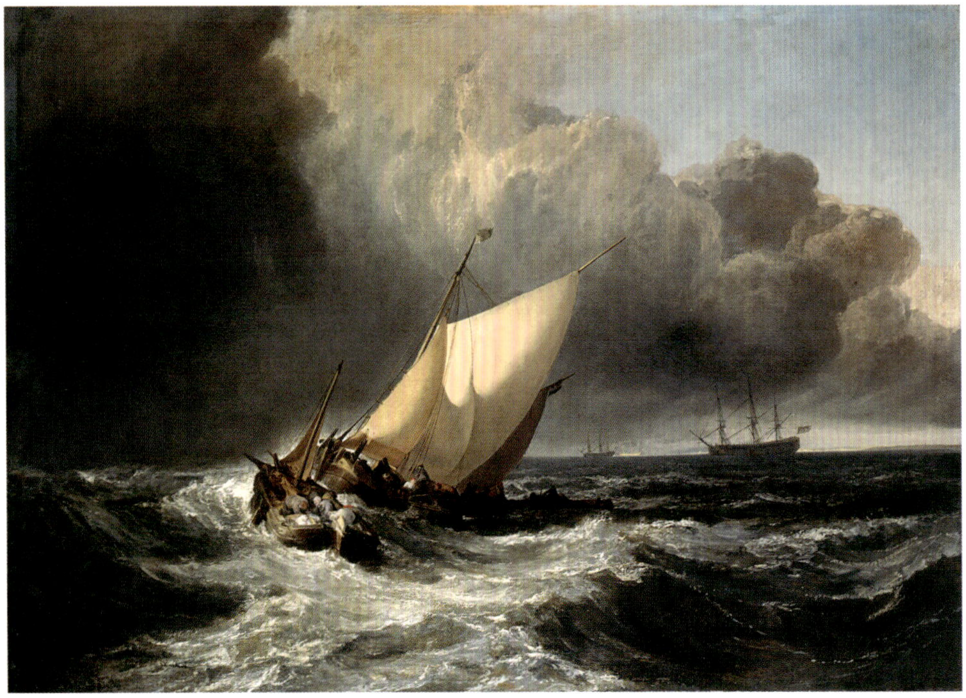

London towards the end of his career, Turner's 'van de Velde' was Dutch through-and-through, and anything but calm.

Following the success of *Dutch Boats in a Gale*, Turner produced two equally challenging seascapes that further explored the artistic and art-historical potential of the sea. *Ships Bearing up for Anchorage* [72] depicts a group of merchant vessels manoeuvring into a strong wind before dropping anchor, a favourite subject of Backhuysen. *Fishermen upon a Lee-Shore, in Squally Weather* [73] extended the artist's interest in the subject of coastal labour by depicting a team of fishermen confronting the daily perils of their work as they struggle to launch their vessel against a powerful onshore wind. Collectively, Turner's early experiments in seascape represent a sophisticated response to a complex and often contradictory history of marine painting. At the same time, they attracted criticism from some for their apparent lack of finish and for demonstrating a '*liberal* stile' that wilfully sacrificed truthfulness for effect – a charge that Turner seems to have relished.[26] Recognizing that no publicity for an artist in search of a reputation is bad publicity, Turner seems to have revelled in his ability to polarize critical opinion in this way. His first seascapes not only established their maker's reputation as the most vital and controversial marine painter of his age, they also contributed to the critical reinvention of a long visual culture of the sea to which he would return, time and again, over the next four decades as he continued to explore what the *Naval Chronicle* foresaw as the 'fine rolling phrenzy of imagination'.

Fig. 6

J.M.W. Turner
Dutch Boats in a Gale
('The Bridgewater Sea Piece') 1801
Oil on canvas 162.5 x 221 (64 x 87)
Private collection, London

Fig. 7

Willem van de Velde the Younger
The English Ship 'Royal Sovereign' with a Royal Yacht in a Light Air 1702
Oil on canvas 180.3 x 144.7 (71 x 57)
National Maritime Museum

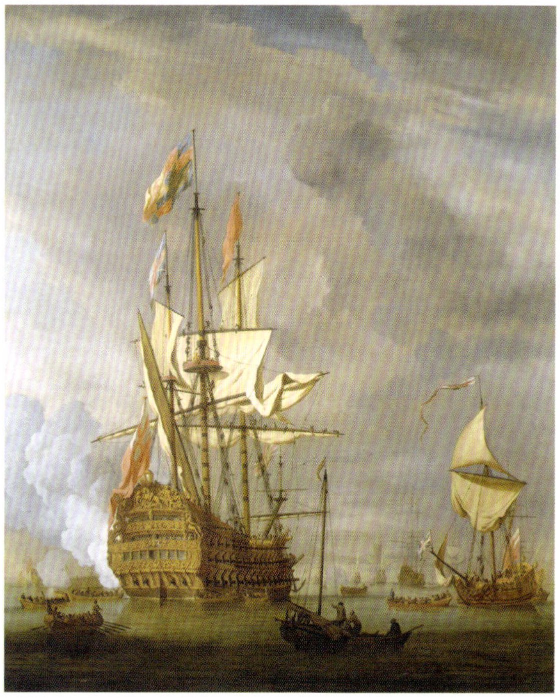

1

Simon de Vlieger

The Beach at Scheveningen 1633

Oil on panel 68.6 x 106.7 (27 x 42)

National Maritime Museum

Gaschke 2008, no. 59

For most of the eighteenth century the Dutch artist Simon de Vlieger (*c*.1601–53) was known in Britain by association, as the one-time master of two more celebrated maritime painters, Jan van de Cappelle and Willem van de Velde the Younger. Towards the end of the century, his posthumous reputation among British painters and collectors appreciated, as widening tastes and a highly developed art market encouraged a more nuanced recognition of Dutch marine and landscape painting. *The Beach at Scheveningen* was among the last works de Vlieger produced in Rotterdam before moving, first to Delft then to Amsterdam, although the same stretch of productive coastline near The Hague remained a dominant theme in the artist's work for the remainder of his career. Almost two centuries later, de Vlieger's calm, silvery seas and expansive skies provided a powerful pictorial model for Turner's romantic evocations of coastal life in England. For his part, Turner visited the small fishing town of Scheveningen in 1817, where he made several sketches of figures and fishing boats on the beach that are similar in outlook to de Vlieger's much earlier compositions (Dort Sketchbook, Turner Bequest CLXII, 24–37a). That Turner shared de Vlieger's interest in the social and economic nexus of contemporary fishing is also evident in *Hastings – Fishmarket on the Sands* [80], one of a group of oil paintings and preparatory studies the artist made of the southern coast of England around 1810.

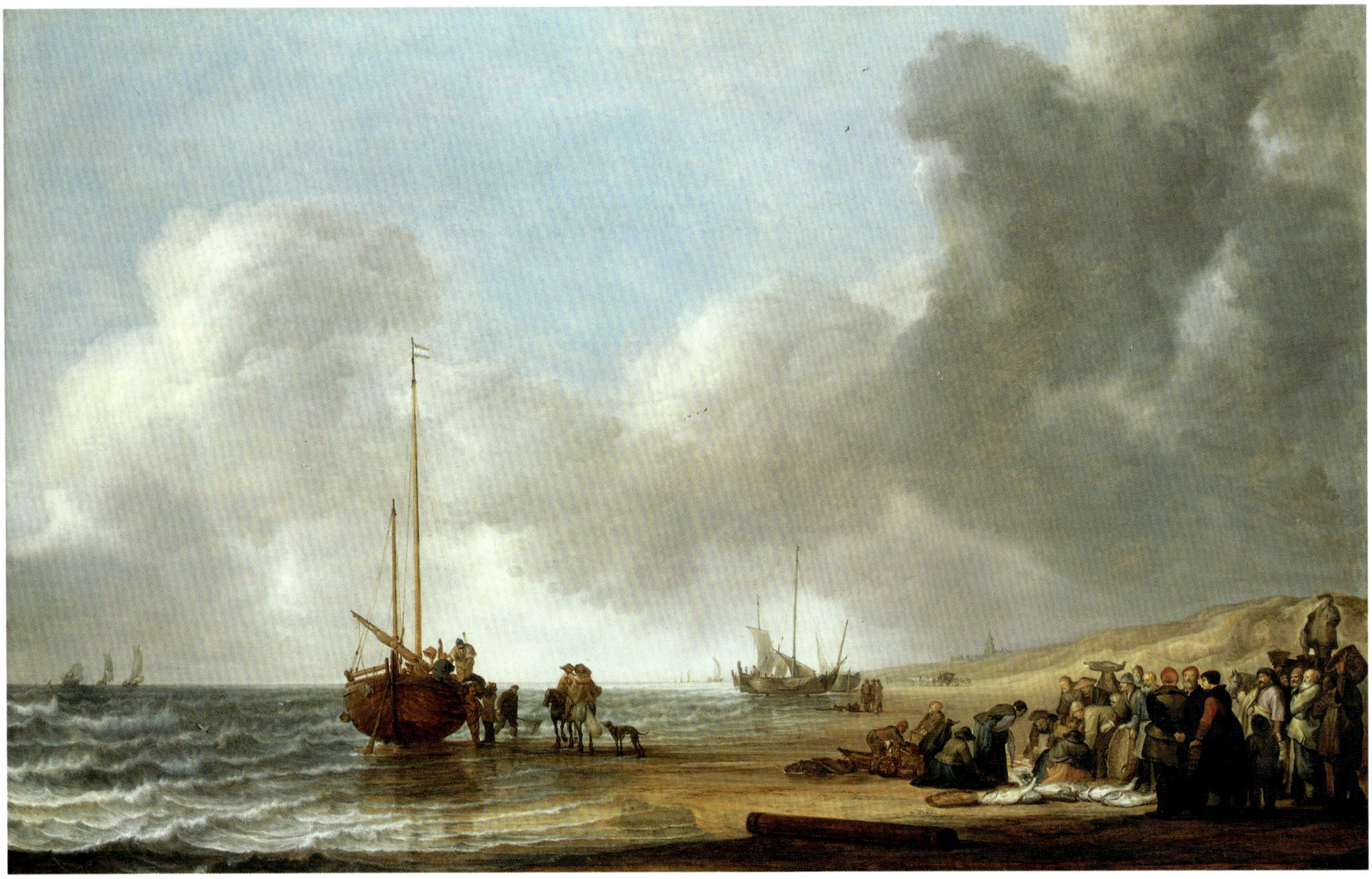

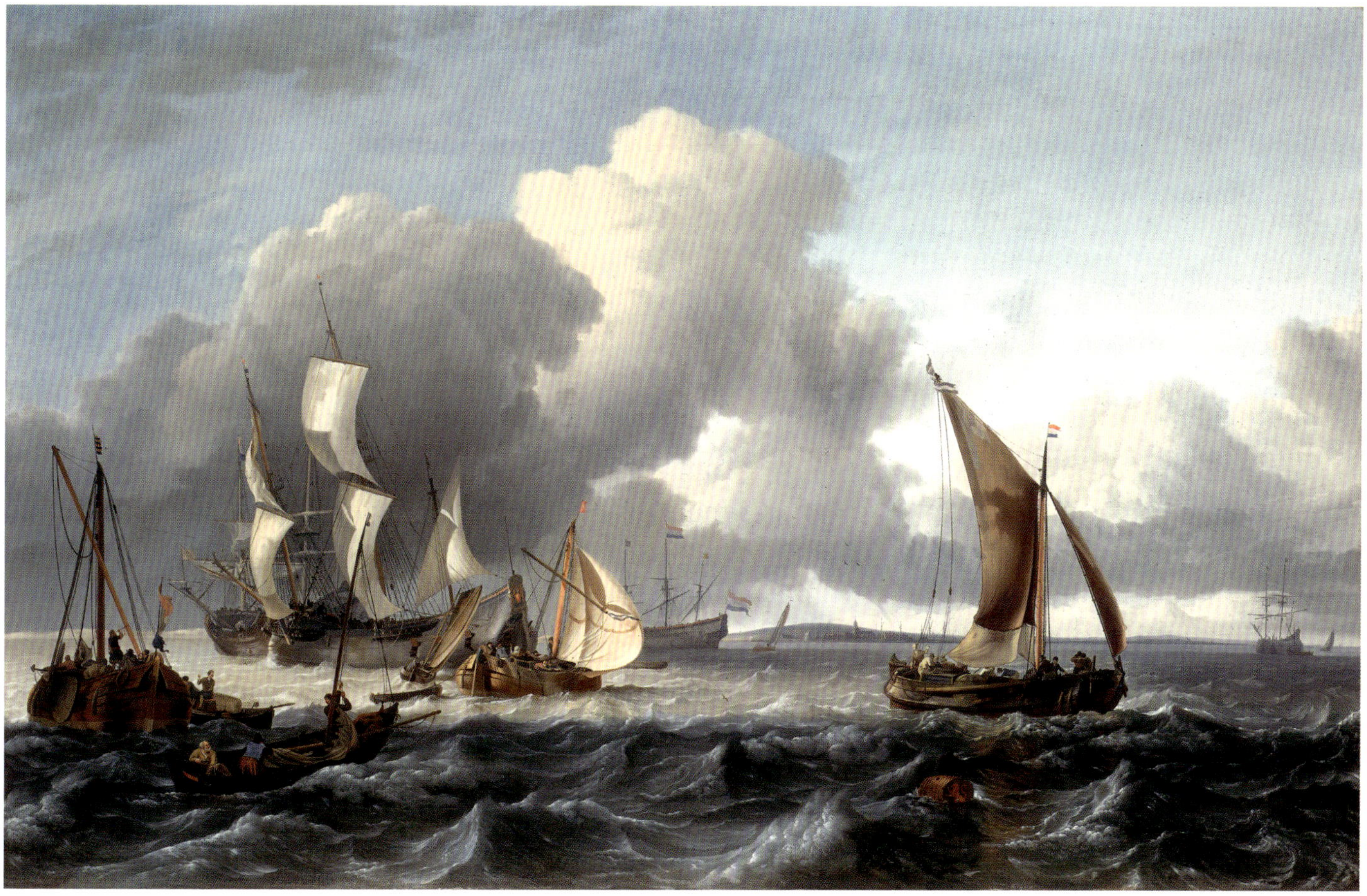

2

Ludolf Backhuysen

The Merchant Shipping Anchorage off Texel Island with Oudeschild in the Distance 1665

Oil on canvas 106.5 x 165 (41⅞ x 65)

National Maritime Museum

De Beer 2002, no. 21; Gaschke 2008, no. 5

Backhuysen (1630/1–1708), by birth a German from Emden, was among the most-admired marine painters of the seventeenth century. Second only to his contemporary van de Velde the Younger in the estimation of British connoisseurs and collectors, his rough and stormy seas were prized above all. Painted around the outbreak of the Second Anglo-Dutch War, and at the height of the artist's career, *The Merchant Shipping Anchorage off Texel Island* represents the roadstead used by the Dutch East India Company at the entrance to the North Sea. Combining an array of fishing and passenger boats with larger merchant and naval vessels, Backhuysen represents the commercial and militarized waters around Texel as a microcosm of the Dutch maritime economy – a self-regulating arena in which the industry and profits of domestic and colonial trade are poised between the natural forces of tide and wind. His celebratory vision of the Dutch Zuiderzee (the large expanse of water that until the twentieth century reached deep into the Netherlands, connecting Amsterdam to the North Sea) later provided a model for Turner's early views of the Thames estuary around the anchorage at the Nore [78].

Backhuysen's working practice gave rise to the enduring fable, later associated with Claude-Joseph Vernet and subsequently adopted by Turner, of the marine painter exposing himself to the wilder side of nature in pursuit of the perfect storm. According to Backhuysen's early biographers, it was a regular event for the intrepid Dutch artist, here relayed in *The Lives of the Most Eminent Modern Painters*:

> As soon as he saw a storm rising, he embraced the critical minute, got on board a vessel, and put out to sea; where he observed and sketched out with his pencil, the forms of the clouds, the stormy skies, and their different effects on the agitated water, the breaking of the waves against the rocks, and the froth and foam of the sea: On his return he shut himself up in his painting room, and from his sketches expressed on his canvas the objects that were then strongly painted in his imagination (Burgess 1754, pp. 102–04).

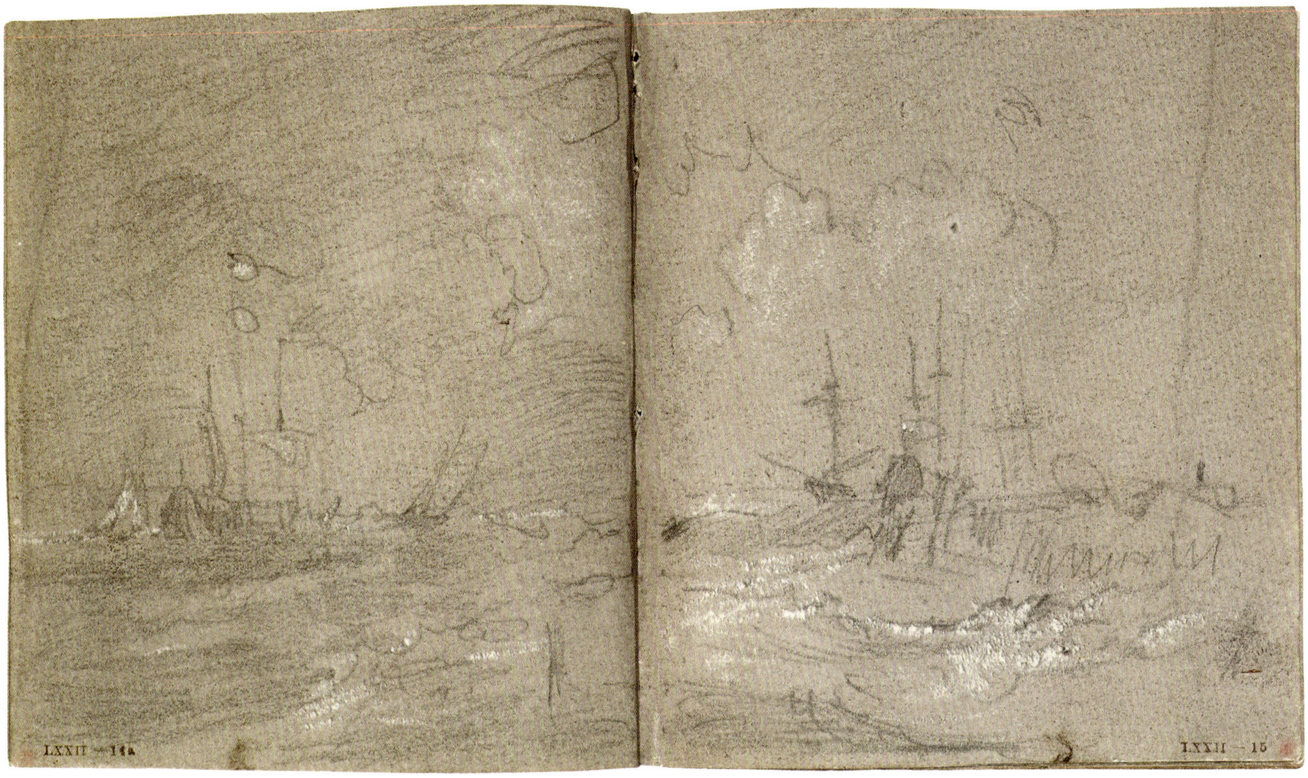

Fig. 8

J.M.W. Turner

A Storm off the Dutch Coast, after Jacob van Ruisdael from the Studies in the Louvre Sketchbook 1802
Pencil on prepared paper 25.8 x 22.8 (10⅛ x 9)
Tate. Turner Bequest 1856

3 (and detail)

Jacob van Ruisdael

The Jetty, or Stormy Weather over a Dyke in Holland 1670s
Oil on canvas 110 x 160 (43¼ x 63)
Musée du Louvre

Slive 2002, no. 653

The short-lived Peace of Amiens of 1802–03 offered a brief respite in the wars with France, making travel to the Continent possible for the first time for many artists of Turner's generation. Among the works in the Louvre that caught Turner's attention during his brief but vital first visit to Paris was a large stormy sea piece by the Dutch landscape and marine painter Jacob van Ruisdael (1628/9–82). True to style, Turner produced an aide-memoire of the painting: a drawing [fig. 8] and a detailed written account. His impromptu sketch provides a valuable real-time record of the artist's first encounter with Ruisdael's work. While his admiration for the Dutch master is evident, more striking is the attention he pays to those formal aspects of Ruisdael's work that he found wanting. Turner records his approval of the ship riding the storm and the 'heavy sombre grey sky', for example, but is critical of the lack of attention the Dutch artist pays to the sea which, though 'finely pencil'd', is 'too brown to allow the idea of it being liquid' (Finberg LXXII 23). Meanwhile, the house that features prominently in the foreground of the original work was thought by Turner to destroy the dignity of Ruisdael's composition and is barely noticeable in his sketch. Such close critical scrutiny reveals the instinctive level at which Turner engaged with the Dutch tradition of marine landscape painting while establishing his early reputation. It has been suggested that in *Calais Pier* [74], painted immediately after (and based in part upon) his first visit to the Continent, Turner consciously corrected the shortcomings he found in Ruisdael's painting (Ziff 1980, p. 168). He returned to the contest several times throughout his career, most visibly by evoking the name and style of the artist in his fictional, reverential coastal scenes *Port Ruysdael* [63] and *Fishing Boats Bringing a Disabled Ship into Port Ruysdael* [fig. 41].

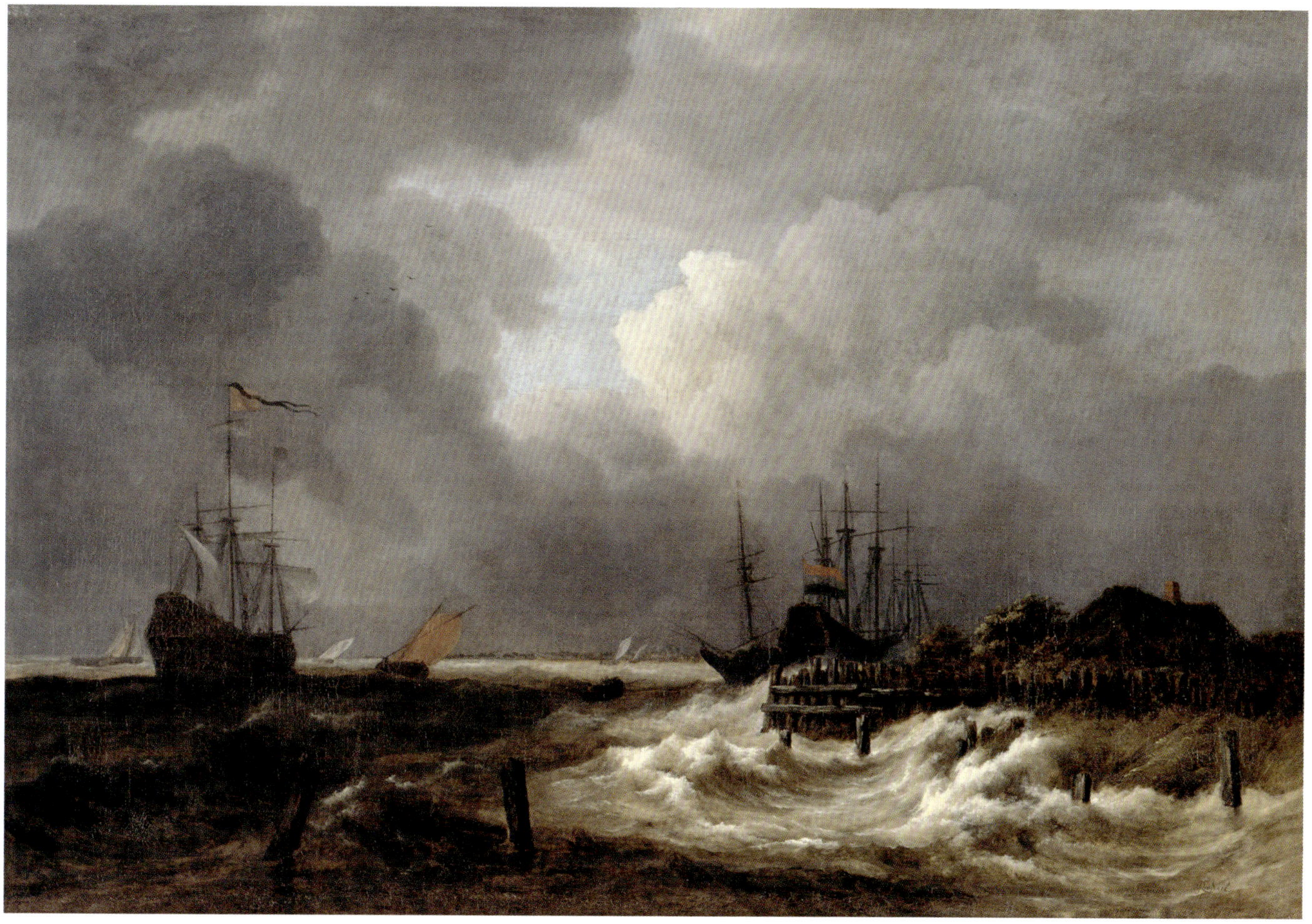

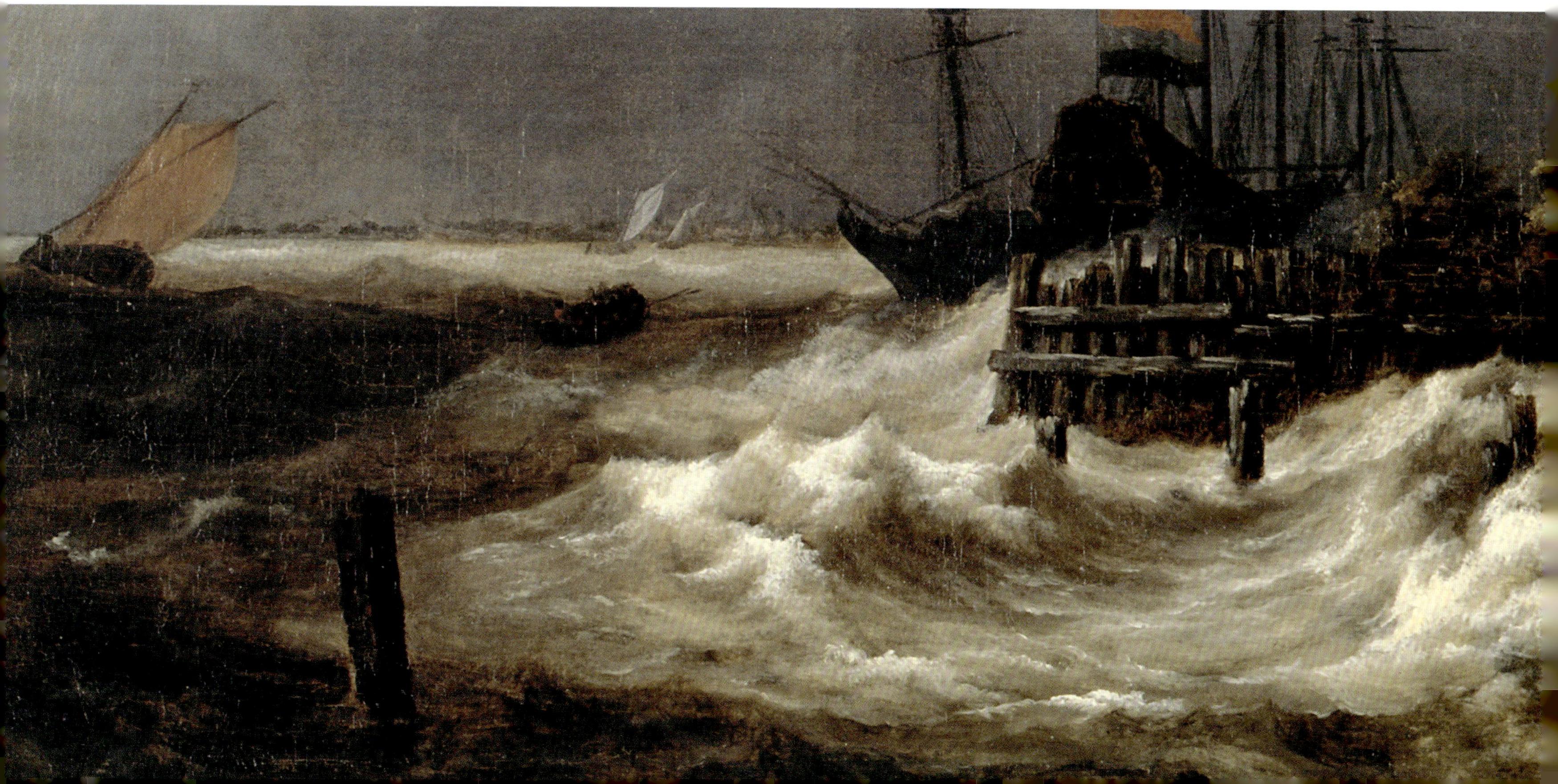

4

Willem van de Velde the Younger
A Calm: A States Yacht, a Barge and many other Vessels under Sail 1659
Oil on canvas 61.7 x 71.7 (24¼ x 28¼)
The Royal Collection

Robinson 1990, no. 31; Shawe-Taylor and Scott 2010, no. 24

This immaculate scene of commercial prosperity and social order, staged upon the shallow waters of the Zuiderzee, is typical of the maritime images van de Velde (1633–1707) produced during the first decade or so of his career – a period of relative peace in an era otherwise defined by a succession of wars between the Dutch and English navies. *A Calm* was one of two early seascapes acquired by the Prince Regent in 1814 as part of an exceptional collection of Dutch and Flemish paintings assembled by the banker Sir Francis Baring. The prominence of the artist's early work at the high end of the art market in the nineteenth century underlines the greater value ascribed by British collectors to van de Velde's Dutch works over the English subjects for which he had been better known for most of the eighteenth century. Following his move to England in the early 1670s, van de Velde's attention turned towards the portrayal of royal yachts and other ships, stripped of the commercial hubbub that enlivened his earlier Dutch calms, and to the sea battles that resumed between the artist's homeland and his adopted country.

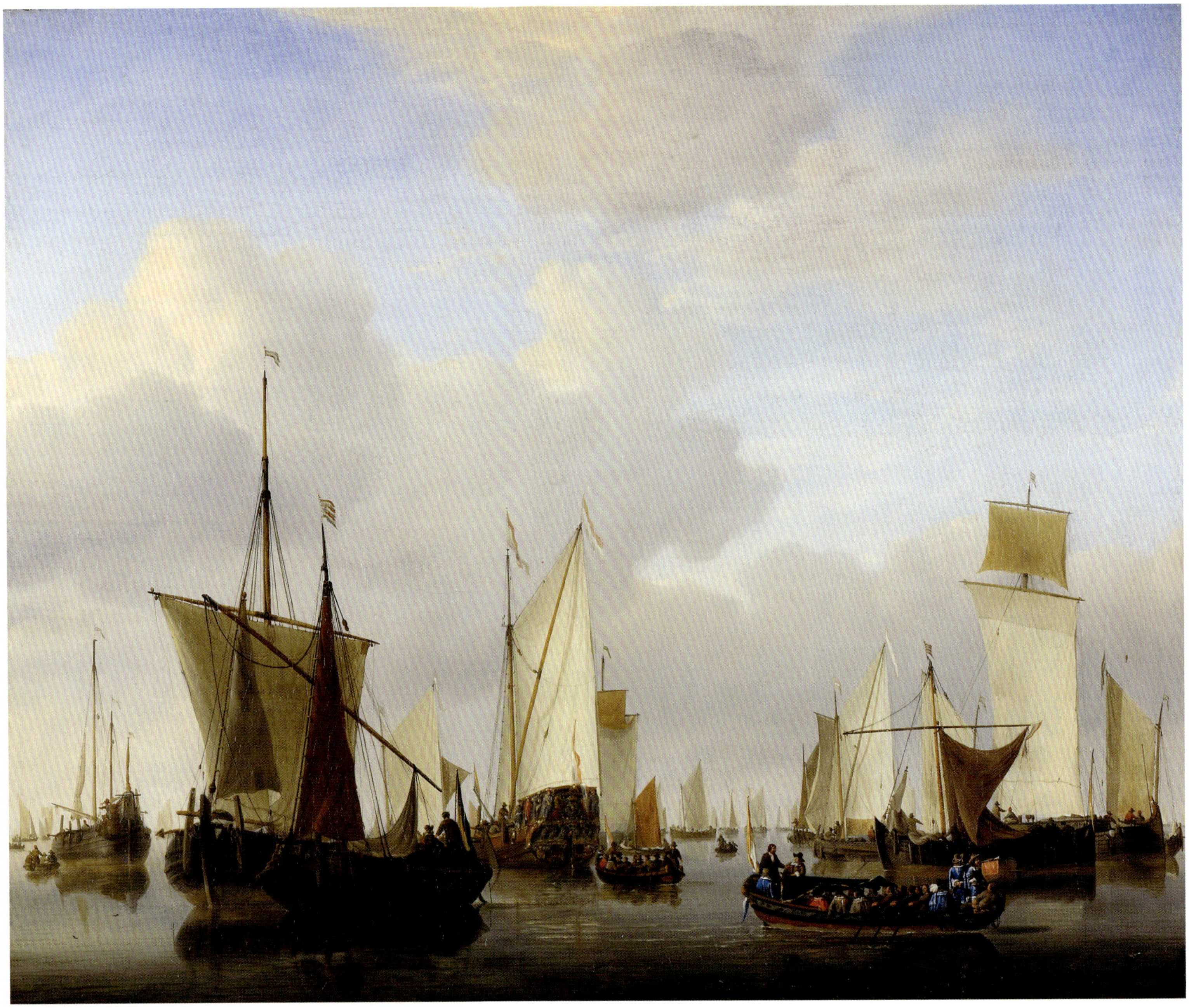

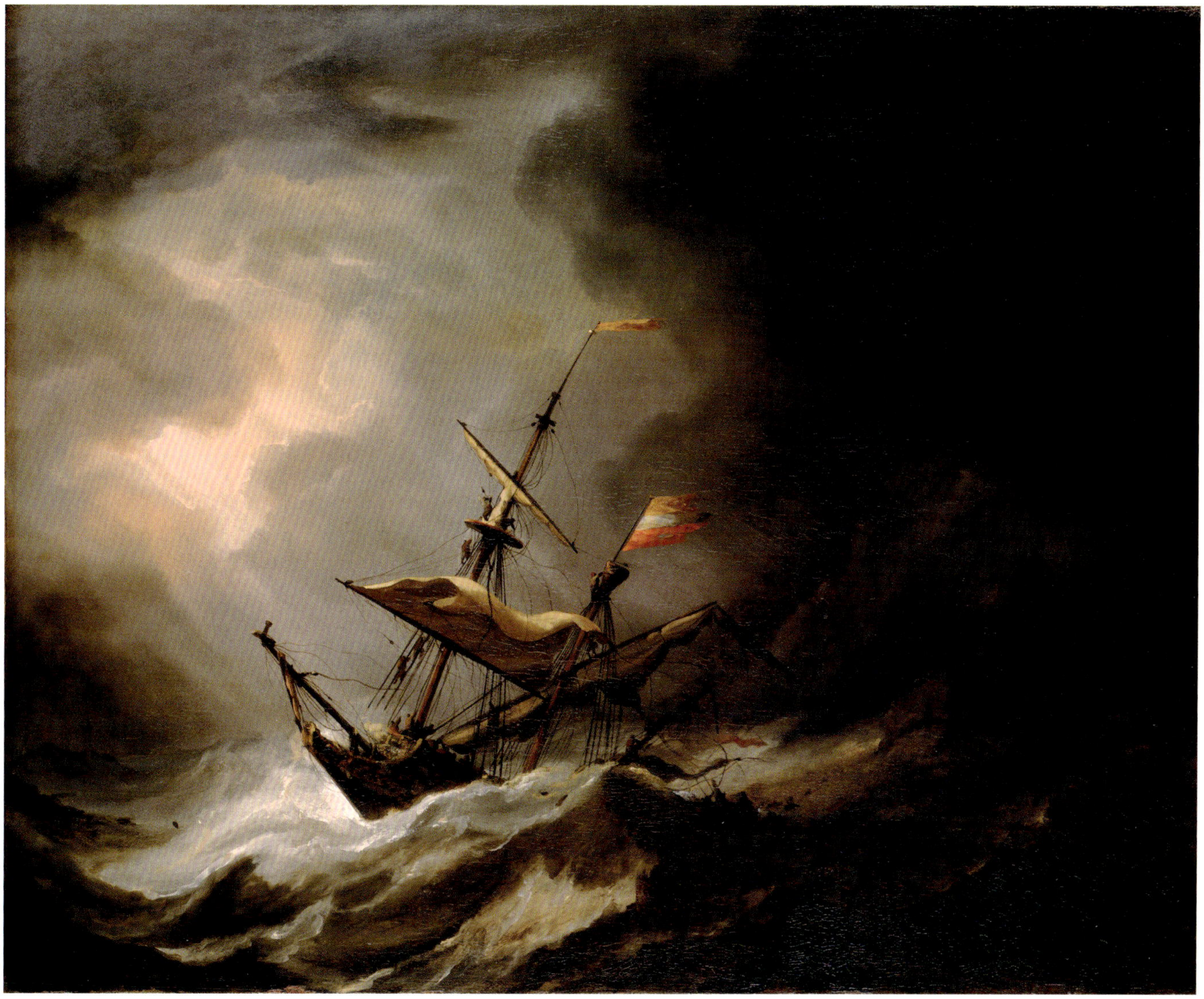

5

Willem van de Velde the Younger

A Mediterranean Brigantine Drifting onto a Rocky Coast in a Storm c.1700

Oil on canvas 63.5 x 76.2 (25 x 30)

National Maritime Museum

Robinson 1990, no. 345

In contrast to the light-infused atmosphere and meticulous brushwork of *A Calm* [4], van de Velde's portrayal of a distressed vessel in the throes of a ferocious storm plays on a violent contrast of light and shade, and a visceral, painterly response to the destructive power of the sea. Ropes snap, masts fail and desperate sailors abandon all hope as the meticulously wrought details of the ship's architecture, the stock-in-trade of the specialist maritime artist, are overwhelmed by heavy, monochromatic layers of paint that mimic the devastating force of a storm at sea. The terrifying prospect of a ship and crew on the brink of disaster proved a popular subject in the Netherlands throughout the seventeenth century, and remained a profitable aspect of van de Velde's repertoire throughout his career in Britain. Typically produced on a small scale for a domestic interior, and often with a corresponding calm in mind, such scenes held an enduring, philosophical appeal that was readily adapted to the tastes of British patrons. Van de Velde's graphic vision of the all-consuming power of the sea continued to fascinate artists and patrons well into the nineteenth century. *A Mediterranean Brigantine Drifting onto a Rocky Coast in a Storm* encapsulates a maritime–sublime aesthetic that was later revived with a showman's eye for drama by Philip James de Loutherbourg [10], and which Turner subsequently reconfigured for the steam age with his controversial painting *Snow Storm – Steam-Boat off a Harbour's Mouth* [131] .

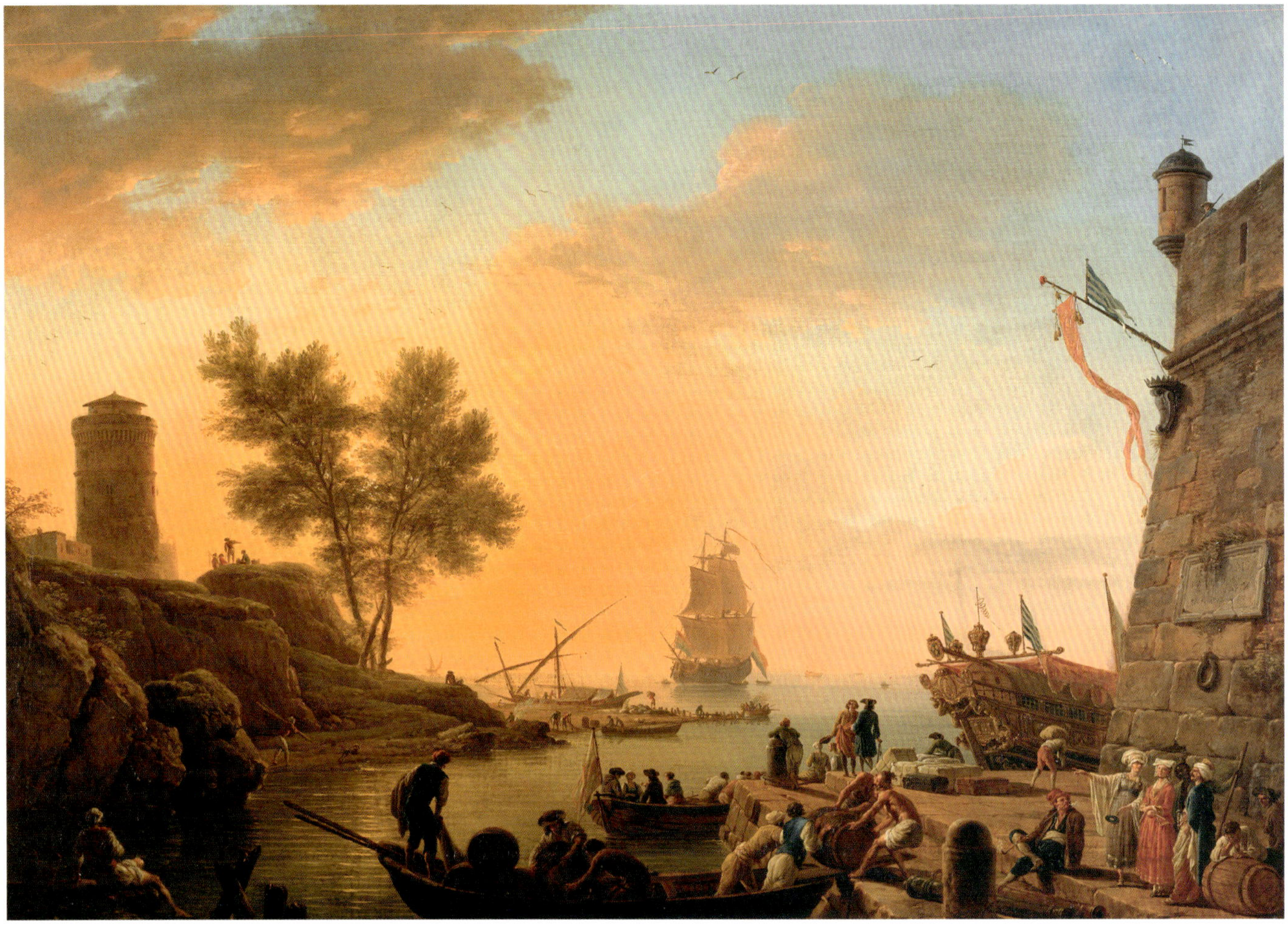

6

Claude-Joseph Vernet
Evening: Harbour Scene with Boats Being Unloaded and Spectators 1751
Oil on canvas 99.1 x 134.6 (39 x 53)
Uppark, West Sussex (National Trust)

7 (and detail)

Claude-Joseph Vernet
Night: Rocky Inlet with Fisherfolk Setting their Nets, Cooking and Drinking 1751
Oil on canvas 99.1 x 134.6 (39 x 53)
Uppark, West Sussex (National Trust)

Ingersoll-Smouse 1926, nos 330–31; Laing 1995, nos 56c–56d

For the eighteenth-century patrons of Claude-Joseph Vernet (1714–89), his pairs and groups of coastal landscapes represented a persuasive alternative to the model of marine painting associated with Willem van de Velde, by reworking the powerful legacy of the seventeenth-century landscape tradition into an accessible, decorative format. In terms of a French painter appealing across the Channel, his output was ideally suited to the British country-house drawing room and the tastes and cultural aspirations of the British Grand Tourists who accounted for around half of his patrons in Rome. Combining the Arcadian beauty of Claude's glowing harbour scenes, the rugged and untamed landscapes of Salvator Rosa, and a wealth of contemporary incident, Vernet's marines evoked his British patrons' memories of their own touristic maritime experiences.

Vernet's vivid representation of natural phenomena by land and sea ranged from the diffused light of a morning sun fighting through a sea fog to the overpowering darkness of an approaching storm. The present *Evening* and *Night* belong to a set of *The Four Times of Day*, commissioned from the artist in 1750 by the English Grand Tourist Benjamin Lethieullier for Uppark, his country seat in West Sussex. *Evening* depicts a fortified harbour at twilight, bustling with end-of-day activity that sees the strenuous unloading of barrels being juxtaposed with the arrival of a party of wealthy travellers, in the soporific warmth of a setting sun; *Night* shows a similar scene in silhouette against a disarmingly bright full moon, with a group of people at the water's edge cooking, drinking and smoking by moonlight. The contrast between the cool raking light of the moon and the warm glow of the cooking fire, a distinctive feature of Vernet's nocturnes, was later evoked by Turner in his first exhibited oil, *Fishermen at Sea* [14].

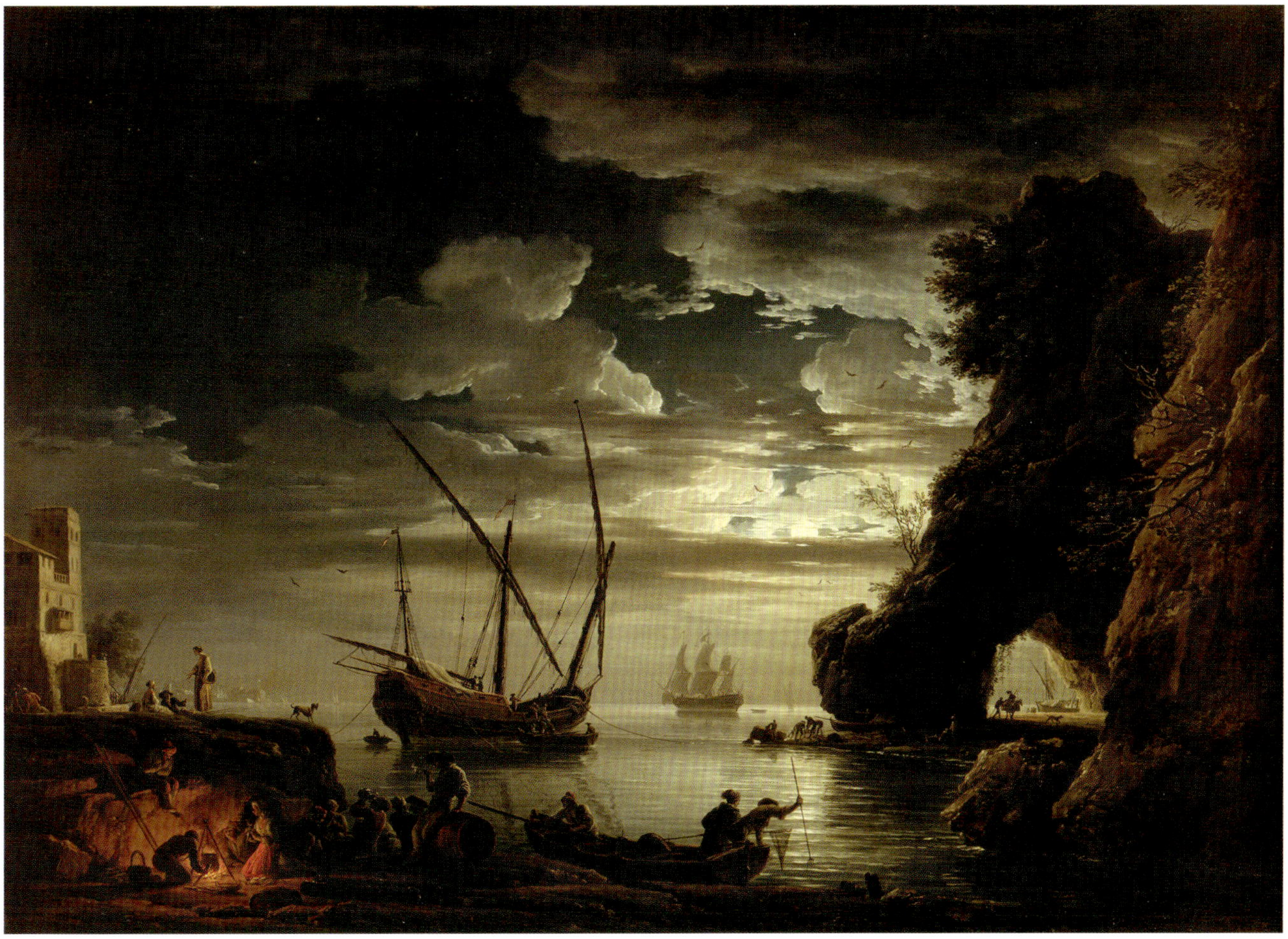

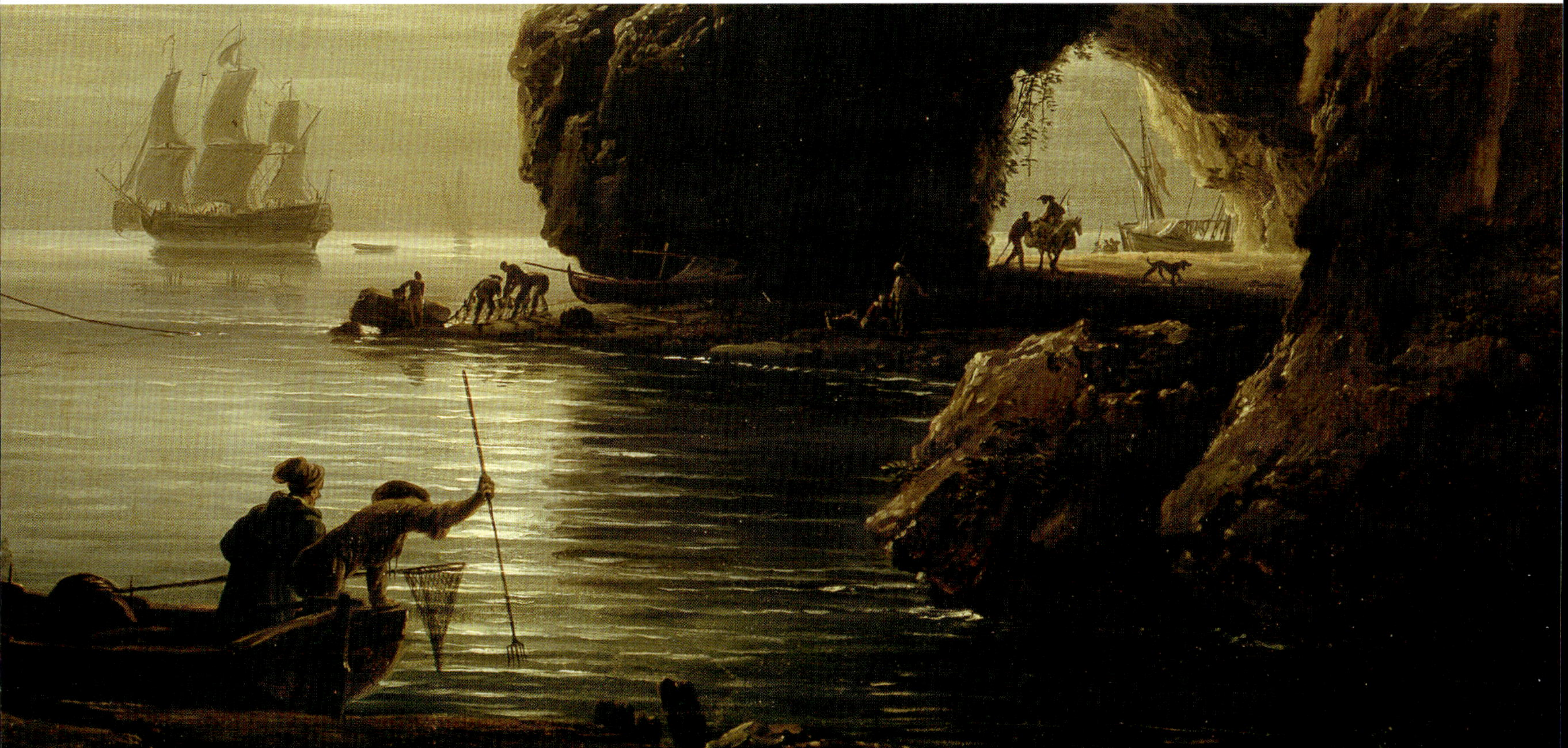

8 (and detail)

Thomas Gainsborough

Coastal Scene 1781

Oil on canvas 100.3 x 127 (39½ x 50)

Private collection

Hayes 1982, no. 127; Rosenthal 1999, pp. 96–99; Rosenthal and Myrone 2002, no. 56

This *Coastal Scene* was one of two maritime subjects that Gainsborough (1727–88) exhibited at the Royal Academy in 1781, the other being *Rocky Coastal Scene with Ruined Castle, Boats and Fishermen* (National Trust, Anglesey Abbey). Also shown that year was his pair of full-length portraits of George III and Queen Charlotte, and a large landscape of the kind that Academy visitors had come to expect from Gainsborough. In a rapturous review, Henry Bate Dudley cited the artist's two sea views as proof of his universal genius, 'for though they are his first attempts in that line, the water is exquisitely painted!' (*Morning Herald and Daily Advertiser*, 1 May 1781). Horace Walpole described the same two sea pieces in a letter to William Mason, a few days after the exhibition had opened, as 'so free and natural that one steps back for fear of being splashed' (Walpole 1904, vol. 11, p. 439).

Gainsborough's sea pieces further distinguished the artist from his great rival and President of the Royal Academy, Joshua Reynolds, and invited comparisons with seventeenth-century Dutch painters, including Jacob van Ruisdael [3] and Jan van Goyen, whose work was becoming better known among British artists and patrons. Two years later, Gainsborough exhibited a larger coastal view, *Sea-piece – A Calm* (National Gallery of Victoria, Melbourne), but despite the critical and commercial success of these first maritime excursions, his enthusiasm for the subject was confined to the early 1780s and, beyond these Academy works, focused on a series of glass-plate transparencies for his experimental 'showbox', in which images were illuminated by candlelight to demonstrate the effects of light. Gainsborough's short-lived artistic interest in the sea pointed towards a form of rustic coastal imagery that was exploited more fully by Philip James de Loutherbourg [10] and George Morland, and which provided an impetus for Turner's earliest maritime watercolours [90]. Turner may also have known Gainsborough's showbox when it was in the possession of his mentor Dr Thomas Monro, who acquired it after Gainsborough's death (Hayes 1982, vol. 2, pp. 506–07).

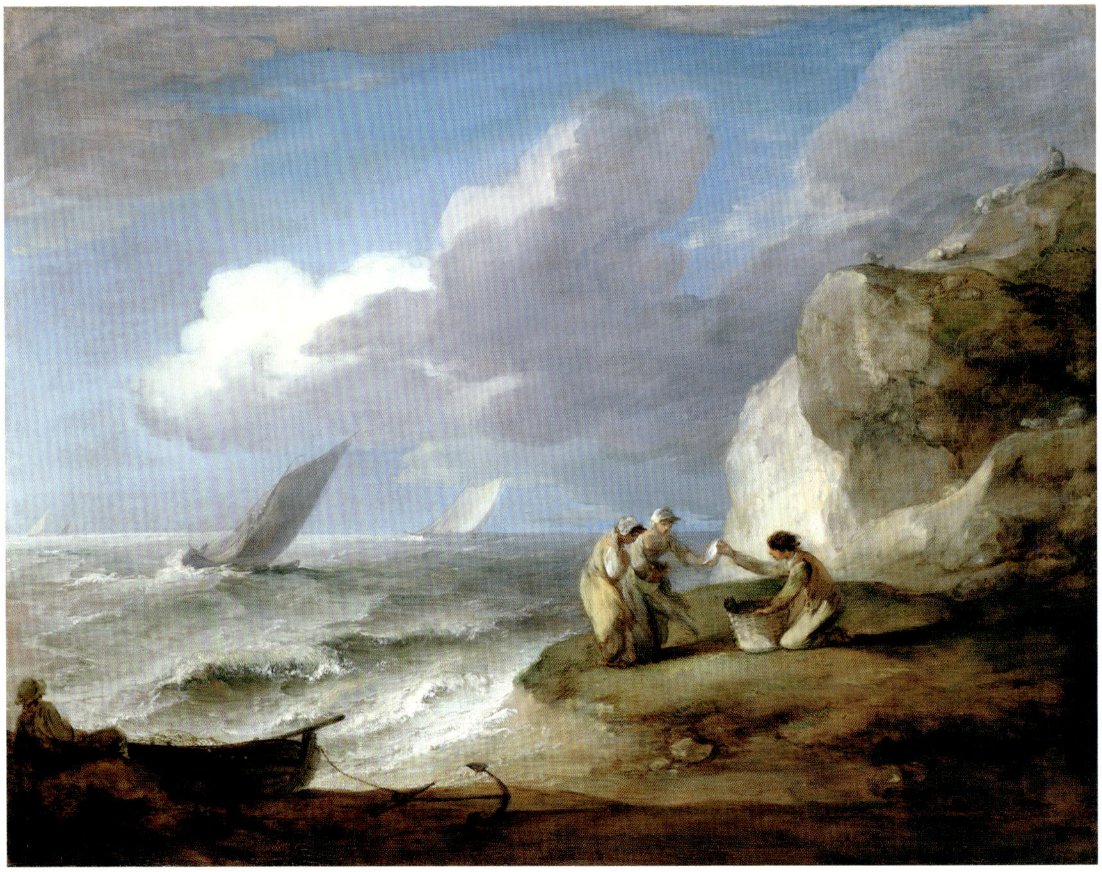

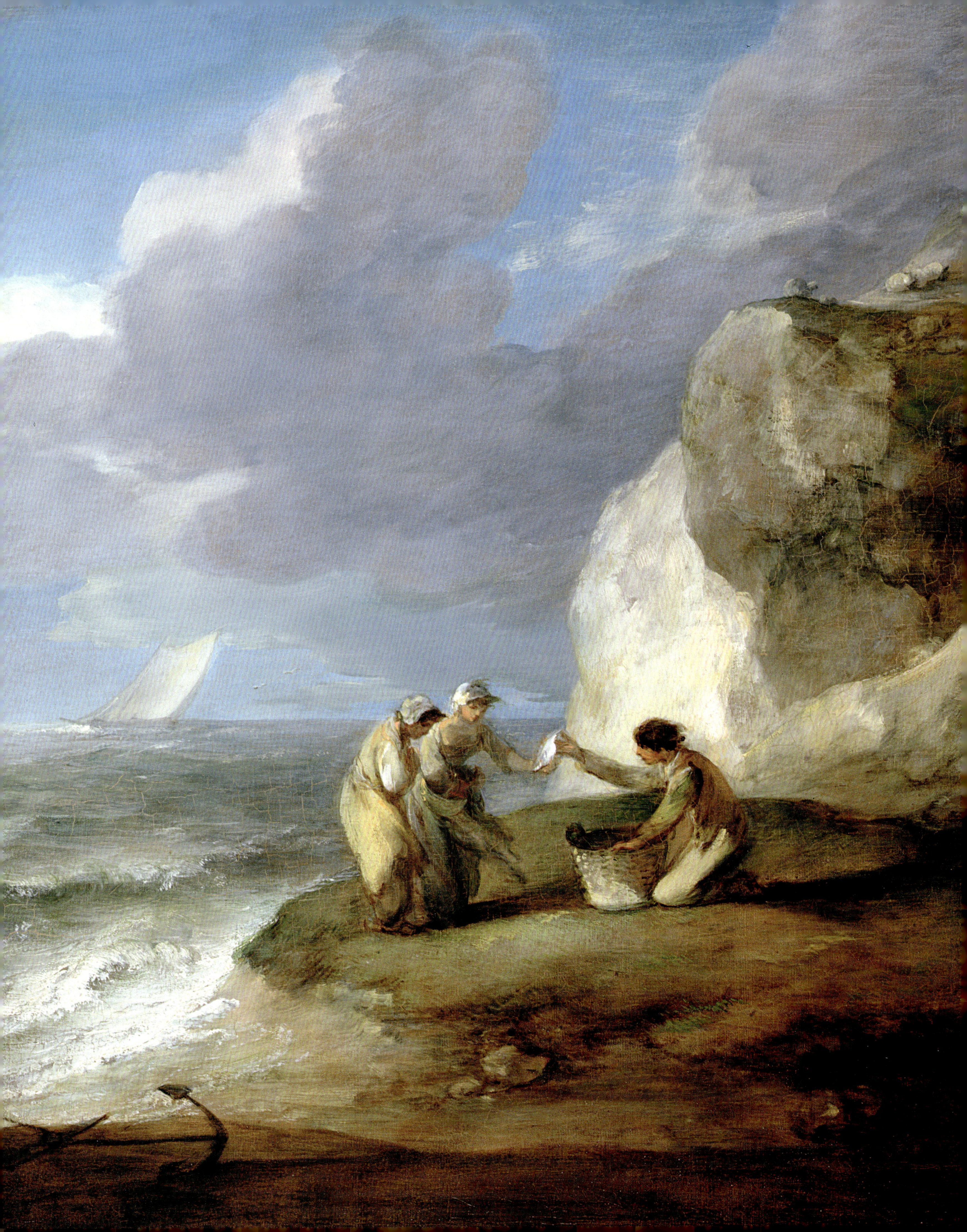

9

William Hodges

A View of Cape Stephens in Cook's Straits with Waterspout 1776

Oil on canvas 135.9 x 193 (53½ x 76)

National Maritime Museum

Quilley and Bonehill 2004, no. 27

In 1772, William Hodges (1744–97) was appointed by the Admiralty to accompany James Cook's second voyage, in search of *Terra Australis*, the fabled Southern Continent. His primary task was to record the places and societies discovered on the way – typically in the form of coastal profiles and other topographical drawings, several of which were later translated into engravings and published to accompany Cook's official account of the expedition. He also produced several small paintings on the voyage but the majority of his related works in oil were done in his London studio after his return. Hodges's finished works strike a balance between reportage and an artistic ambition to imbue the art of landscape and marine painting with the grandeur of religious and mythological epic. To this end, he mediates the crew's real-life experience of the rare and terrifying maritime phenomenon of a waterspout into a classically composed coastal scene, drawing on the popular appeal of the sublime – an approach to viewing and representing the aesthetic of awe, especially from nature – as well as the examples of Claude, Richard Wilson and (specifically here) Gaspard Dughet. *A View of Cape Stephens in Cook's Straits with Waterspout* (the Cape being the tip of D'Urville Island at the north-west entrance to the Cook Strait, New Zealand), is one of four large paintings created as a result of the voyage. Several of Hodges's voyage paintings were exhibited at the Academy in 1776 and 1777. This painting was included in the exhibition of work by deceased British artists at the British Institution in 1817.

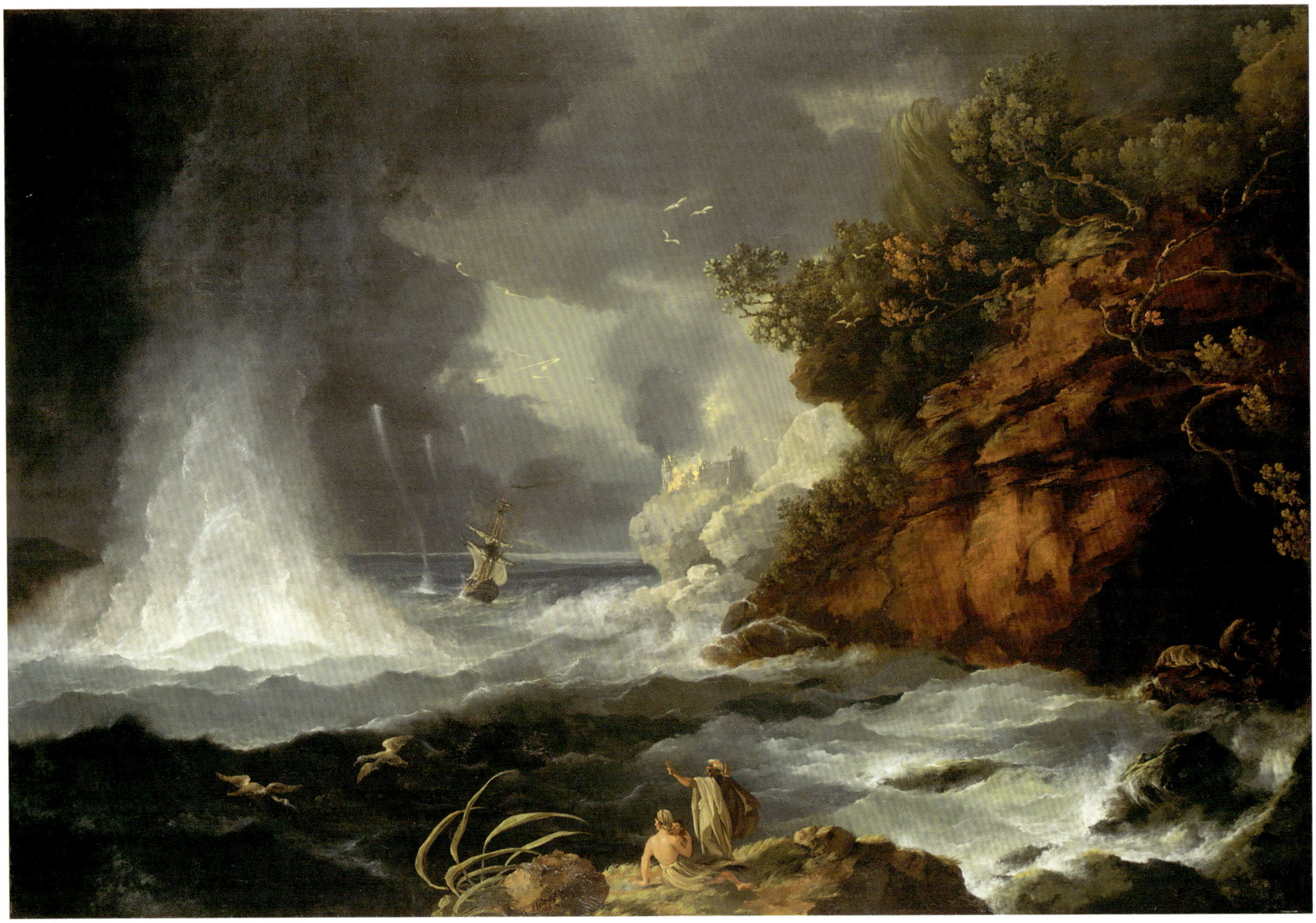

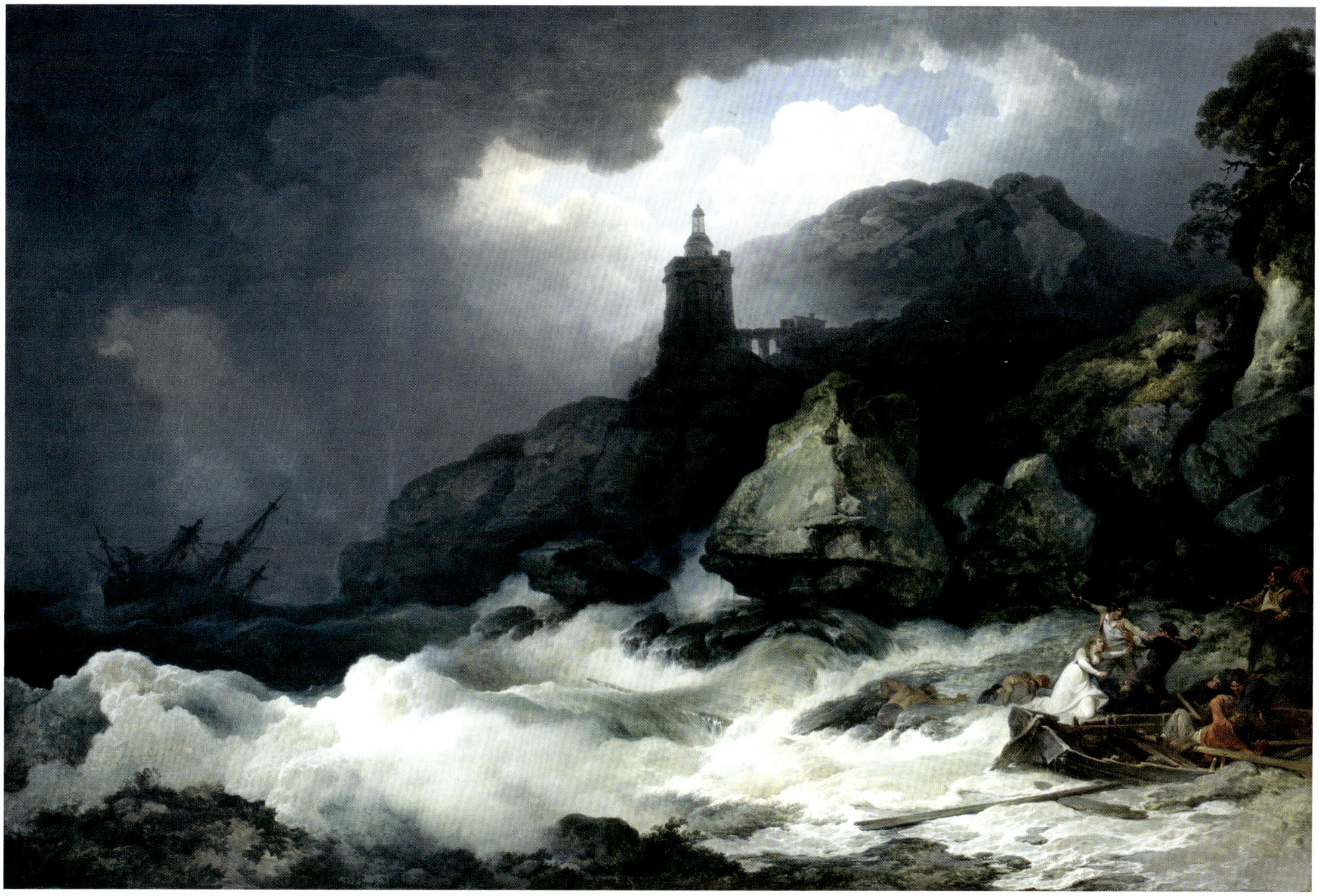

10

Philip James de Loutherbourg
The Shipwreck 1793
Oil on canvas 110.5 x 160 (43½ x 63)
Southampton City Art Gallery

In the 1790s the painter and theatrical scene-designer Philip James de Loutherbourg (1740–1812) returned his attention to the storm-stricken coast and shipwreck subjects that had occupied him thirty years earlier, as a young artist following in the footsteps of Claude-Joseph Vernet in Paris. De Loutherberg's later storms followed the success of the animated disasters and other 'Imitations of Natural Phenomena' of his 'Eidophusikon', a small-scale light-and-sound spectacle that enthralled fashionable London audiences during the 1780s. Such images achieved greater popularity in the light of regular news reports of real disaster at sea, the most notorious of which involved the 'Halsewell', an outward-bound East Indiaman that sank in a blizzard off the coast of Dorset in 1786 with the loss of more than 160 lives, including women and children, and which became a *cause célèbre* of sentimental affect. De Loutherbourg – who represented this in his 'Eidophusikon' that year – extended similar theatrics into the Great Room of the Royal Academy: in 1792 (the year before the present *Shipwreck*) he exhibited three related sea pieces, each more violent than the next, escalating from *Fresh Wind* to *Storm*, and culminating with *Shipwreck*. For his next major shipwreck, de Loutherbourg introduced a further challenge to his audience's capacity for sensibility by combining the terror of a storm at sea with a scene of extreme brutality on shore, as a family of survivors from the stricken vessel are attacked by the wreckers responsible for luring the ship onto the rocks. The inclusion of such a violent episode stepped beyond the usual parameters of the sublime, and may be understood in the context of the escalating violence in France and growing fears within the British Establishment that the Revolution could cross the Channel.

11

Dominic Serres
The Battle of Negapatam, 6 July 1782
1786
Oil on canvas 111.7 x 182.8 (44 x 72)
National Maritime Museum

Russett 2001, pp. 163–70

Few paintings embody the conventions and choreographed violence of eighteenth-century naval warfare as emphatically as *The Battle of Negapatam, 6 July 1782* by Dominic Serres (1722–93). The painting belongs to a group of seven canvases representing the pursuit and repeated engagement of the French East Indies squadron, off the east coast of India, by the corresponding British fleet of Vice-Admiral Sir Edward Hughes, at the end of the American War of Independence. The austere geometry and formal repetition of Serres's painting mark the culmination of a distinctive naval–maritime aesthetic that was valued highly by Britain's powerful eighteenth-century naval elite. At the same time, the artist's close attention to technical detail (underpinned by his first-hand experience of life at sea) demonstrates how far his specialized branch of seascape painting had drifted from the prevailing taste for picturesque landscape.

The naval war in the Indian Ocean proved indecisive but Hughes could claim credit for safeguarding Britain's colonial interests in the East Indies and returned home with a vast fortune in prize money and other perquisites from the campaign. Commissioned for his Essex country seat at Luxborough, the series to which this painting belongs represents the British naval actions under his command as a succession of disciplined and effective encounters. In the same year, William Gilpin mischievously likened the aesthetic violence of such images to the brutal reality of their subject: 'The *line of battle* is a miserable arrangement on canvas' he declared, recalling his impression of Samuel Scott's battle paintings at Shugborough Hall, 'and it is an act of inhumanity in an admiral to enjoin it' (Gilpin 1786, vol. 1, p. 65). Although there is much about Serres's work that the young Turner would reject, or consciously react against, the French-born artist's professional success and commitment to Britain's immediate maritime situation provided a significant benchmark against which Turner's early seascapes were judged.

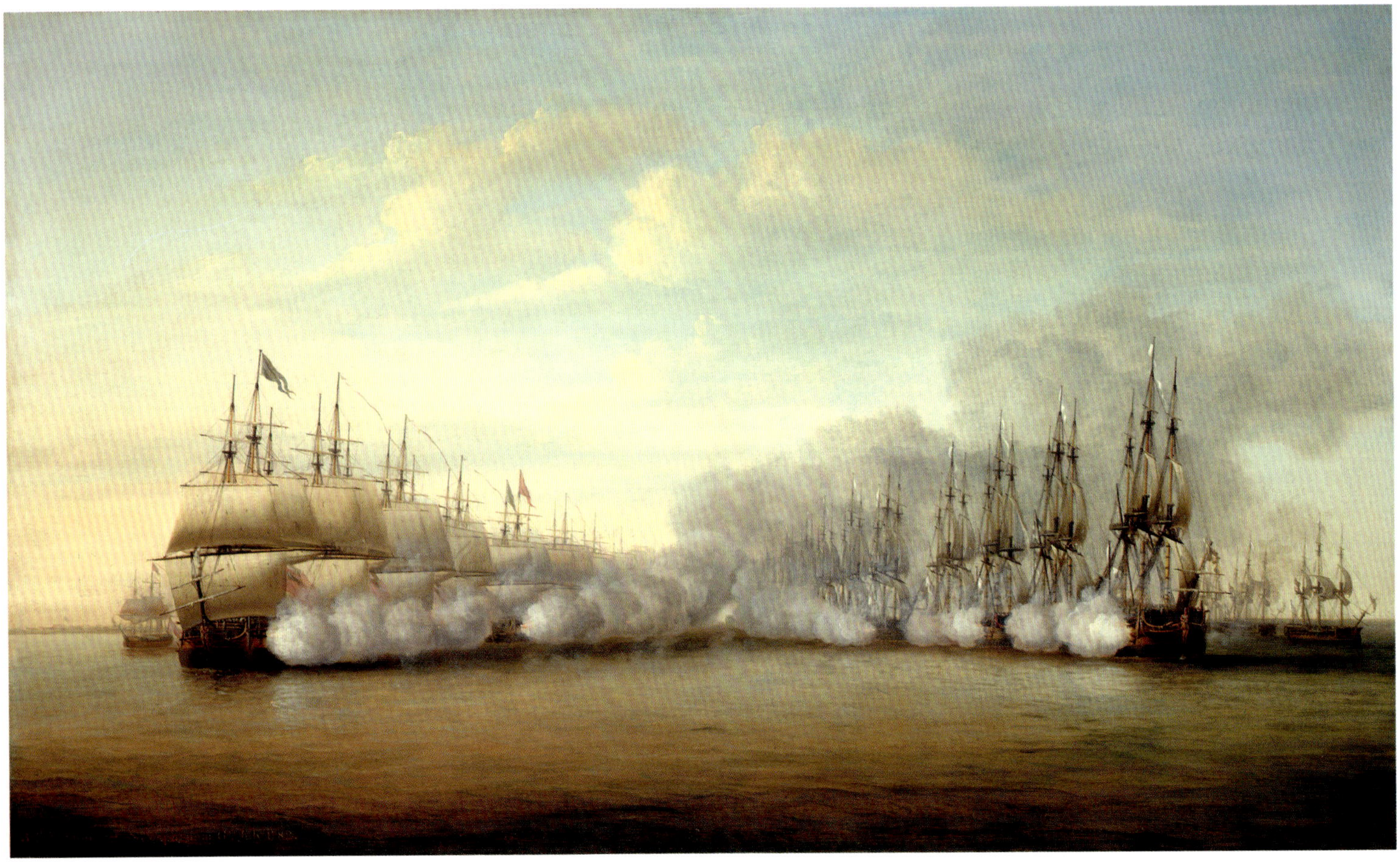

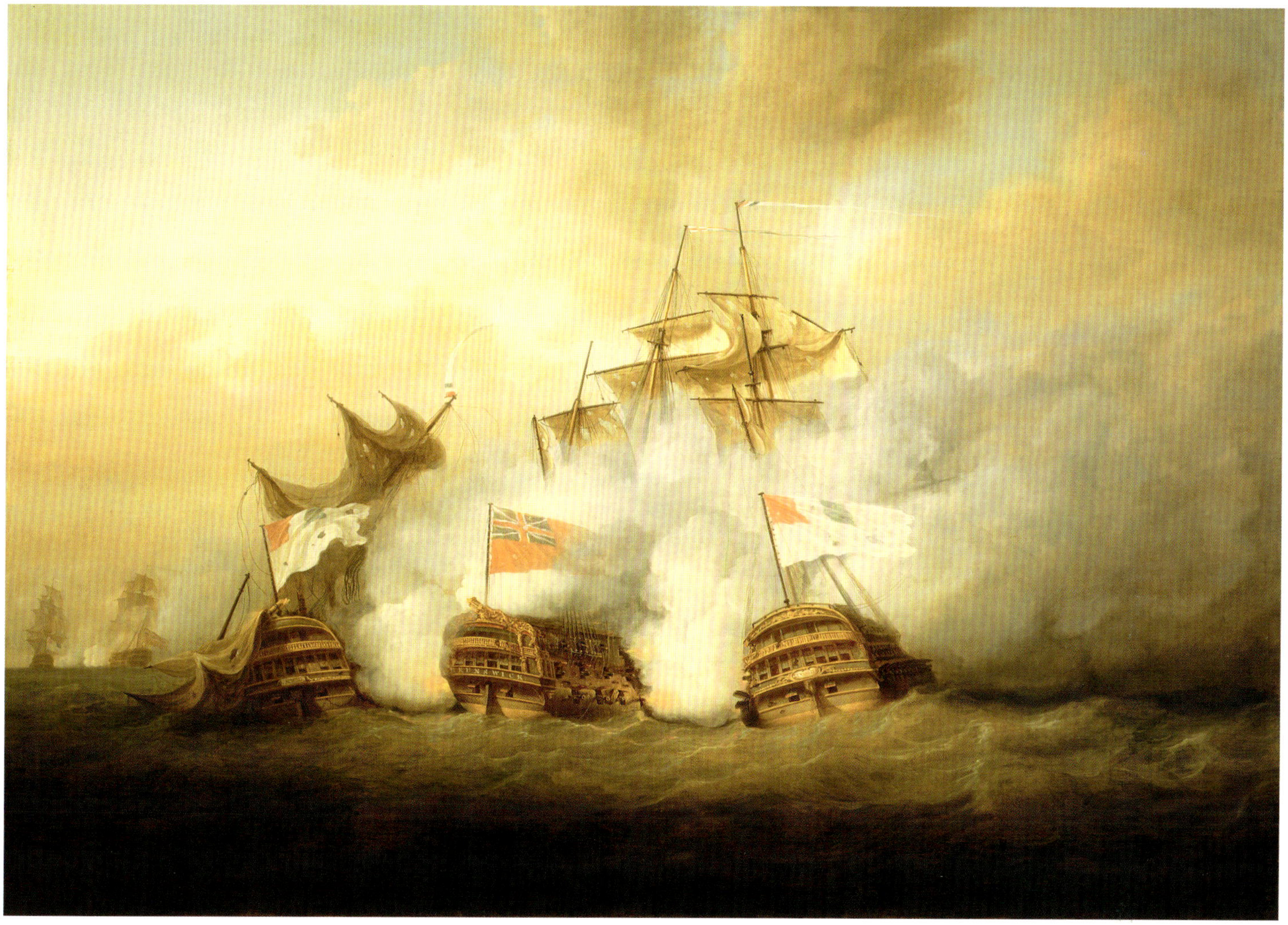

12

Nicholas Pocock

His Majesty's Ship the 'Brunswick' Engaging the 'Vengeur' on the First of June, 1794 1796

Oil on canvas 139.7 x 190 (55 x 74¾)

National Maritime Museum

Cordingly 1986, pp. 74–75, Hughes 2001, pp. 97–148

Pocock (1740–1821) represents the apogee of a distinctive British conception of marine painting that focused on the successive naval encounters of the late eighteenth century. The Third Battle of Ushant, more commonly known to British naval historians as the 'Glorious First of June', was the first major fleet action of the French Revolutionary War, fought 400 miles off the coast of Brittany. Although both sides were able to claim the event as a victory of sorts, the five-day battle culminated in the sinking of the 'Vengeur du Peuple' and the capture of six more French ships by the British fleet under the command of Admiral Lord Howe. The ferocity of the fight and its heavy casualties were reported widely, and within weeks numerous artists claimed to be in the process of making the first, or the most spectacular, or most accurate representation of the battle [53].

Pocock's canvas depicts a climactic encounter between three great fighting machines of eighteenth-century naval warfare. It is an unusually large painting for a sea action between only two or three ships, designed for exhibition and intended to be hung in a prominent position 'on the line' – the most advantageous place from which to be seen within the Great Room of the Royal Academy. The contrast between the carefully delineated naval architecture and an obscuring wall of gun smoke ensures that the critical details of the vessels remain legible, even as they are engulfed by the effects of their own destruction. According to long-standing tradition, Pocock reputedly witnessed the battle at first-hand, recording the encounter in an illustrated journal (now in the collection of the National Maritime Museum, JOD/12). However, the origins of the journal, and thus the assumption that Pocock had been present at the battle, have been convincingly challenged by Eleanor Hughes (Hughes 2001, pp. 97–148). Hughes also offers a closer reading of Pocock's inventive painting in her contribution to this book (pp. 52–55).

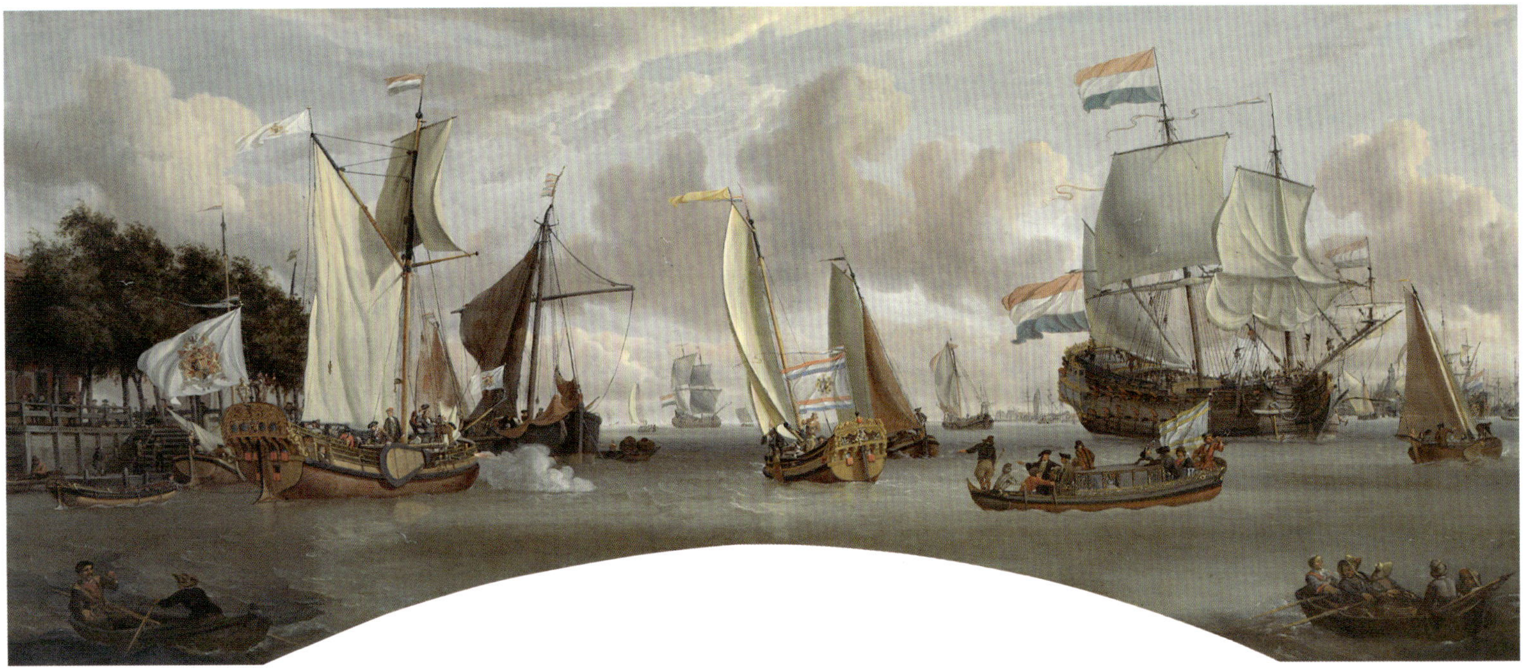

13

Abraham Storck

Ships on the IJ in front of the Tollhouse near Amsterdam c.1690

Oil on canvas 67.5 x 150.5 (26⅝ x 59¼)

National Maritime Museum

Gaschke 2008, no. 43; Quarm 2008; Solkin 2009, p. 231

This painting, also known as *River Scene with Shipping*, was the only identifiable maritime subject in the modest collection of paintings by other artists in Turner's possession at the time of his death. Following the example of Willem van de Velde the Younger and Ludolf Backhuysen in representing the industry and commotion of the Dutch maritime economy, Storck (1644–1708) offers a festive view of a state occasion (probably the arrival of a German prince) at the toll house on the IJ, a stretch of inland water that connected Amsterdam to the Zuiderzee. Relatively few works are known to have been owned by Turner, although the inclusion of Storck's harbour scene indicates that, like many artists, he acquired the work of other painters as part of the working apparatus of his studio. It has recently been noted that Turner used elements of Storck's painting, including the central yacht and the ship on the right, for his historical seascape *Admiral Van Tromp's Barge at the Entrance of the Texel, 1645* [84] (Quarm 2008). However, Turner knew the painting in an altered form, as a conventional rectangle with a more generous provision of sea and sky, after strips of canvas were added to the top and bottom in the early nineteenth century – possibly by a dealer preparing the work for the English market. These later additions were removed in 2007 by the National Maritime Museum's Conservation Department.

14

J.M.W. Turner

Fishermen at Sea 1796

Oil on canvas 91.4 x 122.2 (36 x 48⅛)

Tate

Finberg 1931; Butlin and Joll, no. 1; Warrell 2007, no. 3

Fishermen at Sea has been described as 'a summary of all that had been said about the sea by the artists of the eighteenth century' (Wilton 1987, p. 31). The complexity of Turner's painting was acknowledged when it appeared at the Royal Academy exhibition of 1796, in the reaction of the critic Anthony Pasquin, whose usual satirical mischief was halted temporarily by the painting (see 'The Battle of the Pictures', esp. pp. 52–53). Turner's first exhibited oil painting reveals in an understated style the young artist's command of the Continental tradition of maritime painting. Yet, while studious in its reflections on the art of the distant past, it is also insistent on its contemporary relevance, focusing attention on the south coast of England in a time of war and under the threat of invasion from across the Channel. The ongoing conflict with France, after almost a century of on-and-off hostility, ensured the continued and ever-more-public popularity of pictures of Britain's naval battles. The detailed observation of domestic fishing and the distant coastal profile, most likely Freshwater Bay in the Isle of Wight, are as implicated in the war effort as Pocock's *First of June* [12] exhibited in the same year.

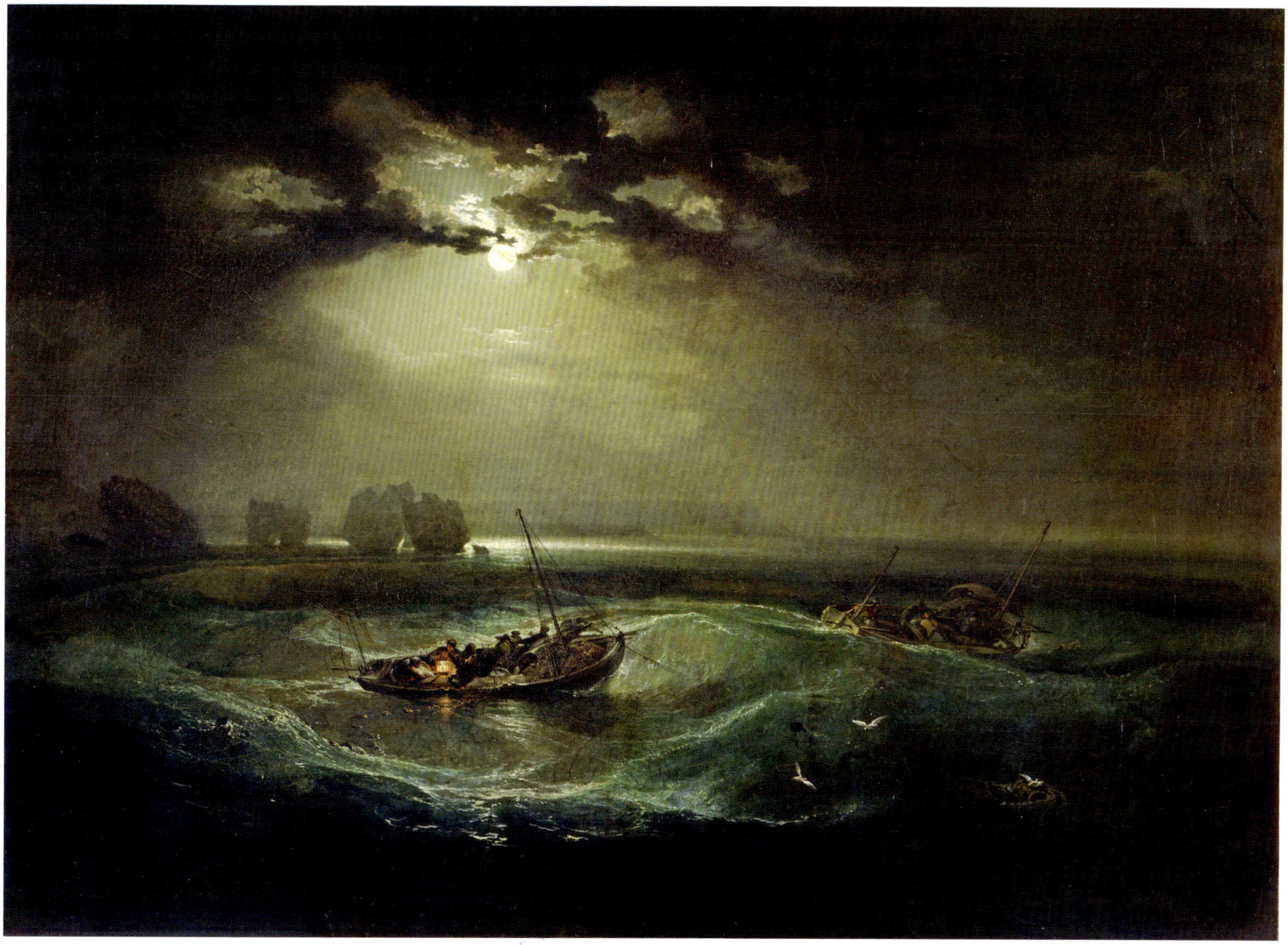

dimension of Turner's 'inconstant, boisterous' coastal swell, it is persuasively, literally translucent. Waves are rendered with shadows at the troughs and scribbles of pale green and blues at their peaks; and for the rest, the artist has simply allowed the buff-coloured ground to show through. In *Fishermen at Sea*, Turner used a similar technique, albeit to a lesser extent, perhaps learned from his contemporaries.

In July 1796, Pocock published a print dedicated 'to the memory of the Brave Captain John Harvey, the Officers & Crew, who fell in the Action, and to the Surviving Officers & Crew of His Majesty's ship the Brunswick' [fig. 9]. This image shows the two ships after the action, the 'Brunswick' in broadside view, her sailors working to repair rigging and hauling in tattered sails. It is a poignant, uncompromising picture with an almost palpable air of weariness, presenting an image of the devastation caused by such an encounter and the labour necessitated in its aftermath, seeming to suggest that war is inescapably a matter of the infliction of physical damage and its consequences. The emotional tenor in Pocock's depictions of the 'Brunswick' is not so far removed from that of *Fishermen at Sea* – the former presenting the realization of a threat that colours the mood of the latter.

The subsequent reception of Turner's debut painting has focused, on the one hand, on the professionalism of its technique and, on the other, on its signalling of Turner's lifelong preoccupation with the theme of man's subjugation to the forces of nature in general, 9
and the ocean in particular. Displayed in 1796, however, the southern coast depicted in *Fishermen at Sea* carried an additional, geopolitical significance. While the precise location of the scene has been debated, and although wartime fears were not at the pitch they would very shortly reach under the threat of direct invasion by Napoleonic forces, the mood set by Turner's solitary fishermen under a moonlit sky, with the English coast stretching into the distance, must also have been coloured by the anticipation of the human threat emanating from the dark, lowering distance as well as that from nature.

J.M.W. Turner
Fishermen at Sea 1796 (detail of [14])

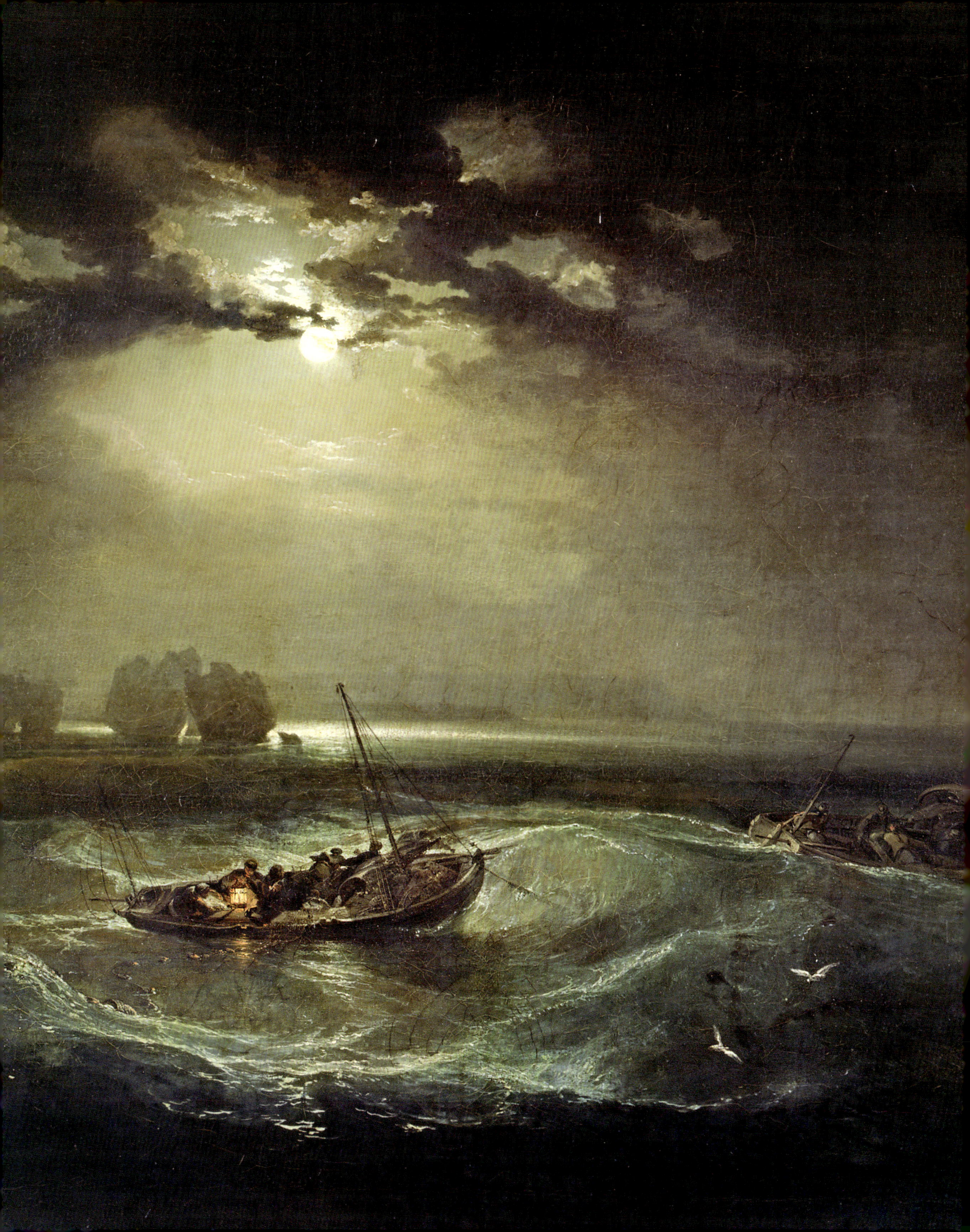

2

'M' FOR MARINE

Christine Riding

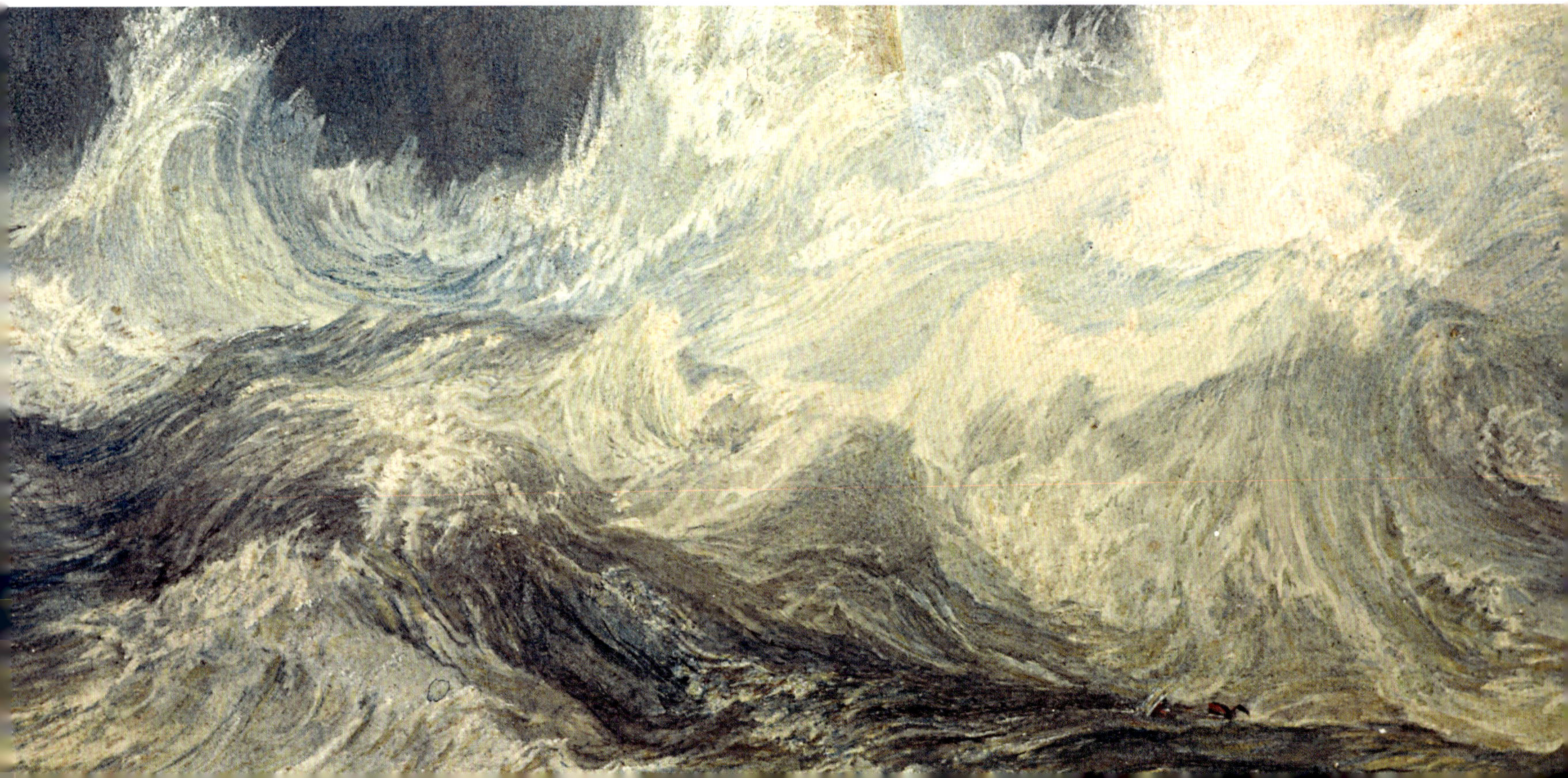

By 1806, Turner was developing ideas for an ambitious print project, to be called *Liber Studiorum* (Book of Studies). It was not only the earliest print series that he engaged in but was also financed entirely by the artist, who in addition oversaw every stage of its production. While Turner's specific intentions are unknown, the *Liber* can be said to function as a manifesto for contemporary British landscape art in general, and for Turner himself as a bold interpreter and innovator of admired traditions, including those associated with marine art.[1] At this point, Turner had been exhibiting paintings and watercolours for some fifteen years. But the impressive list of subscribers and the subsequent commercial success of the large-scale mezzotint of *The Shipwreck* (published 1807) – the first of Turner's paintings to be engraved – indicated the enormous potential for the print market to disseminate and promote his work and ideas further, as well as offering another source of income.

Turner's close involvement with the printmaking process during the *Liber* project meant that he employed and, in effect, trained a group of mezzotint engravers to produce landscapes, seascapes and coastal scenes of the highest quality.[2] Some, including Charles Turner (no relation) and Thomas Lupton, were to work on a number of other projects with Turner that were financed primarily by professional engravers and publishers. Crucially, it was through his extensive involvement with a range of ambitious print projects, and the unprecedented breadth and quality of the watercolours associated with them, that Turner was to achieve an international reputation.

'M' FOR MANIFESTO

The original scope for the *Liber Studiorum* was noted by the engraver John Landseer during a visit to Turner's studio in 1807. In his *Review of Publications of Art*, published the following year, Landseer made reference to a prospectus announcing 'Proposals for the publishing of one hundred Landscapes, to be designed and etched by J.M.W. Turner, R.A., and engraved in Mezzotinto.' The prospectus continues, 'It is intended in this publication to attempt a description of the various styles of landscape, viz., the historic, mountainous, pastoral, marine, and architectural.'[3] These categories would be differentiated by a letter at the top of each published print: 'H' for Historic, 'M' or 'Ms' for Mountainous, 'P' for Pastoral, 'M' for Marine, and 'A' for Architectural. Turner subsequently added a sixth category, 'EP', denoting 'Epic' or 'Elevated Pastoral'. The interrelationship between these various branches of landscape, and the challenge of achieving a numerical balance between them, is suggested by the example of *Dunstanborough Castle*, a coastal scene with a historic landmark, a subject-type well represented in Turner's early work. This plate was first conceived for the 'Marine' category of the *Liber Studiorum* but was eventually published under 'Architectural'.[4]

Initially conceived as a series of one hundred images, Turner's *Liber* project reached only seventy-one prints, published in fourteen parts between 1807 and 1819. In the event, the final marine print was *Entrance of Calais Harbour* [29], published in 1816, although it is not clear how many others, if any, Turner had originally envisaged. From both an intellectual and financial perspective, Turner must have hoped that subscribers would eventually acquire the whole series. However, by identifying 'Marine' as both distinct from and integrated into the broader category of landscape art, he was clearly attempting to define (or redefine) marine art, thus challenging the idea current in certain artistic quarters that maritime subjects were necessarily the preserve of a narrowly defined and specialist genre. The frontispiece to the *Liber Studiorum* [19] demonstrates this integration by including appropriate motifs associated with the marine, such as fish, a sail and oars, among others representing the five remaining categories.

The diverse range of images included in Turner's category of marine art, embracing port and coastal scenes, estuary views and even coastal defences and genre subjects, may have raised a few eyebrows among more established marine artists, such as Nicholas Pocock and John Thomas Serres. In 1805, Serres had published his own illustrated instructional manual of marine painting under the title *Liber Nauticus* [18], including several designs based on the work of his late father, Dominic (d. 1793). The relationship between Serres's project and Turner's is more intriguing (and the differences between them more striking) as Serres had been renting rooms at Turner's Harley Street house.[5] Addressing the 'Amateurs of Marine Drawing', the category of marine art promoted by the *Liber Nauticus* was underpinned by the knowledge and accurate representation of ships, especially those of the navy – the 'floating monuments of British Power'.[6] In stark contrast, Serres devoted only a few diagrams and very little text to methods of representing the sea and the elements in different conditions [fig. 10], although he acknowledged that a proficient marine artist should be 'acquainted with seamanship'.[7]

Given that Serres was at this time Marine Painter to the King (he succeeded his father to the post in 1793) and marine draughtsman to the Admiralty, we might assume that his *Liber Nauticus* represented an official view of the art in naval circles, drawing heavily on the highly successful career and reputation of his father. Not that Turner excluded more conventional and established marine subjects from his *Liber Studiorum*: for example, *Ships in a Breeze* [21 and 22], 'The Leader Sea Piece' [23] and *Calm* [28] all, to a greater or lesser degree, underline his familiarity with the existing conventions of maritime art represented in the *Liber Nauticus*. Naval battle painting, a mainstay of marine art as practised by Serres and Pocock (and even occasionally Turner), did not feature at all in Turner's *Liber* as published. That the category 'Marine' was a slightly baggier term in the wider art world than Serres's publication would have us believe, is demonstrated by Turner's inclusion of *Scene on the French Coast* [20], *Coast of Yorkshire* [24] and *Entrance of Calais Harbour*, which, as coastal and port scenes, look to seventeenth- and eighteenth-century Dutch and French models.

Another point on which the two *Liber* projects found common ground is that marine art, while always informed by the art of the past, engaged primarily with the local and the contemporary. This is reflected in the quotidian and topographical detail that pervades 'Marine' and other categories such as 'Pastoral', and (remembering that Turner's *Liber* project began in about 1806) subjects that are directly concerned with the ongoing Napoleonic War, national defence, ship building and the navy.[8] One of Turner's most contemporary images in this context is *Martello Towers, near Bexhill, Sussex* [26], published in 1811, when some of these defensive forts along the southern coast of England were still under construction. Indeed, *Martello Towers* was later reproduced as one of a series of *Picturesque Views on the Southern Coast of England* (1814–26) – Turner's first collaboration with the brothers William Bernard and George Cooke, who were professional engravers and publishers – underlining the potential transferability between the *Liber*'s marine themes and the British subjects and locations represented in the artist's other, overtly topographical print projects.

As a 'Book of Studies', the *Liber Studiorum* must be understood in parallel with Turner's professional ambitions and standing within the Royal Academy and the Academy Schools in the early years of the nineteenth century. After becoming a full member of the Academy in 1802, Turner was appointed Professor of Perspective in 1807 and presented his first lectures to the Academy students in 1811. Furthermore, as recorded by the landscape artist and diarist Joseph Farington, Turner seems also to have been promoting the idea for a new position, Professor of Landscape Painting.[9] That he sought to address collectors and connoisseurs, as well as artists and students, is indicated by the title he chose for the series, which associated the project with a revered artistic tradition and, by association, with a thriving contemporary trade in old masters in the London art market. It should be noted that this contrasts dramatically with the rather narrow group of 'amateurs' that J.T. Serres had sought to engage through his *Liber Nauticus*.

The *Liber Studiorum* finds some parallels with other recent volumes of engravings after old master collections, such as *The Beauties of the Dutch School*, published in 1793, which showcased the work of leading Dutch land- and seascape painters from the seventeenth century. However, the most immediate model for the *Liber Studiorum* was the prestigious *Liber Veritatis* (Book of Truth) by the seventeenth-century French classicist Claude Lorrain. Initiated by Claude as a register of his compositions, reputedly as a safeguard against imitations and fraud, the *Liber Veritatis* came to represent a study book or, as described by Claude's early biographer Filippo Baldinucci, a book of inspiration for the artist himself.[10] Claude's *Liber* was reproduced by Richard Earlom and published in two volumes by John Boydell in 1777 [fig. 14] (a third volume was produced in 1819), and dedicated to successive Dukes of Devonshire, in whose collection the original drawings were held.[11] Both Turner and Serres would have known the *Liber Veritatis* through Boydell's successful publication (and it is possible that Turner owned his own copy).[12] By the end of the eighteenth century, the number and quality of paintings and drawings by Claude in the private collections of the British aristocracy and landed gentry rivalled any other country in Europe.

MODERN MASTER

Unlike Claude, Turner had always intended his *Liber* to be accessible to a broad public, engaging with Boydell's *Liber Veritatis*, other drawing books and handbooks, such as the *Liber Nauticus* and John Laporte's *The Progress of a Water-Coloured Drawing* (1802), and more generally the luxury print trade. The technique that Earlom had employed for Boydell's *Liber Veritatis* was mezzotint, which, as stated on the title page of the first volume, was thought to be the most appropriate to the original drawings that had been executed by Claude in pen and brown/black washes. Thus Turner's prints in mezzotint

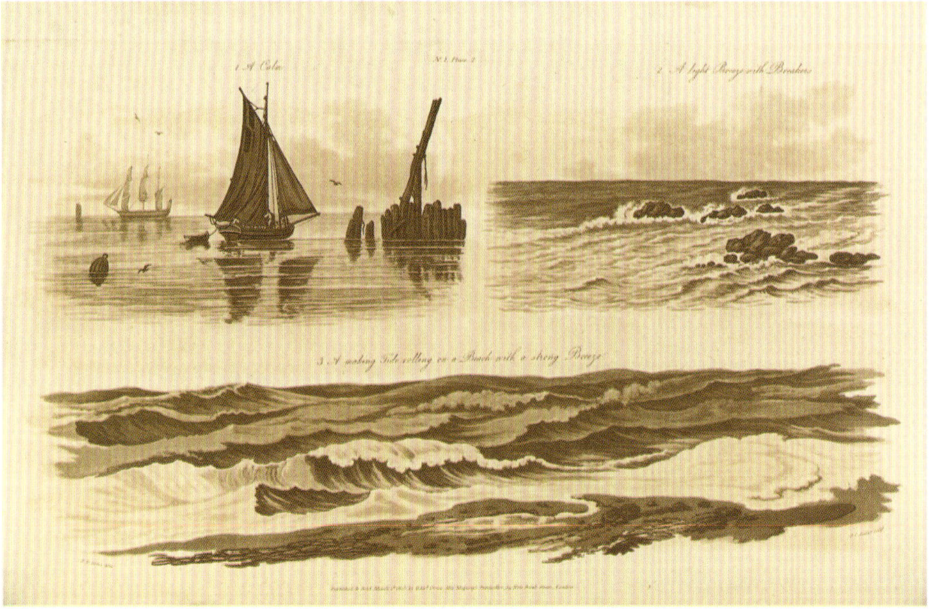

Fig. 10

Dominic Serres the Younger and John Thomas Serres
Liber Nauticus 1805
Aquatint 47.5 x 33 (18¾ x 13)
National Maritime Museum

and his preparatory drawings bear some resemblance to both Claude's originals and Earlom's reproductions. However, the quality of the *Liber Studiorum* prints far outstrips Earlom's – no doubt as Turner intended they should.

Developed from the seventeenth century, mezzotint had the reputation of being the most 'painterly' of print techniques, one that could best represent the painted image, through subtle gradations and velvety texture and effect. Indeed, to an early nineteenth-century viewer, such a technique would have given the contemporary image an artistic pedigree. Given that Turner expended money, time and energy overseeing and correcting every stage of the print production, even learning a number of print-making techniques as the project progressed, we must conclude that for him (as Andrew Wilton has recently observed), printing was not merely mechanical reproduction but a more nuanced process of translation from the original designs, executed primarily in watercolour, to the finished print.[13] On this point, we should be particularly attentive to two of the marine subjects, *Calm* and *Entrance of Calais Harbour*, which were engraved by Turner himself.

Perhaps unsurprisingly, Turner also favoured mezzotint for publishing his paintings, from *The Shipwreck* in 1807 until the late 1820s.[14] Mezzotint had particular associations with marine art in Britain, more specifically through the well-known print series after van de Velde and Peter Monamy published by Elisha Kirkall in the 1720s and 1730s [17]. Through the deliberate fusion of the traditional and contemporary inherent in the marine category – indeed, the whole *Liber Studiorum* project – and by his selection of mezzotint, therefore, Turner was integrating himself seamlessly into this tradition. As published, the *Liber* prints are mezzotint over an etched outline, but Turner was to explore the artistic possibilities of pure mezzotint still further in the 1820s with the so-called 'Little Liber' series. The majority of these are marine subjects [31–38].

Turner's tactic throughout the *Liber Studiorum* was to promote his range as a landscape artist, through original and adapted compositions, and, on a more limited level, to make reference among the plates to specific works and existing patrons. This is particularly marked in the marine category. Turner adapted two known paintings, *Ships Bearing up for Anchorage* (see [21]), owned by the Earl of Egremont, and *Fishing Boats Entering Calais Harbour,* which was probably in Turner's possession at the time (see [29]). And he refers to two further patrons with the so-called 'Leader Sea Piece' [23] and 'Mildmay Sea Piece' [27]. The unpublished plates and preparatory drawings also included adaptations of Turner's first exhibited oil painting, *Fishermen at Sea* [14] and *The 'Victory' Returning from Trafalgar* [fig. 20], painted in about 1806 and owned by his friend and patron Walter Fawkes. Turner's focus on extant works and patrons within the marine category may simply indicate, as Gillian Forrester has suggested, that Turner 'still regarded himself primarily as a painter of marine subjects at that point in his career'.[15] Forrester's suggestion relates specifically to the fact that Turner's early draft design for the *Liber* frontispiece, dating from about 1806 to 1810, had a marine subject as its centrepiece.[16]

Turner's pointed references to individual artistic models and his patrons may have had another purpose. While he had made the transition from promising newcomer to leading artistic talent in a matter of a few years, he had also come under fire from the critics, especially from the influential connoisseur and art patron Sir George Beaumont, whose ire was directed at some of Turner's early exhibited seascapes and classical landscapes. Beaumont's criticisms of Turner largely hinged on the artist's flagrant disregard (as he saw it) of the old master tradition.[17] Such criticism, openly voiced, coupled with the formation in 1805 of the British Institution – a rival exhibiting space to the Royal Academy sponsored by Beaumont and other connoisseurs – may have spurred Turner, as an artist and a committed Royal Academician, into setting out his intellectual and artistic credentials via an ambitious and potentially provocative project such as the *Liber Studiorum*. We might even suggest that the naming of individual patrons within the *Liber* was a signal of support for his approach among discerning collectors of contemporary British art. Thus, we can see how this project deliberately confronted issues surrounding both Turner's work and the status of the British landscape school in comparison with that of the old masters. Beaumont and others also promoted a hierarchy within the old master tradition itself, with the 'ideal' of the classicist tradition, represented by Claude and Nicolas Poussin, taking precedence over the 'lowly' naturalism that was thought to characterize Dutch art, as represented by Willem van de Velde and Aelbert Cuyp. The *Liber Studiorum* integrated all these traditions, making the specific point that old masters ought to be sources of inspiration for contemporary artists, not models to be slavishly copied. Turner, after all, had made this exact point in 1801 with his *Dutch Boats in a Gale* as a pendant to van de Velde's *A Rising Gale* (see pp. 31–35). Although old master models can be detected, the only existing works adapted by Turner in the *Liber Studiorum* are his own.

The artistic tradition most apparent within the marine category is that of the seventeenth-century Dutch school, in particular Cuyp and van de Velde [4 and 5]. However, scholars have discussed the *Liber Studiorum* as a compendium of both past and present artists.[18] Hence allusions can be found to a wide range of contemporary and near-contemporary painters, including Thomas Gainsborough, Paul Sandby, Philip James de Loutherbourg, Thomas Girtin, George Morland and Augustus Wall Callcott. Given Turner's perennial competitiveness, the reference to his peers has also led to the idea of the *Liber Studiorum* as a vehicle for his professional rivalries.[19] Whether a homage or a challenge, the *Coast of Yorkshire*, published in 1811, certainly bears a resemblance to the stormy coastal scenes characteristic of Morland and de Loutherbourg. Similarly, the inclusion of a coastal scene with children playing, entitled *Marine Dabblers* [25], could refer to the kind of figure groups that feature in London river scenes painted by eighteenth-century British marine artists: for example, in Samuel Scott's *A Thames Wharf* (about 1757, Victoria and Albert Museum), or alternatively those populating the coastal scenes of Gainsborough [8] and Morland. Yet the presence of *Marine Dabblers* – with two other genre scenes involving children within the *Liber* – was perhaps a more calculated act, given the death of Morland in 1804 and, soon after, in 1806, the triumphant debut at the Royal Academy by the young genre painter David Wilkie with *Village Politicians* (private collection). Wilkie, it should be noted, enjoyed the support of George Beaumont at this time. Moreover, he was heralded as the heir to seventeenth-century Dutch and Flemish genre painting. On one level, therefore, the inclusion of *Marine Dabblers* acts as a riposte to Wilkie and perhaps the claims made by his supporters, most notably Beaumont.

PICTURESQUE TOURS

The *Liber Studiorum* occupied Turner for at least thirteen years, certainly up to 1819. During this time he was invited to participate in a number of commercial print projects, which were financed primarily by professional engravers and publishers, in particular William Bernard and George Cooke. These have been largely understood as quite separate enterprises from the *Liber Studiorum*. This may be due to the fact that the *Liber*, a high-minded and self-financed project, proved not to be a commercial success and, owing to the paucity of published responses, seems to have been relatively little known during Turner's lifetime. A caveat to the above observation is that the project was admired by some collectors, print connoisseurs and artists, in particular by David Cox, John Sell Cotman and John Constable. Indeed, the *Liber Studiorum* was the starting point for Constable's own mezzotint series, *English Landscape Scenery*, published from 1830 [fig. 11].[20]

The inherent didacticism of the *Liber Studiorum*, and its overall focus on variety of composition and effect, must have informed Turner's approach to more commercial projects, if only to demonstrate how the ideas within the *Liber* could be practically and commercially applied. This is important for two reasons. Firstly, all these projects (to varying degrees) followed and adapted an existing print format, which involved a sequence of topographical views. Such a format, first established in the narrow antiquarian print market, had become more widely disseminated by the end of the eighteenth century through the broader appeal of topographical projects such as Paul Sandby's *XII Views in South Wales* (1775), and Joseph Farington's *Views of Lakes of Cumberland and Westmorland* (1785) and *History of the River Thames* (1794). Certainly Turner's early experience in topographical work would have been invaluable preparation for designing in sets or series of images. Secondly, many of these print projects include marine subjects as defined by the *Liber Studiorum*, for example, in *Picturesque Views on the Southern Coast of England* (1814–26), *The Provincial Antiquities and Picturesque Scenery of Scotland* (1819–26), *The Rivers of England* (1822–26) and *Picturesque Views in England and Wales* (1825–38), or had a specific marine focus, such as *Marine Views* (1822–24), *The Ports of England* (1825–28) and *Picturesque Views on the East Coast of England* (about 1827).

To give some specific examples, *Stangate Creek, on the River Medway* [42] accords with the *Liber*'s marine plate entitled *Calm*; *Ramsgate* [48] and *Sheerness* [49] correspond to *Calais Harbour* and 'The Leader Sea Piece' respectively; and *Dunwich* [50] is a variation on the theme of the *Coast of Yorkshire*. Returning to the same subjects and revising compositions over a period of time was a feature of Turner's artistic practice. A case in point is St Michael's Mount, an impressive landmark on the Cornish coast, which was included in the *Southern Coast* series (the watercolour is dated about 1811), after which Turner exhibited a variation of the composition as a painting at the Royal Academy in 1834 and then adapted and included it in the *England and Wales* series in the late 1830s [52]. Of course, repetition and even replication, especially of such notable landmarks and historic sites, was a feature of topographical art and publishing, a situation that would only become more pronounced as time went on. As one scholar has recently

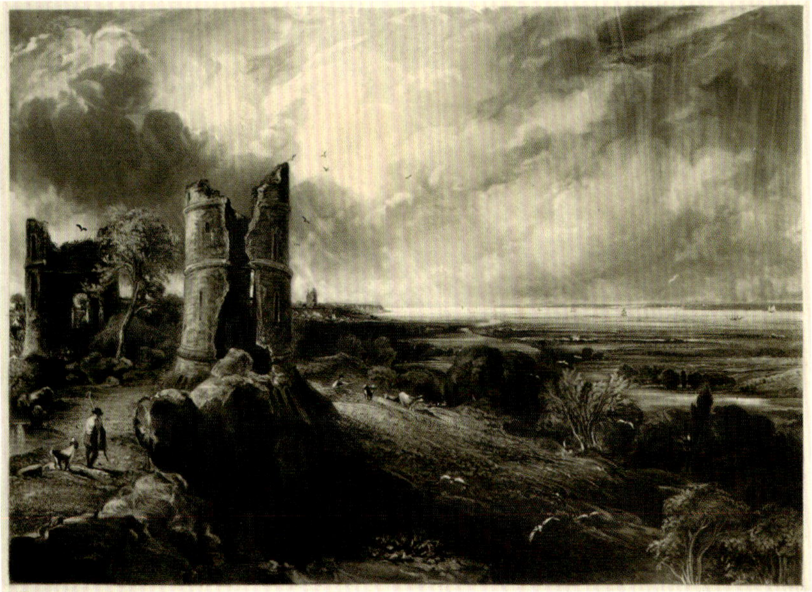

Fig. 11

David Lucas after John Constable
Hadleigh Castle c.1830
Mezzotint and drypoint 26.8 x 36.4 (10½ x 14⅜)
Royal Academy

calculated, fifty-eight out of ninety-six published subjects in Turner's *England and Wales* series can be found in Henry Boswell's *Picturesque Views of the Antiquities of England and Wales* (1796).[21] Turner's challenge, therefore, was to introduce variety into this already established topographical tradition through the example of the *Liber Studiorum*.

That the *Liber Studiorum* was not isolated from the character of other late eighteenth-century topographical print projects, is especially evident in the marine category: all of the prints relate to the coastline of the British Isles except in two instances of the northern coast of France. This can be explained in part by Turner's limited experience of travelling abroad, like many of his contemporaries, prior to the end of the Napoleonic War in 1815. It also reflected a broader trend in the print market for specifically British subjects and the related growth in domestic tourism.[22] The idea of the 'picturesque tour' had been popularized from the late 1760s, above all by the writings of the Reverend William Gilpin, an amateur artist and connoisseur. In his *Observations on the Coasts of Hampshire, Sussex and Kent ... made in the summer of 1774*, published posthumously in 1804, Gilpin noted that,

> In coast scenery ... if its character be preserved distinct, the ideas of grandeur rise very high. Winding bays – view of the sea – promontories – rocks of every kind and form – estuaries – mouths of rivers – islands – shooting peninsulas – extensive sandbanks; and all these adorned occasionally with castles – light-houses – distant towns – towers – harbours – all the furniture of navigation, and other incidental circumstances which belong to sea-coasts, form the rich collection of grand and picturesque materials.

He concluded, 'that a circuit round our own island, to collect the several scenes it presents, would furnish a few volumes of drawings and verbal description, as amusing perhaps, as could be collected from any other coasts.'[23] The wealthy landowner Sir Uvedale Price, a rival exponent of the picturesque in the 1790s, also saw the potential in the coast for both touring and picture making. While the waters of lakes and rivers could offer the viewer an appropriately picturesque experience, Price was particularly taken by the thrill provoked by the sea breaking against rocky outcrops. 'The sublimity of such a picture,' he wrote in *Essay on the Picturesque* (1794), 'absorbs all idea of lesser ornaments; for no one can view the foam, the gulphs, the impetuous motion of that world of waters, without a deep impression of its destructive and irresistible power.'[24]

Despite the ample material highlighted by both Gilpin and Price, the coastline of Britain seems to have been relatively under-represented in both travel guides and in topographical prints at this time. Even in 1814, the writer Richard Ayton could make the claim that, 'While the inlands of England have been so hackneyed by travellers and quartos, the Coast has hitherto been unaccountably neglected, and, if we except a few fashionable watering-places, is entirely unknown to the public.' This state of affairs seemed especially remarkable to Ayton given that 'So many associations flattering to our [national] pride are connected with every view of our seas and shores.'[25] Ayton's comments formed part of his introduction to the first volume of William Daniell's *A Voyage Round Great Britain*, an extraordinarily ambitious print project that contained over three hundred aquatints by the time it was completed in 1825. Daniell's *Voyage* series and the Cookes's contemporaneous *Southern Coast* were to some degree rival projects – the latter was originally planned to depict the whole of the coast of England. Despite covering similar ground, however, the resulting images could hardly be more different (see [fig. 12] and [39 and 40]).

It was the usual practice for landscape artists to make sketching trips, gathering on-the-spot material for present and future projects: Turner, for whom first-hand observation was an imperative, would conduct many such 'working' trips over the summer months, both in Britain and in Europe. However, Daniell's succession of five tours around the coast of Britain was given a heroic gloss via Ayton's introductory text because of the hardships the two encountered en route: 'rapid tides, ground-swells, insurmountable surfs, strong winds, and foul winds, are among the catalogue of horrors on the coast.'[26] Despite the evident

Fig. 12

William Daniell
The Long-ships Light House, off the Lands End, Cornwall 1814
Coloured aquatint 16.2 x 24.1 (6⅜ x 9½)
National Maritime Museum

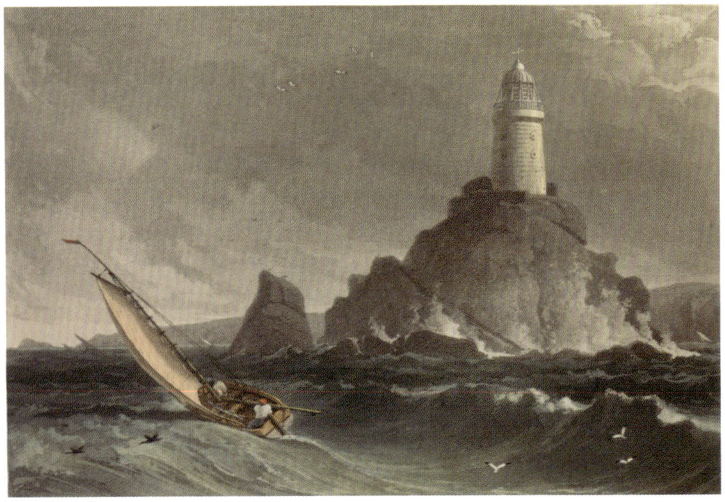

Fig. 13

J.M.W. Turner
Long Ship's Lighthouse, Land's End c.1834–35
Watercolour and bodycolour 28.5 x 43.9 (11¼ x 17¼)
The J. Paul Getty Museum

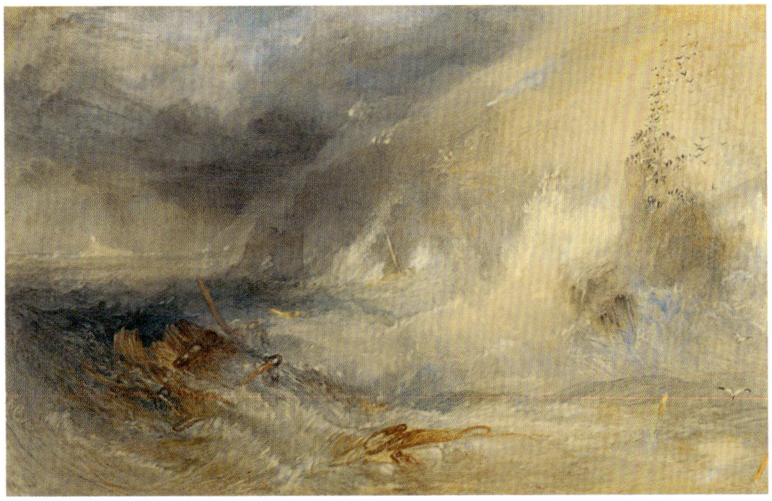

changeability of the coastal climate, Daniell's aquatints as a whole represent a much narrower range of weather conditions than Turner's varied watercolours. The overall tone of Daniell's series also errs towards the documentary and seems to gain authority by the sheer number of images, as he 'maps' the coastline. In contrast, Turner was particularly attentive to the notion of variety within the sequential format, complementing the ever-shifting viewpoints with contrasting times of day and weather patterns, as the viewer moves from one image to the next. Furthermore, in exploring the scenic potential of the coast and the richness of its communities and cultural associations, Turner imbues his coastal scenes with greater narrative depth. In fact, the distance between his approach and that of more conventional topographical projects, including Daniell's, was to become ever greater. The former achieved a high point of sophistication in the 1830s with the *England and Wales* series, in such images as *Long Ship's Lighthouse, Land's End* [fig. 13]. Whereas Daniell's view of the same location [fig. 12] focuses on the commanding presence of the lighthouse – underlining its effectiveness in saving lives – Turner seems to suggest the exact opposite by placing the tower in the distance and introducing wreckage in the foreground (see pp. 100–101).

Even though other established artists were involved in the *Southern Coast* project, it soon was apparent to the Cooke brothers that Turner's illustrations were by far the most innovative and accomplished. As a result, his initial commission for twenty-four watercolours was raised to a total of forty, making Turner the central artistic figure of the whole series.[27] Its critical and financial success encouraged W.B. Cooke to develop further projects during the 1820s with Turner as the sole contributor. Cooke staged a series of public exhibitions between 1821 and 1824 at his premises in Soho Square, London, that showcased Turner's work.[28] In 1821, the display included some prints after the artist's *Southern Coast* works, and from 1822 original watercolours from a number of different series were shown. In that year, for example, *Weymouth, Dorsetshire* [39] was exhibited, and in 1823 the large-scale watercolours of Dover [43] and Margate [45].

Although the original ambition of the *Liber Studiorum* may have been curtailed, Turner's intellectual and financial investment in the project found an outlet through these more commercial initiatives, by underpinning the terms upon which an elevated idea of land- and seascape art could be translated onto the printed page. In turn, as the *Liber Studorium* became more widely appreciated, the prefix 'Liber', increasingly associated with Turner as much as with Claude, began to be used by others to signal a certain type of pictorial series that, in subject and ambition, aspired to the achievements of both artists. For example, *Liber Naturae*, published in 1823–24, was a collection of prints after the work of Turner's early friend and rival Thomas Girtin, and Turner's own *Rivers of France* series was republished in 1853 as the *Liber Fluviorum*.

15

Claude Lorrain

Harbour Scene with a Lighthouse and a Portico c.1638–41

Etching 14 x 19.7 (5½ x 7¾)

British Museum

Mannocci 1988, no. 37

Turner greatly admired Claude (1604/5–82), with whom he had an artistic dialogue that was to last his whole career. His responses to Claude's compositions tended to relate to the earlier artist's biblical and classical landscapes and seaports, reflected in the *Liber Studiorum* by the most overtly 'Claudean' plates within the 'Epic' or 'Elevated Pastoral' category. However, the *Liber Veritatis* contains a small group of contemporary harbour scenes and images of storm at sea and shipwreck, all core subjects in European marine art [fig. 14].

The two etchings by Claude included here are closely related to scenes represented in the *Liber Veritatis*. Like Rembrandt van Rijn, Claude was one of several highly regarded painter-printmakers of the seventeenth century. Thus Turner's *Liber* project benefited from the name and reputation of Claude's *Liber Veritatis*. Furthermore, like Claude, Turner retained creative and commercial control over his work by including printmaking as a central aspect of his artistic practice.

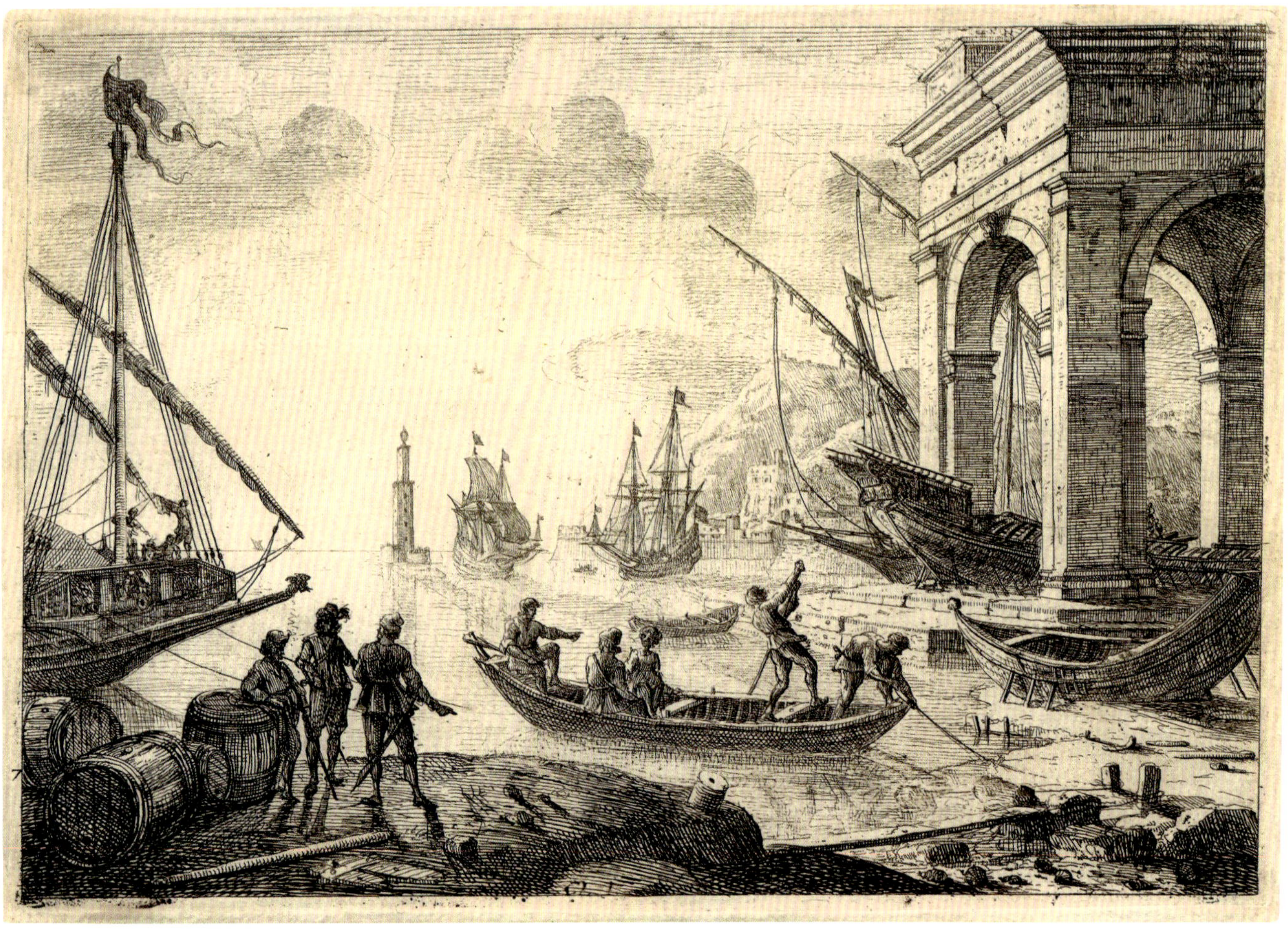

Fig. 14

Richard Earlom after Claude Lorrain
A Sea View in a Brisk Gale
Plate 74 in *Liber Veritatis*, volume 1
Mezzotint 20.8 x 25.9 (8¼ x 10¼)
Published by John Boydell, London, 1777
British Library

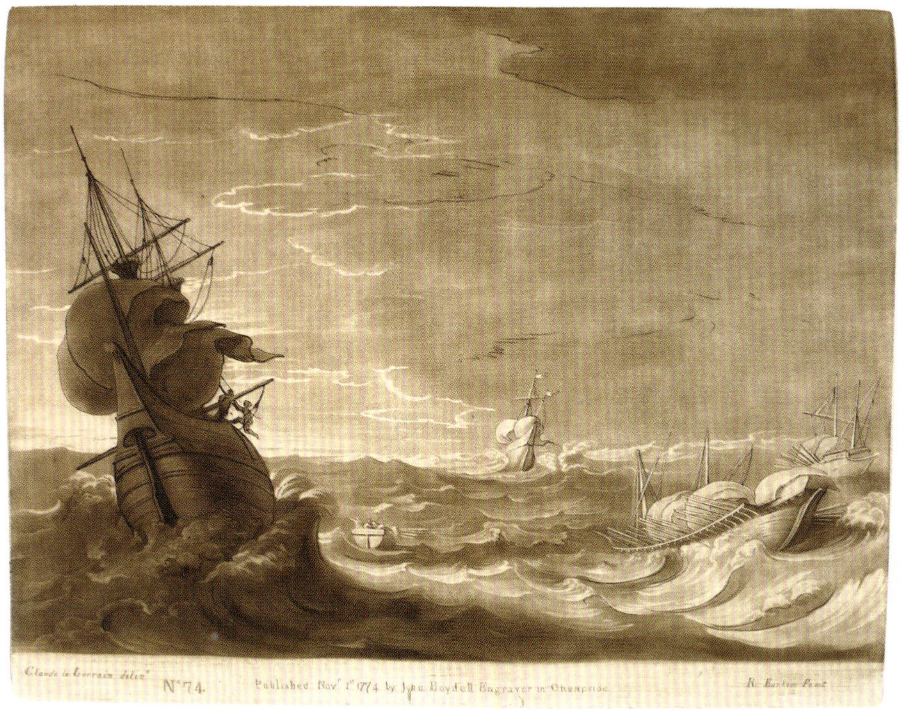

16

Claude Lorrain
The Shipwreck c.1638–41
Etching 12.6 x 18 (5 x 7⅛)
British Museum

Mannocci 1988, no. 35

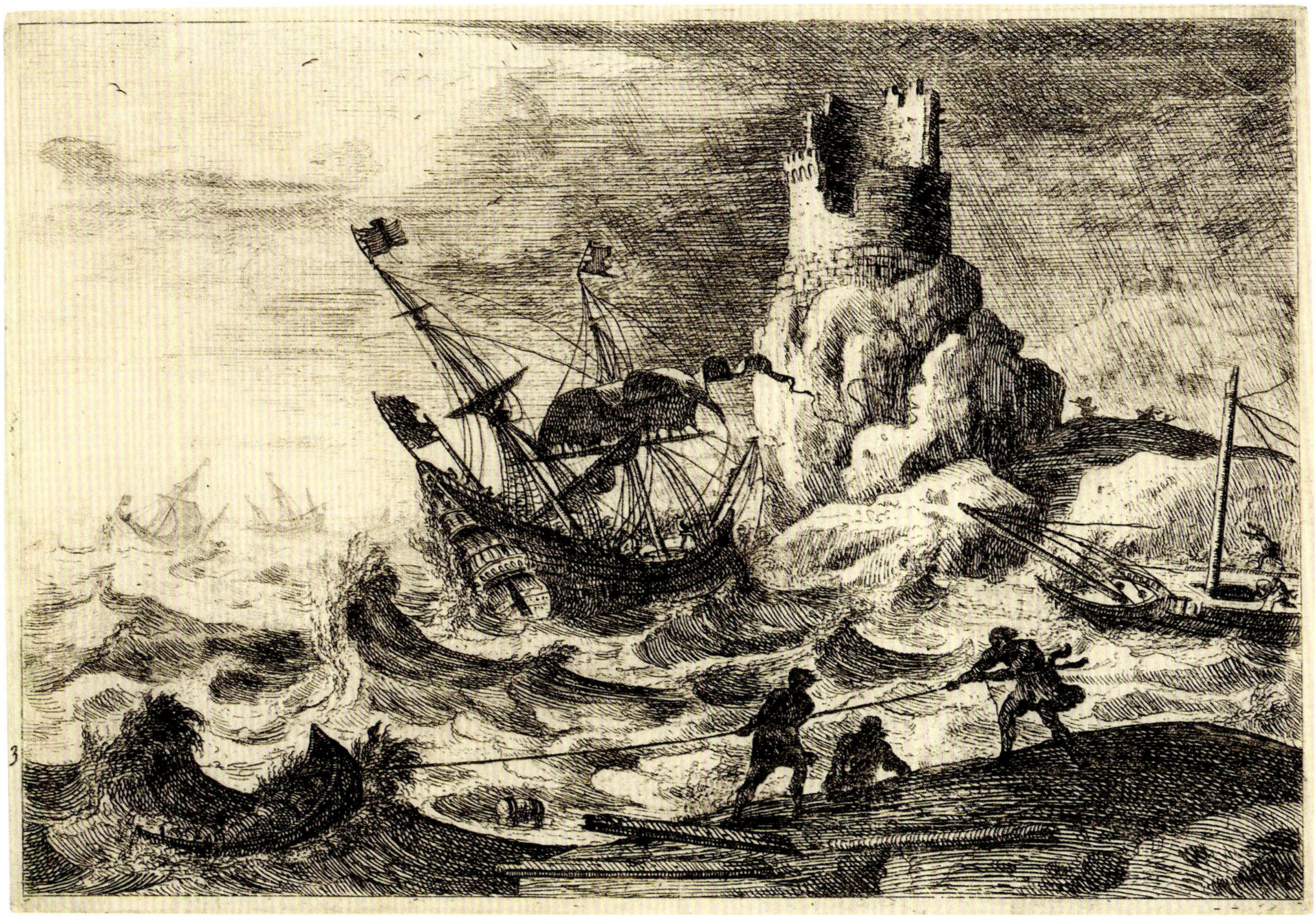

17

Elisha Kirkall after Willem van de Velde the Younger
A Ship Scudding in a Gale c.1726
Mezzotint in green ink 43.2 x 31.1 (17 x 12¼)
National Maritime Museum

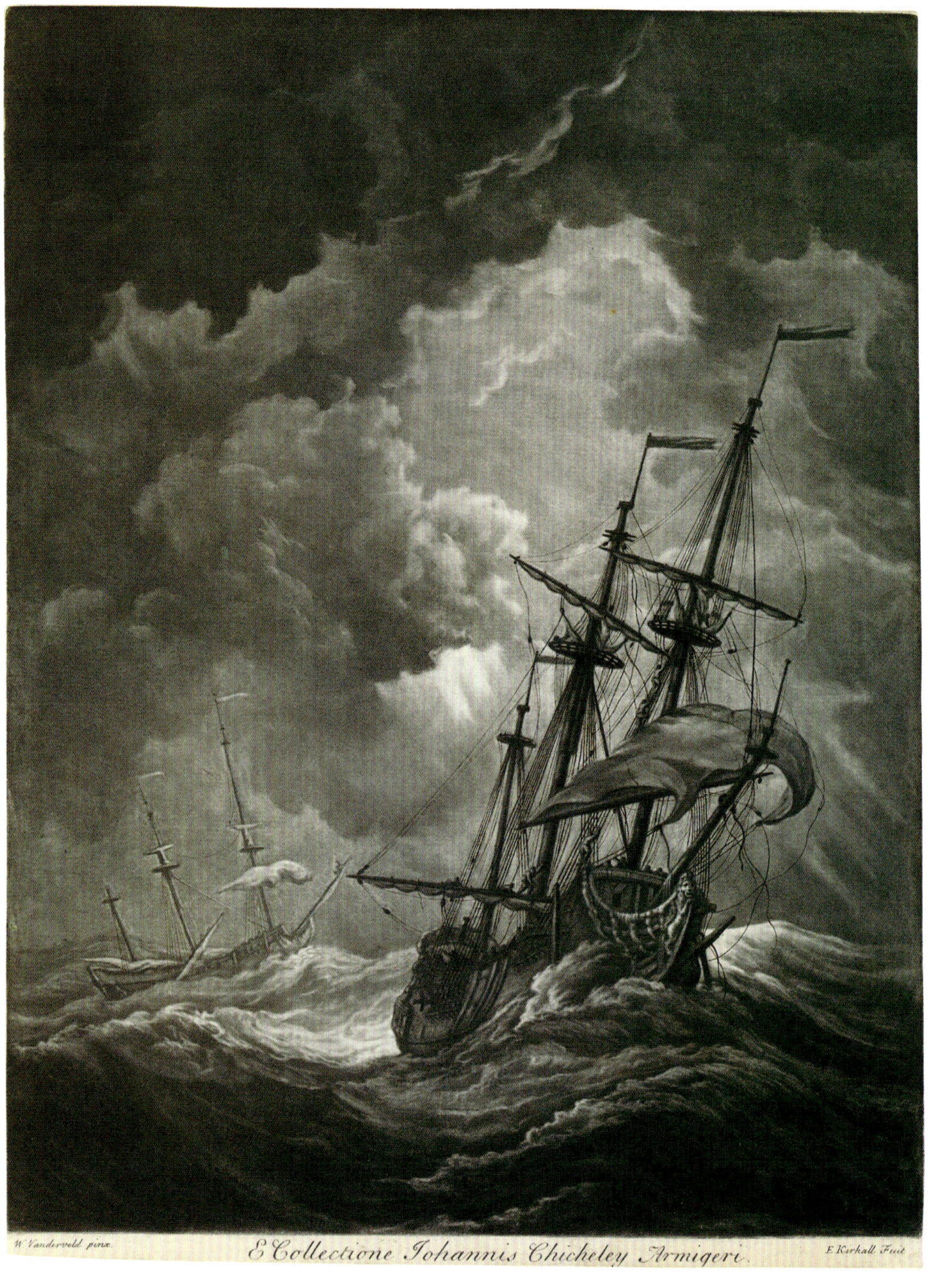

Surprisingly, the work of van de Velde the Younger was rarely (if ever) reproduced during his lifetime. In the years following his death, however, the artist's work became more widely known through prints, especially those published by the inventive printmaker Elisha Kirkall. Taken from a painting formerly in the collection of Sir John Chicheley, an admiral in Charles II's navy, this print forms part of a series of sixteen mezzotints after the younger van de Velde that Kirkall produced and sold by subscription in the 1720s. The series encapsulated the Dutch artist's popularity in England a generation after his death, and showcased the range of his maritime subjects, comprising 'Storms, Calms, Gales, Shipwrecks, Sea-Fights, Moon-Lights, Sea-Ports, &c. Collected from the Closets of the Curious' (*Mist's Weekly Journal*, 27 November 1725). According to the eighteenth-century writer on art George Vertue, Kirkall reportedly made close to £1000 from the project – far more than the value of any of the original paintings – and he followed its success with a similar series of seascapes after Peter Monamy, helping to secure the British artist's reputation as the foremost heir of the van de Velde tradition. Turner openly acknowledged the great importance of the work of van de Velde for his own career, and Kirkall's mezzotint is most probably the image that, later in life, prompted the artist's eloquent and often-quoted response upon seeing a print after the Dutch artist: 'Ah! That made me a painter' (Thornbury 1862, vol.1, p. 8).

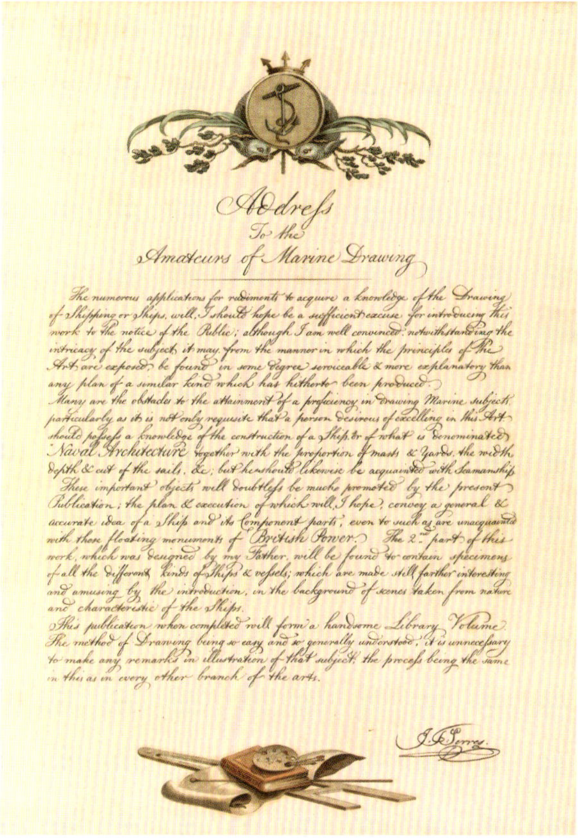

Addreſs
To the
Amateurs of Marine Drawing

The numerous applications for rudiments to acquire a knowledge of the Drawing of Shipping or Ships, will, I should hope be a sufficient excuse for introducing this work to the notice of the Public; although I am well convinced, notwithstanding the intricacy of the subject, it may, from the manner in which the principles of the Art are exposed, be found in some degree serviceable & more explanatory than any plan of a similar kind which has hitherto been produced.

Many are the obstacles to the attainment of a proficiency in drawing Marine subjects, particularly as it is not only requisite that a person desirous of excelling in this Art should poſseſs a knowledge of the construction of a Ship, or of what is denominated Naval Architecture together with the proportion of masts & Yards, the width, depth & cut of the sails, &c; but he should likewise be acquainted with Seamanship.

These important objects will doubtleſs be much promoted by the present Publication; the plan & execution of which will, I hope, convey a general & accurate idea of a Ship and its Component parts, even to such as are unacquainted with those floating monuments of British Power. The 2nd part of this work, which was designed by my Father, will be found to contain specimens of all the different kinds of Ships & veſsels; which are made still farther interesting and amusing by the introduction, in the background of scenes taken from nature and characteristic of the Ships.

This publication when completed will form a handsome Library Volume. The method of Drawing being so easy and so generally understood, it is unneceſsary to make any remarks in illustration of that subject, the proceſs being the same in this as in every other branch of the arts.

J. T. Serres.

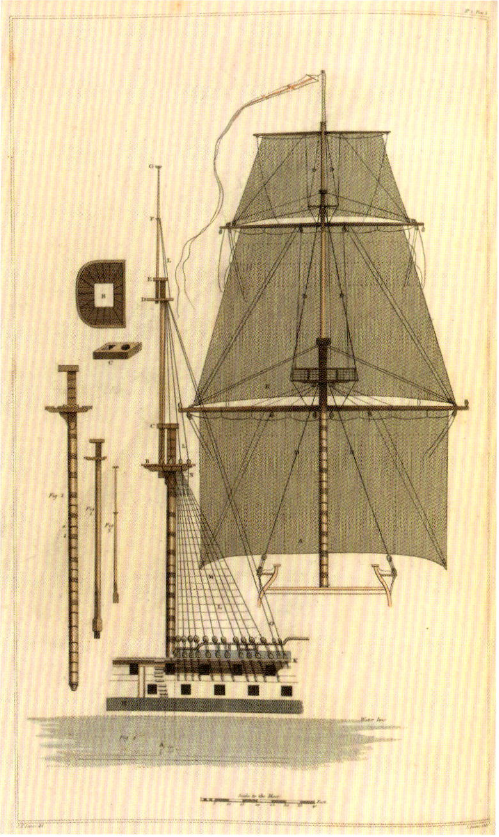

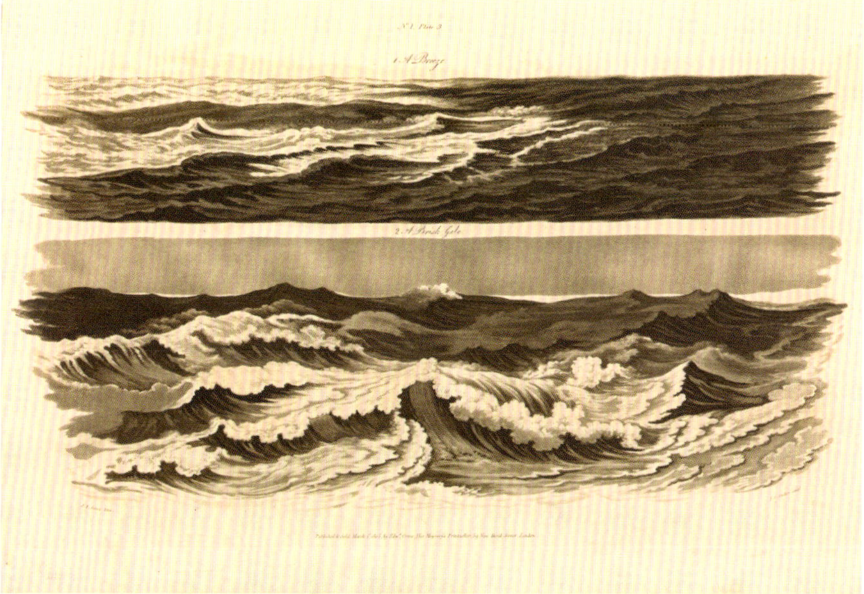

18

Dominic Serres the Younger and John Thomas Serres

Liber Nauticus, and Instructor in the Art of Marine Drawing

Address; Plate 1, Part 1, 'Description of the Masts of Ships'; and Plate 3, Part 1, 'A Breeze' and 'A Brisk Gale'

Engraving and aquatint with watercolour

47.5 x 33 (18¾ x 13)

Published by Edward Orme, London, 1805

National Maritime Museum

Ten plates and two preparatory studies from the *Liber Studiorum* by J.M.W. Turner

By 1816, Turner had published nine plates within the marine category of the *Liber Studiorum*. All are represented here. He made detailed preparatory studies to guide the engravers, using brown tones that correlate visually with the inks used to create the prints [22]. An early sketch for the centre image of the frontispiece (Museum of Fine Arts, Boston; reproduced in Forrester 1996, p. 45) showed a coastal scene with shipping, an indication of how important Turner's identity as a marine artist was at this time. As published, the frontispiece represents the classical myth of the rape of Europa. The subject has maritime associations, given that Europa is abducted by Zeus, in the form of a white bull, across the sea to Crete. A number of compositions seem to have been considered by Turner for the *Liber Studiorum* but were either unpublished or were not made into prints. Two examples are *Moonlight at Sea*, an adaptation of Turner's first exhibited seascape, *Fishermen at Sea* [14], and *The Lost Sailor* (Forrester 1996, no. 84).

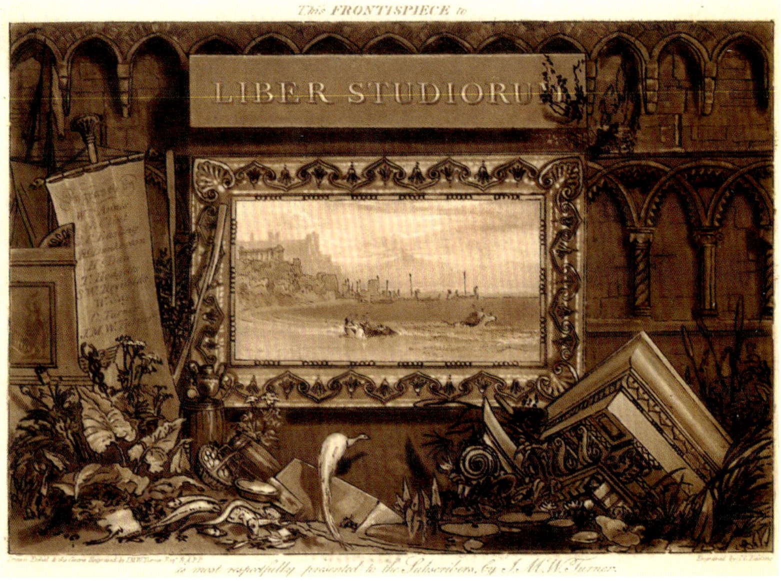

19

Etched and centre image engraved by J.M.W. Turner; remainder of plate engraved by J.C. Easling
Frontispiece 1812
Etching and mezzotint in brown ink,
first published state 18.6 x 26.3 (7⅜ x 10⅜)
British Museum

Rawlinson, no. 1; Forrester 1996, no. 1

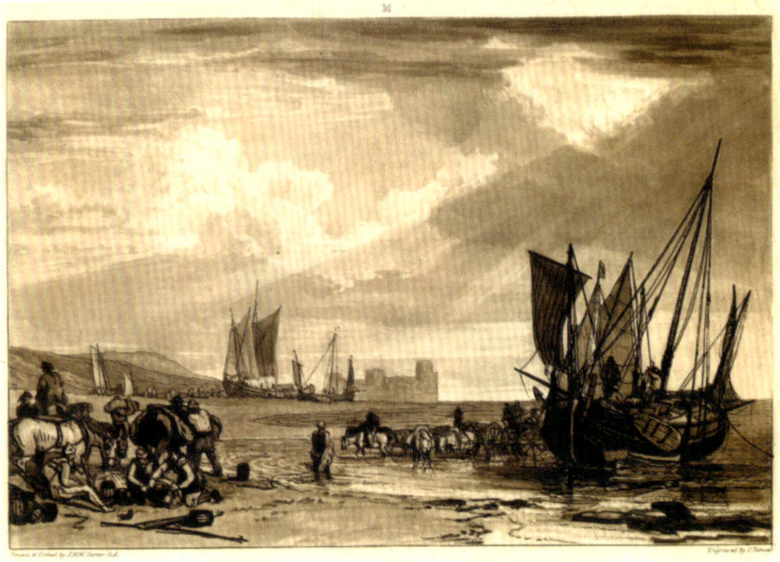

20

Etched by J.M.W. Turner and engraved by Charles Turner
Scene on the French Coast 1807
Etching and mezzotint in brown ink,
first published state 18.2 x 25.9 (7⅛ x 10⅛)
British Museum

Rawlinson, no. 4; Forrester 1996, no. 4

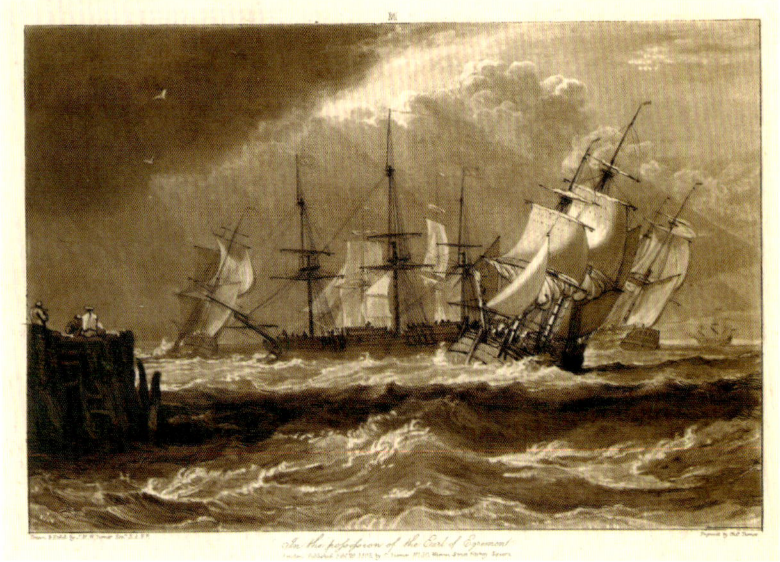

21

Etched by J.M.W. Turner and engraved by Charles Turner
Ships in a Breeze 1808
Etching and mezzotint in brown ink,
first published state 18.2 x 25.7 (7⅛ x 10⅛)
British Museum

Rawlinson, no. 10; Forrester 1996, no. 10

22

J.M.W. Turner

Ships in a Breeze c.1806–07

Watercolour and pencil 18.4 x 26.2 (7¼ x 10⅜)

Tate. Turner Bequest 1856

Finberg CXVI M

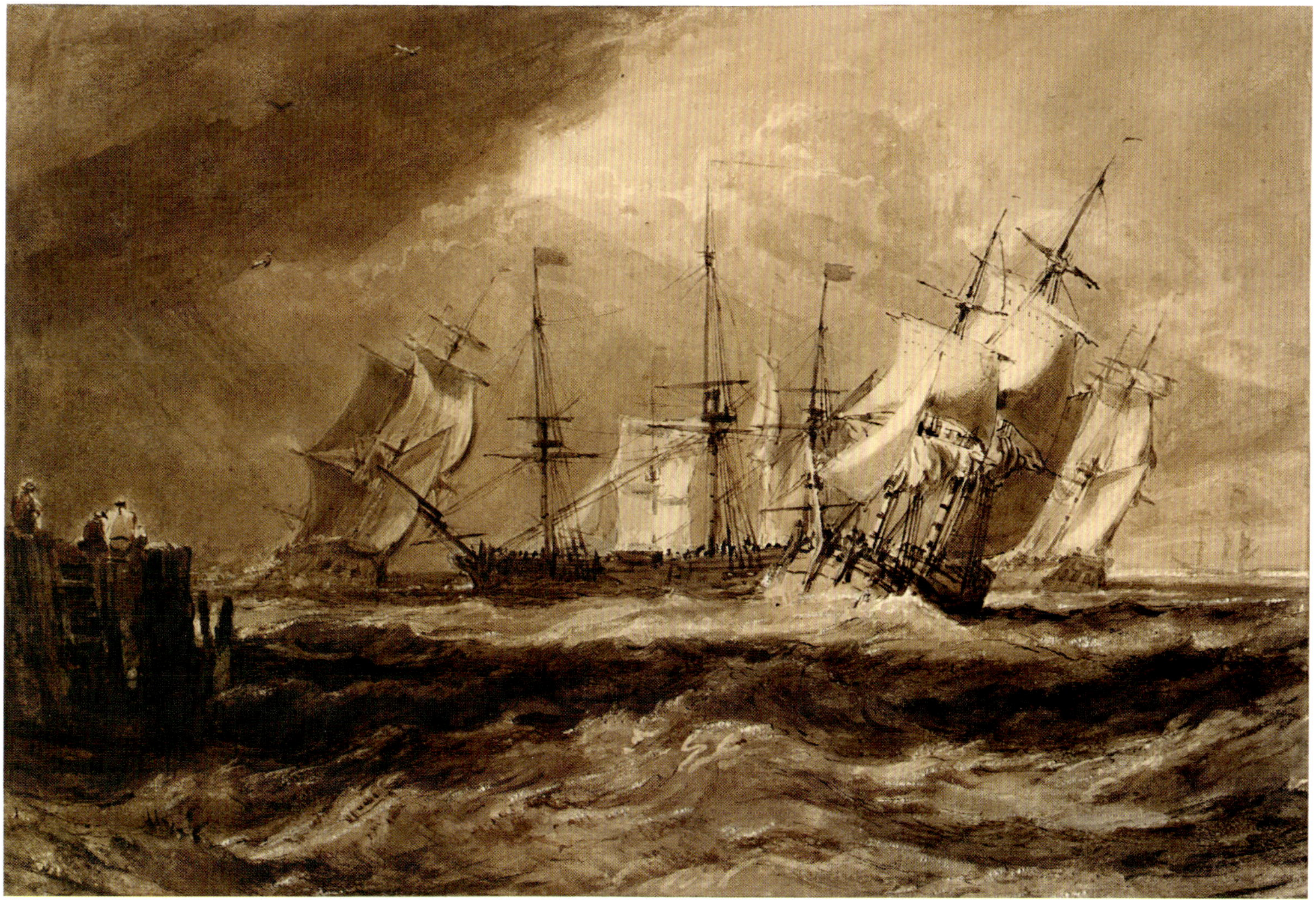

23

Etched by J.M.W. Turner and engraved by Charles Turner
Original Sketch of a Picture for W. Leader, Esq. ('The Leader Sea Piece') 1809
Etching and mezzotint in brown ink, first published state 17.7 x 25.7 (7 x 10⅛)
British Museum

Rawlinson, no. 20; Forrester 1996, no. 20

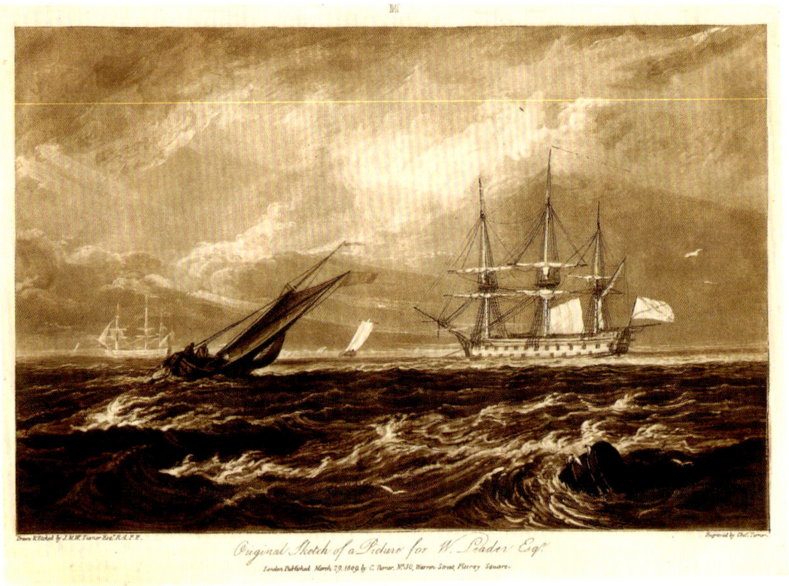

24

Etched by J.M.W. Turner and engraved by William Say
Coast of Yorkshire 1811
Etching and mezzotint in brown ink, first published state 18.1 x 26.6 (7⅛ x 10½)
British Museum

Rawlinson, no. 24; Forrester 1996, no. 24

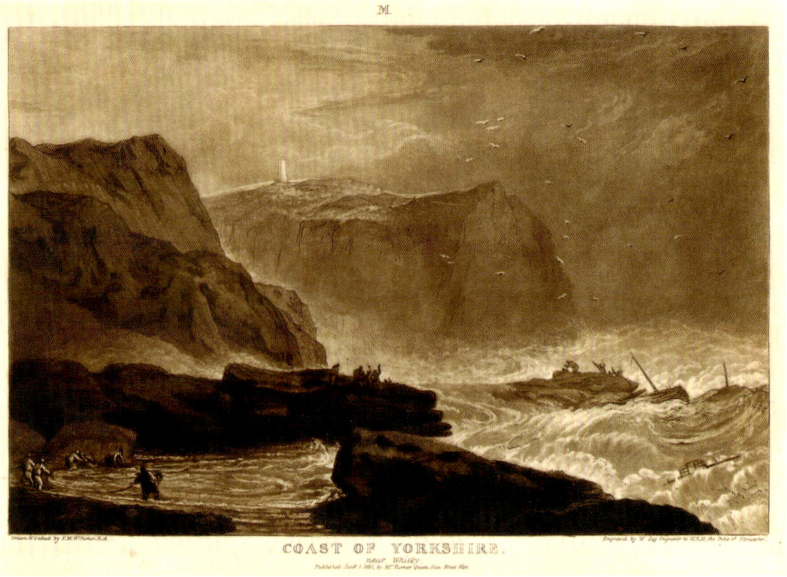

25

Etched by J.M.W. Turner and engraved by William Say
Marine Dabblers 1811
Etching and mezzotint in brown ink, first published state 17.8 x 25.7 (7 x 10⅛)
British Museum

Rawlinson, no. 29; Forrester 1996, no. 29

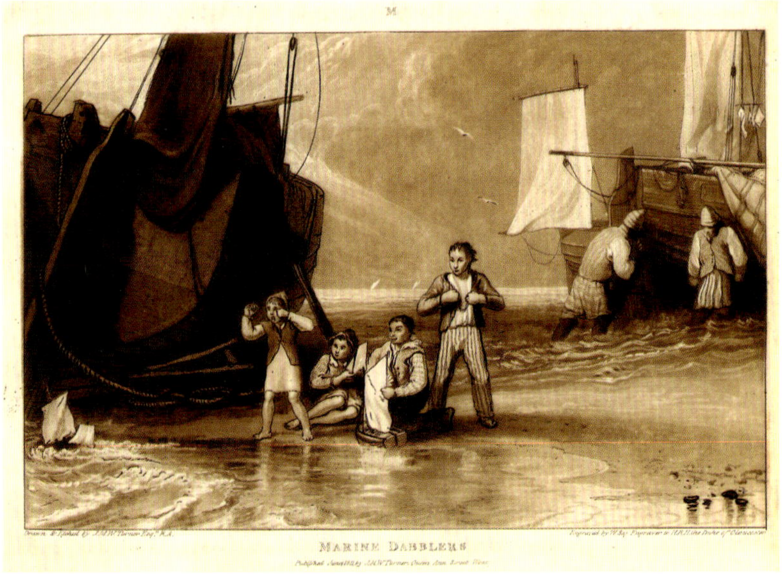

26

Etched by J.M.W. Turner and engraved by William Say

Martello Towers, near Bexhill, Sussex 1811
Etching and mezzotint in brown ink,
first published state 16 x 26 (6¼ x 10¼)
British Museum

Rawlinson, no. 34; Forrester 1996, no. 34

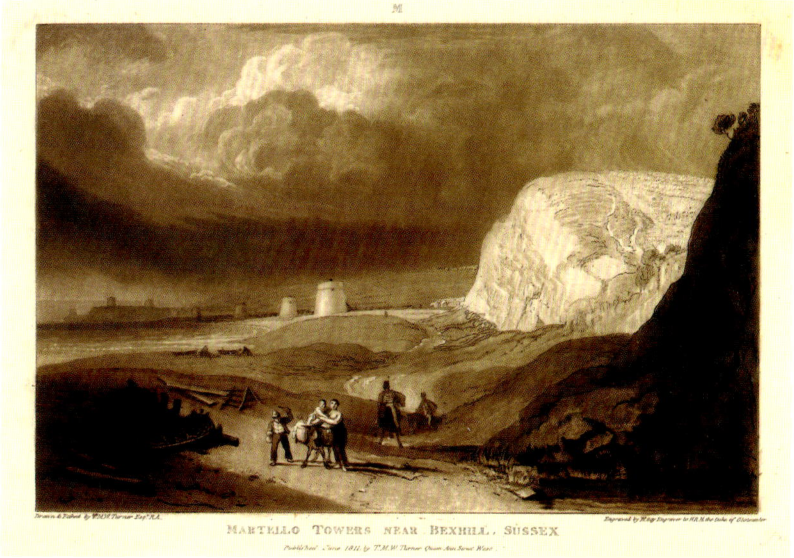

27

Etched by J.M.W. Turner and engraved by William Annis and J.C. Easling

Picture in the Possession of Sir John Mildmay, Bart. ('The Mildmay Sea Piece') 1812
Etching and mezzotint in brown ink,
first published state 18 x 26.5 (7 x 10½)
British Museum

Rawlinson, no. 40; Forrester 1996, no. 40

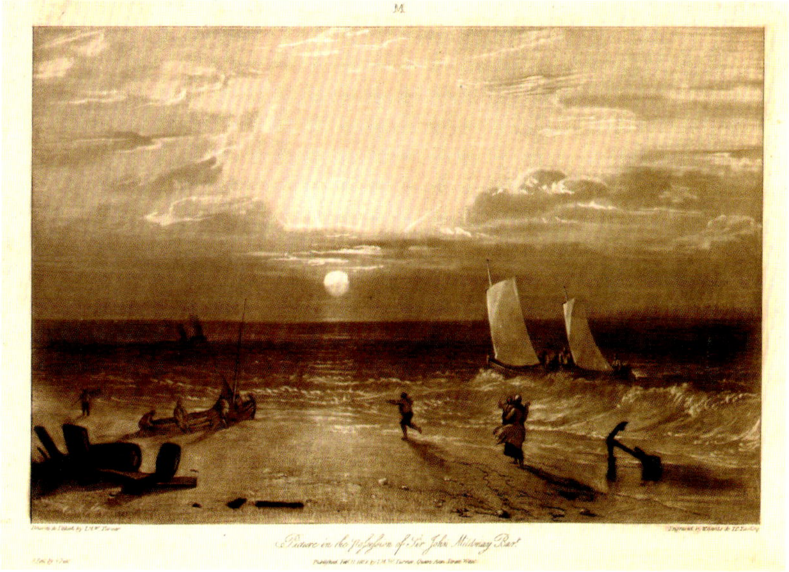

28

Etched and engraved by J.M.W. Turner

Calm 1812
Etching, aquatint and mezzotint in brown ink,
first published state 17.9 x 26.7 (7 x 10½)
British Museum

Rawlinson, no. 44; Forrester 1996, no. 44

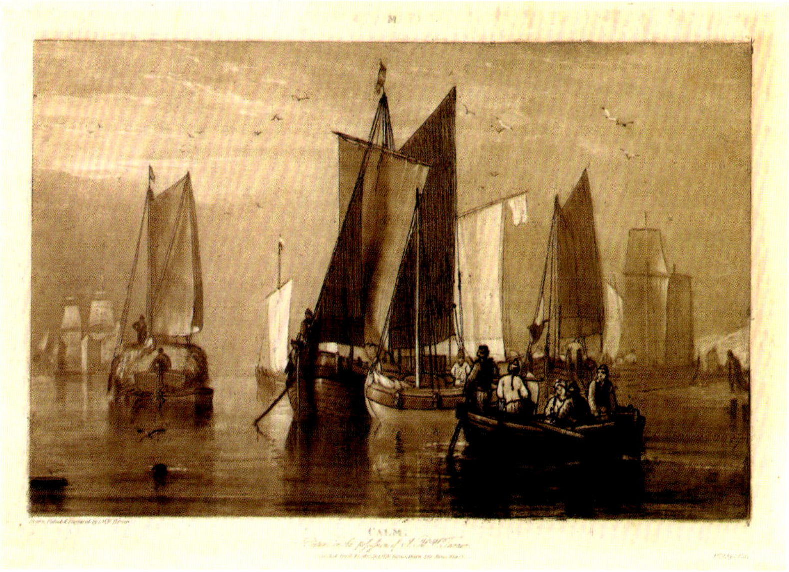

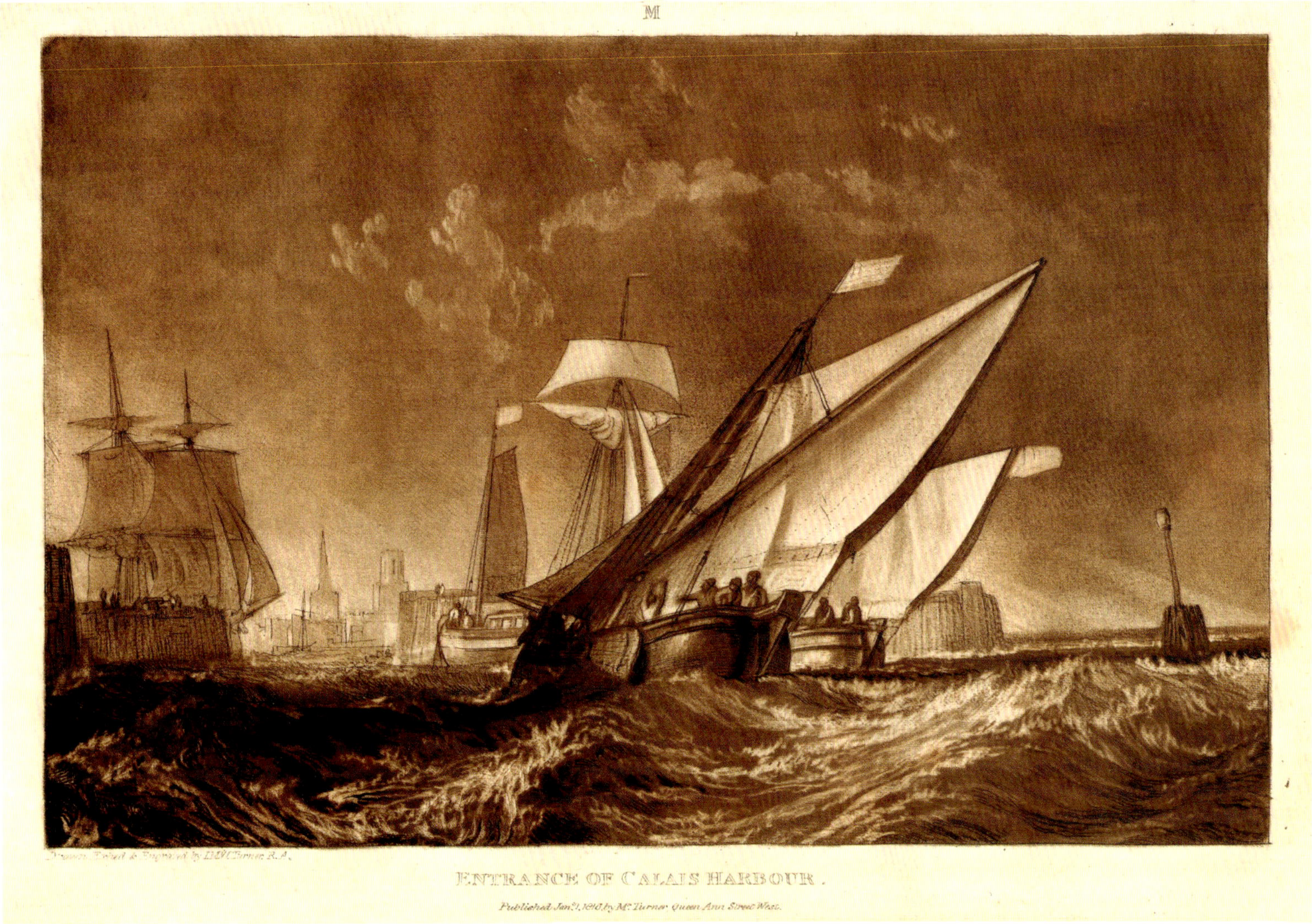

29

Etched and engraved by J.M.W. Turner

Entrance of Calais Harbour 1816

Etching, aquatint and mezzotint in brown ink, first published state 17.9 x 26.6 (7 x 10½)

British Museum

Rawlinson, no. 55; Forrester 1996, no. 55

30

J.M.W. Turner

Moonlight at Sea c.1818

Watercolour 20.9 x 27.6 (8¼ x 10⅞)

Tate

Finberg CXVIII V; Forrester 1996, pp. 150–51

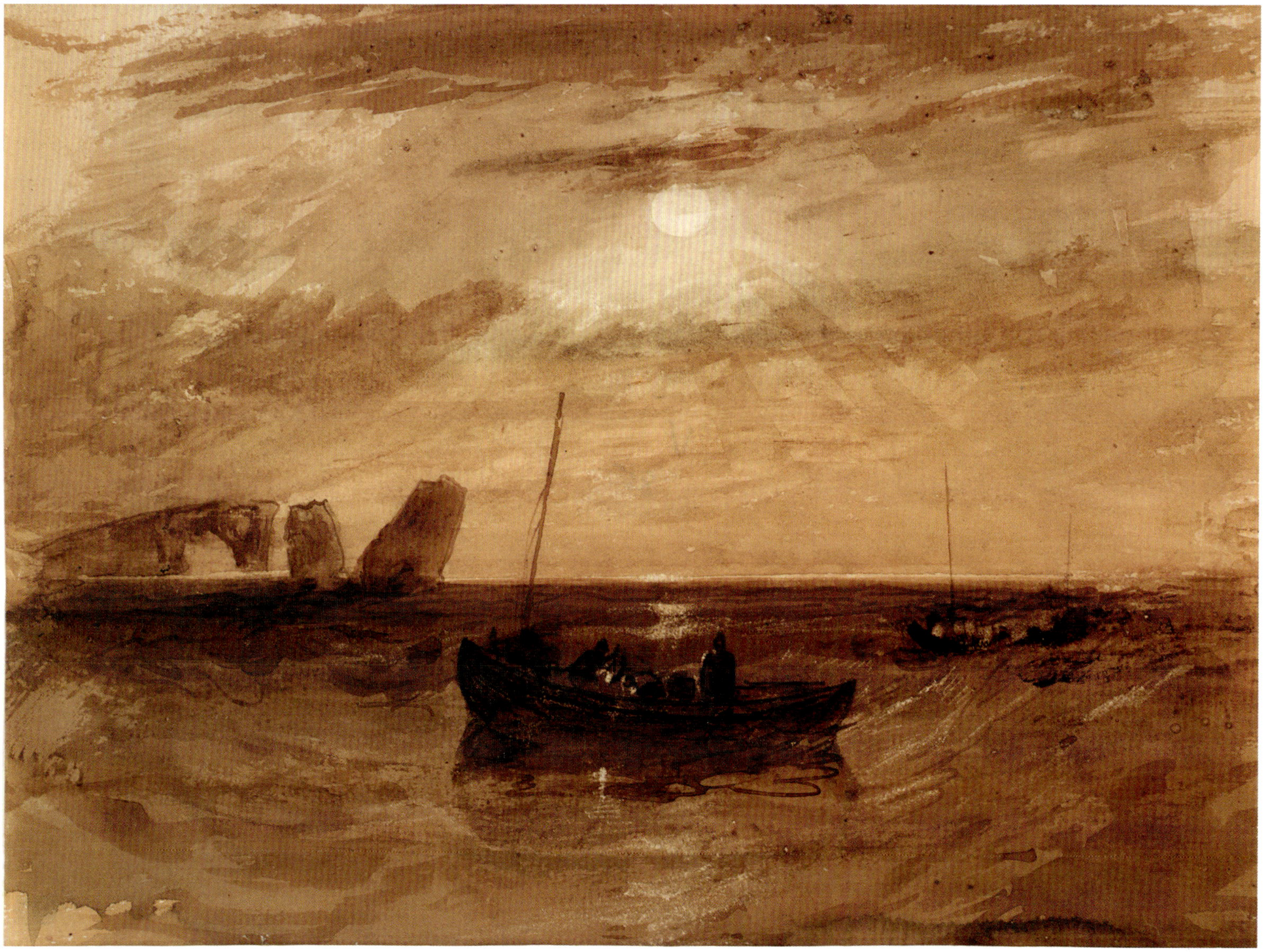

31

J.M.W. Turner
Ship in a Storm c.1826
Mezzotint on steel, engraver's proof
15.1 x 21.3 (6 x $8\frac{3}{8}$)
British Museum

Rawlinson, no. 803; Dupret 1989, no. 5; Lyles and Perkins 1989, no. 521

Six prints and two preparatory studies for the 'Little Liber' series

What Turner's intentions were for the so-called 'Little Liber' prints (or 'Sequels to the Liber Studiorum') is not clear. Few impressions were taken, some were left unfinished and none were published during his lifetime. Most scholars date the works to the mid-1820s, that is, after the *Liber Studiorum* project had ended. Unlike the *Liber Studiorum* prints, which are mezzotint over an etched outline, these works are mezzotint only, allowing Turner to concentrate solely on the gradations of tone and velvety richness associated with the medium. The resulting images, focusing on storm and night scenes, are highly expressive, especially when compared with the more restrained images of the *Liber Studiorum*. Nine of the eleven (or twelve) 'Little Liber' subjects relate to the sea. Included here are preliminary watercolour and pencil studies for *Ship in a Storm* and *Ship and Cutter*. Unlike the drawings for the *Liber Studiorum*, which are in brown tones and highly detailed to guide the engravers, these are freely handled and employ more colourful washes. Some scholars have suggested that *Ship in a Storm* may have formed part of the *Rivers of England* project.

If Turner intended the 'Little Liber' to be published as a group then he may have had a number of other mezzotint projects in mind. In about 1823, for example, the painter John Martin had begun to experiment with mezzotint and was commissioned by the publisher Septimus Prowett for a series of twenty-four prints on the subject of Milton's biblical epic *Paradise Lost* (published 1825–27). This and other print projects were important vehicles for establishing Martin's reputation in Britain and abroad (Myrone 2011, pp. 123–34). W.B. Cooke, with whom Turner was collaborating in the 1820s, published *Gems of Art*, a series of mezzotints after paintings 'by Esteemed Masters of All Ages and All Countries' (1823–25). And in 1826, a mezzotint by F.C. Lewis was published after Francis Danby's *Sunset at Sea after a Storm* [61], a brooding shipwreck subject that had been exhibited at the Royal Academy in 1824 and the British Institution the following year. However, it is perfectly possible that Turner had no intention of publishing the prints at all. In which case, the 'Little Liber' may simply represent the artist's ongoing experimentations with a variety of techniques and media, thus forming part of his ever-expanding cache of sketches, colour 'beginnings' and other reference material.

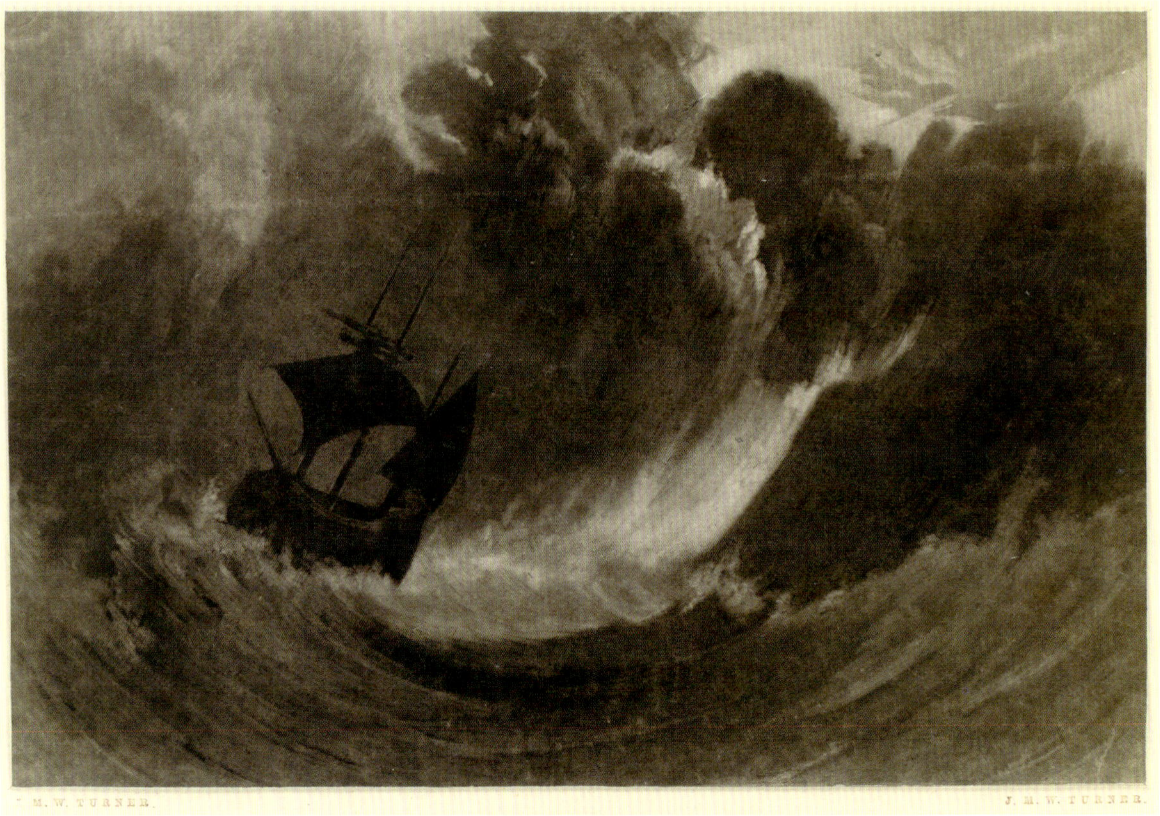

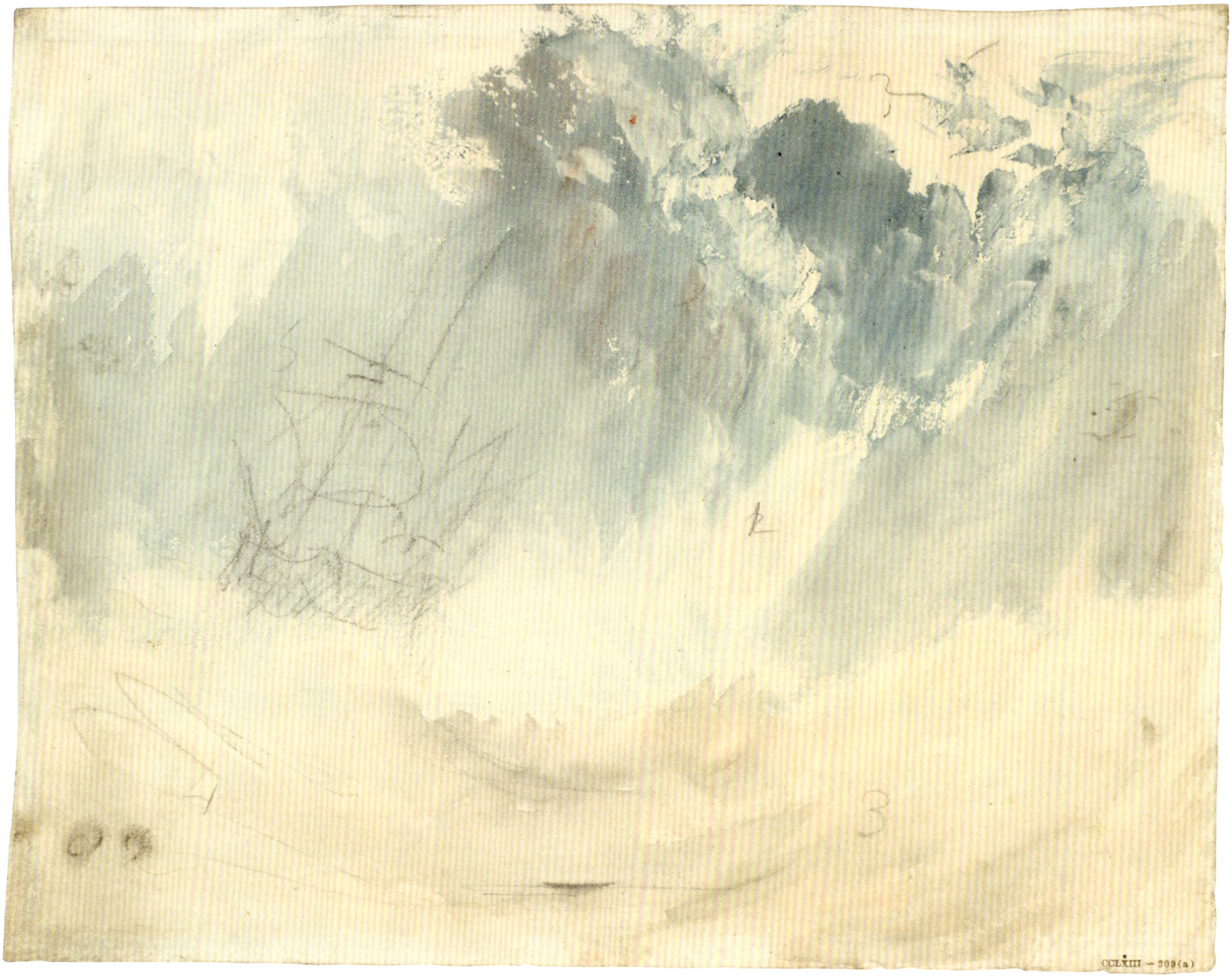

32

J.M.W. Turner

Ship in a Storm c.1823–26

Watercolour and pencil 24.1 x 30 (9½ x 11¾)

Tate. Turner Bequest 1856

Finberg CCLXIII 309a; Wilton, no. 772; Lyles and Perkins 1989, no. 51; Westheider and Philipp 2011, no. 21

33

J.M.W. Turner

Ship and Cutter c.1824

Watercolour and pencil 23.8 x 28.9 (9⅜ x 11⅜)

Museum of Fine Arts, Boston

Wilton, no. 777

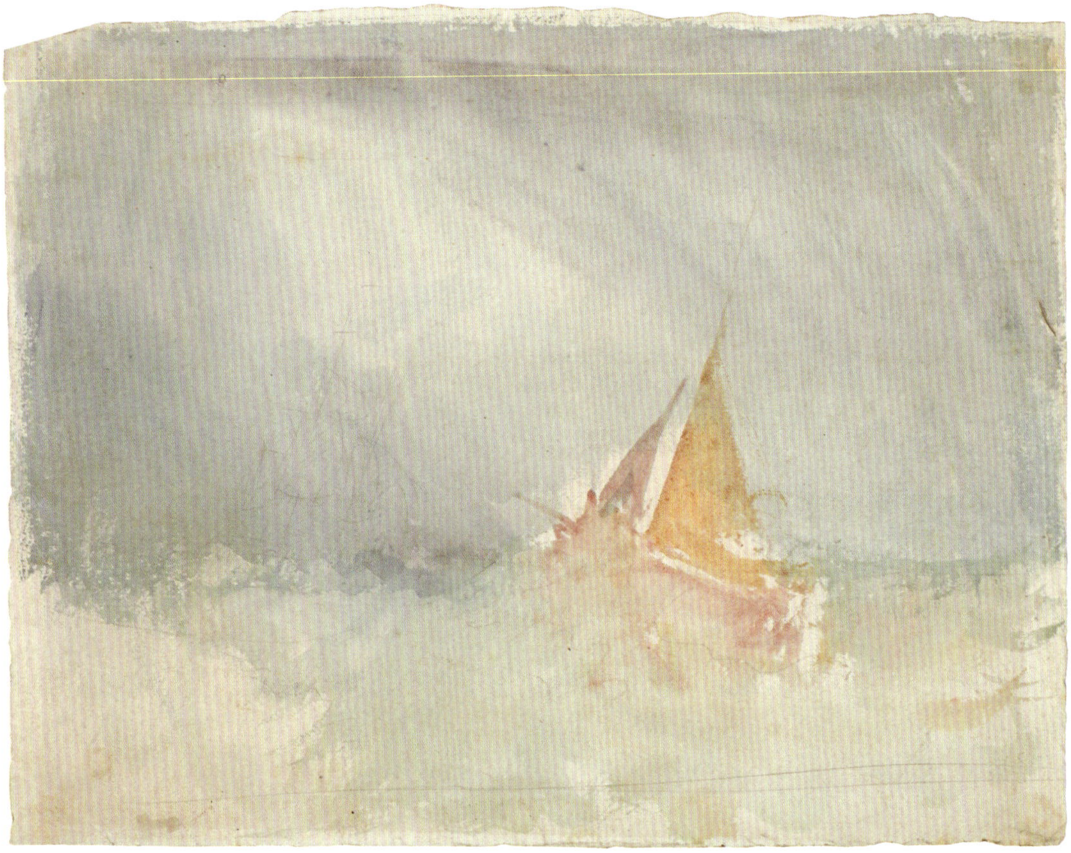

34

J.M.W. Turner

Ship and Cutter c.1825 [late nineteenth-century impression]

Mezzotint on steel 15.4 x 22.2 (6 x 8¾)

Tate

Rawlinson, no. 808; Dupret 1989, no. 10

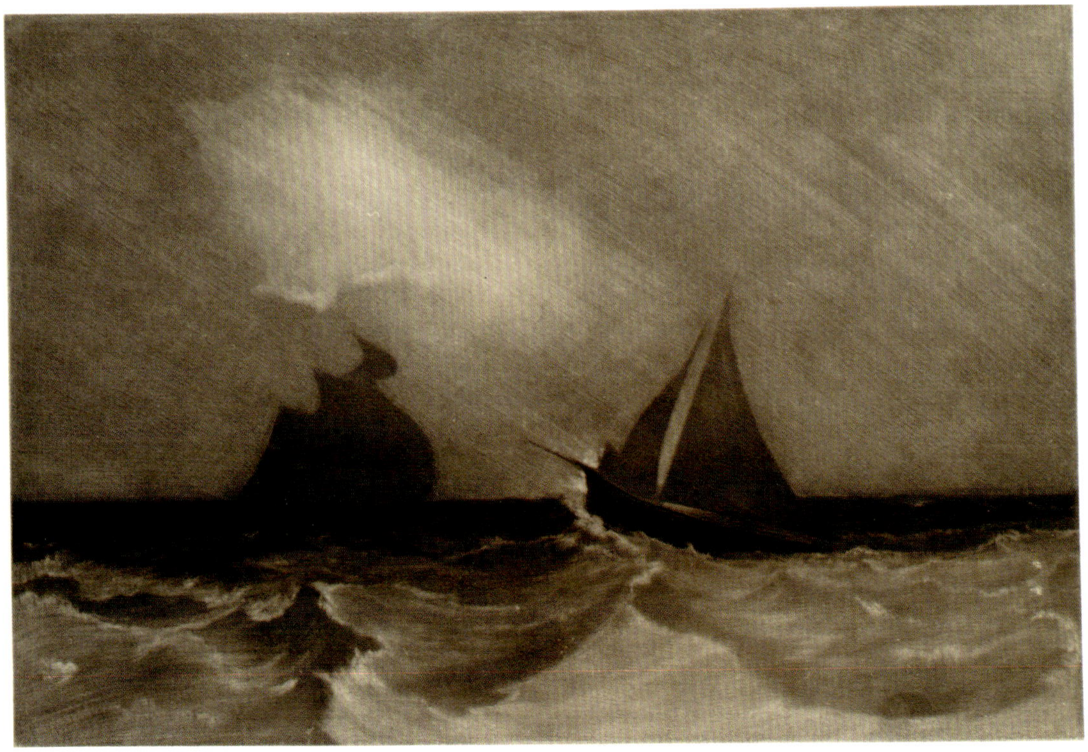

35

J.M.W. Turner

Study of Sea and Sky c.1825 [late nineteeth-century impression]

Mezzotint on steel 15.4 x 21.4 (6 x 8⅜)

Tate

Rawlinson, no. 806; Dupret 1989, no. 8

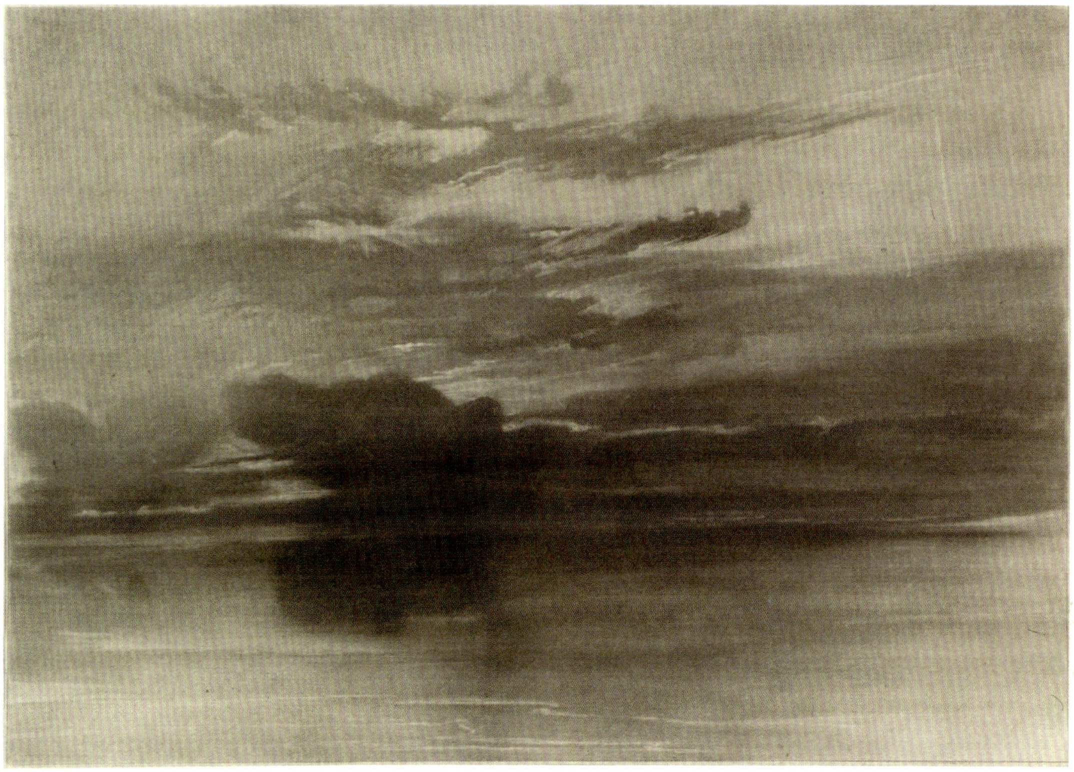

36

J.M.W. Turner

The Evening Gun c.1826

Mezzotint on steel, engraver's proof

19 x 23.3 (7½ x 9⅛)

British Museum

Rawlinson, no. 800; Dupret 1989, no. 2

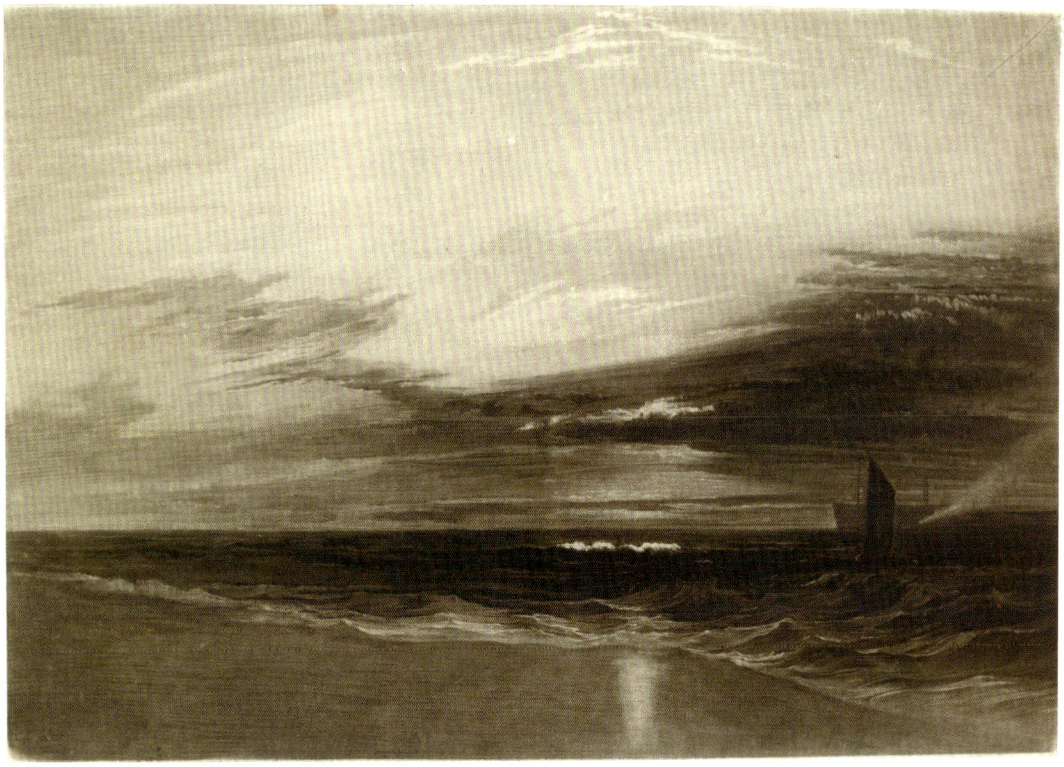

37

J.M.W. Turner
The Mew Stone c.1826
Mezzotint on steel, engraver's proof
19 x 25.3 (7½ x 10)
British Museum

Rawlinson, no. 805; Dupret 1989, no. 7

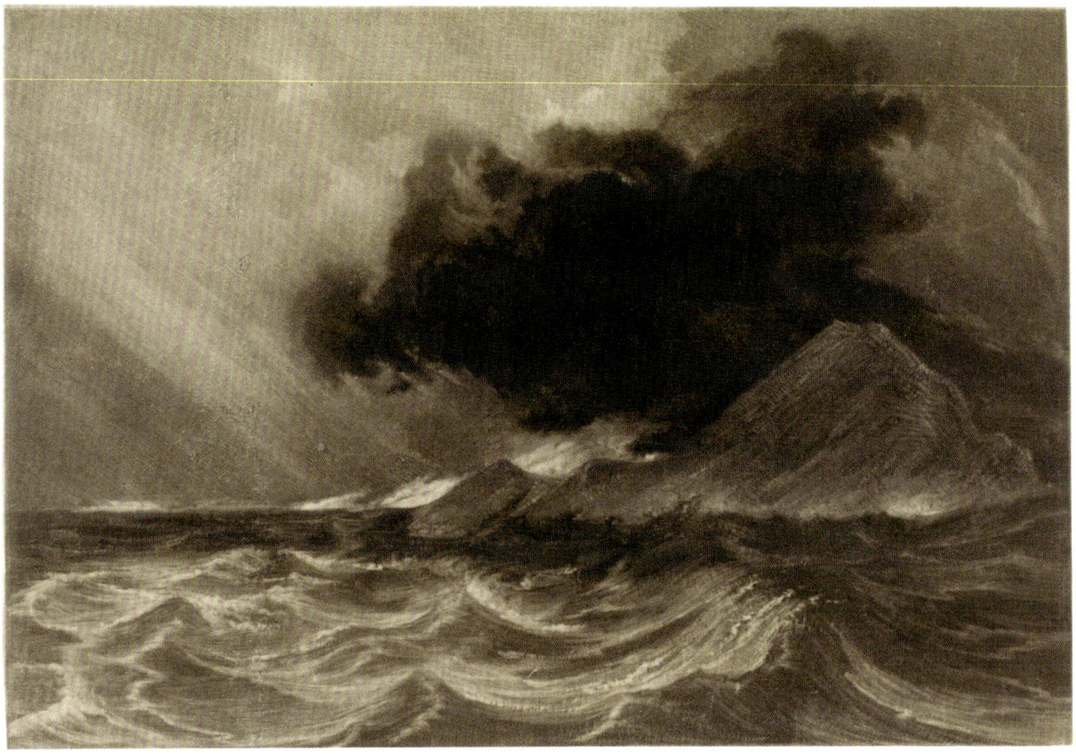

38 (and detail)

J.M.W. Turner
The Medway: Thunderstorm with Rainbow
c.1825
Mezzotint on steel, engraver's proof
19.2 x 25.8 (7½ x 10⅛)
British Museum

Rawlinson, no. 809a; Dupret 1989, no. 12; Forrester 1996, no. 89ii

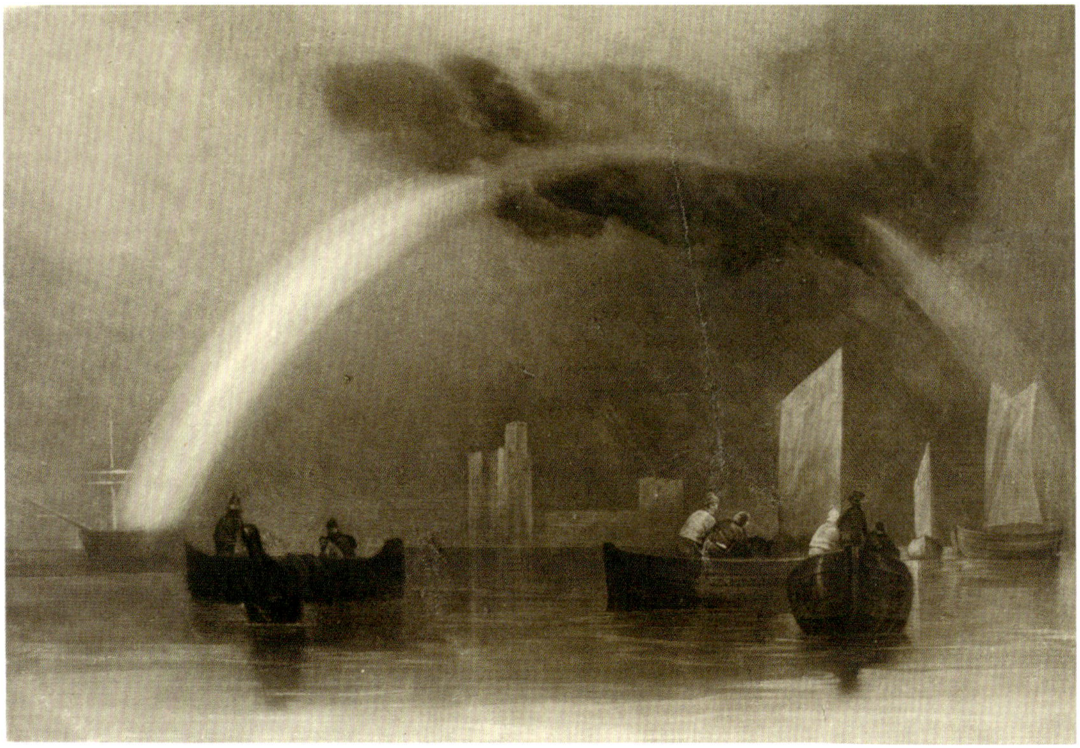

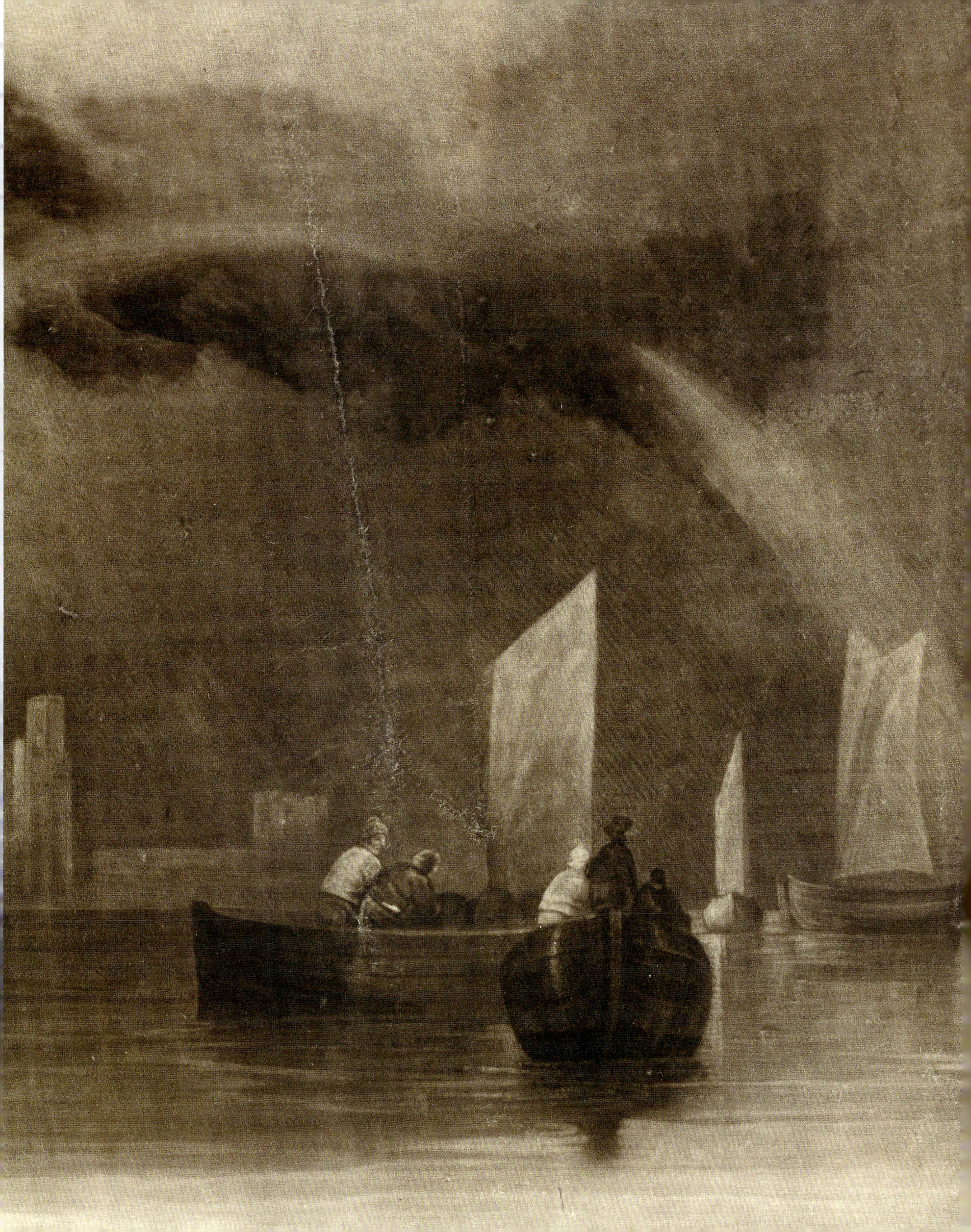

41

J.M.W. Turner
Shields, on the River Tyne 1823
Watercolour 15.4 x 21.6 (6 x 8½)
Tate. Turner Bequest 1856

Finberg CCVIII V; Shanes 1990, no. 77; Warrell 2007, no. 69

These two watercolours formed part of the *Rivers of England* project, which W.B. Cooke seems to have devised as a sequel to the *Southern Coast* project. It was not completed as originally planned, however, probably due to a quarrel between Cooke and Turner over the artist's fees. Unlike the *Southern Coast* series, Turner kept possession of the original watercolours, hiring them out to Cooke to be mezzotinted. Four of the engravers for the series, Thomas Lupton, S.W. Reynolds, Charles Turner and William Say, had worked previously on Turner's *Liber Studiorum*. In the event, sixteen prints were published after Turner, with others after Thomas Girtin and William Collins.

Together, Turner's images (with [68]) demonstrate the variety that he was able to achieve across a series. Indeed, the representation of sunrise, daytime and moonlight, and the contrasting weather conditions and diversity of local industries, could be read as a contemporary British 'Times of Day' in the manner of Claude-Joseph Vernet (see [6 and 7]). Turner reworked the composition of *Shields, on the River Tyne* for a later oil painting, *Keelmen Heaving in Coals by Moonlight*, exhibited at the RA in 1835 [86]. Stangate Creek forms part of the estuary of the river Medway. The hulks, cast in shadow in the distance on the left, are probably Royal Navy ships converted for use as quarantine vessels. Appropriately, the composition and elegiac quality of this image has been compared to Turner's *Fighting 'Temeraire'* [87].

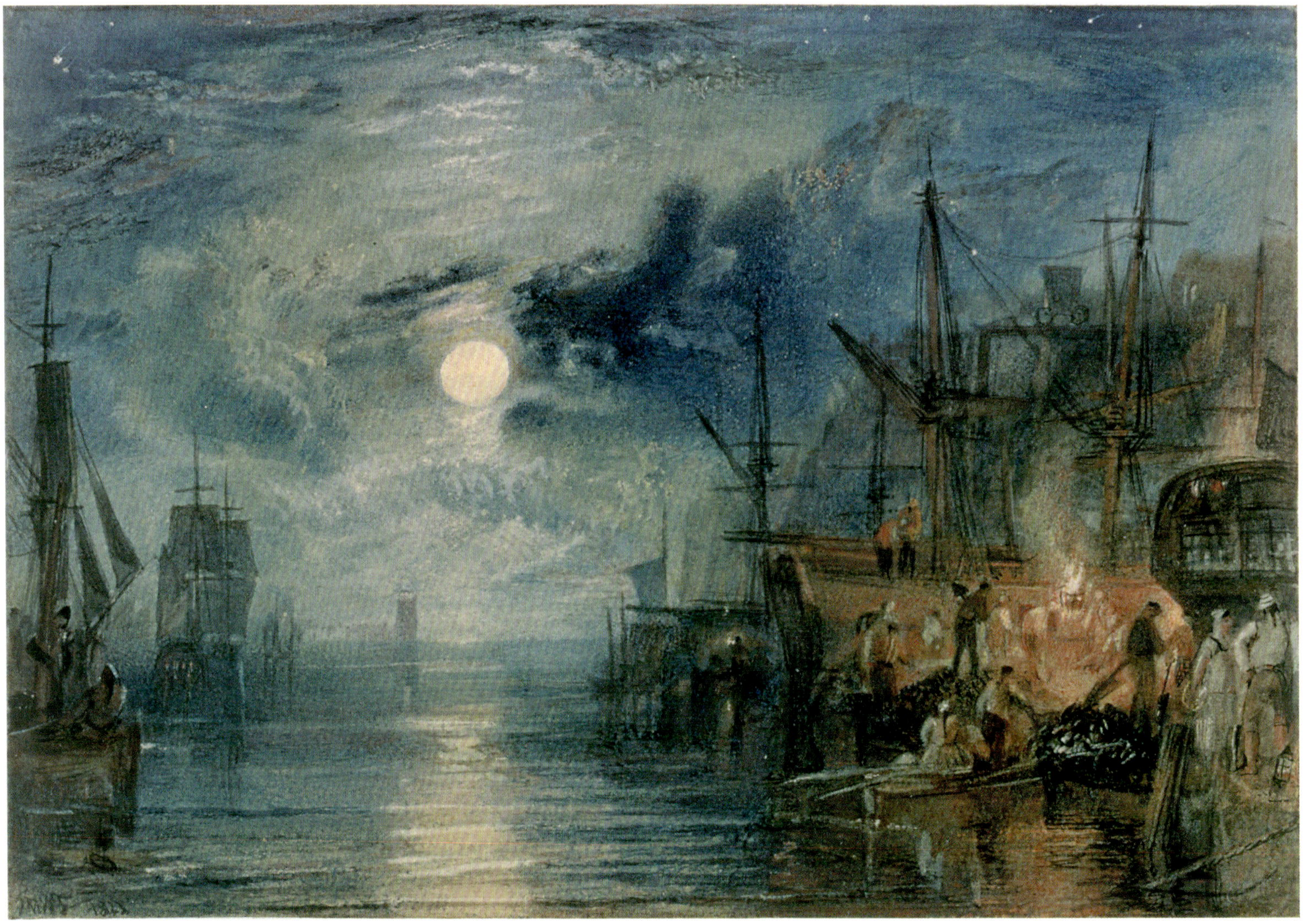

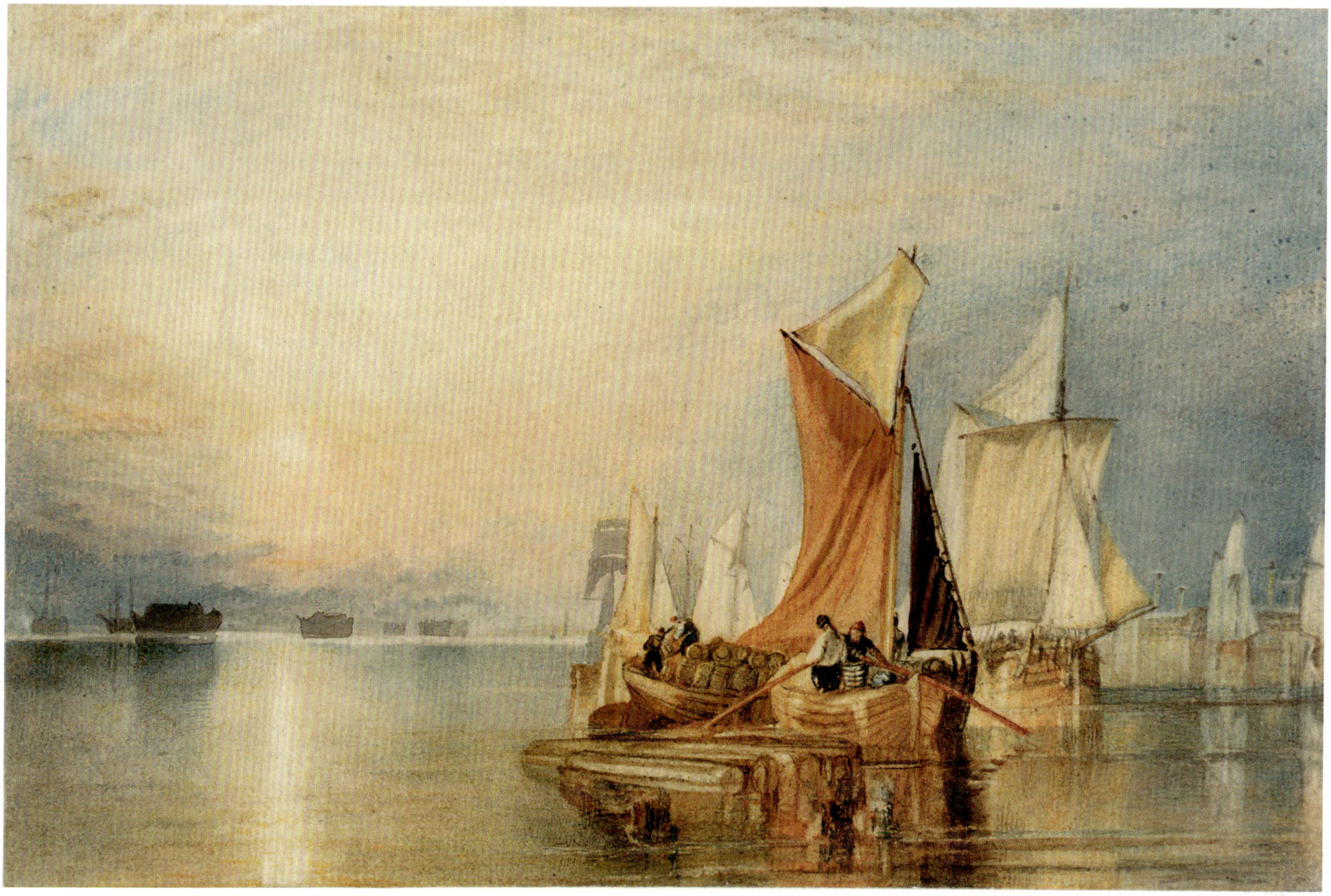

42

J.M.W. Turner

Stangate Creek, on the River Medway

c.1823–24

Watercolour 16.2 x 24 (6⅜ x 9½)

Tate. Turner Bequest 1856

Finberg CCVIII A; Shanes 1990, no. 90; Warrell 2007, no. 68

45

J.M.W. Turner
Sun-rise. Whiting Fishing at Margate 1822
Watercolour 42.6 x 64.8 (16¾ x 25½)
Private collection, UK

Wilton, no. 507; Shanes 1990, no. 57; Noon 2003, no. 158

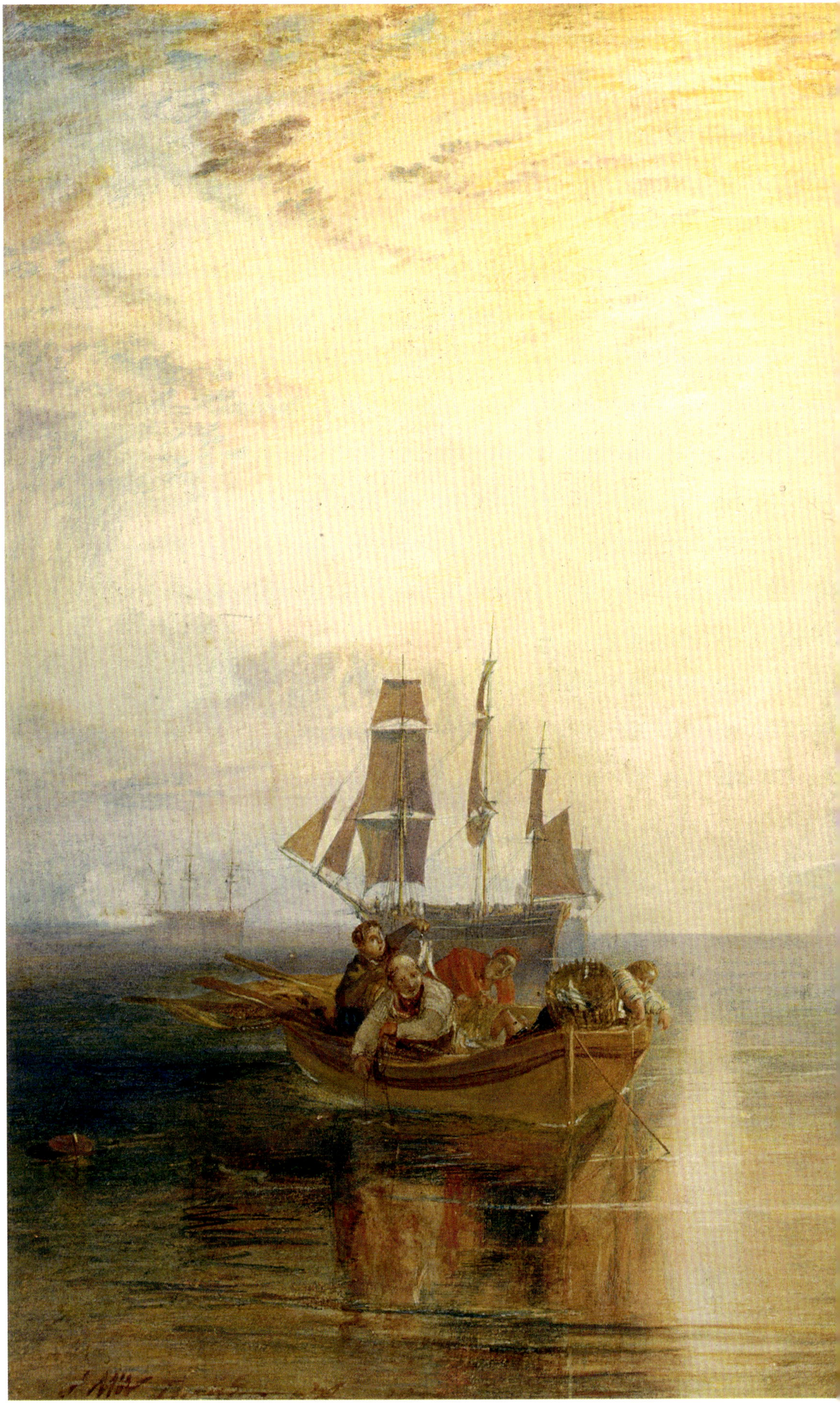

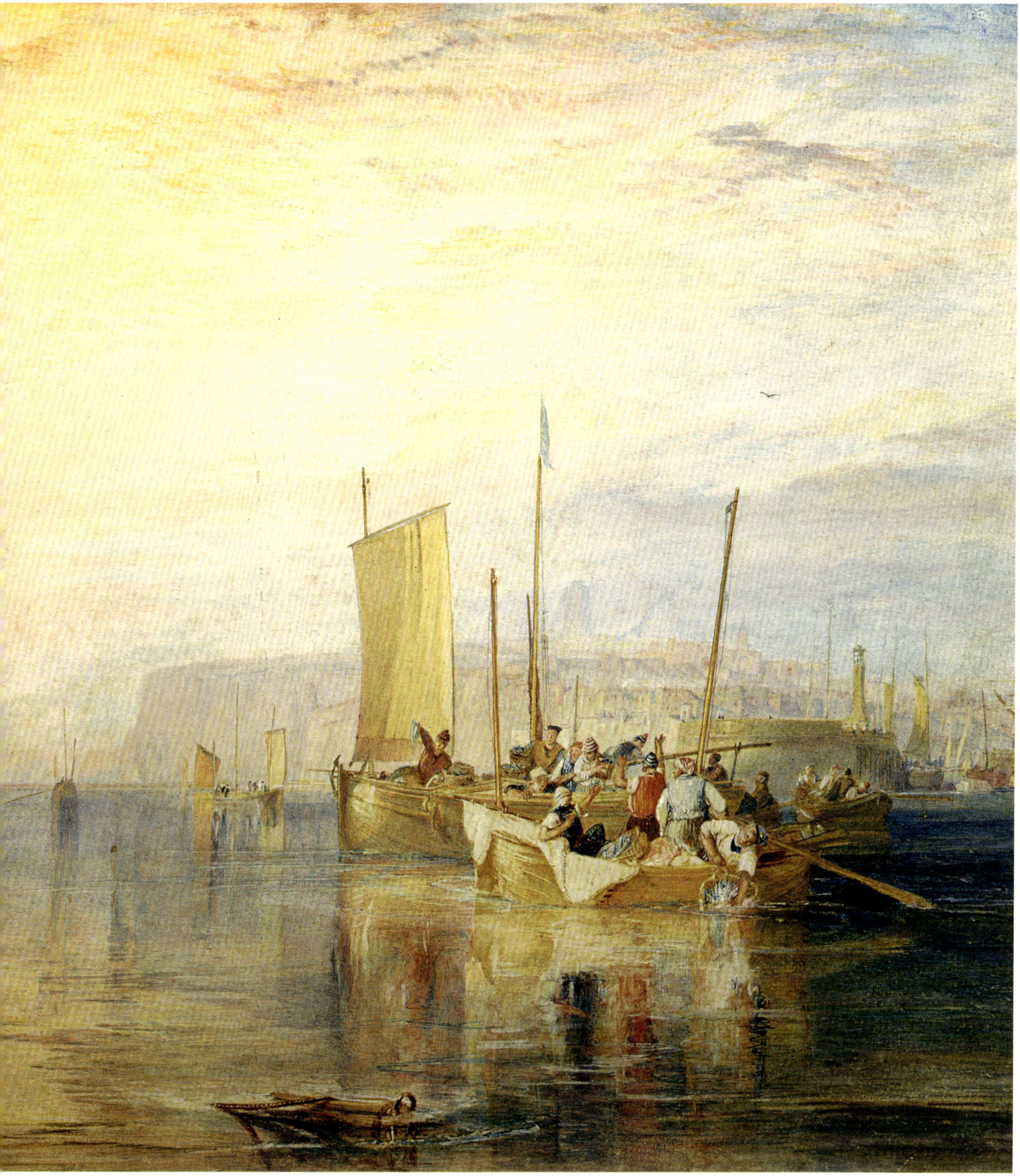

Fig. 15

J.M.W. Turner
The Bell Rock Lighthouse 1819
Watercolour 30.6 x 45.5 (12 x 17⅞)
Scottish National Gallery

The *Provincial Antiquities and Picturesque Scenery of Scotland*, published between 1819 and 1826, was the first collaboration between Turner and the celebrated author and poet Sir Walter Scott. The artist produced ten watercolours with two title-page vignettes to accompany Scott's text. Although Scott selected the subjects, Turner had free rein in devising the compositions. The project proved to be a financial failure. However, Turner worked on two further projects associated with Scott, *Poetical Works* (1833–34) and *Miscellaneous Prose Works* (1834–36).

It was possibly through Walter Scott that Turner gained the commission for a watercolour of the Bell Rock Lighthouse from the civil engineer Robert Stevenson. The structure was designed by Stevenson and built on a partially submerged reef off the coast of Angus between 1807 and 1811. Turner's impressive watercolour was engraved as the frontispiece for Stevenson's *Account of the Bell Rock Lighthouse*, published in 1824.

The Bass Rock, a steep-sided volcanic outcrop, is situated at the mouth of the Firth of Forth, not far from Edinburgh. Its strategic position resulted in its acquisition by Charles II in 1671 and the existing stronghold was remodelled into a royal fortress and prison. Turner had made sketches of the site, from land and sea, during a trip to Scotland in 1818 and made more during another trip in 1822. The resulting image certainly exploits the dramatic potential of the rock, its location and its history. It seems to be lit by a sudden break in the clouds and a lightning bolt cuts through the brooding sky to the right. In the foreground, a small boat attempts to rescue survivors of a wreck floating beside the remains of the ship's mast.

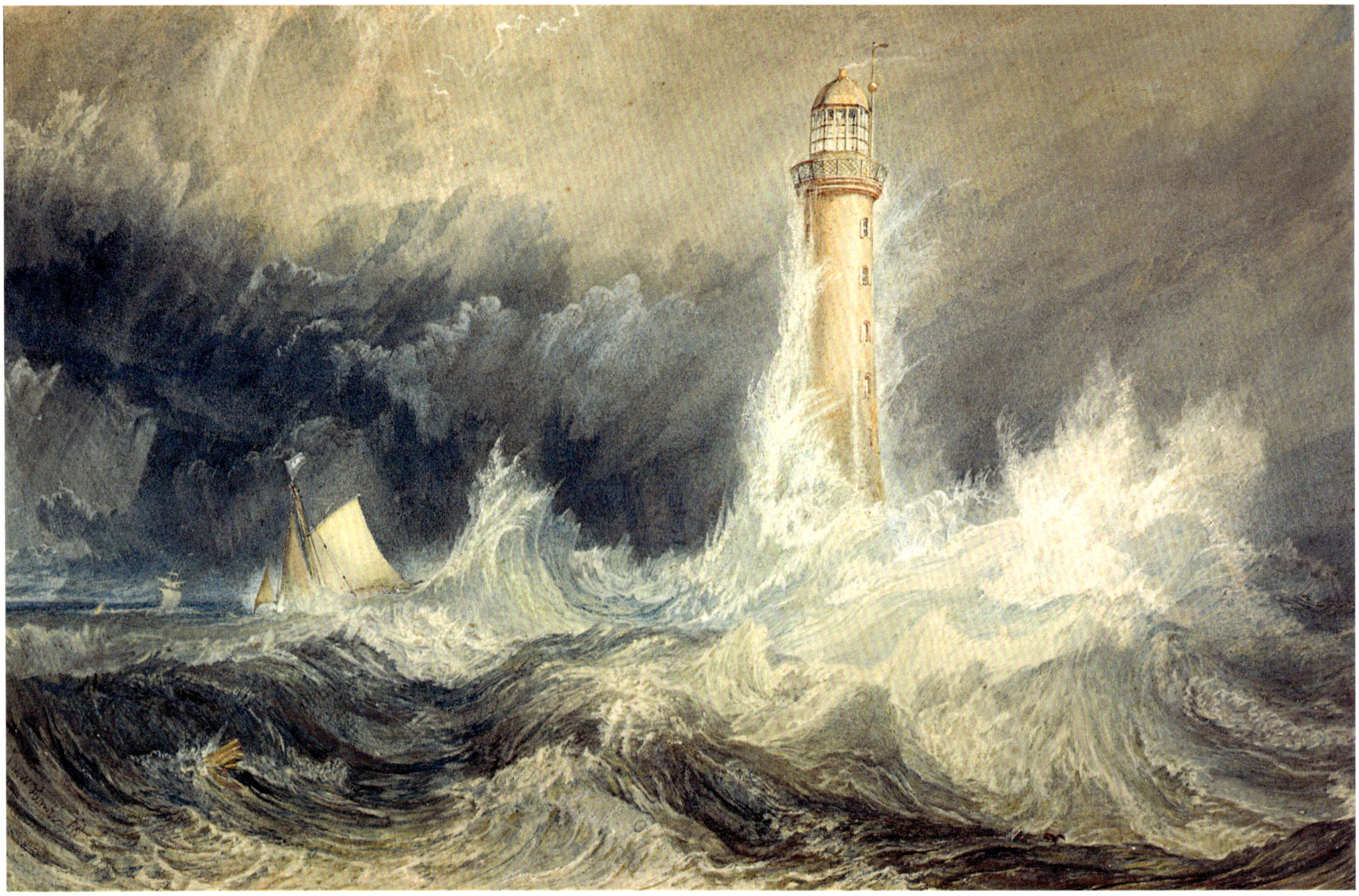

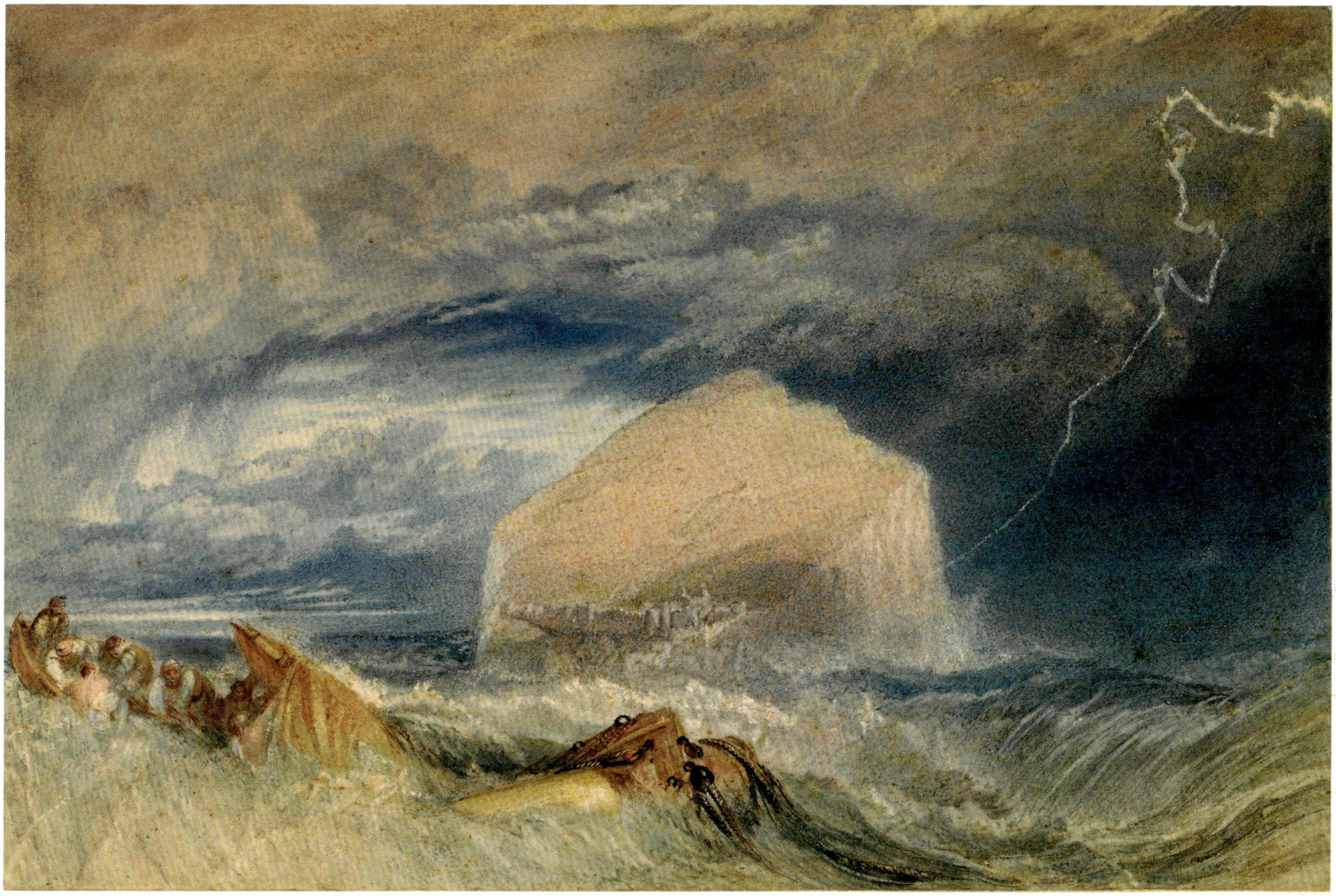

46

J.M.W. Turner

The Bass Rock c.1824

Watercolour 17 x 25.4 (6¾ x 10)

National Museums Liverpool

Wilton, no. 1069; Feather 2010, pp. 190–91

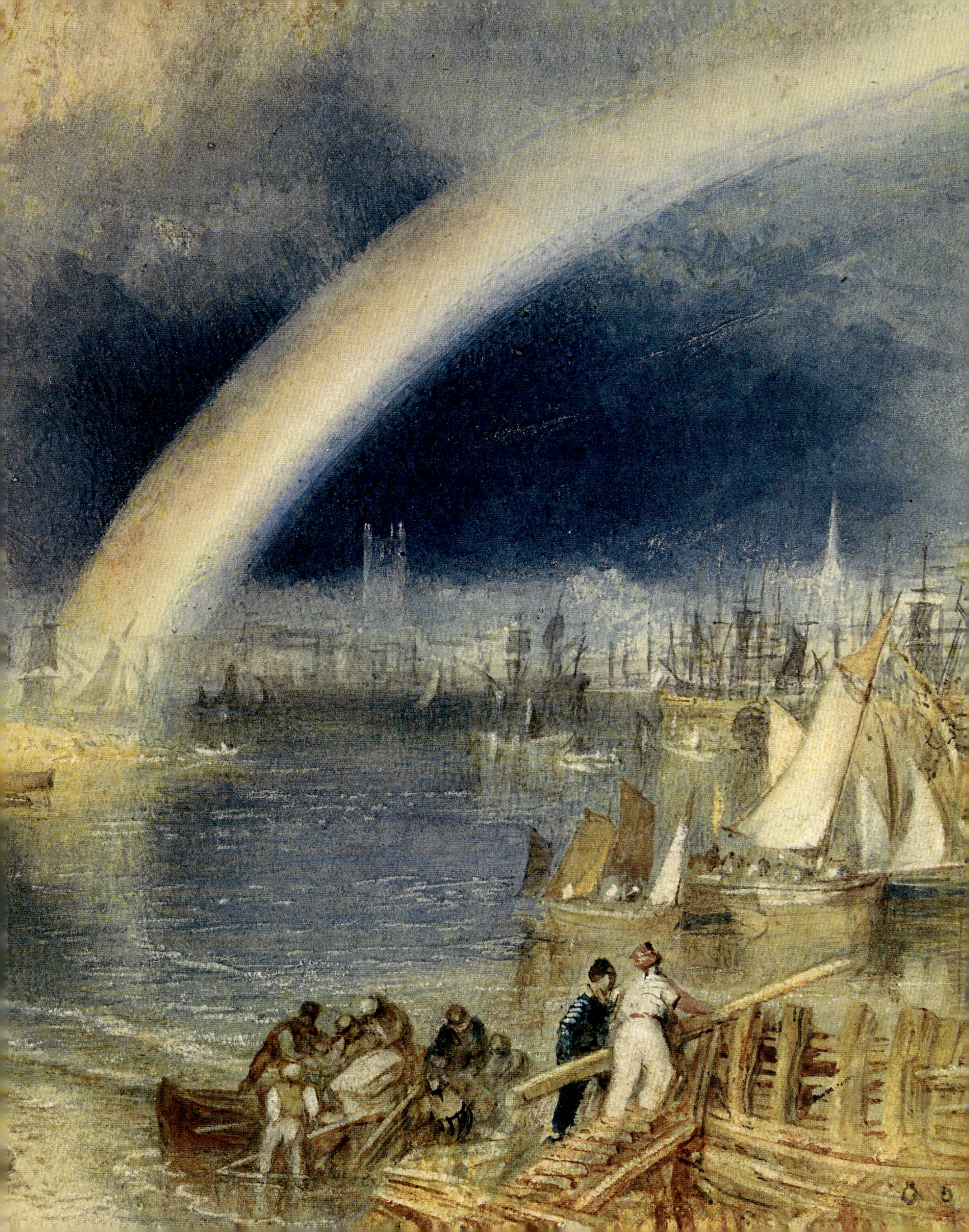

47 (and detail)

J.M.W. Turner

Plymouth with a Rainbow c.1825

Watercolour 16.4 x 24.7 (6½ x 9¾)

Museu Calouste Gulbenkian

Wilton, no. 760

Thomas Lupton acted as both engraver and publisher on *The Ports of England* project, conceived as a sequel to *The Rivers of England*. Its original scope may have been curtailed due to a falling-out between Lupton and Turner in 1828 over the progress of Lupton's mezzotint after Turner's earlier painting *Calais Pier*.

Turner had used the same elevated vantage point seen in *Plymouth with a Rainbow* for his earlier watercolour *Plymouth, with Mount Batten* for the *Southern Coast* series (*c*.1816, Victoria and Albert Museum). Here, the busy port scene has the added drama of a rainbow set against an inky sky as a storm passes.

Ramsgate and *Sheerness* are two of six designs that were published, in 1827 and 1828 respectively. Ramsgate is on the east coast of Kent and has the only Royal Harbour in the country, a title granted by George IV in 1821. In Turner's dramatic watercolour, a boat has left the safety of the harbour, its entrance just visible to the centre left, and is seen buffeted by the wind and waves. Sheerness, long a Royal naval dockyard town, lies at the eastern side of the river Medway in north Kent, with the Nore anchorage to its north-west. The naval two-decker with lowered topmasts, on the right, is probably the Nore guardship.

The 1826 prospectus for *The Ports of England* project stated its author's surprise 'that in a maritime nation like England, immeasurably indebted to her naval achievements for opulence and glory, that a subject so deeply interesting and so intimately connected with her general history as a series of views illustrative of her several Sea Ports and Harbours, should have been to this period neglected' (Thornbury 1862, vol. 1, p. 411). The author, possibly Lupton, may have had in mind Claude-Joseph Vernet's celebrated series of paintings of the ports of France, commissioned by Louis XV in 1753 and engraved in the 1760s. In 1856, the whole of Turner's *Ports* series was published under the title *The Harbours of England*, with text by the art critic John Ruskin.

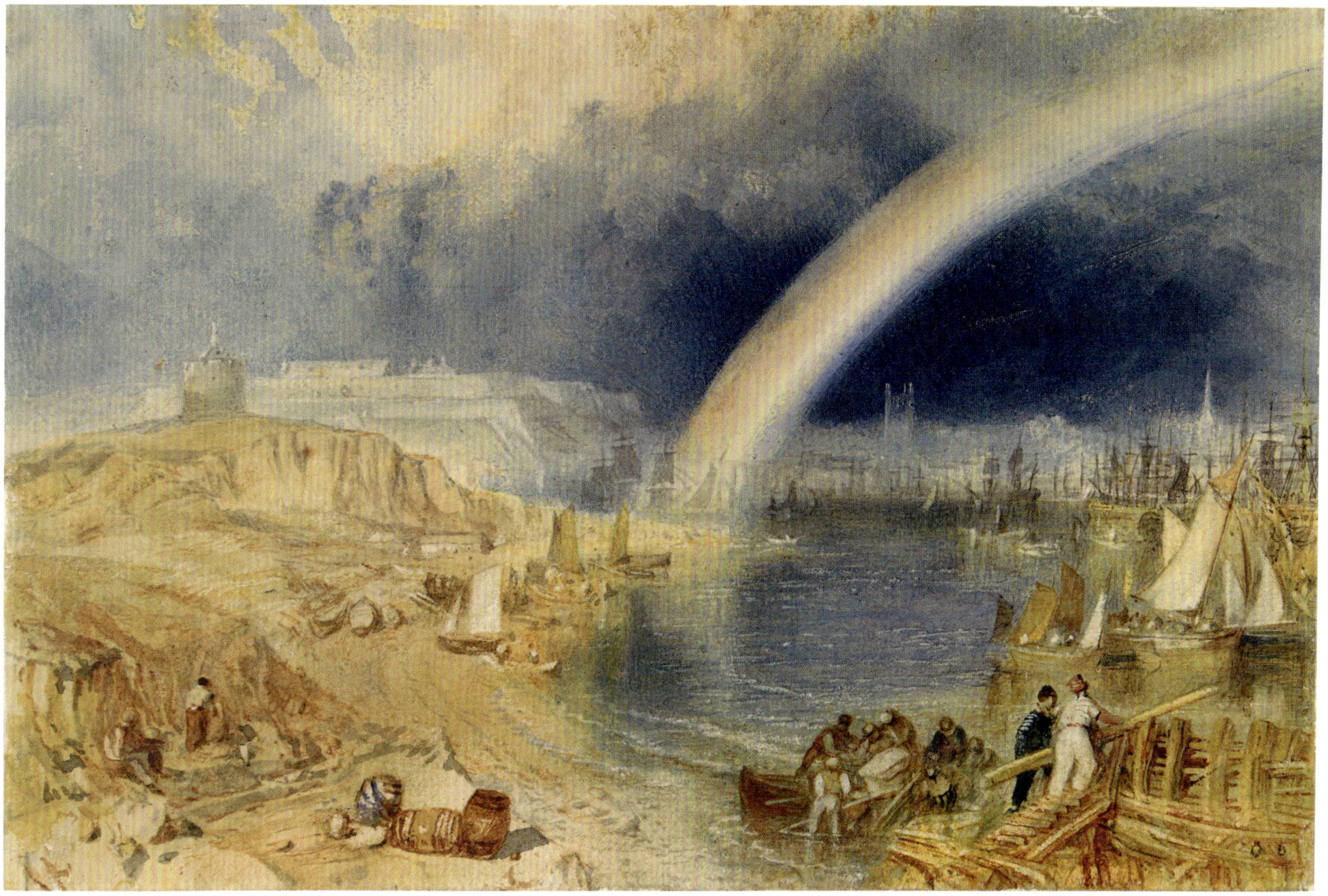

48

J.M.W. Turner

Ramsgate *c.*1825

Watercolour 16.1 x 23.2 (6⅜ x 9⅛)

Tate. Turner Bequest 1856

Finberg CCVIII Q; Wilton, no. 754; Westheider and Philipp 2011, no. 26

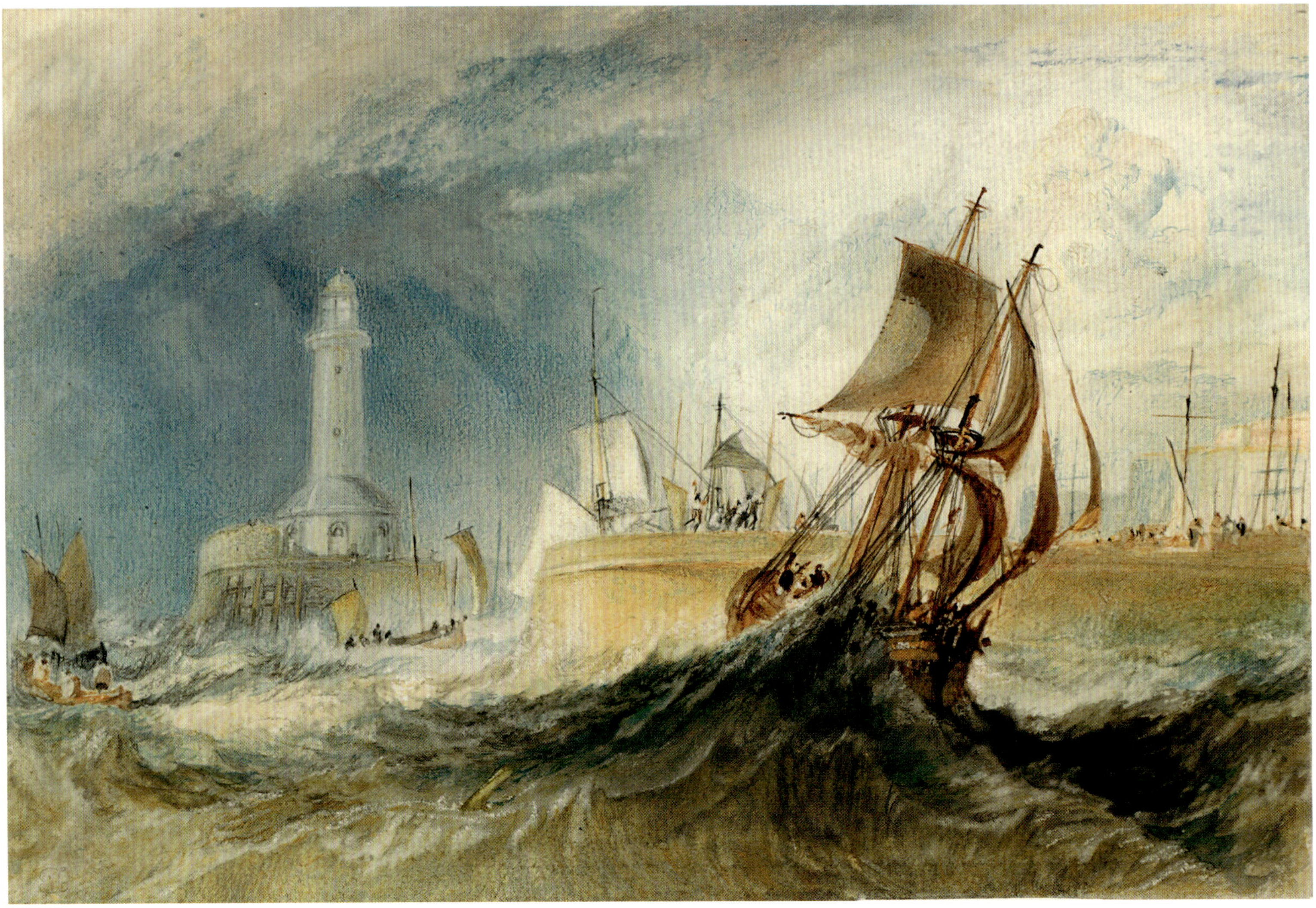

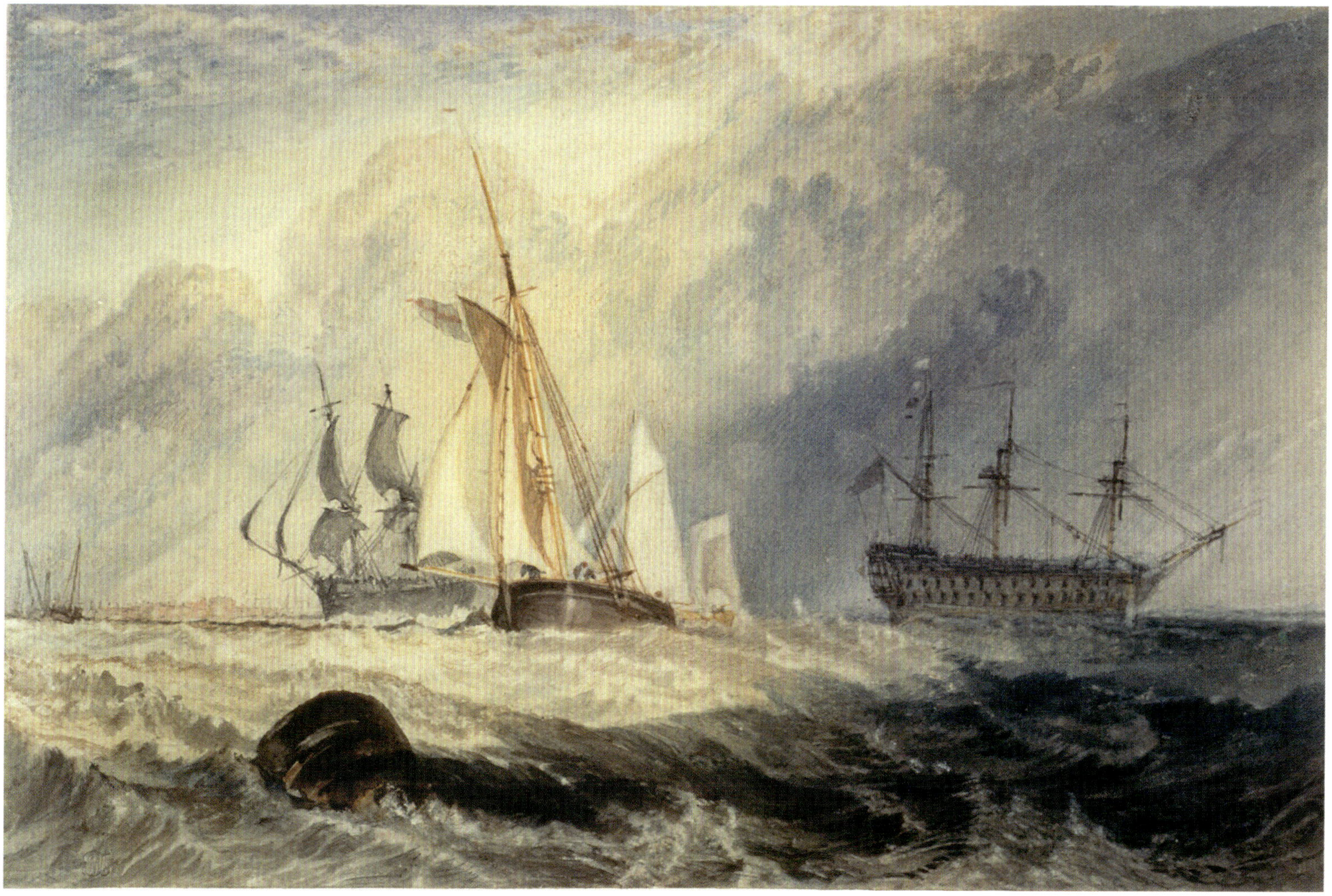

49

J.M.W. Turner

Sheerness c.1825

Watercolour 16 x 23.8 (6¼ x 9⅜)

Tate. Turner Bequest 1856

Finberg CCVIII T; Egerton 1995, p. 53

50 (and detail)

J.M.W. Turner
Dunwich c.1827
Watercolour and bodycolour on blue paper
17.4 x 25.7 (6⅞ x 10⅛)
Manchester City Galleries

Wilton, no. 900

Picturesque Views on the East Coast of England seems to have been planned by W.B. Cooke as a sequel to the *Southern Coast* series. Unlike the other watercolours discussed in this chapter, the *East Coast* works are executed on blue paper. Dunwich, on the coast of Suffolk, had once been a prosperous town but constant erosion by the sea resulted in its economic decline. By the 1820s it was a small fishing village. On the hill, Turner shows the ruins of All Saints Church, the building having been abandoned during the eighteenth century. It was the only ancient church in Dunwich to have survived, until it finally fell into the sea in the early twentieth century. The sense of a doomed community was accentuated in the print version by the inky blackness of the tones and the introduction of a lightning strike.

Turner's image of Great Yarmouth [fig. 22] takes as its theme the participation of the navy in the French Revolutionary and Napoleonic Wars, and its most celebrated hero, Vice-Admiral Nelson. The monument (1817–19) to the right was the first column to be erected in commemoration of Nelson's naval victories and his death at Trafalgar in 1805. In his Devonshire Coast Sketchbook, dated 1811, Turner had bemoaned the lack of a monument in a draft poem he composed while on a sketching trip: 'No monument but yet decks the ground / [Activate] in our hearts but still our eyes / Would pleasing view his Cenotaph arise / On some bold promontory where the western main / Rich with actions ever blesst by fame' (Wilton 1990, p. 175).

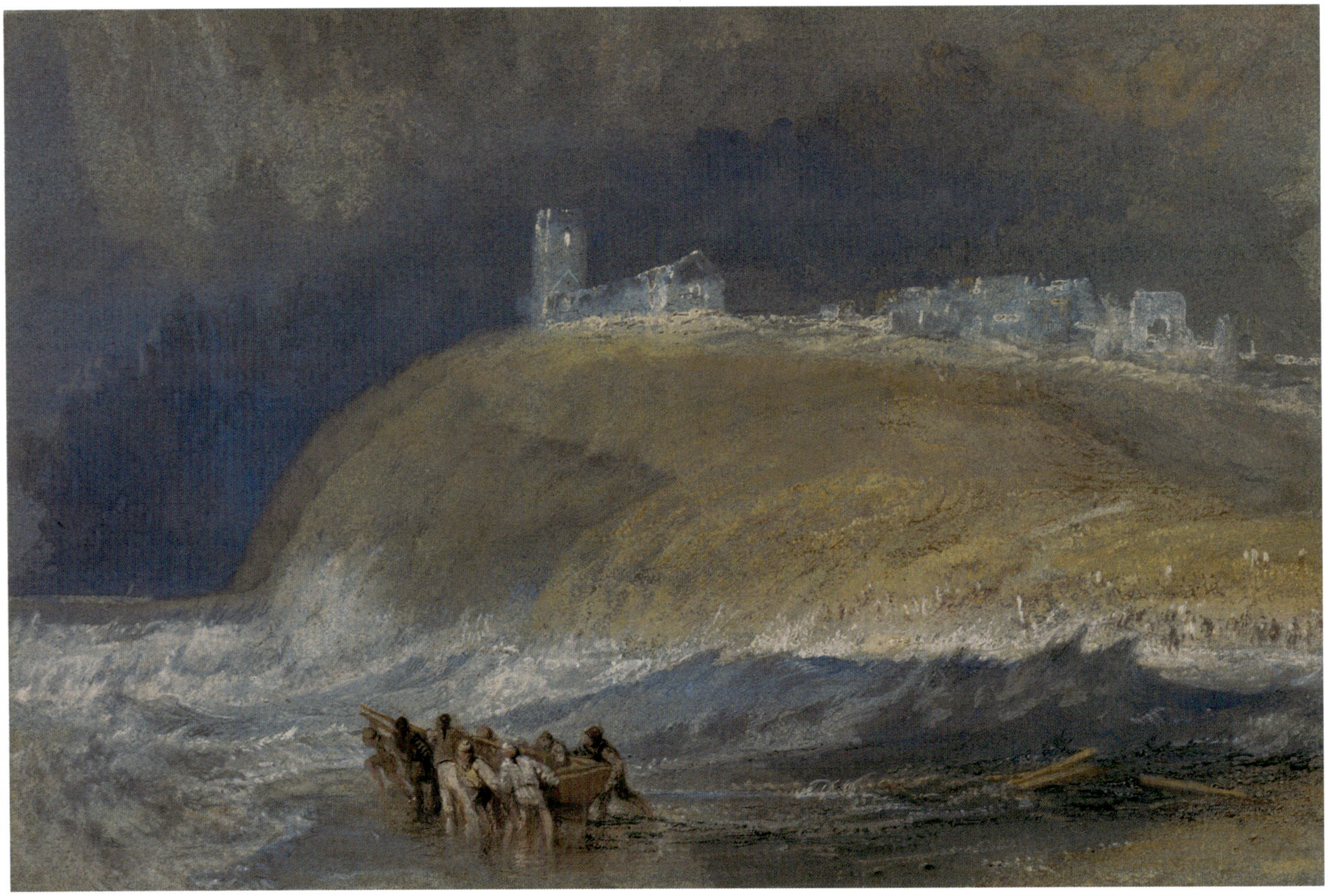

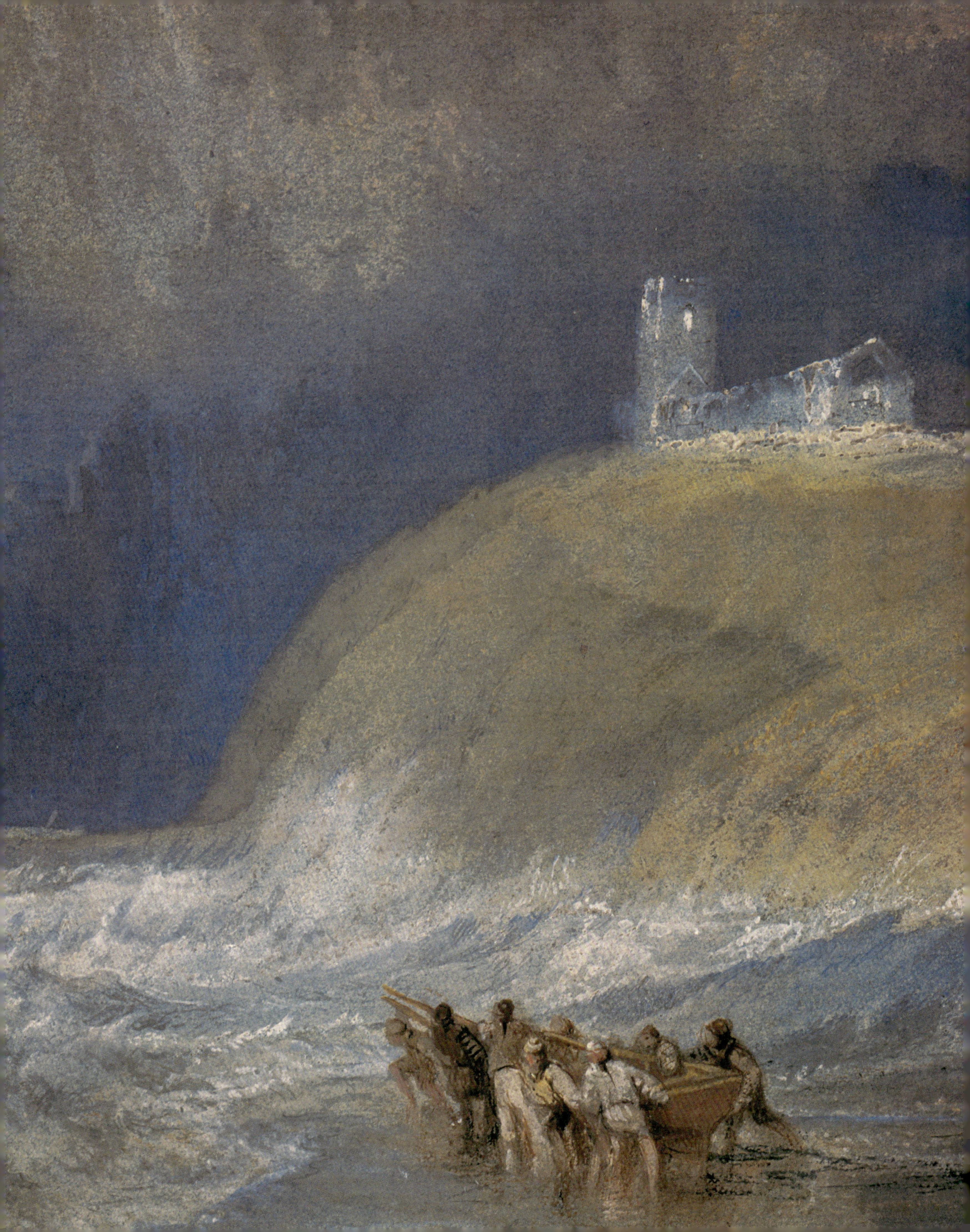

51

J.M.W. Turner

Gosport (Entrance to Portsmouth Harbour), Hampshire c.1829

Watercolour 28.5 x 41.9 (11¼ x 16½)

Portsmouth City Museum

Wilton, no. 828; Shanes 1990, no. 175

Picturesque Views in England and Wales was the most ambitious print project involving Turner during the 1820s and 1830s. Charles Heath, an engraver turned publisher, originally commissioned the artist for 120 works. Owing to a succession of financial problems, however, publication finished in 1838 with only ninety-six plates produced. Unlike the themed series of *The Ports of England*, *The Rivers of England* and *Marine Views*, this one covers almost the full range of landscape subjects open to Turner, from cityscapes and industrial centres to lake, river and coastal scenes, from historic landmarks, peaks and rugged terrains to harbours and fishing villages. In 1829, to encourage interest in the project, Heath exhibited around thirty-eight of Turner's watercolours at the Egyptian Hall, Piccadilly, to favourable reviews. Today they are considered to be one of the artist's most important series of watercolours.

The works illustrated here indicate the range of marine subjects that Turner included. Gosport lies on a peninsula on the western side of Portsmouth Harbour on the south coast of England. Portsmouth was (and is) an important naval base. Ships of the line and other vessels can be seen in the background to the right. From 1812, 'Victory', Nelson's flagship at the Battle of Trafalgar, was stationed here and after 1824 served as port guardship. The art critic John Ruskin, who at one time owned this watercolour, described the scene as a 'delightful piece of fast sailing, whether of boats or clouds' (Ruskin 1878, no. 31).

Longships Lighthouse is positioned off Land's End, Cornwall [fig. 13]. The structure

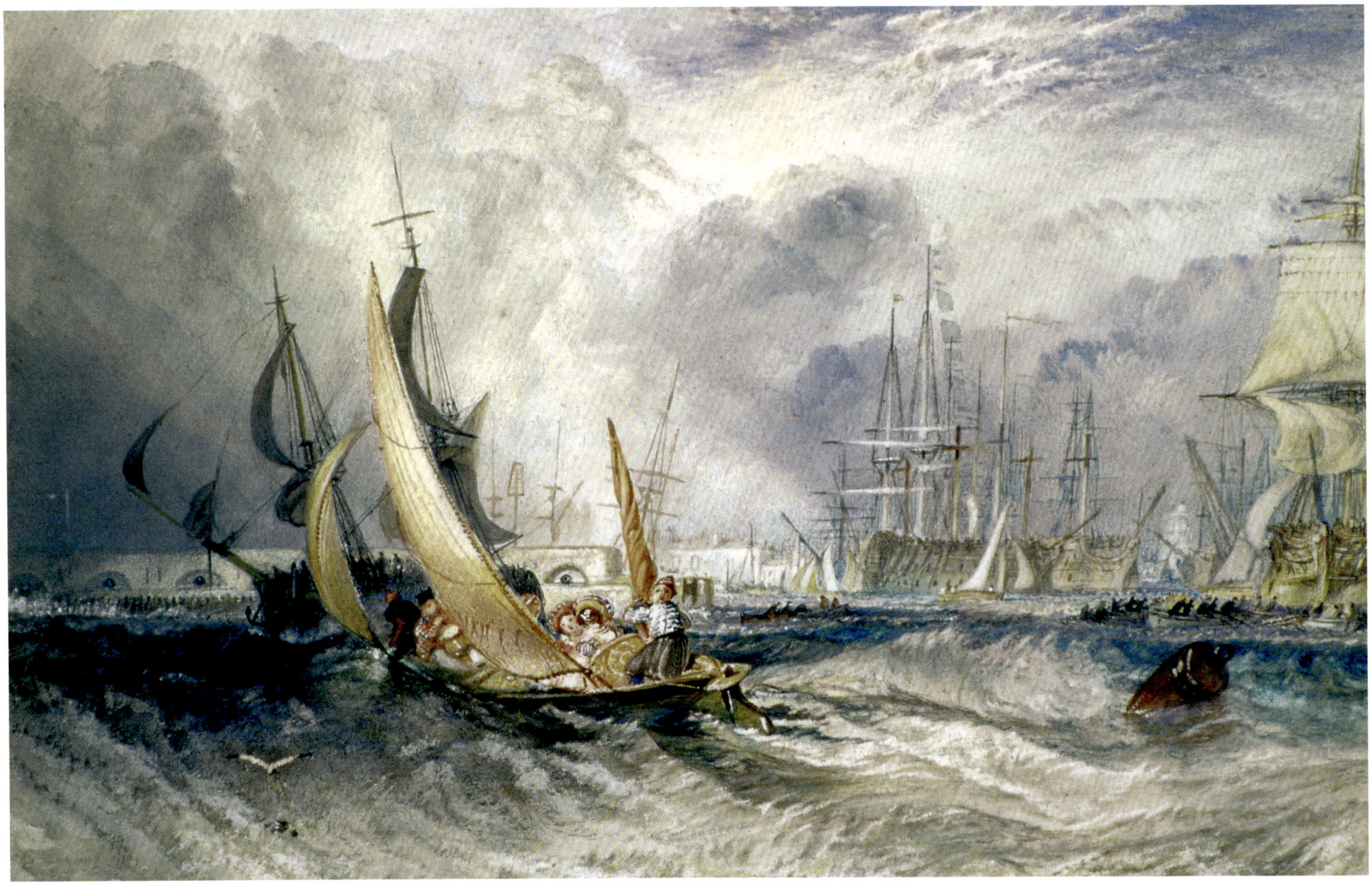

represented here dated from 1795 (the lighthouse was reconstructed in 1875). The lantern, albeit some seventy-eight feet above sea level, was often obscured during storms. Whereas William Daniell showed the lighthouse dominating the scene to the right [fig. 12], in Turner's watercolour the structure is barely visible in the distance to the left, perhaps suggesting its limitations in such perilous conditions. Indeed, in the foreground some wreckage is buffeted by, to quote Ruskin, 'an anarchy of enormous power' (Ruskin 1843, p. 373). In contrast, Turner's representation of St Michael's Mount, a tidal island off the coast of Cornwall, reprises the predominantly pale blues of the *Gosport* watercolour, giving the distant island an ethereal presence. The theme of shipwreck continues, however, with locals in the foreground gathering up wrecked timber to be sold on.

52

J.M.W. Turner
Mount St Michael, Cornwall 1836
Watercolour 30.5 x 43.9 (12 x 17¼)
University of Liverpool

Wilton, no. 880; Shanes 1990, no. 223

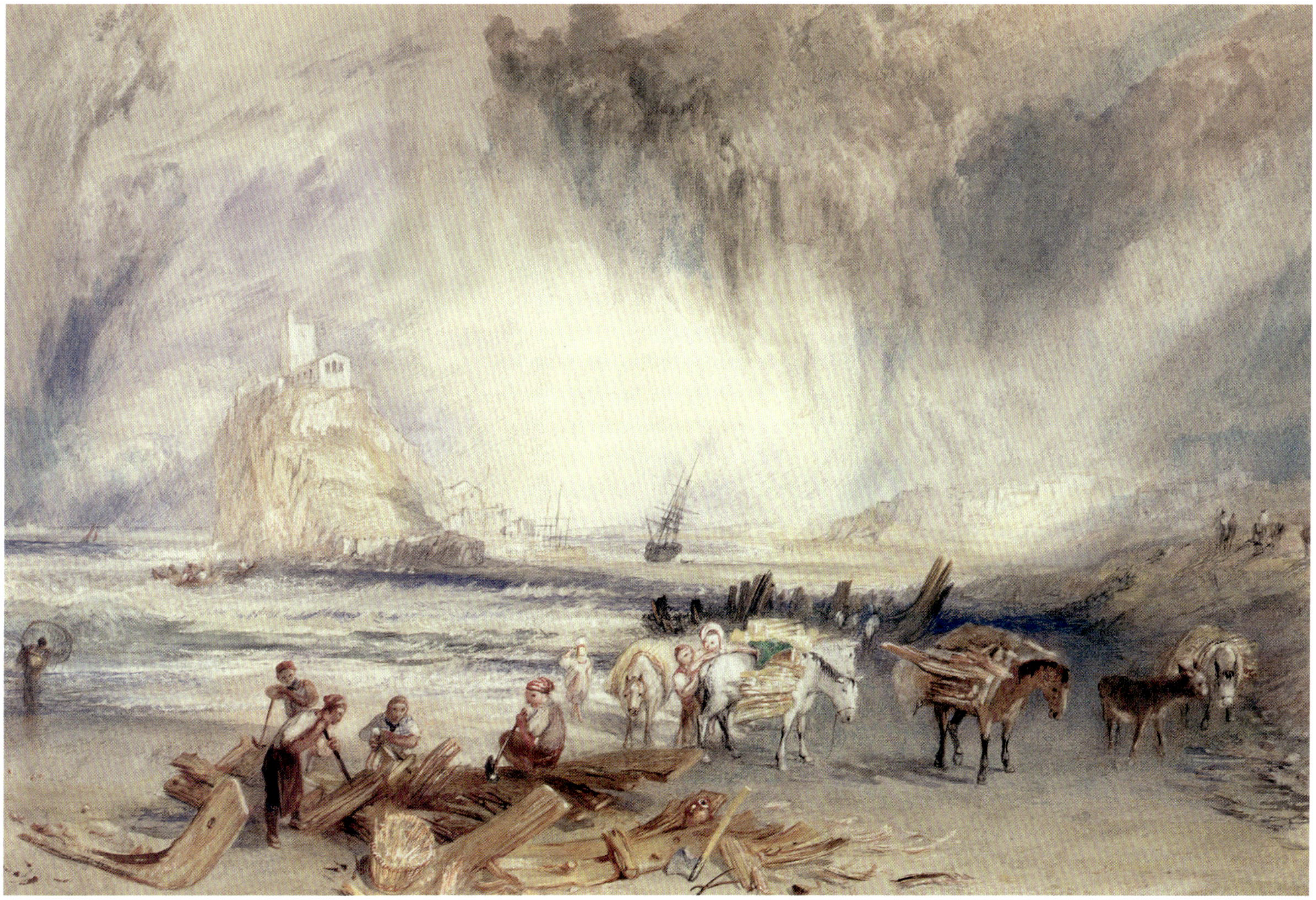

3

TRAFALGAR SQUARED

Christine Riding

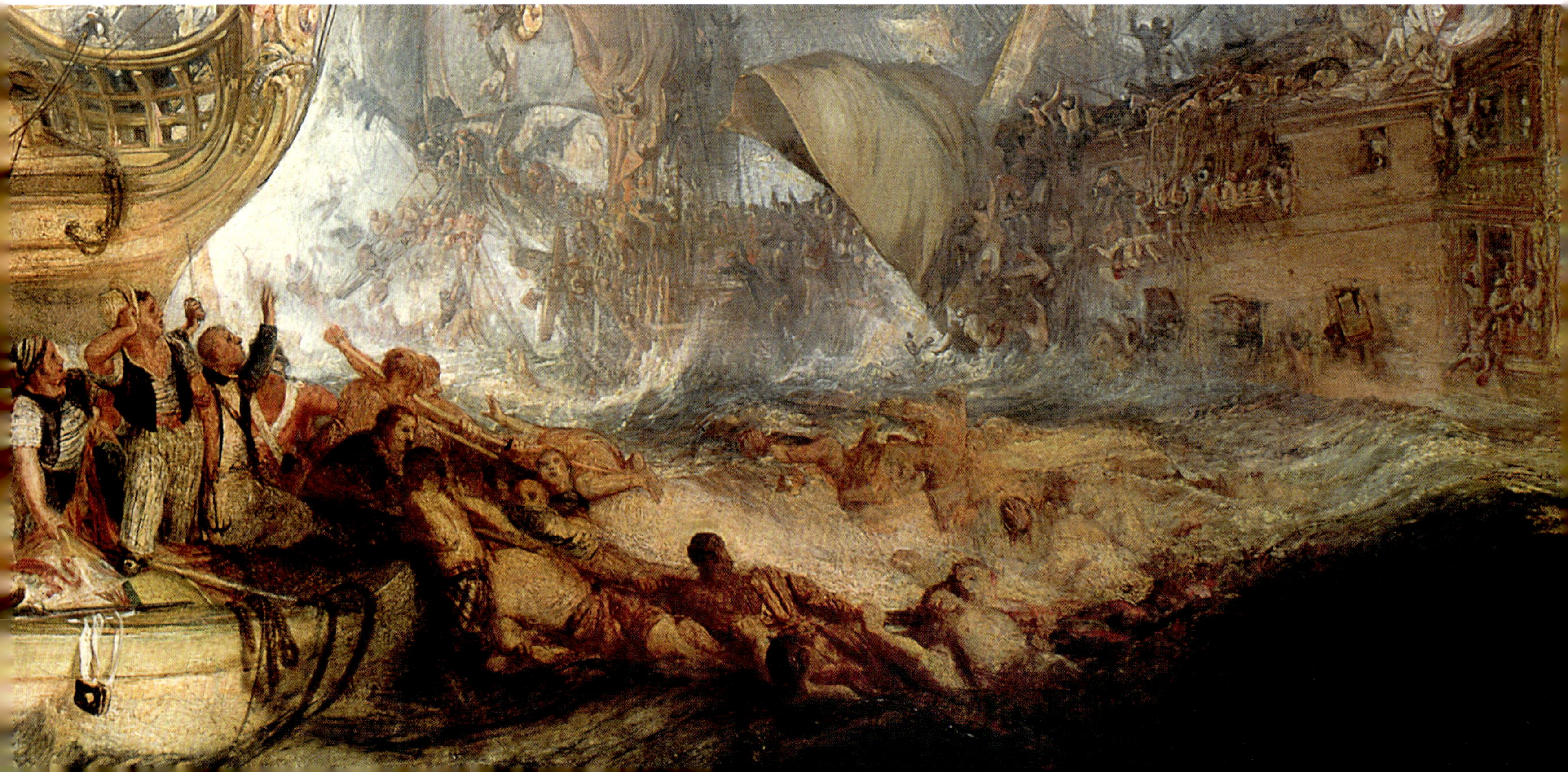

Towards the end of 1822, Turner was commissioned by George IV to paint *The Battle of Trafalgar* [58]. Measuring twelve feet across, it would be his largest work and arguably his most complex and ambitious on the theme of war. As discussed elsewhere (see 'Charted Waters'), battle painting was an established and distinct branch of marine art and yet, despite the extended period of conflict represented by the French Revolutionary and Napoleonic Wars (1792–1815), it was to feature very little in Turner's work. In fact he exhibited only three paintings of contemporary military events: two naval subjects, of the Battles of the Nile (1798) and Trafalgar (1805), and one of Waterloo (1815). All three were speculative ventures. If the depiction of actual battle scenes was of limited artistic interest, in contrast, Turner's engagement with Trafalgar in particular, and the navy more generally, was wide-ranging and profound. It was a subject that he returned to repeatedly in exhibited paintings and watercolours, and in designs for numerous print projects. Above all, his interest in the subject is signposted by three major works that span more than thirty years: *The Battle of Trafalgar, as Seen from the Mizen Starboard Shrouds of the 'Victory'* (1806–08) [fig. 16], *The Battle of Trafalgar* (1823–24) and *The Fighting 'Temeraire', Tugged to her Last Berth to be Broken Up, 1838* (1839) [87].

NELSON, NAVY, NATION

In analysing Turner's responses to Trafalgar, it is important to understand the broader context of British wartime and post-war patriotism, and its associated 'victory culture', at a time when the navy had achieved a unique position within British culture more widely. Late eighteenth- and early nineteenth-century 'naval patriotism', as Timothy Jenks has argued, was not simply a reflection of Britain's 'islandness', or a consequence of naval success and the commemoration of its officer heroes, past and present. Rather, as a hierarchical and relatively meritocratic 'community', the navy had become a potent metaphor for British society as a whole, and a focus for debate around issues concerning 'the nation state' and national identity.[1] The symbols of naval patriotism were its victories, its ships, its commanders and sailors, expressed in popular phrases such as 'heart of oak' and 'wooden walls', which became common currency alongside the cultural stereotype of the honest, nautical jargon-speaking sailor, Jack Tar. The 'ship of state', a universal metaphor, thus resonated powerfully in Britain. All of this is represented in Turner's work.

Of all naval engagements, it was the Battle of Trafalgar, fought on 21 October 1805 against the combined French and Spanish fleets, that defined the relationship between the navy and the nation for the next hundred years. This was primarily because of what the battle as a whole represented: first, it was a decisive and strategic victory that underlined Britain's naval supremacy and signalled to the British public the end of Napoleon's invasion plans; second, for the nature and the conduct of the battle itself, with its emphasis on total victory; and third, that the commander of the British fleet, Vice-Admiral Horatio Nelson, had been killed during the action. Thus Trafalgar came to signify a uniquely powerful fusion of victory, extreme violence, duty and ultimate sacrifice.

In order to galvanize support for the ongoing war, especially in the wake of Napoleon's victories at Austerlitz and Ulm in November and December 1805, the British government sought to gain maximum political benefit from Trafalgar and Nelson's 'death in victory'. The centrepiece of this strategy was Nelson's state funeral in January 1806, a carefully stage-managed event that was calculated to emphasize the navy's centrality to the nation. As a focus of national celebration and mourning, the battle also proved to be the single most important event of the war for the British art world, primarily because of the potential it offered artists for public display and promotion – whether through independent and speculative projects, as part of the regular exhibition culture, through prints, or via competitions and public subscriptions for projects of national, regional and colonial commemoration. Over and above the benefits it could offer individual artists, the Royal Academy of Arts – a highly status-conscious institution – took the opportunity to assert itself as an arbiter of state culture during the war period.[2] This strategy became more evident as the debate around public and official commemoration intensified after 1805. For example, the Academy and the government-appointed 'Committee of Taste' (populated largely by directors of the British Institution) were asked to deliberate over the location and design of Nelson's monument in St Paul's Cathedral. However, state funding – meagre

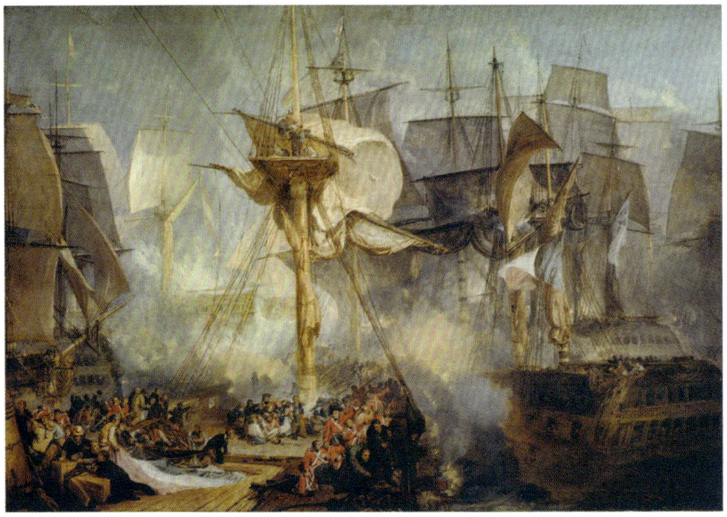

Fig. 16

J.M.W. Turner
The Battle of Trafalgar, as Seen from the Mizen Starboard Shrouds of the 'Victory' 1806–08
Oil on canvas 170.8 x 238.8 (67¼ x 94)
Tate. Turner Bequest 1856

in comparison to that of France – was directed exclusively towards sculptural and architectural commemorative projects.[3] Consequently, those painters who responded to the immediate aftermath of the battle did so from private commissions and competitions, or via public exhibition. It was under these circumstances that Turner produced his first *Battle of Trafalgar* within months of Nelson's funeral, before exhibiting the work at his own gallery in Harley Street. The painting was subsequently reworked by Turner and exhibited again at the British Institution in 1808.

Turner's opportunism was by no means unique. The President of the Royal Academy, Benjamin West, exhibited his *Death of Nelson* in his own gallery in 1806 before exhibiting the same work at the Royal Academy in 1811 alongside its engraved version by James Heath.[4] Such entrepreneurial and market-led strategies had been a feature of the British art scene since the 1760s, following the inauguration of public exhibitions of contemporary art in London: at the Society of Artists from 1761, and at the Royal Academy from 1769. However, the extended war period offered a far greater concentration of topical subjects for artists, particularly after the Battle of the Nile in 1798, which established Nelson as the most successful and celebrated admiral in British naval history. Turner's first battle painting – and the first of his paintings representing a contemporary event – was *The Battle of the Nile*, exhibited at the Royal Academy in 1799 (current location unknown). It was one of five paintings on the same subject in the exhibition that year, alongside two by Nicholas Pocock and two by Robert Cleveley.[5] In the clamour for publicity and financial returns, many artists were willing participants in victory culture and propaganda, underlining art's central role in championing the British cause against the French. By representing contemporary naval events, artists – including Turner – were also open to criticism from beyond the art-interested public; that is, from within the naval community itself.

As stated in the exhibition title for his *Nile* painting, Turner focused on the dramatic explosion of the massive French flagship 'L'Orient' during the battle.[6] We might therefore assume that his composition found some parallels with, for example, Philip James de Loutherbourg's painting of the same subject, exhibited at the RA in 1800.[7] For his next exhibited battle painting, Turner went beyond the conventions of battle imagery to engage with late-Georgian representations of the heroic 'death tableau'. The dying martial hero as a kind of secular martyr was heralded by West's *Death of General Wolfe*, exhibited at the RA in 1770.[8] This was an image that Nelson seems to have been familiar with and, as West was later to claim, the Admiral even expressed a hope that the artist would create his own version, should he die in battle.[9] In 1806, West duly obliged with his *Death of Nelson*, the engraved version of which he promoted as a pair to the financially successful *Wolfe* print [fig. 17]. West had elevated the subject of General Wolfe's death, first, by taking liberties with the historical facts, and second, by utilizing compositional devices from Christian iconography associated with the Passion: for example, when Jesus's lifeless body is lowered from the cross into the arms of his mourners.[10] The approach was acceptable to artists because of the established conventions of history painting, widely held to be the most formally and intellectually challenging of all genres. John Singleton Copley and others developed West's highly successful (if inherently fictionalized) form of heroic representation still further in the 1780s and 1790s, to the extent that by 1805 there existed a ready formula within British visual culture for representing Nelson's death. Indeed, Arthur William Devis brought the quasi-religious 'death tableau' to an extraordinary climax in his sacral *Death of Nelson* of 1807 [fig. 18].

Utilizing these diverse pictorial modes in his first *Battle of Trafalgar*, Turner incorporated West's focus on the figure of the dying admiral, surrounded by officers, sailors and marines, within a broader, more panoramic view of the action, to create a novel pictorial 'middle ground' between the intimacy of the 'death tableau' of contemporary history painting and the more distant viewpoint conventional with naval battle painting, as practised by Nicholas Pocock and others. This Turner achieved by adopting an unusual viewpoint looking down from the mizzen shrouds of the 'Victory' towards the decks of four enormous ships of the line, the British 'Victory', 'Temeraire' and 'Neptune', and the French

Fig. 17

James Heath after Benjamin West
The Death of Nelson 1811
Engraving 50 x 63.5 (19⅝ x 25)
National Maritime Museum

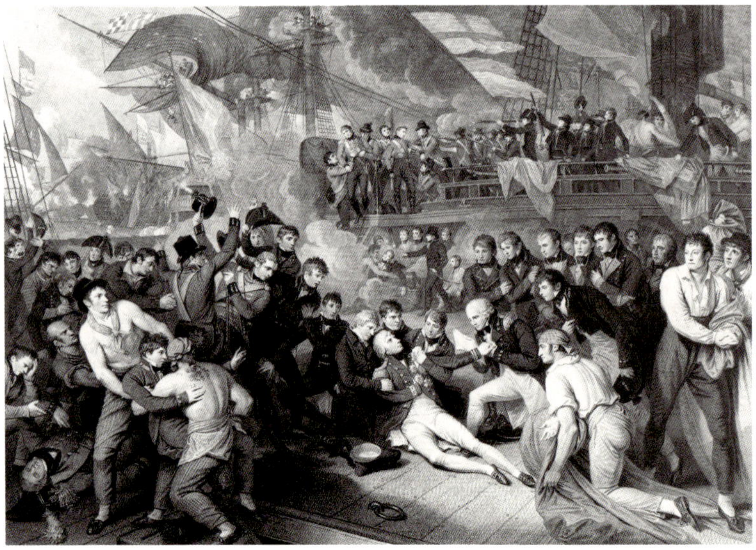

Fig. 18

Arthur William Devis
The Death of Nelson, 21 October 1805 1807
Oil on canvas 195.6 x 261.6 (77 x 103)
National Maritime Museum

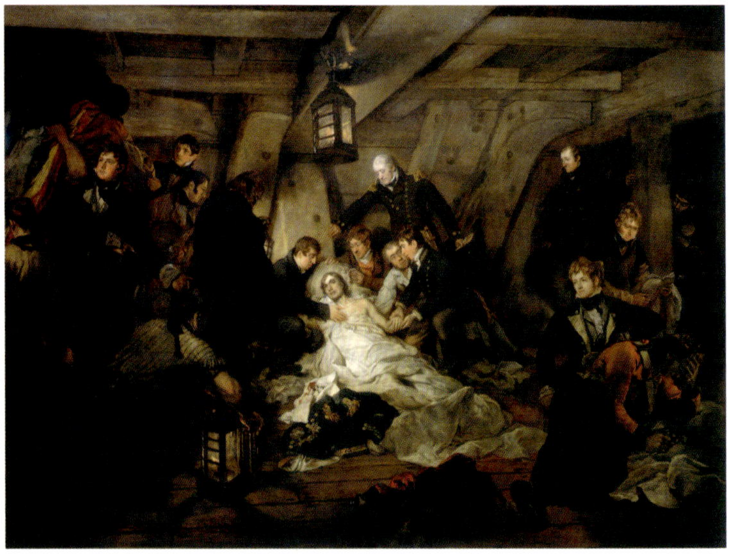

'Redoutable', locked in close combat. The importance of such a view, in shaping an audience's vicarious experience of war at sea, is underscored by the precise title that Turner assigned to the work. Writing in 1796, William Cobbett described the sight of the British fleet at Spithead as follows: 'I had heard of the wooden walls of Old England: I had formed my ideas of a ship, and of a fleet; but, what I now beheld, so far surpassed what I had ever been able to form a conception of, that I stood lost between astonishment and admiration.'[11] Cobbett's apparent difficulty in conceptualizing the fleet off the coast of England neatly underlines how difficult it would have been for many of Turner's contemporaries to imagine major fleet actions, fought for the most part hundreds of miles away.

Furthermore, what Nelson sought at Trafalgar was a decisive outcome. Indeed, just prior to the battle he had stated that it was 'annihilation that the Country wants, and not merely a splendid victory'.[12] This he achieved through battle tactics that forced the fleet into close combat, utilizing the superiority of British guns and rate of fire to devastate enemy ships and crews. The moment Turner chose to represent in 1806 underlined these tactics, the so-called 'Nelson touch'. But the cost of these tactics could also be devastating for the British. As Nelson insisted on leading from the front, he necessarily put himself within range of enemy fire. It was a sniper shot from on board the closely positioned 'Redoutable' that fatally wounded him.

FROM NELSON TO NATION

The immediate impact of Turner's first *Battle of Trafalgar* is not known, owing to the lack of published critical responses. However, the novelty of his approach was discussed at length in the *Review of Art* (1808) by the engraver John Landseer, who categorized the painting as 'new in its kind ... a *British epic picture*'. Drawing parallels with Homer's epic poetry, standard source material for traditional history painting, Landseer noted that Turner had detailed the death of the individual hero, Nelson, and suggested 'the whole of a great naval victory ... in a *single* picture'.[13] When he returned to the subject of Trafalgar in 1822, almost two decades after the event, Turner would again devise a 'British epic picture' but to very different effect and under very different circumstances. Britain was no longer at war, the French army having finally been defeated at the Battle of Waterloo in 1815, and Napoleon had died on St Helena in 1821. In the years after Waterloo, the government continued to debate how best to commemorate the wars, the army and navy, and their respective heroes. But the emphasis had changed since the initial response to Nelson's victory in 1805. Events had proven that Trafalgar was indeed a decisive naval battle and could therefore be perceived, to quote Lord Castlereagh from 1816, as the 'grand point of consummation' for the navy's involvement during the entire war. Accordingly, any national monument to Trafalgar would have to encapsulate this sense of grandeur by commemorating 'the fame of Viscount Nelson, and other officers, seamen and marines, who died gloriously for their country's cause'.[14]

Beyond the deliberations of Parliament, West's successor as President of the Royal Academy, Thomas Lawrence, was engaged in a number of prestigious war-related projects under the patronage of the Prince Regent (George IV from 1820), above all the Waterloo Chamber at Windsor Castle.[15] In addition, the idea of a national gallery of naval art at Greenwich Hospital, first mooted in the 1790s, had gathered momentum under the Hospital's Secretary, Edward Hawke Locker, and George IV gave his royal approval to the project by eventually donating thirty-eight paintings from the royal collection by 1829: these included Turner's second *Battle of Trafalgar* and its earlier pendant, de Loutherbourg's *'Glorious First of June'* [53], which were the last two, sent to Greenwich that year. In this context, it is significant that Lawrence promoted Turner, a fellow Academician, for the royal commission, originally intended for a new scheme at St James's Palace, and that another Academician, George Jones, and Lawrence himself provided the other paintings. Such a move was surely calculated to foreground the Royal Academy and its members. Indeed, the scheme formed part of the King's wider ambitions at St James's, Windsor Castle, Buckingham Palace and the Palace of Westminster to use the visual arts and architecture, with past and present Academicians playing an integral role, as a means of presenting himself as the focus of national celebration, dynastic stability and state culture.[16]

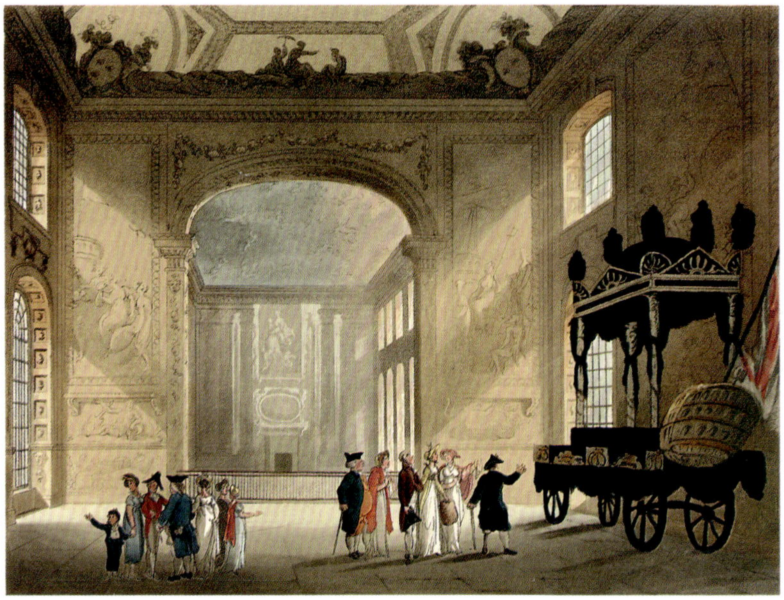

Fig. 19

Thomas Rowlandson and Augustus Charles Pugin
Greenwich Hospital. The Painted Hall 1810
Aquatint and etching with watercolour
23.7 x 27.9 (9⅜ x 11)
National Maritime Museum

By 1822, Turner was a mature and commercially successful artist in his fifties, acknowledged to be the most important landscape and marine painter of his generation. Of course, he was also prone to going his own way in matters of representation. Thus he was at once the obvious choice for such a high-profile commission and, one might argue, a calculated risk. The St James's commission set out a number of important parameters and constraints for Turner, posed by the proposed location of the work within the State Apartment of a royal palace (that is, away from public view), and the pairing with an existing work of art within a highly didactic scheme that, through representations of George III and George IV and the Battles of the 'Glorious First of June', Trafalgar, Vittoria and Waterloo, placed the two most recent Hanoverian heads of state full square with Britain's naval and military success.

Over and above its enormous size, de Loutherbourg's painting is characterized by a number of compositional devices that are also notable in his other naval battle paintings: the ships of the line dominating the upper half of the composition and, in the lower half, the officers directing sailors who are saving fellow and enemy lives. Turner's composition broadly follows this format. However, the two paintings are markedly different. Whereas de Loutherbourg's composition encapsulates the kind of spectacular battle painting he had helped to popularize in the 1790s by emphasizing the movement and dramatic confrontation between two colossal ships, Turner's has a central, static emphasis, dominated by Nelson's flagship 'Victory' (almost to the exclusion of every other ship) with a complex grouping of British sailors in and around small craft, positioned directly below. Hence the central dynamic of Turner's painting is that between the ship and the crew. That this was deliberate is suggested by the marked transition between the two preparatory oil sketches that Turner produced in 1823 (both now in the Tate Collection): from the first, a more conventional image of fleet action, focusing on the relative position of the ships of the line, to the second, that more closely anticipates the finished painting.[17]

At first glance, Nelson is notable by his absence. In reality, he pervades the canvas, not only by association, through the focus on his flagship and the various details Turner incorporated, such as Nelson's famous signal and personal motto, but also through the representation of the battle itself. Indeed 'Victory', and thus Nelson, presides over a scene of annihilation and euphoria. In the background of the painting, as masts shatter and collapse, and clouds of smoke and fire obscure the ships, men of all nationalities are seen falling from the rigging or clinging to wreckage. On one level then, what Turner emphasizes via this modern-day apocalypse – 'gory Trafalgar', as the artist himself described it – is the human cost of the battle, the inevitable outcome, as previously noted, of the 'Nelson touch'.[18] Not that Turner's painting should be read as a rebuke: by the standards of his day, he was a very patriotic man who admired the navy and Nelson in equal measure. Given the almost ethereal presence of 'Victory', presented floating high in the water, Turner might have been evoking Byron's description of Nelson, published in 1819, as 'Britannia's god of war' (*Don Juan*, I, iv). The transition from Turner's first *Battle of Trafalgar*, which focused on the admiral's death in the midst of battle, to this painting and its broader focus, requires further examination.

One important model for Turner in his treatment of war was his own *The Field of Waterloo*, exhibited at the Royal Academy in 1818 (Tate Collection).[19] In contrast to other celebratory images of this epoch-making event, by George Jones and others, Turner's gloomy representation focused on its terrible aftermath, and specifically on the dead and dying from both armies.[20] This focus on the human cost, beyond national divides, was amplified by the excerpt that Turner adapted from Byron's *Childe Harold's Pilgrimage* for the exhibition catalogue, ending with the line: 'Rider and horse – friend, foe, in one red burial blent!' (*Childe Harold*, III, xxviii). While critical responses to Turner's painting varied greatly, two critics, in the *Sun* and *Repository of Arts* respectively, concluded that the painting was a 'terrific representation of the effects of war' and 'more an allegorical representation of "battle's magnificently stern array" than any actual delineation of a particular battle'.[21] That Turner similarly sought to encapsulate the significance of Trafalgar, rather than create a more literal representation of a particular moment in the battle, is underlined by his incorporation of a number of key events from across the action. The stylized quality of the composition also suggests that he intended to create an image that was, like the Waterloo painting, more symbolic or allegorical than strictly historical. We might at this point usefully compare and contrast Turner's *Trafalgar* painting with those by Pocock [54 and 55], commissioned by James Stanier Clarke and John McArthur, founders of the *Naval Chronicle*, for their illustrated biography, *The Life of Admiral Lord Nelson* (1809). The didactic emphasis of Pocock's compositions is explained by the engraved versions being positioned very deliberately with equivalent battle plans, within the publication itself.[22]

In contrast to his *Waterloo* painting, which was a speculative venture, Turner's *Battle of Trafalgar* was a royal commission. Thus we must conclude that the representation was meant by the artist to be broadly celebratory (indeed, Turner travelled to Edinburgh in 1822 primarily to record George IV's state visit).[23] Most commentaries concerning Turner's painting focus on its redisplay at Greenwich in 1829 rather than on the original context of its production earlier in the decade. Returning to the idea of the symbolism of the navy and the 'ship of state', the key to Turner's approach may be found in the contemporary significance of 'Victory', both as a ship and an outcome, in the post-war years. In 1797, the naval mutinies at Spithead, Plymouth and the Nore had caught the navy and the government off guard, and had shaken the comfortable notion of the honest, dutiful seaman of popular culture.[24] The following year, James Stanier Clarke, then a navy chaplain, delivered sermons to the fleet at Spithead that expressly evoked the navy/nation identity. In one, Clarke noted that,

> A Ship, in which so much of your life is past [*sic*], is a just emblem of the social state, or, in other words, of a political government. Here every one has his appointed station. The various gradations of command or obedience are clearly marked; and it is a truth as evident to your understandings, as the meridian sun is to your sight, that, by a joint co-operation of all in their respective departments, of those who command and of those who obey, the vessel is conducted through the waves in safety, appears almost to defy the tempest, and returns rich in spoils or in honour.[25]

Clarke's sermons were first published in 1800. In this context, Turner's numerous representations of the guardship at the Nore, painted between 1806 and 1810, not only signify national defence but also the power and authority of the navy and, by extension, the state [78]. Thus Trafalgar offered a unique opportunity for the final 'rehabilitation' of ordinary sailors, as consenting members of a deeply patriotic, loyal and dutiful 'community'. Indeed, the loyalty that Nelson inspired from those who served under him – as indicated by Nelson's famous description of his officers as a 'Band of Brothers' – was emphasized in reports, narratives and biographical sketches, before and after his death.[26] This loyalty was symbolically re-enacted by the unprecedented participation of the crew of the 'Victory', and Greenwich Pensioners, during Nelson's state funeral, while the funeral carriage itself included a representation of the stern of the 'Victory', alluding to its status as Nelson's flagship and that the ship had brought his body back to England [fig. 19]. Turner had painted the subject of the return of the 'Victory' in about 1806 [fig. 20] and this painting may have been on display in his gallery with his first *Battle of Trafalgar*.

On the one hand, Turner seems to have been engaging with the conventions and visual language of marine art, in particular the ship portrait, as prescribed by J.T. Serres in his *Liber Nauticus*, published in 1805 [18]. Indeed, Nicholas Pocock was commissioned by Clarke and McArthur to paint *Nelson's Flagships at Anchor* [fig. 23], an imagined scene at Spithead, with 'Victory' dominating the composition on the right. On the other hand, if we accept that 'the ship' could represent the state and that the 'Victory' could itself symbolize an outcome of national importance, then any representation of it could achieve significance beyond 'mere' ship portraiture to a contemporary audience. In Turner's painting of 1806, rather than show 'Victory' battle-scarred and with its ensign at half-mast out of respect for the dead admiral (as was indeed the case in 1805), the ship in the centre of the composition is seen off the English coast in full sail, seemingly indomitable and triumphant. This indomitability is emphasized in Turner's second *Battle of Trafalgar*, where 'Victory', bathed in glorious sunlight, presides over the action, with the prominent union flag held up by a member of the crew in the foreground. This seems to be the political and cultural context underpinning Turner's post-war interpretation of the battle: that, despite the destruction and suffering, the navy/nation emerges united and victorious.

WHOSE TRAFALGAR?

The original setting for Turner's second *Battle of Trafalgar* was the rarefied and exclusive domain of a cultured monarch with a specific post-war agenda. Within such an environment, Turner might have expected his highly poetic treatment of Trafalgar to be understood. However, the dominant art-historical narrative associated with this painting is that from the time it was installed in St James's Palace naval officers, seamen and naval historians were united in their disapproval of it, largely on account of its apparent lack of historical accuracy. The discontented, so the story goes, ranged from the king's brother, the Duke of Clarence, the future William IV, who had served as a professional naval officer with Nelson and later became Lord High Admiral, to officer

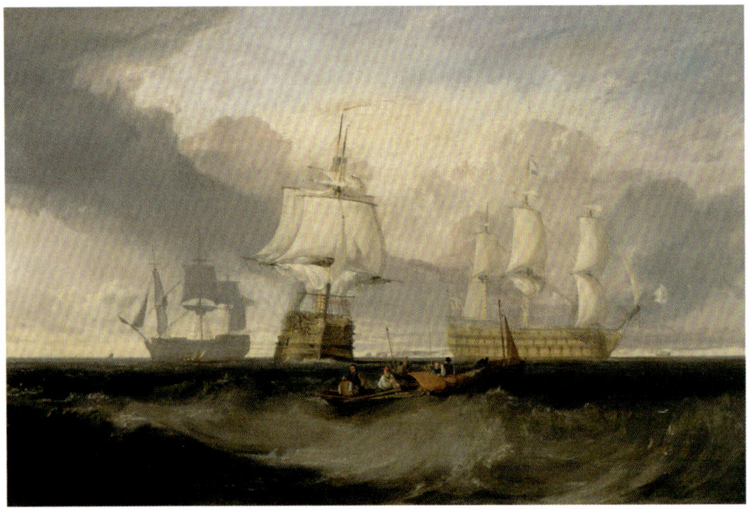

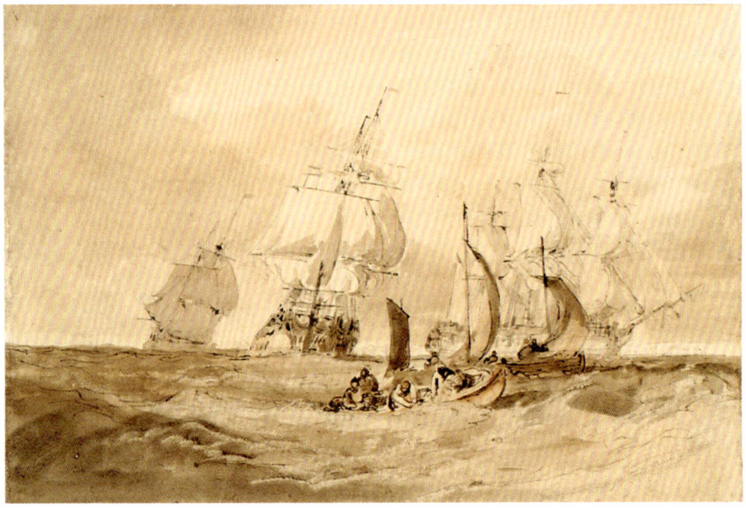

veterans of Trafalgar and, after its inclusion in the Naval Gallery, the Greenwich Pensioners themselves – ordinary seamen, many of whom had served under Nelson at the battle. Would Turner have created the same representation, had he known that the Greenwich Hospital was where it was destined to hang? This must remain a matter of conjecture. However, it is perfectly possible that Turner would have welcomed the engagement with his painting of such a broad-based naval – and public – audience there. He would, for example, have been aware of the controversy surrounding Nelson's funerary monument in 1806, which, with the 2d entrance charge to St Paul's Cathedral, excluded many ordinary sailors, for whom the site had personal and professional meaning.[27] Furthermore, in 1811, Turner had bemoaned the lack of a truly public (i.e. freely accessible) monument to Nelson and Trafalgar.[28] Later he even acknowledged how such a monument could function as a focus for commemoration among the naval community, in his watercolour design of Great Yarmouth [fig. 22]. Here Turner shows ordinary sailors re-enacting a battle with model ships in front of the Nelson monument that had been erected by public subscription by 1819. The first keeper of the monument was a veteran of Trafalgar.

However, remembering that high-ranking naval officers were the main patrons for the kind of battle paintings executed by the likes of Dominic Serres, Pocock and later William John Huggins, there existed at this time a fundamental disjuncture between the expectations of the navy, from whatever rank, and the mainstream art world in matters of representation. As an example, in Jane Austen's *Persuasion*, published in 1818, Admiral Croft critiques the 'incorrect' representation of a boat within a topographical view, hanging in a print

Opposite left Fig. 20

J.M.W. Turner
The 'Victory' Returning from Trafalgar c.1806
Oil on canvas 67 x 100.3 (26⅜ x 39½)
Yale Center for British Art

Opposite right Fig. 21

J.M.W. Turner
The 'Victory' Coming up the Channel with the Body of Nelson c.1807–19
Graphite and watercolour 20 x 28.5 (7⅞ x 11¼)
Tate. Turner Bequest 1856

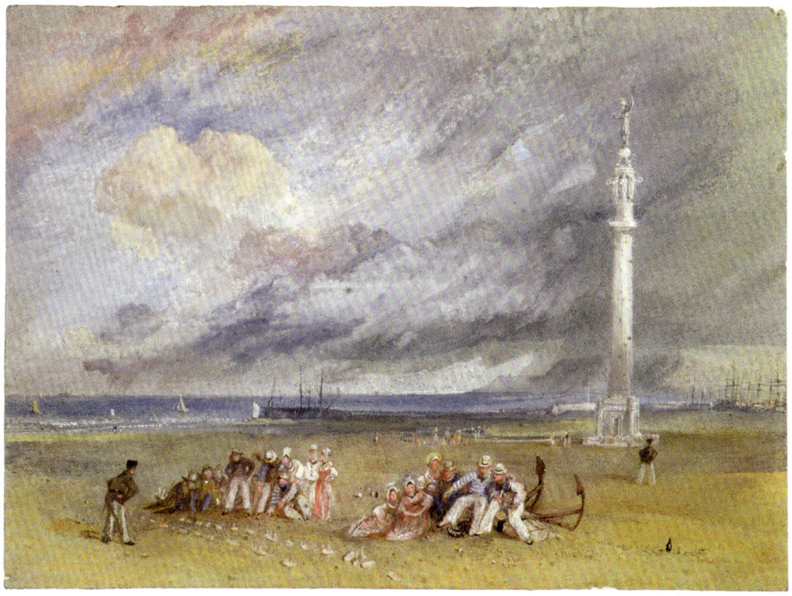

Right Fig. 22

J.M.W. Turner
Yarmouth Sands 1824–30
Watercolour and bodycolour 18.5 x 24.5 (7¼ x 9⅝)
Fitzwilliam Museum

shop: 'Did you ever see the like? What queer fellows your fine painters must be, to think that any body would venture their lives in such a shapeless old cockleshell as that.'[29] Clearly, as a professional sailor, well versed in matters of naval architecture, what the admiral saw in the image was not artistic licence but inaccuracy, pure and simple. Importantly, Austen's brothers were naval officers. Furthermore, John Ruskin's much-quoted encounter with a Greenwich Pensioner in front of Turner's *Battle of Trafalgar*, if authentic, certainly sets up a neat confrontation between the art and navy worlds, just as the art critic's relish in replicating the old sailor's manner of speech – 'Well, sir, it *is* a shame that that thing should be there. We ought to 'a 'ad a Uggins; that's sartain' – introduces the equally potent issue of class.[30]

In 1826, the naval historian William James critiqued Turner's *Trafalgar* at some length. Acknowledging him to be the 'first marine painter of the day', James nonetheless noted that Turner's 'splendid picture' displayed 'scarcely a line of truth'. He continues: 'The principal reason urged for giving to this costly and highly honoured performance so preposterous a character, is that an adherence to truth would have destroyed the pictorial effect.'[31] James concluded that it was a 'national disgrace' that there existed, in 1826, no appropriate representation of Trafalgar, in his estimation at least. Nearly ten years later, Clarkson Stanfield, who had previously served in the merchant and Royal navies, was commissioned by the United Service Club to paint the enormous *Battle of Trafalgar* [fig. 24] as a pendant to another *Battle of Waterloo* by George Jones. The club was created in 1815 for high-ranking officers of the army and navy. The tradition surrounding the creation of Stanfield's painting is that the officers who subscribed to it oversaw its progress, which included those who had fought at Trafalgar. We might, therefore, assume that the result met their demands for technical and historical accuracy and, by being endorsed by serving officers and veterans, represented the kind of battle painting that James had been calling for.[32] Could Stanfield's painting have stirred Turner's competitive spirit, resulting – at least in part – in his last and most celebrated Trafalgar painting, *The Fighting 'Temeraire'*? After all, Stanfield had emerged as one of Turner's artistic rivals in the 1820s, and his *Trafalgar* painting was not only exhibited at the Royal Academy in 1836, but was also from then onwards on permanent display in the club's premises in Pall Mall. This was near to the new buildings occupied by both the National Gallery and the relocated Royal Academy, at the north side of what would soon become Trafalgar Square. By 1843, the now-iconic Nelson's Column would be erected as its centrepiece, the long-awaited culmination of decades of debate over how to commemorate the British navy and its most celebrated hero.

It was at this auspicious moment that Turner caused a sensation, at the Royal Academy in 1839, with his *Fighting 'Temeraire'*. The immediate inspiration for this painting was, of course, the towing of 'Temeraire' – a second-rate ship of the line that had played a central role at Trafalgar – to a ship-breakers yard in Rotherhithe in 1838. Many other war ships had suffered a similar fate. Even so, the subject of Trafalgar had undoubtedly been re-energized by the preparation and laying out of the square from the late 1830s. Given the previous discussion concerning the symbols of naval patriotism, what Turner delivered in 1839 was not simply a topical *coup de théâtre*. This is evident from the comments and above all the allusions made in response to the painting. Turner had taken 'liberties' with the facts of the final journey of the 'Temeraire', as he had previously within his *Battle of Trafalgar*. However, in the environment of the Royal Academy, these details seemed (on the whole) not to have mattered. Indeed, to the critic of the *Literary Gazette*, that the painting went beyond literal representation was self-evident, 'treated as it is historically and allegorically'.

Given the by now standard associations of Trafalgar with ultimate victory and sacrifice, the anthropomorphic analogies made by a number of writers in response to *The Fighting 'Temeraire'* are of particular significance. 'There is something in the contemplation of such a scene,' noted the critic of the *Morning Chronicle*, 'which affects us almost as deeply as the decay of a noble human being. It is impossible to gaze at the remains of this magnificent and venerable vessel without recollecting, to use the words of [Thomas] Campbell, "how much she has done, and how much she has suffered for her country."'[33] The *Spectator* even described the ship and tug boat as 'like a superannuated veteran led by a sprightly boy' and concluded, appropriately enough, that 'this picture ought to be purchased for Greenwich'.[34]

In the event, both *The Fighting 'Temeraire'* and Turner's first *Battle of Trafalgar* formed part of Turner's bequest to the nation. By mid-century, therefore, all three Trafalgar paintings by Turner were in the public domain. However, it was not Turner but Stanfield who would have the final word on Trafalgar in this sequence of artistic responses. In 1844, Stanfield had become the first curator of paintings at Greenwich Hospital. And in 1853, two years after Turner's death, he exhibited *HMS 'Victory' Towed into Gibraltar* [57] at the Royal Academy. While acknowledging that Turner's *Temeraire* and Stanfield's *Victory* are very different images, it is interesting to note that Stanfield chose to focus at this time on the motif of the ship being towed. In this sense, Stanfield's painting not only participated in the ongoing engagement by British artists with the battle and its significance, but was also a timely tribute to Turner himself.

53 (and detail)

Philip James de Loutherbourg

Lord Howe's Action, or the 'Glorious First of June' 1794 1795

Oil on canvas 266.5 x 373.5 (104⅞ x 147)

National Maritime Museum

Quilley 2011, pp. 204–09; Costello 2012, pp. 52–57

Philip James de Loutherbourg was a versatile artist who conducted a successful career in the worlds of theatre, popular entertainment and fine art. By the time of his death in 1812, he had painted many contemporary battle subjects involving the British navy. These, to a greater or lesser extent, followed a successful formula that privileged bold colouring, dramatic contrasts of light and dark and other 'sublime' effects. The popular appeal of such images, whether in painted or engraved form, reflected a broader cultural interest in events relating to the extended war with France. The '*Glorious First of June*', one of de Loutherbourg's largest paintings, was commissioned by the publishers Valentine and Rupert Green as a pair to the artist's earlier *The Siege of Valenciennes*. Both paintings were exhibited at the Historic Gallery, Pall Mall, from March 1795 to promote interest in the prints (the '*Glorious First of June*' print was published in 1799). Both subsequently went on tour. George, Prince of Wales, bought the present painting in the early 1800s for display in Carlton House, underlining the future king's interest in contemporary battle painting (see pp. 124–29).

The 'Glorious First of June' was the first major fleet battle of the French Revolutionary War. De Loutherbourg researched his subject and executed detailed preparatory sketches. His bias towards dramatic effect rather than historical fact, however, is underlined by the central positioning of the British 'Queen Charlotte', on the left, and the French 'Montagne', on the right: the ships engaged during the actual battle but not in this formation. This blatant compositional inaccuracy led to stiff criticism from Lord Howe and Howe's Master of the Fleet, James Bowen. On the extreme left is 'Vengeur du Peuple', sinking after sustained attack from 'Brunswick' (see Pocock's representation [12]). In the foreground, British sailors are assisting the crew of the sinking 'Vengeur', under the direction of naval officers. The motif of 'humanity in victory' not only offered the British public a flattering idea of national character through the navy, but also demonstrated the authority and discipline between those in command and their subordinates.

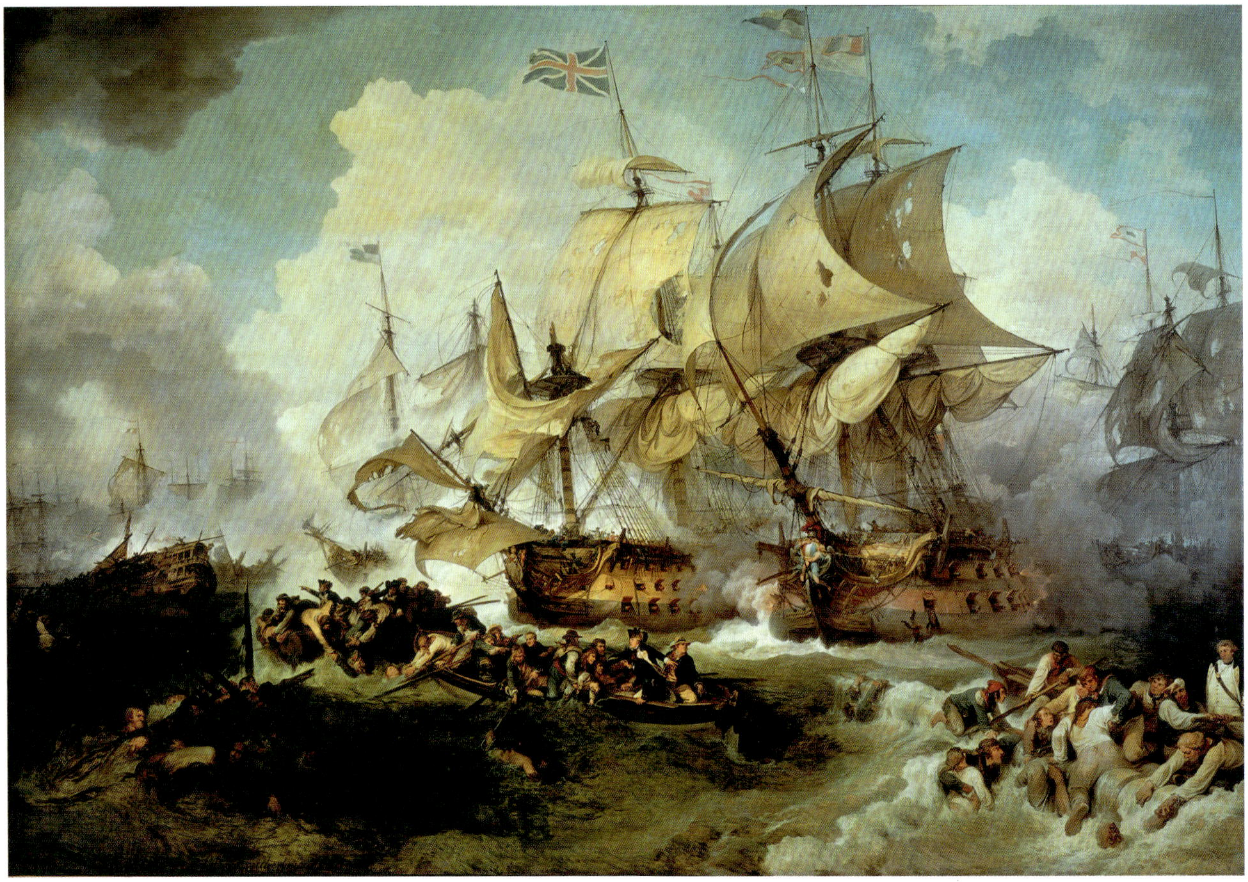

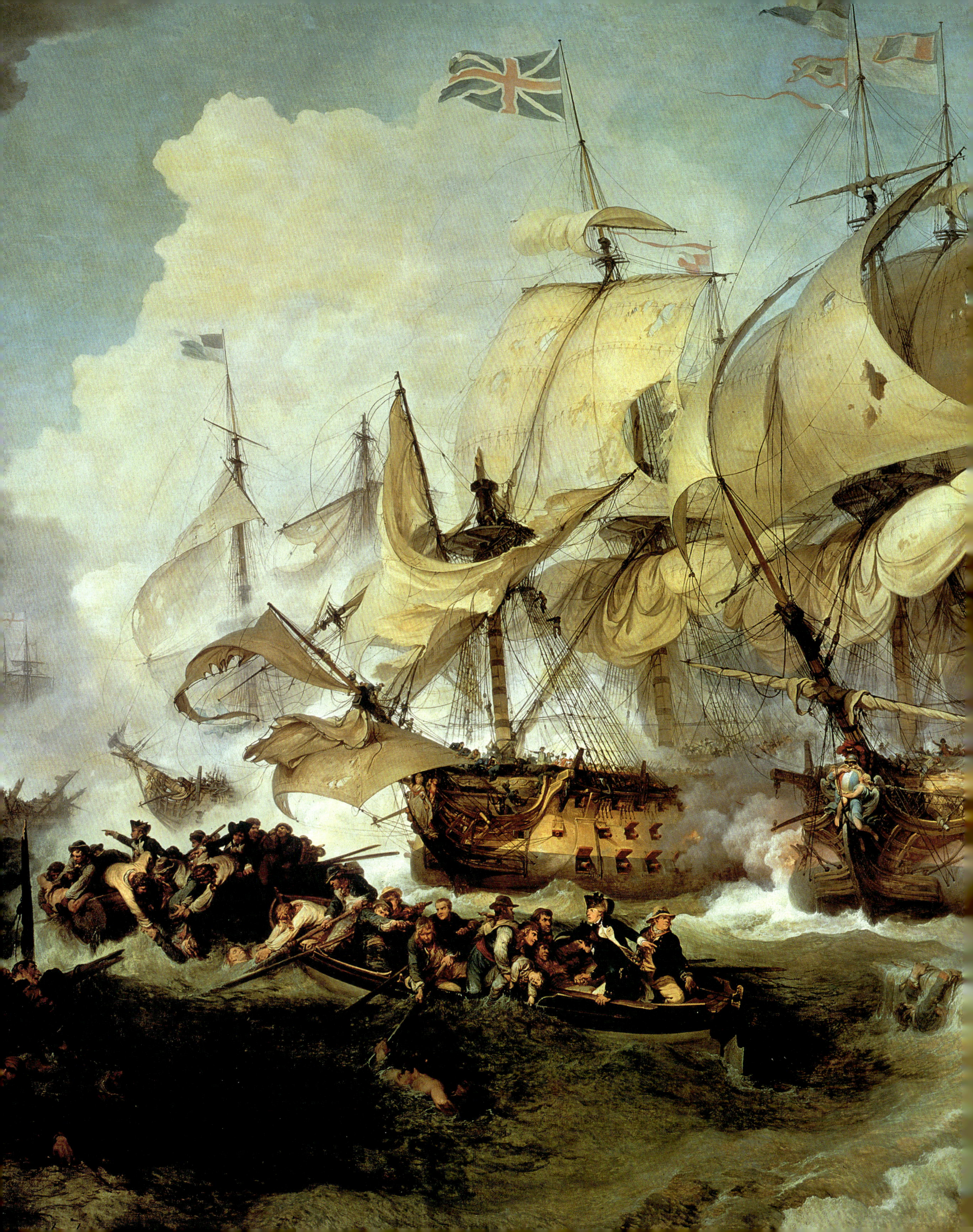

54

Nicholas Pocock
The Battle of Trafalgar, 21 October 1805: Beginning of the Action c.1808
Oil on canvas 71.2 x 101.6 (28 x 40)
National Maritime Museum

The three works illustrated here formed part of a series of six paintings by Pocock to be included as engravings in Clarke and McArthur's *Life of Nelson*, published in two volumes in 1809. Pocock executed two other battle scenes for the book, representing the Nile (1798) and Copenhagen (1801). In the publication, the four images are accompanied by corresponding plans of the battle with a key and a description. This in part explains the programmatic quality of Pocock's compositions, which also evoke the seventeenth-century battle paintings of Willem van de Velde the Elder. Pocock knew van de Velde's reputation as an eyewitness to various battles, and understood the greater authority that the Dutch artist's compositions enjoyed as a result. Here the passage of time from Pocock's first Trafalgar scene to the next is underlined in the painted versions by the change from full daylight at the beginning of the battle to a rose-tinted sunset at its close. Dutch painting was also the model for Pocock's *Nelson's Flagships at Anchor*. The five ships of the line, 'Agamemnon', 'Vanguard', 'Elephant', 'Captain' and 'Victory' are re-imagined as a Dutch 'Calm' [fig. 23].

Clarke and McArthur's *Life of Nelson* was illustrated with numerous other engravings which, viewed together, represent the range of imagery created to celebrate and commemorate the admiral's life and death. In addition to the works by Pocock, Benjamin West's *Immortality of Nelson* (exhibited at the RA in 1807) forms the frontispiece to the first volume and his *Death of Lord Nelson in the Cockpit of the 'Victory'* (exhibited at the RA in 1808) featured in the second with the revised title *Nelson in the 'Victory's Cockpit, Mortally Wounded, Oct 21st 1805*. Both paintings are now in the collection of the National Maritime Museum.

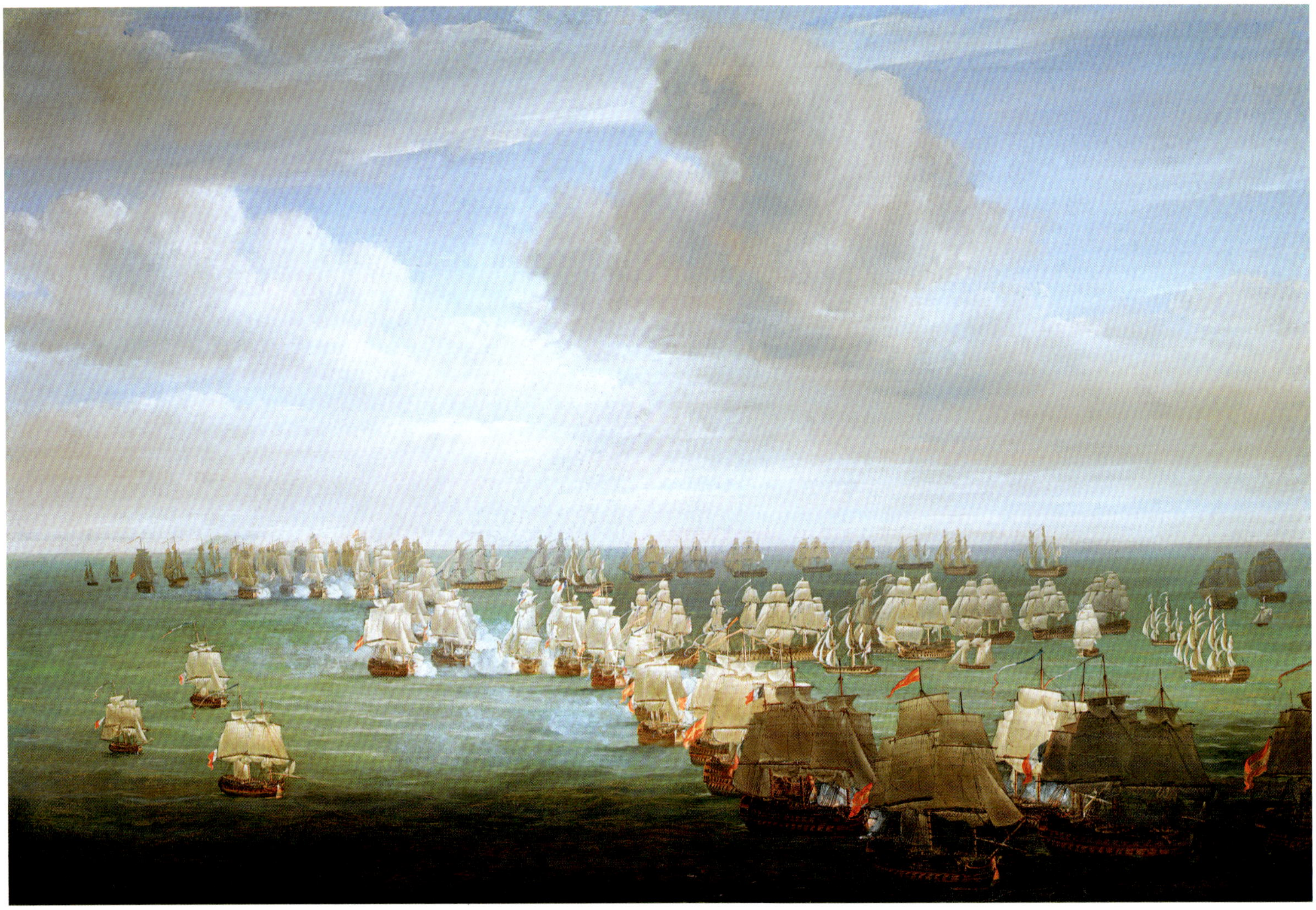

Right Fig. 23

Nicholas Pocock
Nelson's Flagships at Anchor 1807
Oil on canvas 35.6 x 54.6 (14 x 21½)
National Maritime Museum

Below 55

Nicholas Pocock
The Battle of Trafalgar, 21 October 1805: The End of the Action c.1808
Oil on canvas 71.1 x 101.6 (28 x 40)
National Maritime Museum

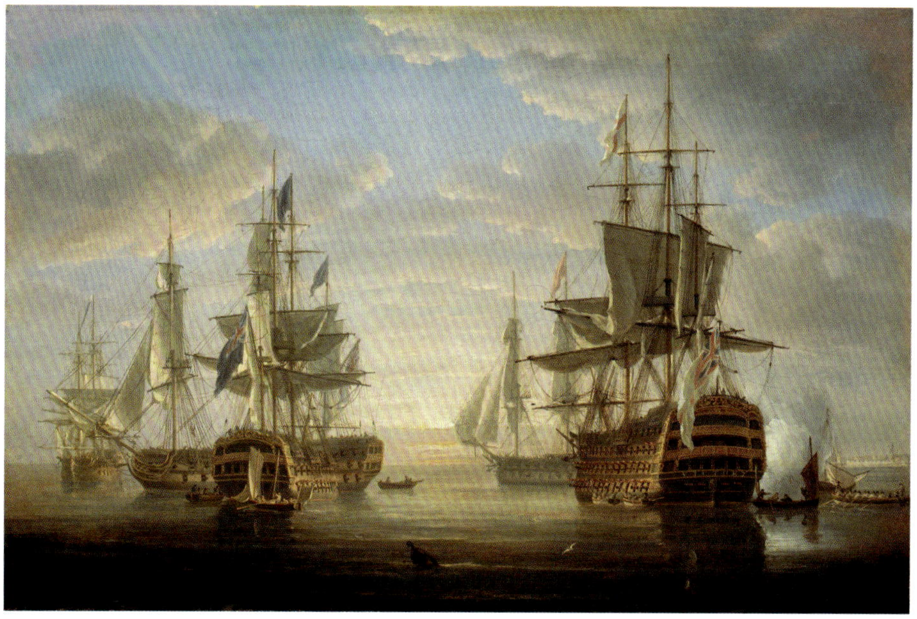

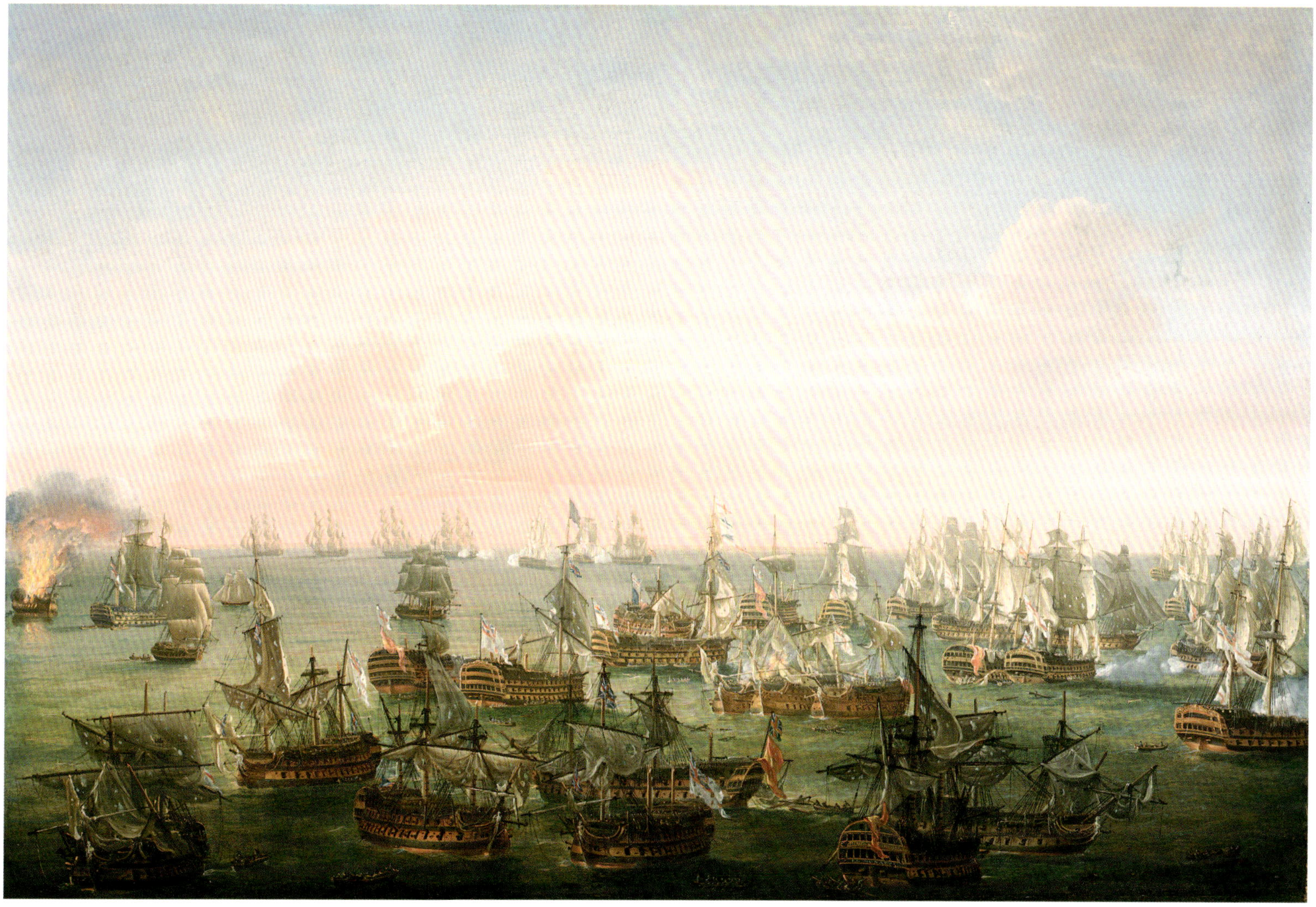

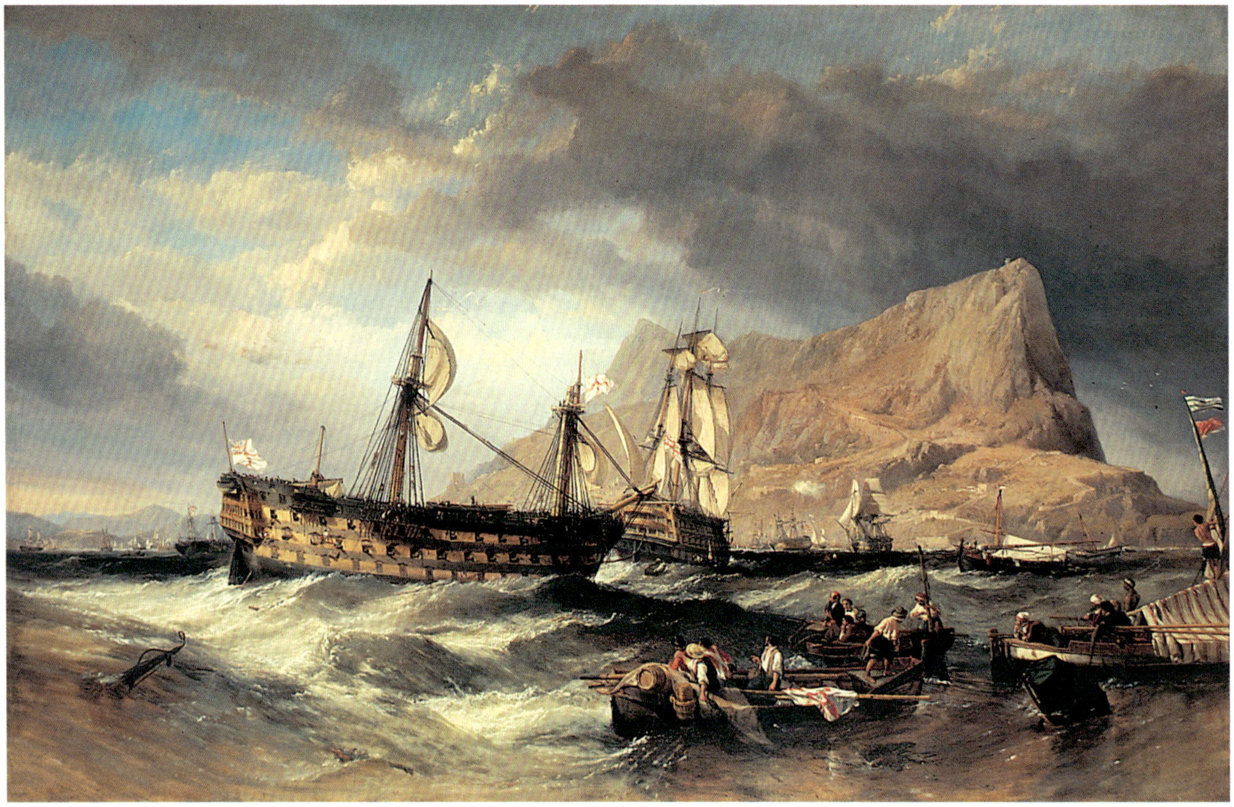

57

Clarkson Stanfield

HMS The 'Victory', with the body of Nelson on board, towed into Gibraltar 28th October, 1805, seven days after the Battle of Trafalgar 1853

Oil on canvas 176 x 262 (69¼ x 103⅛)

Somerleyton Hall, Suffolk

Van der Merwe 1979, no. 304

In 1808, Clarkson Stanfield (1793–1867) entered the merchant navy and in 1812 he was pressed into the Navy as an able seaman. For the next two years he served at Sheerness on the guardship 'Namur', under Captain Charles Austen (brother of the novelist Jane Austen). By 1818, Stanfield had become a professional painter and was engaged in the same year under John Thomas Serres, scenic director at the new Coburg Theatre (now the Old Vic), one of many engagements he undertook in the theatre world. Impressed by one of his exhibited paintings, William IV, the 'sailor king', commissioned from Stanfield views of Portsmouth and Plymouth, the subject of the latter changed to the royal opening of New London Bridge in 1831. Stanfield was elected a member of the Royal Academy in 1835, and in 1844 was appointed the first curator of the Naval Gallery at Greenwich Hospital, to advise on acquisitions (all by gift) and the maintenance of the collection and the Painted Hall.

This large painting is the second of three Trafalgar-related paintings by Stanfield, the first being the *Battle of Trafalgar* [fig. 24] commissioned by the United Service Club, completed in 1836, and the third, *HMS 'The Defence' and her Prize, 'El Sant Ildefonso'*, exhibited at the RA in 1863 (now at the National Gallery of Victoria, Melbourne). The present painting was commissioned by Sir Samuel Morton Peto, the railway contractor who had erected Nelson's Column. A markedly less elegiac representation than Turner's *Fighting 'Temeraire'*, Stanfield's *Victory* was nonetheless lauded by critics at the Royal Academy in 1853 for its dramatic power. Seventeen years later, the *Art Journal* described this and Stanfield's celebrated shipwreck scene, *The Abandoned* (1856, current location unknown), as evidence that the artist 'had smouldering within him the ardour of poetic fire'.

58

J.M.W. Turner

The Battle of Trafalgar, 21 October 1805

1823–24

Oil on canvas 261.5 x 368.5 (103 x 145⅛)

National Maritime Museum

Butlin and Joll, no. 252; Quilley 2011, pp. 228–46; Costello 2012, pp. 51–57

After receiving the royal commission in late 1822, Turner embarked on an unusual amount of practical research for this painting. In addition to the sketches he had made of the 'Victory' in December 1805, for his first *Battle of Trafalgar* [fig. 16] and for *'Victory' Returning from Trafalgar* [fig. 20], he borrowed a plan of the ship from the Admiralty and asked the marine artist J.C. Schetky to make further sketches of the 'Victory' at Portsmouth. He also made two compositional oil sketches. Moreover, the numerous paintings and watercolours he had created up to 1822 demonstrate the artist's extensive knowledge of naval architecture. In 1818, for example, he created a detailed representation in watercolour of a massive 'first rate' and other vessels, allegedly in a matter of hours [81].

The finished painting here combines a number of incidents from different times during the battle. The falling mast, perhaps an allusion to the dying Nelson, bears his white vice-admiral's flag, while code flags spelling 'd-u-t-y' – both the last word of his famous signal to the British fleet at the beginning of the battle ('England expects that every man will do his duty'), and the last words Nelson reportedly spoke ('Thank God I have done my duty') – are flying from the mainmast. On the right is the French 'Redoutable', surrendered and sinking (in fact the ship went down in the storm after the battle). Beyond the 'Victory' on the left are the Spanish 'Santísima Trinidad' and the French 'Bucentaure', flagship of Admiral Villeneuve. 'Temeraire' is on the far right, all but concealed by battle smoke. In the foreground, British seamen try to save fellow and enemy crew from the bloodied sea, which is strewn with rigging and other wreckage. Fragments of Nelson's motto, *Palmam qui meruit ferat* ('Let him who has earned it bear the palm'), can be seen below the water's surface.

The battle was fought off Cape Trafalgar, a headland near Cádiz on the southern coast of Spain. Although Turner never visited Spain, he had made his first extended visit to Italy in 1819, an experience that was transformative for the artist, both in the range of his subject matter and use of colour. In Turner's *Trafalgar* painting, the luminosity of the sky and sun-bathed ships, in sharp contrast to the shadowy darkness below, may be a fitting allusion to the battle's 'Mediterranean' setting.

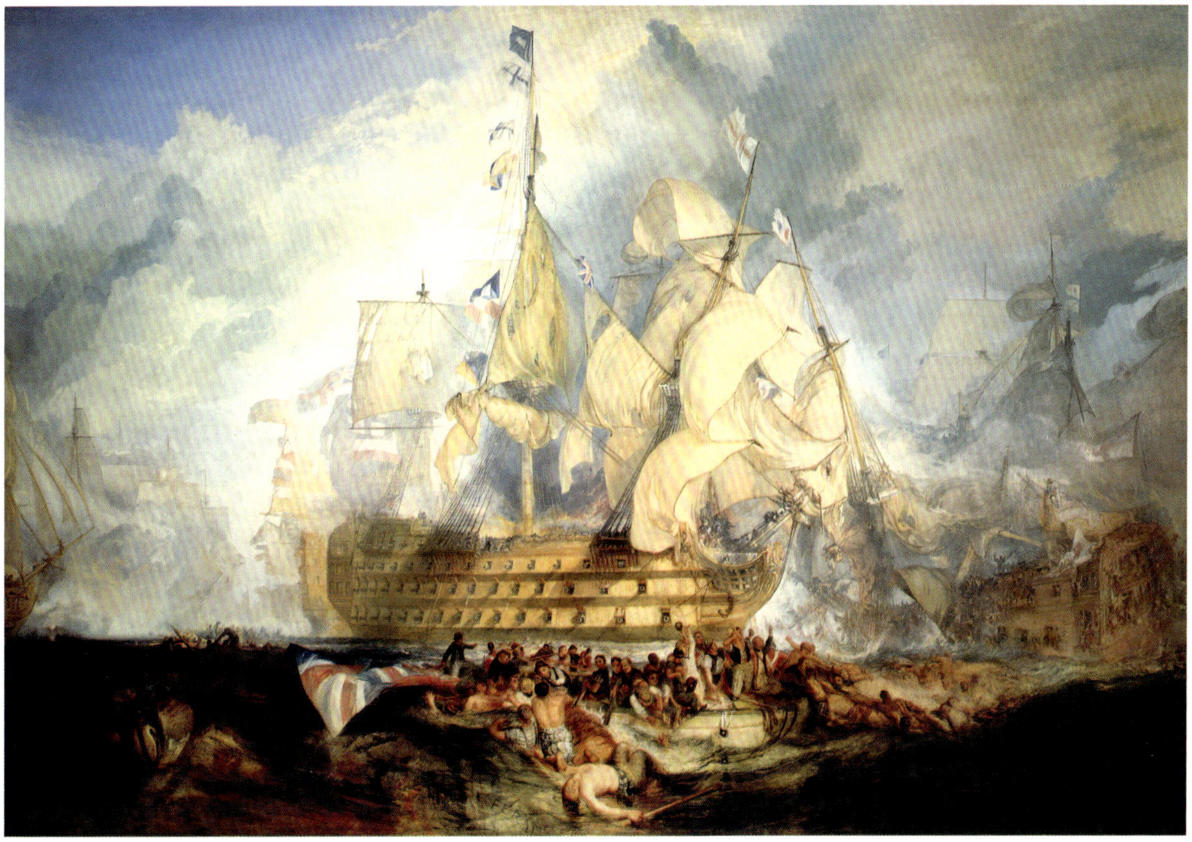

Turner's *Battle of Trafalgar* at the National Gallery of Naval Art

Cicely Robinson

In 1829, Turner's monumental painting *The Battle of Trafalgar, 21 October 1805* [58] was moved from its original and intended location at St James's Palace to the recently opened National Gallery of Naval Art, or Naval Gallery, situated in the Painted Hall of the Royal Naval Hospital at Greenwich. The transferral of Turner's largest painting from a royal palace to a retirement home for old and maimed seamen has been a determining factor in the subsequent critical reception of the work. Overwhelmingly, it has been regarded by art historians as an act of royal rejection: a demotion for a painting that had failed to live up to expectations as part of the redecoration of the state rooms of St James's Palace.

The painting had been commissioned by George IV in 1822 as a pendant for Philip James de Loutherbourg's *Lord Howe's Action, or the 'Glorious First of June' 1794* [53] – a work that had been acquired for the royal collection after initial public exhibition at the Historic Gallery in Pall Mall (a stone's throw from the palace), followed by public touring, and which was also given to Greenwich in 1829.[1] At St James's, these two large battle pieces hung alongside paintings by George Jones of the land battles of Vittoria and Waterloo, and full-length portraits of George III and IV, as part of a larger display of British victory that directly aligned the nation's military prowess with the strength, continuity and security of the Hanoverian lineage. In the years following 1815, the battles of Trafalgar and Waterloo became synonymous with British victory. Together, they presented a statement of total martial dominance on land and sea that was illustrative of George IV's wider commemorative cultural patronage in the wake of the French Revolutionary and Napoleonic Wars. As Prince Regent, George had initiated what was to become the Waterloo Chamber at Windsor Castle in 1814, commissioning Thomas Lawrence to paint a series of portraits depicting all the key figures involved in ending the war. This gallery positioned royal portraits alongside a collection of leading military commanders, diplomats and heads of state, forging an inextricable link between the British monarchy and the men directly involved in the defeat of Napoleon.[2] And in 1822, while the redecoration of St James's Palace was underway, George IV commissioned John Soane to create a new Royal Entrance for the Palace of Westminster, with the intention of locating other grand-scale images of Trafalgar and Waterloo on either side of the Royal Gallery there.[3]

In the absence of any government-funded war memorials in the years immediately after the conflict, George IV adeptly situated himself at the centre of a series of commemorative projects. Through his involvement in a number of art institutions, including the Royal Academy and the British Institution, as well as the appointment of Denis Dighton in 1815 as his military draughtsman, he constructed an identity as *the* patron of British commemorative military painting. The British Institution ran two related competitions while George IV was involved as its Royal Patron. In 1815, the Institution offered 1000 guineas for the best finished sketch of a subject connected with the British army in Spain, Portugal or France. After British victory at Waterloo, the Netherlands were promptly included within this geographical remit. George Jones won second prize, and the following year was commissioned to work his sketch of Waterloo into a full-sized painting for Chelsea Hospital.[4] In 1825, a second competition requested finished sketches of the naval battles of the Nile and Trafalgar – this time with the intention of donating the winning entries to the new Naval Gallery at Greenwich. Samuel Drummond won the commission for his representation of the Battle of Trafalgar, but because Lord Bexley had recently presented Arthur William Devis's *Death of Nelson* [fig. 18] to Greenwich, Drummond was instructed to change the subject of his painting to represent Lord Duncan's victory off Camperdown in 1797.[5] The donation of battle paintings to Greenwich and Chelsea emphasizes the prestigious status of these two complementary locations. As royal charities, both institutions exemplified monarchical support for the veterans of national victory, and the gift of two high-profile works of art underlined the extent of the King's involvement in the commemorative and cultural redevelopment of the nation in the wake of a prolonged war.

When George IV first received a proposal for the formation of a National Gallery of Naval Art at Greenwich Hospital, he 'instantly approved' and became its founding Royal Patron.[6] The Painted Hall at Greenwich Hospital already had strong royal associations. Originally designed by Christopher Wren as a dining hall for the naval pensioners, the lower hall was elaborately decorated by James Thornhill in the early eighteenth century with a scheme on the ceiling that centres on the Stuart monarchs William and Mary enthroned in Heaven and surrounded by a host of mythological virtues. In the upper hall, George I is shown surrounded by his extended family, in a pictorial proclamation of the security of the Hanoverian succession. Thornhill's decorative scheme is supported throughout by symbols of maritime prowess, including a British man-of-war and a Spanish galleon, which enact a narrative of naval conquest and capture at either end of the main hall. It was in this setting that Nelson's body lay in state from 5 to 7 January 1806, and where his funeral carriage was displayed until 1826 (see [fig. 19]). With such an emphasis on the relationship between state and navy, it is hardly surprising that when a collection of naval art was proposed in 1823 (or, rather, revived from 1795) to commemorate and memorialize 'the distinguished exploits of the British Navy', the Directors of Greenwich Hospital suggested that there could not be 'a more proper Repository'.[7]

When the National Gallery of Naval Art opened to the public in 1824, it was the first 'national' collection to be

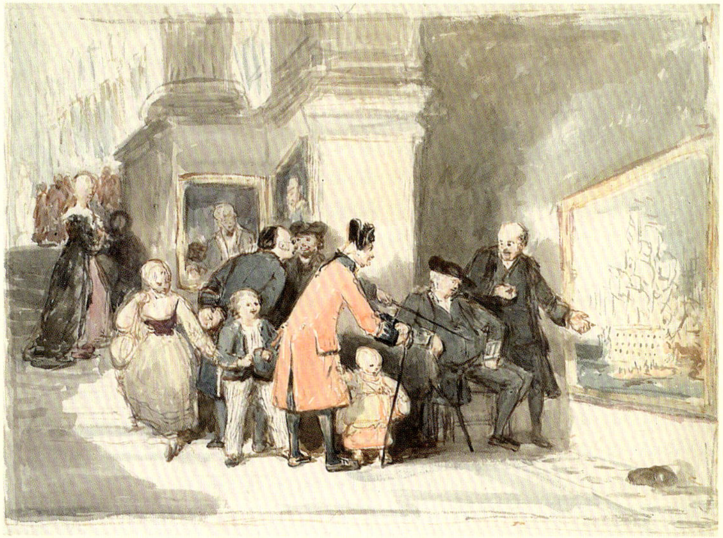

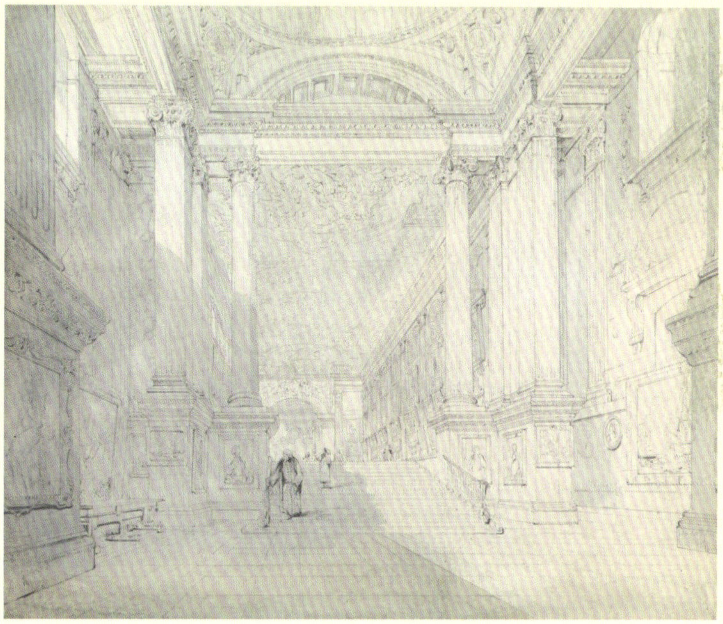

Top Fig. 25

John Burnet
Sketch for *A Tale of Trafalgar* showing a Greenwich Pensioner, a Chelsea Pensioner and other visitors in the Painted Hall after 1829
Watercolour 44.5 x 59.5 (17½ x 23½)
National Maritime Museum

Above Fig. 26

John Scarlett Davis
The Painted Hall of Greenwich Hospital, from the Vestibule 1830
Pencil with grey-blue wash 37 x 42.5 (14⅝ x 16¾)
National Maritime Museum

Overleaf and p. 129

J.M.W. Turner
The Battle of Trafalgar, 21 October 1805 1823–24 (detail of [58])

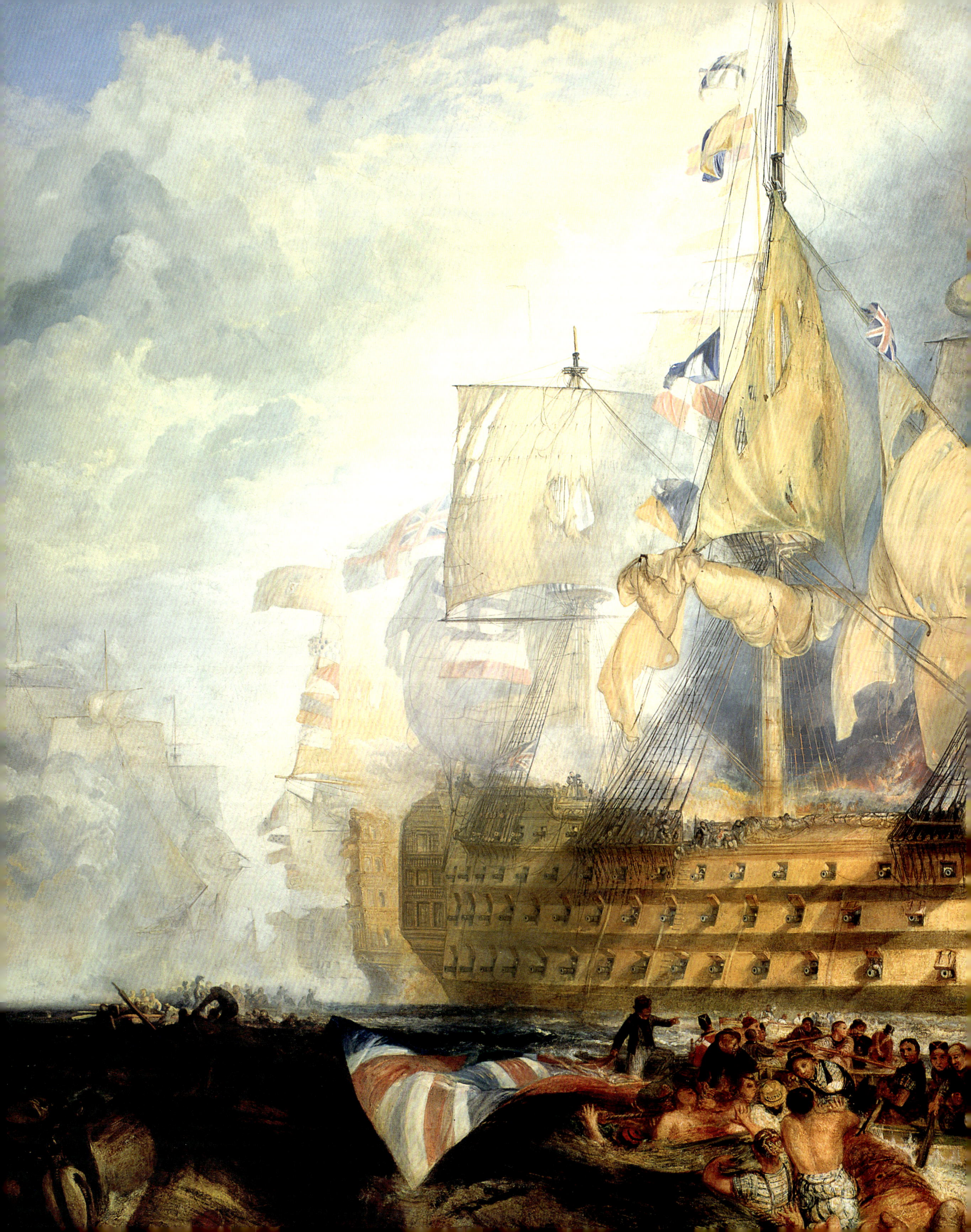

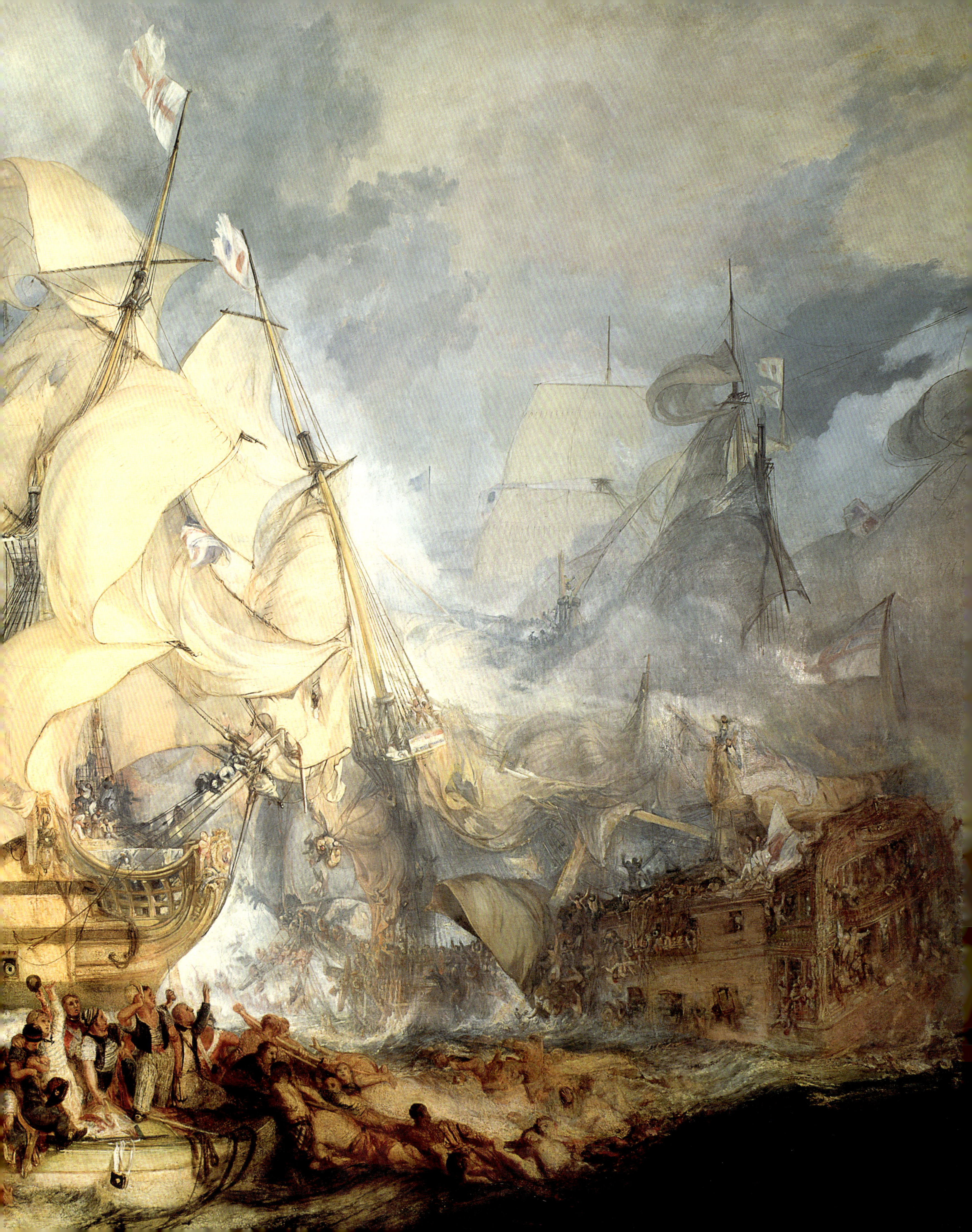

acquired and exhibited for the general public, predating the opening of the nascent National Gallery by a matter of weeks.[8] During the first five years of the gallery's existence, George IV donated no less than thirty-eight paintings to the Naval Gallery from the royal collection, including two important groups of earlier naval portraits, by Peter Lely and Godfrey Kneller, which extended the historical reach of the Hospital's small pre-existing holdings back to the Dutch and French Wars of the late seventeenth century. In making such a prestigious gift, George IV can be seen to have actively associated himself with the statement of monarchical endurance and naval prowess already firmly established both within the Painted Hall and the Royal Hospital as a whole. When Turner's *Trafalgar* and de Loutherbourg's '*Glorious First of June*' were moved from St James's Palace to the Naval Gallery in August 1829 – the King's last two gifts – they marked the culmination of an extensive and high-profile royal endorsement of the project. The Greenwich Hospital board minutes record their wish to 'convey to His Majesty their grateful acknowledgments for these further marks of his Royal favour to the Institution'.[9]

A drawing of the Painted Hall made by John Scarlett Davis in 1830 [fig. 26] (the earliest known visual record of the Naval Gallery) illustrates the prime location that these two works were given when they arrived at Greenwich. In Davis's drawing, the paintings are shown on display on either side of the vestibule: the '*Glorious First of June*' was hung to the left of the entrance, with Turner's *Trafalgar* located directly opposite on the right. Thus positioned, they were the first and last works that visitors to the Naval Gallery would have seen. Together they framed the gallery space with the first and last major naval victories of the recent Revolutionary and Napoleonic Wars, constructing a symmetrical narrative of national triumph and commemoration. It would have been immediately clear to visitors that the Naval Gallery was, primarily, a commemorative pantheon for Britain's recent naval achievements and the individuals responsible for them. Full-length statues of Admiral Sir John Jervis, Earl St Vincent, and Admiral Richard, Earl Howe, were positioned either side of the '*Glorious First of June*'; on the other side, those of admirals Lord Nelson and Duncan framed Turner's *Trafalgar*. These sculptures were plaster copies from the four admirals' monuments in St Paul's Cathedral.[10] By forming an association with St Paul's, the arrangement in the vestibule carried greater commemorative resonance. In the wake of British triumph over the French, this was a rare opportunity to assert, in an entirely secular context, both the exemplary personal virtues and hierarchical, Establishment authority of the heroes concerned, as integral to national success.

Meanwhile, within the vestibule, the towering presence of the ships in de Loutherbourg's and Turner's battlescapes glorified the dominance and sheer monumental magnificence of the British fleet. However, visitors to the Naval Gallery encountered these paintings at close quarters, with the wreckage of the battle, and the more immediate and horrific spectacle of dead and drowning men, at eye level. When viewing Turner's *Trafalgar* in this context, visitors would have met the petrified, wide-eyed gaze of the sailor in the immediate foreground head on (see detail opposite). The body of this anonymous sailor, positioned at the edge of the picture plane in an inverted crucifix position, was effectively lowered out of the canvas and into the gallery space. This deposition-like action memorialized the real body of the anonymous naval martyr in a quasi-religious manner.

The veneration of the navy and its most celebrated hero would reach its apogee in the upper hall, where a collection of Nelson's relics was put on display. The Duke of Clarence, later William IV, initiated this trend in 1828 when he presented the coat Nelson wore at the Battle of the Nile to the Naval Gallery. Later, in 1845, Prince Albert donated Nelson's blood-stained coat from Trafalgar. A number of other Nelsonic artefacts were subsequently added to this display in the upper hall, including his pigtail, cut off after his death. Collectively, these items formed a secular reliquary that performed an intercessional role between the public and this national naval martyr.

The Greenwich Hospital Pensioners were a prominent spectacle within the Naval Gallery, with chosen Pensioners selected (and paid from entry fees) to 'show the Hall' and collection to general visitors. In the wake of the recent conflicts, many of these men had personal experiences of both Nelson and the Battle of Trafalgar. In John Burnet's sketch for *A Tale of Trafalgar*, for example [fig. 25], a Greenwich Pensioner is shown standing before Turner's *Trafalgar* in the vestibule of the Naval Gallery, recounting his personal involvement to an audience of visiting Chelsea Pensioners and members of the public. Within the gallery space, the physical presence of the naval veterans, and the 'living memory' that they re-enacted on a daily basis to visitors, offered a human connection to the events on display.[11] In recounting personal narratives of Trafalgar, the Pensioners would have further assisted in making Turner's tableau of the action a tangible narrative of sacrifice and national duty. Simultaneously, the inclusion of Turner's *Trafalgar* within the gallery space provided a pictorial focus against which their personal naval mythologies could be played out. Its centrality to the pantheon of national naval supremacy embodied by the Gallery became even more prominent before Turner's death. For in 1845–46, as part of an overall renovation and rearrangement of the display, both the *Trafalgar* and its de Loutherbourg pendant were relocated from the vestibule to the main hall. A watercolour by L.H. Michael of the Naval Gallery in 1865 (National Maritime Museum) depicts these two monumental assets positioned as the central paintings on, respectively, the south and north walls of the main hall.

We should challenge any assumption that the Naval Gallery was a minor display, isolated from the cultural and intellectual London metropolis. Instead, this extensive public attraction, situated within the prestigious complex of Greenwich Hospital, functioned as a site for naval commemoration and a significant forum for the exhibition of contemporary naval art. George IV's donation of Turner's painting, along with a large group of highly acclaimed naval portraits from the royal collection, cannot be simply dismissed as the result of a royal whim, or as a shameless attempt to raise an ailing royal profile. In the years after Waterloo, George IV had demonstrated his interest in the visual commemoration of the nation's military achievements as a way of supporting the development of contemporary British art. With the foundation of the Naval Gallery at Greenwich he evidently recognized an opportunity to relocate some of the most powerful contemporary works in the royal collection – including Turner's *Battle of Trafalgar* – to the centre of a national naval commemorative project.

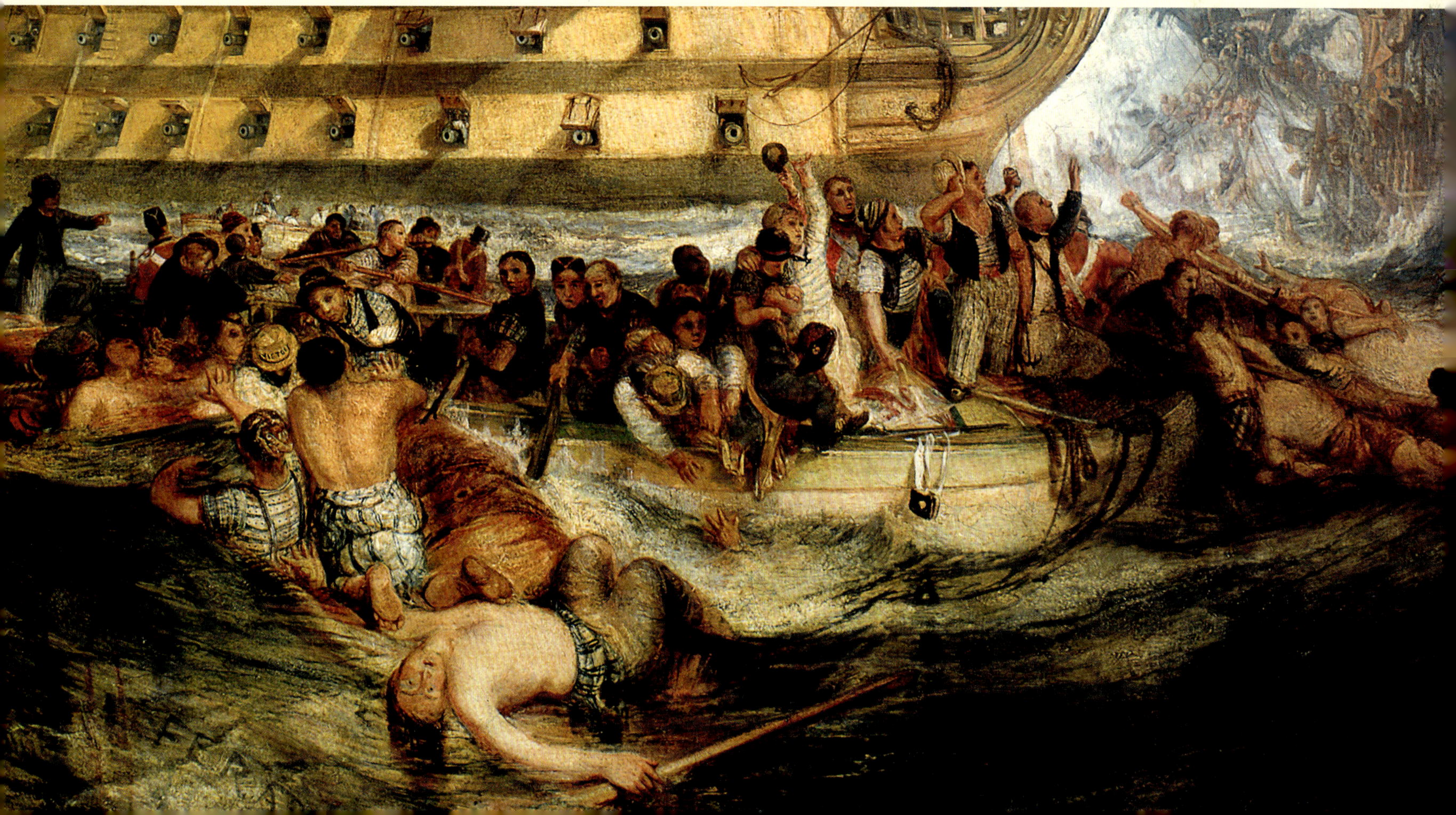

4

CONTESTED WATERS

Richard Johns

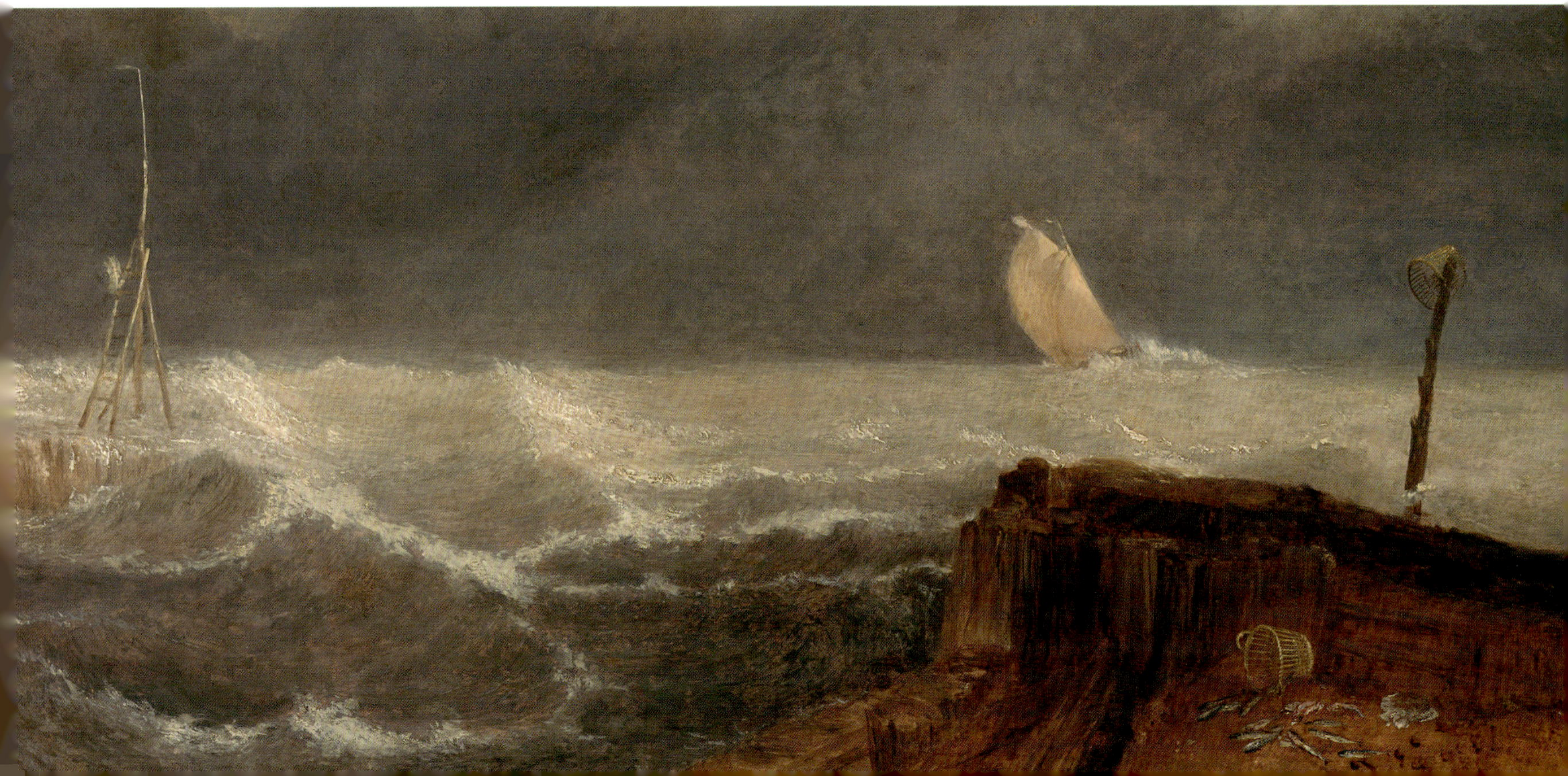

Between 1825 and 1827, the works Turner submitted to the annual Royal Academy exhibitions included three large maritime oil paintings, the first he had shown for six years. Scenes of arrival and departure at different foreign ports, they drew on the artist's experience of travelling by sea during recent sketching tours to the Continent. *Harbour of Dieppe (Changement de Domicile)* of 1825 was followed a year later by a river scene, *Cologne, the Arrival of a Packet Boat. Evening*, and in 1827 by *'Now for the Painter' (Rope) – Passengers Going on Board* [59]. As well as evoking the harbour scenes of Claude and Claude-Joseph Vernet, all three paintings relate, both in composition and subject matter, to some of Turner's most celebrated earlier works.[1] *'Now for the Painter'*, for example, a work inspired by the artist's departure from Calais at the end of his most recent trip abroad, playfully invokes *Calais Pier* [74], which commemorated his arrival at the same French port at the beginning of his first, formative visit to the Continent in 1802. Moreover, by showing passengers approaching and boarding an outgoing packet boat, with a distant prospect of the port town to the right, the same picture also purposefully echoes the central motif (though not the calm conditions) of his more recent highly acclaimed work, *Dort, or Dordrecht, the Dort Packet-Boat from Rotterdam Becalmed* of 1818 [fig. 1].

A strong thematic continuity is thus evident in Turner's maritime subjects from one decade to the next, but the artist's work from the mid-1820s bore conspicuous differences in painterly technique, above all a heightened register of colour. One reviewer described *Harbour of Dieppe* as 'the most splendid piece of falsehood'; another as a 'brilliant experiment upon colours, which displays all the magic of skill at the expence [*sic*] of all the magic of nature'.[2] The following year the reviewer for the *Literary Gazette* looked wide-eyed at the 'glitter and gaud of colour' of *Cologne* – an effect that he judged better suited to a 'fairy scene' than a picture of a modern river port. And in 1827, the same critic saw in *'Now for the Painter'* an exaggerated style that he described as 'much of the ultra both in effect and colour'.[3] As a group, these works provide an apt metaphor for a turning point in Turner's career. At the moment when he had unquestionably arrived as an artist (and by the mid-1820s he was by some distance the most renowned and highly remunerated in Britain) he changed course, making his intentions clear in the title of the work with which he launched this departure – *'changement de domicile'*.

'MUCH OF THE ULTRA'

The technical innovation of *Harbour of Dieppe*, *Cologne* and *'Now for the Painter'* can be attributed in part to two related aspects of Turner's recent experience: first, his extended travels on the Continent following the end of the Napoleonic War in 1815; second, a deeper engagement with the creative and commercial possibilities of the medium of watercolour. In August 1819, Turner left England for his first, long-anticipated trip to Italy – a journey that had been virtually impossible for many years while Europe was at war. He had made a brief foray across the French-Italian border during his first Continental visit seventeen years earlier but this time, over the course of six months, he was able to take in each of the major Italian cities, including a visit to Venice and an extended stay in Rome. Like so many artists before him, he became immersed in the light and colour of the Italian countryside, and he spent long days studying the vestiges of ancient Rome and the art and architecture of the Italian Renaissance. He returned laden with sketchbooks, filled with drawings and watercolour studies that provided a source for his work for many years. The lure of Italy helps to explain both the temporary hiatus in Turner's Academy marine paintings during the early 1820s – his oils of the period were predominantly views of Rome and other classicizing Italian landscapes – and the greater luminosity of the paintings that marked his return to the genre from 1825. However, this luminosity was also a result of his experimentation with watercolour, a medium that had become an increasingly important part of his output.

Turner produced around 1800 finished watercolours during his career. This prolific output was facilitated by the scale and relative speed of working on paper, and he exploited the freedoms of the medium to produce images that could be as challenging in composition and narrative complexity as his most contentious works in oil. During the early decades of the nineteenth century watercolour was at the height of its popularity and featured every year in the Academy shows. It was overshadowed by the greater number of larger oil paintings on display, and generally confined to the lesser rooms with prints and other works on paper, but the establishment of various sketching clubs and exhibiting societies around the turn of the century extended the reach and improved the status of watercolour among a broader constituency of artists and patrons. Turner's early involvement in the informal academy established by Dr Thomas Monro in the 1790s brought him into contact with some of the most talented watercolourists of the age, including Thomas Girtin, his most serious rival in the medium before his death in 1802, and a young watercolourist from Norwich, John Sell Cotman [67].

Turner's rise to the head of a thriving national school of watercolour in the years that followed was confirmed by the exhibition of Walter Fawkes's collection at his London town-house in Grosvenor Place in 1819–20, which centred on a room hung with around sixty of the artist's works on paper, including *A First Rate Taking in Stores* [81] and *Loss of an East Indiaman* [82]. His work also predominated in the displays organized by the engraver-publisher W.B. Cooke in the early 1820s, which featured several of his larger *Marine Views* (see '‘M’ for Marine', esp. pp. 63–67). Addressing the artist in his role as Professor of Perspective at the Royal Academy (and maintaining the old usage of 'pencil' for 'brush'), the critic of the *London Chronicle* declared in 1819 that watercolour 'is *par excellence* English, no continental pencil can come near the force, freedom, and nature of our professor's'.[4] It was through his original works on paper and, increasingly, via the prints that were made after them, that Turner's reputation spread far beyond the London art world during his lifetime. Collectors, connoisseurs and other artists in France and further afield were familiar with these more portable works long before they knew his oil painting at first-hand. Turner produced many watercolours for various series of engraved and published views that aimed to provide a comprehensive pictorial survey of the edges of the British Isles – either as part of a collaborative project or, as with the ambitious *Picturesque Views in England and Wales* [51 and 52], begun in 1825, as their sole artist. During the first twenty years or so of his career, he travelled extensively within the British Isles and and charted much of the coast as part of this work. In many of his early seascapes, including *Fishermen at Sea* [14] and *Sheerness as Seen from the Nore* [78], he scrutinized the inshore waters around the southern coast with a vigilance prompted by war and the recurring threat of invasion, investing the fishermen who plied them with a heroic demeanour. Following the final defeat of Napoleon's army at the Battle of Waterloo and the resumption of trade and communication with France, the British coast itself became the subject of renewed artistic interest. No longer a frontier of war, the seaside developed into a site of amusement and picturesque encounter, where history, coastal industry and leisure combined in a new, patriotic and deeply romanticized image of life by the sea.

The successive series that contributed to the re-conception of the country's coastline were distinctly commercial projects. In response to a competitive market, Turner adopted an ever more experimental approach to the medium, capitalizing on the greater availability and convenience of ready-to-use pigments, which during his lifetime transformed watercolour from a laborious and expensive specialist practice into an affordable and eminently transportable art form. Exploiting the full range of colours that had recently become available from specialist merchants, he worked in brighter blues, deeper greens and, above all, radiant chrome yellows to dramatic effect. The saturated blue and scratched highlights of the sea, and the lighter washes of the sky that suggest both distance and depth in his view of *Weymouth, Dorsetshire* from around 1811 [39], attest to Turner's deft manipulation of the watery medium. Colour is used to different effect to capture the deep but momentary reflections in the calm water of *Sun-rise. Whiting Fishing at Margate* [45]; and the restless layering of blues and greys gives the deep swell and brooding sky a sense of urgency in *The Mouth of the River Humber* [68].

In the mid-1820s Turner translated the intense colour tones and translucency of his watercolour to his exhibited work in oil. The characteristic, heavily impastoed surface of *Calais Pier*, for example, is replaced in *'Now for the Painter'* with layers of translucent glazes that mimic the techniques of his recent work on paper to capture the luminosity of air and water, and the reflection of boats and people on the surface of the sea. The liberal use of opaque white paint – which prompted Sir George Beaumont to liken his attempt to represent tumultuous water in *Calais Pier* to 'the veins on a Marble slab' – gives way to the full spectrum of watery hues that the *Literary Gazette* described, with some trepidation, as 'much of the ultra'.[5]

In fact, Turner had already conjured a similarly prismatic effect, at once scientific and poetic, to very different ends in his *Battle of Trafalgar*, his sole royal commission, completed in 1824 [58]. On that occasion, bright tones were employed to convey the debris of battle on and just below the surface of the water in the foreground, but such a departure from the more conventional, sober palette of the painted sea was deemed inappropriate by many for so monumental a subject. On that occasion, Turner's 'love of excess of light and attractive colour' was simply too much for a subject of such grand character, which was better suited to 'the sublime conceptions that rested upon subdued tones'.[6] Whether or not the Academy critics approved of the beguiling effects of Turner's latest marine paintings, they agreed that they stood apart, not only from the artist's earlier work in the genre but also from the other seascapes on show, produced by a group of talented younger painters for whom Turner was both a model and a rival.

PASSENGERS

Following the early public success of *Dutch Boats in a Gale* [fig. 6], Turner had nurtured a reputation as Britain's foremost marine painter, an artist equal in stature to the great luminaries of seventeenth-century Dutch maritime art. The most consistent challenge to this pre-eminence came from Augustus Wall Callcott, an artist who at the height of his career was regarded by many as the equal of Turner as a painter of the sea.[7] Just four years his junior, Callcott joined the Royal Academy Schools in 1797 and began his professional career soon afterwards as a portrait painter under the tuition of John Hoppner. By 1805 he had abandoned 'face painting' and, with a growing reputation as an accomplished landscape artist, was singled out as the painter most likely to 'press hard upon Turner'.[8] The two artists shared a number of influential patrons and around 1807 Callcott was commissioned by Thomas Lister Parker to paint a replica of an estuary scene by Turner that he owned, *Sheerness and the Isle of Sheppey, with the Junction of the Thames and the Medway from the Nore* (NGA, Washington).[9]

Callcott emerged as a serious challenger to Turner a few years later with a series of large-scale river and harbour scenes painted in the Dutch manner, which included the sensational canvas *The Entrance to the Pool of London* (1816) [fig. 27]. The result of another commission, this time from the third Marquess of Lansdowne, Callcott's *Pool of London* was modelled closely on *The Maas at Dordrecht* by the seventeenth-century Dutch painter Aelbert Cuyp (NGA, Washington), a work that had only recently been acquired by Abraham Hume, a founding member of the British Institution. Cuyp was barely known in Britain before the mid-1700s but by the end of the century his calm harbour scenes were among the most sought-after of all Dutch paintings, more highly regarded even than the finest works by Willem van de Velde. The large canvas from Hume's collection had been a highlight of the Institution's old masters exhibition in 1815, and Callcott's confident reworking of the scene into a modern Thames subject was widely regarded as a triumph for the artist over his living rival, Turner.

Years later, John Ruskin, keen to erase any sense of real competition with Turner, consigned Callcott to the margins of British art history by judging him a thoroughly pedestrian artist; a mere follower, who 'painted everything tolerably, and nothing excellently'.[10] At the time, however, the response to Callcott's work was far more positive. William Henry Pyne, writing for Rudolph Ackermann's *Repository of Arts* in 1816, declared unequivocally that '[of] this species of style we think this the very best picture we ever saw', while William

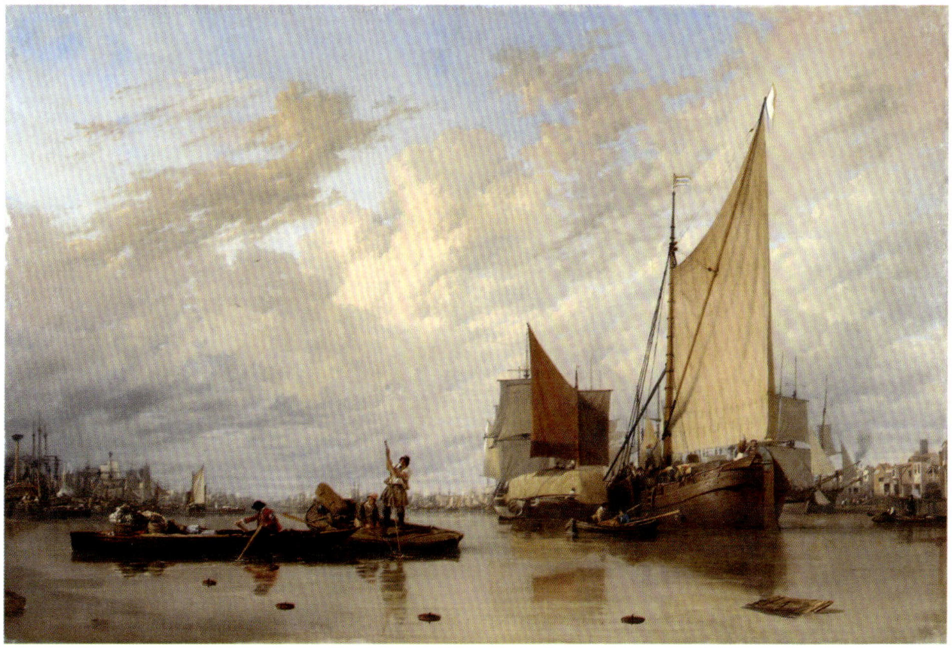

Fig. 27

Augustus Wall Callcott
The Entrance to the Pool of London 1816
Oil on canvas 153 x 221 (61.2 x 88.4)
Bowood House, Wiltshire

Hazlitt was bold enough to suggest a changing of the guard, such that 'Mr. Turner may now take useful lessons from Mr. Callcott, instead of Mr. Callcott from Mr. Turner.'[11] Turner reportedly also praised the picture by suggesting that his rival ought to have been given five times the 200 guineas that Lord Lansdowne had paid for it. Two years later, he responded to the combined challenge of Cuyp and Callcott with the glowing *Dort*, a powerful restatement of his ability to outshine his contemporaries by taking a fresh look at the art of the past.[12]

Thereafter, the two artists' careers took very different trajectories. Following the success of *Pool of London*, Callcott was much in demand, and although he worked slowly (each painting typically took around six months to complete) he maintained a highly successful practice, presenting himself as a painter of and for the Establishment. By catering for a more conservative taste in maritime imagery, and by consistently undercutting Turner on price, Callcott achieved a level of official recognition (including a knighthood in 1837) that eluded his older rival. However, the two artists remained allies within the Academy and lifelong friends, with Turner's usual belligerence tempered, it seems, by the distinct character of their individual success. Thus as Turner embarked on his 'brilliant experiment upon colours' in the 1820s, Callcott remained committed to producing the type of works with which both artists had made their name at the beginning of the century. In fact, Callcott's *Heavy Weather Coming on, with Vessels Running to Port* [62], exhibited in the same show as Turner's more vibrant '*Now for the Painter*', had been commissioned by Lord Egremont as a pendant to Turner's *Ships Bearing up for Anchorage* of 1802 [72], a reminder of the enduring importance of Turner's early sea pieces as a model for established and aspiring artists and their patrons during the 1820s.

In the same decade a new generation of marine painters began to make a name for themselves by painting the sea in what may broadly be described as a Turnerian manner. Among these younger contenders was George Chambers, who worked in the coastal trade from Whitby from the age of ten before becoming a painter in his teens. Following the example of Nicholas Pocock and others before him, Chambers forged his youthful experiences of life at sea into a successful (if relatively brief) career as a marine artist, painting the kind of coastal vessels on which he had worked as a boy. After moving to London in 1825, he contributed to the British Institution exhibition in 1827, and in the following year displayed his work at the Royal Academy for the first time. A later view of his home town of Whitby [fig. 28] reveals the extent to which Chambers was guided by Turner's use of strong tonal contrasts and loose brushwork in pursuit of atmospheric effect. In 1836, Chambers was commissioned to paint two large historical naval battles for the National Gallery of Naval Art – a copy of Benjamin West's *Battle of La Hogue, 1692* and a composition of his own making, *The Bombardment of Algiers, 27 August 1816*, both of which hung within sight of Turner's epic *Battle of Trafalgar* in the Painted Hall of Greenwich Hospital. For Chambers, as for his peers, battle painting was no longer the mainstay of the marine genre but an occasional departure from more peaceable subjects, either to commemorate past glories or, as with *The Battle of Navarino, 20 October 1827*, which George Philip Reinagle showed in the Academy exhibition just a few months after the event, as a public reminder of Britain's continued appetite for imperial adventure.[13]

The end of war with France also allowed for an unprecedented artistic exchange between Britain and France – two nations that had defined their own cultures in opposition to each other during many years of hostility. The long-awaited opportunity for more extensive and safer travel, including the inauguration of the first regular steam-packet service linking Dover and Calais, encouraged a cross-pollination of art and ideas between the artistic centres of London and Paris.[14] A leading figure in this exchange was the Anglo-French painter Richard Parkes Bonington. English by birth, Bonington moved to France with his family at the age of fifteen. While living in Calais, within sight of the Kent coast, he trained in the English manner of watercolour with Louis Francia [69] (a French artist who had spent the war years in England) before moving to Paris. During the early 1820s, Bonington's and Turner's itineraries crossed as they each separately explored and painted the French coast. In the summer of 1825, Bonington visited London in the company of Eugène Delacroix and other French artists, where he encountered Turner's work, including *Harbour of Dieppe*.[15] The following year, Bonington's work was exhibited in London for the first time, at the British

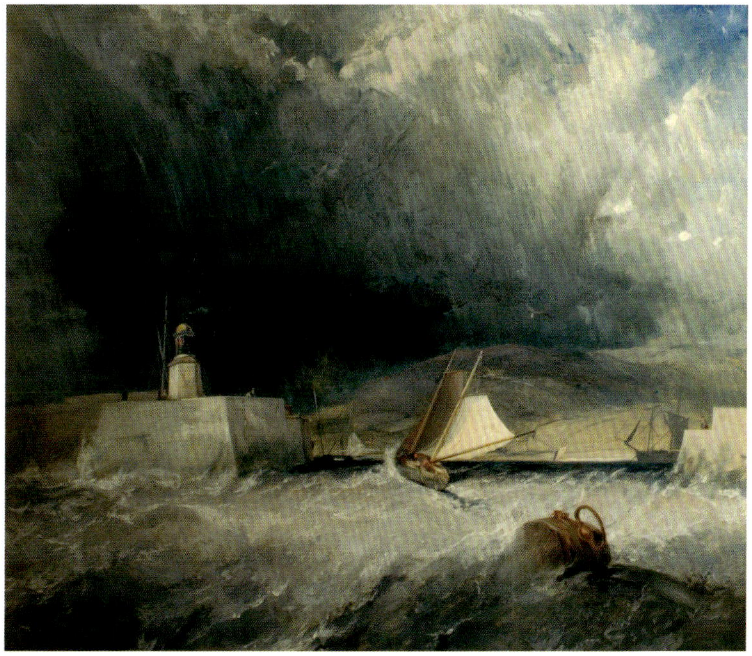

Fig. 28

George Chambers
Whitby Harbour 1836
Oil on canvas 101.6 x 132.1 (40 x 52)
Nottingham Castle Museum

Institution, followed in 1827 by a small painting titled *Scene on the French Coast* at the Royal Academy.

Chambers and Reinagle painted the sea in ways that invited comparison with Turner's work of the previous two decades and, along with Bonington, Francis Danby and Clarkson Stanfield, were capable at times of posing a serious challenge: from the coastal scenery charted by Bonington and the sublime effects pursued by Reinagle and Danby [61], to the maritime spectacles created by Stanfield (none more spectacular than his huge *Battle of Trafalgar* [fig. 24] which, at almost fifteen feet across, dominated one wall of the Academy exhibition in 1836 before being moved to its permanent home at the United Service Club). Yet despite the variety in the work of these artists, and the revived sense of competition that they brought to the London art world, some contemporary observers remained suspicious of the artistic merits of marine painting, which they regarded as a predictable, repetitive genre, of interest only to sailors and a small band of specialists. 'When you have seen about a dozen varieties of sea-pieces you have seen all that can be painted,' wrote the *New Monthly Magazine* in 1827 in a review of Callcott's *Heavy Weather*. 'Sea-painters, we know, will deny this utterly, and no one among them has so good a (seeming) right to deny it as Mr. Callcott. But it is true nevertheless.'[16]

When Turner submitted his first works to the Royal Academy in the 1790s, the Academy itself was a generation old and possessed of all the apparatus and accessories of a mature institution: the annual rituals of exhibition had been established, a receptive audience was in place, and a critical vocabulary had been developed by a new breed of art critic.[17] It was within this inherently competitive environment that Turner had earned a reputation for working independently from the established conventions of British marine painting. He was notoriously secretive about his practice and uncomfortable with the notion that his art was in any sense imitable. He refused to allow other artists to sketch from the paintings on display in his own gallery; and when he felt that Samuel Owen [70], a prolific specialist in pictures of shipping in watercolour and a fellow contributor to *Picturesque Views on the Southern Coast of England*, was leaning too heavily in his direction, Turner reportedly sent a prickly note requesting that in future Owen 'draw from his own resources, and not from his'.[18]

Turner permitted only his most trusted patrons and friends to watch him at work, except, of course, when performing on his own terms under the staged conditions of the Academy varnishing days, when exhibiting artists were permitted to bring their brushes and palette into the galleries to make any final adjustments to their work before the doors were opened to the public.[19] The power of a colour well placed was demonstrated most dramatically a few years later, in an often-cited incident during the varnishing days of 1832, when Turner enlivened the brooding grey sea of *Helvoetsluys* [fig. 29] with a 'shot' of red paint (deftly fashioned at the last minute into a buoy) in order to upstage Constable's much larger *Opening of Waterloo Bridge*. On that occasion, Turner's performance was not only one of painterly bravura but also a provocative contrast between the pomp of Constable's overwrought Thames pageant (which he had struggled for years to finish) and the understated economy of his own work. Unlike Turner, Constable never fully embraced the art of the sea, although his occasional artistic excursions to the coast resulted in a group of works that introduced new challenges for the genre (see 'Constable, Brighton and the Sea', pp. 158–61).

Turner's adeptness at using the Royal Academy exhibition as an opportunity for personal promotion, even (or especially) at the expense of his fellow artists, is epitomized by his submission of *'Now for the Painter'* and *Port Ruysdael* [63] in 1827. The long, descriptive title of the former painting carries an additional, punning jibe at the expense of the young Clarkson Stanfield who had 'missed the boat' the previous year when he failed to complete the work (to be called *Throwing the Painter*) that he had hoped would secure his reputation as a serious rival of Callcott and Turner. By contrast, *Port Ruysdael*, in its subject, muted tones and reverential title, explicitly resumed a dialogue with an older tradition of Dutch marine painting that Turner had aligned himself with thirty years earlier. It is a deliberately austere, abstracted painting in comparison with *'Now for the Painter'*, which declared an artistic departure in a different direction, one that left the artist's fellow passengers struggling to stay on board, and which perhaps left them behind altogether.

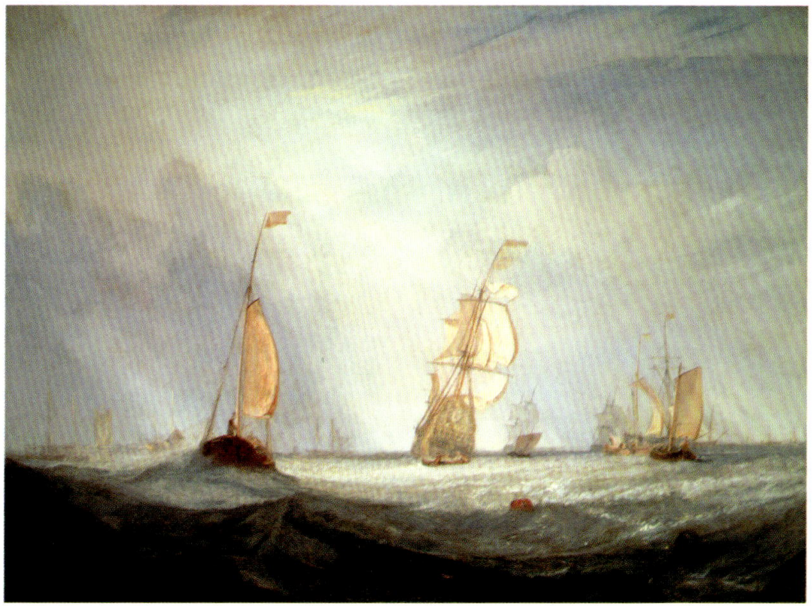

Fig. 29

J.M.W. Turner
Helvoetsluys; – the City of Utrecht, 64, Going to Sea 1832
Oil on canvas 91.4 x 122 (36 x 48)
Tokyo Fuji Art Museum

59

J.M.W. Turner
'Now for the Painter' (Rope) – Passengers Going on Board 1827
Oil on canvas 174.3 x 223.5 (68⅝ x 88)
Manchester City Galleries

Butlin and Joll, no. 236; Warrell 1997, pp. 172–78; Hamilton 2003, pp. 13–15

The curious, disjointed title plays on the double meaning of the word 'painter', a nautical term for a type of rope used for tying-up or towing a boat. It was first explained by the artist's biographer Walter Thornbury as a joke between Turner and his fellow-artist Augustus Wall Callcott [62], made at the expense of the emerging marine painter Clarkson Stanfield, who had failed to complete a painting (to be called *Throwing the Painter*) in time for the previous year's exhibition. Callcott had poked fun at Stanfield's overstretched ambition in 1826 by extending the title of his own painting to *Dutch Fishing Boats running foul in the endeavour to board, and missing the Painter Rope*. The following year with *'Now for the Painter' (Rope)*, Turner mischievously extended the pun to signal his public return to maritime subjects, eight years after his last open sea painting. As well as answering Callcott and Stanfield – one an established artist at the height of his career, the other a younger artist with a growing reputation – *'Now for the Painter'* may also be understood as a response to the recent arrival on the scene of another precocious young marine artist working in a Turnerian mode, George Philip Reinagle [60]. The artist's reference to 'passengers going on board' raises the stakes by reminding all his rivals that they remained mere passengers, following in his wake.

The critical response was mixed, however. 'And now for the artist!' declared the playful critic of the London *Literary Gazette* (2 June 1827), full of praise for Turner's work. 'Though this, as well as many others of his performances, has much of the ultra both in effect and colour, it evidently arises from an exuberance of imagination; and there is "method in the madness," if such it may be called.' Others felt that Turner had overreached himself in his pursuit of visual effect – that the 'ultra' observed by the *Gazette* signalled a self-defeating disjuncture between observation and execution. 'Mr. Turner's pictures are every thing they should be, except natural,' complained the *New Monthly Magazine and Literary Journal*, 'they want a charm that all their power of imagination and execution cannot make up for, much less conceal' (1 July 1827).

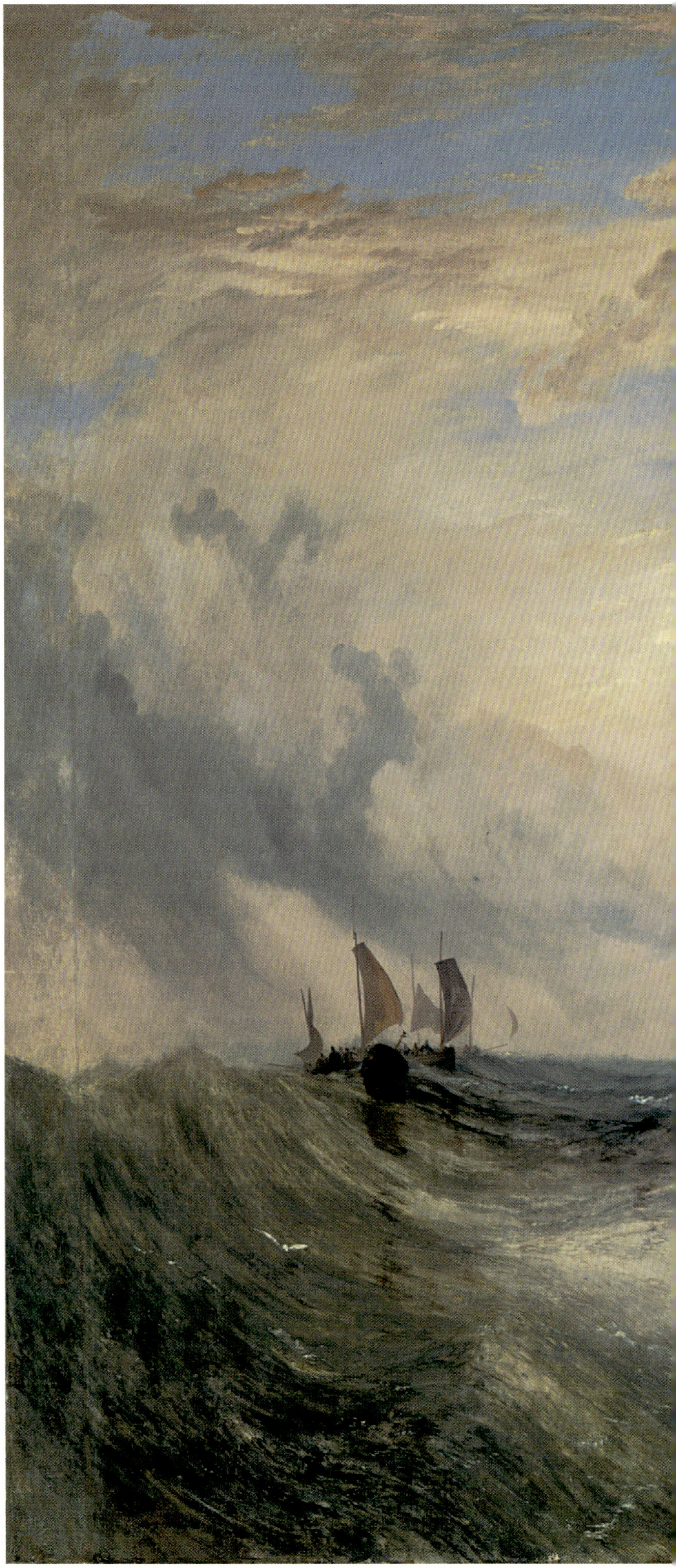

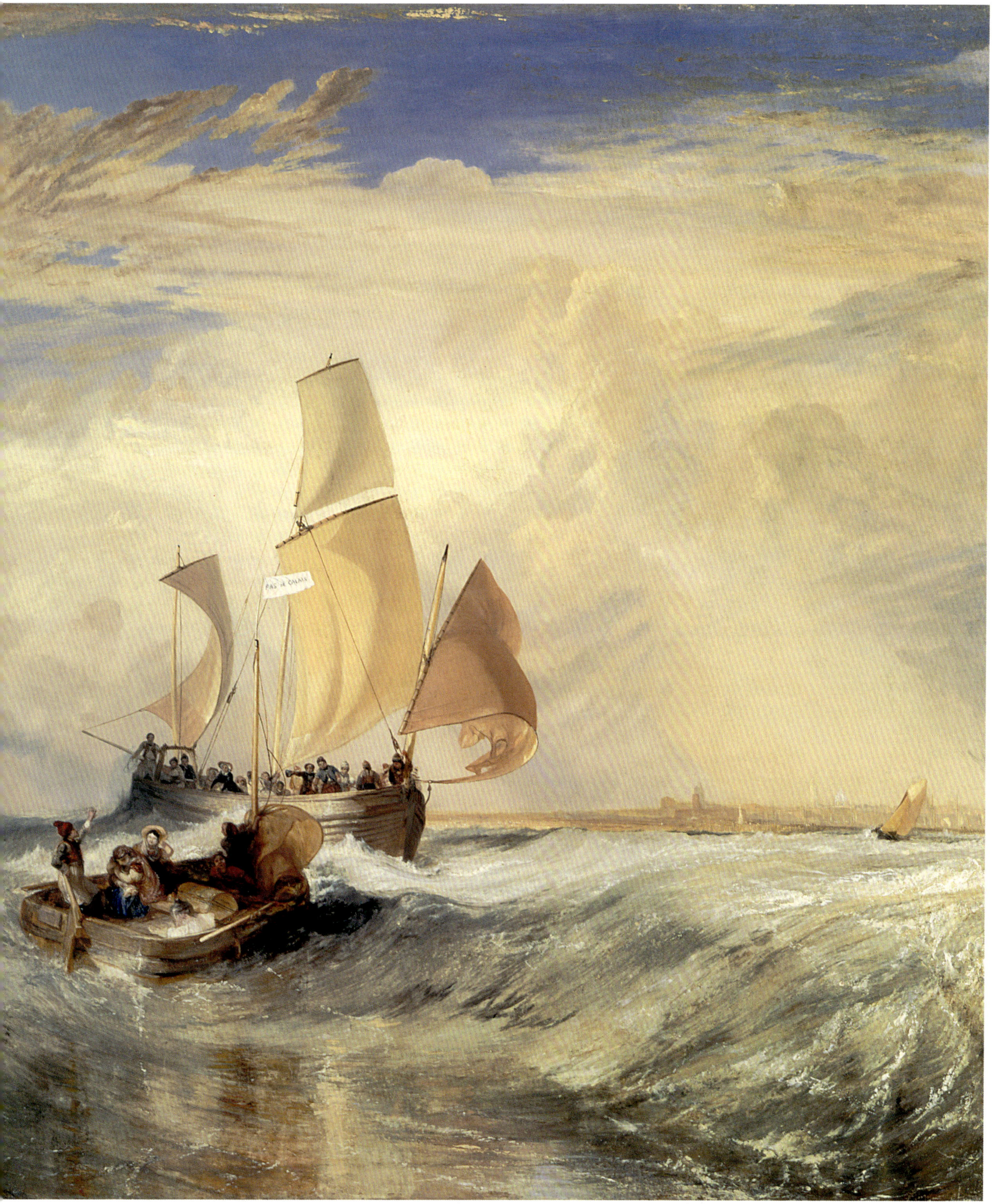

60

George Philip Reinagle
A First Rate Man-of-War, Driving on a Reef of Rocks, and Foundering in a Tempest 1826
Oil on canvas 102 x 127.2 (40⅛ x 50⅛)
Royal Albert Memorial Museum

George Philip Reinagle (1802–35), following in the footsteps of his father, Ramsay Richard, and grandfather Philip, began his career painting portraits and the occasional landscape, alongside copies of seventeenth-century Dutch seascapes. The influence of artists such as van de Velde and Backhuysen is plain to see in *A First Rate Man-of-War*, one of Reinagle's first original naval subjects. The poetic image of a ship overwhelmed by the elements indicates a first-hand knowledge of van de Velde's storm scenes, such as *A Mediterranean Brigantine Drifting onto a Rocky Coast in a Storm* [5]. The violence with which the sea confronts the viewer suggests that Reinagle was also responding to the more recent challenge of Turner's vision of maritime disaster in *The Shipwreck* [75]. The drama and universal appeal of *A First Rate Man-of-War* prompted one reviewer at the Royal Academy exhibition of 1826 to praise its 'tempest-tost character, upheaving spray, electric flashing, &c' (*Examiner*, 2 July 1826). The critical success of the work encouraged Reinagle to focus exclusively on maritime subjects for the rest of his short career. He was working from his father's premises in London's Fitzroy Square (54 Upper Charlotte Street) when he painted *A First Rate Man-of-War*. The following year, he accompanied the Mediterranean fleet under the command of Admiral Edward Codrington and witnessed the Battle of Navarino at first-hand from on board the naval sloop 'Mosquito'. Reinagle produced several exhibition paintings based on the battle, as well as a successful series of lithographs, which brought both the event and the artist to wider attention. He died at the age of thirty-three in 1835.

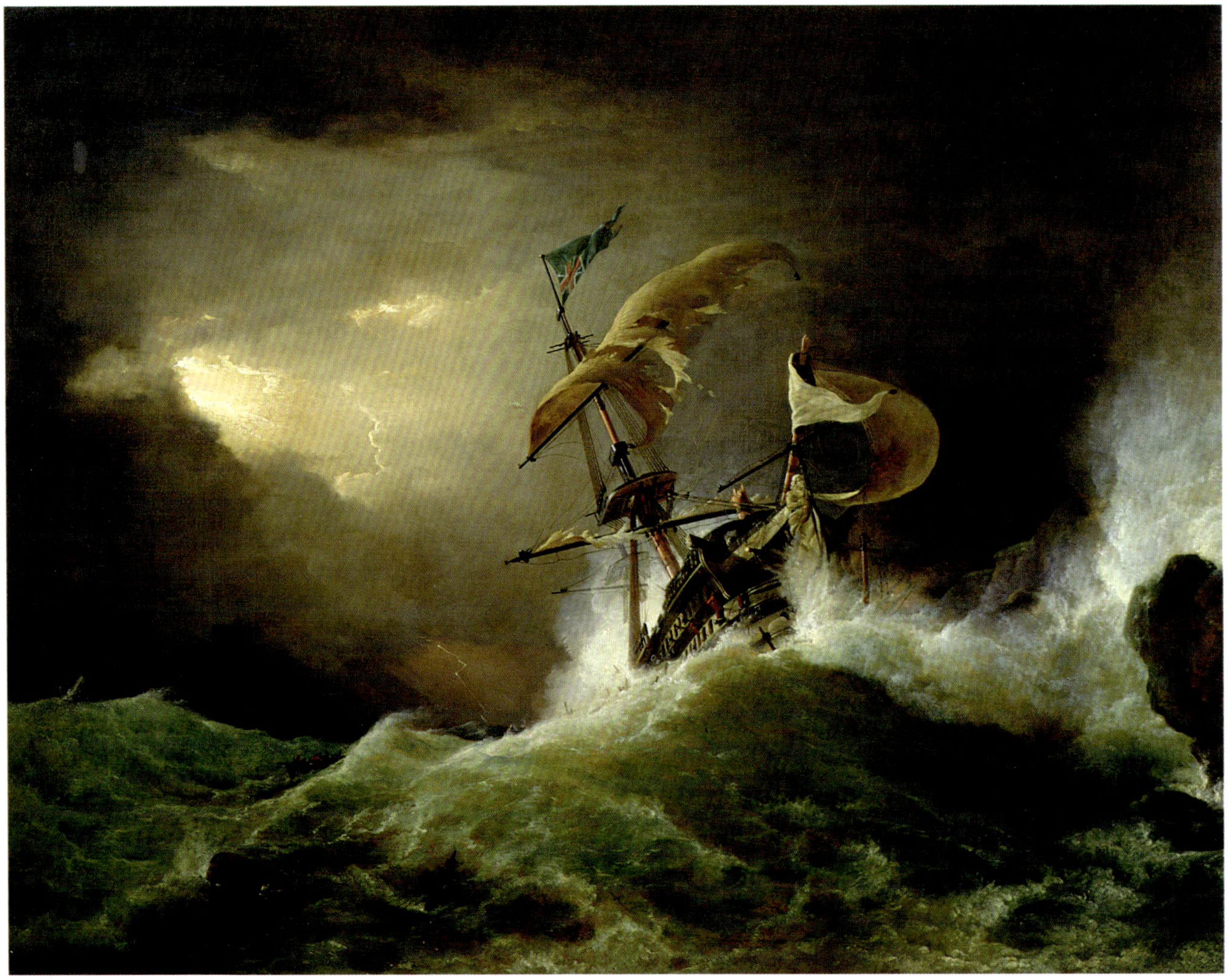

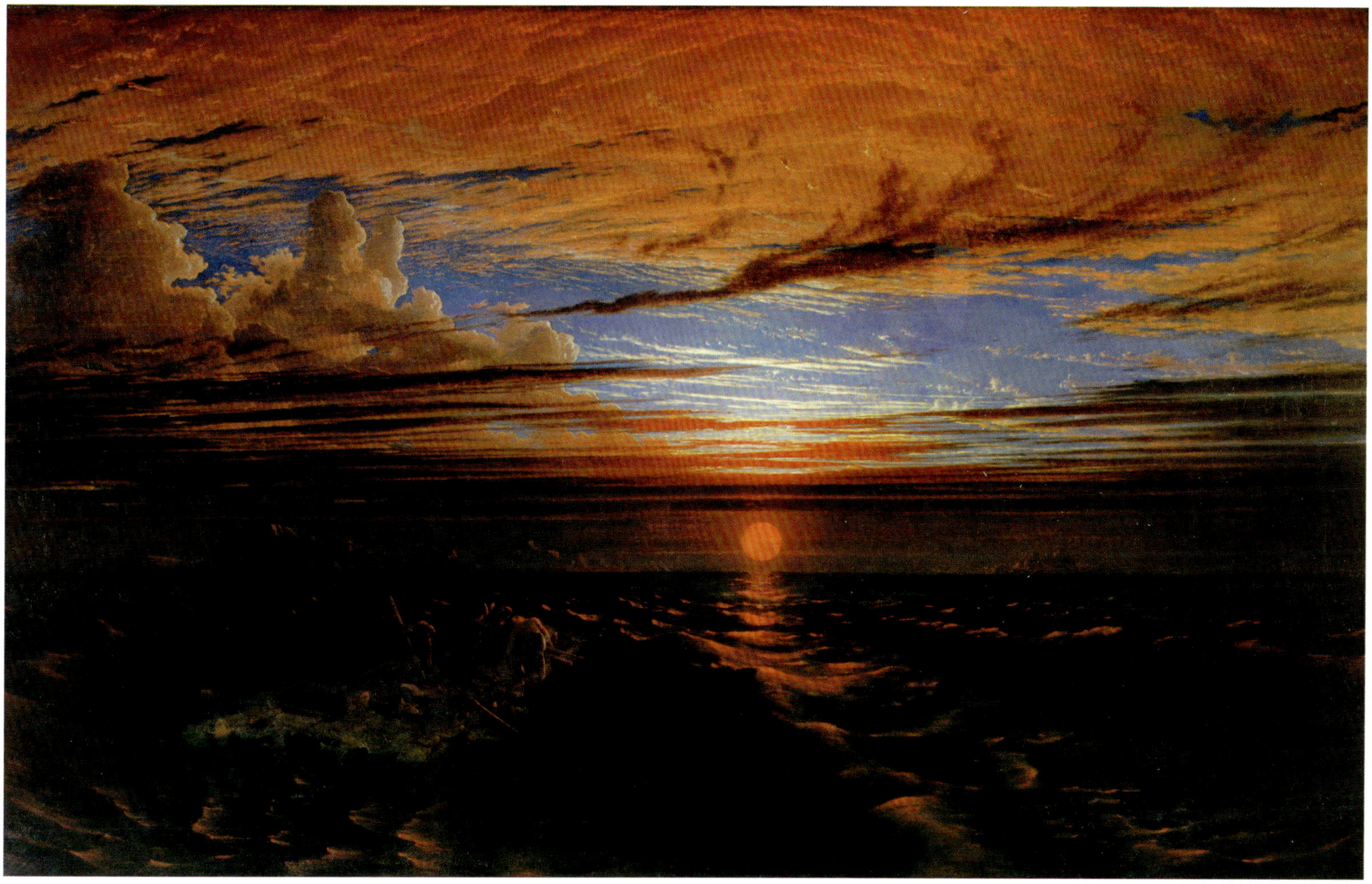

61

Francis Danby

Sunset at Sea after a Storm 1824

Oil on canvas 85.4 x 117.4 (33⅝ x 46¼)

Bristol Museums and Art Gallery

Noon 2003, no. 28

Born in Ireland, Danby (1793–1861) travelled to England in his youth and lived for several years in Bristol, where he established a reputation for producing imaginative, 'poetical' landscapes. From 1820, he regularly sent pictures for exhibition in London. *Sunset at Sea after a Storm* was his most successful work to date. It was bought by the painter Thomas Lawrence, who reportedly paid Danby twice the price he had asked for the painting. As President of the Royal Academy, Lawrence's endorsement helped to secure Danby's reputation, encouraging him to move to London. Reviewing the Academy exhibition, the *Literary Magnet* described the painting as 'the most extraordinary picture in the collection; such a peculiar distribution of black, blue, red, and yellow in streaks, certainly never was placed upon canvas before' (1824, p. 424).

Many of Danby's other landscape and biblical paintings may be considered more overtly Turnerian in subject; but with its theme of maritime disaster, coupled with the artist's unconventional use of colour, *Sunset at Sea after a Storm* comes closer than any other work to matching Turner's imaginative exploration of the sublime potential of the sea. The veiled sight of a raft of exhausted shipwreck survivors drifting into the sunset recalls Géricault's *Raft of the Medusa* (Musée du Louvre), one of the most complex and devastating images of maritime catastrophe in the history of Western art, and a painting that also had a visible impact on Turner's work. Géricault's enormous canvas had been exhibited in Paris in 1819 and to great acclaim the following year at the Egyptian Hall in London. Whether or not Danby knew the painting at first-hand, its reputation was such that he must have intended his audience to draw a parallel between the two images. Danby's work was reproduced in 1826 as a mezzotint dedicated to Lawrence.

62 (and detail)

Augustus Wall Callcott
Heavy Weather Coming on, with Vessels Running to Port 1827
Oil on canvas 115.5 x 169 (45½ x 66½)
Petworth House, West Sussex (National Trust)

Fig. 30

Augustus Wall Callcott
Dead Calm, Boats off Cowes Castle c.1827
Oil on canvas 89 x 119 (35 x 46⅞)
National Maritime Museum

The 1820s were a productive decade for Callcott (1779–1844). Previously he had tended to exhibit just one work each year, but *Heavy Weather Coming on* was one of four paintings submitted to the Academy in 1827. Together with *Bruges, from the Ghent Canal*, a marine townscape in the manner of the seventeenth-century Dutch artist Aelbert Cuyp, it was praised highly in the *Literary Gazette*, albeit without the sense of excitement that Turner's works inspired in the same reviewer (see [59]). *Heavy Weather* and *Bruges* presented 'the most powerful contrast: the turbulence of the elements in the one, and the quiet, Cuyp-like effect in the other, are master-works in this department of painting. But when did we ever see a performance of this artist which had not the stamp of nature, mature practice, and judicious selection?' (2 June 1827).

As a young landscape painter, Callcott had enjoyed the patronage of several influential collectors, including Sir John Leicester and Richard Payne Knight. As his attention turned increasingly towards the sea, his reputation became more closely tied to Turner's, and for several years the two artists maintained a friendly rivalry. Sir George Beaumont famously rejected both artists as 'white painters' on account of their painterly approach to the sea – a charge to which Turner responded by buying more white paint. Callcott took his revenge by contributing to two satirical spoof catalogues of Beaumont's British Institution exhibitions in 1815 and 1816. *Heavy Weather Coming on*, also known as *A Seapiece, with a Dutch Fishing Boat Coming in, and Men of War in the Distance*, was acquired by the Earl of Egremont to hang alongside Turner's *Ships Bearing up for Anchorage* [72]. Among Callcott's other exhibited works in 1827 was an Italianate take on the English coast, *Dead Calm, Boats off Cowes Castle* (a location that Turner painted to great effect after a visit later the same year [83]). A smaller version of Callcott's *Cowes* painting, illustrated here, was formerly in the Egremont collection and was acquired by the National Maritime Museum in 1946.

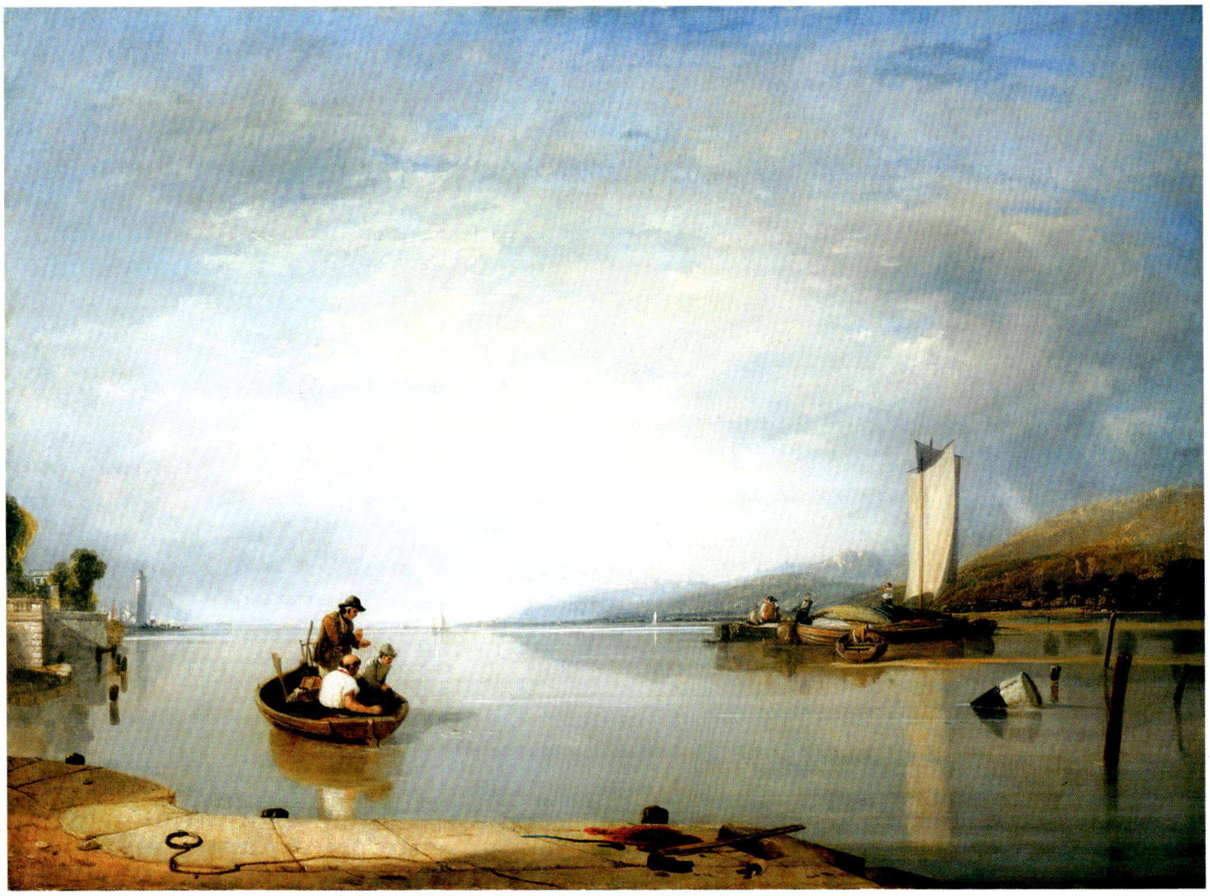

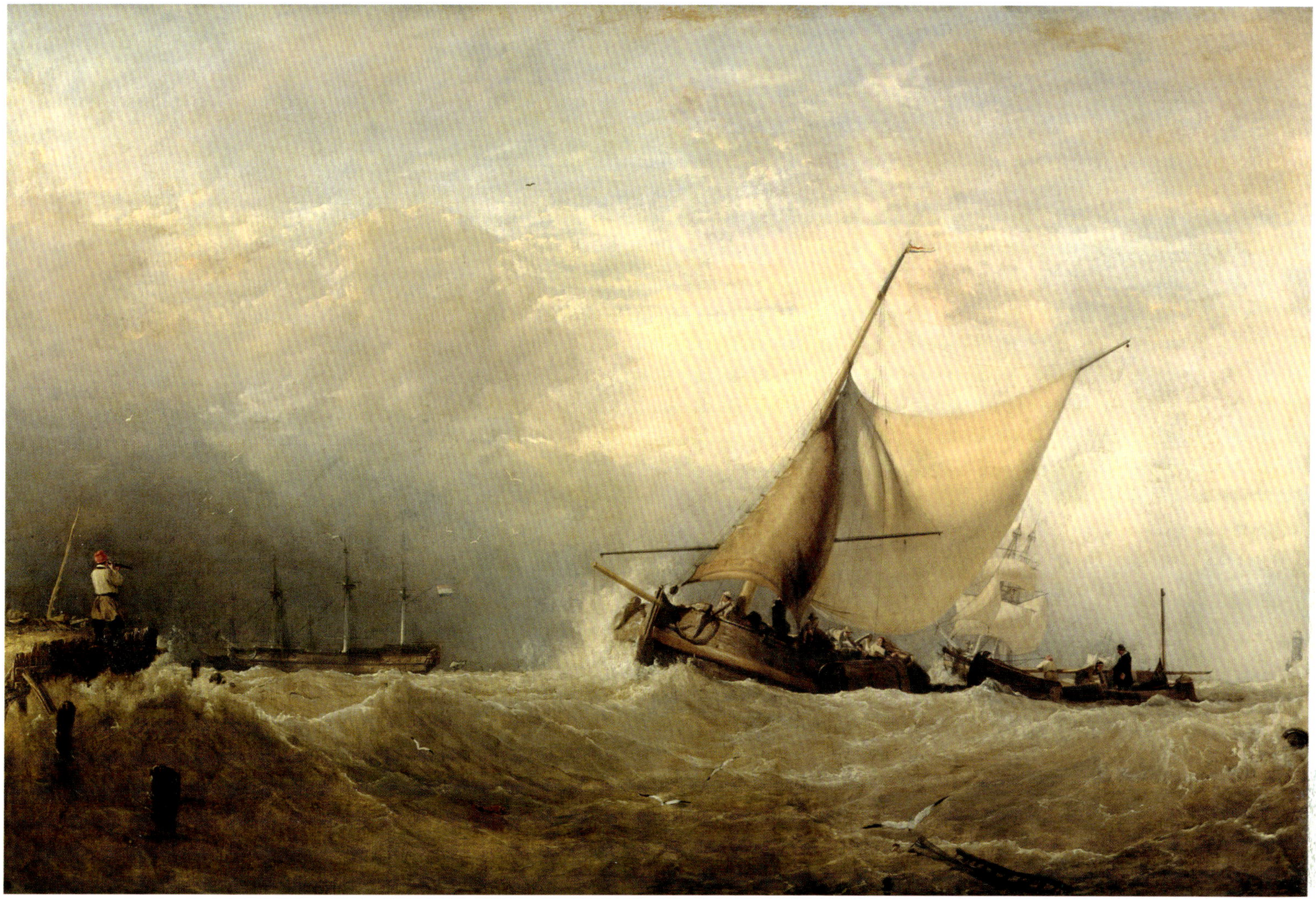

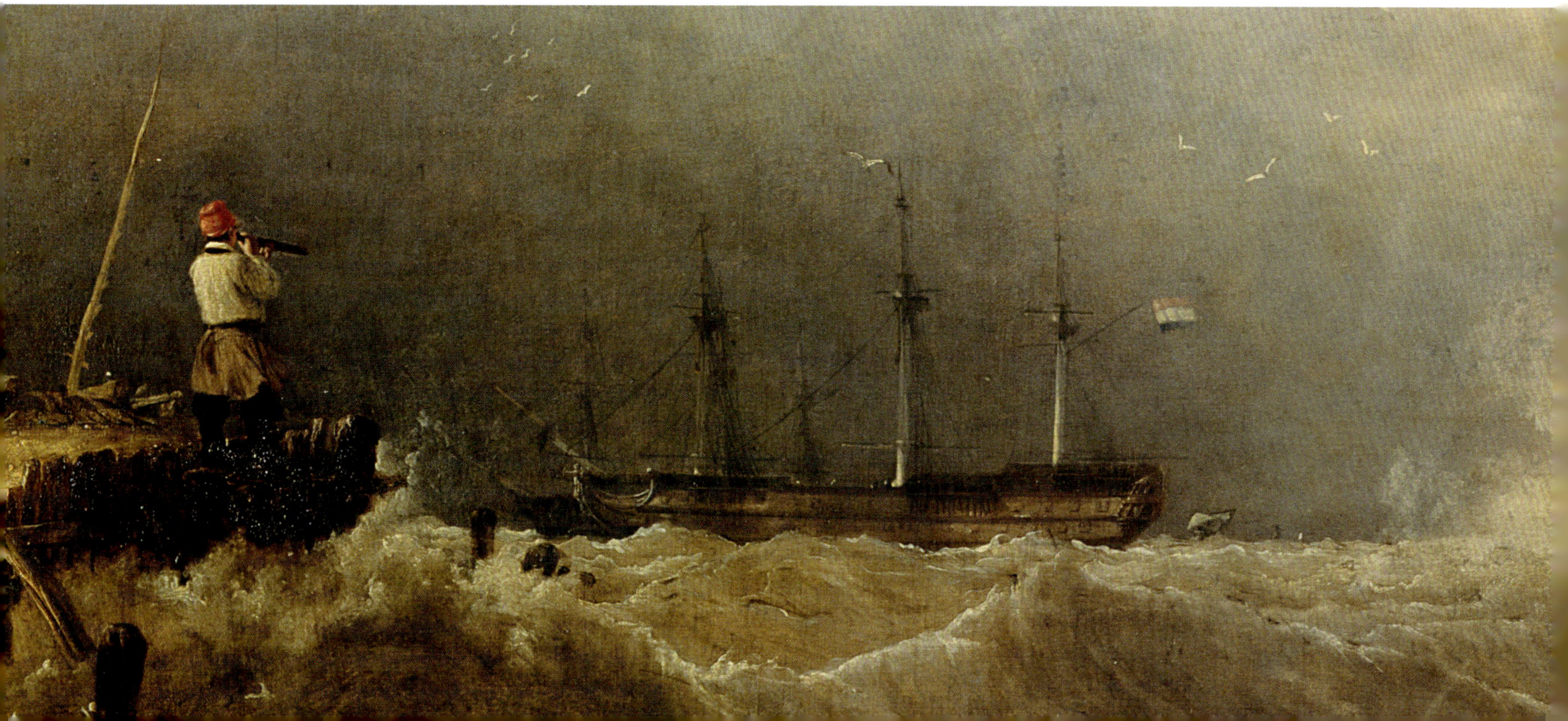

63

J.M.W. Turner

Port Ruysdael 1827
Oil on canvas 92.1 x 122.6 (36¼ x 48¼)
Yale Center for British Art

Butlin and Joll, no. 237; Solkin 2009, pp. 182–83

This is the first of two paintings by Turner set off the coast of the fictive Dutch harbour, invented by Turner to conflate artist and art in a playful homage to Jacob van Ruisdael. The other, *Fishing Boats Bringing a Disabled Ship into Port Ruysdael*, now in the Tate Collection, was exhibited at the Royal Academy in 1844 [fig. 41]. Throughout the eighteenth century, Ruisdael's landscapes had been highly prized by British painters, including Joshua Reynolds and Thomas Gainsborough. In the nineteenth, the artist's seascapes also became well known to a wider audience in Britain. Turner had made a close study of *The Jetty, or Stormy Weather over a Dyke in Holland* [3] at the Louvre in 1802; another painting, *Rough Sea at a Jetty* (Kimbell Art Museum, Fort Worth, Texas) was sold through the London art market in 1826 and it is likely that Turner had the opportunity of studying other examples of Ruisdael's work at first-hand in British collections. Where *'Now for the Painter'* indicated a radical departure from the accepted tones of marine painting, *Port Ruysdael* signalled a renewed and deeper engagement with the Netherlandish tradition that had been so important at the beginning of Turner's career. On the basis of this work, the *Examiner* agreed, likening Turner to 'the best of the Dutch marine painters' (1 July 1827).

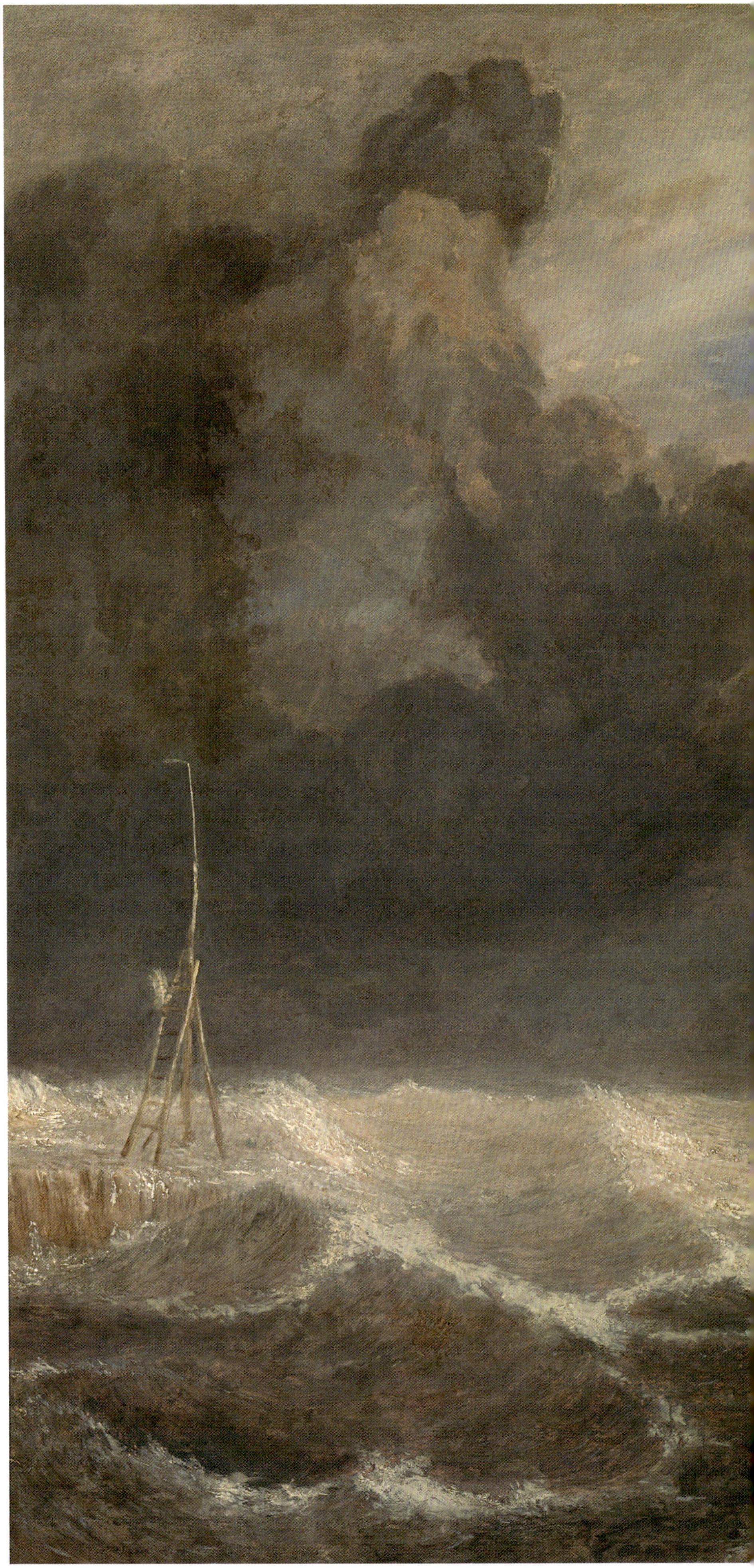

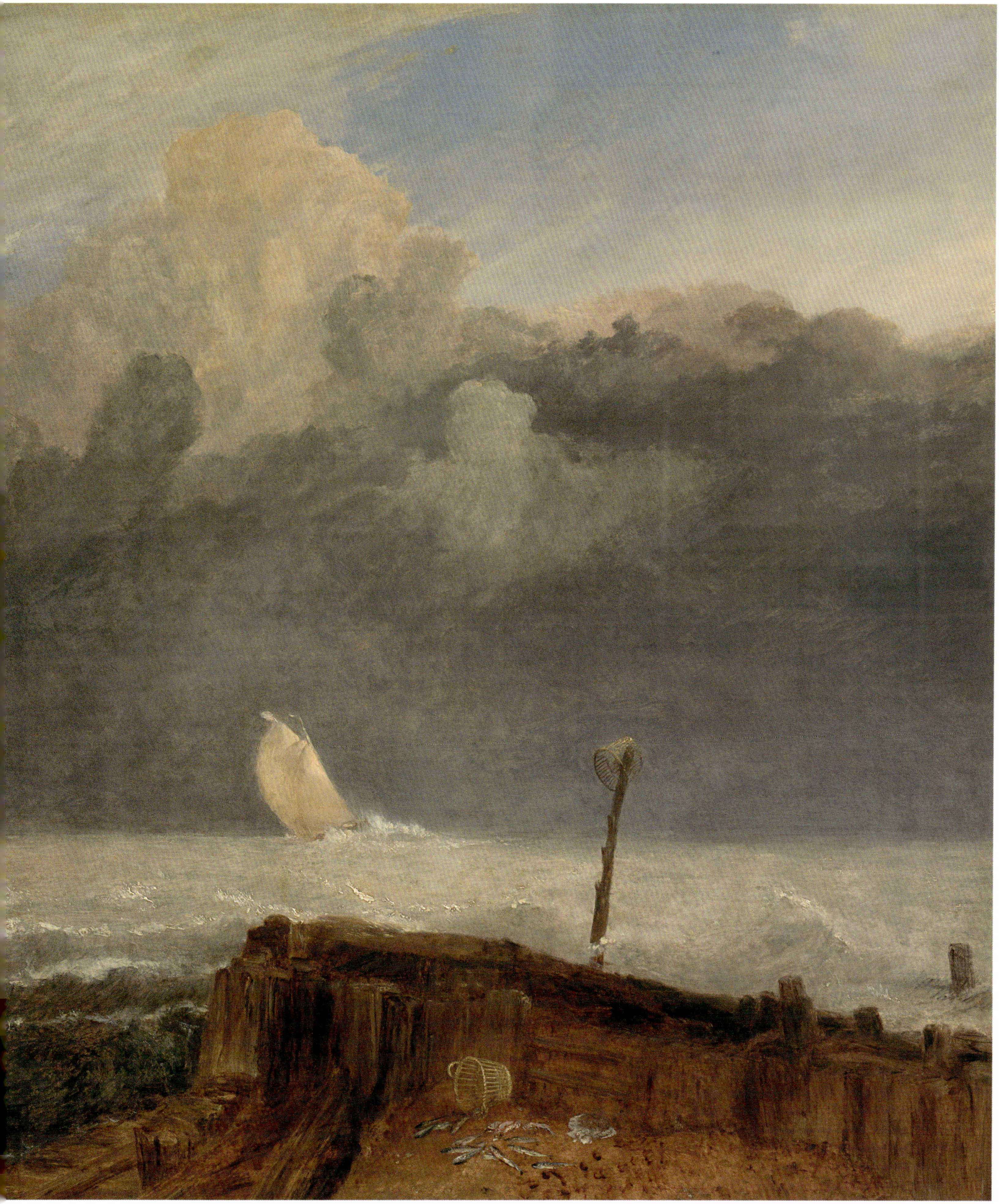

Opposite 64

John Constable
Chain Pier, Brighton 1827
Oil on canvas 127 x 183 (50 x 72)
Tate

Lyles 2006, no. 51

Below Fig. 31

J.M.W. Turner
Brighton from the Sea c.1828–30
Oil on canvas 63.5 x 132 (25 x 52)
Tate and the National Trust (Petworth House)

John Constable's large canvas is the only full-scale painting that resulted from his visits to Brighton in the 1820s. Constable (1776–1837) regarded the town's newly developed seafront as an artificial place, far less noble a subject for art than the cultivated fields of Suffolk. Brighton was 'Piccadilly ... by the sea-side', a place of novelty and confusion, and his visits there were overshadowed by his wife's illness. Nevertheless, he was drawn to the beach and to the spectacle of the recently opened Royal Suspension Chain Pier 'with its long & elegant strids [*sic*] into the sea a full 1/4 of a mile' (Constable 1968, p. 171). Constable described the 'dandy jetty' to his patron the Reverend John Fisher as an extension of the fashionable visitors who promenaded noisily along Marine Parade. Perhaps the artist saw, in the throng of seaside tourists, the same behaviour shown by the crowds who attended the annual exhibition at the Royal Academy. Although placed at a distance in his composition, the pier dominates the scene, at once obscuring and emphasizing the horizon. The subject and composition are unusually modern for Constable. As with all of the artist's 'six-footers', *Chain Pier, Brighton* was the result of much study and countless drawings and oil sketches, and the heavily worked surface of the finished painting betrays the many hours of labour that went into its making.

Turner painted the same subject under rather different circumstances, as one of four landscapes commissioned by the Earl of Egremont for the long dining room of his country seat at Petworth. The other works in the group were two prospects of the park at Petworth and a view of the Chichester canal. The choice of Chichester and Brighton is explained by Egremont's financial interests in both towns, as an investor in the canal and the Chain Pier, two monuments of the new industrial age. Turner undoubtedly had Constable's recent painting of the same subject in mind. Even more than Constable, Turner allows the powerful horizontal presence of the pier to set the tone of the painting. However, taking his view from the east, and from the sea, Turner sets the pier in silhouette against a fiery sunset that casts the distant prospect of Brighton's seafront buildings in a golden haze. The pier was built as a landing station for the steam and sail packet-boat traffic with France, and it is this aspect that Turner's work emphasizes over Constable's uneasy encounter with the modern pleasure beach.

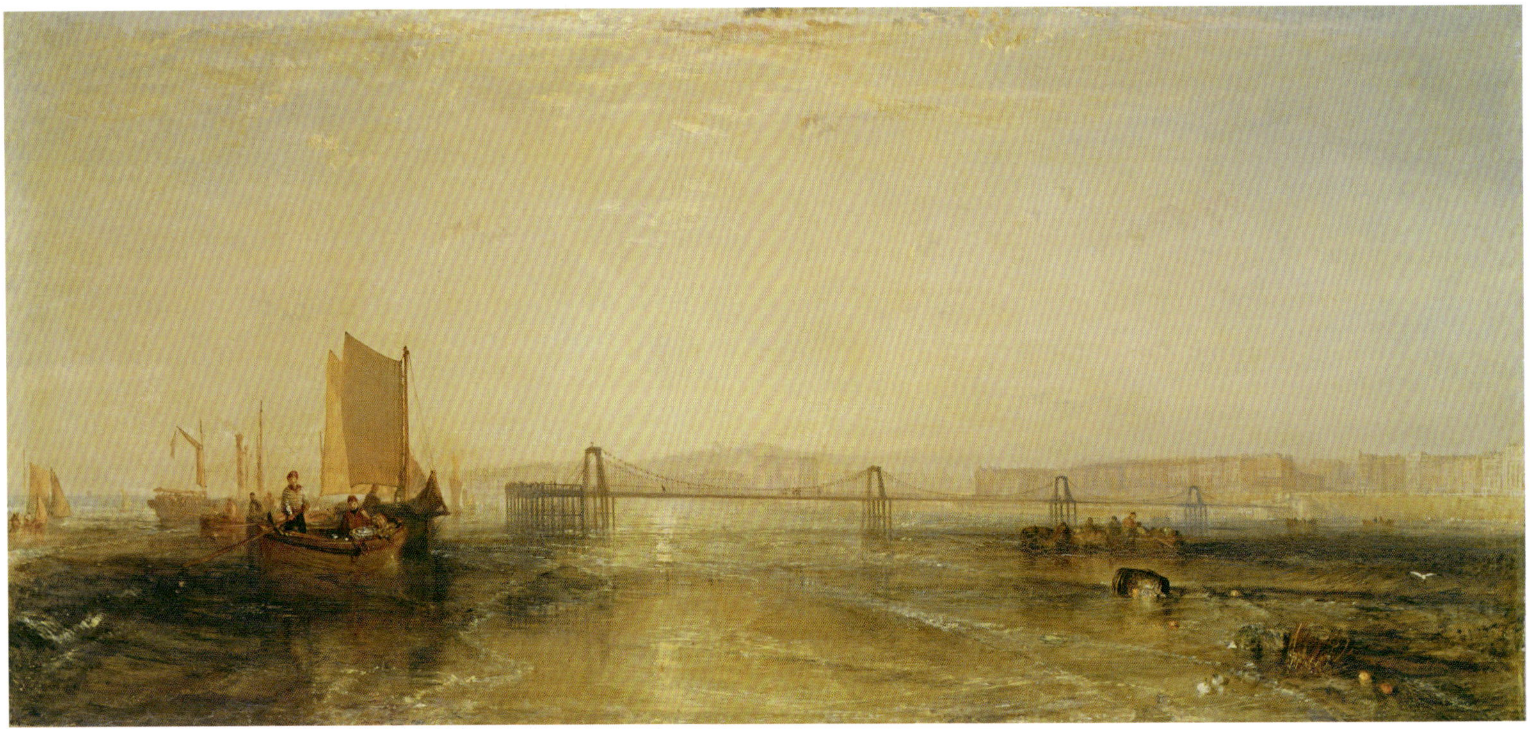

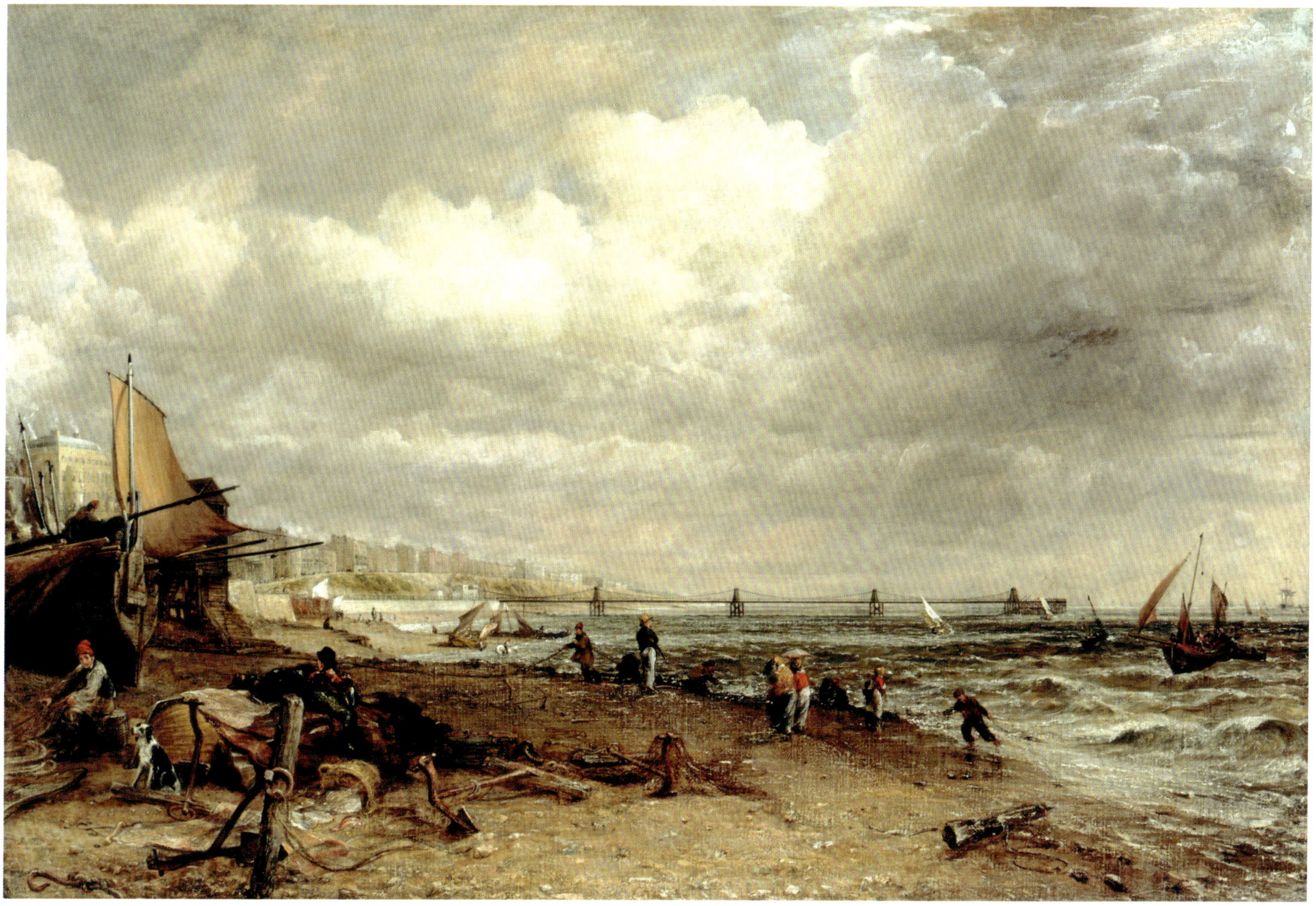

65

Richard Parkes Bonington
Ships at Anchor c.1825
Oil on millboard affixed to canvas
35.8 x 30.7 (14⅛ x 12⅛)
National Museums Liverpool

Pointon 1985, fig. 55; Noon 2008, no. 180

This view of maritime trade and coastal life in northern France, where Bonington (1802–28) lived, was probably painted shortly after he had first visited London. The vertical format, unusual for a marine subject, echoes the forms of the windless sails on the coastal trading vessel, set against an expansive sky and shimmering calm sea. This elegant effect is emphasized by Bonington's understated technique of applying vertical brushstrokes for the sails and sky, horizontal for the water and everything below the horizon (Noon 2008, p. 216). Made on a pre-prepared board for a domestic setting, this intimate painting stands apart from the larger canvases favoured by Bonington's contemporaries in Britain. Despite the obvious differences between Bonington's work and Turner's oil paintings of the same period, *Ships at Anchor* reveals a shared interest in seventeenth-century Dutch models, especially the port scenes of Jan van de Cappelle and the smaller, jewel-like calms of van de Velde (see, for example, [4]). For following his own path, drawing on his earlier experience of working in watercolour, Bonington has since been recognized as one of Turner's most original rivals in the art of marine painting.

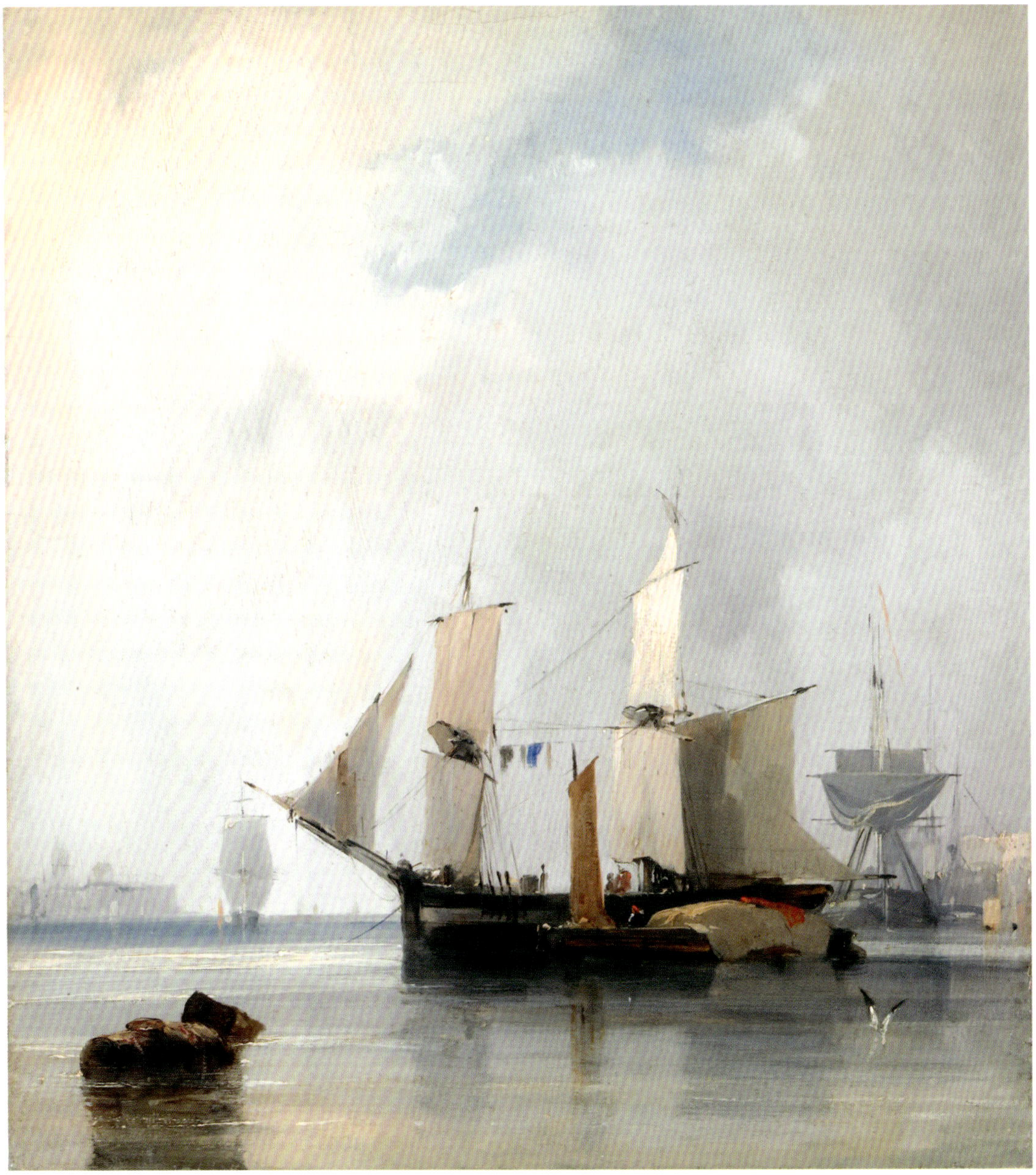

66

Richard Parkes Bonington

Near St-Valery-sur-Somme c.1824–25
Oil on canvas 80 x 121 (31½ x 47⅝)
Anglesey Abbey, Cambridgeshire (National Trust)

Noon 2003, no. 126; Noon 2008, no. 177

In the 1820s, Turner and Bonington turned their attention to the coasts of Britain and France respectively, and to the fishing communities that had lived on opposing sides during years of war. While Turner made a close study of the southern coast of England, Bonington travelled extensively along the northern coast of France, observing the life of local fisherfolk and documenting the ebb and flow of their lives by the sea. This scene has been identified as the beach near the small fishing village of St-Valery-sur-Somme on the Picardy coast, although, as with Turner's views around Hastings [80], topographical detail is not the artist's priority. The work shows signs of being altered several times, giving it an unfinished appearance that is most apparent in the composition of the family group and horse in the foreground. Bonington painted *Near St-Valery-sur-Somme* at the height of his career in France. A related composition, possibly *A Fishmarket near Boulogne* (Yale Center for British Art) or *Coast Scene with Fisherfolk* (Tate Collection), was awarded a gold medal at the Paris Salon in 1824. Critics noted Bonington's unfinished style: 'His paintings are, from a distance of several feet, the accent of nature, but they are, in truth, only sketches' (cited in Noon 2008, p. 198). Two years later, the artist exhibited two paintings at the British Institution (including *Coast Scene with Fisherfolk*) to universal acclaim.

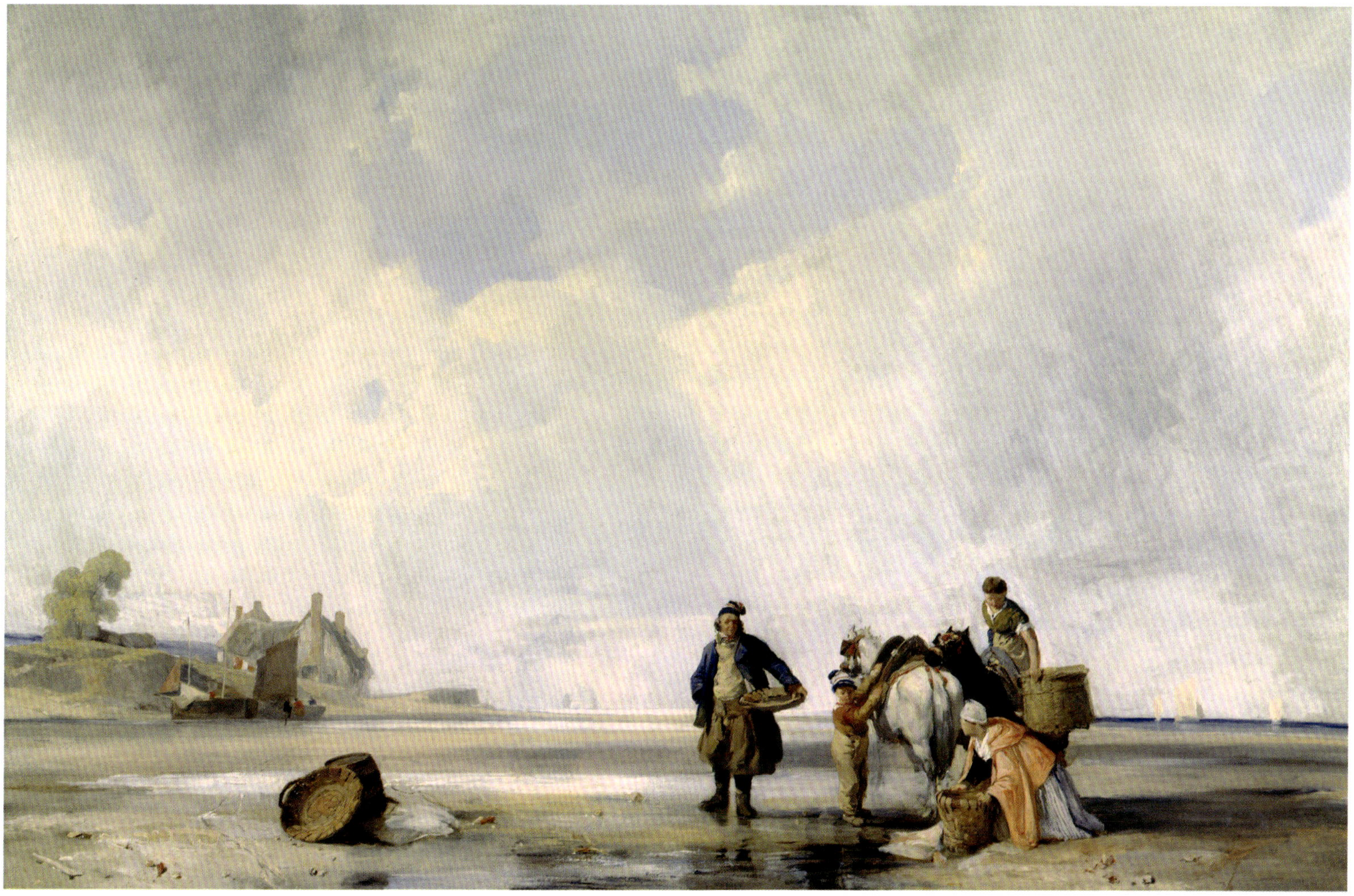

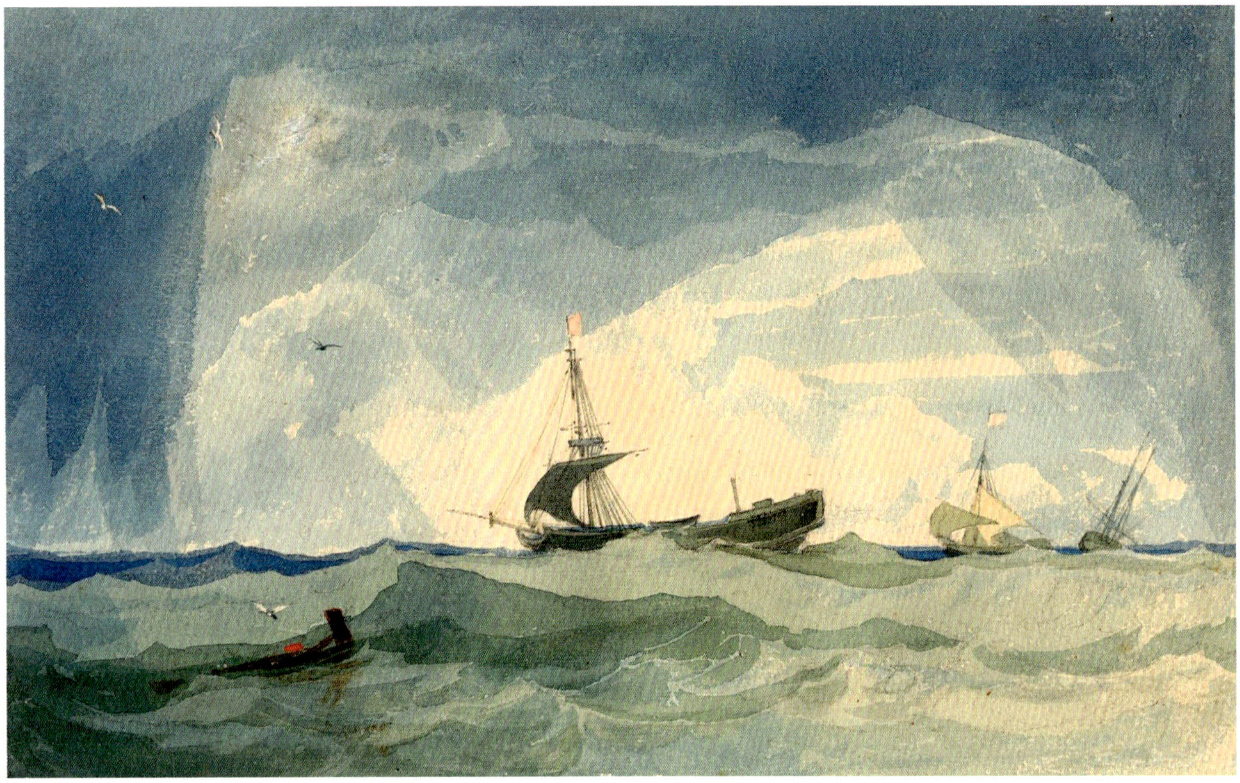

67

John Sell Cotman
A Dismasted Brig c.1810
Watercolour 20.1 x 31 (7⅞ x 12¼)
British Museum

Recognized as one of the most innovative watercolourists of his generation, John Sell Cotman (1782–1842) first met Turner as a teenager in the 1790s through the patronage of the physician Dr Thomas Monro, a keen collector of art who encouraged artists to meet regularly, work and exchange ideas at his house in Adelphi Terrace, London. When Cotman returned to his home town of Norwich to set up a drawing school after several years living and working in London, he produced a number of shipping scenes in oil and watercolour based on the Norfolk coast. It is likely that *A Dismasted Brig*, among the most celebrated of Cotman's marine subjects, was made during this productive period. Cotman was prominent among a generation of artists in watercolour (alongside Turner, Louis Francia, Thomas Girtin and others) who embraced the physical properties of the medium to produce a new kind of land- and seascape that owed little to the more tactile character of oil painting. Cotman's distinctive use of broad, regular washes of colour for the sea and sky embodies this new aesthetic in a way that seems wholly in tune with his maritime subject. He also studied, and made his own work based on, Turner's *Liber Studiorum* (for example, *Sea View (Fishing Boats)* in the Norwich Museum). There is a close similarity in composition between *A Dismasted Brig* and 'The Leader Sea Piece', one of the earlier marine subjects to be published as part of the *Liber* [23].

68

J.M.W. Turner

The Mouth of the River Humber c.1824–25

Watercolour 16.2 x 24.2 (6⅜ x 9½)

Tate. Turner Bequest 1856

Finberg CCVIII R; Shanes 1990, no. 87

In the early 1820s, Turner's continued interest in marine subjects focused on the creative and commercial possibilities of watercolour. *The Mouth of the River Humber* is one of eighteen watercolours that he prepared for W.B. Cooke's *Rivers of England*, possibly planned as a sequel to the successful and ongoing *Picturesque Views on the Southern Coast of England* (see pp. 63–67). Turner's approach to the elements in these works drew on his earlier marine oils, especially in the dramatic tonal contrast within and between sea and sky, but the layering of broad washes of watercolour allowed an even greater freedom in representing the elusive, intangible yet overwhelmingly powerful weight of the elements. The techniques that Turner perfected while working for Cooke had a profound effect on his later works in oil. More immediately, Turner's *Southern Coast* and *Rivers* influenced his fellow artists – especially the watercolours of Bonington. There is no evidence to suggest that the two artists met during Bonington's visit to England in 1825, but they were by this time familiar with each other's work. Bonington owned proofs of the prints after Turner's *Rivers* (and *Margate* from the *Marine Views* series, see [45]) and it is likely that he also knew the original watercolours.

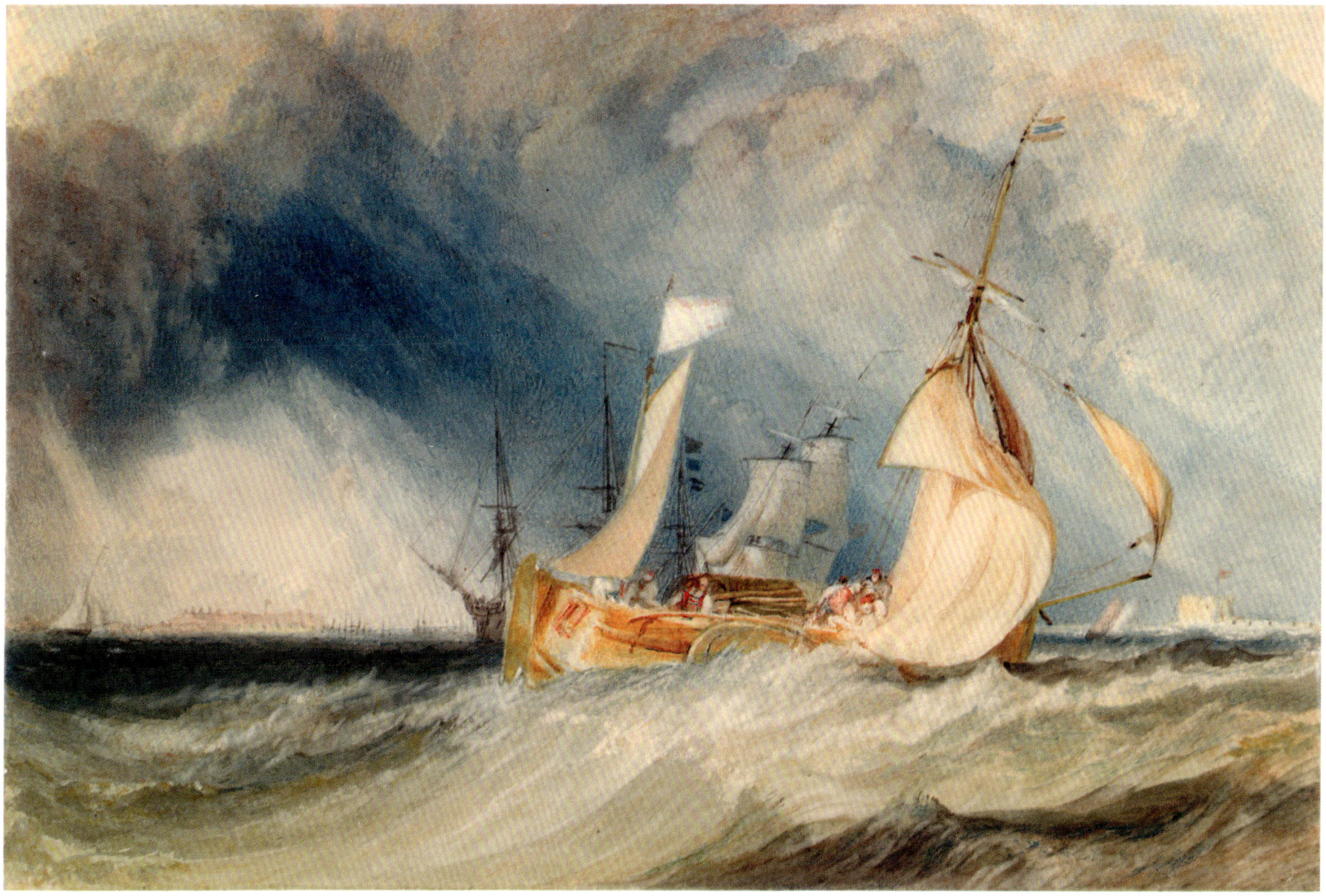

69

François Louis Thomas Francia
Running before the Wind c.1810
Watercolour 14.6 x 9.5 (5¾ x 3¾)
Yale Center for British Art

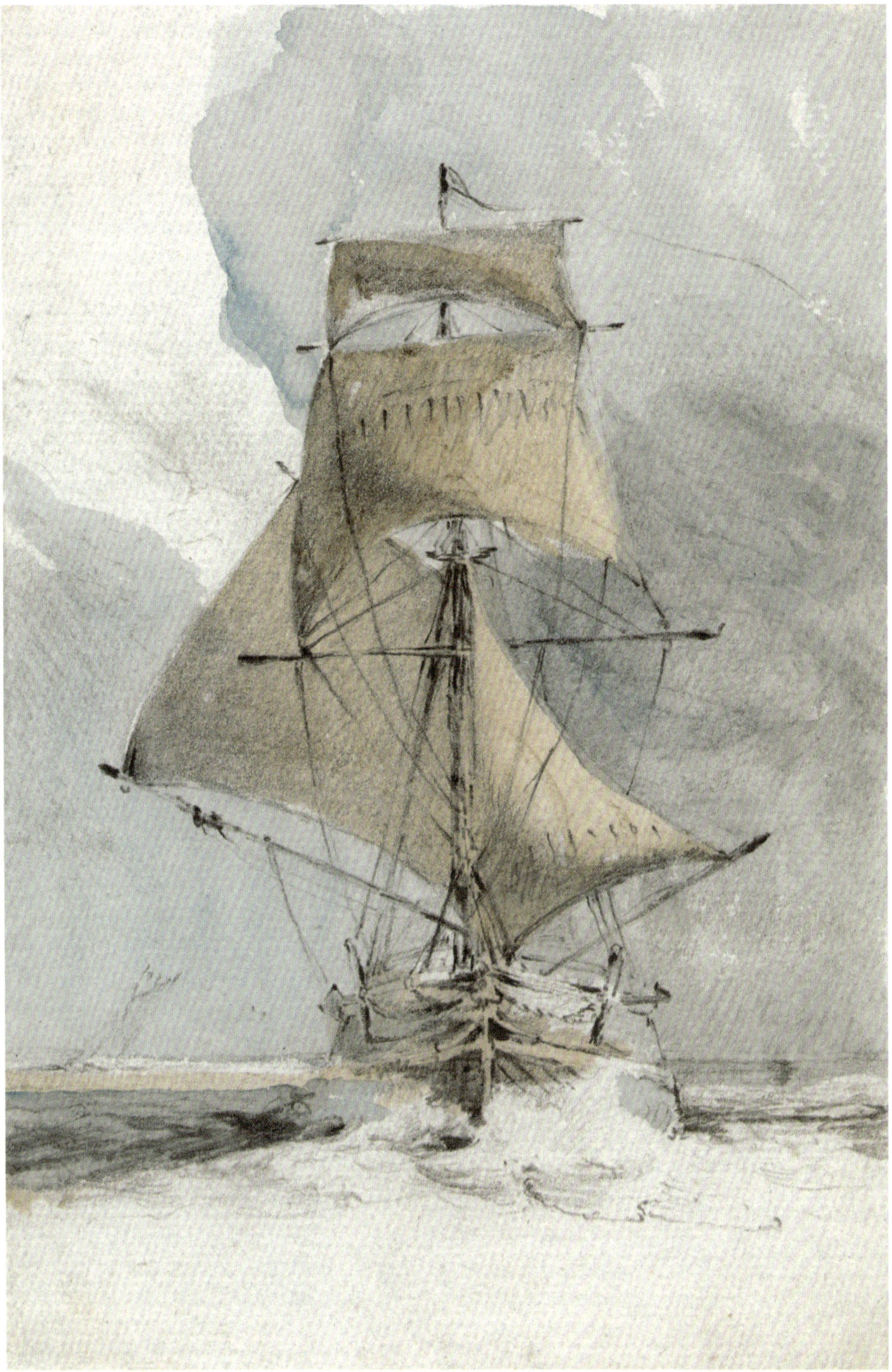

Born in France, Louis Francia (1772–1839) moved to England with his family as a child and trained in London. He began to exhibit watercolours at the Royal Academy in 1795, around the time that Turner's earliest public works in the medium were beginning to attract the attention of critics and a broader public. Francia was a well-connected and sociable artist. He joined the Sketching Society established by Thomas Girtin in 1799 and was involved in several other watercolour societies, although he did not succeed in his ambition to become more closely associated with the Royal Academy. *Running before the Wind*, a small but highly effective bow-view of a cutter in full sail, shows the artist at his most economical. It was probably made as a study for a larger composition. In 1816, Francia returned to Calais where he met the young Richard Parkes Bonington, training him in the English style of watercolour that he had learned in London.

70

Samuel Owen

Shipping on a Stormy Day c.1810
Grey wash over pencil 38.7 x 50.8 (15¼ x 20)
Yale Center for British Art

The greater availability of the pigments and associated paraphernalia of watercolour painting around the turn of the nineteenth century, combined with new ways of exhibiting and selling works on paper, helped to transform the medium from a laborious, highly specialist practice into a popular and commercially viable art form. London's artists' suppliers, or colourmen, were typically involved in other aspects of the business: providing a full range of materials and guidebook and instructional literature; selling the work of aspiring artists in their shops; and even employing them directly. Richard and Thomas Rowney were perfume and cosmetic merchants, but began selling artists' materials around 1800 and counted Turner among their most loyal customers. Rudolph Ackermann was another figure at the heart of the watercolour economy. In 1795, he opened a shop called the Repository of Arts in the Strand, from where he sold prints and books as well as all manner of artists' materials. He also ran a thriving publishing business from the back of his shop.

Samuel Owen (1768/9–1857) exhibited a handful of maritime subjects at the Royal Academy during the 1790s and early 1800s, but in 1808 turned his energies towards the recently founded Associated Artists in Water-Colours, one of several exhibiting societies formed around the beginning of the century with the aim of raising the status of the medium. Other exhibitors included David Cox, Louis Francia [69] and William Westall. Owen shares with Francia a broad handling of the brush and a keen eye for technical maritime detail, as well as a visible debt to Turner's early work on paper. The use of grey wash in *Shipping on a Stormy Day* emphasizes the atmospheric effect of the scene, while drawing attention to the ship at the centre – its pitch and closely delineated rigging observed with a mariner's eye. Owen's work was more widely known in print, including a series of eighty-four views of the Thames published by W.B. Cooke between 1809 and 1811. He later collaborated with William Westall and Ackermann to produce *A Picturesque Tour of the River Thames* (1828).

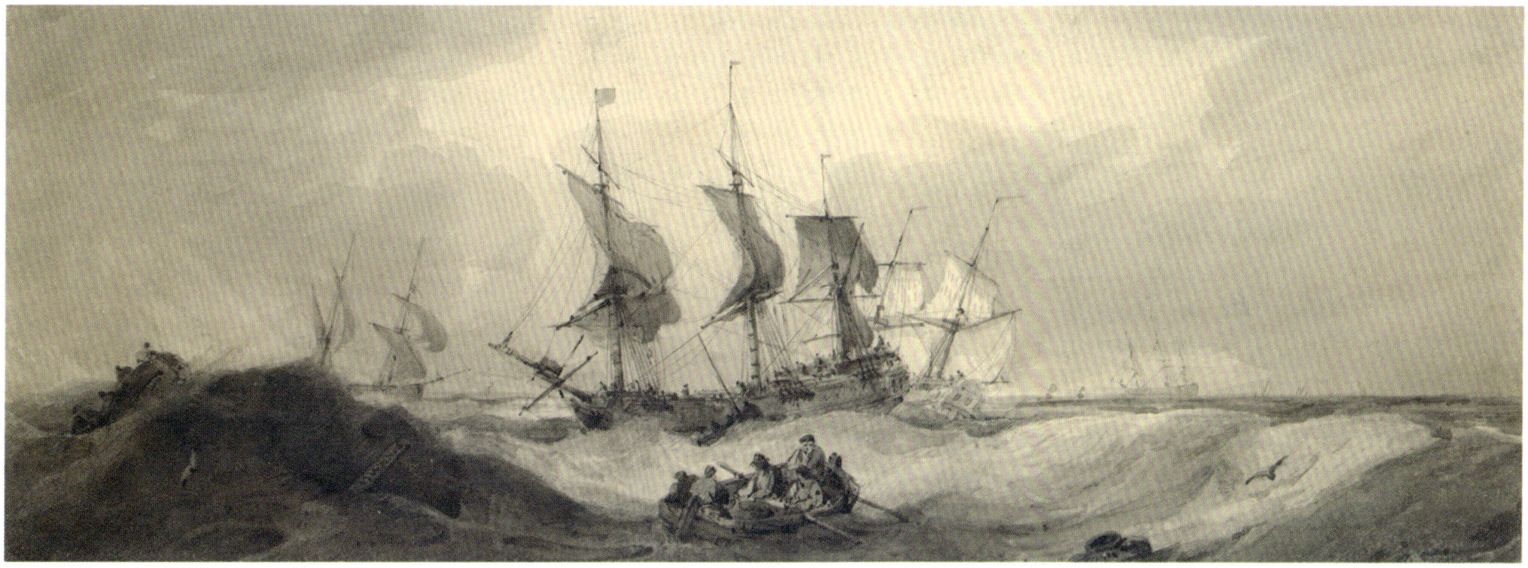

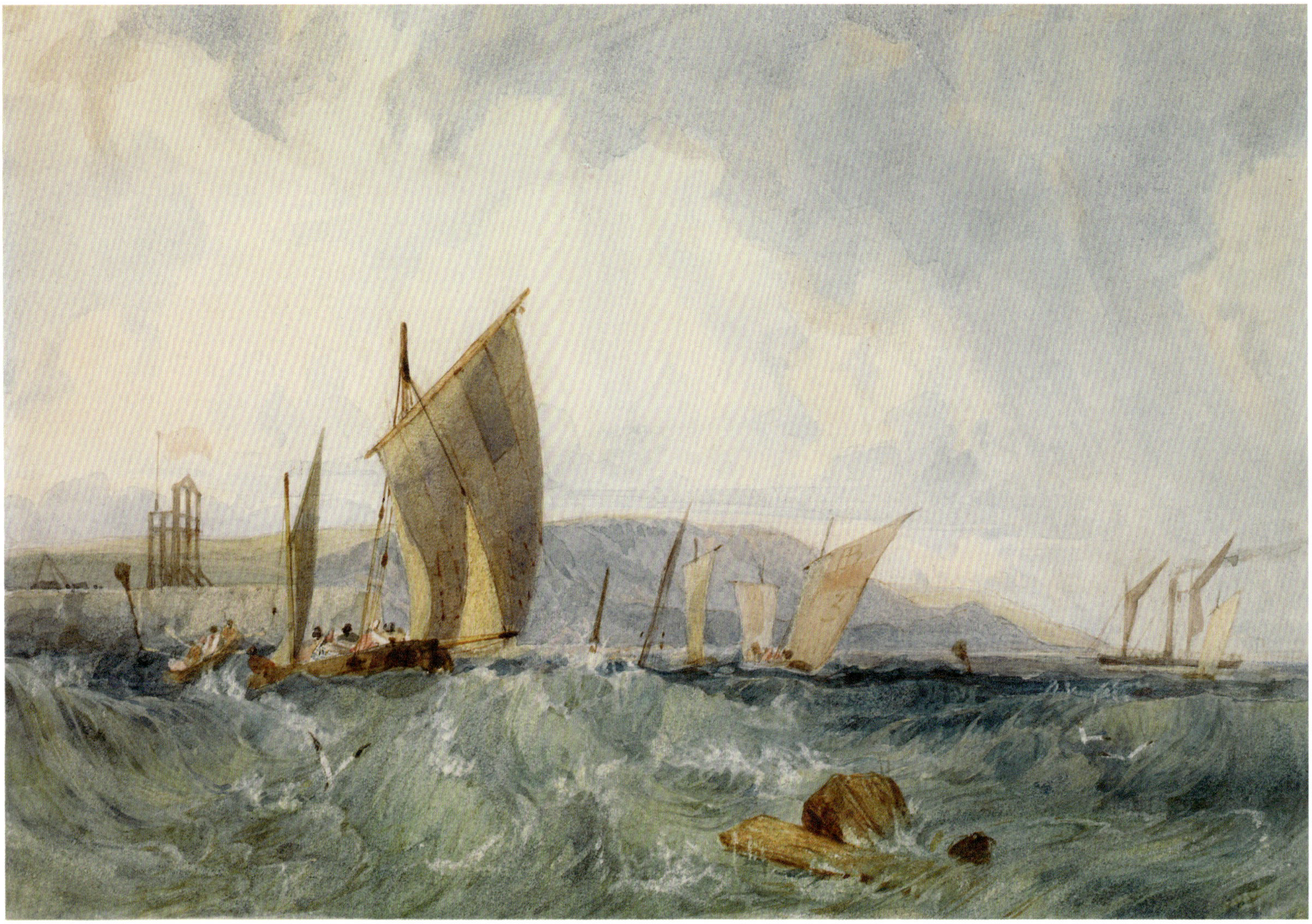

71 (and detail)

Richard Parkes Bonington
Fishing Boats and a Paddle Steamer, Boulogne c.1825
Watercolour 18.3 x 25.2 (7¼ x 9⅞)
National Maritime Museum

Noon 2008, no. 78

Bonington's picturesque view of fishing boats and a paddle steamer in choppy waters was painted shortly after the first regular steamboat services were established between England and France. Previously identified as a view of Dieppe, the prospect more closely resembles the topography and jetty at Boulogne, as suggested by an old inscription on the reverse. The large wooden framework flying a faded red flag at the end of the jetty, on the south side of the harbour entrance, is a navigational landmark, also used to indicate the tides to steamers entering the port. This relatively late example of the artist's watercolours of the Normandy coast suggests a first-hand knowledge of Turner's work of the period, especially in its treatment of the agitated sea. The artist animates the sea with vigorous brushstrokes – a few nervous scratches within the thicker layers of paint evoking the foam of tumultuous waves – and the figures rendered with a simple economy. This view was taken after Bonington's first adult visit to London in 1825, although it is likely that he already knew Turner's work in engraved form. Since his early death from tuberculosis at the age of twenty-six, Bonington has been recognized as an artist who successfully fused British and French approaches to marine and genre painting, and whose work had a lasting influence on both sides of the Channel.

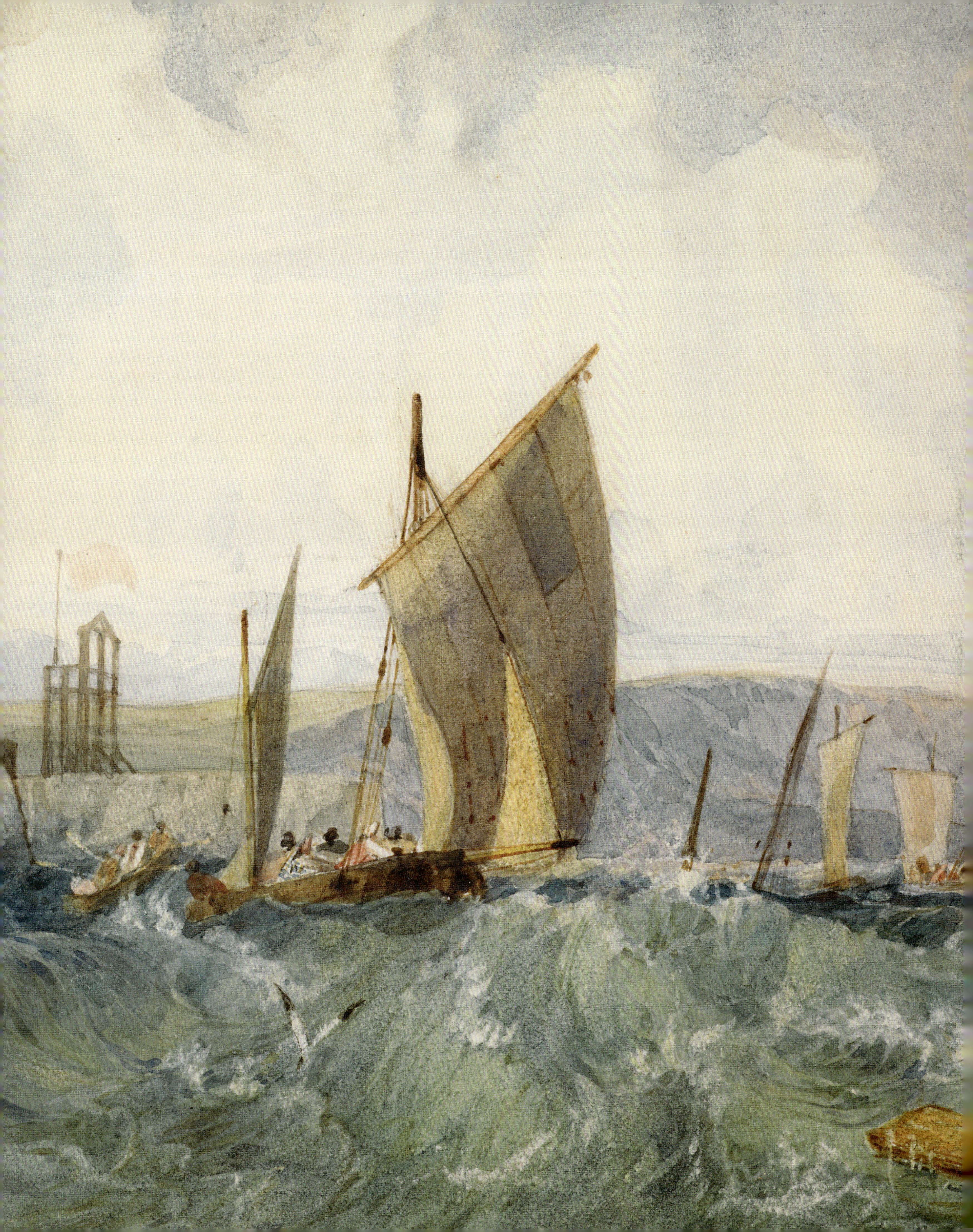

'Turner, Calcott and Collins will not like it': Constable, Brighton and the Sea

Anne Lyles

John Constable, Turner's greatest rival in the art of landscape, is not generally thought of as a painter of the sea. His best-known marine subject, *Chain Pier, Brighton* [64], shown at the Academy in 1827, is not characteristic of his previously exhibited output, nor did it serve to steer his work in a new, maritime direction. However, coastal and marine subjects form an important part of Constable's full range as a landscape painter, especially when his oil sketches, prints and drawings are taken into consideration. He was familiar with the sea, shipping and river transport from boyhood. His father, a Suffolk corn miller and coal merchant, depended on barges for carrying cargoes up and down the river Stour and on sailing vessels for transporting them onwards by sea between Mistley on the Stour estuary and the port of London. Some of the artist's earliest known drawings are marine subjects copied from drawings or prints in the style of Dominic Serres or Robert Cleveley.[1] He also made youthful studies of boat-building yards and of warehouses and shipping on the river Orwell.[2]

Constable's first direct experience of the open sea took place in the spring of 1803 when he spent nearly a month on board an East Indiaman, the 'Coutts', captained by a friend of his father. The ship was sailing to China but Constable joined it only for the short stretch of its journey between London and the Downs (off Deal in Kent). The sketches he made of the shipping he observed along the estuaries of the Thames and Medway have been likened in style to the drawings of Willem van de Velde the Younger. Some fifty of these are known today.[3] When the 'Coutts' moored briefly at Gravesend, Constable went ashore and walked to Chatham to see the men-of-war, including Nelson's flagship, 'Victory', finishing a major refit, just two years before the Battle of Trafalgar. Constable described 'Victory' as the 'flower of the flock, a three decker of (some say) 112 guns – she looked very beautifull [*sic*], fresh out of Dock and newly painted'.[4] He mentioned making sketches of the ship in three views, which have been identified with three drawings that appeared on the London market in 2003.[5] He used these sketches when working on a finished watercolour of the naval engagement at Trafalgar for exhibition at the Royal Academy in 1806, the same year that Turner exhibited his first Trafalgar-related painting at his own gallery.[6] However, Constable's watercolour passed unnoticed by the critics and it was to be some years before he sent a marine subject for exhibition again.

Constable was always attracted to painting the sea. When Maria Bicknell, his future wife, was staying in Bognor in 1812, he told her that 'a sea coast is always a subject enough for a pencil [brush]'.[7] Indeed, it was usually when a coastal area had strong personal associations that Constable tended to see its artistic potential. When on honeymoon in Dorset in 1816, and staying with his friend John Fisher in Osmington, he often painted the views from isolated stretches of the beach nearby. His remarkable oil sketch of *Weymouth Bay* (Victoria and Albert Museum), made at speed as a thunderstorm was approaching, was to become the basis of a larger exhibition canvas that he probably showed at the British Institution in 1819.

It was, of course, the coastal resort of Brighton that was to feature so significantly in Constable's personal life when, between 1824 and 1828, he and his family paid extended visits there in the hope of finding a cure for

Maria's tuberculosis. His initial reaction to the town was unfavourable. As Richard Johns has noted (p. 148), Constable referred to it in disparaging terms in a now famous letter to John Fisher:

> Brighton is the receptacle of the fashion and offscouring of London. The magnificence of the sea, and its ... everlasting voice, is drowned in the din & lost in the tumult of stage coaches – gigs – 'flys' &c – the beach is only Piccadilly ... by the sea-side ... there is nothing here for a painter but the breakers – & sky.[8]

Constable made many striking oil studies of sea and sky from the beach at Brighton, generally looking westwards away from the resort towards Hove and Shoreham [fig. 32].[9] However, only two years after writing this letter to Fisher, he also embarked on painting the large 'six-foot' canvas of the recently opened Chain Pier, having previously dismissed the 'trimmed and neat appearance & the dandy jetty' of this section of the beach near Marine Parade as 'still more unnatural'. Not only does the modern pier seem an odd choice of subject for Constable in the light of these remarks, but it also seems especially unsuitable given that, in the same letter, he had vented his prejudices against coastal scenes in general:

> [T]hese subjects are so hackneyed in the Exhibition, and are ... so little capable of that beautifull sentiment that landscape is capable of ... that they have done a great deal of harm to the art ... [I] call to your recollection that we have Calcott [*sic*] & Collins – but not Wilson or Gainsborough.

Yet Constable was nothing if not contradictory. In the early 1820s he had again started to paint and exhibit coastal scenes, albeit on a much smaller scale than *Chain Pier*, given that modest, 'cabinet'-scale pictures were generally easier to sell. Indeed, so readily saleable did these small coastal subjects of *Harwich Lighthouse* and *Yarmouth Jetty* prove, that Constable was to make three versions of each of them.[10] One of the replicas of *Yarmouth Jetty* was sold to the Anglo-French dealer John Arrowsmith in 1824, as part of a package

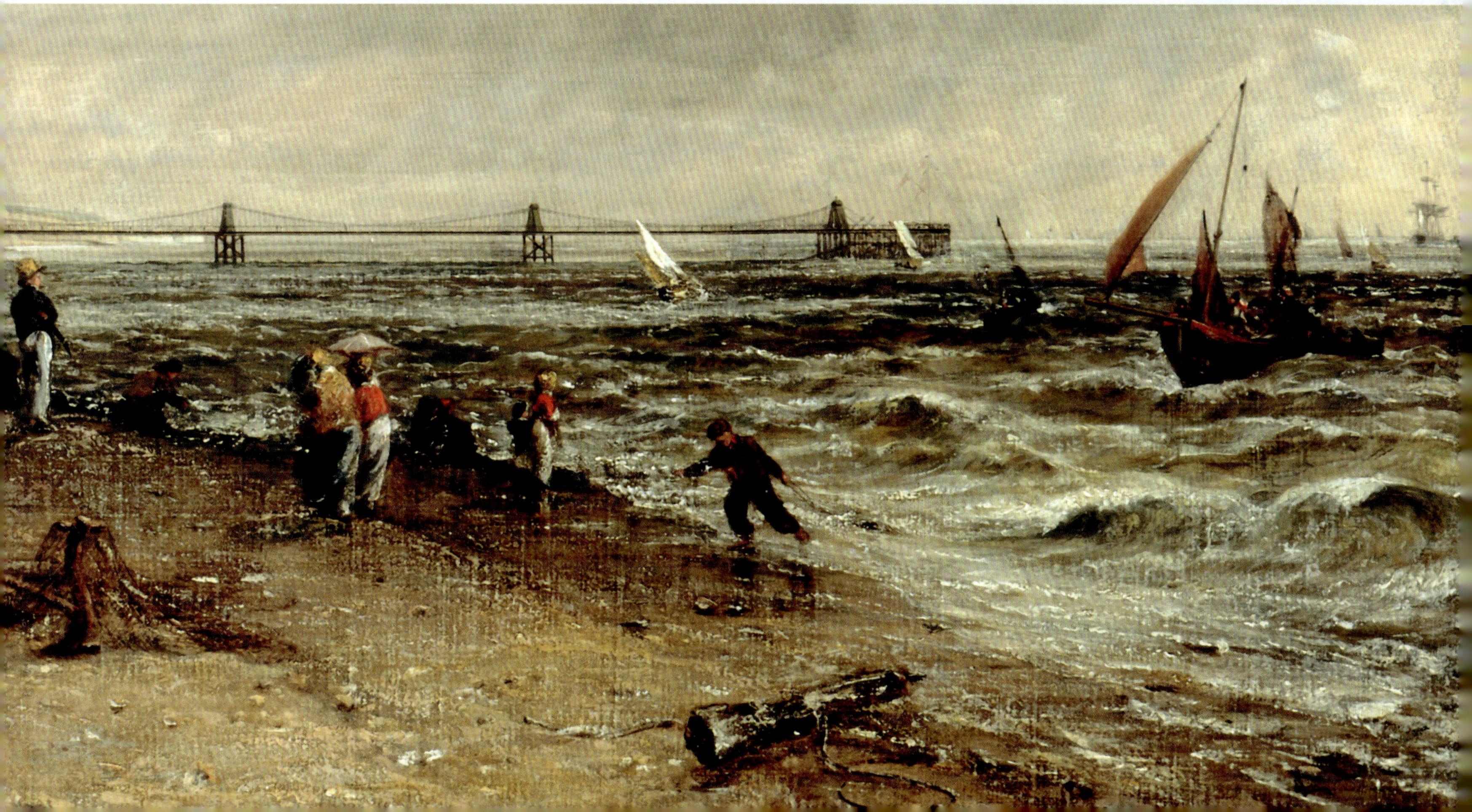

Preceding page

John Constable
Chain Pier, Brighton 1827 (detail of [64])

Fig. 32

John Constable
Hove Beach c.1824
Oil on paper laid on canvas 29.8 x 49.2 (11¾ x 19⅜)
Victoria and Albert Museum

Fig. 33

J.M.W. Turner
Brighton Beach, with the Chain Pier in the Distance
c.1827; reworked 1843
Oil on canvas 90.2 x 122 (35½ x 48)
Tate. Turner Bequest 1856

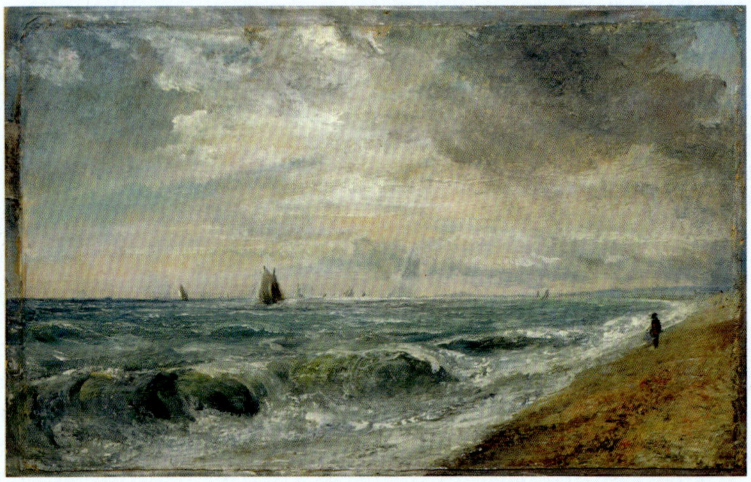

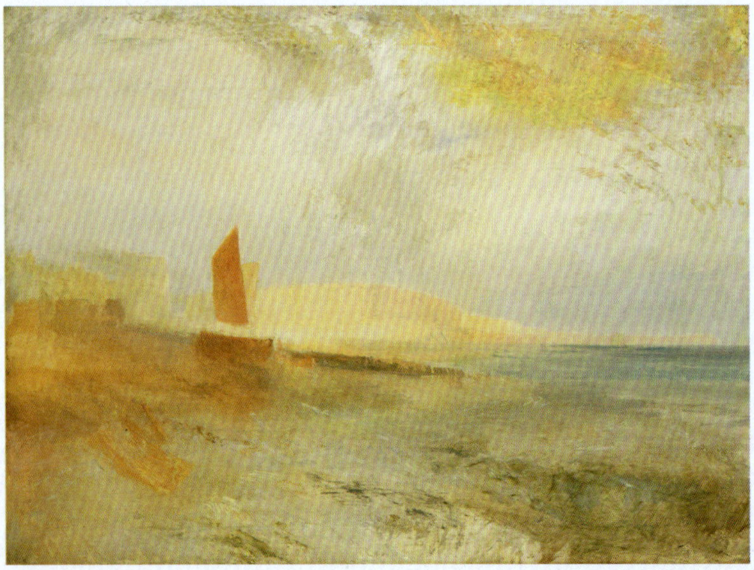

that included two of the artist's large Suffolk six-footers, the *Hay Wain* and *View on the Stour*.[11] Arrowsmith seems to have been so keen on Constable's marine subjects that in the same year he also commissioned him to make twelve drawings of Brighton boat and beach scenes with a view to publishing engravings of them in Paris, though nothing seems to have come of this project.[12]

By 1825 Constable, partly encouraged by Fisher, was increasingly feeling the need to diversify his subject matter away from the large river Stour scenes he had been painting since 1819, the year in which *The White Horse* had won him election as an Associate Academician. He may well have thought that to paint a coastal subject on the scale of *Chain Pier* would serve to demonstrate his versatility as a landscape painter and increase his chances for election as a full Academician. It was a risky strategy though, in terms of how both the critics and his fellow artists might respond to his change of direction. Fisher anticipated the problem in a letter to his wife about Constable's *Chain Pier*, noting that 'Turner, Calcott [*sic*] and Collins will not like it' – meaning they would surely regard it as an intrusion into their own territory.[13]

As far as Turner was concerned, Fisher's prediction seems to have been remarkably accurate. When 'provoked' in this manner, Turner's usual response was to paint a similar subject by way of riposte, or to find other, more theatrical ways to outdo his rival. When Turner began painting a view of the Chain Pier for Lord Egremont a year after Constable's picture, he showed the view from the opposite direction and also from the sea with the pier extending boldly across the viewer's line of vision rather than featuring as a detail in the far distance [fig. 31]. In presenting the subject this way, Turner may have deliberately tried to disguise the influence of Constable's version. For his first exploration of the subject (as pointed out by Ian Warrell) seems to have been a large colour study showing the scene exactly from Constable's viewpoint, and with a prominent orange-red sail in much the same position in the left foreground [fig. 33].[14]

The reactions of Augustus Wall Callcott and William Collins to Constable's *Chain Pier* are not recorded. Certainly,

Constable took a very different – and more challenging – approach to his subject than they were wont to do. As Andrew Hemingway has observed, by using strong contrasts of colour and light and shade, Constable has deliberately drawn attention in *Chain Pier* to the distinction between old and new, adding an element of dramatic tension to the picture, and engaging directly with the 'modern' seaside in a way that distinguishes his approach from the more traditional representations of Callcott and Collins.[15] A fisherman, an anchor, drying nets and an upturned basket of skate in the left foreground contrast with details such as the fashionable visitors braving the blustery conditions on the beach, the recently opened Albion Hotel on the left and the houses on Marine Parade picked out in sunlight beyond it. Constable has created a memorable portrait of a coastal town at a key moment of historical transition.

Constable's *Chain Pier* divided the critics. One dubbed it 'a capital local landscape', another 'one of his best works', but a further critic argued that it only served to highlight how much better suited his style of painting was to rustic landscapes.[16] Whether or not Constable took this latter review to heart, he produced no further marine subjects for exhibition during his lifetime. However, he did continue to paint views in watercolour of scenes along the Sussex and Kent coasts in the 1830s. Nor did he neglect to include marine subjects in the important print-publishing venture he embarked on around this time. *English Landscape* was intended by Constable as a pictorial overview of his work and, like Turner's *Liber Studiorum* (by which it seems partly to have been inspired), it also had a didactic purpose in its attempt to represent a comprehensive range of landscape types. Whereas Turner's approach was to define landscape by category, including the designation 'M' for Marine, Constable's aim was mainly 'to display the phenomena of the chiaro'scuro of nature', as he put it on the title page of the second edition in 1833. To this end he gave his subjects subtitles that were intended to demonstrate nature under different weather conditions and in different moods. Of the twenty-two prints engraved by David Lucas and published in *English Landscape* during Constable's lifetime, three were pure marines: *Yarmouth Pier* (to demonstrate 'Morning Breeze'), *Sea Beach, Brighton* ('Windy Noon'), and *Weymouth Bay* ('Tempestuous Evening'). A fourth scene, *The Nore, Hadleigh Castle*, includes an extensive view looking out towards the Thames estuary and the Nore (he gave this print the subtitle 'Morning after a Stormy Night'). Like Turner, Constable would carefully monitor the progress of the engraved image as it emerged from the plate, and there are many 'proof' impressions of the prints for *English Landscape* and related images in which he and Lucas gradually resolved the correct balance of light and shade. In a slightly larger version of *Hadleigh Castle*, for example [fig. 11], the glimmering stretch of water on the far horizon, where a number of sailing ships ply back and forth along the Nore sands, is particularly well rendered.

Turner and Constable did not often meet, though Turner went out of his way to call on his rival and congratulate him when, in February 1829 and while still grieving for his wife, he was finally elected a full Academician. The Earl of Egremont tried to get the two artists together at Petworth in September 1834 but Turner arrived after Constable had left. C.R. Leslie and his family were staying there at the time, and Constable had rigged-up a model sailing ship for the young Robert Leslie. When Turner arrived and saw the toy boat, he is alleged to have muttered that Constable knew nothing about ships and proceeded to re-set the rigging.[17] As already noted, Constable was certainly familiar with the sea and sailing vessels, and could draw or paint them as well as any artist, with the possible exception of Turner himself.[18] Turner's comment at Petworth was surely uttered in the context of a long-standing rivalry between the two painters, a rivalry perhaps first and most acutely provoked by the exhibition of *Chain Pier* in 1827. Rivalry, of course, cuts both ways. In 1825, Constable had told Fisher how pleased he was that his artistic reputation was 'dayly gaining ground' and how deeply he felt 'the honour of having found an original style & independent of him who would be Lord over all – I mean Turner'.[19] With *Chain Pier*, Constable had briefly moved into Turner's territorial waters and, temporarily, had thrown him off his bearings.

5

TURNER ON SHOW

Philippa Simpson

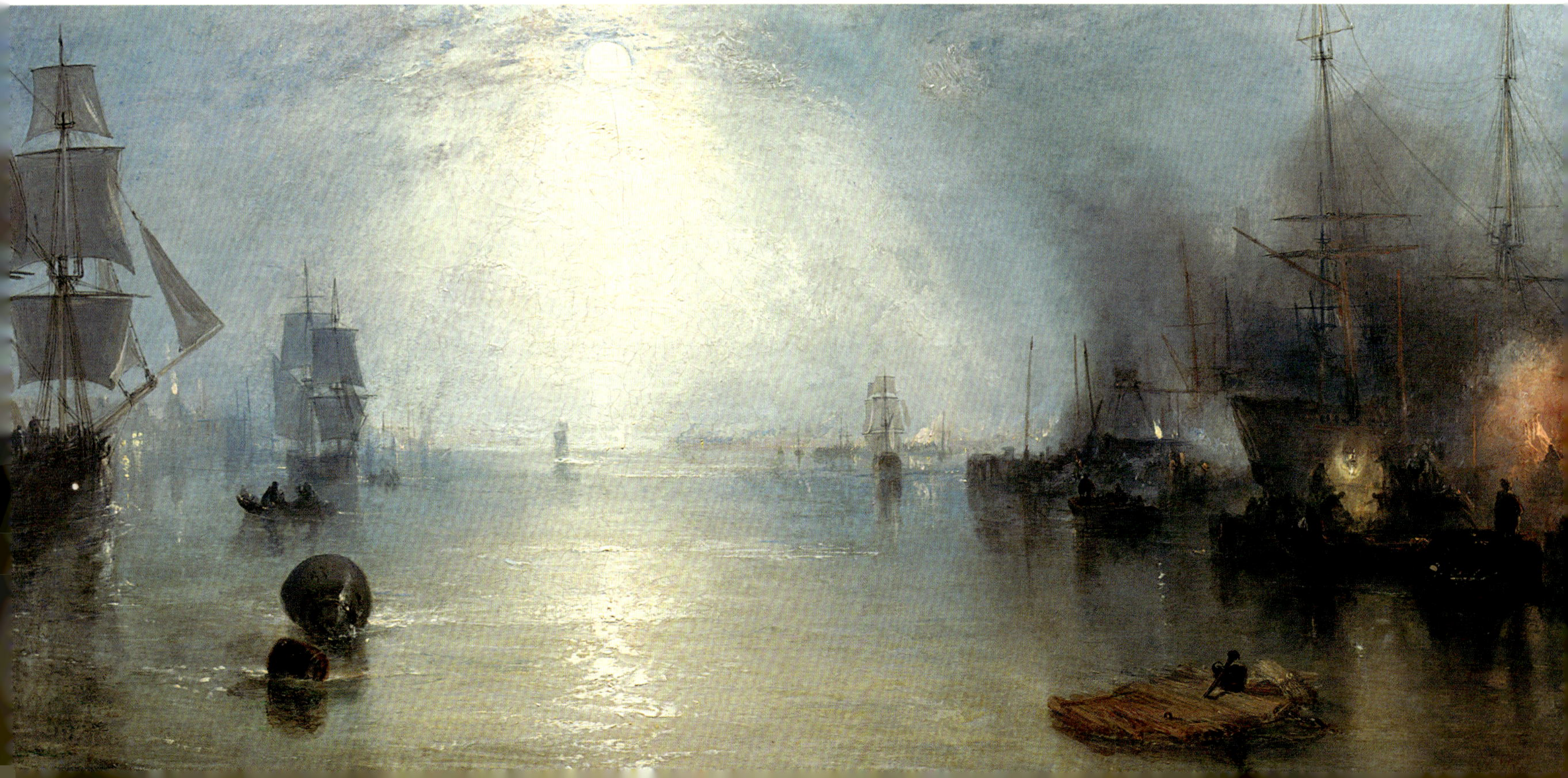

Shortly after his death on 19 December 1851, until his funeral at St Paul's Cathedral on 30 December, J.M.W. Turner's body lay in state in the centre of the gallery he had constructed next to his house in Queen Anne Street, London, surrounded by the paintings he had chosen to leave to the nation. It is not clear whether this was arranged according to Turner's own request but the ritual could not have been more appropriate. Since his earliest years the artist had been a keen self-publicist and this final 'exhibition' underscores a crucial aspect of his work's reception – the central place of the man himself. From his first submission to the Royal Academy summer exhibition to this final display in his own gallery, Turner strategically constructed both a reputation for his paintings and a persona for himself, at the heart of which were his pictures of the sea.

SEA AND CELEBRITY

Turner's first brush with publicity came at a young age, when his proud father would charge visitors a shilling to see works by his precocious son pinned up in his barber shop. For the same price, art lovers could have visited the Academy exhibition, London's only major display of contemporary art and an essential platform for any artist hoping to establish a reputation [fig. 34]. Joining the Academy Schools in 1789, aged just fourteen, Turner entered the brutally competitive fray of these exhibitions enthusiastically and, determined to command the attention of the 90,000 people who attended annually, selected as his first exhibited oil painting a dramatic seascape, *Fishermen at Sea* [14]. While functioning to announce a new talent, the submission of this one work was also tantamount to Turner defining himself as a sea painter.

In the final decades of the eighteenth century, comparatively few seascapes appeared at the RA, predominantly by the same few artists, including Dominic Serres [11], Nicholas Pocock (for example, [12]) and Robert Cleveley, who had secured their livings with images of the British fleet engaged in battle or under royal inspection. *Fishermen at Sea*, by contrast, did not rely upon accurate detail or patriotic sentiment to attract an audience, but rather drew attention to the facture of the painting itself. With its turbulent waves and intricate light effects, the picture allowed Turner to display a virtuoso handling of material, clearly designed to catch the eye. The theatrical moonlight emanates towards the viewer and renders the scene a pattern of stark tonal contrasts, recalling the back-lit transparencies then in vogue at printsellers around London. 'As a sea-piece', wrote one critic, 'this picture is effective ... The colouring is ... natural and masterly; and the figures, by not being more distinct and determined, suit the obscure perception of objects, simply seen through the gloom of night, partly illumed.'[1] Over half a century later, Turner's obituarists recalled the first reactions to *Fishermen* that seemed to herald a new mode of sea painting, 'remarkable for its truth and novelty' and 'excessively refreshing after the wearisomeness of [Abraham] Pether's moonlights, and [George] Barret's smiling landscapes'.[2]

Encouraged by these early responses, Turner regularly exhibited paintings of the sea at the RA over the next ten years, achieving a notable success with *Dutch Boats in a Gale* [fig. 6], commissioned as a companion piece to a picture by the celebrated Dutch sea painter Willem van de Velde. Much larger than its model, and with a heightened energy of handling, this painting announced Turner's ambition to overshadow not only his contemporaries but also the most revered old masters. But despite being ' a peculiar favourite of the spectators',[3] this tour de force fell victim to a circumstance that was to become all too familiar to Turner, the luck of the hang. It was a common complaint that the summer exhibitions were dominated by images of fashionable faces, and one critic noted that the 'water (surrounded with such a mass of glaring portraits as hang all round it) does not appear sufficiently tinctured with green'.[4] Turner was increasingly obliged to consider his sea pictures as participants in a battle for popular appeal, a challenge to which he became ever more alert. In 1804, the Royal Academician Joseph Farington recalled Turner's anxiety about *Boats Carrying out Anchors and Cables to Dutch Men of War, in 1665* [fig. 35] being hung directly underneath a

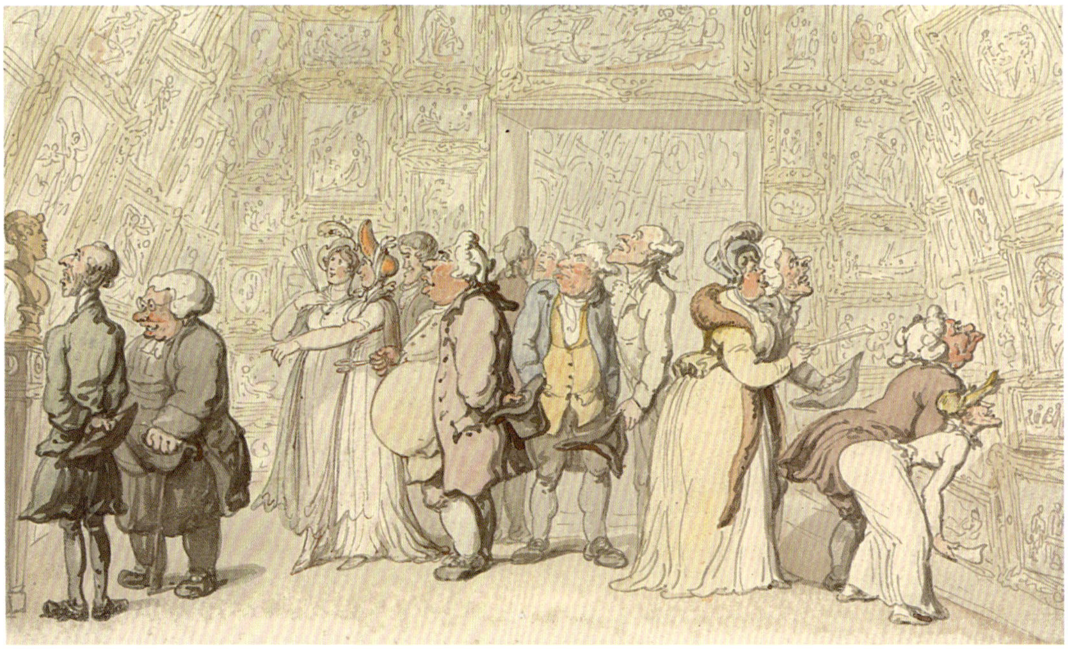

Fig. 34
Thomas Rowlandson
Viewing at the Royal Academy c.1815
Watercolour with pen and grey and brown ink over graphite
14.6 x 24.1 (5¾ x 9½)
Yale Center for British Art

particularly eye-catching portrait by John Singleton Copley containing a dazzling expanse of white drapery. Turner must have realized that his own extensive use of white to evoke churning waters would appear muddy and dull by comparison, but he had learnt a valuable lesson.[5] Almost thirty years later, on seeing Constable's brightly coloured *Opening of Waterloo Bridge* hung next to the more muted *Helvoetsluys* [fig. 29], Turner used the varnishing day (the time allowed for artists to make last-minute adjustments to their works before the exhibition opened) to add a small but conspicuous paint mark to his sea, which he then shaped into a red buoy. Constable, recognizing that this simple gesture made his own heavily worked painting look ridiculously overblown, famously declared that Turner 'has been here, and fired a gun'.[6]

Turner tactically built upon the celebrity acquired by *Dutch Boats* with two exhibits the following year; *Ships Bearing up for Anchorage* [72] and *Fishermen upon a Lee-Shore* [73], both of which, despite heavy working, create the impression of a scene speedily recorded. The unusual orientation of *Fishermen upon a Lee-Shore* in particular, looking diagonally along the beach at the floundering boat, adds to this sense of immediacy by positioning both artist and viewer as helpless onlookers. The work was declared 'a masterly performance' that would 'impress and delight the spectator', but the same critic struggled to reconcile the emotive force of the work with familiar modes of 'reading' a painting. 'We wish to feel it for men', he wrote, 'whose ... daily occupations ... expose life to such imminent peril, and we regret that ... the boat and its tenant convey but a faint idea of the *action*.'[7] For this critic, Turner's lack of finish, or rather his use of painterly

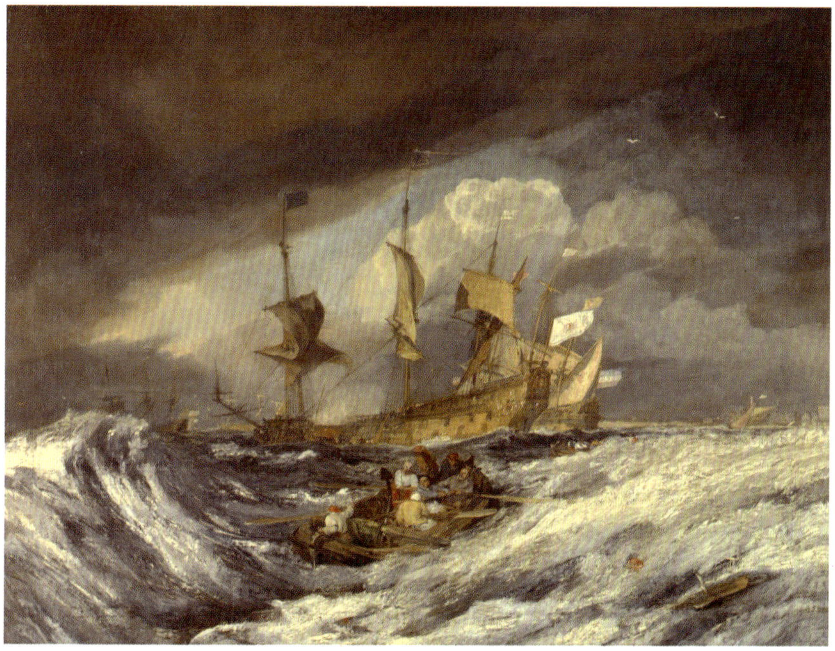

Fig. 35

J.M.W. Turner
Boats Carrying out Anchors and Cables to Dutch Men of War, in 1665 1804
Oil on canvas 101.5 x 130.5 (40 x 51⅜)
Corcoran Gallery of Art

materiality as a narrative tool, functioned as a barrier to full empathetic engagement. Immediacy was achieved at the cost of legibility: the work may be appreciated as an 'admirable sketch', but not as a 'finished picture'.[8]

Criticism of this sort was to haunt Turner throughout his career, but the artist's rejection of traditional notions of technical accuracy can be understood as an experiment with an alternative mode of visceral 'realism'. It was in fact not an art critic but an author in the *Naval Chronicle* who expressed the conflict between these two approaches to the art of the sea most clearly:

> Marine Painting is at present ... cramped, and greatly confined to portraits of particular ships, or correct representations of particular actions ... all who are unacquainted with the intricate anatomy of ships, or the various magnificence of the Ocean, are ill qualified duly to appreciate the labours of the Marine Painter, who moves in a space of peculiar Grandeur, and Sublimity.[9]

According to the professional seaman, both observation and imagination were crucial to picturing the sea in any meaningful way, a combination powerfully evident in *Calais Pier* [74], which Turner sent to the RA in 1803. This work, exceptionally dynamic both in style and in subject, presented a view of the sea that was emphatically personal. In 1802, the artist had taken advantage of a peace treaty between Britain and France to join a horde of tourists travelling across the English Channel. On arrival, the high winds and choppy waters made for a traumatic landing – 'Nearly Swampt' wrote Turner as he recorded the experience in a series of rapid sketches, which he subsequently worked up into a finished painting. This was one of many seascapes by Turner that engaged with current affairs, and he displayed it with a title giving the exact location, insisting on his personal experience of the place and its specific political significance. Just a few days after the opening of the exhibition, however, the peace treaty was dissolved. For visitors to the Academy that year, the stormy seas might just as well have symbolized the renewed hostilities as the short-lived burst of travel between the two countries.

The power of *Calais Pier* relied both on the contemporary political resonance of the subject and in the visceral immediacy of its execution. The view is one of a participant in and observer of the scene, as the route into the picture (the pier) leads to nothing but a churning sea and a mass of costume and limbs. Increasingly in his seascapes, Turner was adopting the persona of artist-traveller, the quintessential Romantic figure who belongs nowhere and everywhere. Parallels between this definition of the artist and contemporary ideas of the sailor are rife. As Geoff Quilley has observed, the sailor was conceived simultaneously as national hero and dangerous maverick: the man with the 'heart of oak' who could quickly become a mutinous threat to society.[10] The sailor, then, was a loaded analogue for the painter, and the personal engagement with the sea expressed so boldly in Turner's early exhibited oils is heavily suggestive of his own identification with that paradoxical figure of patriotism and fierce independence.

The image of Turner as an outsider was later substantiated by reports of his surliness and secrecy concerning his private life, behaviour greatly at odds with earlier figures, such as Joshua Reynolds and Thomas Gainsborough, who had promoted their residences as social hubs, frequented by nobility, gentry and fellow artists.[11] The gallery that Turner opened in 1804 attached to his home was not in the model of these elite ateliers, but functioned rather as a defiant assertion of his marginality. Indicating that he saw this space as a direct alternative to the Royal Academy, Turner provocatively issued invitations to Academicians on the day of the opening dinner for the summer exhibition of that year.[12] Upon arrival, visitors passed through the house before entering a space made to Turner's own design, over sixty-feet long and twenty wide. Great pains were taken to ensure the best display conditions, including top lighting, an idea borrowed from no less a model than the new Louvre museum. The method for diffusing the light, however, bore a certain Turnerian finesse. The effect was 'got by the simplest means', recalled one early visitor, 'a herring net was spread from end to end just above the walls, and sheets of tissue paper spread on the net'.[13]

The very fabric of life at sea thereby infiltrated the normally rarefied space of the gallery, an impression that surely complemented the display of the enormous and dramatic *Shipwreck* [75], one of the first works to be shown there. The banking waves and unbalanced composition mark this out from the more controlled composition of works such as *Dutch Boats in a Gale*, while the rough application of paint exacerbates the sense of urgency expressed in the desperate efforts of the sailors. Painted on a canvas of almost exactly the same dimensions as *Calais Pier*, *The Shipwreck* of 1805 can be seen as expanding upon its themes of direct encounter and personal jeopardy, which are here elevated into a universal language of sea and vessel. These ideas were to be revisited five years later, in another work of the same scale, *The Wreck of a Transport Ship* [76]. Although this latter work was not publicly exhibited until 1849, it can be understood as a further development of Turner's simultaneously aggressive and immersive approach to picturing the perilous volatility of the sea, which reached its apogee in *Snow Storm – Steam-Boat off a Harbour's Mouth* [131]. When considered together, these three works – *Calais Pier*, *The Shipwreck* and *The Wreck of a Transport Ship* – trace an increasing interest in both confronting and unsettling the viewer with the raw power of the ocean, transposed into the rough and frenetic application of liquid paint.

Described by one reporter as having been painted in Turner's 'grandest and best style', *The Shipwreck* was the first of his works to be engraved and was later referred to as evidence that 'no marine painter ever painted with so sailor-like a mind as Turner'.[14] Within a few years of its execution, Martin Archer Shee (future President of the Royal Academy) classified *The Shipwreck* as a work that had 'surpassed the most applauded efforts of living Genius in every other country of Europe'.[15] Under some pressure to live up to this growing repute, Turner next turned his attention to matters of the greatest current interest, and in 1806, just a year after the event, exhibited *The Battle of Trafalgar, as Seen from the Mizen Starboard Shrouds of the 'Victory'* [fig. 16]. This work was shown first at his own gallery, then in 1808 at the recently established British Institution, which functioned both as a contemporary exhibition space and as a site for artists to study from the old masters.

Established to encourage the 'higher branches' of painting – in particular history painting – the British Institution would have seemed the perfect arena for this image of recent naval victory, and in preparation for this more public platform, Turner is recorded as making many alterations to the work, achieving 'a broader principal light ... more vigour and richness of colour, and every where more expression of space'. The author of this description, the engraver and critic John Landseer, referred to the work as the first of its kind – a '*British epic picture*' – and likened the artist to no less a figure than the Ancient Greek poet Homer. The success of the painting, for Landseer, resided in its immediacy. Turner, like Homer before him, had 'detailed the death of *his* hero, while he has suggested the whole of a great naval victory, which we believe has never before been successfully accomplished ... in a *single* picture'.[16]

The intensely crowded composition, however, which to modern eyes seems poignantly to capture the confusion and destruction of battle, struck the wrong tone for contemporary viewers steeped in a mood of national celebration. 'If Mr. Turner would stand on the poop of the Victory', wrote one critic, 'with a picture frame the size of his own placed before him ... he would there see, that so many objects could not be crowded together under so small an angle as it would subtend.'[17] The sense that this lack of clarity prevented the work from functioning as an appropriate commemoration was exacerbated by the display directly opposite of a model by the renowned sculptor Matthew Wyatt, for a monument dedicated 'to the memory of the immortal Nelson'. The model showed its hero surrounded by personifications of Britannia, Fame and Death, and it was said that 'all the figures, considered *separately* have much sense, and are *grouped* in a masterly manner. This Monument is designed for a *central* situation in some public building.'[18] Turner's attempt to capture the heat of the battle, in contrast, lacked (at least to some contemporaries) the objective distance required to translate such a historic event into neutralized, timeless allegory.

SEA AND STYLE

Turner was not to return to battle painting for over ten years, and his next submission to the British Institution, the elegiac *The Sun Rising through Vapour* [79], met with greater approval. With its warm tones, this idealized scene of coastal industry was said to 'have a truly magical appearance, from any of the rooms'.[19] This, and another version of the subject that Turner had exhibited at the Royal Academy two years earlier [fig. 37], indicate a new direction in his style. Attracting attention not through dynamic handling or theatrical subjects, but with a richly coloured palette and the arresting quality of a finely rendered reflective surface, Turner seems to have achieved a confidence in his abilities that did not need to declare itself quite so loudly. The gentler tone of these paintings led the way to later pictures, such as *Dort, or Dordrecht, the Dort Packet-Boat from Rotterdam Becalmed* of 1818 [fig. 1], in which Turner was said to have transcended 'all his contemporaries'.[20] But even with his cultural collateral apparently at a peak, Turner was not an artist to rest on his laurels. Over the next few years he continued to exhibit works that thrilled and baffled audiences in equal measure, often within the same exhibition.

In 1827, two contrasting pictures were submitted to the Royal Academy, *'Now for the Painter' (Rope) – Passengers Going on Board* [59] and *Port Ruysdael* [63], which were praised in the *Examiner* for constructing an immersive experience for the viewer: 'he at one glance transports our recollections to the sea, and to its freshening influence. To stand on the solitary beach of *Port Ruysdael*, and contemplate the airy and aqueously moving scene before him ... the thoughtful observer would enjoy an ocean of maritime and sentimental pleasure.'[21] Another reviewer, however, struggled to reconcile what was seen to be the excessively mannered style of *'Now for the Painter'* with the undeniable potency of the work as an evocation of the sea:

> This is one of Mr. Turner's clever extravagances ... [It exhibits] that innate love of exaggeration which the persons who possess it term a knowledge of *effect*, and which means neither more nor less than that the real external world is not what it should be ... Mr. Turner's

pictures are every thing they should be, except natural; and in wanting this latter quality, they want a charm that all their power of imagination and execution cannot make up for, much less conceal. In the picture before us ... nothing can be more skilfully painted than the water. It is transparent, liquid, and in actual motion, so far as effect is concerned; but still it is not like the water of Vandervelde, of Backhuysen, or of nature; and the reason is, that the artist has essayed to make it more like 'real water' than that of either of the above.[22]

This failed attempt to condemn the work in exact terms reveals a paradox at the heart of Turner's endeavour in painting the sea. In his efforts to evoke a lived experience of the ocean, he was obliged to reject conventional models. But it was these models that had come to define what was 'real'. Turner's paintings elicited the right reactions, perhaps, but through the wrong means – or, as one writer put it, 'there is "method in the madness," if such it may be called'.[23]

Although the title *'Now for the Painter'* has long been accepted as a punning in-joke at the expense of a rival, Clarkson Stanfield, who had failed to finish his own picture 'Throwing the Painter' in time for the summer exhibition the previous year, it inescapably inserts the artist himself into the scene. As exiles from France returning to Britain pass from the smaller boat to the

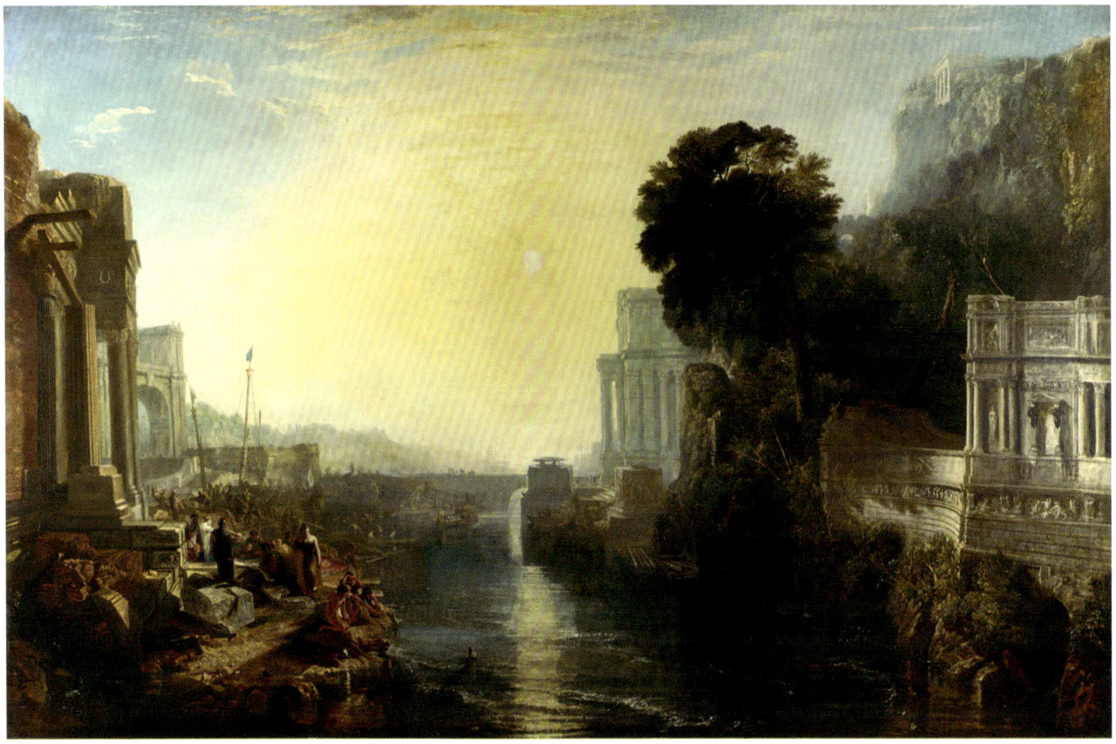

vessel bound for home, it can be implied that the painter is one of those caught between territories, stranded in an indeterminate space. At this stage in his career, having secured a major royal commission and established himself as Professor of Perspective at the Royal Academy, Turner's carefully constructed 'nonconformist' persona benefited enormously from this deliberate self-representation as a man of the sea. Jack Tar stereotypes had positioned the sailor as a figure of alternative, often opaque, social codes, whose moral and behavioural ambivalence was mitigated only by his dedication to king and country. Turner's defiant appearance within the Academy, dressed in a shabby overcoat and refusing to adopt the graces expected of a professor, chimed meaningfully with the personal vision he expounded in his charged, immediate images of the sea.

Responses to Turner's *Admiral Van Tromp's Barge at the Entrance of the Texel, 1645* [84], shown four years after *'Now for the Painter'*, testify to the success with which the artist had promoted the ocean as his natural habitat. Telling comparisons were drawn between this and another of Turner's submissions, *Watteau Study by Fresnoy's Rules*, a small interior of an artist's studio intended as a homage to the French painter Antoine Watteau. *Admiral Van Tromp's Barge*, wrote one reviewer, was 'Turner himself ... He is great at sea, and has a mastery over the waves worthy of Neptune'. *Watteau Study*, however, was a failure, since 'there is a story to tell here by means of human beings, and Turner never could tell a story by

Fig. 36

J.M.W. Turner
Dido Building Carthage 1815
Oil on canvas 155.5 x 230 (61¼ x 90½)
National Gallery. Turner Bequest 1856

Fig. 37

J.M.W. Turner
Sun Rising through Vapour: Fishermen Cleaning and Selling Fish before 1807
Oil on canvas 134 x 179.5 (52¾ x 70⅝)
National Gallery. Turner Bequest 1856

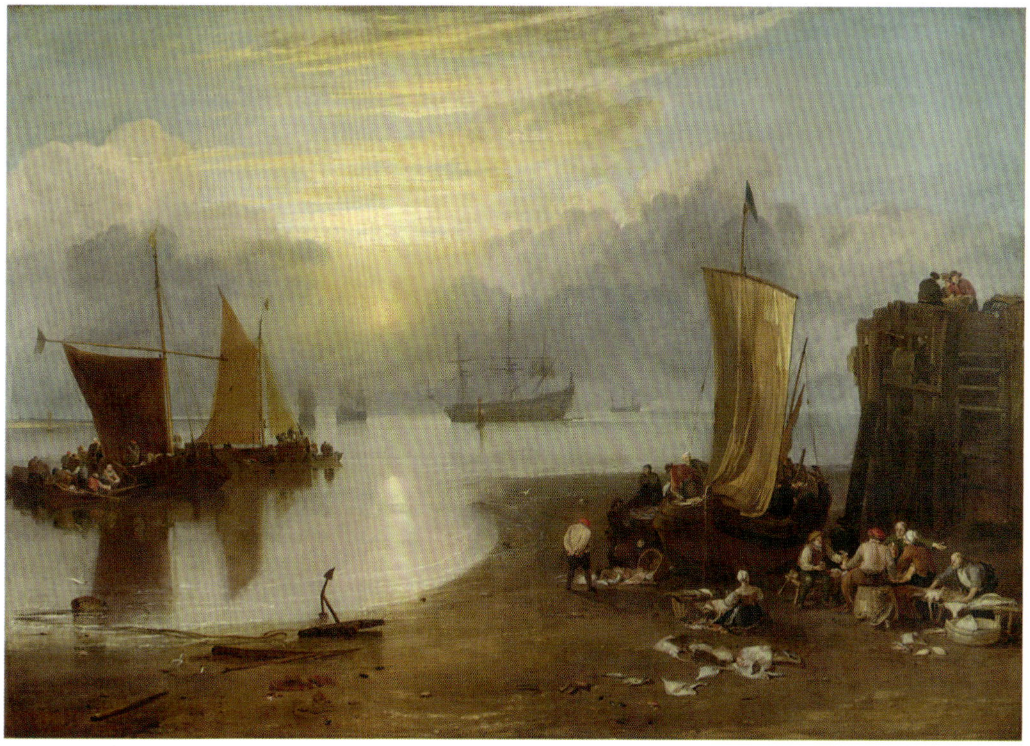

such agency in his life; the troubled sea, the stormy sky and the ruined temple are the material with which he has attained his glory?'[24] Or, as another writer more succinctly put it: 'Admiral von Tromp's Barge ... Mr. Turner at home ... Watteau study by Fresnoy's rules ... Mr. Turner not at home.'[25]

However, it would be another eight years before Turner would produce the painting that, in large part, came to establish his reputation. When it was exhibited in 1839, *The Fighting 'Temeraire', Tugged to her Last Berth to be Broken Up* met with rapturous responses and was later described as having won 'golden opinions from all sorts of men'.[26] Showing a vessel that had fought in the Battle of Trafalgar and then long sat as a hulk and guardship at Sheerness before being towed to Rotherhithe to be broken up, the picture was rich with patriotic nostalgia. But the contemporary 'truth' of the scene did not prevent Turner from employing full artistic licence to amplify its emotional resonance, having the sun setting in what would in reality have been the east, and reinstating masts and rigging that had already been removed. Even the title was an invention – known by the crew as the 'Saucy Temeraire', Turner's new epithet was to prove so effective that by the time of his death it was believed to have been the name given to the ship by the sailors: testament to how synonymous Turner had become with real life at sea.[27] Despite the apparent romanticism of the image, however, much of the symbolism remains ambiguous: does it mourn the loss of a fighting ship, or celebrate a new age of steam power? Does the white flag signify final surrender, or herald a new era of peace? Exhibited alongside pictures of *Ancient Rome* and *Modern Rome*, the *Fighting 'Temeraire'* can be understood as a reflection, without resolution, upon the decline of empire.

This complex dialogue between past and present was to preoccupy Turner throughout his late career, and was poignantly expressed in two pendant pieces, produced in 1834 and 1835: *Venice: The Dogana and San Giorgio Maggiore* [85] and *Keelmen Heaving in Coals by Moonlight* [86]. Both works were painted for the Manchester businessman Henry McConnel. Together these pictures showcased Turner's skill in rendering light effects and his ability to tackle disparate subjects. Pairing a scene of startling modernity with a nostalgic paean to the crumbling glories of Venice was powerfully suggestive of Britain's new industrial age as the successor to the magnificence of the Italian city in its heyday. It also identified Turner as an artist fully engaged with the realities of current maritime commerce, which he was able to translate into a classicized artistic idiom (drawing in particular on the works of Claude Lorrain), producing works that would appeal to the nobility and gentry as well as to the new market growing in the industrial cities of the North.[28]

Soon after, Turner produced a painting that responded to the newest advances in maritime technology. *Rockets and Blue Lights* [130], exhibited at the Royal Academy in 1840, shows ships employing recently invented distress flares in a scene that registers the peril of the vessel – which is all but subsumed by sea and spray – and the beauty of the illuminations. However, when the work was shown the following year at the British Institution, along with *Snow-Storm, Avalanche and Inundation – a Scene in the Upper Part of Val d'Aouste, Piedmont* (1837), opinion was starkly divided. 'Wonderful as examples of colour – prodigious as eccentric flights of genius. They would be equally effective, equally pleasing, and equally comprehensible if turned upside-down', wrote one bemused critic, while another lamented that 'this once talented gentleman could not be induced to leave the space they occupy to the junior exhibitors ... One would imagine, that Mr. Turner had left his studio for the kitchen, and discarded his oil, pigment and brushes, to paint with the contents of the cruet-stand.'[29] But one reviewer thought them 'two striking examples of Mr. Turner's highly imaginative art. More poetical than natural, and yet so founded on nature, that even the most daring departures astonish more than they offend us ... There is a sweep and confusion, a drift and strife of elements, dashed in with so masterly a hand, that we forget the parts that are extravagant in admiration of the whole.'[30] A comparison between this review and those of *Fishermen at Sea* and *'Now for the Painter'*, cited above, suggest that in some circles at least, the reception of Turner's work had developed from a struggle to define their method to an easier acceptance of their effect.

Turner re-used the title *Snow Storm* in 1842 for a painting that was not only an experimentation in style but was also a vehicle for asserting, once again, his direct experience of life at sea. Originally exhibited with the full title *Snow Storm — Steam-Boat off a Harbour's Mouth making Signals in Shallow Water, and going by the Lead. The Author was in this Storm on the Night the 'Ariel' left Harwich*, Turner claimed the work was a result of observations he had made while strapped to the mast of a ship.[31] Whether true or not, Turner's self-mythology was to become vital to the subsequent reception of his marine paintings. His final exhibited works included two that were to impress upon the minds of viewers an image of the artist as a man haunted by his experience of the sea: *The Wreck Buoy* [88] and *Wreck of a Transport Ship*, both painted early in his career (about 1807 and 1810 respectively) but kept in private collections and not publicly displayed until 1849. *The Wreck of a Transport Ship* was included in an exhibition at the British Institution of 'Deceased British Artists and Ancient Masters' two years *before* Turner's death. Indeed, it is recalled that, following an enquiry concerning the name of the ship depicted, Turner staged an appearance at the rooms, proclaiming, 'now you cannot say that I am a Deceased British Artist, or how could I give you the information you require'.[32] Determined up to the last to prove the vitality both of himself and of his work (the visit was surely intended to draw further attention to the picture as an honoured anomaly among works by older masters), Turner made clear that his painting of a wreck was at once deeply personal and powerfully relevant.

Due to its age, in the context of the old master exhibition, *The Wreck of a Transport Ship* can be seen to have functioned as a historic record of an earlier style. Not so in the case of *The Wreck Buoy*, however. More than forty years after it was first exhibited, this picture was extensively repainted by Turner over six days, in preparation for its appearance at the Royal Academy just a few months before the British Institution show. It emerged a quite different work. Adding the wreck buoys (which warned sailors of sunken ships) and the rainbow (described in Turner's fragmentary poem *Fallacies of Hope* as a false symbol of optimism), the picture was transformed into a consideration of the ultimately destructive nature of the sea, a fact that did not go unnoticed by his contemporaries. Five years after Turner's death, in a publication of his prints called *The Harbours of England*, his great champion John Ruskin referred to *The Wreck Buoy* as the last picture he painted 'before his noble hand forgot its cunning'. Ruskin then went on to describe his impressions of the artist in relation to this work:

> I am well persuaded that, from ... when first he saw a ship rent asunder, he never beheld one at sea without, at the same time, in his mind's eye, seeing her skeleton ... But he had seen more than the death of a ship. He had seen the sea feed her white flames on souls of men; and heard what a storm-gust sounded like, that had taken up with it, in its swirl of a moment, the last breaths of a ship's crew. He never forgot either the sight or the sound.[33]

It is hard to know whether the association of Turner with marine painting prompted biographers to construct an image of the artist as an experienced seaman, or whether informal anecdotes during his lifetime encouraged positive reactions to his sea painting (at least in his earlier years), but the conflation of Turner with life at sea quickly became commonplace after his death. He was said to have travelled by sea whenever possible, and obituaries and early biographies were filled with stories of his taste for sailing, on one memorable occasion exclaiming 'That's fine! – fine!' during a particularly rough journey while another artist and a soldier who was accompanying them were vomiting at the bottom of the boat.[34] One of his earliest biographers, Walter Thornbury, repeatedly referred to Turner as 'half a sailor', having been brought up by the Thames, watching boats coming in and out of the docks. 'Long afterwards his morality was regulated by the sailor's standard', Thornbury complained, 'Yet the training had its value ... It was this early love for ships and sailors that led him to paint so many storms and shipwrecks.'[35]

While these posthumous texts appear as so much myth-making, they find some substantiation in Turner's bequest to the nation of two key paintings: *Dido Building Carthage* [fig. 36] and *Sun Rising through Vapour*. In his will, Turner instructed that this pair of paintings be treated as distinct from the body of his work and displayed in perpetuity alongside two works by his artistic hero, Claude Lorrain. By his own instruction, therefore, his reputation as a British artist within a wider European canon was to be established upon the display of two pictures with the sea at their heart. Years later, when Turner took part in his final exhibition [fig. 38], that of his own body in the gallery hung with herring net, he was described in more than one obituary as a stout man with a highly coloured complexion, altogether 'somewhat sailor-like'.[36]

Fig. 38

George Jones
Turner's Body Lying in State, 21 December 1851 c.1851
Oil on millboard 14 x 23 (5½ x 9)
Ashmolean Museum

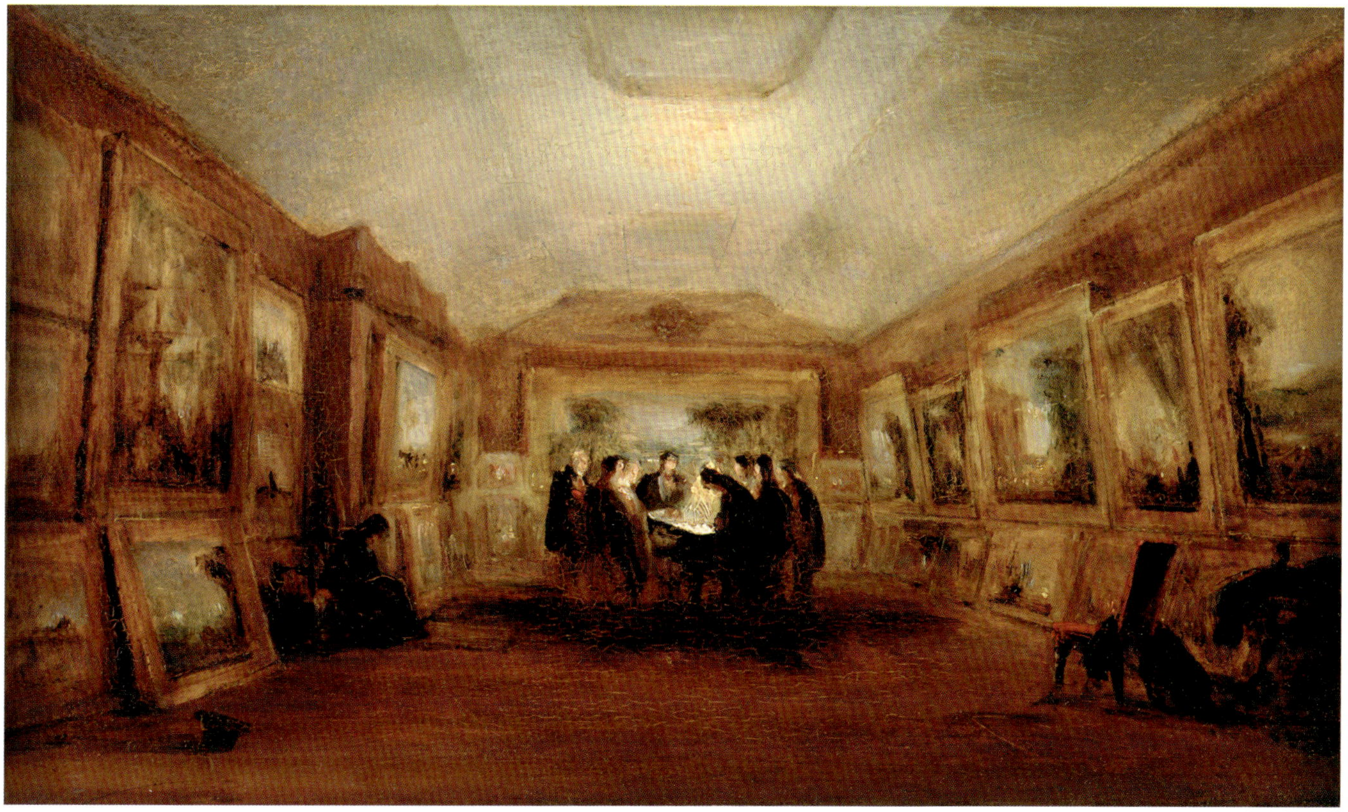

72

J.M.W. Turner
Ships Bearing up for Anchorage
('The Egremont Sea Piece') 1802
Oil on canvas 119.5 x 180.3 (47 x 71)
Tate and the National Trust (Petworth House)

Butlin and Joll, no. 18

This is the larger of two maritime subjects that Turner exhibited in the hope of building on the critical and commercial success of the previous year's *Dutch Boats in a Gale* [fig. 6]. It extends the artist's close encounter with Dutch marine painting of the seventeenth century. The subject of ships lying at anchor was one favoured especially by Ludolf Backhuysen [2]. Turner's focus on the sequential movements of ships turning into the wind before dropping anchor (the subject of several sketches and studies of the previous two years), combines a studied compositional elegance with a level of technical observation that seems designed to appeal to a specialist maritime audience. However, by locating the vessels in the far-to-middle distance, Turner leaves the majority of the picture space open for his principal concern: a close painterly study of the elements.

The sale of the painting to the third Earl of Egremont confirmed Turner's artistic ascendancy and signalled the beginning of a long and fruitful association with one of the era's most prominent patrons of contemporary British painting. In 1802, the year this painting was exhibited, Turner was also elected a full member of the Royal Academy, the same year in which he restyled himself 'J.M.W. Turner RA' (this is the first work signed by the artist with his full and familiar initials). A variant of *Ships Bearing up for Anchorage* was one of the first marine images produced for the artist's *Liber Studiorum* [21], with the revised title *Ships in a Breeze*.

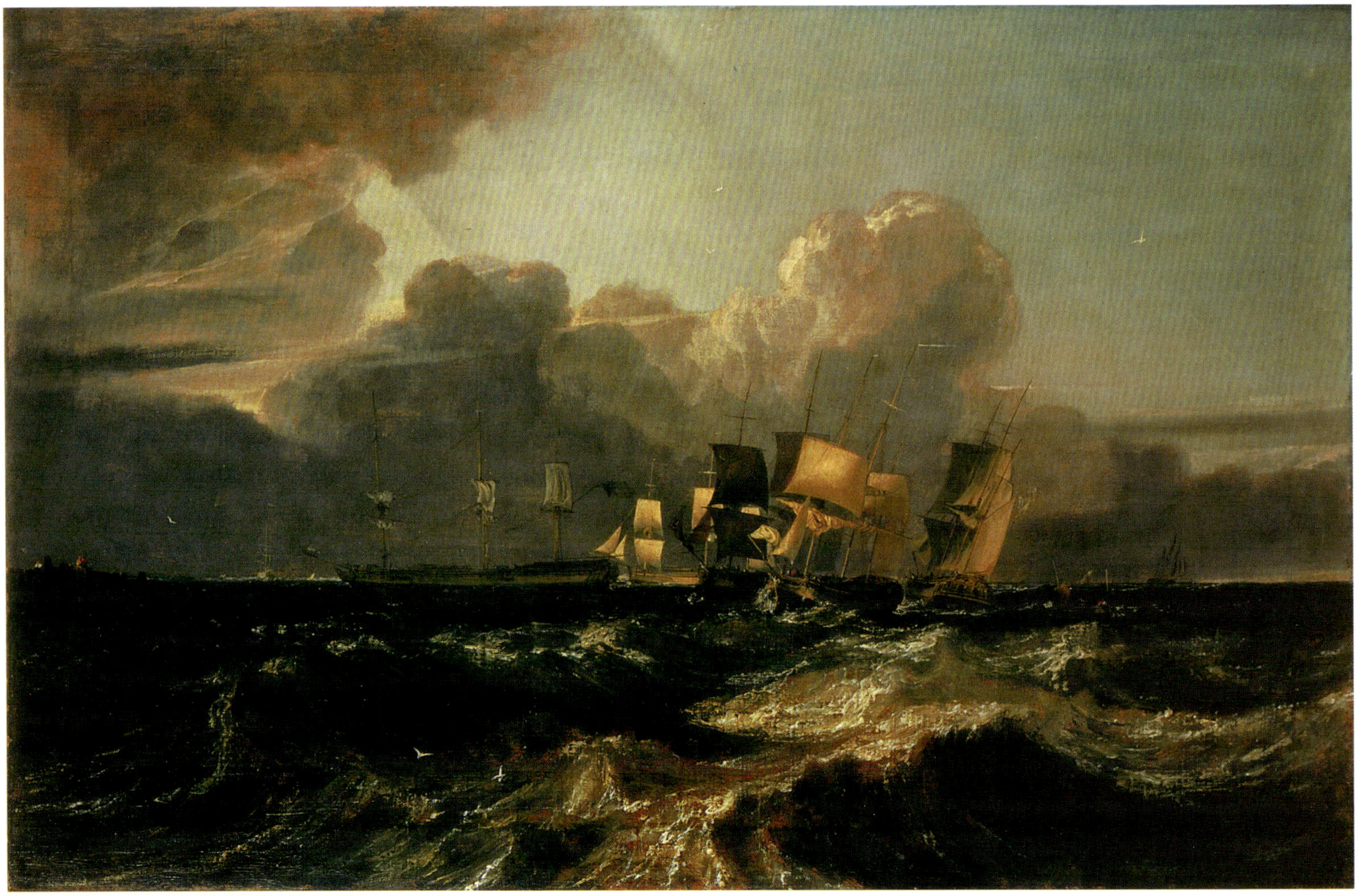

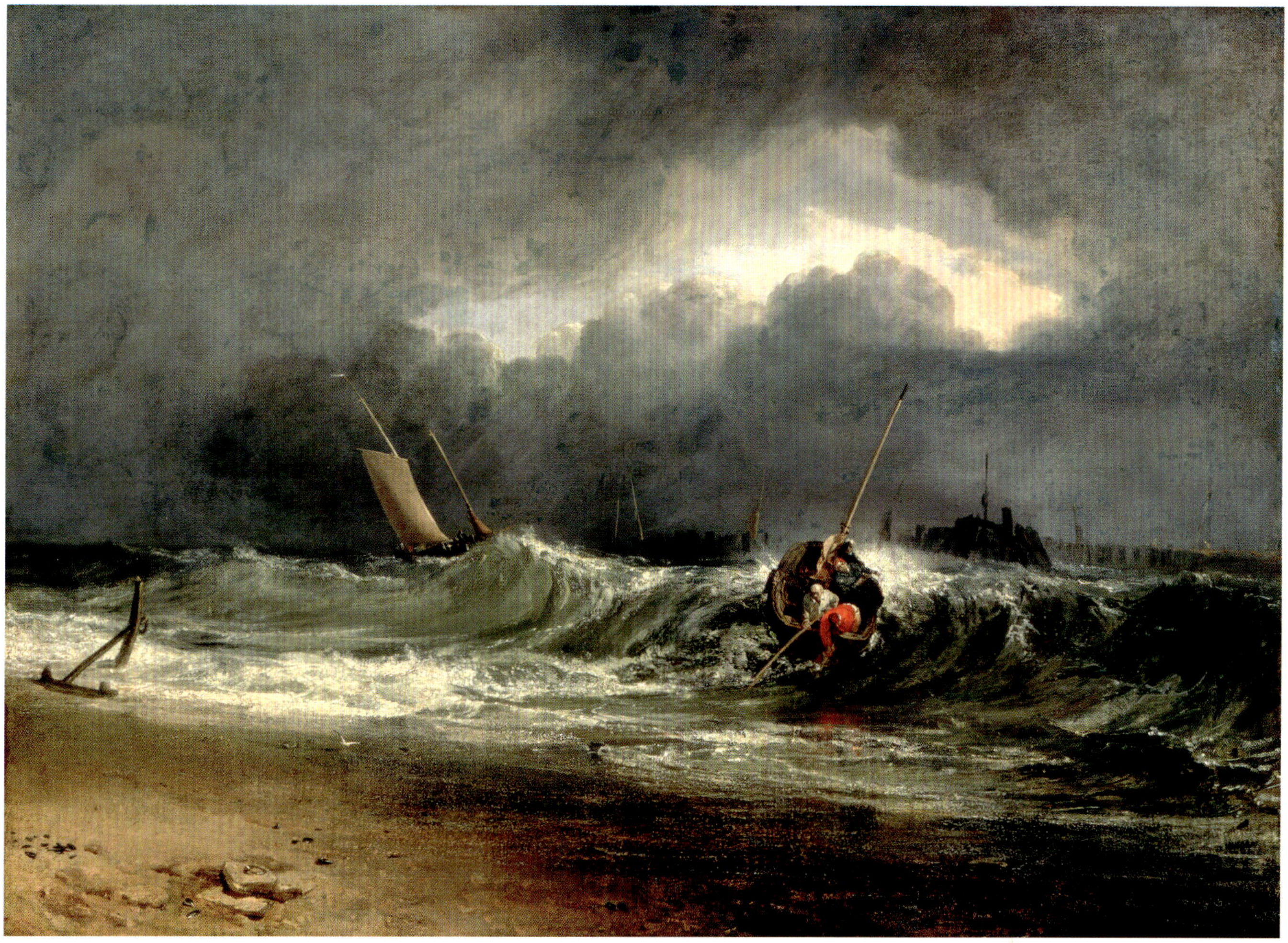

73

J.M.W. Turner

Fishermen upon a Lee-Shore, in Squally Weather 1802
Oil on canvas 91.4 x 122 (36 x 48)
Southampton Art Gallery

Butlin and Joll, no. 16

A lee shore in squally weather is a perilous situation, for the risk of being driven onto the shore is high. The image of a vessel struggling against an onshore wind had more often been deployed by marine artists since the seventeenth century as a portent of maritime disaster (see, for example, [5]). Such dangers are faced by the fishermen in Turner's painting as an everyday part of life, as they strain to launch their boat into an unforgiving, unpredictable sea. The heroic demeanour of Turner's coastal labourers was applauded by the reviewer of the *Monthly Mirror*, who described *Fishermen upon a Lee-Shore* as a 'masterly performance', notable not only for the 'massive roll of the waves' that governs the formal structure of the painting, but also for the empathy it inspired for the fishermen 'whose necessary and daily occupations of livelihood expose life to such imminent peril' (June 1802). However, in keeping with the broader critical response to Turner's work at the time, the same reviewer also expressed growing unease at the lack of detail in the artist's work – a 'creeping vice' that he urged the artist to correct. Another critic described the same painting as 'indeterminate and wild'; a third registered the work's unfinished appearance by calling it 'a very admirable sketch' (both reviews cited in Butlin and Joll 1984, pp. 14–15). Such language was already becoming commonplace among Turner's respondents as they grappled with his unorthodox pursuit of painterly effect. The motif of the breaking wave that lies at the heart of the painting was a source of extraordinary creativity for Turner, to which he returned throughout his career. The following year, he painted a companion subject, *A Coast Scene with Fishermen Hauling a Boat Ashore* (Iveagh Bequest, Kenwood House), which shows a similar group of fishermen returning safely to shore.

74

J.M.W. Turner
Calais Pier, with French Poissards Preparing for Sea: An English Packet Arriving 1803
Oil on canvas 172 x 240 (67¾ x 94½)
National Gallery. Turner Bequest 1856

Butlin and Joll, no. 48; Egerton 1998 NG472

'Our Landing at Calais. Nearly swampt.' This was how, in the margins of a sketchbook, Turner recalled his first journey across the English Channel in 1802. The voyage had been made possible by the temporary cessation of hostilities between Britain and France during the short-lived Peace of Amiens, and the adventure that ensued became the subject for one of Turner's largest and most sophisticated marine paintings. All of Turner's early coastal and marine landscapes were shaped in one way or another by the wars with Revolutionary and Napoleonic France, but *Calais Pier* is among the most autobiographical of the artist's responses. Turner's comic characterization of the French fishermen attempting to land, and their raucous wives on the windswept pier, combines allusions to the low humour and bawdy incident of Dutch genre painting and Hogarthian satire with the fishmarket scenes of other Dutch artists, including Simon de Vlieger [1]. The result is one the artist's most ambitious figure groups and the first in a series of three major maritime storm scenes that Turner made during the first decade of the nineteenth century, followed by *The Shipwreck* [75] and *The Wreck of a Transport Ship* [76].

Calais Pier was one of a dwindling number of maritime subjects at the Academy in 1803. It appeared alongside two works by Nicholas Pocock – a painting of the East India Company's ship 'Rockingham' in a storm, and a post-action portrait of the disabled and captured French ship 'Guillaume Tell' – that demonstrated how far Turner's conception of the sea had drifted from the established conventions of marine painting. On hearing the artist's intention to charge considerably more for the painting than the £250 he had received from the Duke of Bridgewater for *Dutch Boats in a Gale*, Joseph Farington described him as 'confident, presumptious – with talent' (Farington, vol. 6, p. 2030). But the painting was not welcomed wholeheartedly – primarily, it seems, on account of Turner's extraordinarily gestural (and, in the eyes of his critics, slap-dash) use of white paint in the foreground. Sir George Beaumont likened the sea in Tuner's painting to 'the veins on a Marble slab', while another critic thought Turner's thickly painted sea more closely resembled 'pease soup'. An audience used to looking through the picture plane, unencumbered by the physical attributes of paint, was now asked to navigate and take account of Turner's conspicuous and tactile painted surface before responding to the subjects beyond.

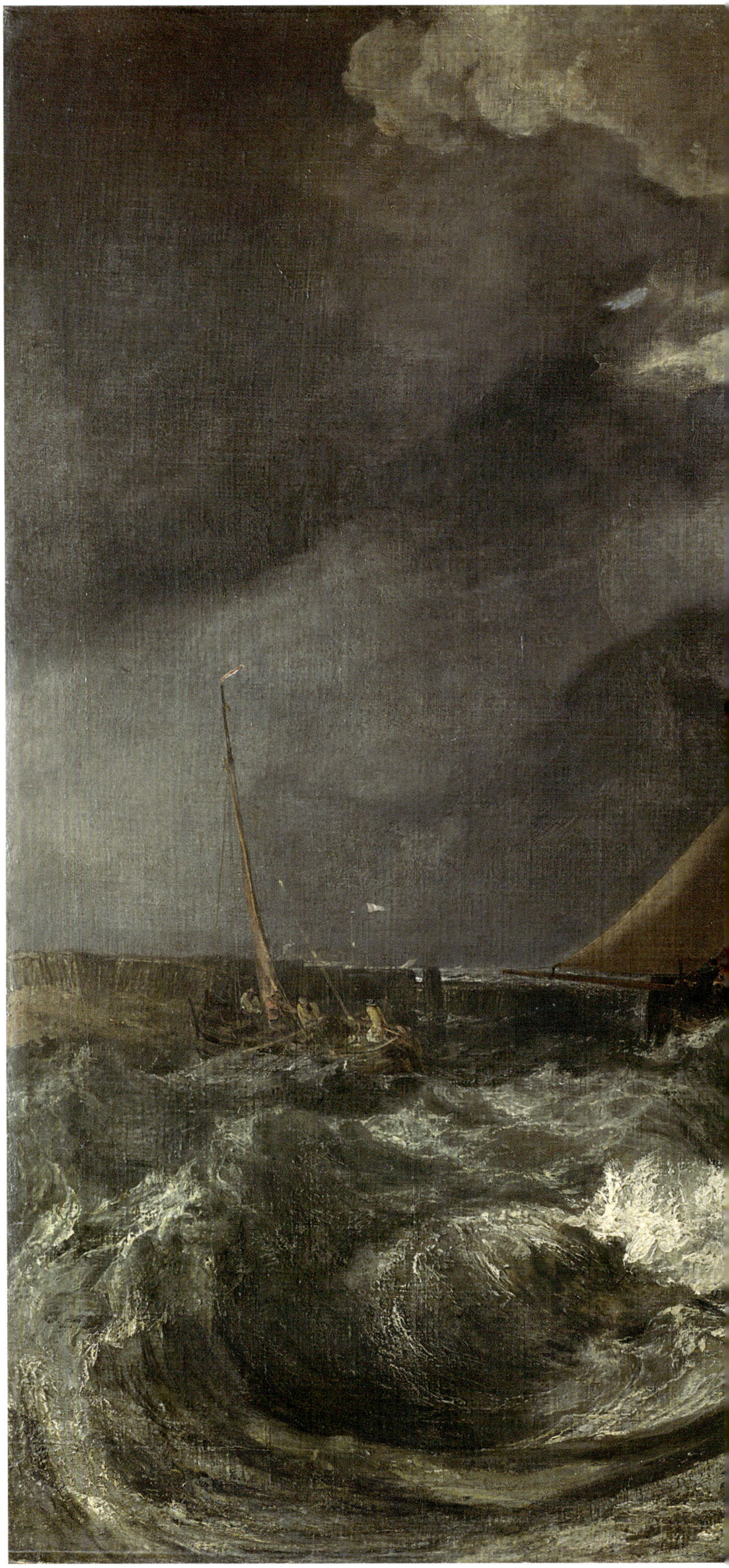

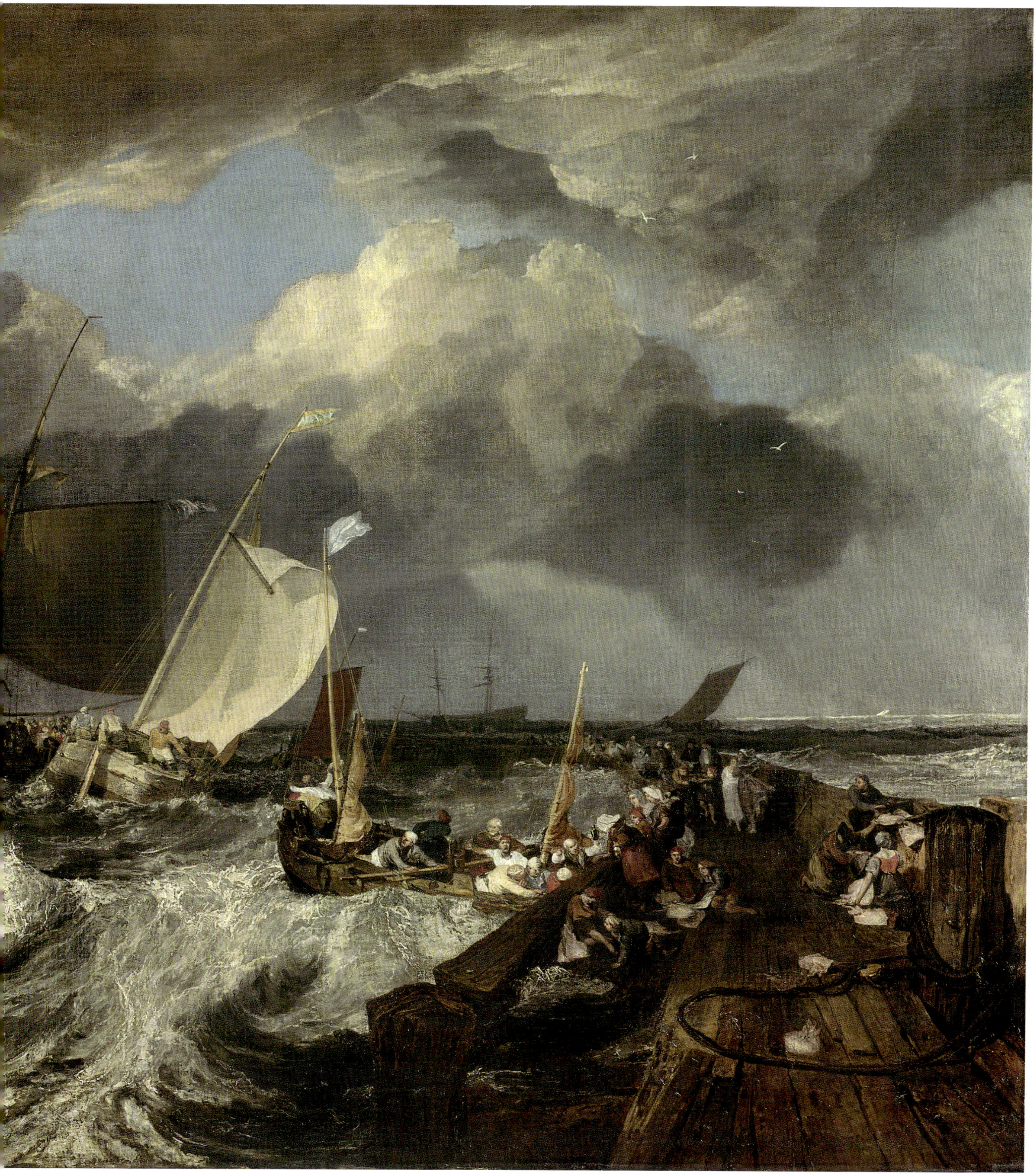

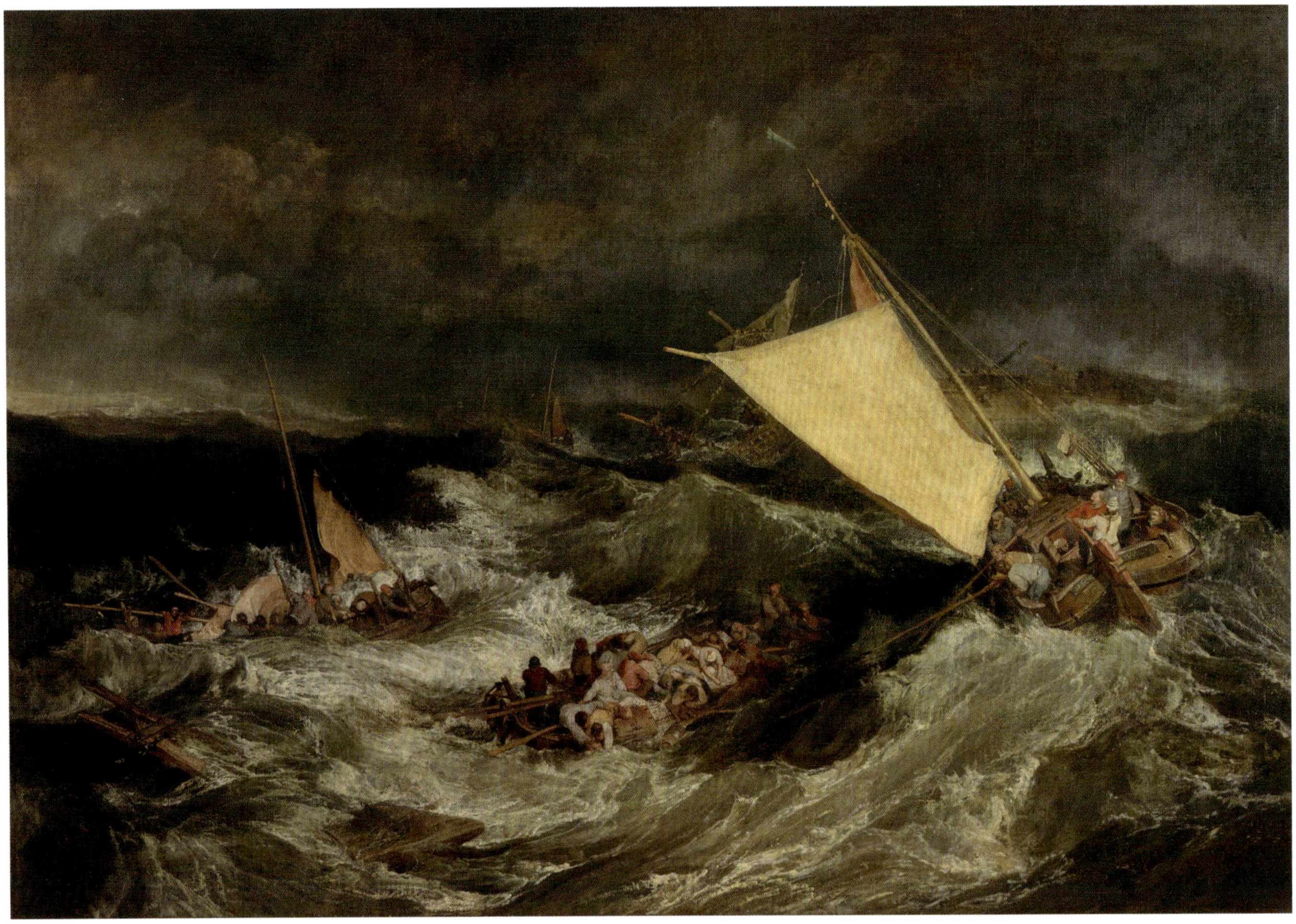

75

J.M.W. Turner
The Shipwreck 1805
Oil on canvas 170.5 x 241.5 (67⅛ x 95⅛)
Tate. Turner Bequest 1856

Butlin and Joll, no. 54; Spencer-Longhurst 2003, esp. pp. 10–13; Costello 2012, pp. 73–84

In 1805, Turner chose not to submit any works to the Royal Academy's annual exhibition. His decision to disassociate himself from the environment in which his reputation had been won over the previous ten years was part of a more widespread antagonism between the artist and his fellow Academicians. The year before, he had opened his own specially designed gallery at his home in Harley Street, which for several years became the principal public arena for the display of his paintings. *The Shipwreck* remained on display in Turner's gallery while subscriptions were taken for the forthcoming mezzotint of the work. The resulting print, engraved by Charles Turner, proved a great success and marked the beginning of a long and creative engagement with the print market for Turner. The painting followed soon after the republication, in 1804, of William Falconer's epic poem of the same title, and the involvement of Nicholas Pocock as illustrator of that edition may have provided an added incentive for Turner's choice of subject. However, the success of both the painting and the poem depended on the perennial threat of real disaster at sea, most recently the sinking of the 'Earl of Abergavenny' off Weymouth in February 1805, whose victims included the ship's captain, John Wordsworth, brother of the poet William Wordsworth.

The Shipwreck draws on a long pictorial tradition of maritime disaster that was most closely associated at the time in Britain with work of Philip James de Loutherbourg [10]. Turner abandons the classical conventions of landscape painting favoured by de Loutherbourg and others, in order to confront the viewer directly with a fearsome tempest-tossed sea littered with the debris of the wrecked ship. It was Turner's most emphatic exploration of the maritime sublime to date. Despite the desperation of the scene, however, the principal (and often overlooked) emphasis of Turner's painting is the attempted rescue of survivors, not abject disaster.
In this way, *The Shipwreck* extends the heroic portrayal of fishermen seen in several of the artist's other works from around the same time.

76

J.M.W. Turner

The Wreck of a Transport Ship c.1810

Oil on canvas 172.7 x 241.2 (68 x 95)

Museu Calouste Gulbenkian

Butlin and Joll, no. 210

The Wreck of a Transport Ship is arguably the most brutal of Turner's marine paintings – a chaotic vision of total loss. 'No ship or boat could live in such a sea,' Admiral William Bowles is reported to have remarked upon seeing the work at the British Institution in 1849 (see Butlin and Joll 1984, p. 116). Artists rarely depicted the sea at its most destructive, preferring instead to focus on the critical moments of danger immediately before the ship is wrecked (and thus when there appears still to be a chance of escape), or the eerie tranquillity of the morning after. This devastating scene followed more than ten years of marine painting by Turner, during which the perils of the sea had been a recurring theme, signalling the daily danger faced by every fisherman, sailor and civilian who set sail. Leo Costello goes further, suggesting that *The Wreck of a Transport Ship* also prefigures the pictorial deconstruction that became so characteristic of the artist's late style (see pp. 196–201).

The painting was acquired in 1810 for the collection of Lord Yarborough, possibly as the result of a commission. It is not recorded as having been exhibited at the time of its completion, but it did appear to great acclaim on two occasions towards the end of the artist's life: at the British Institution in 1849; and again at the Royal Society of Arts in 1851, a few months before the artist's death, under the more descriptive title *The Wreck of 'Minotaur', Seventy-four, on the Haak Sands, 22nd December 1810*. Turner never confirmed whether or not the painting had been inspired by the loss of the 'Minotaur', or any other incident.

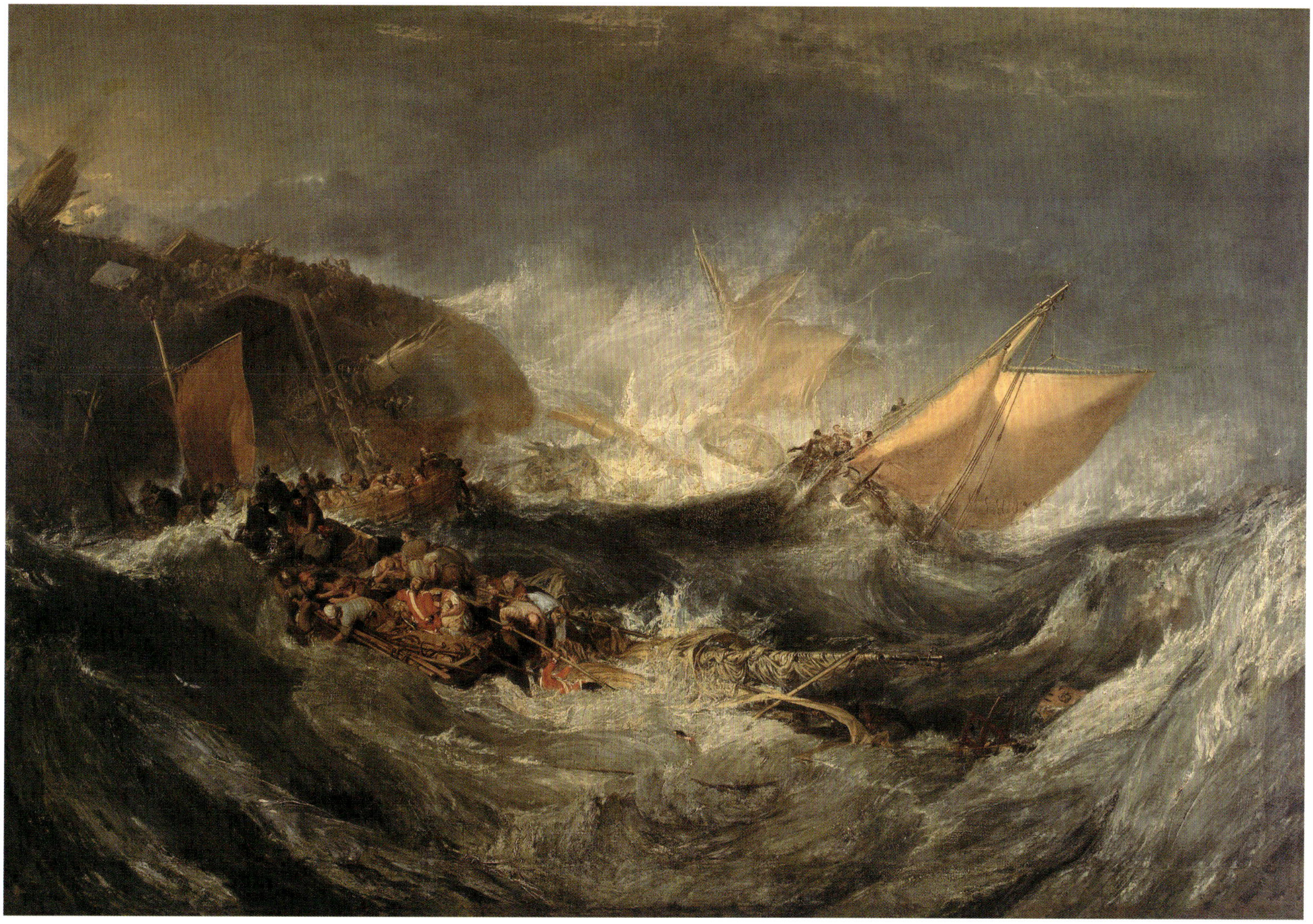

77

J.M.W. Turner

Pembroke Castle: Clearing Up of a Thunder-Storm 1806

Watercolour 64 x 104.5 (25¼ x 41⅛)

University of Toronto

Wilton, no. 281

The ruined castles that guard the Welsh coastline provided the subject for some of Turner's most enduring works in watercolour. At once picturesque and rich in narrative association, they provided him and his contemporaries with an opportunity to explore a romantic notion of Britain's ancient past. *Pembroke Castle: Clearing Up of a Thunder-Storm*, one of Turner's largest and most ambitious works in the medium, locates the ancient stone monument at the centre of a vibrant scene of contemporary coastal industry, a theme that preoccupied him at the time. From the close observation of the still life of fish in the foreground, to the parting sky and rolling waves, to the architectural prospect of the castle itself, it is a confident assertion of the artist's command of watercolour, designed to hold its own in an exhibition environment. Turner toured Wales on several occasions, and in 1801 exhibited an alternative view of the castle, on that occasion with a thunderstorm approaching (the watercolour's current location is unknown). David Hill has argued that the titles and dates of these two watercolours have been switched in modern times, and that the present work is that exhibited in 1801 (see Hill 1985). About 1829, Turner produced a variation of the same view, this time with a greater focus on the fishermen unloading their catch in the foreground, which was engraved in 1831 by Thomas Jeavons for *Picturesque Views in England and Wales*.

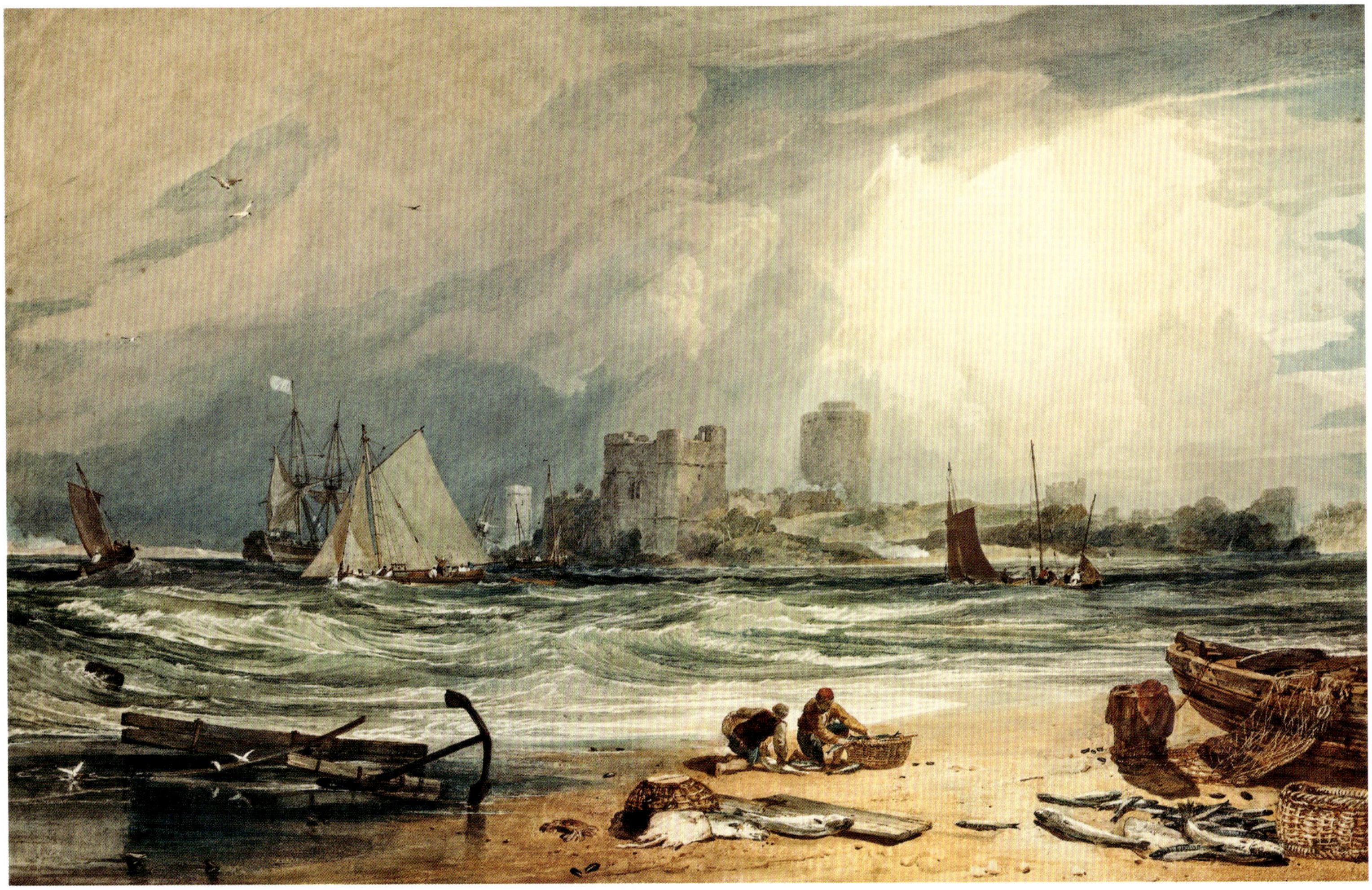

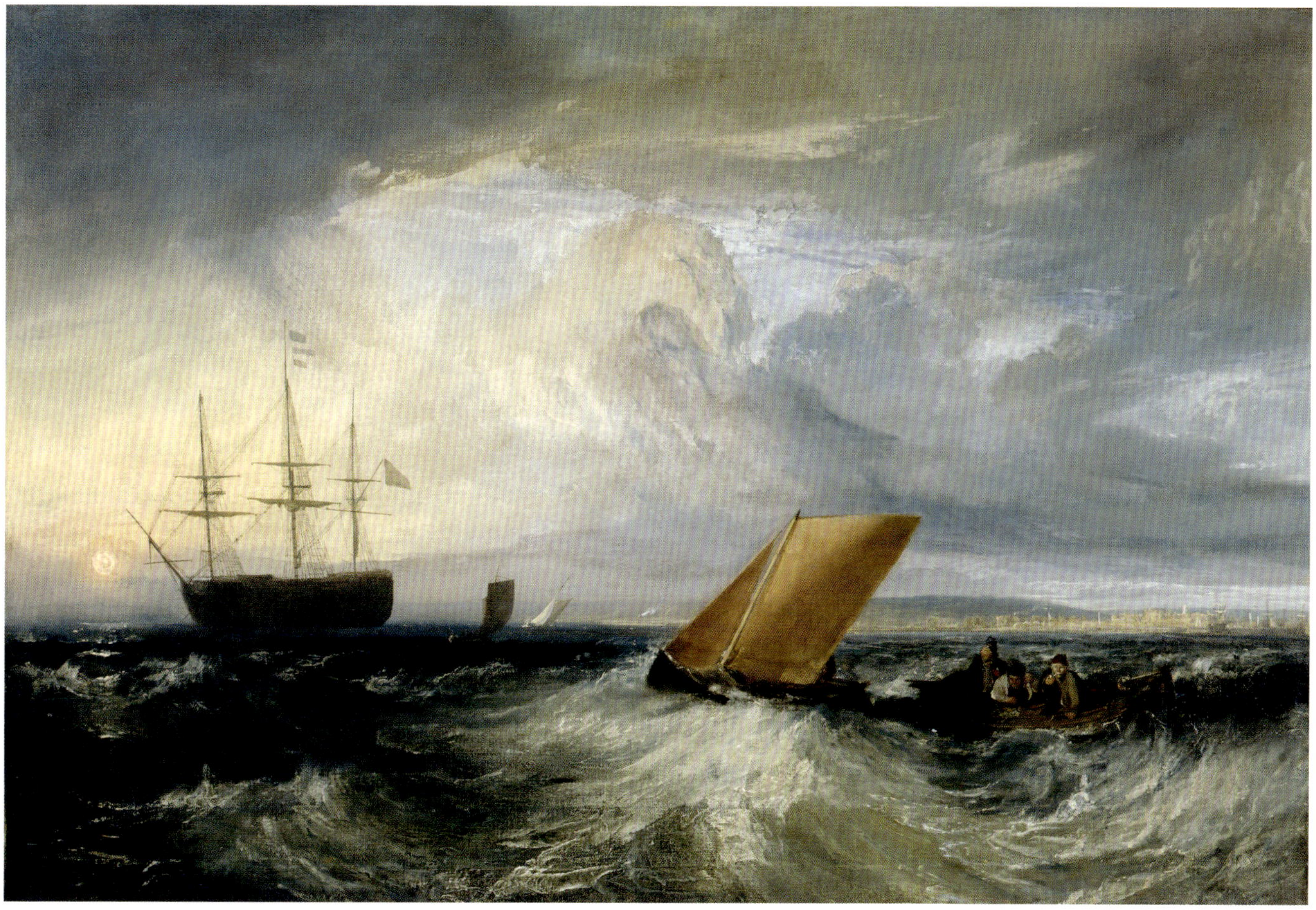

78

J.M.W. Turner

Sheerness as Seen from the Nore c.1808
Oil on canvas 105.4 x 149.8 (41½ x 59)
Museum of Fine Arts, Houston

Butlin and Joll, no. 76; Warrell 2007, no. 35

This is one of a series of paintings of the Thames estuary that Turner exhibited at his own gallery in the years following the decisive British victory at the Battle of Trafalgar. The painting is a variation of the Dutch manner that predominated during the first decade of Turner's professional life, characterized by a steep, buffeting sea in the foreground, a distant view of the English coast and an anchored ship of the line between the two. More specifically, the descriptive title and distant landmarks locate the scene on or about the Nore, a shoal formed by the converging currents where the rivers Thames and Medway meet the North Sea. The Nore had been an important fleet anchorage for the Royal Navy since the seventeenth century. More recently, it had also been the site of a violent mutiny that ended with the execution of twenty-nine British sailors and the flogging or deportation of many more. It was also where Turner joined thousands of others to witness the return of the 'Victory' with Nelson's body on board after the Battle of Trafalgar. The collective memory of these contrasting moments of naval discipline and deference gave Turner's marine views of the Nore a powerful contemporary resonance that has since been largely forgotten.

Moreover, the direct encounter with fishermen at work on the English coast extends a theme introduced in earlier works, including *Fishermen at Sea* [14]. The methods used by Turner's fishermen, the fish they catch and the boats that carry them represent a form of domestic-level industry that underpinned Britain's coastal economy around the turn of the nineteenth century, and which was soon to be challenged by more commercial methods of production. Three years after Trafalgar, Turner seems to foreground and to celebrate the heroic contribution to the war effort made by these coastal labourers – not least by constructing a viewpoint on a level with the fishermen. Together with another estuary subject, *Purfleet and the Essex Shore* (private collection), exhibited in Turner's gallery in the same year, the *Examiner* described *Sheerness as Seen from the Nore* unequivocally as 'the finest sea-pieces ever painted by a British Artist' (8 May 1808).

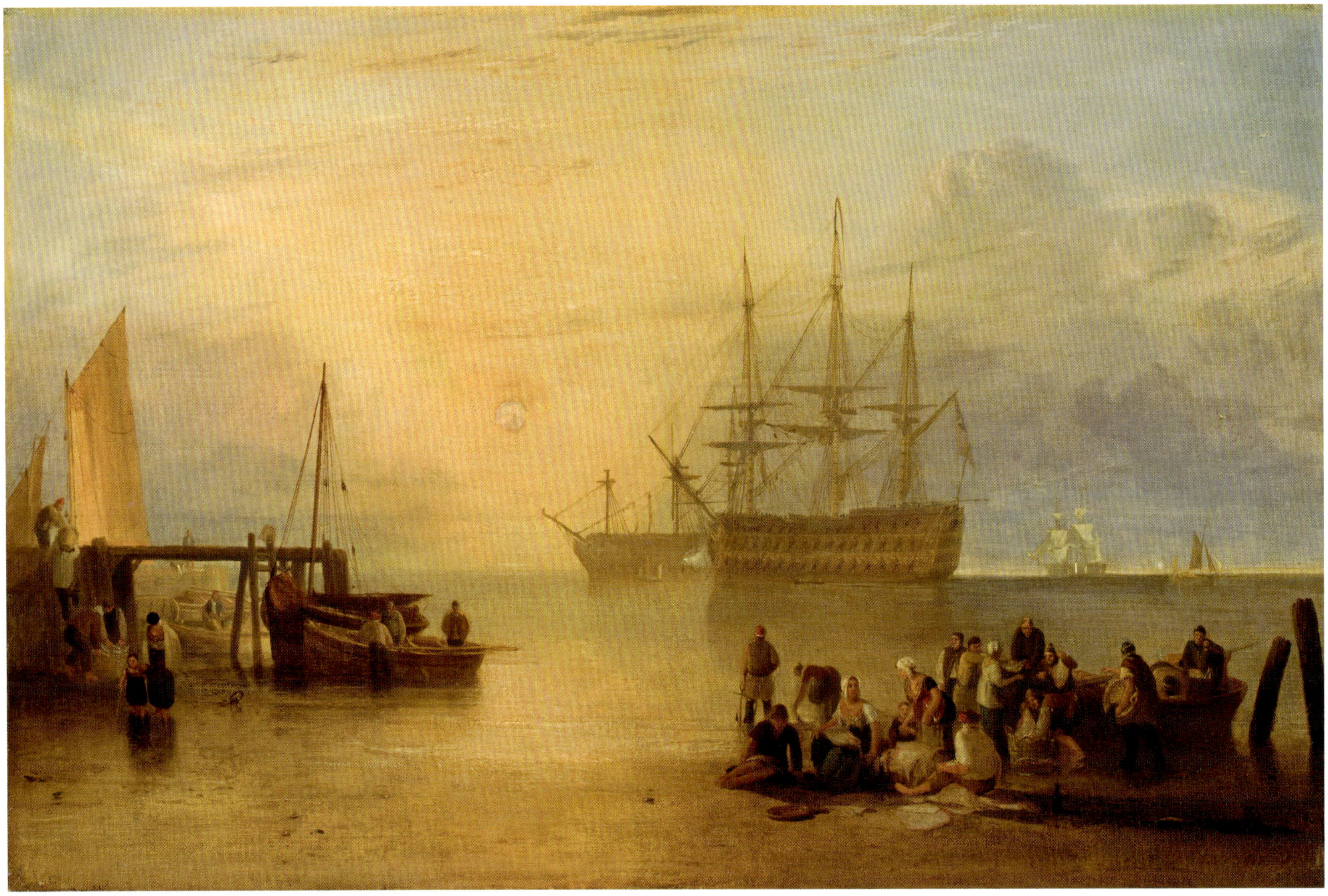

79

J.M.W. Turner
The Sun Rising through Vapour 1809
Oil on canvas 69 x 102 (27⅛ x 40⅛)
Barber Institute of Fine Arts

Butlin and Joll, no. 95; Spencer-Longhurst 2003, no. 7

The Sun Rising through Vapour is among the more brooding of the patriotic marines that predominate in the first full decade of Turner's professional career. The rising sun throws the entire scene into silhouette in a way that seems to emphasize the formal and symbolic relationship between the commercial activity on the seashore – the landing and selling of a day's catch – and the towering warships in the middle distance. Taken as a group (or viewed over successive years in the artist's gallery) Turner's early seascapes attest to his range and artistic ambition, encompassing different times of day and weather conditions, and constructing an art-historical pedigree that identified his practice with both the Dutch and the Italianate traditions of coastal landscape. One of the smallest of Turner's exhibited seascapes, *The Sun Rising through Vapour* is similar in subject (though substantially different in detail) to a painting exhibited with virtually the same title at the Academy two years earlier, now in the collection of the National Gallery, London [fig. 37]. The present painting was bought by Walter Fawkes, who may have commissioned the subject as a pendant to *The 'Victory' Returning from Trafalgar* [fig. 20], a work of identical size that Fawkes had recently acquired from the artist. It was first shown at Turner's gallery in 1809.

80

J.M.W. Turner

Hastings – Fishmarket on the Sands 1810
Oil on canvas 91 x 120.6 (35⅞ x 47½)
Nelson-Atkins Museum of Art

Butlin and Joll, no. 105; Spencer-Longhurst 2003, pp. 38–39; Warrell 2007, no. 44

Like *The Sun Rising through Vapour* [79], exhibited the previous year, *Hastings – Fishmarket on the Sands* evokes a venerable Dutch tradition exemplified by the calm, productive coastal scenes of Simon de Vlieger [1]. Turner's view is traditionally identified as Hastings, which toward the end of the eighteenth century had emerged as an alternative to Brighton and Margate as a fashionable seaside resort. When, as a result, the town prospered, the social divisions between the developers and the fishing community became more conspicuous. Turner's romanticized vision of British coastal life, created in the first instance for a London audience, endows the seaside fishmarket with a sense of tranquillity and order that was at some remove from the busy, divided and fast-growing fishing town. Historically, the fishing communities of Hastings and surrounding towns had been at the front line of British coastal defence, never more so than during the French Revolutionary and Napoleonic Wars. The popularity of the subject was demonstrated by other artists as well, most notably in a large, patriotic view of the fishmarket at Hastings that Joshua Cristall exhibited to critical acclaim at the Society of Painters in Water Colours in 1808 (now at the Victoria and Albert Museum), which shows a crowded but impeccably ordered vision of Britain's wartime coastal economy.

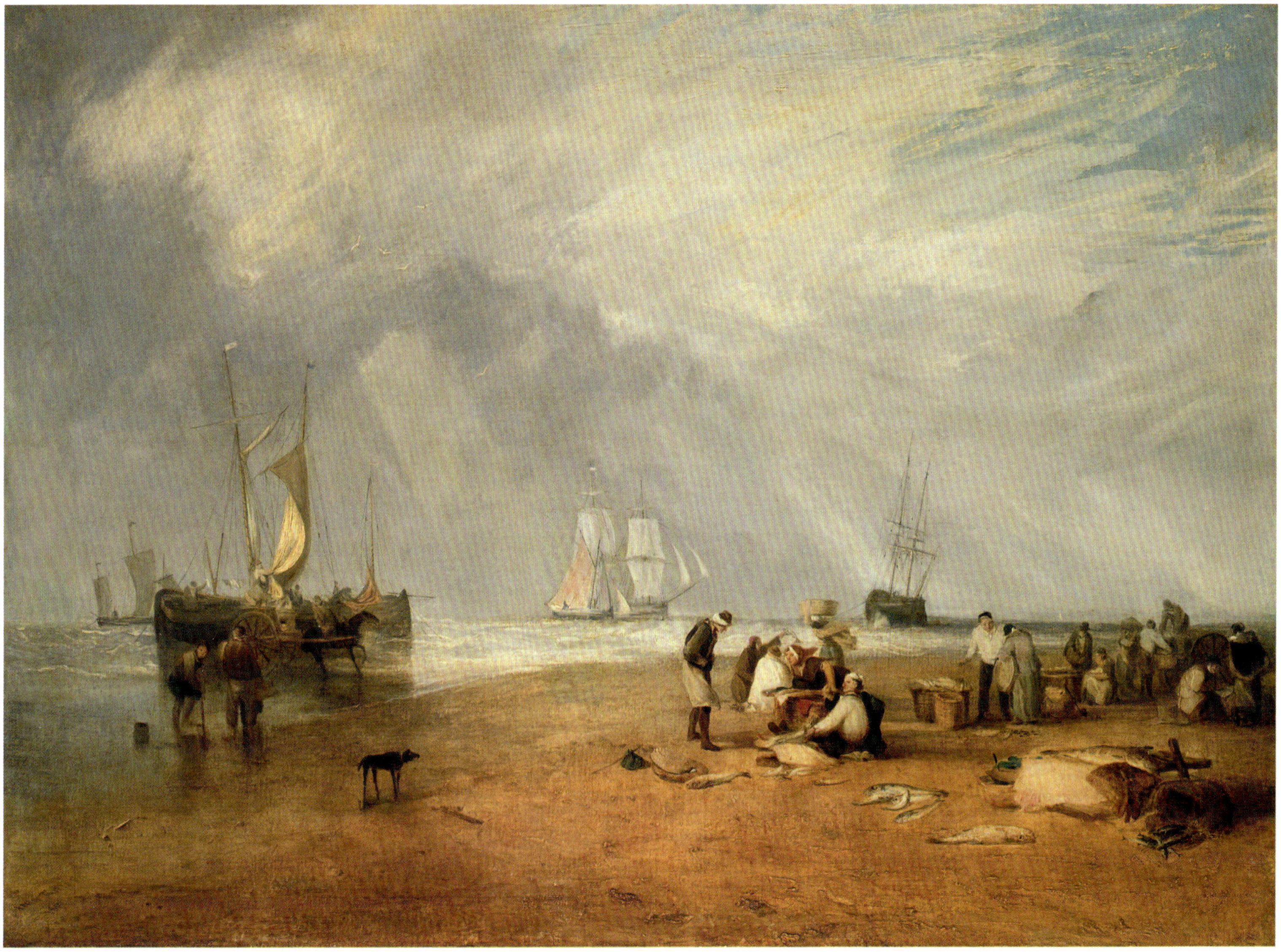

81

J.M.W. Turner
A First Rate Taking in Stores 1818
Watercolour 28.6 x 39.7 (11¼ x 15⅝)
Cecil Higgins Art Gallery and Bedford Museum

Wilton, no. 499; Shanes 2001, pp. 13–15; Joll 2002, pp. 270–71; Smiles 2006, pp. 175–76; Warrell 2007, no. 56

Turner's finished watercolours were even more widely known during his lifetime than his work in oil, thanks to the growing opportunities to exhibit works on paper beyond the Royal Academy and the British Institution. *A First Rate Taking in Stores* was first shown alongside *The Loss of an East Indiaman* [82] in a privately organized show of Walter Fawkes's collection in 1819–20 at his residence in Grosvenor Place, London. The watercolour was reportedly made one morning during the previous winter, while Turner was staying with Fawkes at Farnley Hall, after the artist's host had asked him for a drawing to demonstrate the scale of a man-of-war. Turner responded to the friendly challenge by drawing three ships that are vastly exaggerated in relation to the people and other smaller vessels. The 'first-rate' on the right towers over the supply boats at its side, its crew is dwarfed by the over-sized gun ports, and even the page is too small to contain the ship, which spills beyond our view. Turner's playful response to Fawkes's request also conveys a serious message by emphasizing the symbolic grandeur and superhuman force of a 100-gun ship of the line.

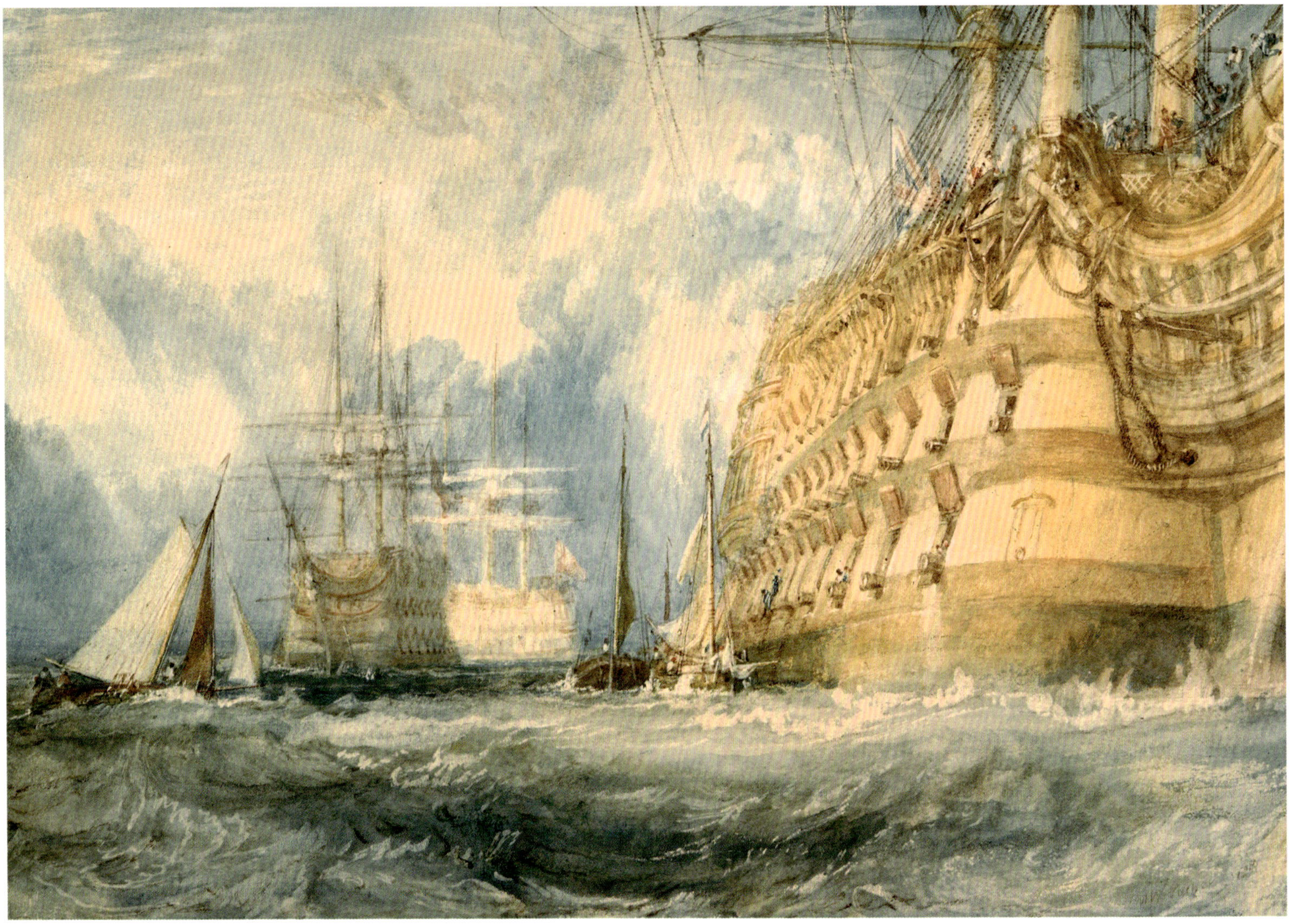

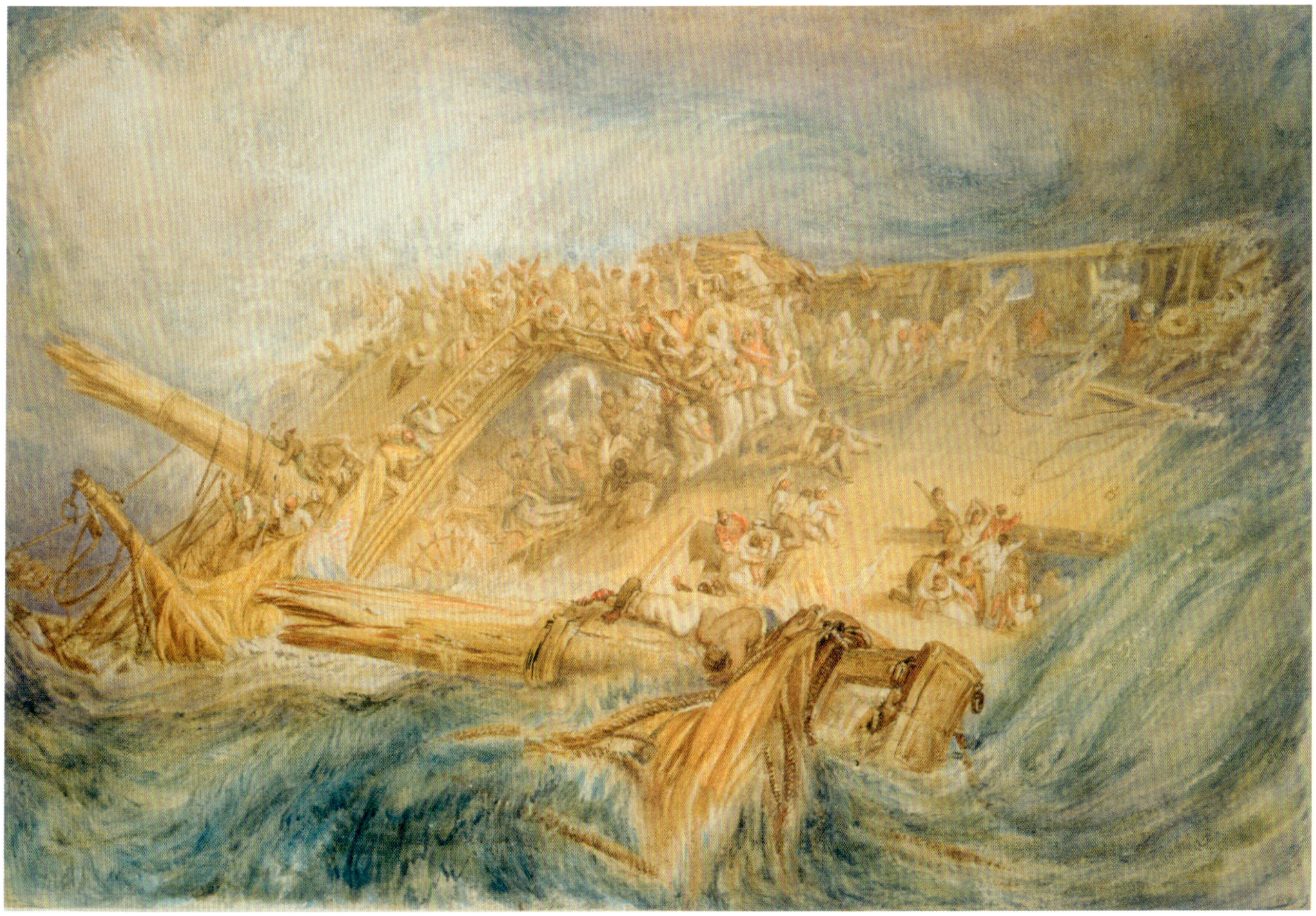

82

J.M.W. Turner

The Loss of an East Indiaman c.1818

Watercolour 28 x 39.5 (11 x 15½)

Cecil Higgins Art Gallery and Bedford Museum

Wilton, no. 500; Shanes 2000, p. 135; Shanes 2001, pp. 13–5; Joll 2002, pp. 271–72

First exhibited as part of Walter Fawkes's collection at his house in Grosvenor Place, *The Loss of an East Indiaman* harks back to the sinking of the 'Halsewell' in 1786, one of the most infamous shipwrecks of the eighteenth century. On a small sheet of paper, and in a medium that was more often associated with a lightness of touch and the picturesque view, Turner creates a devastating image of maritime sublimity that focuses on the point of no return – when the enormous merchant ship is overwhelmed and consumed by the sea.

The subject may have been chosen to complement *A First Rate Taking in Stores* [81], thus inaugurating a contrast between war and peace, calm and storm. It is among the most violent of any of the artist's shipwreck scenes and, as with *A First Rate Taking in Stores*, conveys a sense of the ship's enormous scale by adopting a relatively low viewpoint, extending the vast sinking hull beyond the edges of the picture. Both watercolours were exhibited together on a second occasion during Turner's lifetime, at the Music Hall in Leeds in 1839.

88 (and detail)

J.M.W. Turner
The Wreck Buoy c.1807; reworked 1849
Oil on canvas 92.7 x 123.2 (36½ x 48½)
National Museums Liverpool

Butlin and Joll, no. 428

This painting was the final seascape that Turner exhibited at the Royal Academy and his only submission in 1849. He had not shown any works in 1848, having exhibited (among others) a number of Venetian scenes and his four whaling paintings in 1845 and 1846 (see [139]). It would be tempting, therefore, to view *The Wreck Buoy* as a final statement of the artist's lifelong engagement with the sea. Instead, the history of the painting is anything but straightforward. It was initially completed about 1807, bought some time after 1830 by H.A.J. Munro of Novar, then reworked by the artist for the Academy's summer exhibition in the late 1840s. Munro was one of Turner's most important patrons and a close friend. He had agreed to send the painting from his estate in Scotland to London but seems to have been dismayed, at least initially, by what the artist then did. In his reference to *The Wreck Buoy*, Turner's early biographer, Walter Thornbury, tells us that it was 'an early picture, on which Turner spent six laborious days, quite at the end of his life, much to Mr. Munro's horror; but it came out gloriously with a whitened misty sky and a double rainbow' (Thornbury 1862, vol.1, pp. 232–33).

The addition of the rainbow and a much heightened contrast of light and dark obscures a different seascape. It is likely that it was a Thames estuary scene similar to those exhibited in the artist's gallery in the early 1800s (see [78]). Interestingly, Turner had reworked another early painting, *The Hero of a Hundred Fights* (Tate Collection), his only Academy exhibit in 1847. In their *catalogue raisonné* of Turner's oil paintings, Butlin and Joll suggest that most of the reworking of that painting was done during the varnishing days, Turner having been provoked by the juxtaposition of his work with Daniel Maclise's large-scale history painting, *The Sacrifice of Noah* (Leeds City Art Gallery). In a letter to Clarkson Stanfield, Ruskin commented on the poor position of Stanfield's painting in the exhibition display, but noted that the hanging committee 'had served Turner worse ... there is nothing in his picture but even colour, and they must needs put Maclise's rainbow side by side with it' (cited in Butlin and Joll 1984, p. 245). Two years later, Turner submitted *The Wreck Buoy* for exhibition having added a spectacular rainbow.

Given Turner's perennial competitiveness, this may simply represent the last of many such episodes played out in the public arena of the Royal Academy. However, we might also interpret the reworking of *The Wreck Buoy* as emblematic of his interest in elevating marine art through poignant allusions to the past or making references to biblical and classical subject matter. Using Maclise's painting as a recent reference point, it is possible that Turner sought to explore (not for the first time) the theme of fallacious hope and the threat of disaster at sea, here through the symbolism of the rainbow. In Judeo-Christian tradition, the rainbow represents God's covenant with mankind after the deluge, pledging that the Earth would never again be destroyed by a great flood. The fact that Turner juxtaposes the rainbow with a wreck buoy and evidence of a shipwreck adds a further layer of complexity to this enigmatic late work. Indeed, Turner had exhibited *Shade and Darkness – The Evening of the Deluge* and *The Morning after the Deluge* (Tate Collection) in 1843. The latter was accompanied by the following lines from his own unpublished poem *Fallacies of Hope*, which makes a reference both to Noah's ark and the elusiveness of the rainbow:

> The ark stood firm on Ararat; th' returning sun
> Exhaled earth's humid bubbles, and emulous of light,
> Reflected her lost forms, each in prismatic guise
> Hope's harbinger, ephemeral as the summer fly
> Which rises, flits, expands, and dies.

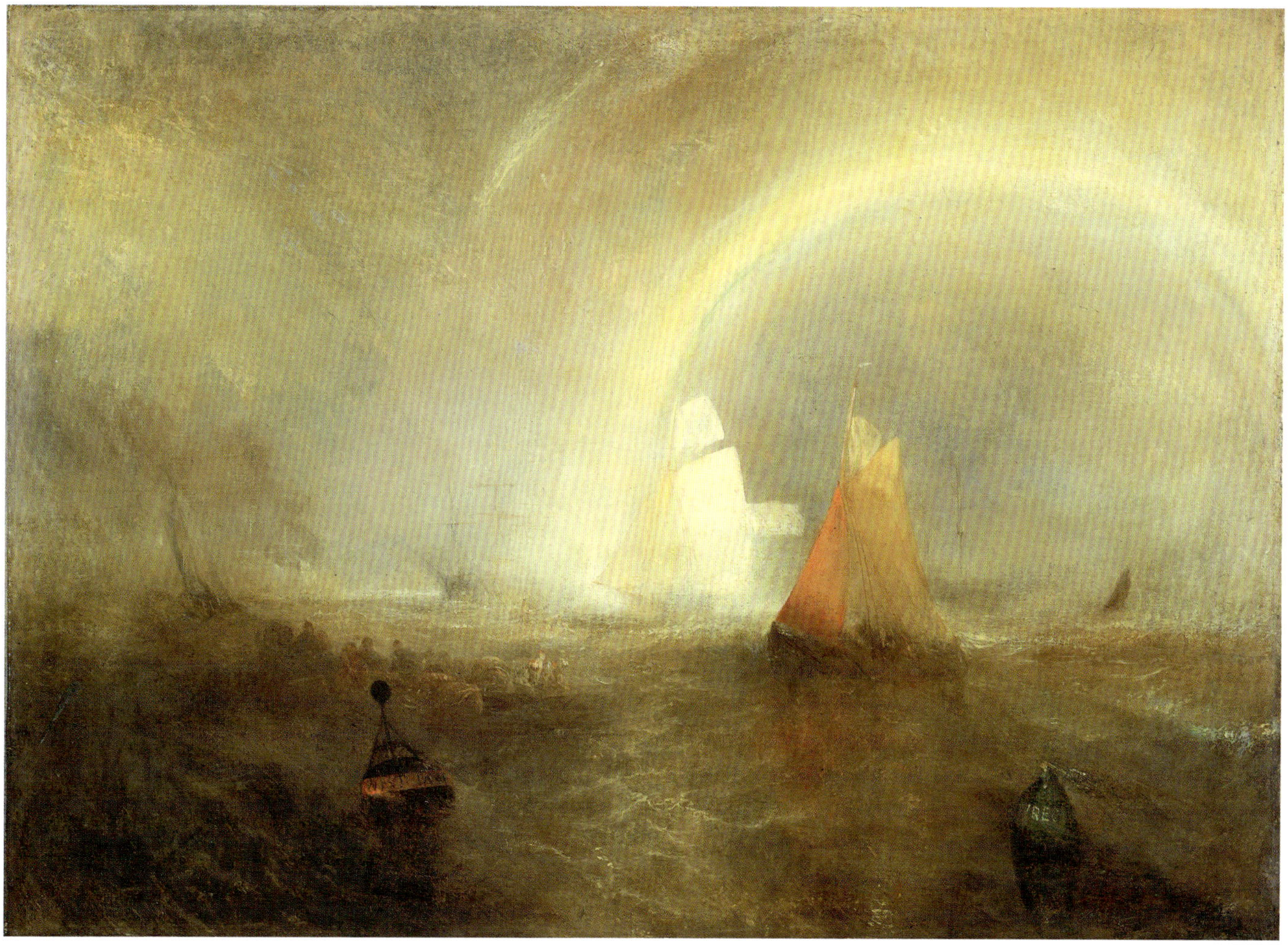

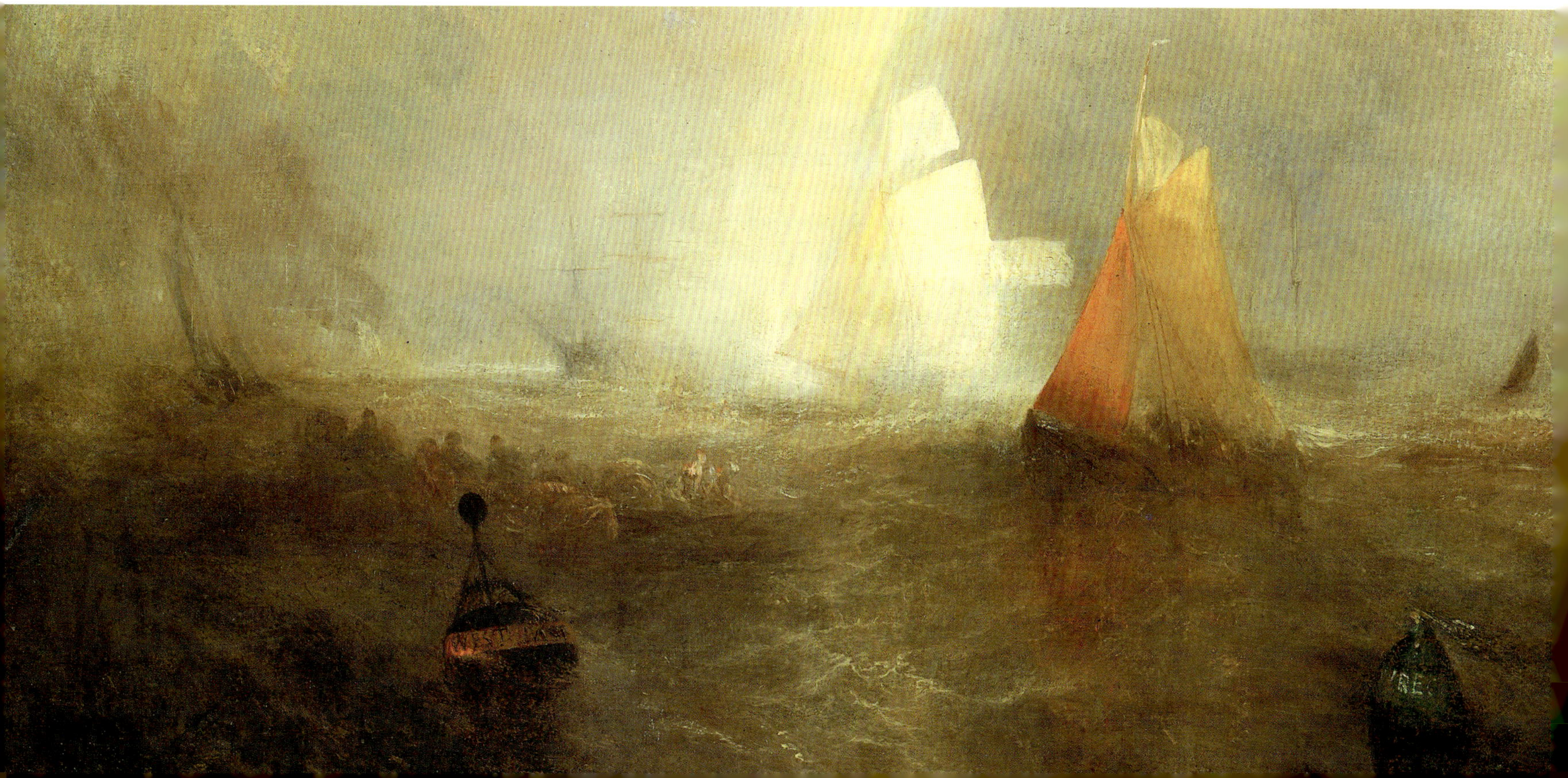

'Tearing and Desolating': Dissolution and Decomposition in *The Wreck of a Transport Ship*

Leo Costello

Reviewing Turner's *Wreck of a Transport Ship* (*c*.1810) [76] at the British Institution exhibition in 1849, the *Spectator* called the painting 'a partial foretaste of that dissolution which now decomposes all Turner's works even before they reach the canvas'. Critics often invoked a rhetoric of decline during the last decade of Turner's life in response to his increasingly loose handling and obscure subject matter. It is unusual, however, to see this marshalled in response to a painting from so early in his career. Such retrospective comments far more often provided viewers with the opportunity to lament the artist's descent from the more 'natural' work of his early career. Indeed, the same review called another early work, *The Festival upon the Opening of the Vintage of Macon*, first exhibited in 1803, 'a modest copy of the thing seen,' that 'would surprise many who know only Turner's later eccentricities, by the substantial power which it displays.'[1]

On the other hand, just a year after Turner's death, *The Wreck of a Transport Ship* was cited by writer John Burnet as an example of the artist's incomparable ability as a painter in oil: 'When we hear people talk of the drawings of Turner, compared with a work of this kind, it seems a farce. His drawings may be imitated, and have been imitated successfully; but no one has yet given the smallest idea of a work such as this.'[2] Together these responses indicate the extraordinary degree to which Turner's seascapes continued to be a site for the elaboration of competing views of his production and legacy. The *Spectator*'s account is further interesting because it connects *The Wreck of a Transport Ship* to what followed in Turner's career. Later viewers, by contrast, have been more inclined to consider the painting as a kind of summation of his marine subjects of the previous decade. Martin Butlin and Evelyn Joll, the compilers of the *catalogue raisonné* of Turner's paintings, suggest, for instance, that the work 'marked the culmination of a decade of painting grand seascapes', a view shared by a number of subsequent scholars.[3]

As a means of assessing the ongoing ambivalence the painting has provoked, as well as both its predictive and retrospective qualities, I would like to take seriously the *Spectator*'s idea of this painting, and Turner's oeuvre as a whole, as informed by some prior state of dissolution. Negative though it is, it captures very well the degree to which decomposition and dissolution were central to Turner's depictions of the sea. If a combination of creativity and destruction informs these paintings, moreover, then a similar mixture also structured Turner's approach to creating his own reputation, as well as fostering a British school of painting.

A number of factors combined in the first decades of the nineteenth century to make Turner's seascapes particularly important to his developing career. First, seascapes had become increasingly prominent as a means of negotiating and creating British national and imperial identity.[4] Second, these depictions emerged in an increasingly competitive artistic environment, something that created considerable concern among aesthetic theorists, who worried that the private demands of the marketplace might overwhelm the public concerns of history painting. Royal Academician (and future President of the Royal Academy) Martin Archer Shee summed up these concerns as follows:

> The emulation excited by an exhibition is rarely influenced by general and comprehensive views; occupied with local and partial objects, it becomes a rivalry not of positive, but comparative excellence; not of the merits of Art, but the manner of the school. Instead of contending with the great masters, we are obliged to contend with ourselves.[5]

This placed ambitious artists such as Turner in a kind of double bind, for they needed at once to strive to build their own reputation in a combative marketplace, while also attempting to serve the cause of British art, and even art in general.

Within this competitive exhibition space, artists in the nineteenth century increasingly resorted to using dramatic effects, loose brushwork and high-key colours to attract attention on the crowded walls of the Academy exhibitions.[6] Given this combination of factors, it is not surprising that Turner was drawn so consistently to the sea as a subject during the first full decade of his exhibiting career. Seascapes offered a subject that at once allowed him to demonstrate a full range of formal and technical innovations while treating subjects of considerable public interest at a time of war. In particular, Turner used seascapes as a means of distinguishing himself among his contemporaries and measuring himself against the old masters, fastening particularly on images of destruction. In doing so, his ambition was to establish a reputation as the painter of the sea *par excellence* and in the process nurture a uniquely British school of painting.[7] But, as the *Spectator*'s response proves, this was a risky proposition – not least because the means by which Turner pursued his ends could lead some to believe that he was destroying the bases of artistic composition and tradition, and thus the very British school he proposed to lead.

Part of the development that so many scholars have detected in Turner's seascapes, up to the *Wreck of a Transport Ship* in 1810, is an increase in the intensity of the formal and thematic representation of destruction. Whereas many of the pictures from the first half of the decade show a scene of implied or impending destruction, such as *Dutch Boats in a Gale* [fig. 6] and *Calais Pier* [74]; with *The Shipwreck* [75] and *The Wreck of a Transport Ship* we see Turner composing a picture by means of decomposition; that is, depicting ships violently breaking apart. It is clear that he was aware of the defining role such depictions played in his career. Barry Venning has noted that Turner saw both water and shipwrecks as personal and professional metaphors.[8] Later in his career, Turner even referred to *Dutch Boats in a Gale* as a work that 'launched my Boat'.[9] In 1806, Turner selected *The Shipwreck*, his most vivid image of destruction to date, as the first of his pictures to be engraved for publication. The extensive number of drawings of shipwrecks in his sketchbooks of these years underlines the importance of this theme for the artist.[10]

Unusually for Turner, there is direct archival evidence that he was actively thinking about the means of representing dissolution and destruction in precisely these years. When he visited the Louvre in 1802, he looked closely at Nicolas Poussin's *Winter, or The Flood*, and his subsequent analysis of the painting speaks to this precise point. Turner criticizes Poussin for failing to give sufficiently intense visual form to a world being enveloped in water. 'The lines,' he writes:

> are defective as to the conception of a swamp'd world and the fountains of the deep being broken up. The boat on the waterfall is ill-judged and misapplied, for the figures are placed at the wrong end to give the idea of falling. The other boat makes a parallel with the base of the picture, and the woman giving the child is unworthy [*sic*] the mind of Poussin, she is as unconcerned as the man floating with a small piece of board. No current or ebullition (in the water), although a waterfall is introduced to fill up the interstices of the earth – artificially, not tearing and desolating, but falling placidly in another pool.[11]

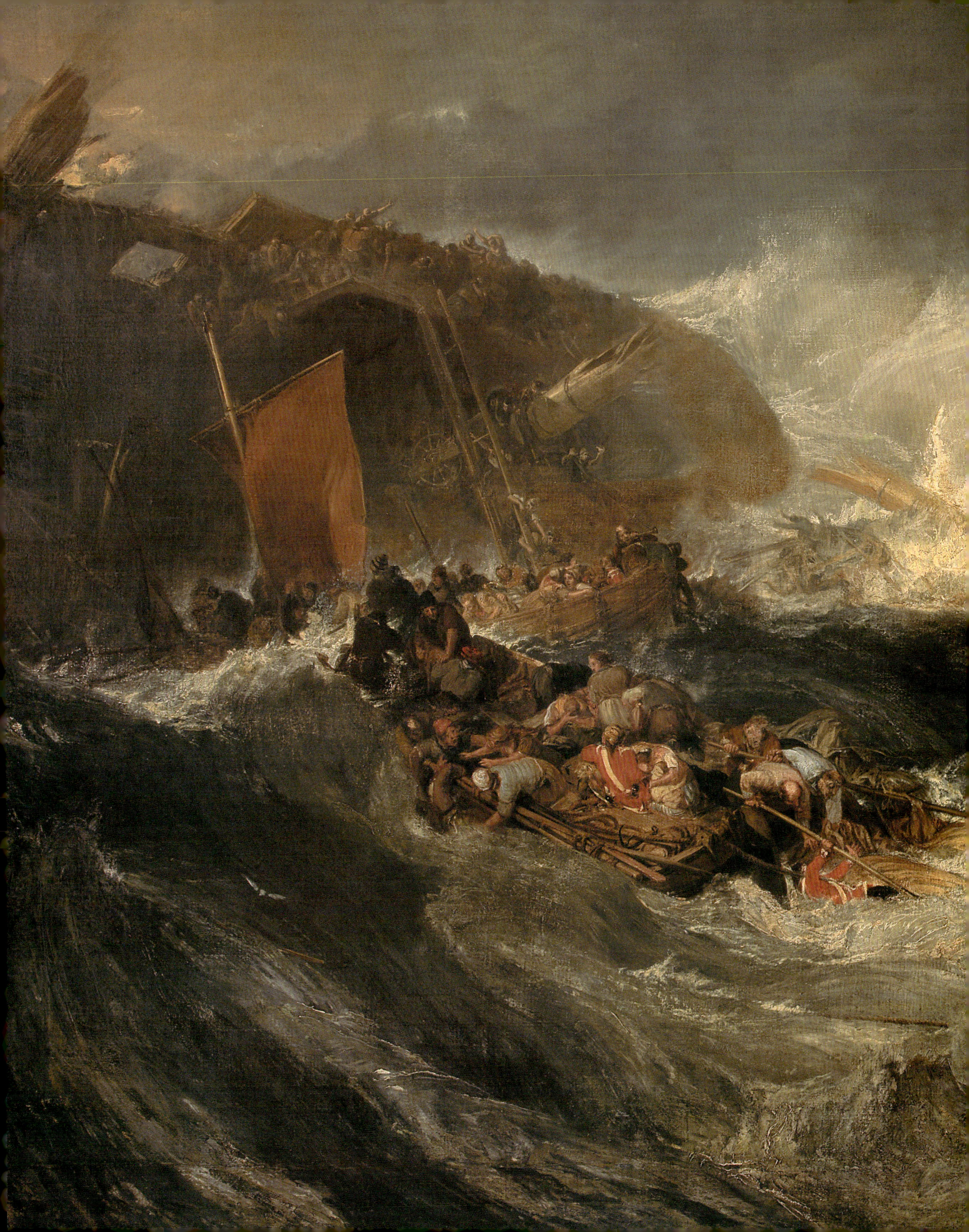

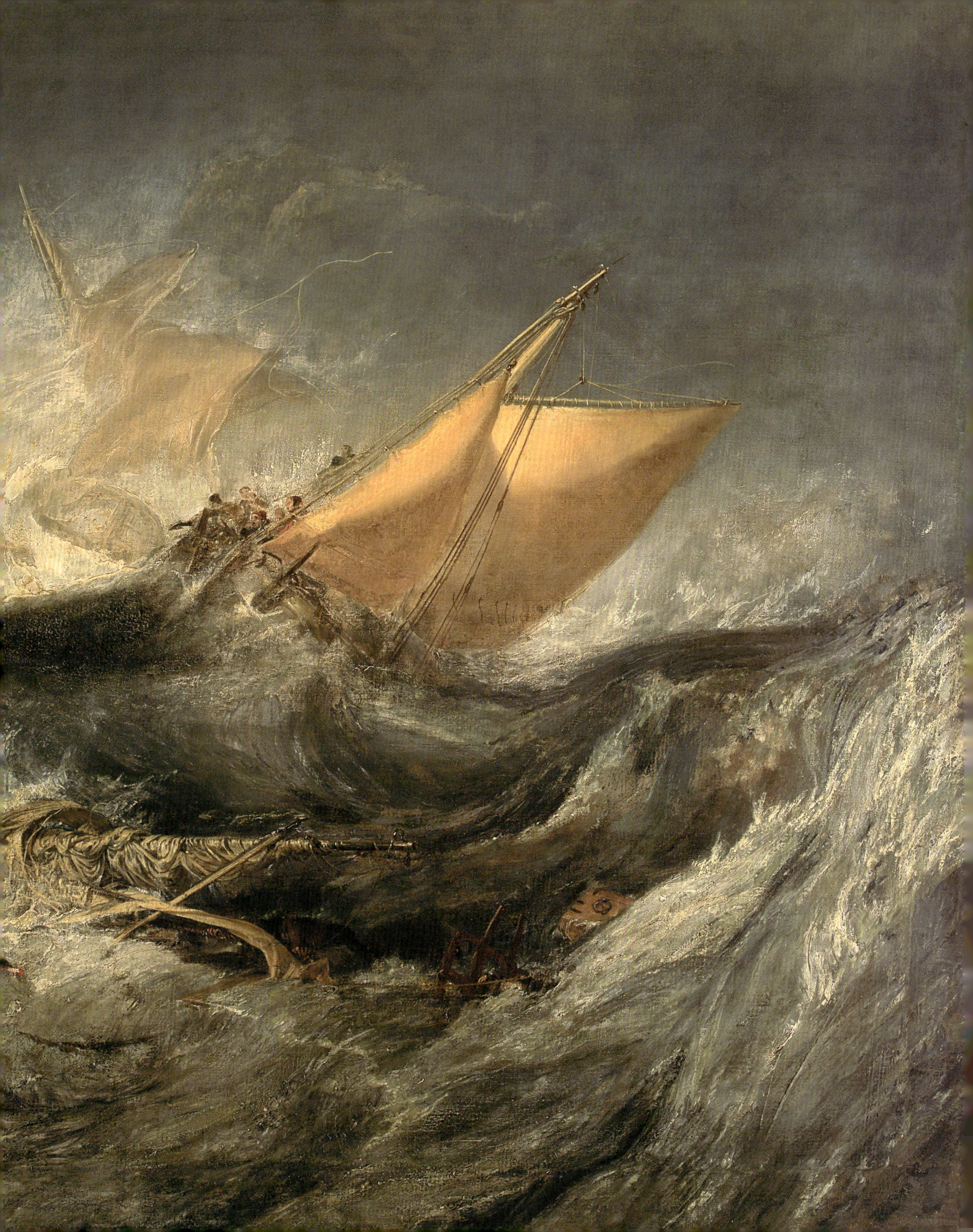

Turner is critical of the formal failings of Poussin's work, invoking the stability caused by parallel lines, and the lack of movement and energy in the representation of a cataclysmic theme. This we might expect from Turner, but he is also very attentive to thematic questions – not just the position of the figures, but also their actions, their emotional responses, or lack thereof. I have elsewhere discussed the relation of this extraordinary passage to *The Shipwreck*, but here I would like to note how fully *The Wreck of a Transport Ship* responds to Turner's analysis of Poussin's work.[12] This is not to say, of course, that it is reducible to that response in the Louvre from some years before, but rather that the writing can offer an effective means into the taut dynamics which underpin Turner's (de)composition.

In the first place, we might note the lifeboat in the foreground, which gashes diagonally across the picture plane, rather than aligning with the horizontal bottom edge of the canvas. This vessel is closer to us than its counterpart in *The Shipwreck*, and also more crowded with figures, allowing us to concentrate on their actions. The lifeboat is perilously angled on the steep wave and thus seems to combine the two boats from Poussin's painting. Throughout the picture, we see figures reaching, grabbing, clinging, attempting to hold on to a boat, an oar, another arm, or merely a piece of wreckage. Many of these gestures are similar to ones in Poussin's painting, but they appear infinitely more desperate here, appropriate to figures perched everywhere on the edge of an abyss.[13]

Indeed, Turner highlights this kind of positioning throughout the picture: look at the figures along the top edge of the tilting ship in the back left, the two men at the very top of the lifeboat cresting the wave in the foreground, and the figures on the left edge of the fishing boat in the right middle ground. All of them are silhouetted against a more broadly painted background of sky or water. This helps to explain the particular dichotomy in the picture between large areas of canvas filled with depictions of sweeping natural elements in which there are no definite, stable forms, and the areas of almost hyper-specific detail.[14] *The Wreck of a Transport Ship* is at once filled with incident and also suffused with a growing, terrifying emptiness. The stakes here are heightened even from *The Shipwreck*. Whereas in the earlier picture, the foundering ship rolls away from us in the background, here it looms ominously over us, dramatically increasing the vertiginous closeness of the waves, which are also steeper and taller than in *The Shipwreck*.

It is in this respect, that *The Wreck of a Transport Ship* also looks ahead to paintings in Turner's later career. While he stopped painting seascapes for much of the next decade, the watercolour *The Loss of an East Indiaman* [82] reprises many of the same elements and details, now taking us closer to the foundering ship itself. It also preserves the sense of figures perched on the edge of an abyss, such as those silhouetted along the elevated starboard rail, about to be subsumed into the swirl of water and air. In its stark, even abject, sense of the terror of a world falling apart, *The Wreck of a Transport Ship* also looks ahead to seascapes such as the unfinished *Disaster at Sea* (Tate Collection) and, of course, *Slavers* [fig. 46]. Thus, the *Spectator* may have been right – in ways other than the reviewer intended – in proclaiming that, in *The Wreck of a Transport Ship*, we see 'a partial foretaste of that dissolution which now decomposes all Turner's works even before they reach the canvas'. Indeed, it was out of such a prior state of dissolution and decomposition that Turner built his career as a painter of the sea.

Preceding page

J.M.W. Turner
The Wreck of a Transport Ship c.1810 (detail of [76])

Opposite

J.M.W. Turner
The Shipwreck 1805 (detail of [75])

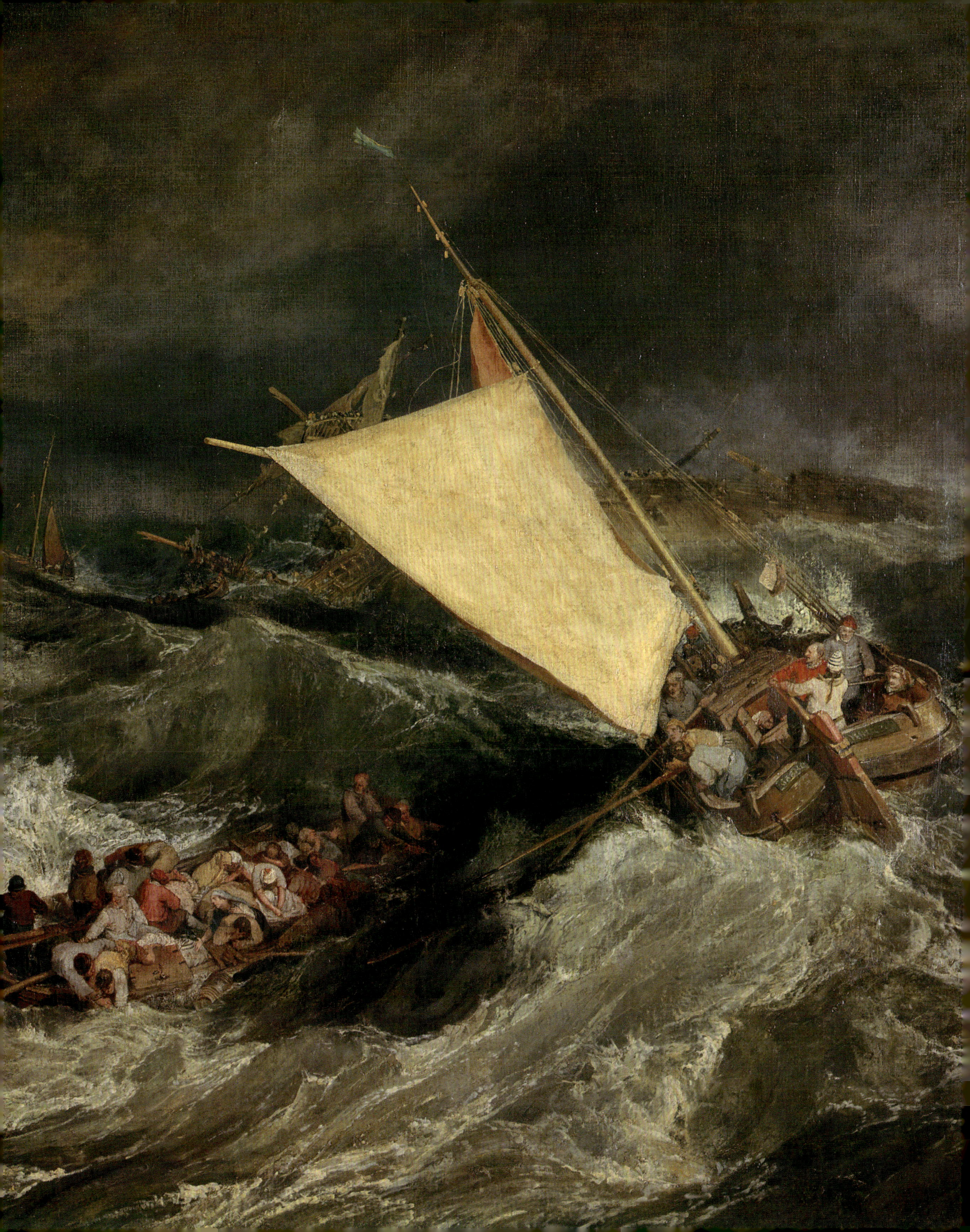

6

IMAGINING THE SEA

Richard Johns

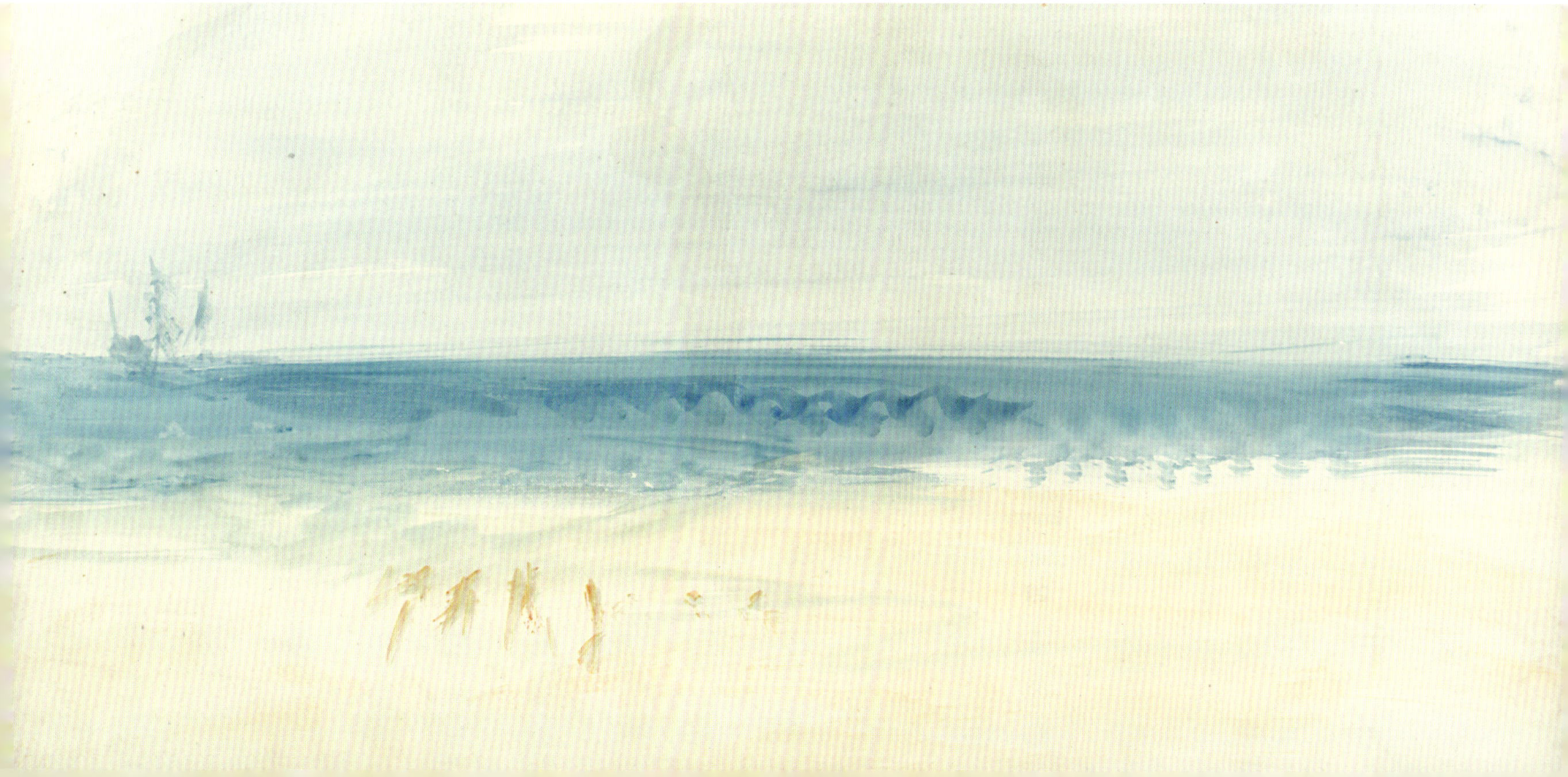

A broad sweep of cobalt blue, applied across a wet page with a few strokes of a loaded brush, sets the scene [106 and detail opposite]. The dampness of the paper gives the artist a valuable few seconds to manipulate the vibrant watercolour before it dries: enough time to add a disorderly flourish with the tip of the same brush (without pausing to adjust the colour) to indicate a fully rigged ship sailing into the picture from the left; and to work a neater, calligraphic pattern into the blue to suggest the rolling breakers of an agitated but unthreatening sea. The lightest of washes above and below denote the sky and a sandy beach, while a handful of darker yellow marks towards the bottom of the page indicate something else. But what? The carcass of a wrecked fishing boat? A group of figures? It is not clear, but the marks are just sufficient to animate the foreground, as the waves and the three-masted ship above draw the blue sweep away from the viewer towards a distant horizon. With an economy that few artists have been able to match, Turner invokes a coastal landscape – a kind of marine view that he had created countless times before, in all manner of ways. *Blue Sea and Distant Ship* probably dates from the early 1840s, though there is not much to distinguish it from similar works of ten or even twenty years earlier. It belongs to a group of several hundred rapidly made and highly expressive watercolours, sometimes referred to collectively as colour 'beginnings', that form part of the huge body of preparatory studies, unfinished work and related items from Turner's studio that became part of the national collection after his death.

If such works are experiments, as they have often been described, they are only so in the loosest sense of the word, as exercises in imagination. After a lifetime of experiencing and imagining the sea, there was little practical value to be learned from such experiments, which seem to convey their maker's undiminished delight in the materials and techniques of his profession, and in the process of transforming unadulterated colour into a boundless seascape. The more elemental of Turner's late watercolour sketches are often invoked in relation to the avowedly non-figurative painting that emerged and flourished during the twentieth century, for whose protagonists the process of making art was celebrated as an end in itself. Yet, for all their abstract appeal to modern eyes, *Blue Sea and Distant Ship*, and other watercolours and oil paintings made in the same spirit, remain unapologetically figurative. A more rounded view of the work that Turner produced in his studio, away from the public eye, reveals a far greater variety of imagery reaching across his whole career. Some of it is experimental, some even verges on the incomprehensible, but much of it is more conventional in subject and technique, and more clearly grounded on the pedagogic traditions of the Royal Academy and the principles of land- and seascape painting that had been established during the previous century.

Since Turner's death in 1851, the extent of his practice has become more fully understood and appreciated in step with the stages by which the work he left behind has been catalogued and conserved to ever more exacting standards. In the past fifty years, especially, this once-hidden aspect of Turner's enterprise has shaped his posthumous international reputation at least as much as any of the oil paintings that were finished and exhibited during his lifetime. The private world of Turner's sketchbooks and studio has been investigated, exposed and selectively called upon as evidence in the shifting assessment of the painter's long-term significance for the history of art. This is nowhere more apparent than in those drawings and watercolours that are concerned with the sea. At the same time, the Turner Bequest continues to serve a biographical purpose: the subjects depicted and the many handwritten annotations, observations and memoranda that are scattered throughout provide an essential, if at times elusive, source of information about the artist's many journeys around Britain and Europe, the places he saw and the works by other artists he deemed worthy of visual record.

BEQUEST

Turner had made clear his intention to leave around a hundred finished oil paintings to the National Gallery (upon the fulfilment of variously interpreted criteria regarding how and where they should be displayed), but he made no explicit provision for the vast quantity of preparatory and unfinished material that filled his West End gallery at the time of his death.[1] As a result of this uncertainty and a poorly drafted will, the fate of Turner's estate, including the full contents of his studio, was mired in a legal challenge by the artist's extended family that dragged on for five years. The finished oil paintings that he had intended to leave to the nation – a representative selection which, with an eye on posterity, he had extended and refined over several years – already ensured that he would become (as he remains) the most comprehensively represented British artist in any national collection. With the addition of around 180 other oils that were deemed by the artist's executors to be unfinished (the precise figure varies according to the definition of 'finished') and more than 19,000 drawings, watercolour studies and other works on paper spanning more than fifty uncommonly productive years, the legally determined Turner Bequest of 1856 grew into an unprecedented and unwieldy testimony of a creative life.[2]

John Ruskin was the first to impose a semblance of order on the Bequest, in ways informed by his own impassioned vision of the artist as a purveyor of divine truth through his engagement with the natural world. Named as one of Turner's original executors, he stood down when the will was contested, but once the court case had been determined, he set about preparing an unofficial catalogue for the inaugural exhibition of works selected from the Bequest, which opened at London's Marlborough House in 1856.[3] Selections from Turner's studio gradually became known to a wider public through a series of further displays, in London and beyond. Also selected by Ruskin (or otherwise informed by his ideas on the artist), these emphasized Turner's experiential and imaginative response to nature too, and endorsed Ruskin's rigid chronological assessment of the artist's creative ascent, maturity and decline.[4] A second show at Marlborough House, dedicated to works on paper, included a selection of sketchbooks and, for the first time, a small group of preparatory sketches, or 'trials of effects for pictures'. However, there was only a handful, as Ruskin (who had yet to explore and appreciate the Bequest as fully as he later would) concluded that while such works might be useful to students, 'they are not in general interesting'.[5] A few seascapes in oil that were presumed unfinished were included in the displays of the Turner Bequest during the nineteenth century, including *Fire at Sea* (also known as *A Disaster at Sea*, Tate Collection), in which the artist revisited the subject of storm and shipwreck that had done so much to secure his reputation in the early 1800s as a painter of the sublime sea.[6] A lone unfinished or abandoned marine painting today called *Seascape: Folkestone* (the only one of its kind known to exist outside of the Turner Bequest, or found shortly thereafter), has also been identified as the work included in the winter exhibition of 'Old Masters and Deceased Masters of the British School' at the Royal Academy in 1894 as *Storm off the Forelands*.[7]

As part of the same process of uncovering and ordering the Bequest within the context of Turner's working methods, Ruskin also included several of the artist's unpublished mezzotints and related studies in the early displays at Marlborough House. Among them was the pairing of a watercolour study and mezzotint proof of *Ship in a Storm* [31 and 32] from the so-called 'Little Liber' series of prints. The juxtaposition revealed how Turner approached mezzotint, not merely as a means of reproduction but as an essential part of the picture-making process, during which an image could continue to develop in keeping with the new limits and possibilities of the medium.[8] However, the majority of Turner's preparatory and otherwise unresolved work remained almost hidden, neither catalogued nor exhibited in earnest, until twentieth-century interest in his practice in the round made it increasingly visible.

Turner was known for being secretive about his methods and means. Those few who saw him draw or paint outside of the walls of the Academy and whose impressions have been recorded, recall with excitement the variety and inventiveness of his technique. Manipulating the pigment in every way imaginable, he would even plunge whole sheets of paper into a bath when working in watercolour, as he conjured an image into existence. On one celebrated occasion, Hawkesworth Fawkes, the eldest son of his patron Walter Fawkes, recalled his amazement on seeing Turner create from memory a richly detailed watercolour of a man-of-war [81] within a few hours – pouring, tearing, scratching and scrubbing 'in a kind of frenzy' until the final, detailed image emerged in time for lunch.[9] Others, too, likened Turner's finished watercolours to the work of a magician who could bring forth poetical views onto the page, as if from nowhere. However, there is a marked difference between his finished watercolours, which he was able to sell as quickly as he could make (and of which, as a result, he kept relatively few), and the many thousand watercolour sketches he produced for his own purposes, about which he was even more guarded. As Ruskin tirelessly worked his way through the residuum of Turner's career, preparing for display those works he regarded as exemplary and consigning others to tin boxes, he became the first to appreciate the full extent of his brilliant and at times chaotic artistic life.

DRAWING

Among Turner's belongings during his second visit to Scotland, in 1801, was a small sketchbook treated with a tinted wash that could be scratched away to reveal the white paper beneath. Thus prepared, and armed with a single brush and a colour, the artist was able repeatedly to model the infinitely complex surge of North Sea waves breaking on Dunbar beach. One such wave [99] reappeared a year or so later on the walls of the Royal Academy, much embellished and combined with the contents of another sketchbook [93] but in essence unchanged, as the central motif of *Fishermen upon a Lee-Shore, in Squally Weather* [73]. Among the many other sketchbooks and torn pages in the Bequest is a series of pencil studies recording the pitch and roll of boats in a rough harbour [96–98], one of which is annotated in the artist's typically indecipherable hand with what appear to be colour notes for an anticipated painting. The same vessels continue their struggle against the elements (with the designated colours now in play) in *Ramsgate* [48], *The Mouth of the River Humber* [68] and other finished watercolours that Turner produced in the mid-1820s for the *Ports and Rivers of England* series. These examples, all apparently made (or, at least, begun) out of doors, form part of a traditional picture-making process that Turner practised at the Royal Academy Schools, in which repeated sketches made in front of the motif (whether a fishing boat in a busy estuary or a nude model in the life class) were studiously developed into a composed and finished work of art, whether in oil, watercolour or print.

Drawing was an essential part of Turner's early artistic training and remained integral to his practice throughout his working life, largely filling the majority of more than 280 sketchbooks that he accumulated in his studio as a working repository of ideas. However, despite the prevalence in the Bequest of drawing in pencil, chalk and other dry media, his work as a draughtsman has until recently received relatively little attention from scholars. Perhaps this is because it has been seen to represent a more conventional aspect of his career compared to his singular work in watercolour; or because the drawn line becomes visibly less apparent in his later, more expressively painterly and indistinct work.[10]

The so-called Calais Pier Sketchbook [100] is especially pertinent to a consideration of Turner as an artist of the sea, as it contains some of the most complex and rewarding preparatory marine studies from the early part of his career. The large-format volume of blue paper contains much more than the early workings of the eponymous oil painting, *Calais Pier* [74], which the artist exhibited in the summer of 1803. Filled over the course of several years, its pages show Turner studiously committing his first thoughts on various subjects to paper – in chalk and charcoal, and in pen. Alongside several academic figure studies and designs for biblical and mythological subjects, the sketchbook includes initial ideas for some of his most important seascapes from the first five decades of the nineteenth century, including compositional studies for *Ships Bearing up for Anchorage* [72] and the National Gallery's *Sun Rising through Vapour* [fig. 37]. The purpose of such designs, it seems, was something akin to 'invention' in the old, eighteenth-century meaning of the word, when a figment of the artist's imagination first assumes a pictorial form, when speed and a lightness of touch are of the essence, and before the niceties of detail are determined. His later, more colourful watercolour sketches may have fulfilled a similar purpose.

Turner rarely travelled without a pencil and pocket-sized sketchbook to hand, but increasingly the majority of his watercolour sketches and compositional studies were made in the studio or, when travelling, in his lodgings after a long day exploring and observing. They are filtered by memory, simplified and reconfigured by the physical properties and artist's handling of the medium.[11] Turner's familiarity with the tinted drawings produced by watercolourists of the late eighteenth century informed his earliest coastal marine subjects (for example, [90]), in which the vessels, rocks and trees, and even the principal forms of sea and sky, are delineated in pencil before being modelled with watercolour. *Shipping at Sea, with a Distant Fort* [89], probably made in his early twenties during a journey through Wales (a context that can be gleaned only from the other contents of the sketchbook of which it is a part), dispenses with pencil altogether, replacing line with a succession of increasingly deeper watercolour washes to register in silhouette the position and rigging of two naval ships and a smaller coastal vessel. At first glance, a watercolour thought to represent the Eddystone

Lighthouse [fig. 39] gives the impression of having been made rapidly in front of the subject. It appears in a sketchbook interleaved with numerous pencil drawings of West Country scenes and other landscapes, and is dated (tentatively, as with so much in the Bequest) to the early 1810s, when Turner made several visits to the Devon coast. But the lighthouse (the third, completed in 1759 by John Smeaton) is situated twelve miles off Plymouth, and the image, a night scene, is one of three that show the structure at different times of day and in various stages of a storm. The effect of immediacy is fabricated safely on dry land, heightened by the storm of watercolour that Turner conjured around the remembered outline of the isolated tower.

NEW WAVE

Prominent within the Bequest is a group of late and atmospheric seascapes, painted in oil on board or canvas, that seem to transcend the preparatory function of the majority of the other sketches it includes, and which blur the distinctions between a finished and unfinished work of art, confounding all modern attempts to assign anything as certain as a title or even a subject. They are among the most evocative (and provocative) of all of Turner's productions, and much about them, including the artist's hopes for their future preservation and display, is clouded in uncertainty. They include *Seascape with Storm Coming On* [125] and *Seascape with Distant Coast* [126], two of a series of canvases that were first taken seriously and fully incorporated into the permanent Bequest during the first half of the nineteenth century, having previously remained rolled up in the basement of the National

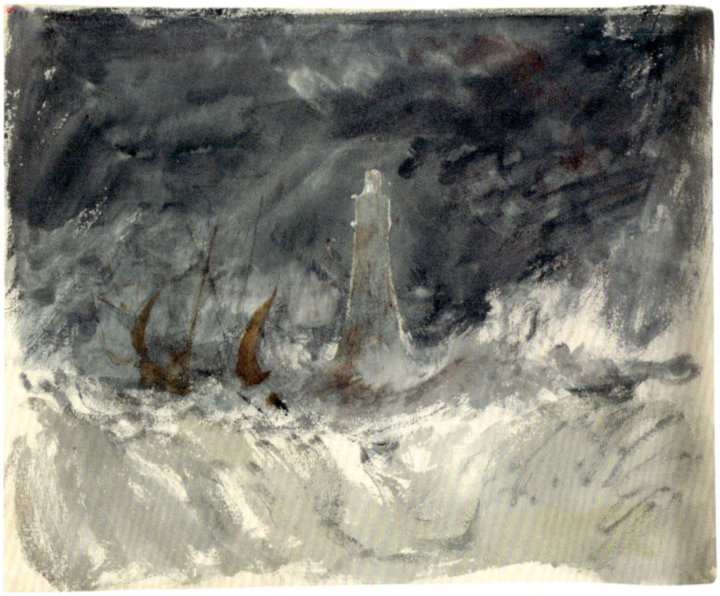

Fig. 39
J.M.W. Turner
Eddystone Lighthouse from the Vale of Heathfield Sketchbook *c.*1810–16
Watercolour and pencil 18.1 x 22.8 (7⅛ x 9)
Tate. Turner Bequest 1856

Fig. 40
John Constable
Rainstorm over the Sea *c.*1824
Oil on paper, laid on canvas
23.5 x 32.6 (9¼ x 12⅞)
Royal Academy

Gallery. These later exercises also include *Calm Sea with Distant Grey Clouds* [123], one of a group of chromatically complex but austere paintings that lay unnoticed for more than a hundred years after the artist's death and which were only formally accessioned in 1972. Other artists among Turner's contemporaries produced oil sketches that are comparable in their expressive power. Constable's open-air study of a thunderous rainstorm witnessed from Brighton beach is a good example [fig. 40], and he, too, could fashion a convincing seascape from little more than a pencil line for a horizon. But unlike Turner's intensely private exercises, such images are more readily identified with the public work for which Constable is better known, often as part of the development of a conventionally 'finished' work of art.

With few exceptions, these late marine studies (usually described as 'unfinished', if only for want of a more appropriate word) focus on that essential maritime motif – the wave. It was a phenomenon that Turner had attempted to capture in countless sketches throughout his working life and which had been a defining aspect of his public seascapes from the beginning. From the luminous, threatening swell of *Fishermen at Sea* [14] to the tumbling wall of water that crashes through *Fishermen upon a Lee-Shore, in Squally Weather*, and to the white, storm-tossed waters of *The Shipwreck* [75], the visible action of the wind and tide was the driving force behind a series of seascapes that effectively reinvented the genre while raising their maker to the highest level of artistic achievement. The hoard of canvases that Turner produced during the last ten years of his life indicate that, towards the end (a period that Ruskin characterized as one of decline and increasing incomprehension), the anonymous, unrelenting churn of the sea became the focus of deep self-reflection.

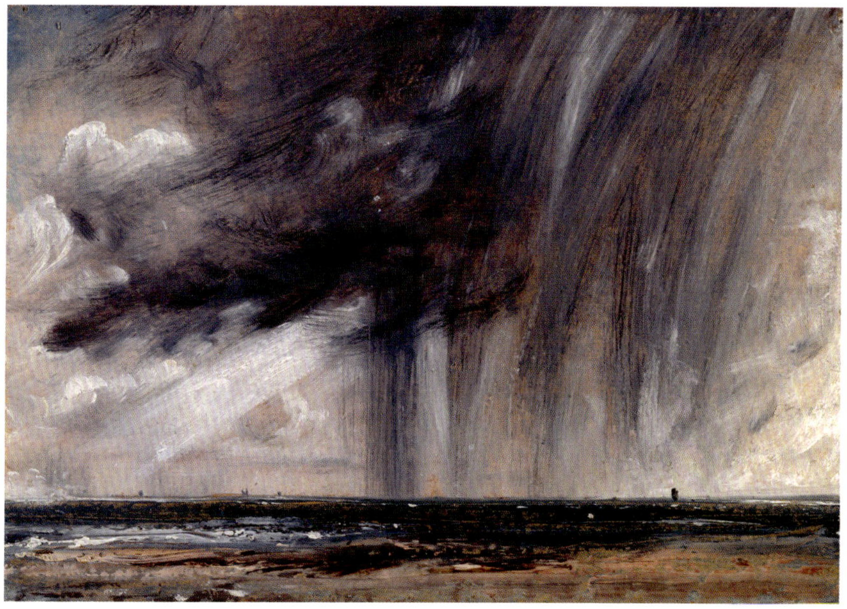

Following the completion of A.J. Finberg's monumental inventory of the Bequest in the early part of the twentieth century, and the physical relocation of the work from the National Gallery to the Tate (then, for several decades, to the British Museum), Turner's private world became the subject of renewed study. As the contents of his studio became more widely known, his posthumous identity was increasingly constructed around the shifting priorities and new formal challenges of the contemporary twentieth-century art world, which valued repetition and championed the abstract, the provisional and the raw as signs of untamed creativity.[12] As a result, a very different artist emerged – one that would have been unrecognizable to his contemporaries. Turner was re-imagined as a progenitor of modern art; first of Impressionism, then of post-war abstraction.

The late twentieth-century reinvention of Turner found its clearest expression with an exhibition curated by Lawrence Gowing and Monroe Wheeler for the Museum of Modern Art in New York in 1966.[13] As one dedicated to an artist who had been dead for more than a hundred years (and who thus lay outside any commonly accepted definition of 'modern' art in 1960s America), the show was unprecedented for MoMA, an institution more readily associated at the time with American abstract work on a heroic scale. Within this transatlantic context, Turner was defined more clearly than ever as a modern creative force. With a strong focus on his late and unfinished work, including a tranche of previously unseen examples from the Bequest, he was presented as an artist whose most vital works explored what Gowing called 'the intrinsic visual character of painting with a directness that anticipated the studies of modern painters'.[14] The re-emergence of a body of later works that appeared to be even more abstracted than anything previously known from Turner only enhanced the notion that he had single-handedly released painting from the conventions and expectations of the Victorian art world: it was as if they had come straight from the artist's studio.

For any historical understanding of Turner's late work such associations are, of course, anachronistic. Moreover, in recent years the twentieth-century reinvention of Turner as a proto-modernist has itself become the subject of historical enquiry, rejected by some as an inappropriate assessment of an artist who remained committed to the traditions and aspirations of the Royal Academy throughout his working life.[15] In 1974–75, two important London exhibitions – one a 'blockbuster' at the Royal Academy – marked the bicentenary of Turner's birth and prompted a renewed interest in all aspects of the Bequest.[16] More recently, with the advent of digital technology and the gradual realization of a long-standing ambition to conserve and catalogue the entire collection, the Turner Bequest is now more accessible than ever before.[17] These near-ideal conditions allow the possibility of a deep insight into the private side of Turner's working life;

the myriad techniques he employed and the papers, pigments and other materials that were available to artists during the first half of the nineteenth century. Nonetheless, the visual challenge of those later, unfinished paintings persists, as does the notion of Turner's instinctive modernity. However misleading, the latter remains attractive (and is encouraged by museums and galleries, and in the media) precisely because the critical apparatus of modern and contemporary art provides a value language that these extraordinary late works otherwise seem to lack. It provides a framework for their intense play of colour as a primary occupation, for the deep engagement with material and process that is evident in much of Turner's studio work, and his fascination with repetition and expressive gesture. The 'indistinct' (especially where it is deployed in such an expressive manner as, for example, in the Whalers Sketchbook [113–116]) has come to define Turner's reputation: restless in his work, ceaselessly creative, and an artistic producer whose output seems to transcend the historical circumstances of its production.

Although Turner is not known to have sold any of his preparatory works, or watercolours or paintings that he might have considered unfinished, a substantial number did find their way into private collections following his death. Of these, several have subsequently been acquired by various public collections (for example, [108 and 118]). More recently, in July 2012, a watercolour study of a storm at sea was sold at auction in London. The grey and blue sketch is comparable in size, tone and style with several of the so-called colour 'beginnings' (for example, [103]) that form part of the Turner Bequest. The sketch was advertised as 'the first idea' for one of the artist's most powerful late seascapes, *Staffa, Fingal's Cave* [128], and much of the pre-sale information directed potential buyers towards this alluring connection.[18] The compositional association with *Staffa*, coupled with an impeccable provenance that reached back to the mid-nineteenth century, ensured considerable interest in the work, and in the event the single sheet sold for a little over £120,000. The exceptionally high critical and commercial value placed on Turner's preparatory works is only partly explained by their evident aesthetic and technical qualities. Equally important is the mythical status of Turner's private studio practice, as a result of which such 'beginnings' have come to represent something essential and immediate about the artistic process. In the context of Turner's reputation as a painter of the sea, it is notable that such a brisk sketch, one of several thousand similarly ephemeral works by him on paper (albeit one of only a few that could ever appear on the market), far surpassed the record amount paid for a finished oil painting by the most prominent and successful marine painter among Turner's contemporaries, Augustus Wall Callcott.[19] If such a disparity tells us anything, it is that history (like the market) is fickle, and that the art of the past is always and inevitably reinvented according to the desires of the present.

89

J.M.W. Turner
Shipping at Sea, with a Distant Fort
from the Dolbadarn Sketchbook
1799–1800
Watercolour 13.1 x 7.8 (5⅛ x 3)
Tate. Turner Bequest 1856

Finberg XLVI 115 a

Turner's economical depiction of different types of shipping in this early watercolour suggests a first-hand knowledge of both the subject and the art-historical tradition of marine painting. It is likely, for example, that he already had a good understanding of the drawing practices of the Willem van de Veldes (the Elder and the Younger), as well as other dedicated ship painters of the seventeenth and eighteenth centuries. By contrast, the distinctive architectural motif in this image is based on a landmark that Turner had never seen in person, the sixteenth-century Belém Tower located a few miles west of Lisbon. He would have been aware of the tower's imposing architecture through paintings and prints by other artists, including his friend, the mariner and marine painter J.T. Serres, who had painted the structure in 1793. Turner also used the silhouette of Belém Tower in one of the later watercolours he painted for Walter Fawkes, *Man-of-War, making a Signal for a Pilot off the Tagus* (*c*.1819, Sheffield Galleries and Museums Trust). His ideas at the time may also have been guided by his friendship with Serres in other ways. In 1805 Serres published the *Liber Nauticus* [18], a detailed instructional manual (based largely on the work and reputation of his father, Dominic), which included several compositional models for aspiring marine painters.

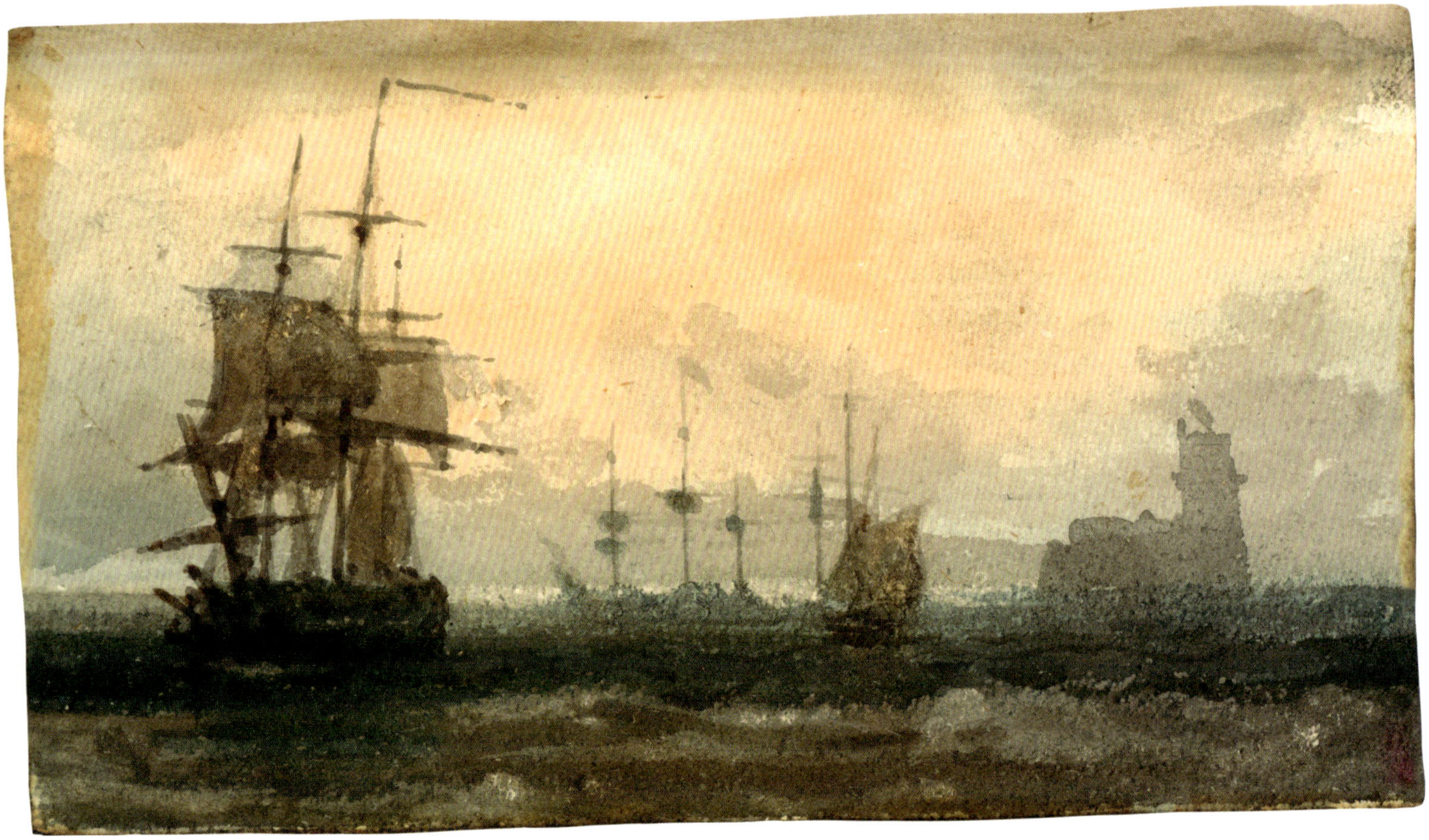

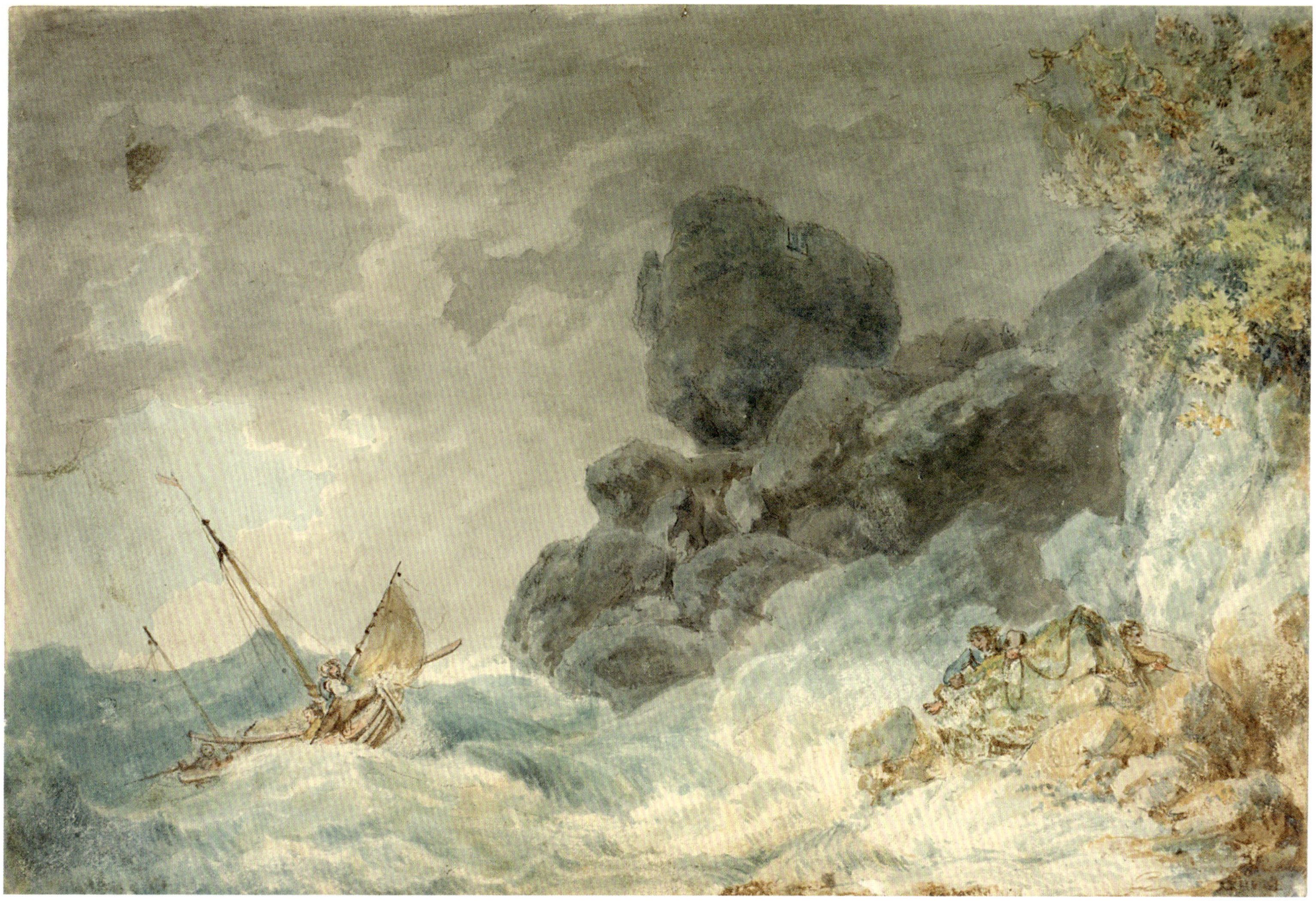

90

J.M.W. Turner

A Rocky Shore, with Men Attempting to Rescue a Storm-Tossed Boat c.1792–93

Pencil and watercolour

16.2 x 23.2 (6⅜ x 9⅛)

Tate. Turner Bequest 1856

Finberg XXIII R

Turner's earliest recorded marine watercolours, produced when he was a teenager, emulate the type of stormy coastal scenes most readily associated at the time with Philip James de Loutherbourg [10]. Turner's practice soon departed from the relatively conventional techniques of *A Rocky Shore*, but the theme of shipwreck and rescue remained prominent in his work over the next fifty years.

91

J.M.W. Turner

Shipping at the Mouth of the Thames c.1806–07

Oil on canvas 85.7 x 116.8 (33¾ x 46)

Tate. Turner Bequest 1856

Butlin and Joll, no. 175

These two unfinished sea pieces, both still in Turner's studio at his death, indicate the different techniques he employed during the early part of his career. Working in oil, he begins with several layers of under-painting: the principal colours are blocked-in over a pale prepared ground, and the sea and sky are modelled with various thinly applied base colours. At this stage, the composition is fixed, but there is more work to be done before the final highlights are added. When working on a much smaller scale in watercolour, by contrast, the artist progresses from light to dark, using the palest wash over the white paper to indicate the sails of the boat in the centre, and introducing successively darker tones, broadly applied, to represent the rolling sea and precipitous sky. In later years, Turner experimented with different techniques across both media in a quest to replicate the spontaneity and indistinctness of watercolour in his larger oil paintings. Both of these works follow a compositional pattern found in several of Turner's early Thames subjects, with fishing and other smaller boats in the foreground and a larger vessel in the middle distance. However, although the oil painting shown here has previously been identified as the Thames estuary off Sheerness, it has recently been suggested by Ian Warrell that the land in the distance is an offshore view of Margate.

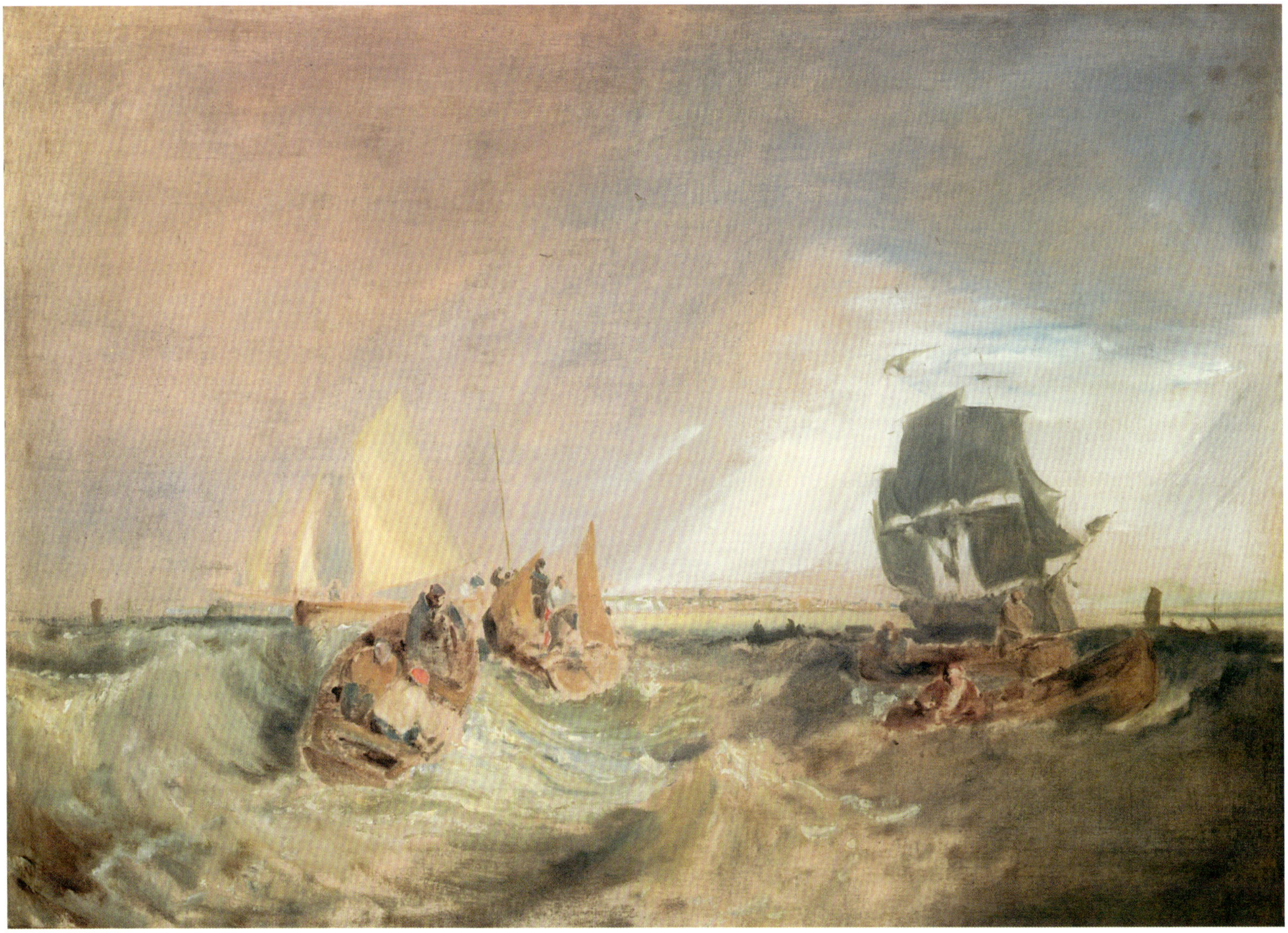

92

J.M.W. Turner

Study for Sheerness c.1824

Watercolour 17 x 24.4 (6¾ x 9⅝)

Tate. Turner Bequest 1856

Finberg CCLXIII 266

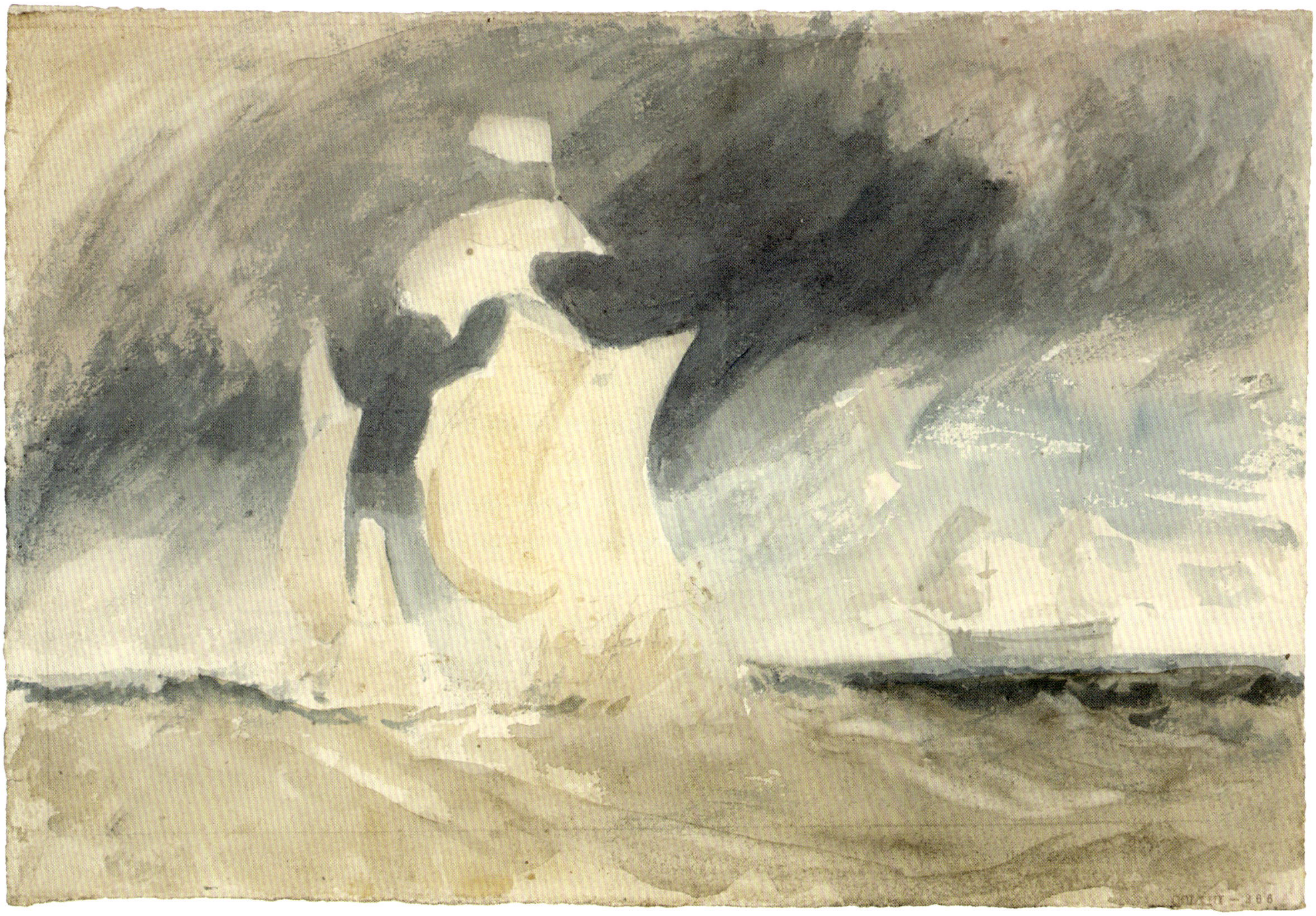

93

J.M.W. Turner

Fisherman Hauling a Boat, with Shipping beyond Breakers from the On a Lee Shore (2) Sketchbook 1800–01
Pen and ink with wash on grey ground
11.7 x 18.2 (4⅝ x 7⅛)
Tate. Turner Bequest 1856

Finberg LXVIII 4

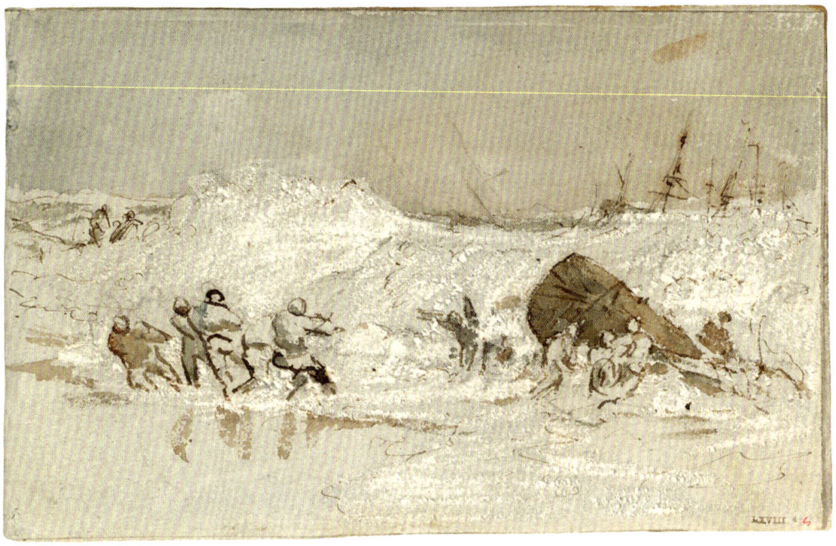

The exertions and perils of coastal fishing were of great interest to Turner for many years. In this shoreline study, fishermen struggle to land on a relatively steep beach, the gradient of which causes the incoming waves to 'dump' onto the shore. Turner scratches through the pre-prepared grey ground to depict the wall of surf that is causing the coastal labourers so much trouble. This and several other studies in the same sketchbook formed the basis of *Fishermen upon a Lee-Shore* [73] of 1802.

94

J.M.W. Turner

Study of 'The Shipwreck' from the Shipwreck (1) Sketchbook *c.*1805
Pen and ink with grey wash
11.8 x 18.5 (4⅝ x 7¼)
Tate. Turner Bequest 1856

Finberg LXXXVII 16

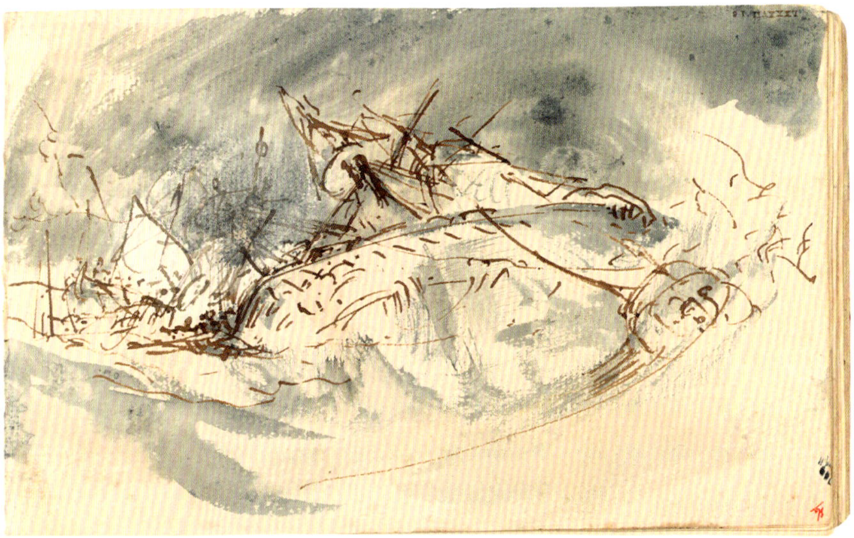

95

J.M.W. Turner

A Shipwreck from the Shipwreck (2) Sketchbook *c.*1805
Pen and ink 11.9 x 18.9 (4¾ x 7½)
Tate. Turner Bequest 1856

Finberg LXXXVIII 17

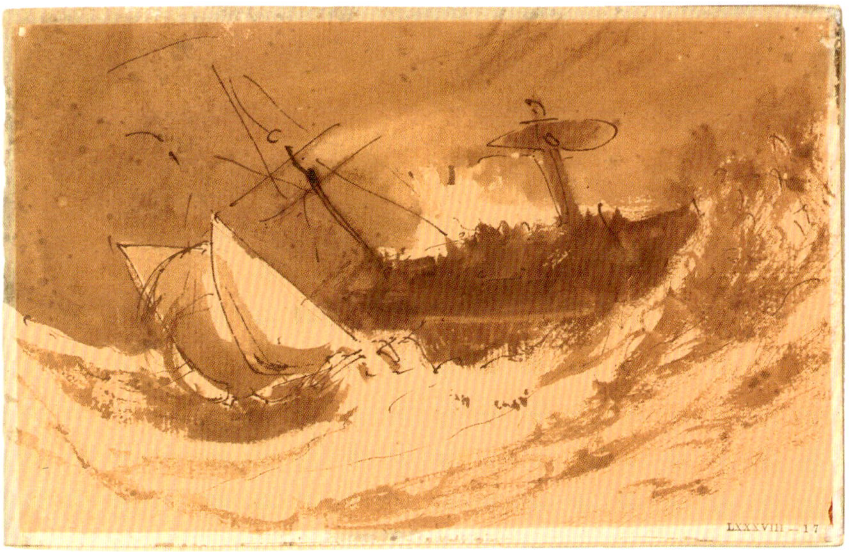

A pair of sketchbooks relating to *The Shipwreck* of 1805 [75] reveal the genesis of one of Turner's most successful early works. Both books comprise a series of compositional drawings showing different stages of a wreck, made as the artist began working on his epic painting. The first includes a list of subscribers to the mezzotint print that Charles Turner made after the painting in 1807. The paper was originally white but has discoloured as a result of heavy exposure to light during the decades following Turner's death.

Three marine studies by J.M.W. Turner

96

Study of a Boat c.1822
Pencil 12 x 20.4 (4¾ x 8)
Tate. Turner Bequest 1856

Finberg CCIII F

97

Study of a Boat c.1822
Pencil 10.6 x 20.4 (4⅛ x 8)
Tate. Turner Bequest 1856

Finberg CCIII G

98

Study of a Boat c.1822
Pencil 10.8 x 20.3 (4¼ x 8)
Tate. Turner Bequest 1856

Finberg CCIII E

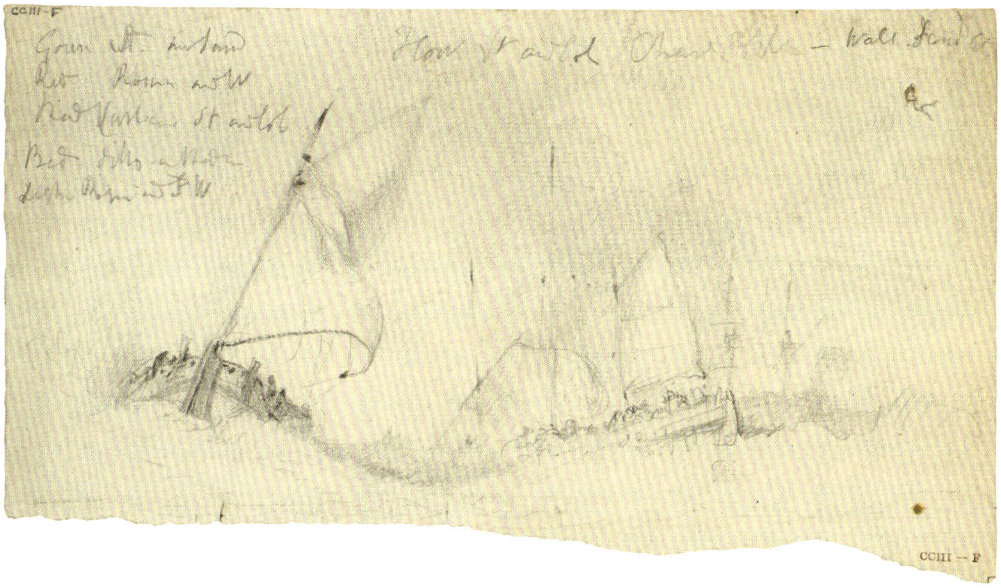

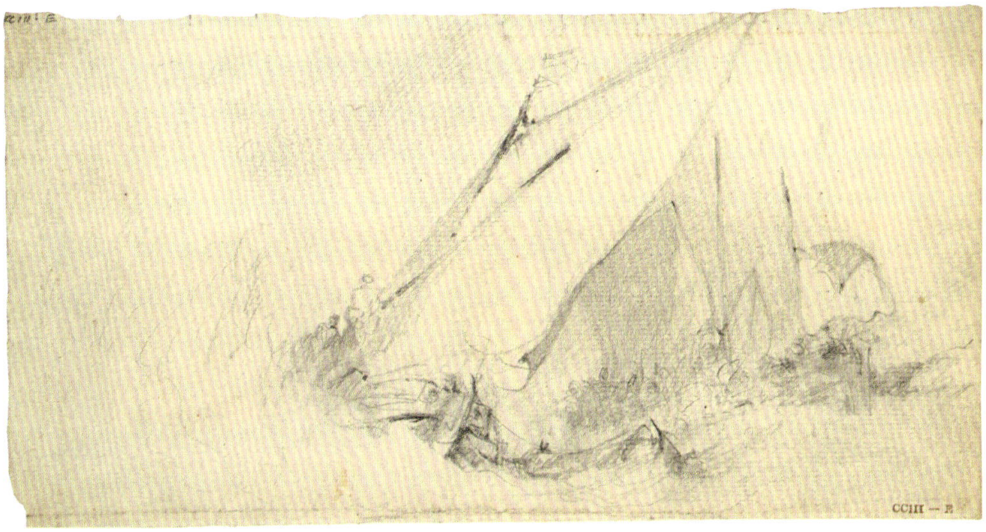

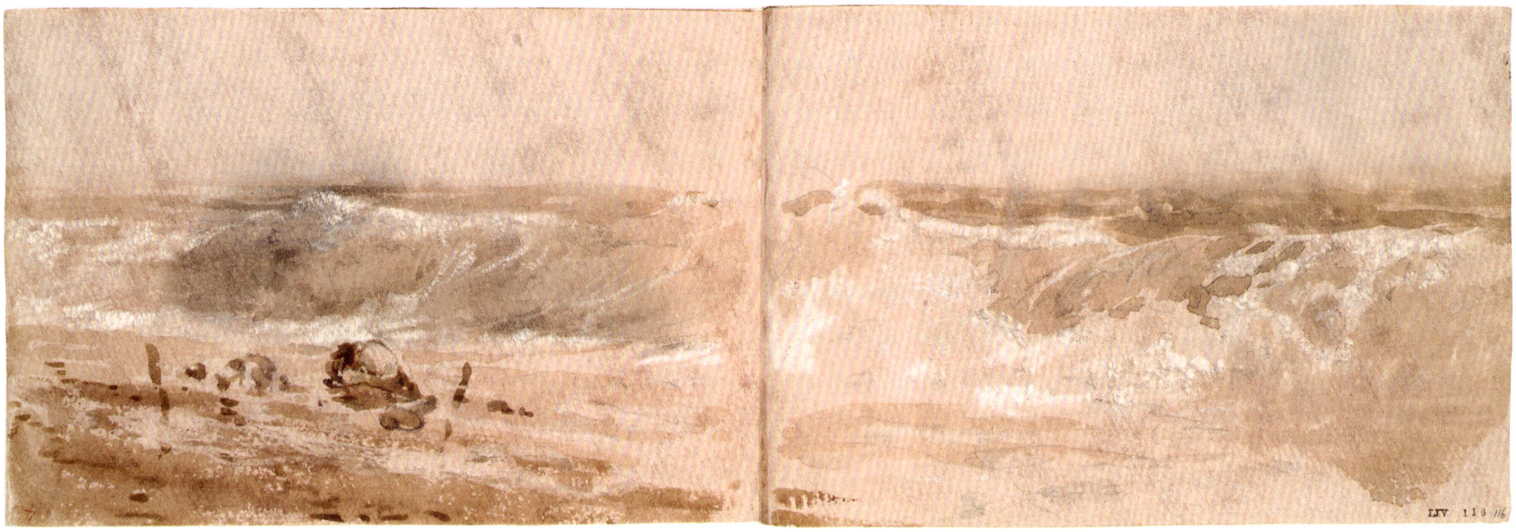

99

J.M.W. Turner

Study of Waves Breaking on the Shore
from the Dunbar Sketchbook 1801
Brown wash on a pink ground
11.5 x 16.2 (4½ x 6⅜)
Tate. Turner Bequest 1856

Finberg LIV 115a–116

Turner routinely experimented with different materials and techniques, tailoring his approach to suit his subjects. During a visit to Scotland in his mid-twenties he prepared the pages of this sketchbook with a rough pink ground, which not only stiffened the paper, making it better suited for outdoor use, but also allowed him to scratch through the tinted surface with the back end of his brush or fingernail to reveal the brilliant white paper beneath. In this way, with a simple brown wash, Turner was able to produce sophisticated observational studies of North Sea waves breaking on the beach. It is an example of picture making at its most efficient.

Few other painters had made such a concerted effort to study the elusive forms of the sea, prompting one writer on art to observe that, before Turner, British artists had habitually painted the sea 'more like japanned tea-boards' than anything approaching the restless 'ever-changing element' (see 'The Battle of the Pictures', pp. 52–55). As a result of his close and repeated studies, Turner ensured that the sea and its forces became as much a part of his pictorial narratives as the people and vessels that trespass across its surface. This early study reveals the artist's interest in the elusive and repetitive rhythm of waves breaking on the shore, an infinitely variable motif that featured in early paintings such as *Fishermen upon a Lee-Shore* [73], and which became the subject of close personal study in his later, unfinished canvases.

100

J.M.W. Turner

Study for a Sea Piece, with Small Boats in Choppy Water from the Calais Pier Sketchbook 1799–1805

Pen and ink with wash and extensive black and white chalk on blue paper 43.3 x 27.2 (17 x 10¾)

Tate. Turner Bequest 1856

Finberg LXXXI 9

The principal purpose of this remarkable drawing is apparent in the swirling, heavily worked and rubbed interlacing lines of black and white chalk, which suggest the surface and depth of a turbulent sea and stormy sky, sacrificing detail for an overall effect of movement. The large-format sketchbook is made with relatively inexpensive blue paper and contains a whole range of subjects: figures drawn from life, details of landscape and mythological compositions, and several studies relating to some of the artist's most important early seascapes, including *Calais Pier* and the early sea pieces he painted for the Duke of Bridgewater and the Earl of Egremont. An inscription in pen on the left-hand side of the drawing shown here reads 'Study not Painted 1805'.

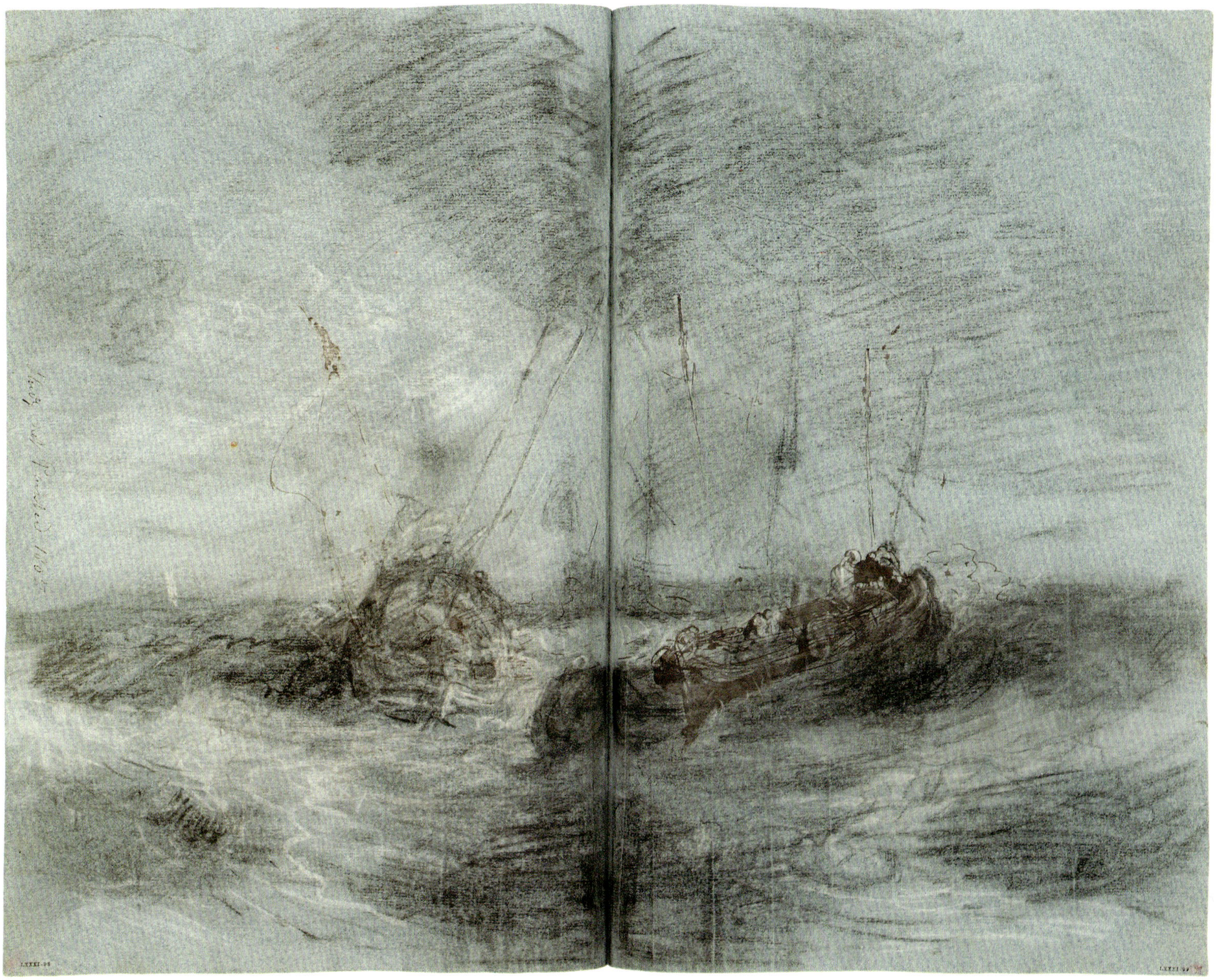

101

J.M.W. Turner

A Sea Piece – A Rough Sea with a Fishing Boat c.1820–30

Watercolour 20 x 29.5 (7⅞ x 11⅝)

Yale Center for British Art

Wilton, no. 767

This poetic preparatory study (a rare example of its kind outside of the Turner Bequest) sees the artist returning to a theme that had provided the subject for his Academy debut in oil [14] and which he went on to explore repeatedly during the first two decades of his career: the plight of coastal fishermen persevering against the elements, never far from danger. Here, the theme is expressed in its simplest form, the principal compositional elements articulated with a subtle juxtaposition of primary colours against a dark, brooding sea.

During the mid-1820s, Turner worked on a sequel to the *Rivers of England* series, six plates of which were published as mezzotints by Thomas Lupton during his lifetime under the title *The Ports of England*. Although it contains no visible landmarks, this watercolour has been identified as one of a group of preparatory works for the *Ports* series, several of which include fishing boats and other vessels teetering on a rough or squally sea in the foreground.

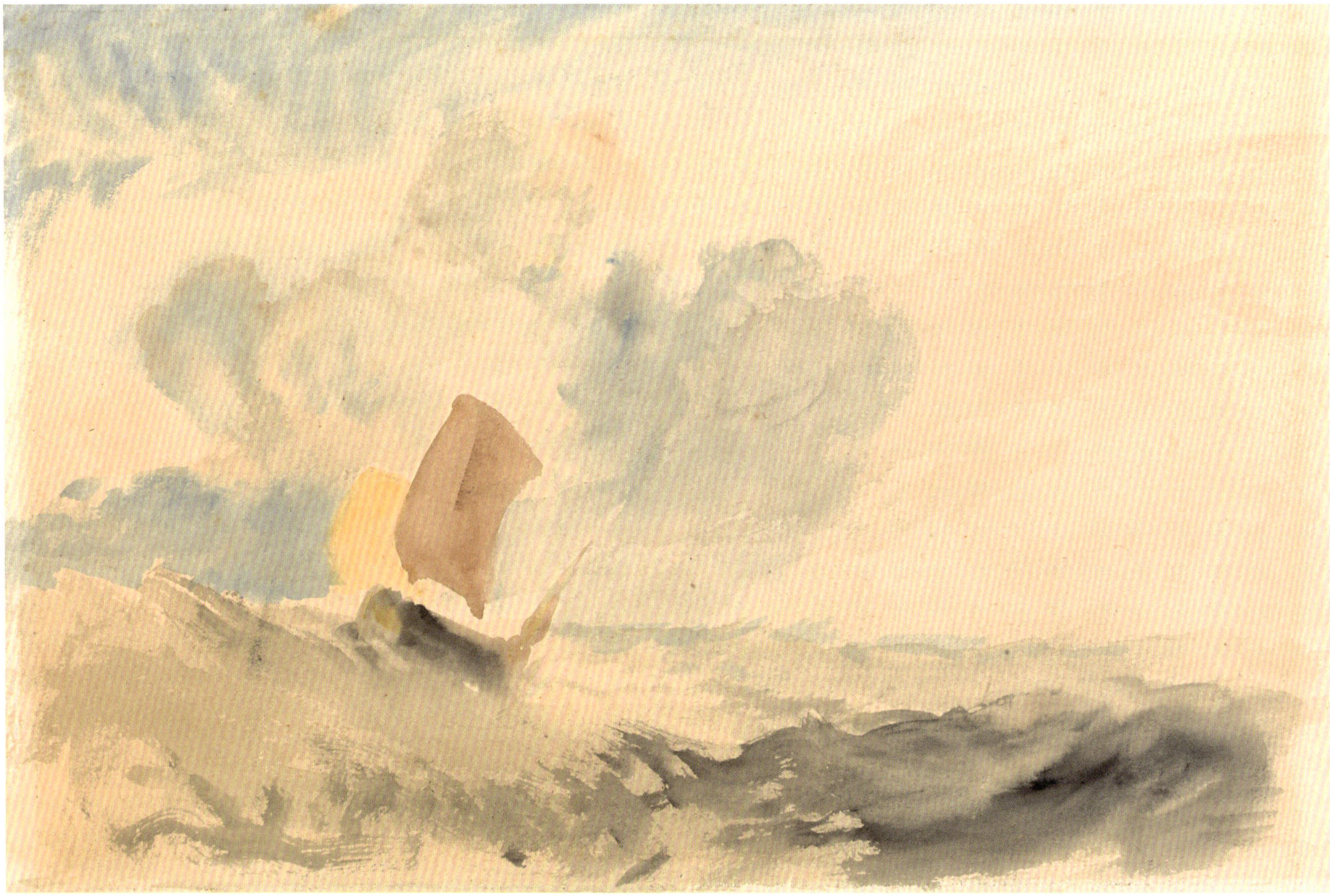

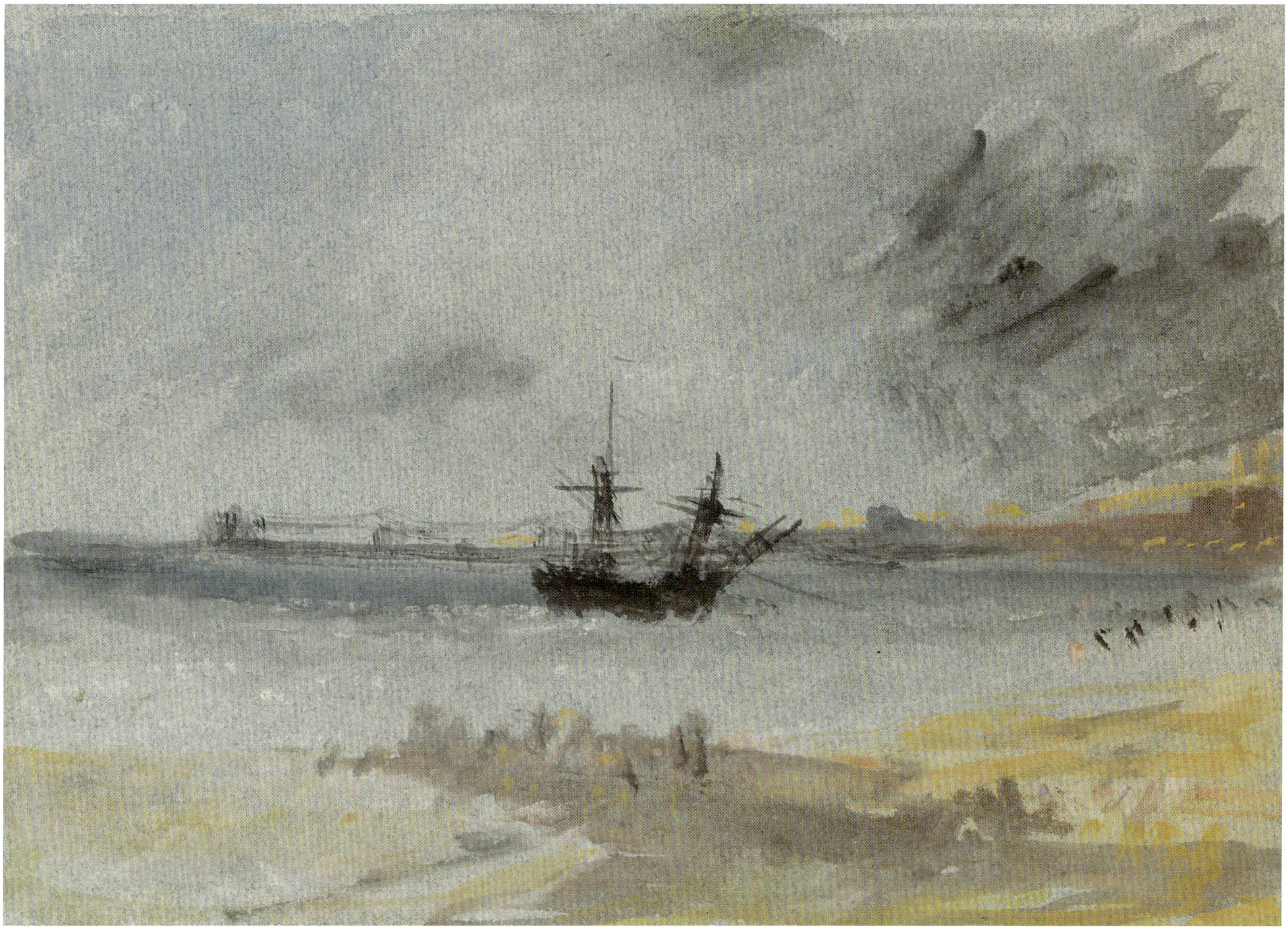

102

J.M.W. Turner

Ship Aground, Brighton c.1828–30
Watercolour and gouache on blue paper
14 x 19.4 (5½ x 7⅝)
Yale Center for British Art

Wilton, no. 917

This is one of over a hundred drawings that Turner made under the patronage of the third Earl of Egremont from 1827, distinguished as a group by the artist's use of paper torn from larger sheets of blue wrapping paper. This unusual choice of material proves especially effective for the marine subjects in the group, where Turner allows the colour of the paper to set the tone of the sea and sky.

Ship Aground, Brighton relates most obviously to *Brighton from the Sea* [fig. 31], one of four finished oil paintings that Turner painted for the Earl's dining room at Petworth House in the late 1820s. In other ways, the theme and composition were developed by Turner a year or two later in his enigmatic oil painting *Fort Vimieux* [fig. 43], which featured in the Royal Academy exhibition of 1831.

This selection of watercolour studies shows Turner at his most experimental. They employ a startling range of colours, from subdued greys to pale pinks and electric blues, and see the artist dragging his fingers across the saturated page, flicking paint from his brush and even immersing the page in water in search of ever more inventive results. By working in watercolour on wet paper (a technique sometimes known as 'wet-on-wet'), Turner allowed the colours to bleed in unexpected ways, creating an ephemeral effect that mimics the fluid interaction of sea and light at different times and in different weather conditions: sky and sea merge, ships and figures are merely suggested, as he focuses entirely on the aquatic possibilities of his medium.

103

J.M.W. Turner
Study of Sea c.1820–30
Watercolour 14.3 x 21.7 (5⅝ x 8½)
Tate. Turner Bequest 1856

Finberg CCLXIII 314

104

J.M.W. Turner
Firing Rockets on the Coast after 1830
Watercolour with pencil 22 x 28.9 (8⅝ x 11⅜)
Tate. Turner Bequest 1856

Finberg CCCLXIV a 134

105

J.M.W. Turner
Ship at Sea c.1830–35
Watercolour and bodycolour with pencil 19 x 27.3 (7½ x 10¾)
Tate. Turner Bequest 1856

Finberg CCLXIII 226

106

J.M.W. Turner
Blue Sea and Distant Ship c.1843–45
Watercolour 28.2 x 44.4 (11⅛ x 17½)
Tate. Turner Bequest 1856

Finberg CCCLXV b 21

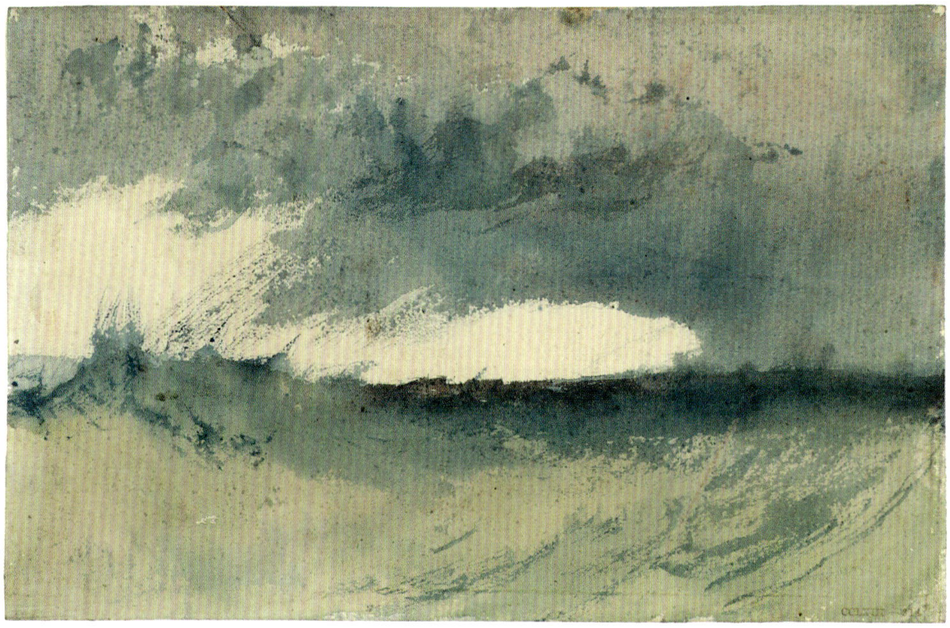

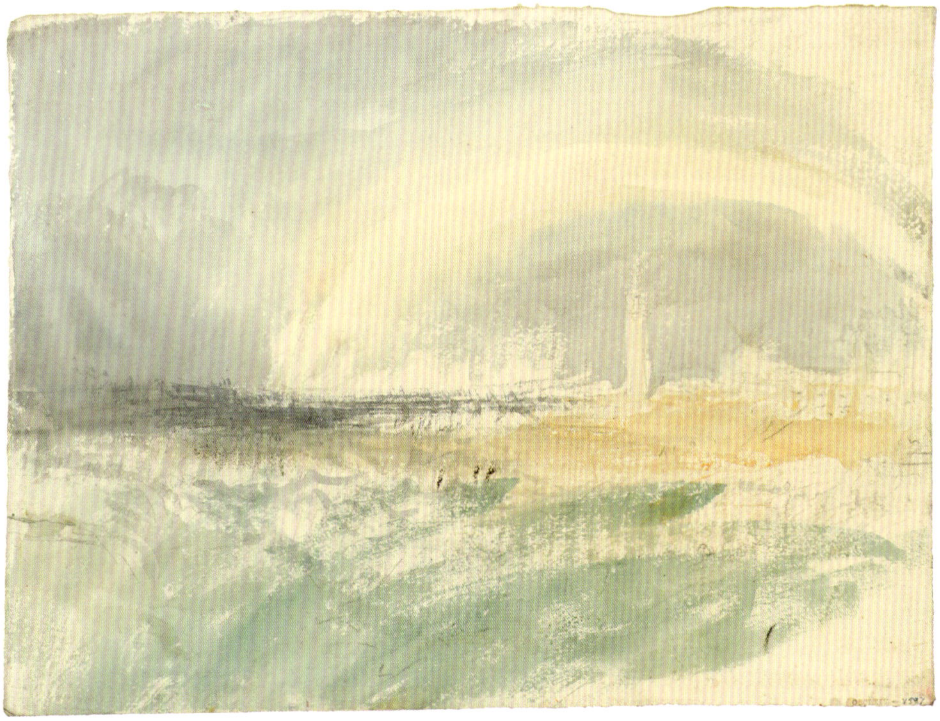

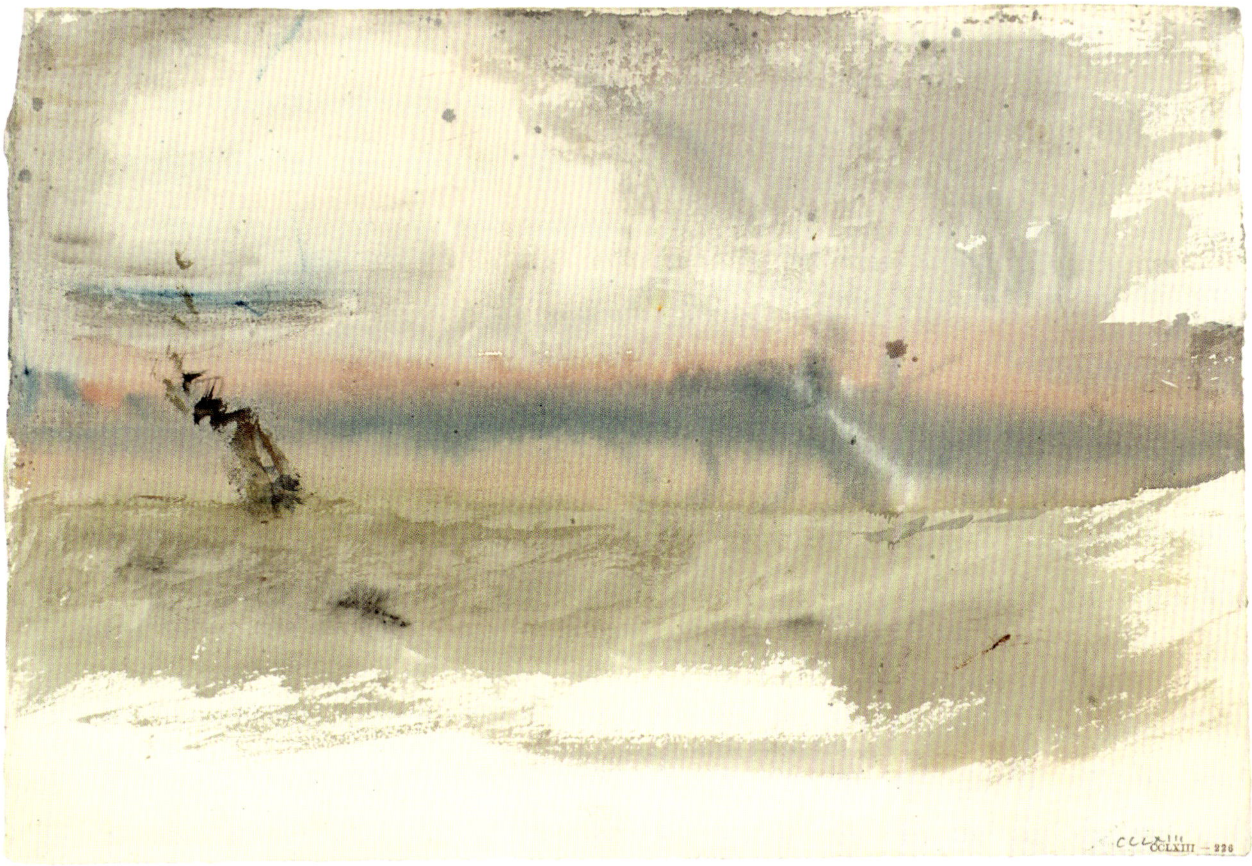

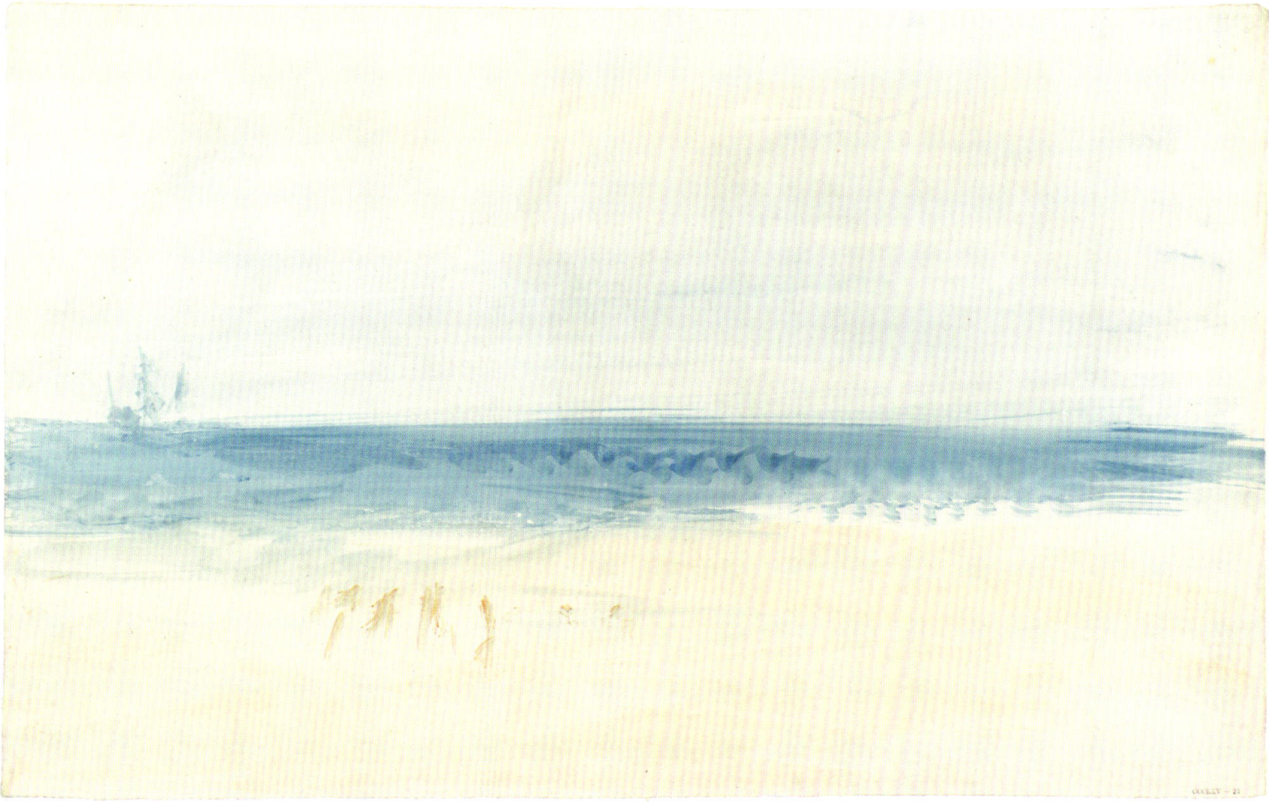

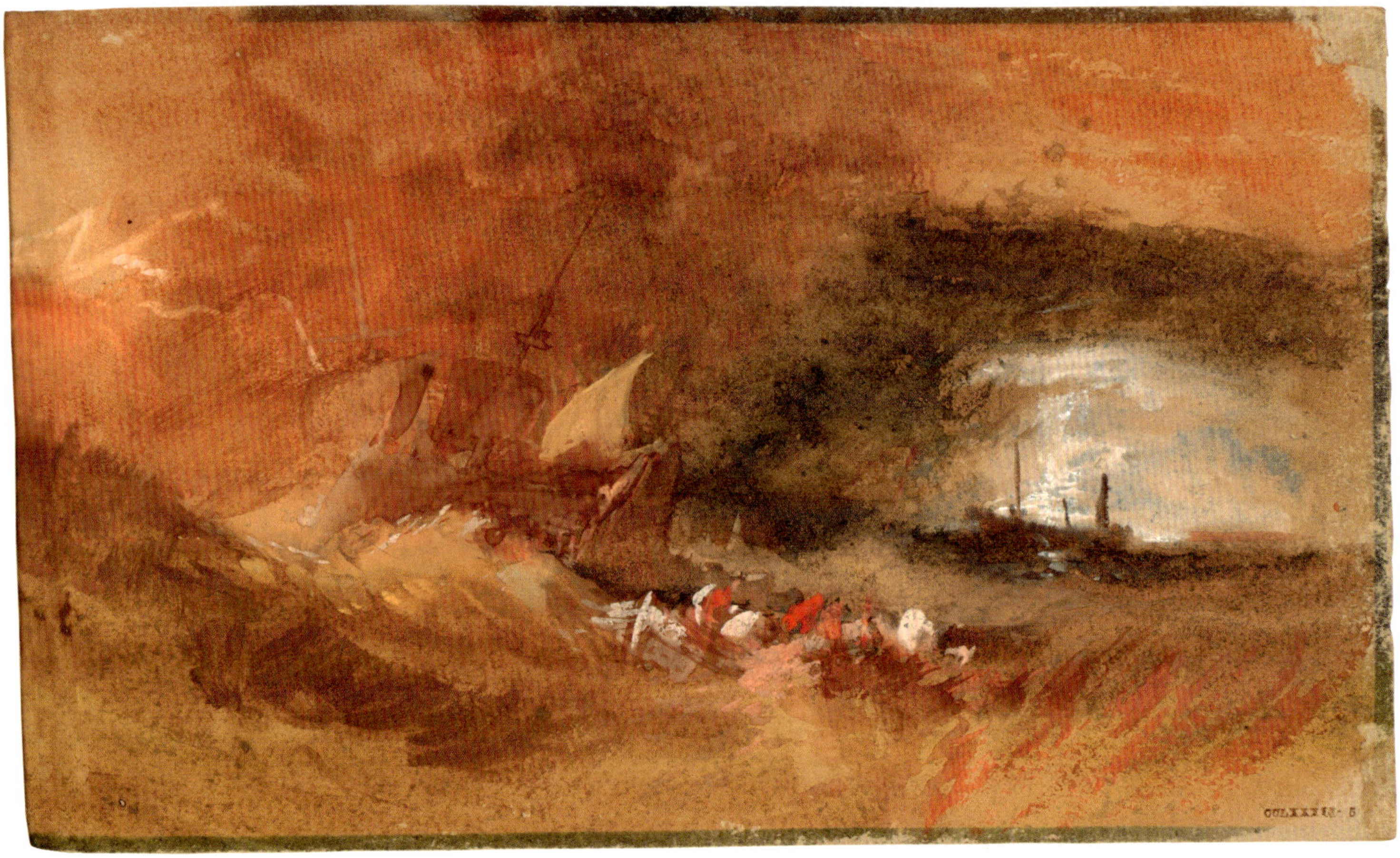

107

J.M.W. Turner
Ships in a Storm, with Lightning from the Fire at Sea Sketchbook *c.*1834
Watercolour and bodycolour
13.9 x 22.8 (5½ x 9)
Tate. Turner Bequest 1856

Finberg CCLXXXII 5

A page from a sketchbook, with a handful of increasingly detailed and violent scenes of a ship on fire after a lightning strike. Despite their small size, they recall the violence and destructiveness of *The Wreck of a Transport Ship* [76] and served as preliminary material for an unfinished painting, *Disaster at Sea* (Tate Collection). The best pages from the Fire at Sea Sketchbook (including this one) were removed by John Ruskin for display over several decades, causing some of the colours to fade.

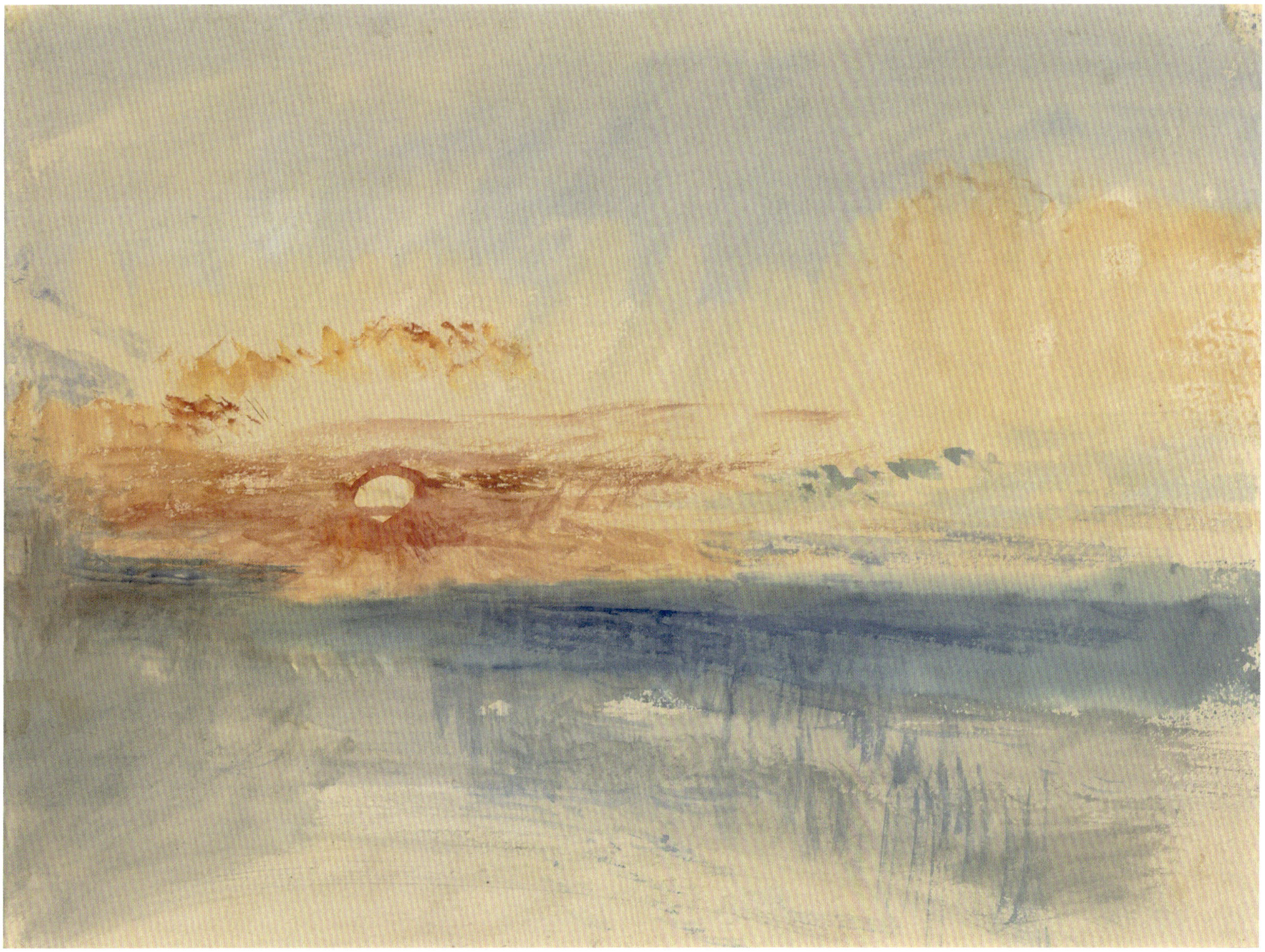

108

J.M.W. Turner

Sunset on Wet Sand c.1840–45
Watercolour 23 x 29.7 (9 x 11¾)
Manchester City Galleries

Wilton, no. 1415

This vibrant watercolour was probably made while Turner was staying at Margate during the 1840s, although the location is not identifiable from any landmarks. However, the sole focus of the image is not the seaside town but the ever-changing relationship between the sea, sand and sun – the chromatic effects of fiery sunlight against the wet sand of a receding tide. The fleeting impression is captured using unmixed primary colours. Though this and other studies like it bear comparison with some of the more colourful of Turner's finished oil beach scenes, such as *Calais Sands at Low Water – Poissards Collecting Bait* (1830, Bury Art Gallery and Museum), it is unlikely that this drawing was made with a finished watercolour or oil painting in mind. Rather, it belongs to a group of reflective studies that Turner made towards the end of his career, after studying the sea for half a century or more.

Four pages from the Ambleteuse and Wimereux Sketchbook by J.M.W. Turner

109

A Storm Clearing Up 1845
Watercolour with pencil 23.8 x 33.7 (9⅜ x 13¼)
Tate. Turner Bequest 1856

Finberg CCCLVII 3

110

Sunset at Ambleteuse c.1845
Watercolour with pencil 23.9 x 33.5 (9⅜ x 13¼)
Tate. Turner Bequest 1856

Finberg CCCLVII 9

111

Storm Clouds, Looking out to Sea 1845
Watercolour 23.8 x 33.6 (9⅜ x 13¼)
Tate. Turner Bequest 1856

Finberg CCCLVII 12

112

A Harpooned Whale 1845
Watercolour with pencil 23.8 x 33.6 (9⅜ x 13¼)
Tate. Turner Bequest 1856

Finberg CCCLVII 6

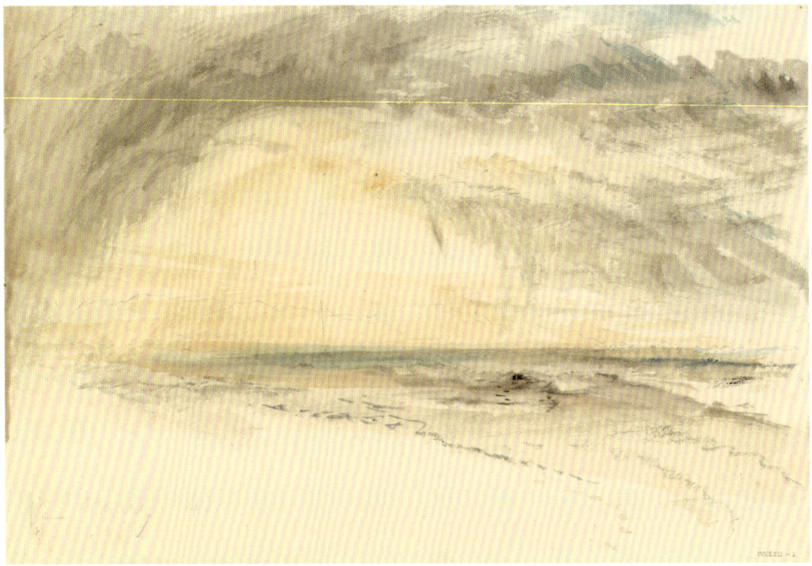

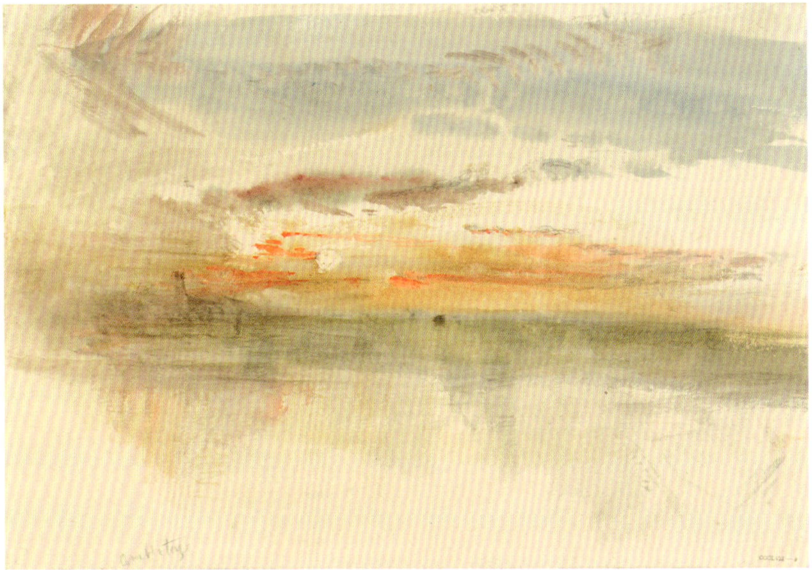

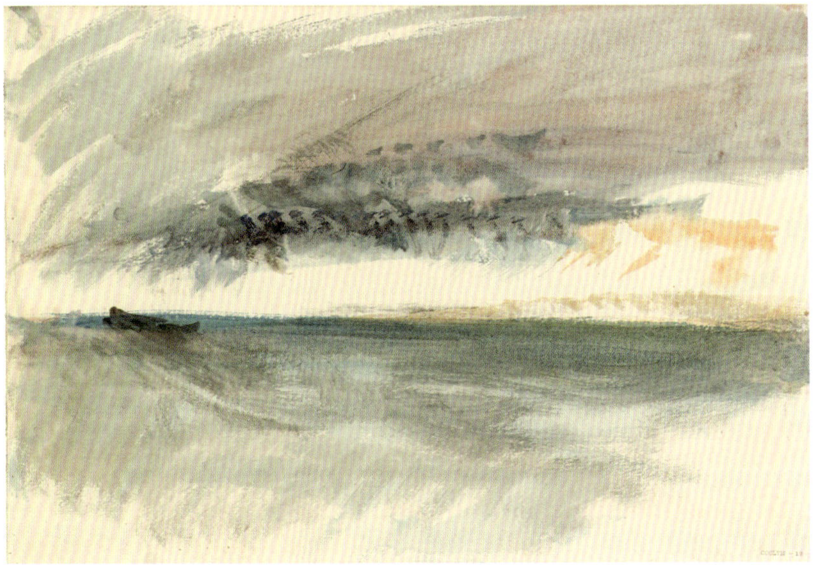

The Ambleteuse and Wimereux Sketchbook includes a sequence of beautifully preserved marine studies resulting from the artist's brief visit to France in 1845 (one of the works [109] is dated by the artist in pencil 12 May 1845). The majority do not relate to finished paintings but seem to have been made as impressions of light and colour, taken from the beach at Ambleteuse. Exceptionally, however, *A Harpooned Whale* also belongs to a series of whaling studies and oil paintings that Turner produced in the mid-1840s [139]. In this study, the tail of one whale lashes the air. Another lunges forward as flashes of blood-red pigment stain the otherwise pale page. It is inscribed in Turner's hand: 'I shall use this'.

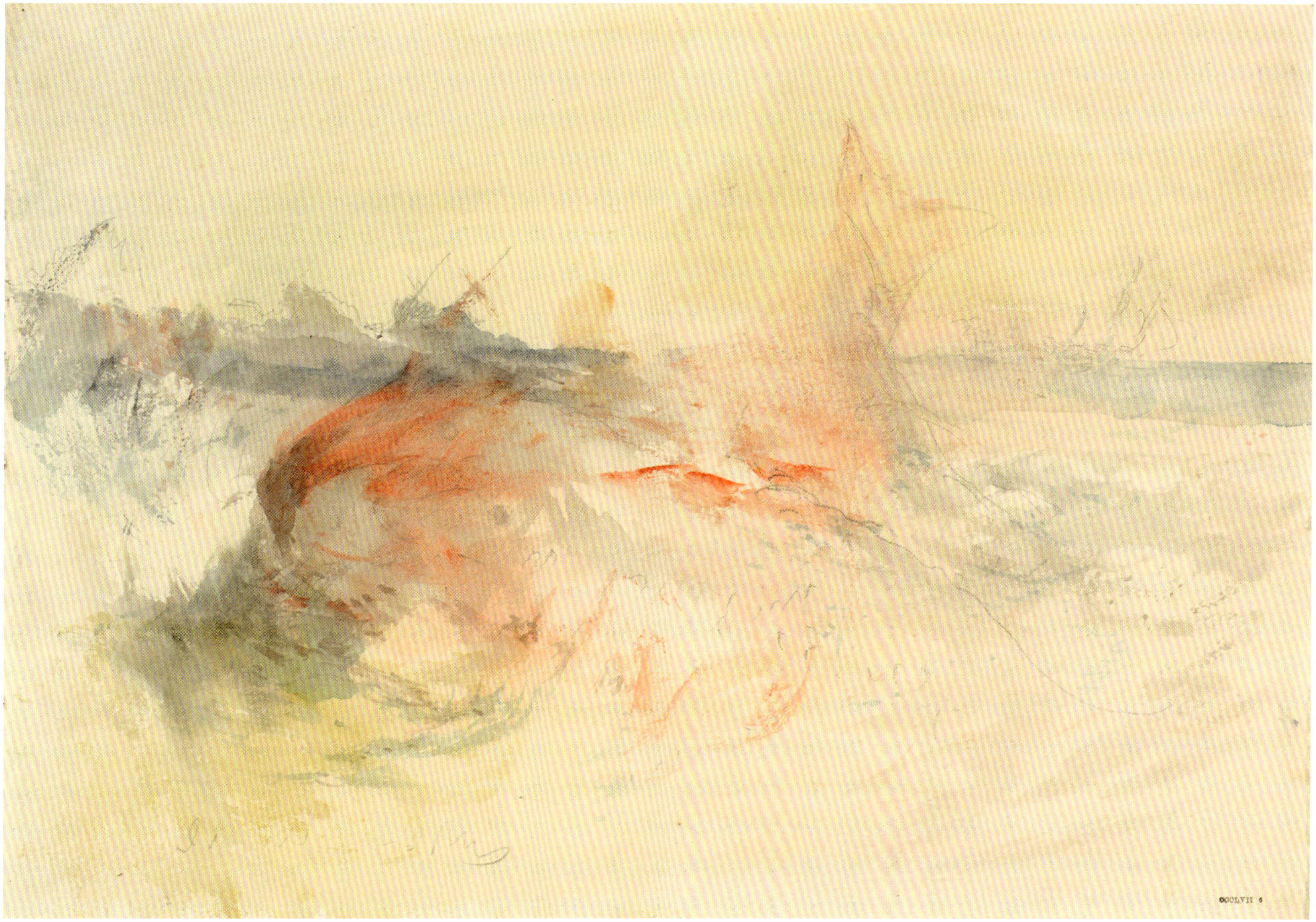
CCCLVII 6

Four pages from the Whalers Sketchbook by J.M.W Turner

113

Whalers at Sea at Sunset c.1845
Chalk and watercolour 22.2 x 33 (8¾ x 13)
Tate. Turner Bequest 1856

Finberg CCCLIII 11

114

Whalers at Sea c.1845
Chalk and watercolour 22.2 x 33 (8¾ x 13)
Tate. Turner Bequest 1856

Finberg CCCLIII 12

115

Sea Piece with Figures in the Foreground c.1845
Chalk and watercolour 22.1 x 33.1 (8¾ x 13)
Tate. Turner Bequest 1856

Finberg CCCLIII 13

116
Whalers c.1845
Chalk and watercolour 22.1 x 32.9 (8¾ x 13)
Tate. Turner Bequest 1856

Finberg CCCLIII 14

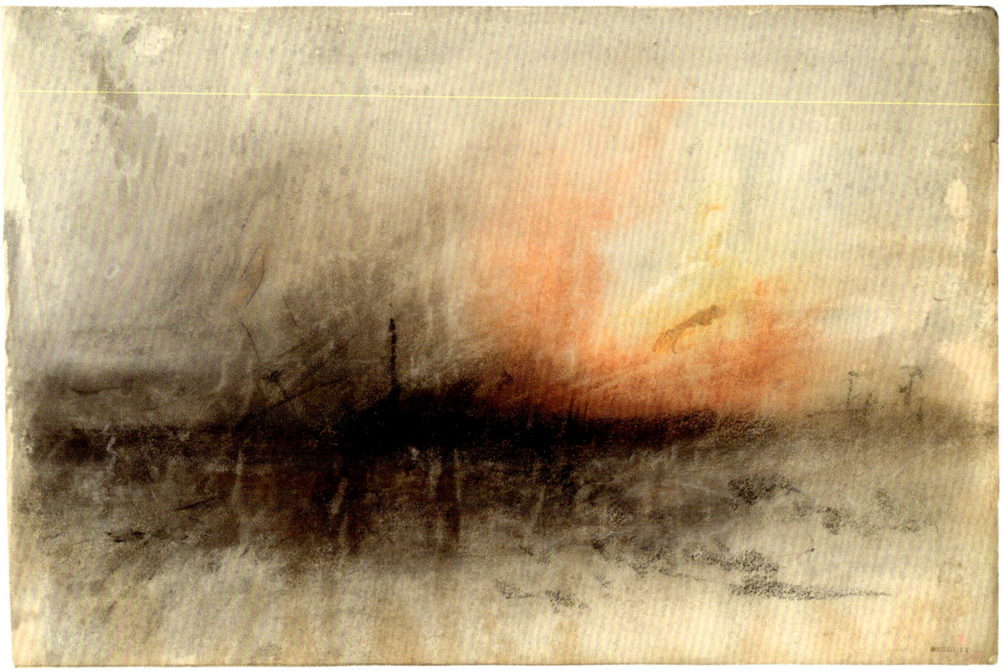

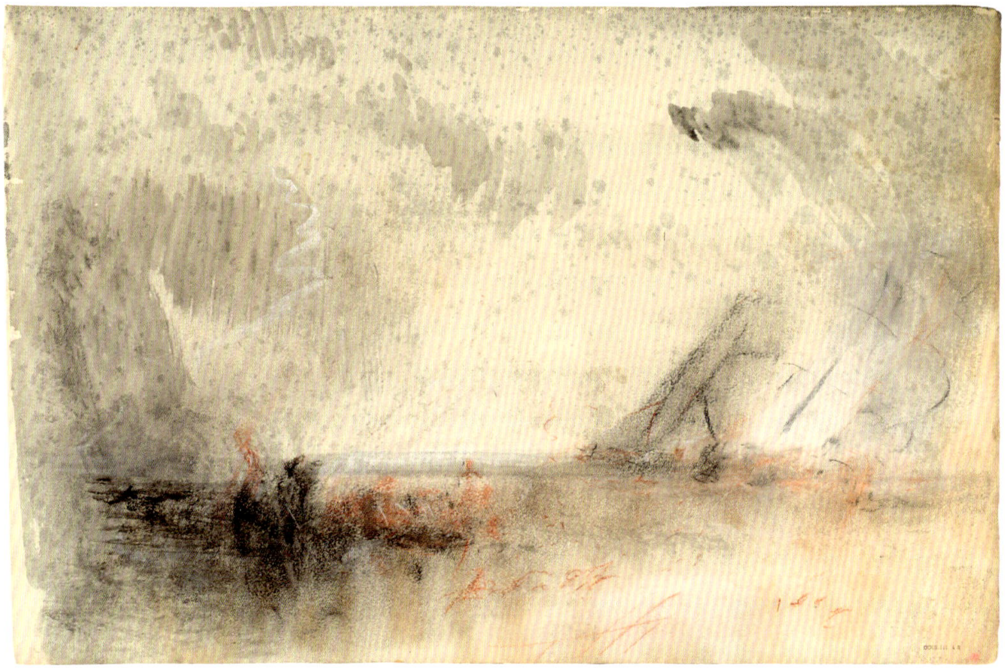

Four pages from a sketchbook that originally included sixteen mixed-media studies of a whale hunt, made in preparation for a series of finished oil paintings that Turner produced in the 1840s. Although individual images are hard to discern, his use of different coloured chalks combined with watercolour washes effectively conveys the urgency and underlying violence of the hunt. The whale itself remains elusive. The indistinctness of Turner's images has been exaggerated by water damage and subsequent spotting, caused by the Thames flood of 1928.

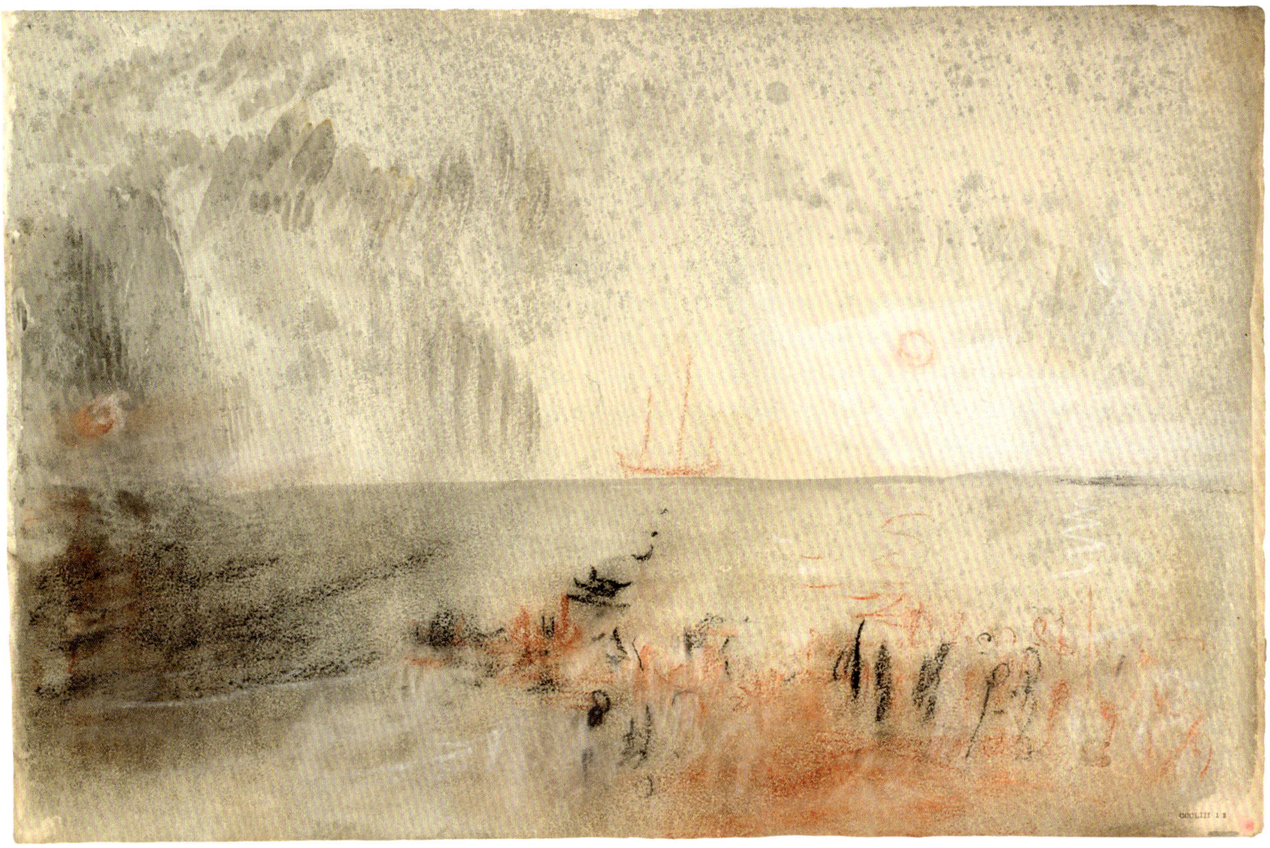

117

J.M.W. Turner
A Steamer off Ostend c.1840
Watercolour 24.8 x 36.4 (9¾ x 14⅜)
National Museums Liverpool

Wilton, no. 1409; Feather 2010, p. 200

For many years this moody, indistinct watercolour was thought to represent the Yarmouth Roads anchorage off the Norfolk coast. However, the distant shoreline has recently been associated with *Ostend* (Neue Pinakothek, Munich), an oil painting that Turner exhibited in 1844, and with a small group of views that the artist made while passing through that Flemish port town on his return journey from a tour of the Continent in the summer of 1840. The precise location is of secondary importance to the combined effects of sea, sunlight and smoke – the last produced by the steamboat on the far left of the picture. These details, together with the relatively dark tones used, also call to mind one of Turner's most contentious paintings, exhibited around the same time, *Snow Storm – Steam-Boat off a Harbour's Mouth* [131] (Warrell 2007, p. 192).

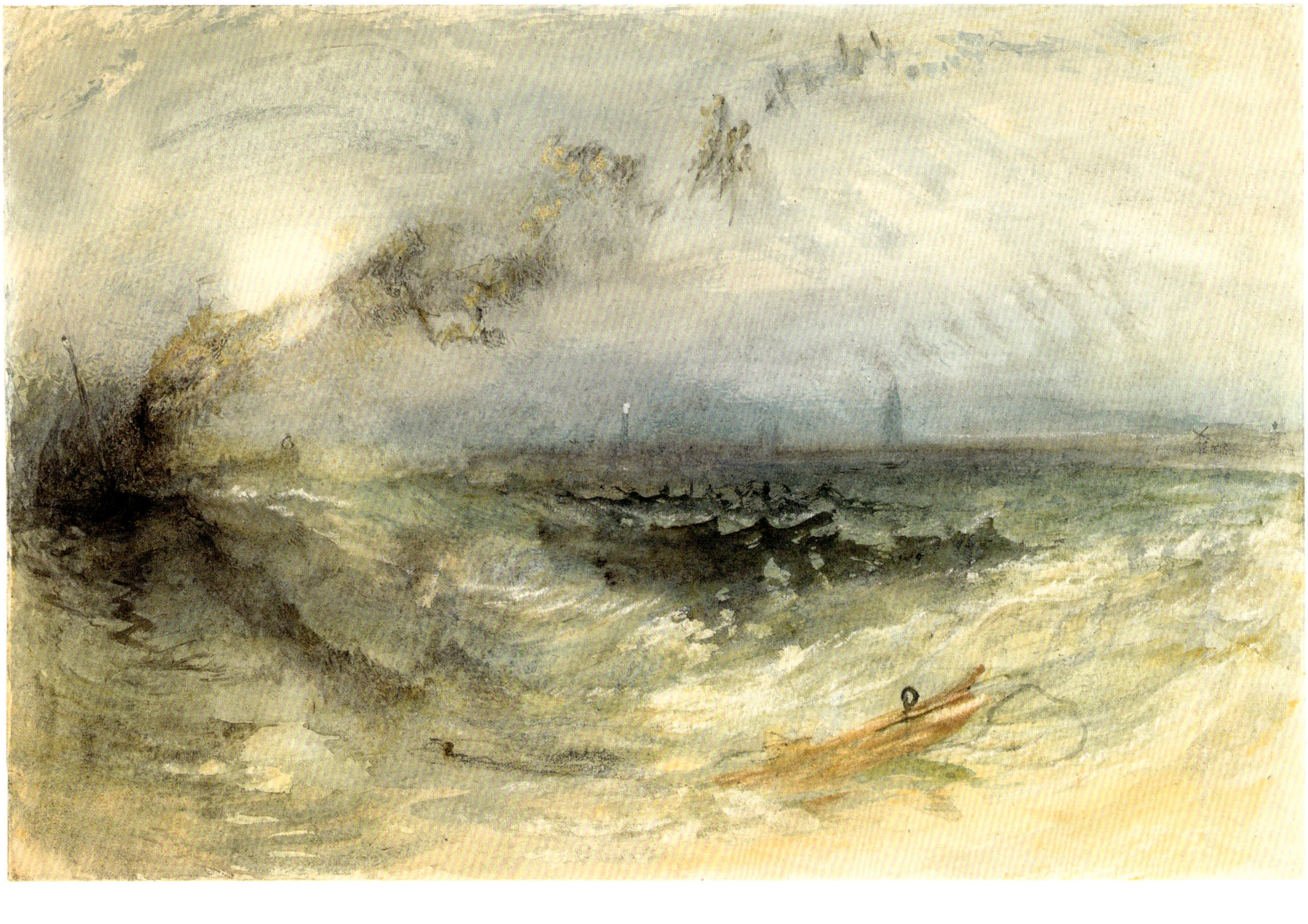

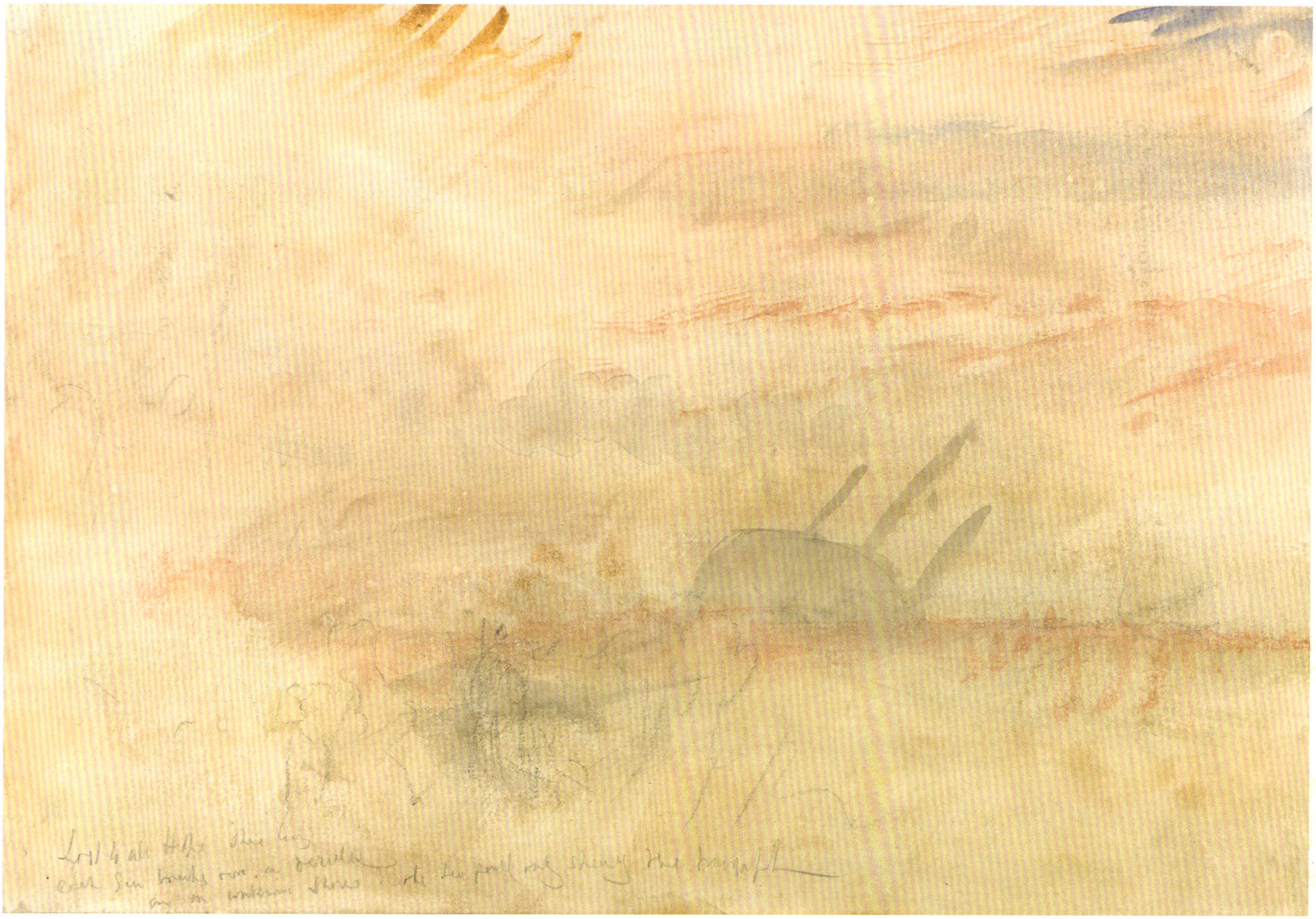

118

J.M.W. Turner

Lost to All Hope *c.*1845–50

Watercolour with pencil 22.9 x 32.4 (9 x 12¾)

Yale Center for British Art

Wilton, no. 1425

A poetic reflection on a theme that had occupied Turner throughout his career, this sparse image of a wrecked and abandoned ship is given greater pathos by a fragmentary inscription scrawled along the lower left of the page. Written in the artist's hand, it reads: 'Lost to all Hope she lies / each sea breaks over a derelict / on an unknown shore the sea folk only sharing the triumph'. The use of slightly tinted paper enhances the melancholic mood of the scene, giving the sky a pinkish undertone, against which the broken vessel is suggested with a light grey wash, with three bare poles for the spars. Even less distinct are the figures in the foreground (the 'sea folk' identified in Turner's inscription), who are merely suggested by a few pencil marks.

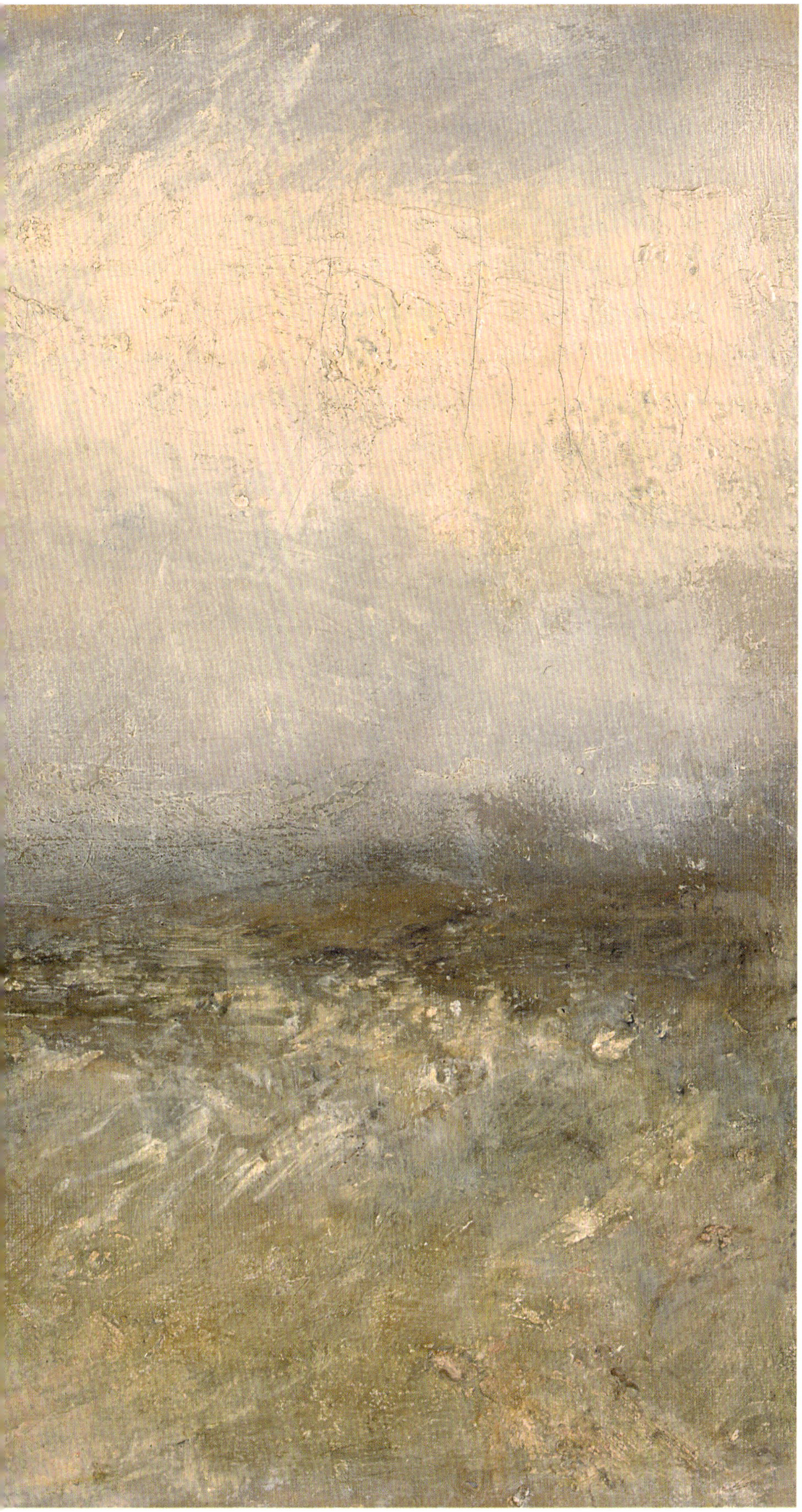

119

J.M.W. Turner
Off the Nore: Wind and Water c.1840–45
Oil on paper, laid on canvas 30.5 x 46
(12 x 18⅛)
Yale Center for British Art

Butlin and Joll, no. 476

Painted on paper that has been mounted on canvas and framed, this work exemplifies the blurring between finished and unfinished in Turner's later work – a difference of perception that has as much to do with the presentation of a work and the expectations of the viewer as with the intentions of the artist. Although this example includes no discernible topographical markers, the modern title associates the work with the mouth of the Thames and with a series of earlier paintings that helped to define Turner's reputation around the turn of the nineteenth century (see, for example, [78]). Before it was acquired for the Paul Mellon Collection in 1978, *Off the Nore* was thought to be lost; it was last sighted at the turn of the century and thereafter known only from a photograph.

Four marine oil sketches by J.M.W. Turner

These belong to a group of fourteen oil sketches that lay unnoticed among the Turner Bequest until the 1960s, when they were rediscovered in a parcel of uncatalogued material. Together with the artist's unfinished oil paintings and last watercolour studies, they have been celebrated as among his most innovative works. In their extreme abstraction they relate broadly to some of Turner's later exhibited seascapes, such as *Rockets and Blue Lights (Close at Hand) to Warn Steam Boats of Shoal Water* [130], and confirm the importance of the sea – now virtually devoid of meaningful human activity – as a focus for his imagination. Whether or not Turner intended them to be seen, or even kept beyond his lifetime, they encapsulate the extraordinary breadth of his long career as a painter of the sea.

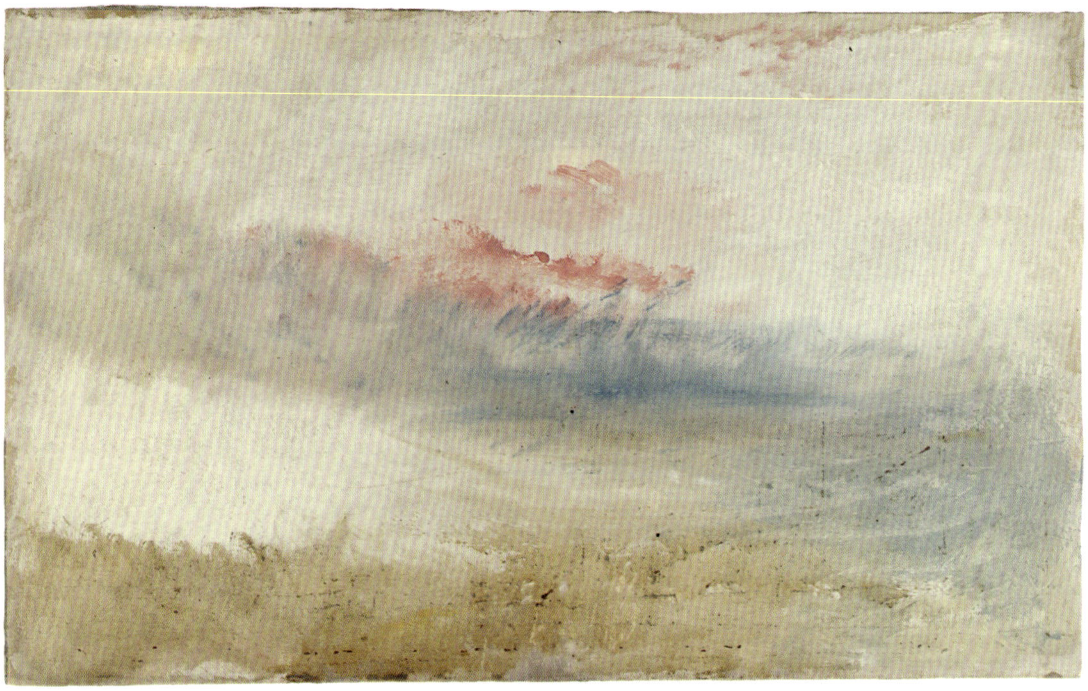

120

Red Sky over a Beach c.1840–45
Oil on board 30.5 x 48 (12 x 18⅞)
Tate. Turner Bequest 1856

121

Ship in a Storm c.1840–45
Oil on board 30.3 x 47.6 (11⅞ x 18¾)
Tate. Turner Bequest 1856

122

Sea and Sky c.1840–45
Oil on board 30 x 45.9 (11¾ x 18⅛)
Tate. Turner Bequest 1856

123

Calm Sea with Distant Grey Clouds c.1840–45
Oil on board 30.1 x 48 (11⅞ x 18⅞)
Tate. Turner Bequest 1856

Butlin and Joll, nos 488–490 and 492;
Parris 1999, nos 4–6

124

J.M.W. Turner
Waves Breaking against the Wind c.1840
Oil on canvas 60.4 x 95 (23¾ x 37⅜)
Tate. Turner Bequest 1856

Butlin and Joll, no. 457

Among the contents of Turner's studio at the end of his life were several enigmatic canvases that relate closely to the many watercolour studies he made during the 1830s and 1840s. These works eschew the usual perspectival and compositional conventions that allow a painting to be 'read' as a view into pictorial space. Instead they favour a more immersive experience, shaped by subtle changes of colour, with light surface touches that merely indicate the forms of sea and sky – unconventional methods that found a fuller, more public expression in some of Turner's last exhibited works.

Although the precise circumstances in which these canvases were made remains elusive – even their assumed date is informed by a modern interpretation of Turner's progression towards ever more impressionistic and abstract forms – it is likely that they include some of his final work. Whether Turner regarded them as works-in-progress, stand-alone experiments, or unfinished and abandoned canvases, they attest to the extraordinary path that his career had followed, leaving the impression of a lifelong creative engagement with the sea that remained, inevitably, incomplete.

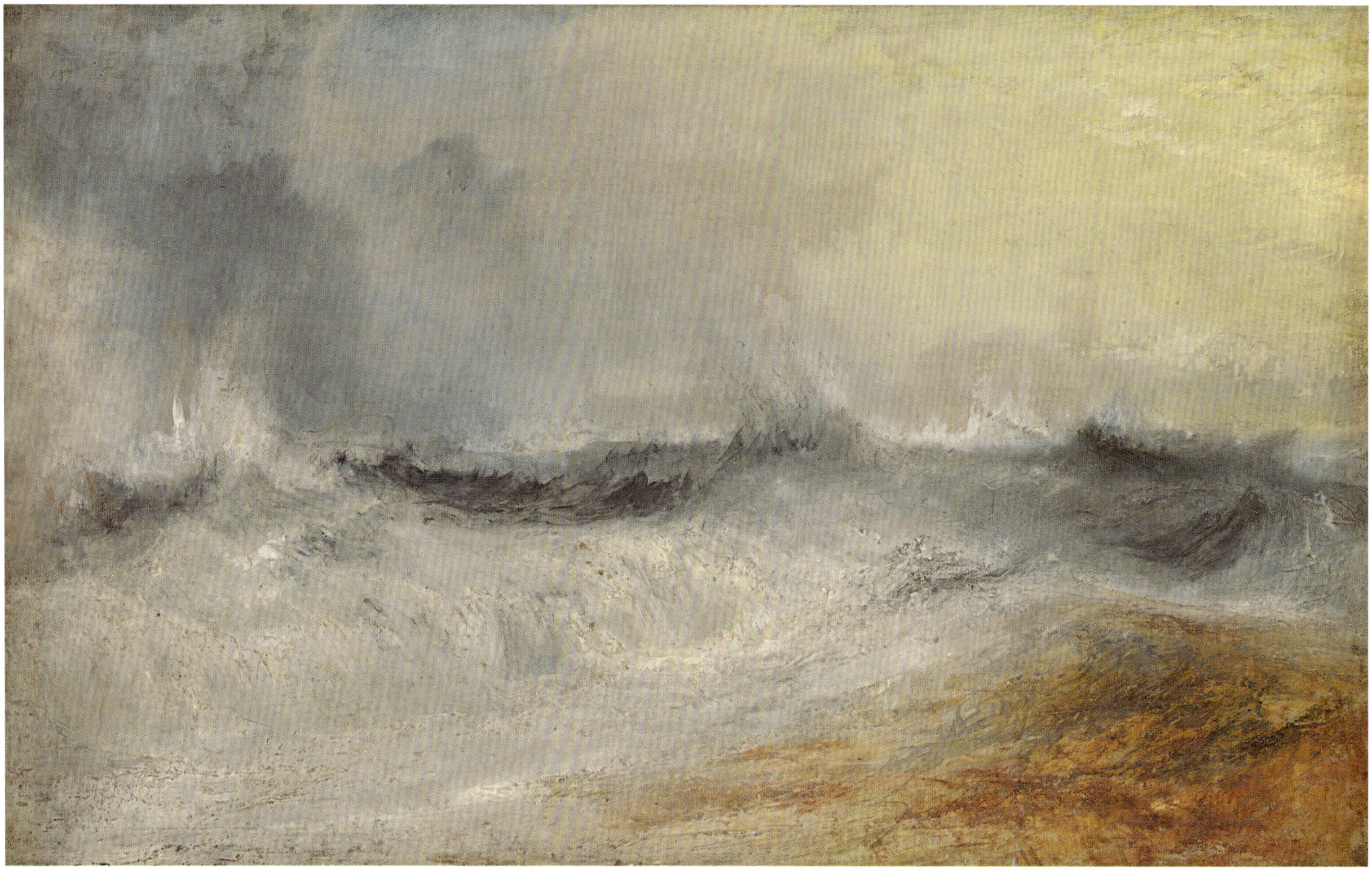

125

J.M.W. Turner

Seascape with Storm Coming On c.1840

Oil on canvas 91.4 x 121.6 (36 x 47⅞)

Tate. Turner Bequest 1856

Butlin and Joll, no. 466

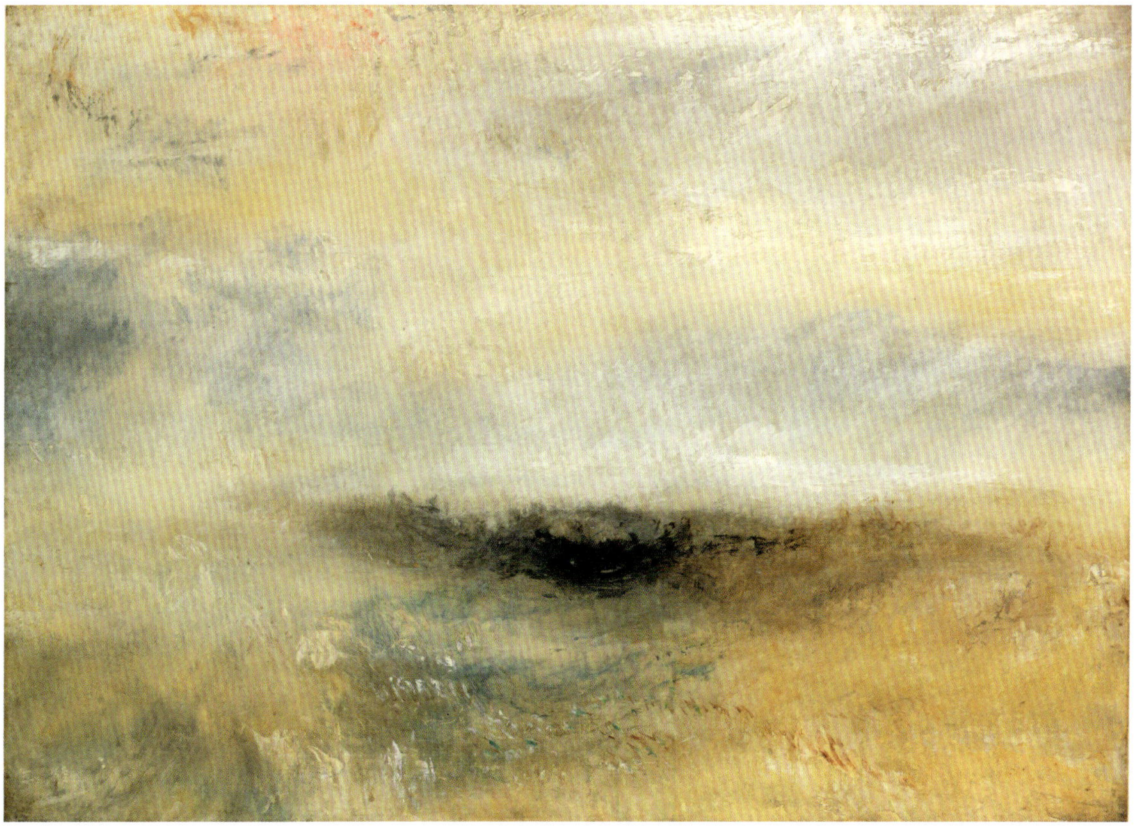

126

J.M.W. Turner

Seascape with Distant Coast c.1840

Oil on canvas 91.4 x 121.9 (36 x 48)

Tate. Turner Bequest 1856

Butlin and Joll, no. 467

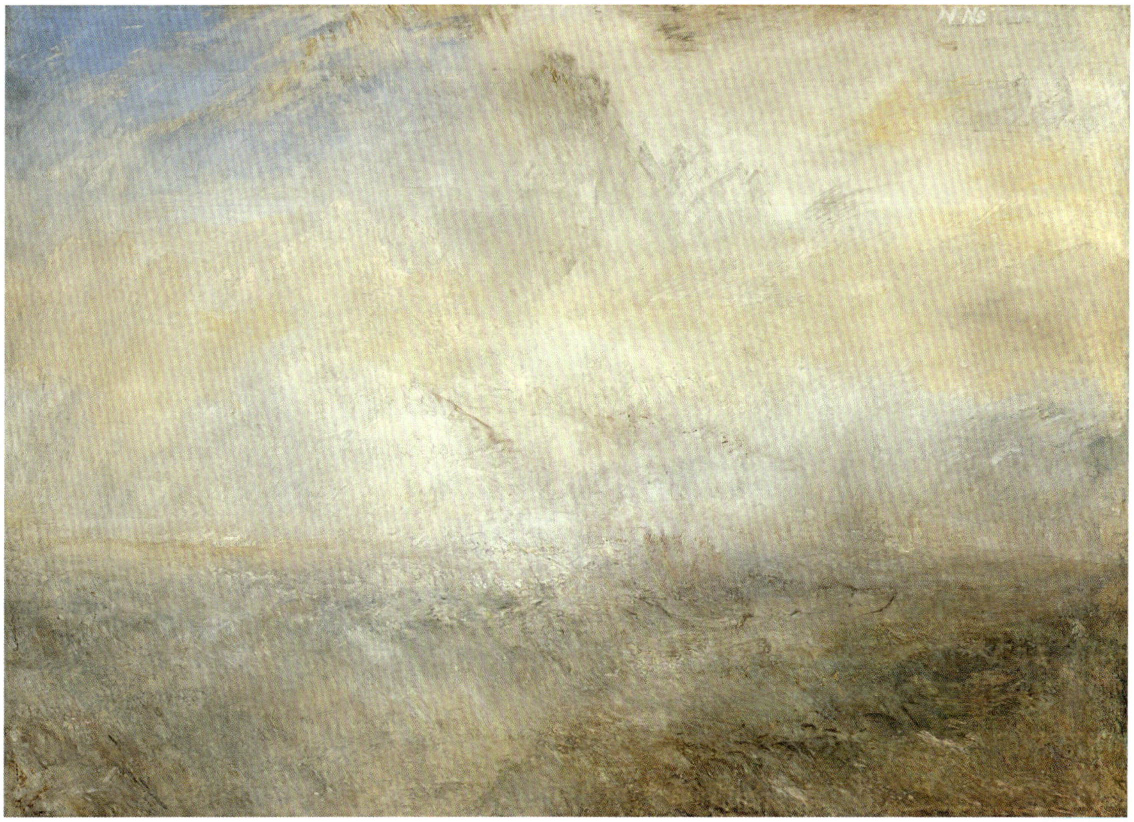

127

J.M.W. Turner
A Wreck, with Fishing Boats c.1840–45
Oil on canvas 91.4 x 122.2 (36 x 48⅛)
Tate. Turner Bequest 1856

Butlin and Joll, no. 470

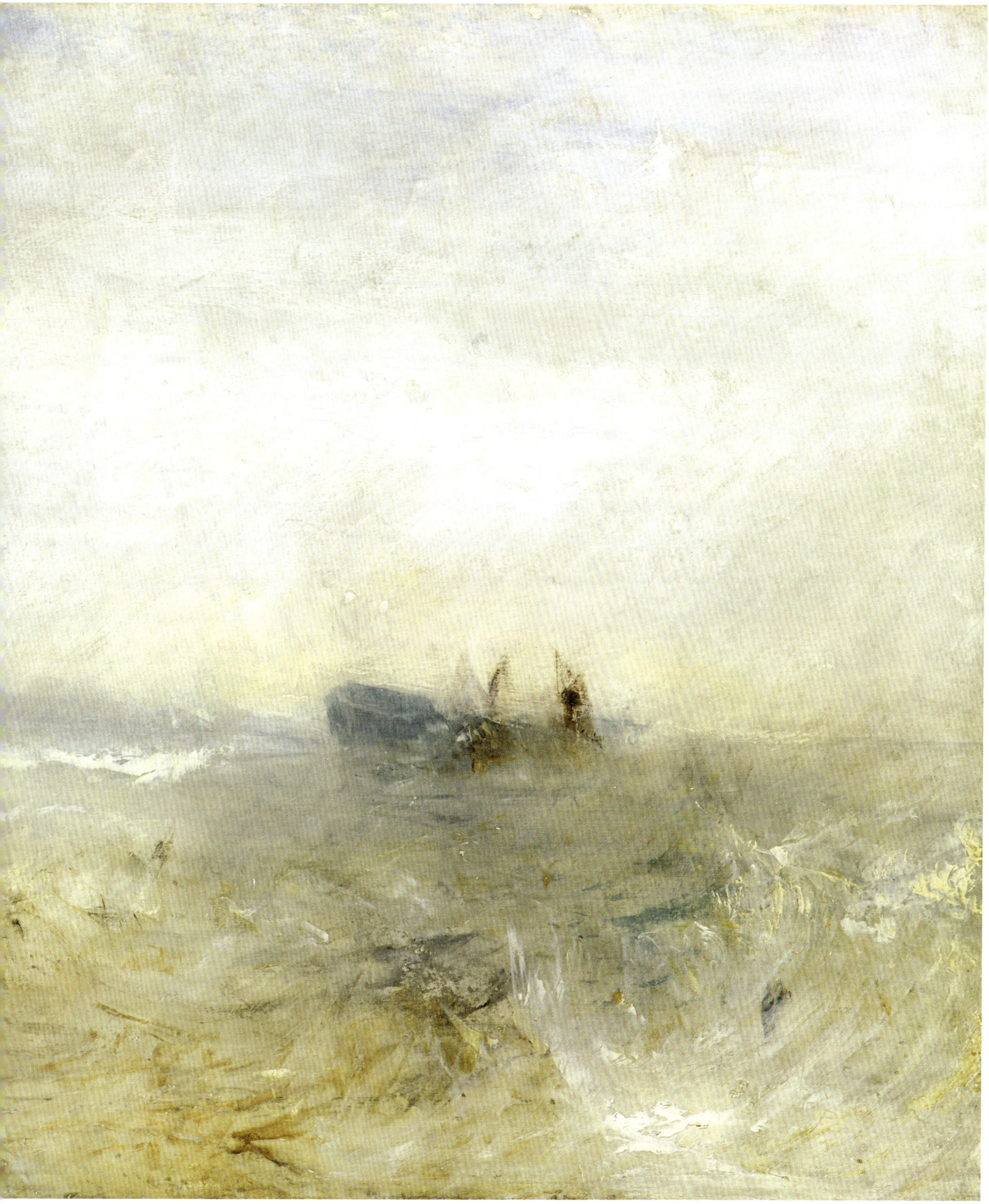

7

MAKING WAVES

Christine Riding

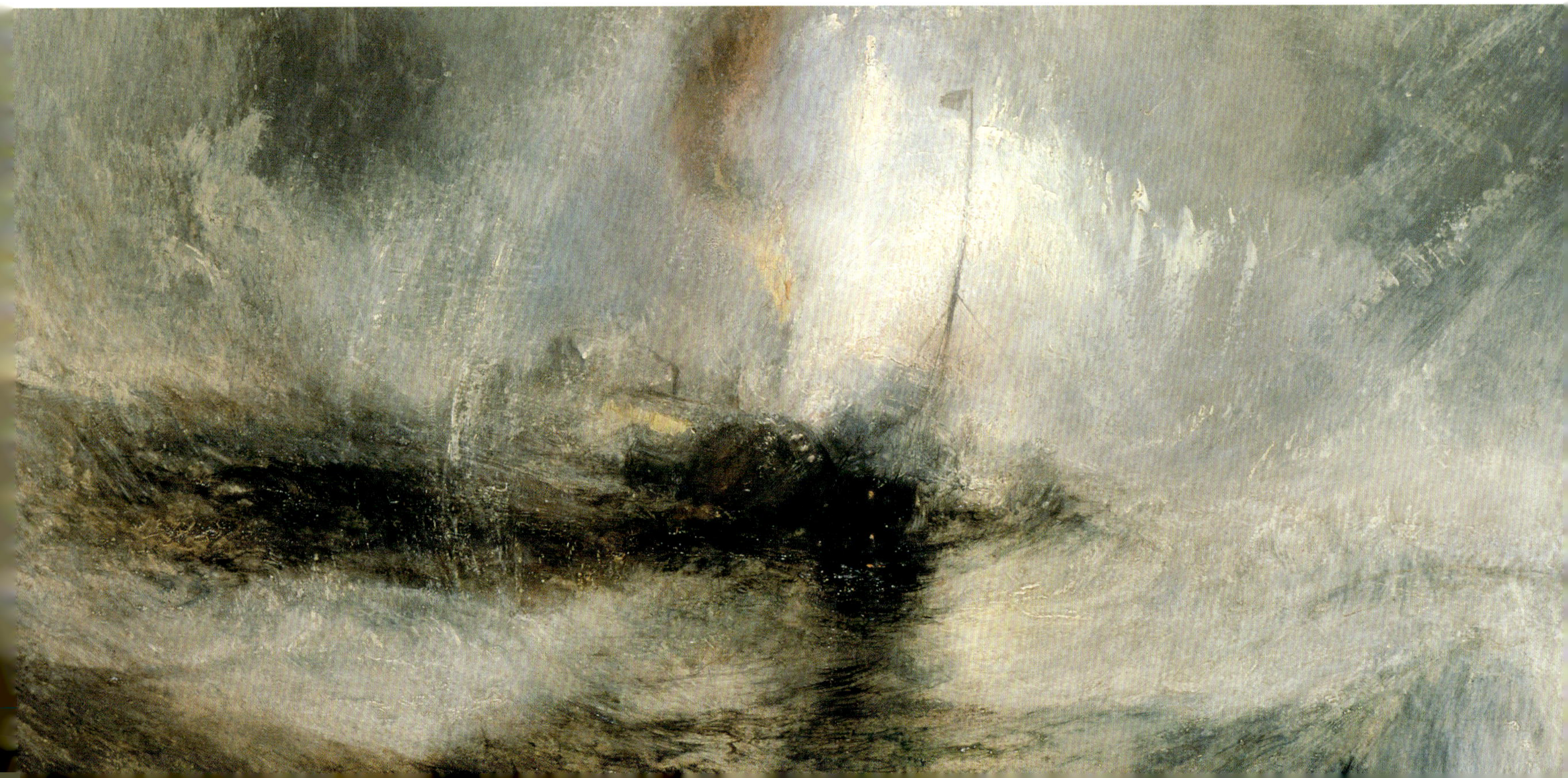

As Turner entered his sixties in 1835, he had cause to be satisfied with his career thus far. He had been at the forefront of his profession for over thirty years and his astute engagement with the art market (in particular print culture) and management of his personal finances had made him independently wealthy. Far from resting on his laurels, however, he continued to develop and diversify his artistic practice, giving fresh impetus to themes and subjects that had preoccupied him from his youth. This is above all true of the sequence of extraordinary marine paintings he exhibited into the mid-1840s, *The Fighting 'Temeraire'*, *Slavers Throwing overboard the Dead and Dying*, *Rockets and Blue Lights*, *Snow Storm – Steam-Boat off a Harbour's Mouth*, *Peace – Burial at Sea* and the 'Whaling' series of 1845–46. All of these underline that the sea continued to be a primary site through which he explored such perennial themes as mortality, loss, cruelty and hope, while at the same time extolling man's perseverance and ingenuity in confronting the overwhelming power of nature.

It has often been stated that Turner, of all his contemporaries, was the landscape artist who embraced the modern world, detailing industrialization and technological advances that were considered by many to be unsightly and thus inappropriate subjects for high art. Turner's focus on modern steam travel is a case in point, heralded by *Staffa, Fingal's Cave* [128], in which the plucky steamboat is dwarfed by its dramatic surroundings. Turner was to develop this juxtaposition still further in his *Rockets and Blue Lights* [130] and *Snow Storm – Steamboat off a Harbour's Mouth* [131] in the early 1840s. However, it was not the subject matter that progressively exercised Turner's critics but the increasingly broad brushwork and focus on gradations of colour over clear outlines that characterized many of his later works. Indeed, *The Fighting 'Temeraire'* and a number of Turner's Venetian subjects were the only outright critical successes of this period. Of course, Turner was no stranger to controversy but the sheer volume of adverse (even satirical) comment during these years is remarkable, although we should note that there were also reviews that acknowledged, in admiring tones, the vitality and pioneering quality of his approach.

One result of these attacks was the intervention of John Ruskin who, from the first volume of *Modern Painters* in 1843, was to offer a comprehensive re-evaluation of Turner's work, in particular his later output, positioning him incontrovertibly as the most important landscape painter in Western art. Another was Turner's own intervention in securing a place in history, primarily through his substantial bequest of works to the national collection and, importantly, the provision for their public display after his death in 1851.

PAST, PRESENT AND FUTURE

In September 1844, Turner's *Fighting 'Temeraire'* [87] was on show at the print-publisher Joseph Hogarth's premises in Great Portland Street, London. The loan by Turner of this critically acclaimed painting, away from his gallery in nearby Queen Anne Street, was in connection with the engraving of it by James Tibbets Willmore, published in 1845. It is perhaps surprising, given its rapturous reception at the Royal Academy in 1839, that it took six years for an engraved version to appear and that the painting itself remained unsold. This seems not to have been for want of trying by various art collectors. In 1845, the genre painter C.R. Leslie, of American parentage and a frequent visitor to Turner's gallery, was asked for assistance by the American collector James Lenox in acquiring one of the Turner's works. In his posthumously printed *Autobiographical Recollections* (1860), Leslie wrote: 'I replied, that his [Turner's] rooms were full of unsold works, and I had no doubt he would part with one.' Lenox left the choice of picture to Leslie. 'I called on Turner,' Leslie continues, 'and asked if he would let a picture go to America. "No; they won't come up to the scratch." I knew what he meant, for another American had offered him a low price for the "Téméraire" [*sic*].'[1] In the end, Leslie chose *Staffa, Fingal's Cave*, a painting he had 'admired more than most of his works' from the time it was exhibited in 1832. It was the first of Turner's paintings to travel to America and Leslie later recalled how, following news of the painting's arrival in New York, Turner had asked him how Lenox liked the picture: '"He thinks it indistinct" [I answered]. "You should tell him," he replied, "that indistinctness is my fault."'[2]

In this oft-quoted (and occasionally misquoted) comment, Turner seems to have admitted, perhaps with a degree of irony, to the main attribute that had made his recent paintings 'unintelligible' to many of his contemporaries. Adverse criticisms directed at a number of Turner's exhibited works at this time were couched in terms of 'absurd extravagances' and 'eccentric flights of genius' in which 'nothing is distinguishable'. One critic in 1841 even suggested (only half joking) that the artist's paintings would be no less legible hung upside-down.[3] However, *Staffa* had been broadly admired in 1832, one critic praising its 'sublimity of vastness and solitude'.[4] When it was finally sold in 1845, Turner was seventy years old and for some time his thoughts had focused on the issue of his posthumous reputation and legacy. This focus would manifest itself, above all, in a substantial bequest of autograph works, ultimately comprising the oil paintings and watercolours, as well as the sketchbooks and other works on paper that filled his London house. Turner's earliest will of 1829 had stipulated that two of his paintings should hang in perpetuity with two by Claude in the National Gallery (see 'Turner on Show', p. 175). This was subsequently amended and expanded, with later revisions to the will stipulating that the rest of the 'finished Pictures' would be displayed together in a designated space to be called 'Turner's Gallery'.[5] Thus, when Lenox visited Turner's Queen Anne Street gallery in 1848 and attempted, unsuccessfully, to buy *The Fighting 'Temeraire'*, the artist had already resolved on giving the painting, along with many others in his possession, to the nation.[6]

How strategic Turner was in determining the fate of individual paintings – whether to keep or to sell – is difficult to determine. The *'Temeraire'*, a painting that he famously described in 1844 as his 'darling', was clearly central to his thinking. *'Now for the Painter'* [59], however, was bought from Turner in the year of his death. In the event, Turner's bequest included works from his early career, notably *Calais Pier* [74] and *The Shipwreck* [75], through to his most contentious marine paintings of the 1840s, thus offering a comprehensive overview of his output in that genre. Turner perhaps had in mind recent donations of paintings by wealthy collectors, notably those of John Julius Angerstein and George Beaumont, to the nascent National Gallery in the 1820s, and Robert Vernon's bequest of British works in the 1840s, which included four paintings by Turner. Of these, *The Dogano, San Giorgio, Citella, from the Steps of the Europa* was the first of Turner's paintings to be displayed at the Gallery, from December 1847. In addition, Turner's fellow Academicians Thomas Lawrence and Francis Chantrey, who died in 1830 and 1841 respectively, had both made provision for the development of the national collection, and the architect John Soane had negotiated an Act of Parliament in 1833 to preserve his house and collection – which included *Admiral Van Tromp's Barge at the Entrance of the Texel* [84] – as a museum for the benefit of 'amateurs and students'.[7] Meanwhile, Turner's monumental *Battle of Trafalgar* [58] had been on public display in the National Gallery of Naval Art in the Painted Hall of Greenwich Hospital since 1829. This prestigious scheme of some three hundred works predated the National Gallery and, albeit specifically naval in theme, showcased British marine painting, thus providing more than a hint to Turner as to how he could situate himself within a broader narrative of Western art (see 'Turner's *Battle of Trafalgar*', pp. 124–29).

In attempting to manage his posthumous reputation, Turner seems to have deliberately revisited or even confronted his own earlier work. In 1838, for example, he exhibited *Fishing Boat with Hucksters Bargaining for Fish* (Art Institute of Chicago) at the British Institution, the year after his *Dutch Boats in a Gale* of 1801 [fig. 6], a work of comparable subject and composition, had been displayed at the same venue alongside the painting by van de Velde that had inspired it. Six years later, in 1844, *Port Ruysdael* [63] was bought by Elhanan Bicknell, almost twenty years after it was first exhibited. In the same year, Turner revisited the imaginary port that he had named after the celebrated seventeenth-century

Dutch artist with *Fishing Boats Bringing a Disabled Ship into Port Ruysdael* [fig. 41], and reprised another historical theme of the early 1830s with *Van Tromp, Going About to Please his Masters* (J. Paul Getty Museum). He also seems to have been spurred by the sale of *Port Ruysdael*, *Helvoetsluys* [fig. 29], *Wreckers – Coast of Northumberland* and three other paintings to Bicknell, whose commercial wealth was based on the sperm-whale fishery, to begin his innovative 'Whaling' series in 1845 [139]. Bicknell was at the time amassing an impressive collection of modern British art, including works by Turner, Callcott and Stanfield, which he hoped to bequeath to the nation.[8]

On one level, Turner was continually refreshing previous themes and subjects, even as he continued to explore new ones, such as *Whalers*. Whether he liked it or not, it is also clear that Turner was being compared with his younger self (often to the detriment of his more recent work) through retrospective displays and published reviews. The *Literary Gazette*, for example, in response to *Whalers* at the Royal Academy in 1845, noted that: 'There are atmospheric effects of magical talent; but after all, we would rather possess one of Mr. Turner's earliest works, when he did not think of subliming truth, than three of the most brilliant of these imaginations, created with all his mastery of art.'[9] Similar comments can be found in other exhibition reviews and commentaries published in the years after the artist's death. Thus in his 'Memoir' of 1852, Peter Cunningham could state that, 'Whoever wishes to possess a single Turner will, if he has true taste, take care to secure, if he can, a picture of a period before 1820. For no painter, in his later style, will be found at times to have thrown both nature and art into more extraordinary convulsions than he has done.'[10] Such opinions offer a poignant context for Turner comprehensively reworking an early

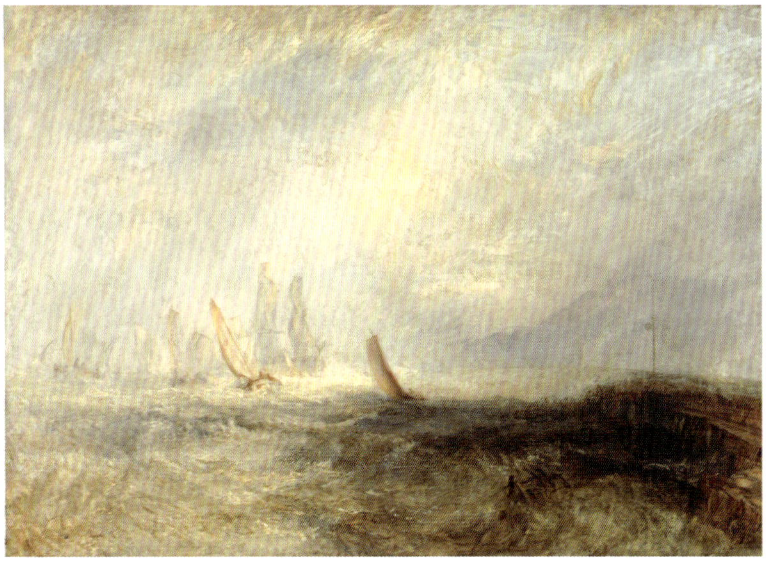

Fig. 41

J.M.W. Turner

Fishing Boats Bringing a Disabled Ship into Port Ruysdael 1844

Oil on canvas 91.4 x 123.2 (36 x 48½)

Tate. Turner Bequest 1856

seascape and exhibiting it as *The Wreck Buoy* in 1849 [88]. His *Wreck of a Transport Ship* of 1810 [76] was shown to critical acclaim at the British Institution in the same year – in an exhibition of 'old masters'. One can only guess at Turner's thoughts on being designated a living 'old master'. However, given his long-standing promotion of a national school of landscape art, he must have been gratified by the fact that the paintings were retained after the exhibition closed, as reported by the *Spectator*, to be 'copied by students of both sexes'. The resulting works were exhibited near the originals and according to the same report there were thirteen copies alone after Turner's painting.[11]

The prospect that future generations of artists might study Turner's approach to landscape art had prompted his ambitious *Liber Studiorum*, a project which emphasized that the role of past masters was to inspire originality in contemporary practice, rather than serve as a model to be slavishly imitated. The bequest, with its provision for a designated display space, can thus be seen as an even more ambitious extension of that earlier project. In terms of marine painting, we can see how Turner was acting in the 1830s and 1840s as his own 'past master', resulting in works that were not only varied in their subject matter and formal qualities but, as exemplified by the contrasting critical fortunes of *The Fighting 'Temeraire'* and *Snow Storm – Steam-Boat off a Harbour's Mouth*, could also in turns delight and revolt, inspire and provoke. One might argue that by including both of these paintings in his bequest, Turner was guaranteeing that the precise nature of his artistic legacy would remain unresolved and thus continually debated. It was the very fluidity of Turner's artistic identity and its ability to accommodate a variety of artistic concerns and approaches that was to have the greatest impact in the second half of the nineteenth century and beyond. That the *'Temeraire'* and *Snow Storm* are both marine paintings is pertinent here, especially given the autobiographical context of the latter and the claims it thus appears to make on behalf of the artist as an interpreter of the natural world.

THE ARTIST AS HERO

Today, *Snow Storm* has the reputation of being one of the most groundbreaking of Turner's works. Far from marking an abrupt departure from his earlier artistic practice, however, the painting can be understood as one of the last in a long line of works that engaged with the Dutch tradition, as exemplified by van de Velde and Backhuysen.[12] It was also the last of a sequence of exhibited paintings focusing on ships in distress, a theme that Turner made his own with some of his earliest explorations of storm at sea, most powerfully in *The Shipwreck* and *Wreck of a Transport Ship*. Such thematic continuities should not obscure the innovative nature of *Snow Storm*. In comparison to the earlier works, which, for all their dynamism, remain pictorially legible, there is relatively little here for the viewer's eyes to focus upon. In fact, the whole surface of the canvas has erupted into swirls of paint, deliberately obscuring our view of the steamboat and harbour. Turner had explored such effects in *Rockets and Blue Lights (Close at Hand) to Warn Steam Boats of Shoal Water*, exhibited in 1840, a painting that bears comparison, if only in subject and composition, with the much earlier painting *Fishermen upon a Lee-Shore* [73]. While these later images of embattled steamboats are similarly tinged with uncertainty of outcome, the effect is achieved primarily through the greater 'indistinctness' of the brushwork.

Turner's innovative approach in 1842, as has often been mentioned, was made additionally befuddling (and thus provocative) by the title, lengthy even by Turner's standards, which accompanied the painting in the Royal Academy exhibition catalogue: *Snow Storm – Steam-Boat off a Harbour's Mouth making Signals in Shallow Water, and going by the Lead. The Author was in this Storm on the Night the 'Ariel' left Harwich*. For some critics, the title only served to exaggerate the abstraction or 'indistinctness' of the image. 'Where the steam-boat is – where the harbour begins, or where it ends – which are the signals, and which the author in the *Ariel*,' bemoaned a reviewer in the *Athenaeum*, 'are matters past our finding out.'[13] And a critic in the *Art Union* even concluded that 'the Artist meant the title and the subject as a sarcasm upon the style.'[14] Many scholars have attempted to associate Turner's elusive painting with a specific maritime event. However, there is no evidence that a ship of that name left that port on that date in those weather conditions. Despite this, the claims and allusions made in the title – and the (self) mythology that subsequently accrued around the image itself – have morphed into one of the most enduring episodes of Turner's biography. Indeed, the painting's 'meaning' was considerably extended via an exchange, recorded by Ruskin in 1857, between the artist and the Reverend William Kingsley, whose mother had been absorbed by the sight of *Snow Storm* during a visit to Turner's gallery. Having told the artist about his mother's response to the painting, Kingsley relayed their conversation (according to Ruskin) as follows:

> [Turner] then said, 'I did not paint it to be understood, but I wished to show what such a scene was like; I got the sailors to lash me to the mast to observe it; I was lashed for four hours, and I did not expect to escape, but I felt bound to record it if I did. But no one had any business to like the picture.' 'But,' said I, 'my mother once went through just such a scene, and it brought it all back to her.' 'Is your mother a painter?' 'No.' 'Then she ought to have been thinking of something else.'[15]

If we take this exchange to be broadly authentic, then there is certainly a defiant tone in Turner's comments, firstly in not wanting to be 'understood' (apropos his critics?) and secondly, in the privileged position he assigns to the 'painter' over an 'ordinary' spectator.

Turner's reference to 'the Author' in the title of *Snow Storm* indicates a desire to be personally associated with the scene depicted. He had playfully alluded to himself on a previous occasion in the title of *'Now for the Painter'*, but such instances are rare in his work. Why he additionally chose to identify himself as the 'Author' rather than the 'Artist' or 'Painter' of *Snow Storm* remains a matter of conjecture. The literary inflection of Turner's choice is useful, however, when unpacking the cultural (and specifically maritime) associations of the rest of the title. First, the name of the ship is perhaps a reference to Ariel, the spirit character from Shakespeare's *The Tempest*, a play that begins with a shipwreck; or to the poets Byron and Shelley, the latter having drowned in 1822 during a storm in a boat called 'Ariel'.[16] Turner's lifelong exploration of painting and poetry as 'sister arts' is discussed elsewhere (see 'Introduction', esp. pp. 12–19), but although commentators made references to both poets in relation to him, it was Byron who Turner engaged with most consistently, appending fragments of his poetry to exhibited paintings. Furthermore, Byron's poetry and biography (the two were often interchangeable) gave the compulsion to travel a heroic aura that was to resonate throughout the nineteenth century. In *Childe Harold's Pilgrimage*, a poem Turner knew well, Byron reflected on the epic nature of travelling by sea:

> Once more upon the Waters! yet once more!
> And the waves bound beneath me as a Steed
> That knows his rider. Welcome to their roar!
> Swift be their guidance, wheresoe'er it lead!
> Though the strained mast should quiver as a reed,
> And the rent canvas fluttering strew the gale,
> Still must I on; for I am as a Weed,
> Flung from the rock, on Ocean's foam to sail
> Where'er the surge may sweep, or tempest's breath prevail.[17]

Turner was well aware of Byron's reputation for seafaring and, importantly, misadventure at sea. Thus, unlike William Wordsworth, who was also a renowned traveller, Byron deliberately 'ran risks, courted danger and discomforts', and castigated what he saw as the small-minded, touristic scope and ambition of his fellow poets Wordsworth, Robert Southey and even Samuel Taylor Coleridge.[18] There was, of course, a degree of competitiveness and dramatization behind Byron's self-identity as the reckless traveller and the same might be said of Turner, certainly so by 1842. By then, he was undoubtedly one of the most travelled artists in Europe and his various sketching tours, published in the 1830s under the titles *Turner's Annual Tours*, had further enhanced this aspect of his artistic identity and celebrity. The first volume of his views of the Seine, also known as *Wanderings by the Seine* (1834), begins with a description written by the journalist Leitch Ritchie of the traveller leaving his or her native shores: 'in mid-channel the vast sea is spread out before, behind, and around us – without beginning and without end – when the heavens and the waters are only separated by the line of the visible horizon, which describes a circle, whereof we ourselves are the centre.'[19] That Turner sought to encourage the notion of himself as an experienced and fearless artist-traveller towards the end of his life is underlined by a letter he wrote in 1845 to James Lenox, in which he recounted his hazardous journey to Staffa, off the western coast of Scotland, in 1831. A 'strong wind and head sea' had delayed the steamboat landing at the uninhabited island, where Turner and others travellers scrambled into Fingal's Cave, 'not very pleasant or safe when the wave rolls right in'.[20]

The lengthy title of *Snow Storm* thus goes beyond simply reinforcing the primacy of personal observation and familiarity with nautical matters in marine art to embrace a new and powerful Romantic notion of creative endeavour. Furthermore, it also made specific links with a particular brand of artistic heroism associated with the sea. One might state that, by the mid-nineteenth century, misadventure (or deliberately putting oneself in the way of danger) had become a rite of passage for any self-respecting marine artist: hence the references made in biographies to Dutch painters seeking out storms at sea to inform their art. In 1834, a critic had evoked the idea of Backhuysen's habit of 'putting to sea in the most tempestuous weather' in his review of Turner's *Wreckers – Coast of Northumberland*.[21] One of the best-known artistic anecdotes in the early nineteenth century was the 'conversion' of Claude-Joseph Vernet from budding history painter to fully fledged marine artist, during his journey from his native Avignon to Rome in 1734. Having succumbed to the sublime spectacle of the Mediterranean, his first experience of the sea, Vernet departed from land and became engulfed by a raging storm. What happened next was dramatized by the artist's biographer, Léon Lagrange, as follows:

> [He] assumes a position of honour; he has himself tied to the mast of the ship, and, head held high, he continues to dominate the elements that assault him. How beautiful it is, this drunken genius! The artist reveals himself to himself, receiving with joy the terrible caresses of the sea, this baptism of the waves from which he emerges as a marine painter.[22]

Lagrange's biography was published in 1864, at a moment when the motif of being 'tied to the mast of the ship', courtesy of Ruskin and others, was firmly associated with both Turner and Vernet.

THE ARTIST AND THE SEA

Given the far-reaching impact of Ruskin's *Modern Painters*, it is interesting to note that his defence of *Snow Storm*, published in 1843, should specifically evoke the heroic identity of the 'artist in the storm'. In the chapter entitled 'Of water, as painted by Turner', Ruskin famously described the painting as 'one of the very grandest statements of sea motion, mist, and light that has ever been put on canvass, even by Turner'. He continues,

> Of course it was not understood; his finest works never are; but there was some apology for the public's not comprehending this, for few people have had the opportunity of seeing the sea at such a time, and when they have, cannot face it. To hold by a mast or a rock, and watch it, is a prolonged endurance of drowning which few people have courage to go through. To those who have, it is one of the noblest lessons of nature.[23]

Towards the end of his career, Turner was thus being absorbed into a long tradition associated specifically with marine artists, one that placed a premium on first-hand experience and heroic misadventure. The attraction of such a tradition for Turner, above all in the contested years of the 1840s, may in part relate to the prominence of British and French marine artists in the eighteenth and nineteenth century, who, like Dominic Serres, Nicholas Pocock, William John Huggins and Stanfield, had been at sea in merchant service or the Royal Navy, and the assumed accuracy and thus authority that their images had as a result. Indeed, according to Ruskin, Turner's poetic but 'inaccurate' *Battle of Trafalgar* at Greenwich Hospital was compared unfavourably by the institution's naval Pensioners to Huggins.[24]

Perhaps of greater significance is the inclusion of *Peace – Burial at Sea* [fig. 42], Turner's homage to his friend and earlier rival David Wilkie, in the same exhibition as *Snow Storm*. Wilkie had died on board the steamship 'Oriental' on 1 June 1841, returning from the Near East, and was buried the same evening off Gibraltar. The painting was paired in the exhibition with *War – The Exile and the Rock Limpet* (Tate Collection), the exile in question being Napoleon Bonaparte. However, that both *Burial at Sea* and *Snow Storm* are marine paintings, similarly dominated by a cool palette and a steamer at their centre, coupled with a shared theme of mortality, makes the links between these two paintings additionally poignant. On the one hand, the images reprise the time-honoured juxtaposition of 'calm' and 'storm' of traditional marine art; on the other, given that a contemporary British painter is literally and metaphorically at the heart of each, they serve as emphatic statements concerning the centrality of art to the nation. Both paintings were bequeathed to the National Gallery.

If *Snow Storm* was conceived by Turner as a kind of manifesto, then its inclusion in his bequest is of vital importance. Reviled and mocked in 1842, by the 1870s it could be seen as an integral part of Turner's legacy, at a moment when he was by far the most-represented artist in the national collection. Ralph Nicholson Wornum, who was from 1855 the Keeper and Secretary of the National Gallery, noted in 1875 that the collection was 'happily rich in the great sea-pieces of Turner, as in other of his works'. 'The pictures,' he continued, 'are distinguished for their variety and individuality. He is clearly the prince of painters of the English school, in marine as in other landscapes.'[25] The paintings Wornum listed included *Calais Pier*, *The Shipwreck*, *Sun Rising through Vapour* [fig. 37], the early *Battle of Trafalgar* [fig. 16], *The Fighting 'Temeraire'*, *Snow Storm* and the later *Port Ruysdael*. These paintings, in Wornum's estimation, were 'sufficient to immortalize the name of any painter'.[26]

Wornum's comments formed part of a series of articles on the National Gallery collection published in the monthly art periodical *The Portfolio*. The editor was the writer and critic Philip Gilbert Hamerton, who commissioned the accompanying illustrations. The circumstances are revealing here, not least because Hamerton refers to them in his *Life of J. M. W. Turner, RA*, published in 1879. There he describes the visit to the National Gallery of 'several eminent French etchers' who were 'perfectly familiar with the old masters, and with as much modern art as may be seen in Paris'.[27] According to Hamerton, having seen the collection, they 'asked to be employed in the interpretation of Turner' and specifically with 'those daring experiments in light and colour'.[28] The published images were after *Burial at Sea*, *The Fighting 'Temeraire'* and later *Port Ruysdael*, and two late Venetian paintings, *The Sun of Venice* and *The Approach to Venice*. 'It was not mere critical approbation', Hamerton continued,

> not merely the respectful attention usually given to a great master, it was the passionate enthusiasm with which highly educated and very sensitive persons acknowledge a new, strange, irresistible influence in the fine arts, the sort of enthusiasm which was awakened by the verses of Byron and the violin-playing of Paganini.[29]

He concluded that 'these pictures have the one great power of all genuine works of art, as distinguished from simple imitations of nature, the power which excites and arouses the artistic susceptibilities.'[30]

By the time Hamerton's biography was published, both Aestheticism and Impressionism were having a profound impact on perceptions of art. Indeed, *Snow Storm* was called upon the previous year, in 1878, during the celebrated libel trial of Whistler versus Ruskin. The painting was used as evidence specifically to underline the inconsistencies of Ruskin's passionate defence of Turner's late style and his vilification of Whistler's nocturnes – in particular, *Nocturne in Black and Gold – The Falling Rocket* of 1875 – despite the comparable indistinctness of the two artists' work.[31] Ironically, the subject and formal qualities of Whistler's painting may have had their origins in his early interest in Turner's late seascapes, and the ephemeral effects of rockets falling. He made a watercolour copy of a chromolithograph after *Rockets and Blue Lights* in 1855.

As the appreciation of Turner's distinctive 'indistinctness' continued to grow, the great range and variety of his marine subjects offered myriad pointers for a new generation of artists who, like Whistler, followed the British painter's restless example by exploring new and self-consciously modern ways of representing the sea.

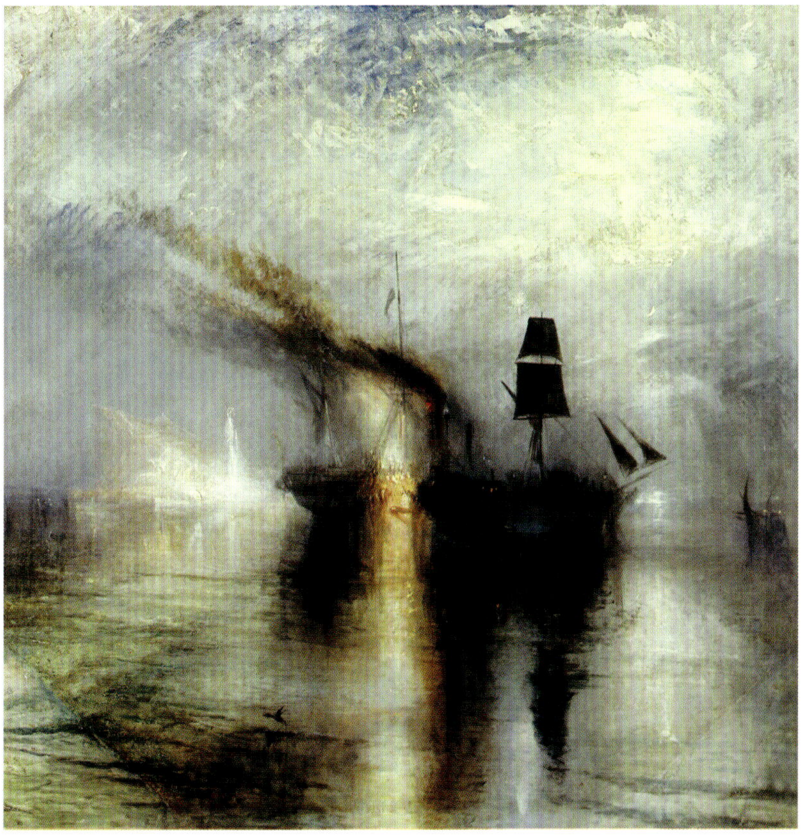

Fig. 42

J.M.W. Turner
Peace – Burial at Sea 1842
Oil on canvas 87 x 86.7
(34¼ x 34⅛)
Tate. Turner Bequest 1856

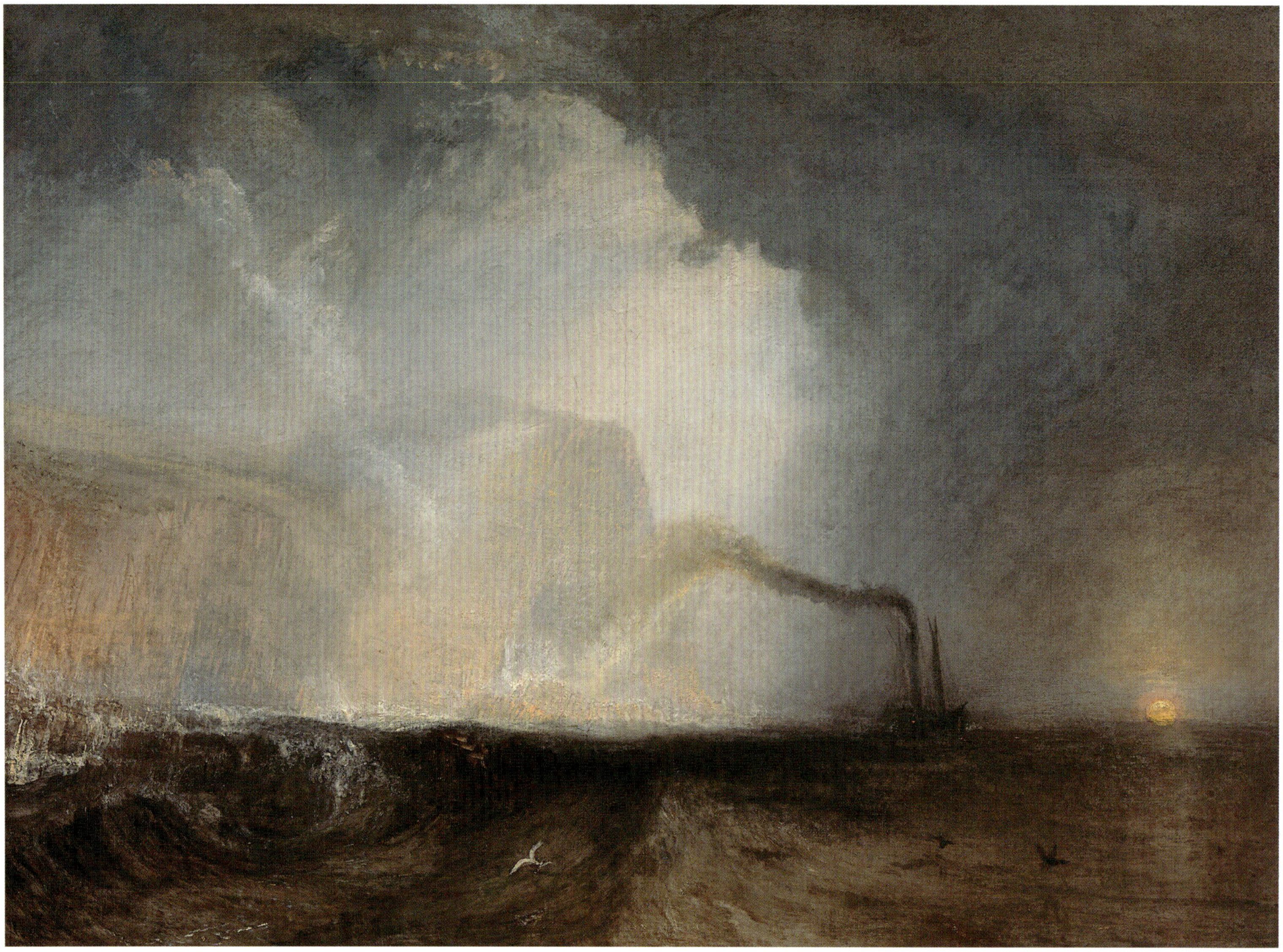

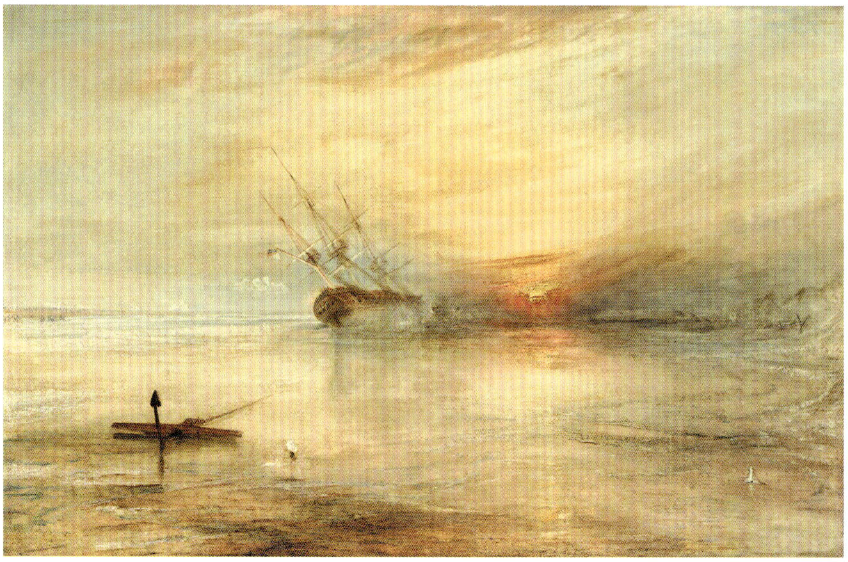

128

J.M.W. Turner
Staffa, Fingal's Cave 1832
Oil on canvas 90.8 x 121.3 (35¾ x 47¾)
Yale Center for British Art

Butlin and Joll, no. 347; Warrell 2007, no. 102

Fig. 43

J.M.W. Turner
Fort Vimieux 1831
Oil on canvas 71.1 x 106.7 (28 x 42)
Private collection, USA

In 1831, Turner visited Staffa, a Hebridean island off the west coast of Scotland, as part of a sketching trip, gathering material for *The Poetical Works of Sir Walter Scott* (1833–34). He had collaborated with Scott, already a celebrated writer and poet, in the 1820s, on *The Provincial Antiquities and Picturesque Scenery of Scotland* (see [fig. 15]). Turner's sketches from this tour can be found in the Staffa Sketchbook in the Tate Collection, which includes numerous representations of Fingal's Cave, a unique sea-cave formed of polygonal basalt columns with a 227-foot cavern. In his travel journal, *A Cruise Around Scotland in 1814*, Scott described entering the cave as follows:

> The stupendous columnar side walls – the depth and strength of the ocean with which the cavern is filled – the variety of tints formed by stalactites dropping and petrifying between the pillars ... the dreadful noise of those august billows so well corresponding with the grandeur of the scene – are all circumstances elsewhere unparalleled (Scott 1839, pp. 331–32).

Turner seems to have been equally impressed by it and clearly relished the inhospitable weather that only served to heighten his experience of the island. In a letter to James Lenox, who acquired the present painting in 1845, Turner recounted that a number of passengers refused to journey on to the nearby island of Iona 'at all hazards' and, in order to compensate 'the displeased', the captain took the steamboat around Staffa three times. 'The sun getting towards the horizon,' he wrote, 'burst through the rain-cloud, angry, and for wind.' The painting appears to represent the scene as Turner described it, with the steamboat positioned near the brooding skies and setting sun on the right, and the cave entrance bathed in light on the left.

Fingal's Cave had been 'discovered' in 1772 by the botanist and traveller Sir Joseph Banks. By that time (according to Banks) the site had already become associated in Scottish legend with the ancient warrior-king Fingal and his poet son, Ossian. In the 1760s, Ossian was credited as the author of a number 'rediscovered' epic poems of which *Fingal* was the most famous. These chronicled the doomed world of this Scottish hero, thus imbuing Staffa by association with a mystical aura. On the advice of Scott, William Daniell had visited Staffa and devised a number of images for his *A Voyage Round Great Britain* (1814–25). They included a view from inside Fingal's Cave looking out to the sea. Turner took a similar viewpoint for the design he created for Scott's *Poetical Works*, which was engraved and published as the frontispiece for volume ten in 1834. In Turner's painting, the eeriness of the island and its mythical associations are emphasized by contrasts of light and dark, vaporous and murky, with the indistinctness of the cave suggestive of the 'presence' of the legendary king. In the Academy exhibition catalogue of 1832, Turner appended a quotation from Scott's *Lord of the Isles* (1815), a poem describing Scotland's struggle for independence from England, leading up to the victory by the Scots at Bannockburn in 1314. The quotation chosen by Turner describes Fingal's Cave, thus conflating national legend and history: 'nor of a theme less solemn tells / That mighty surge that ebbs and swells, / And still, between each awful pause, / From the high vault an answer draws.' Felix Mendelssohn's evocative 'Hebrides Overture (Fingal's Cave)', composed after the young composer's trip to the island in 1829, was premiered in London on 14 May 1832, the week after the Royal Academy exhibition opened with Turner's painting on display.

In 1850, James Lenox acquired his second painting by Turner, *Fort Vimieux* [fig. 43], which had been exhibited at the Royal Academy in 1831. It was accompanied in the catalogue by an excerpt from *Naval Anecdotes* (but possibly authored by Turner himself) concerning a British cruiser that had become stranded on the coast of France in 1805 and had been bombarded from the nearby fort. As a naval scene relating to the Napoleonic War, the painting has some relationship to *The Fighting 'Temeraire'*, as does the focus on a warship and, in general terms, the composition. This may explain Lenox's interest in *Fort Vimieux*, given his attempts to acquire Turner's *'Temeraire'* several years earlier.

Below left Fig. 44

Thomas Birch
Engagement between the 'Constitution' and the 'Guerrière' 1813
Oil on canvas 71.1 x 92 (28 x 36¼)
Museum of Fine Arts, Boston

Below right Fig. 45

Frederic Edwin Church
Coast Scene, Mount Desert 1863
Oil on canvas 86.7 x 121.9 (34⅛ x 48)
Wadsworth Atheneum

Opposite 129

James Hamilton
Old Ironsides 1863
Oil on canvas 153.4 x 121.9 (60⅜ x 48)
Pennsylvania Academy of Fine Arts

James Hamilton (1819–78) was an Irish-born American marine painter and printmaker. He was a lifelong admirer of Turner and advised Thomas Moran to study the English artist (see [133]). By the 1860s, Hamilton was often described as the 'American Turner', primarily because of such paintings as *Foundering* (1863, Brooklyn Museum of Art) and *Old Ironsides*. These works are very similar in composition, with a clear formal relationship both to storm scenes by Turner (see, for example, *The Shipwreck* [75]) and to the Dutch tradition of marine art, as represented by van de Velde (see [5]). Over and above these shared artistic models, both paintings also achieved a powerful symbolic resonance in the 1860s through their historical references, at a time when the idea of American nationhood was severely tested by the Civil War (1861–65).

Old Ironsides refers to the nickname of the 'Constitution', a frigate in the American navy, which had been launched in 1797 and named by the President, George Washington, after the Constitution of the United States of America. The ship became famous during the Anglo-American War of 1812. Thomas Birch (1779–1851), America's first marine painter, produced a series of canvases based on the single-ship actions of 1812 between the American and British navies. These had resulted in five unexpected and thus celebrated victories for the new republic. Birch's painting represented here [fig. 44] documents the first of these, the defeat of the British frigate 'Guerrière' by the 'Constitution' off the coast of Nova Scotia. In his history of the American navy, first published in 1839, James Fenimore Cooper explained the euphoria that greeted these successes as follows: 'So deep had been the effect produced on the public mind by the constant accounts of the successes of the English over their enemies at sea, that the opinion ... of their invincibility on that element, generally prevailed' (Cooper 1840, vol. 2, p. 85). He later wrote *Old Ironsides* (1853), a patriotic biographical sketch that underscored the place of the 'Constitution' in America's foundation narrative. In Hamilton's painting, the conventional 'ship of state' analogy is thus made more poignant through the associations provoked by the named ship, a strategy that Turner had used to powerful effect in *The Fighting 'Temeraire'*. While Hamilton's painting makes explicit reference to a national crisis, the relentless pounding of the sea against the American coastline could also serve as a comment on contemporary events. Indeed, *Coast Scene, Mount Desert* [fig. 45] by Frederic Church, painted in the same year as *Old Ironsides* and similarly influenced by Turner, was exhibited at the Albany Sanitary Fair, an event organized in 1864 to raise funds for the Unionist war effort (Wilton and Barringer 2002, p. 150).

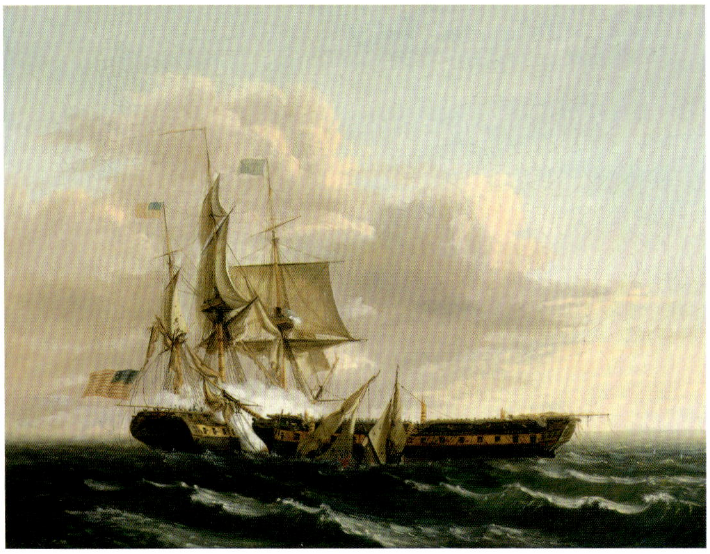

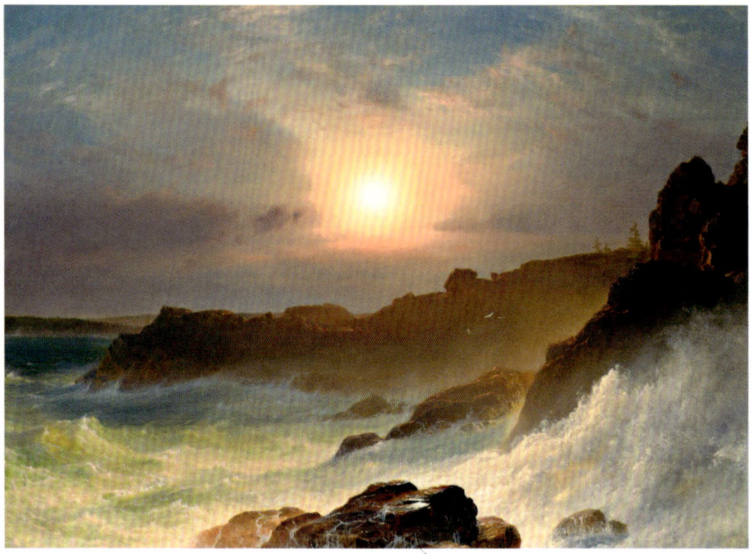

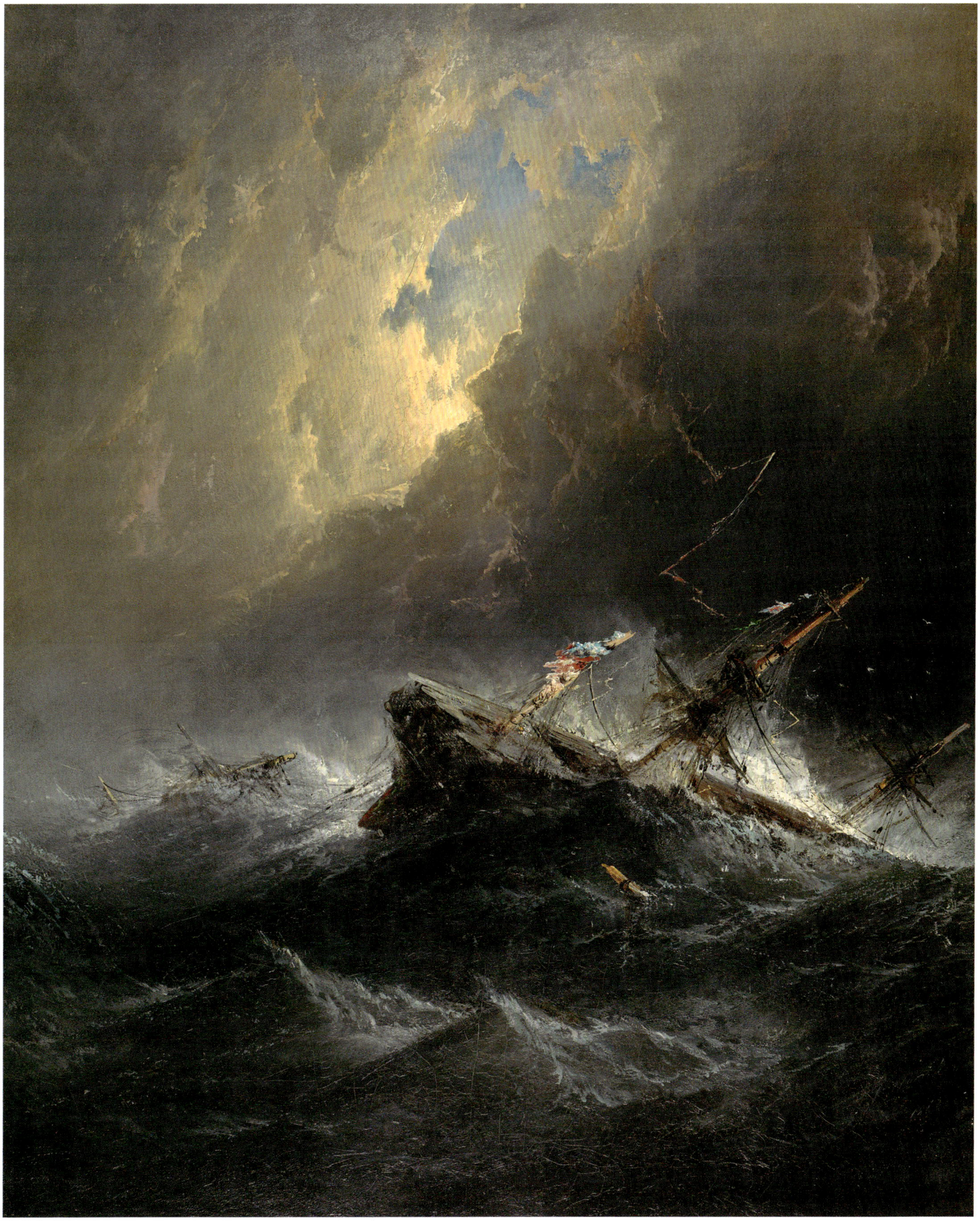

131

J.M.W. Turner
Snow Storm – Steam-Boat off a Harbour's Mouth 1842
Oil on canvas 91.4 x 121.9 (36 x 48)
Tate. Turner Bequest 1856

Butlin and Joll, no. 398; Warrell 2007, no. 136

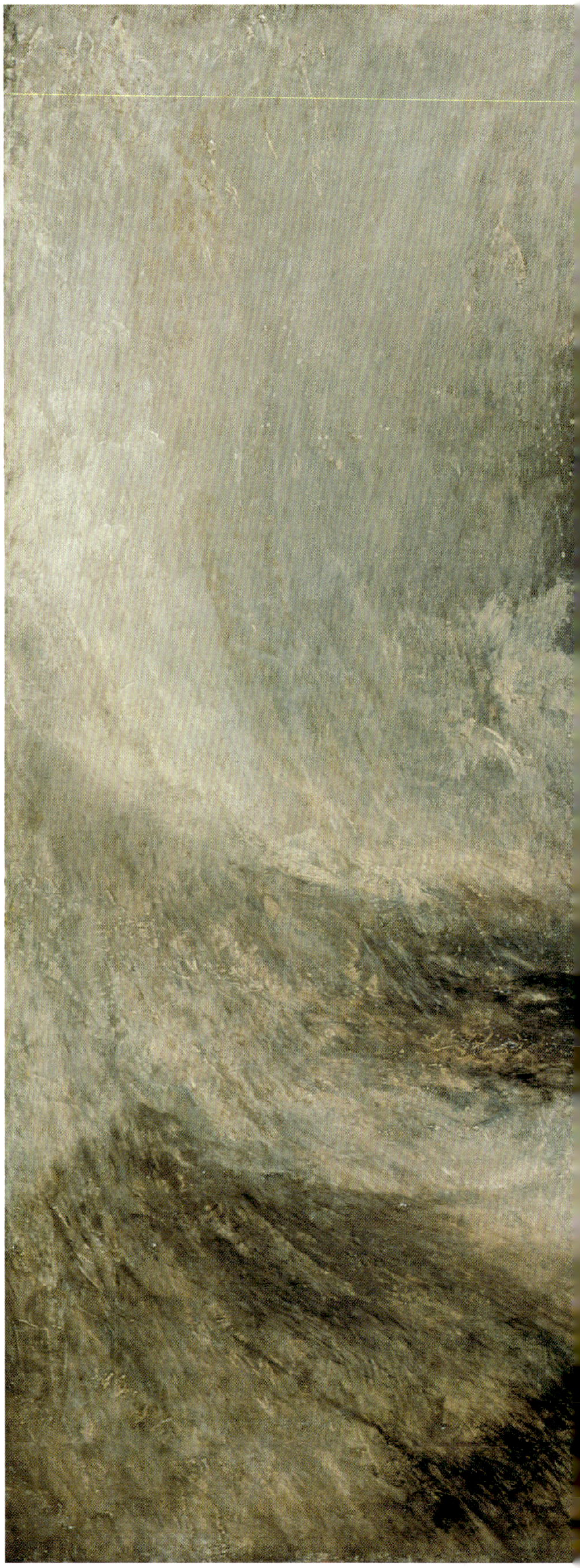

Turner exhibited three paintings at the Royal Academy on the subject of snow storms: *Snow Storm: Hannibal and his Army Crossing the Alps* (1812, Tate collection), *Snow-Storm, Avalanche and Inundation – a Scene in the Upper Part of the Val d'Aouste, Piedmont* (1837) and the present painting, exhibited in 1842. Albeit representing very different subjects, all three focus on man's vulnerability in the face of the sublime forces of nature. This is underlined above all by the dramatic vortex that dominates each composition, suggesting overwhelming elemental motion. In the painting of 1842, this compositional device has been exaggerated to such an extent that reviewers of the Royal Academy exhibition (perhaps wilfully) found the image too indistinct to decipher, despite the long and highly specific title given in the catalogue. The critic in the *Art Union* observed, 'Through the driving snow there are just perceptible portions of a steam-boat labouring on a rolling sea; but before any further account of the vessel can be given, it will be necessary to wait until the storm is cleared off a little. The sooner the better' (1 June 1842).

Other exhibits did not fare any better. Turner's other contemporary marine subject, *Peace – Burial at Sea* [fig. 42] also provoked the critics, primarily because of the juxtaposition of the cool hues of the sea and sky with the deep blackness of the steamer, in sharp contrast with its pendant painting, *War – The Exile and the Rock Limpet*, composed of fiery reds and yellows. 'He is successful as ever in caricaturing himself,' noted the *Spectator*, 'in two round blotches of *rouge et noir*' (7 May 1842). The reviewer seems to have been making an additional quip at Turner's expense by alluding to Stendhal's *The Red and the Black*, published in 1830. The novel chronicles the attempts of Julien Sorel, a delusional young man of modest means, to rise in Parisian society, only to fall victim to his passions. Such diatribes represent quite a contrast with the reception of Turner's two Venetian subjects in the same display. The reviewer in the *Athenaeum* thought them 'among the loveliest, because least exaggerated pictures, which this magician (for such he is, in right of his command over the spirits of Air, Fire, and Water) has recently given us. Fairer dreams never floated past poets' eye' (Butlin and Joll 1984, vol.1, p. 223). These paintings were also promptly sold: *Campo Santo, Venice* (Toledo Museum of Art) was acquired at the exhibition by Elhanan Bicknell and the other, *The Dogano, San Giorgio, Citella, from the Steps of the Europa* (Tate Collection), by Robert Vernon. This became the first Turner to hang in the National Gallery, as part of Vernon's gift in 1847.

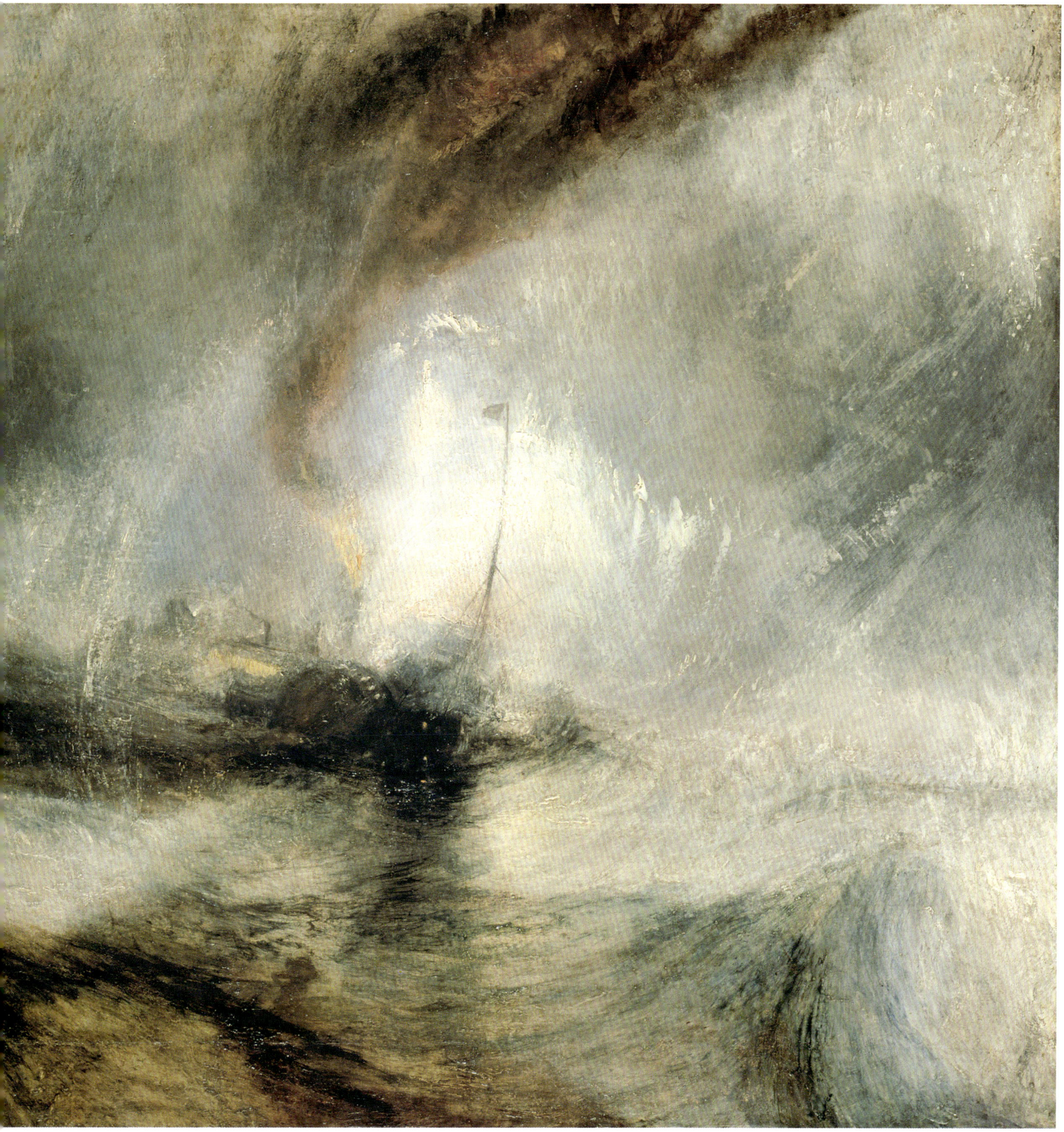

132

John Singer Sargent
Atlantic Storm 1876
Oil on canvas 58.5 x 81.5 (23 x 32⅛)
Curtis Galleries

Cash and Ormond 2009, pp. 44–47, fig. 51

As a mature artist, John Singer Sargent (1856–1925) was a renowned portrait painter. His early interest, however, was in landscape and marine painting. He made two seascapes in 1876, *Atlantic Sunset* (private collection) and *Atlantic Storm*, and three small and delicate oil studies, *The Derelict* and *Mid-Ocean, Mid-Winter* (both in private collections), and *Seascape* (The Annapolis Collection). Most of these works focus on the seemingly endless expanse of the ocean, in a manner that is comparable to the work of Whistler, Courbet and others. The exception is *Atlantic Storm*, which takes as its subject the very human experience of a modern transatlantic crossing. The composition is highly innovative, with the viewer looking along the deck towards the stern, as the steamship pitches upwards. Two passengers can be seen struggling on the left. Beyond, the ship's wake maps its progress through the mountainous waves. Sargent had experienced a rough passage on his return from America to Europe in 1876. Although he made sketches of the steamship 'Algeria' and the movement of the sea for this painting, he seems to have been working largely from memory.

While first-hand experience was the starting point for *Atlantic Storm*, it is possible that Sargent was also seeking to emulate the work of earlier artists, in particular that of Turner. In about 1876, he made a sketch (now in the collection of the Museum of Fine Arts, Boston) of Turner's *The Shipwreck* [75], which he may have seen on display at the National Gallery or, alternatively, copied from a print. Sargent's scrapbook, which contains drawings made from his first two Atlantic crossings, also includes a print after *Calais Pier* [74] pasted onto one of the pages (The John Singer Sargent Scrapbook, Metropolitan Museum of Art). Furthermore, Sargent may have been drawn to the composition of *Snow Storm – Steam-Boat off a Harbour's Mouth* [131] and its autobiographical associations, especially if he also knew the story of Turner having experienced the storm, tied to the mast of the ship.

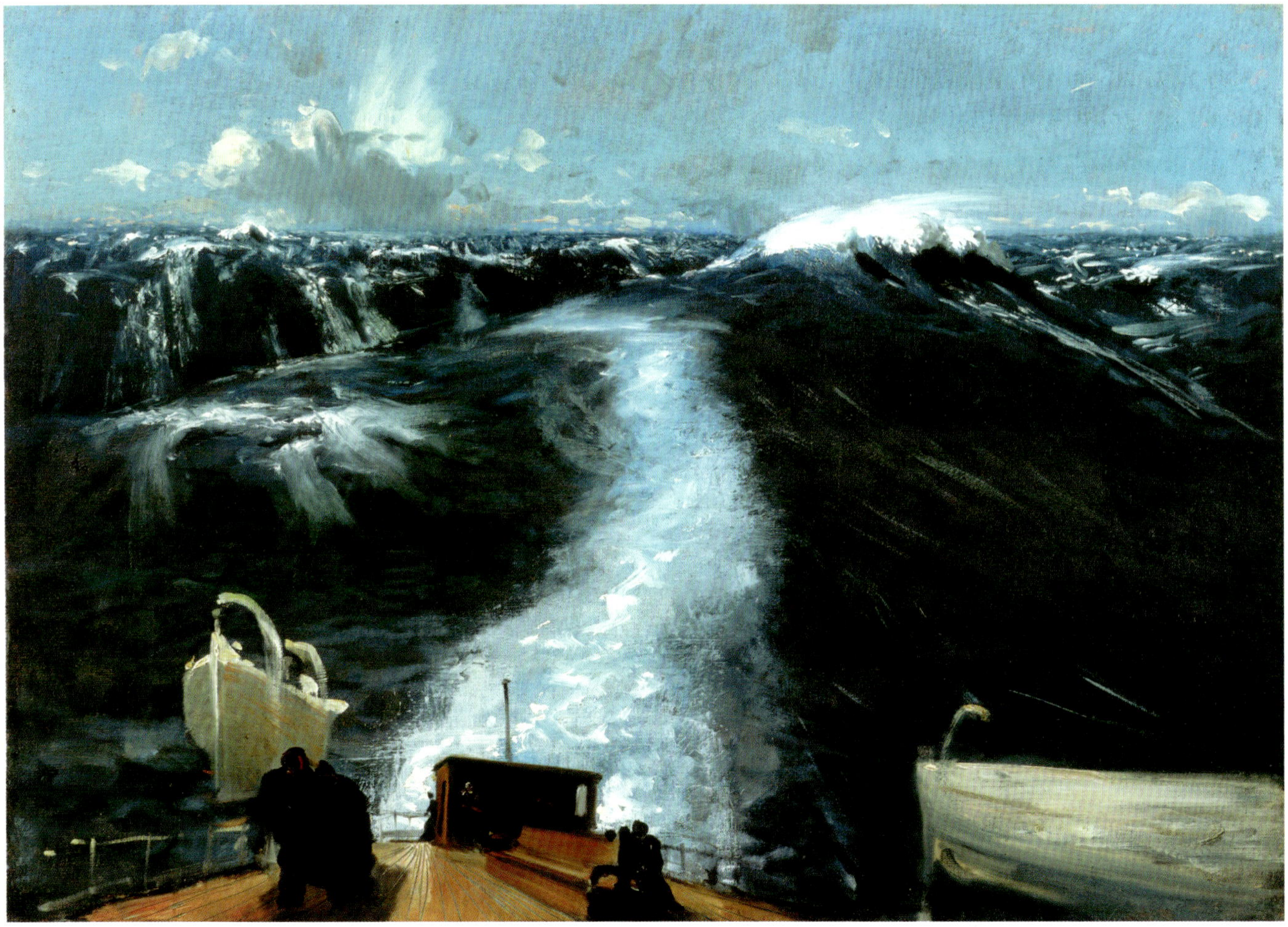

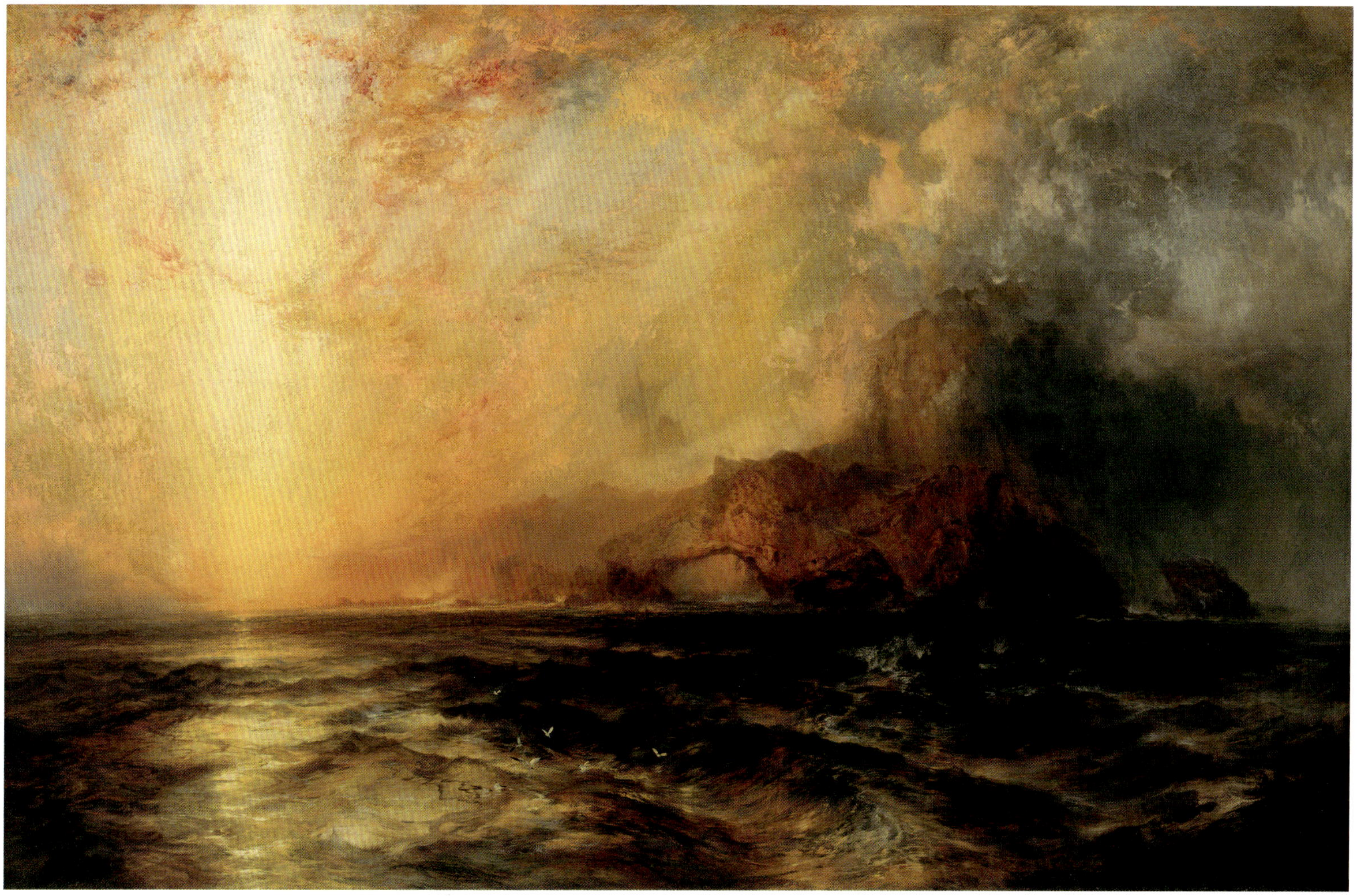

133

Thomas Moran

Fiercely the red sun descending / Burned his way along the heavens 1875–76

Oil on canvas 84.8 x 127 ($33\frac{3}{8}$ x 50)

North Carolina Museum of Art

Wilton and Barringer 2002, no. 97

Thomas Moran (1837–1926) was an American painter and printmaker. He was encouraged to study Turner by fellow artist James Hamilton [129], resulting in the colouristic style and the poetic emphasis of his early works. The present painting is a case in point. The subject is taken from Henry Wadsworth Longfellow's *The Song of Hiawatha*, which was an immediate success when it appeared 1855. Intentionally epic in scope, the poem follows the adventures of Hiawatha, a legendary Native American leader. Moran had executed two earlier paintings on the subject, *Hiawatha* (1867–68, Philbrook Museum of Art) and *Hiawatha and the Great Serpent* (1867, Baltimore Museum of Art). This painting represents the opening passage of part IX, which describes a sunset over Lake Superior: 'Fiercely the red sun descending / Burned his way along the heavens, / Set the sky on fire behind him, / As war-parties, when retreating, / Burn the prairies on their war-trail.'

All three Hiawatha paintings use Turner as a reference point. Like many of his contemporaries, Moran was most familiar with the English artist through engravings (he owned copies of Turner's *Liber Studiorum*) and was 'stunned by the radiance' of the paintings and watercolours he saw at the National Gallery during a visit to London in 1862 (Spassky 1985, p. 520). The works on show at this time would have included *Ulysses Deriding Polyphemus* [fig. 3] and *The Fighting 'Temeraire'* [87]. Andrew Wilton has proposed that Moran also made specific formal references here to Turner's *Staffa* [128] and *Slavers* [fig. 46] (Wilton and Barringer 2002, p. 146). Both works were in American collections by this time. In terms of subject matter, *Staffa*, and its association with Scottish legend, and *Ulysses*, representing an episode from Homer's *Odyssey*, find obvious parallels with the legend of Hiawatha.

134

Gustave Le Gray

The French Fleet at Cherbourg, 5 August 1858

1858

Albumen print laid down on card

30.9 x 41 (12⅛ x 16⅛)

The Royal Collection

Aubenas 2002, no. 160

Gustave Le Gray (1820–84) trained as a painter in Paris, for a time in the studio of the history painter Paul Delaroche, before taking up photography in 1847. He was to become a renowned innovator in the new art form, notably for his use of two negatives to make a single picture, which, in his seascapes, allowed him to achieve a tonal balance between sea and sky. Le Gray completed two series of French coastal scenes and seascapes, the images taken in Normandy (1856–57) and on the Mediterranean coast (1857). Both sets are represented here: *Solar Effect – Ocean* represents a view from the northern coast and *The Great Wave, Sète* shows the jetty of the port of Sète on the southern coast.

Le Gray's seascapes were exhibited to critical acclaim in London and Paris. In February 1857, a reviewer in the *Journal of the Photographic Society* wrote effusively: 'We stop with astonishment before M. Le Gray's "Sea and Sky", the most successful seizure of water and cloud yet attempted. The effect is the simplest conceivable.' The receptiveness to Le Gray's images in London may have come from the correspondence between his work and the tradition of British marine and landscape art, as practised by Turner, Constable and others, and the association commentators often made between photography and prints. Furthermore, mezzotint (a technique deployed by both Turner and Constable, and known in France as 'the English manner') was thought to correlate closely with photographic prints, primarily because of its emphasis on gradations of tone and lack of hard outlines (Aubenas 2002, pp. 223–24). Le Gray explored the artistic possibilities of the depopulated seascape, thus focusing on formal contrasts and effects, through such motifs as the breaking wave and the horizon. Indeed, it has often been suggested that the late seascapes of Gustave Courbet [fig. 48] show the influence of Le Gray, as well as of Turner and Constable. Furthermore, in his series of images of the French and British fleets, taken during Queen Victoria and Prince Albert's state visit to France in 1858, Le Gray gave fresh artistic impetus to the tradition of the naval review.

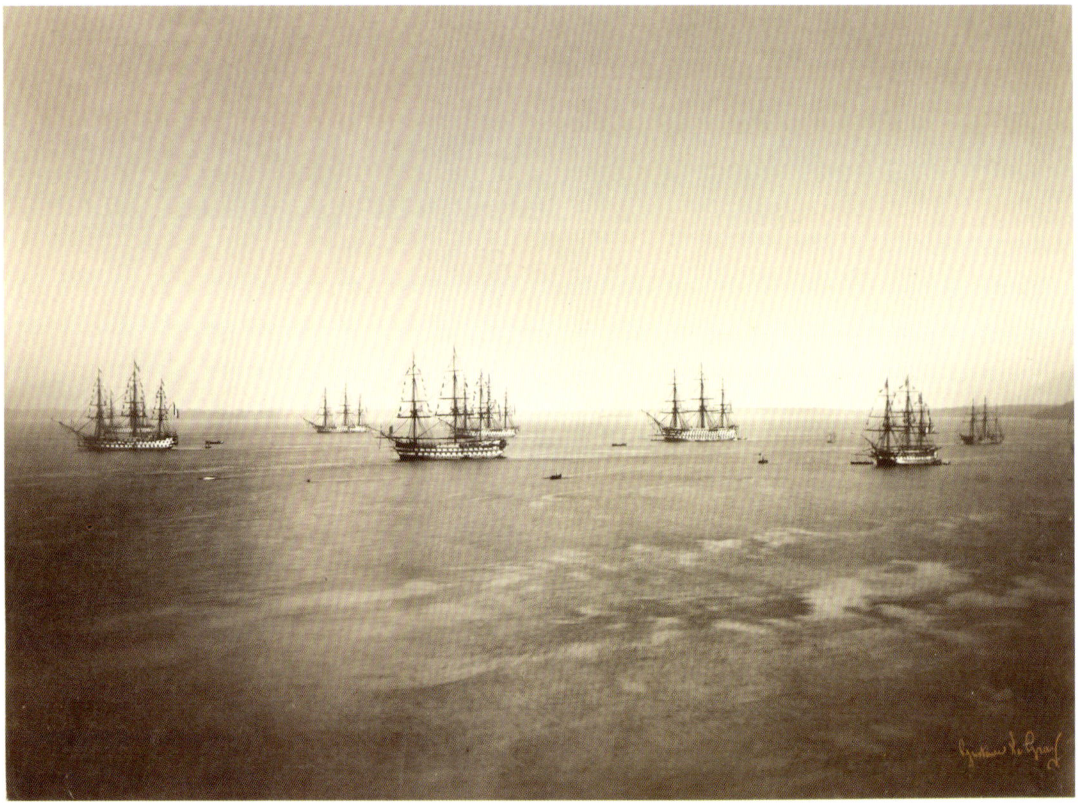

135

Gustave Le Gray
Solar Effect – Ocean 1857
Albumen print from two collodion-on-glass negatives 31.3 x 40.5 (12⅜ x 16)
Victoria and Albert Museum

Aubenas 2002, no. 121

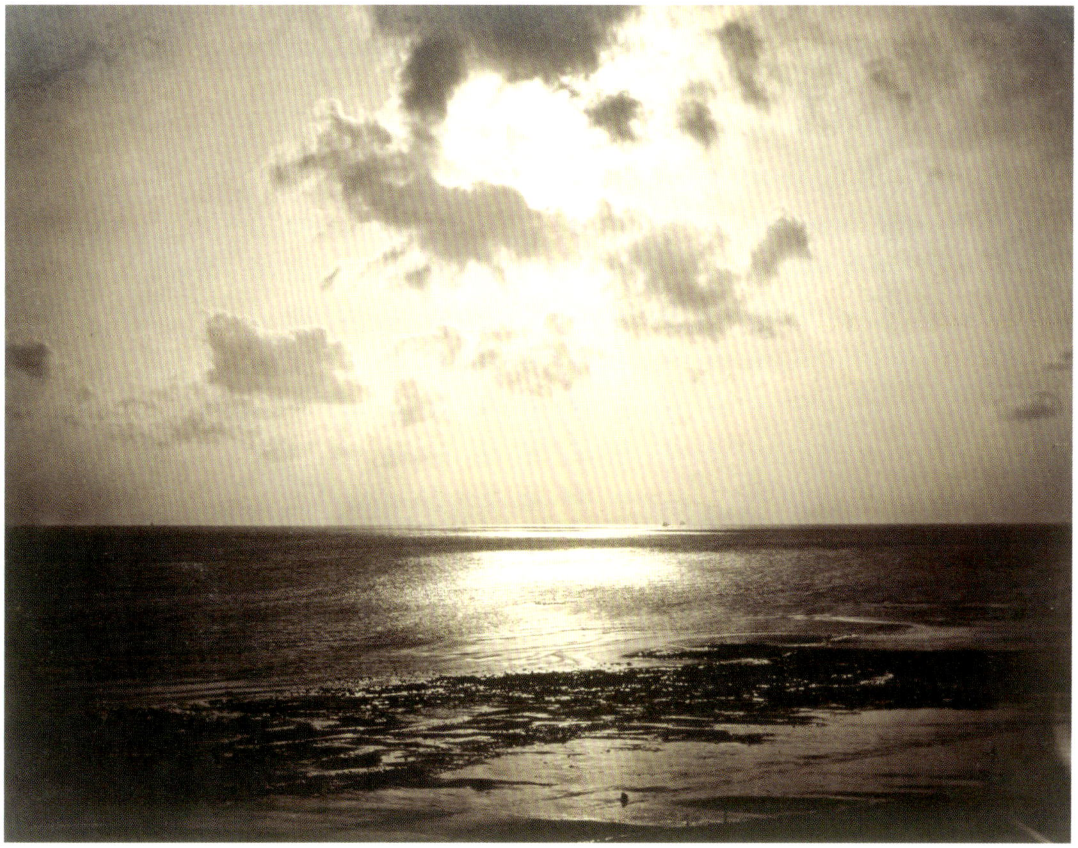

136

Gustave Le Gray
The Great Wave, Sète 1857
Albumen print from two collodion-on-glass negatives 34.3 x 41.2 (13½ x 16¼)
Victoria and Albert Museum

Aubenas 2002, no. 134

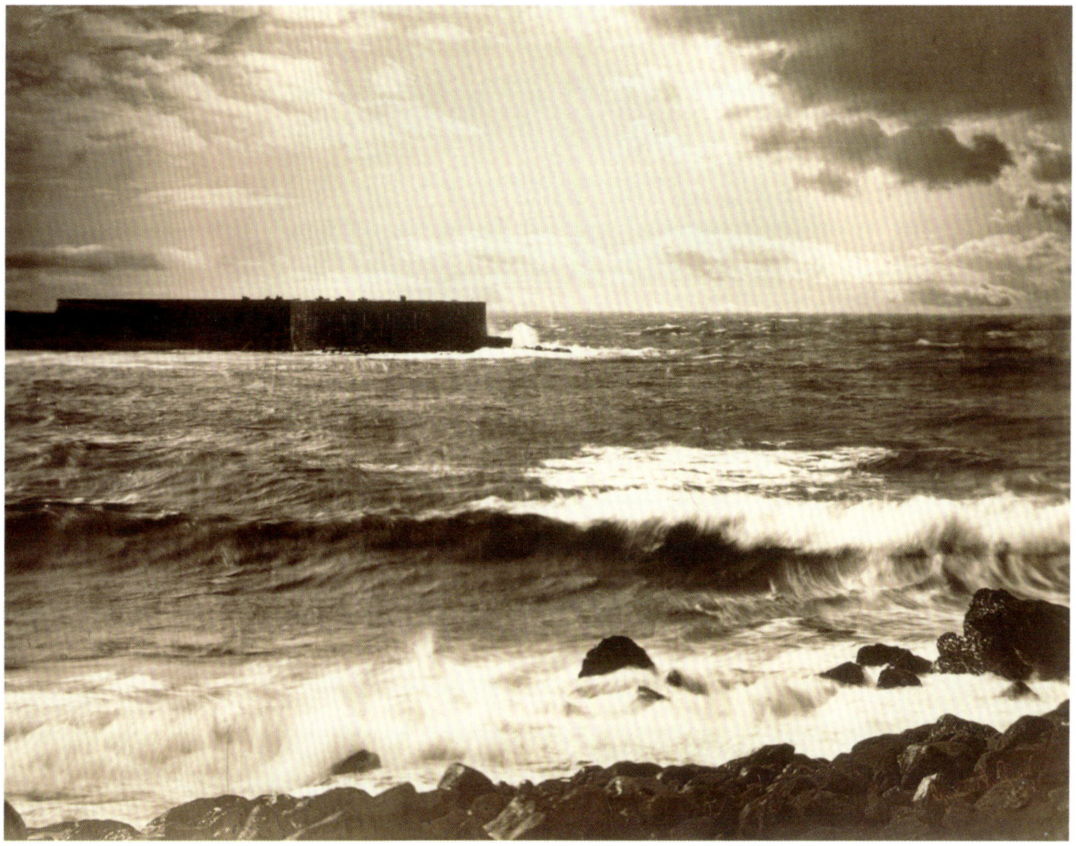

Fig. 47

Édouard Manet

The Battle of the U.S.S. 'Kearsage' and the C.S.S. 'Alabama' 1864
Oil on canvas 134 x 127 (52¾ x 50)
Philadelphia Museum of Art

The word 'crepuscule' (or twilight) refers to the time of day immediately before sunrise or after sunset, which results in a distinctive quality of ambient light. Whistler (1834–1903) attempted to capture the effect, primarily through subtle colour harmonies. This painting was admired when it was exhibited at the French Gallery, Pall Mall, in 1867. A reviewer in the *Athenaeum* thought the artist had given 'an aspect of sleepy motion to the vessels, and ... conveyed to the spectator the rolling, seemingly breathing, surface of the sea with a power that is magical' (Dorment and MacDonald 1995, p. 118).

The understated quality of Whistler's representation might encourage us to view it as an atmospheric harbour scene, devoid of narrative content. However, Valparaiso, the principal harbour of Chile, had been the scene of naval drama in 1866, having first experienced a blockade and then bombardment by the Spanish navy. Whistler had travelled to South America to assist the Chilean cause. By the time he arrived, British, American and French navy ships were also present, as a 'neutral' peacekeeping force. In the event, albeit outraged by the actions of the Spanish, these fleets were obliged to withdraw. Whistler's painting represents the beginning of this retreat, on the evening of 30 March. The scene thus represents a stark contrast with the tradition of European battle painting. The 'sleepy' atmosphere evoked by Whistler (and noted in the review quoted above) corresponds to the impotence of the foreign fleets as they prepare to leave the harbour. Rather than the epic naval representations of the past, this one finds greater parallels with the powerlessness of the warships in Turner's *Fort Vimieux* [fig. 43] and *The Fighting 'Temeraire'* [87].

Whistler's early seascapes are often compared to those of his contemporary Édouard Manet. However, in his first known seascape, *The Battle of the U.S.S. 'Kearsage' and the C.S.S. 'Alabama'* [fig. 47], Manet can be seen to have reinvigorated the traditional battle painting. His epic yet thoroughly modern representation responds to an engagement between two American ships off the coast of Cherbourg during the American Civil War.

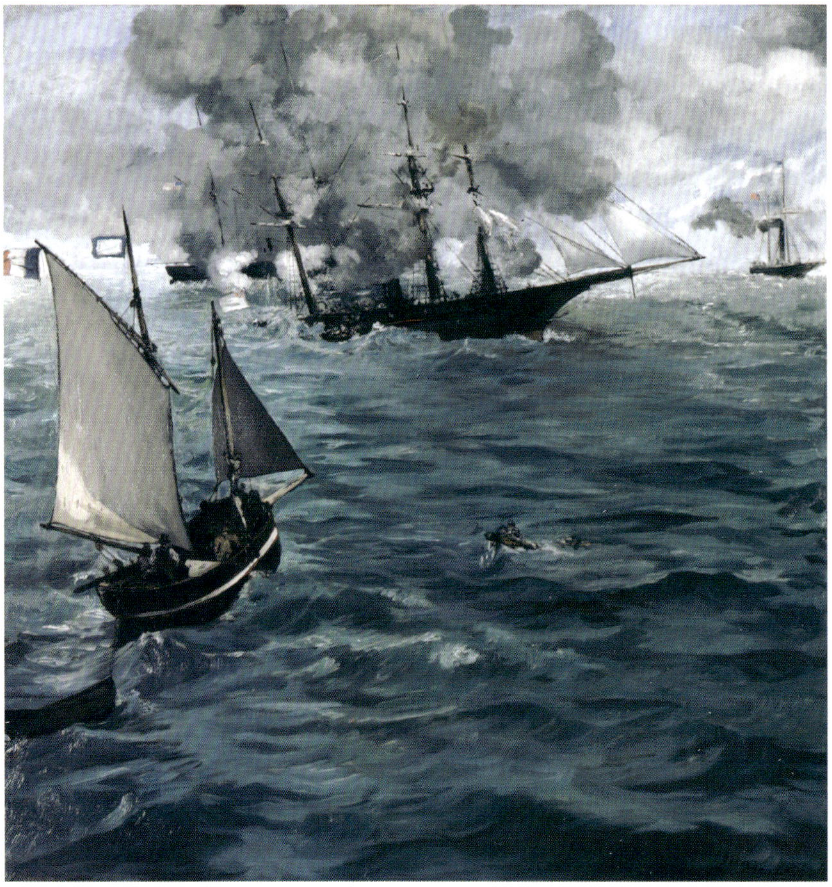

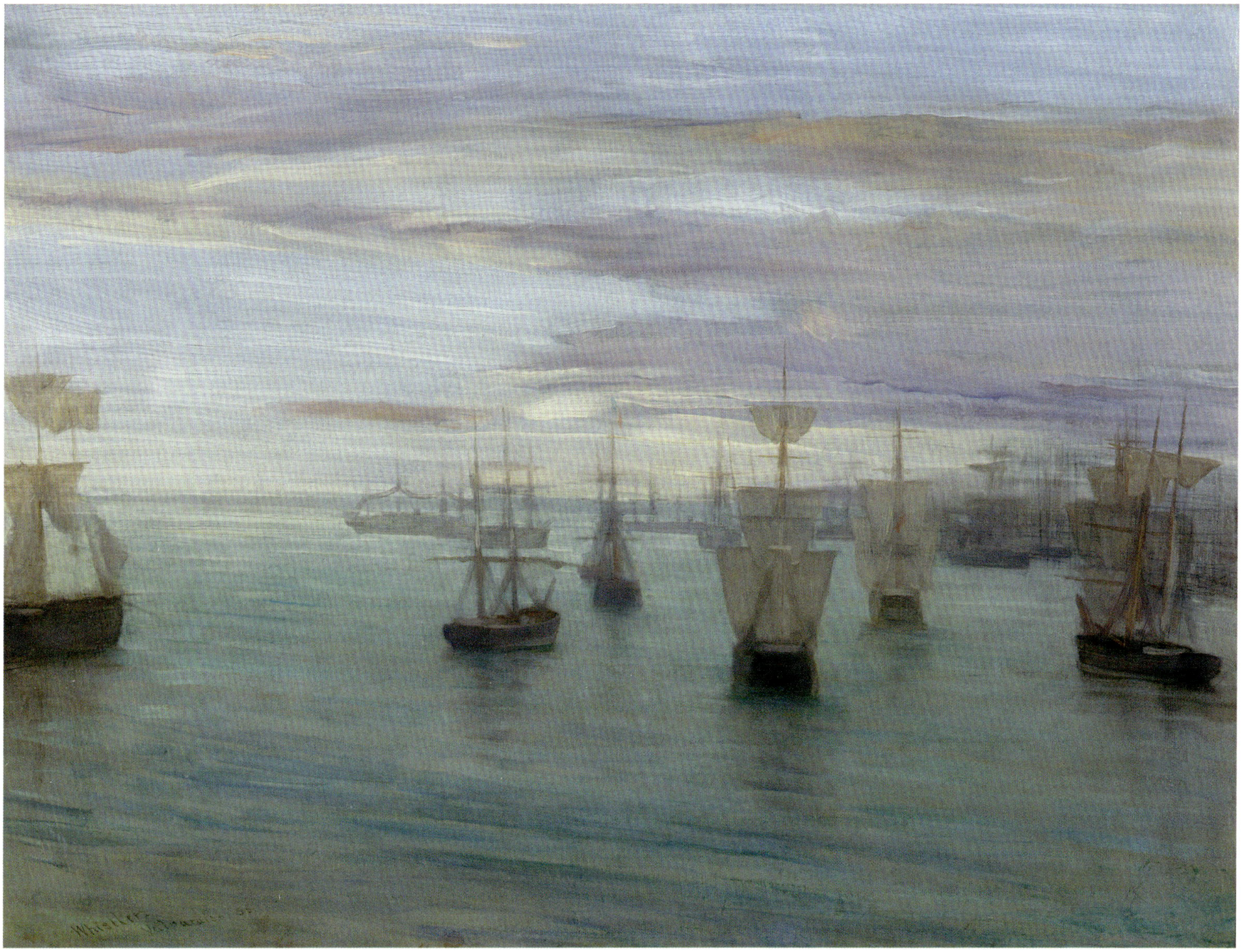

137

James McNeill Whistler

Crepuscule in Flesh Colour and Green: Valparaiso 1866

Oil on canvas 58.6 x 75.9 (23⅛ x 29⅞)

Tate

Dorment and MacDonald 1995, no. 44

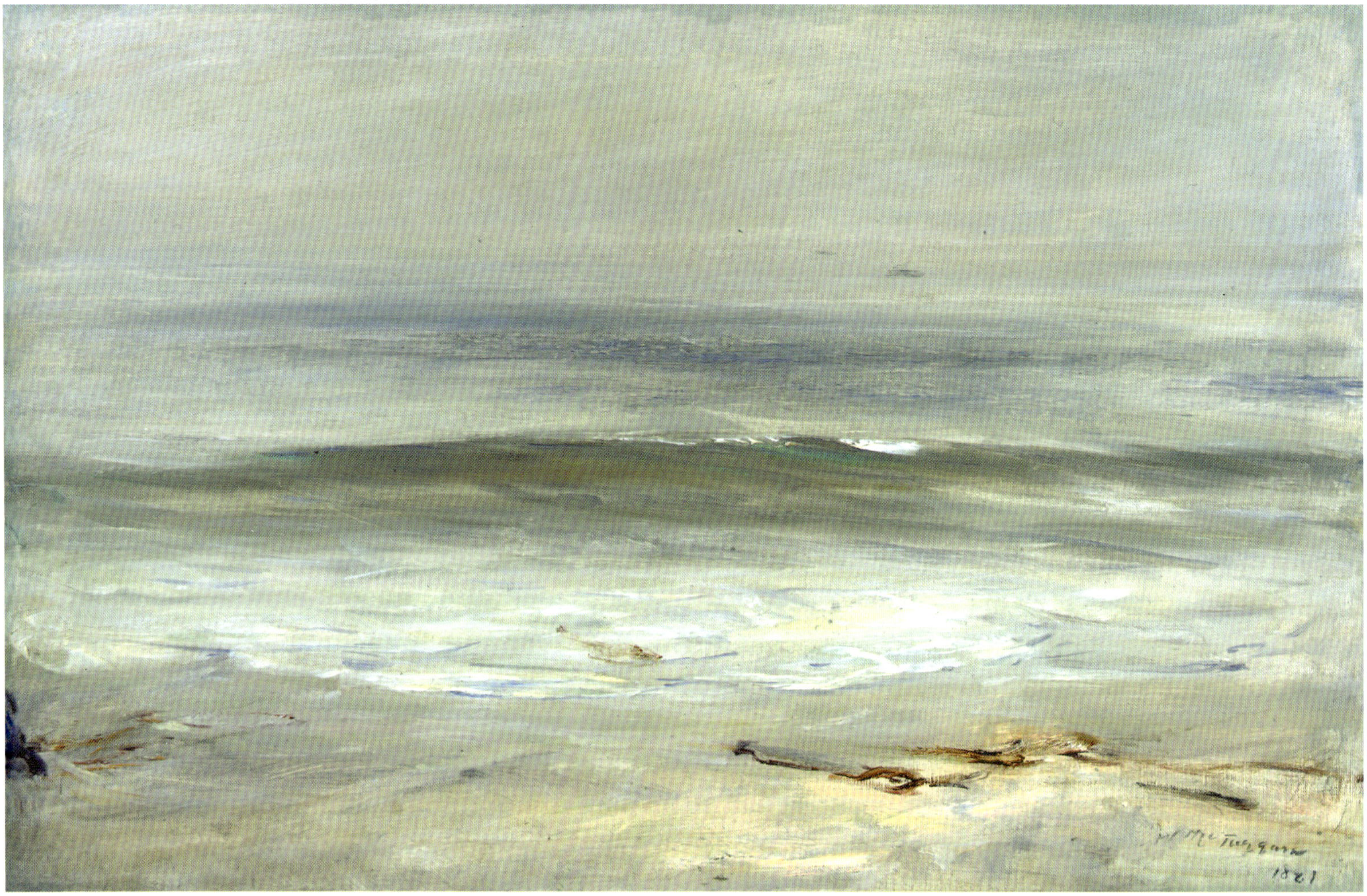

138

William McTaggart

The Wave 1881

Oil on canvas 62 x 92 (24⅜ x 36¼)

Kirkcaldy Museum and Art Gallery

Kvaerne 2007, p. 155

William McTaggart (1835–1910) specialized in marine painting for most of his long career. Today he is often described as a Scottish Impressionist. From the late 1860s he began to focus on coastal scenes and seascapes, initially responding to The Hague School, and then to Whistler, with whom he was sometimes compared in the 1870s and 1880s. On seeing Whistler's paintings for the first time, McTaggart is recorded as saying that 'They were beautiful colour, but they were also something new' (Kvaerne 2007, p. 151). His increasingly broad and expressive style of painting also underlined an interest in Turner and Constable, although McTaggart's early biographer, the art historian Sir James Caw, suggested that Turner was 'more an inspiration than an influence' (Caw 1917, p. 20).

McTaggart had many opportunities of seeing Turner's work. Like Whistler, he visited the Manchester Art Treasures exhibition in 1857 and regularly made trips to London. After Henry Vaughan donated his collection of Turner watercolours to the National Gallery of Scotland in 1900, McTaggart also made a point of visiting the gallery every January, when they were on display. Like many of his other seascapes, *The Wave* was painted on the coast at Machrihanish, a village in Argyll, western Scotland.

The subtlety of McTaggart's approach greatly impressed Caw. Summarizing the artist's contribution to marine painting, he wrote:

> In its own way indeed 'The Wave' is a rendering of the sea's haunting fascination that he never surpassed ... the under-sense of greatness has been so finely felt by the artist and set down with such consummate and unobtrusive art, that the whole strength and vastness of the wide sea are vividly and subtly suggested (Caw 1917, pp. 80–81).

McTaggart's technique has been likened to Whistler's work, especially in his 'nocturnes'. Its simplicity also bears comparison with Turner's many watercolour sketches and oil studies of the sea (see [124 and 125]) as well as Courbet's *L'Immensité* [fig. 48]. During the late 1850s and 1860s Gustave Courbet's unconventional seascapes were an important model for Whistler, as demonstrated by *Harmony in Blue and Silver: Trouville* (Isabella Stewart Gardner Museum), which in 1866 Whistler gave the title of *Courbet – on sea shore*.

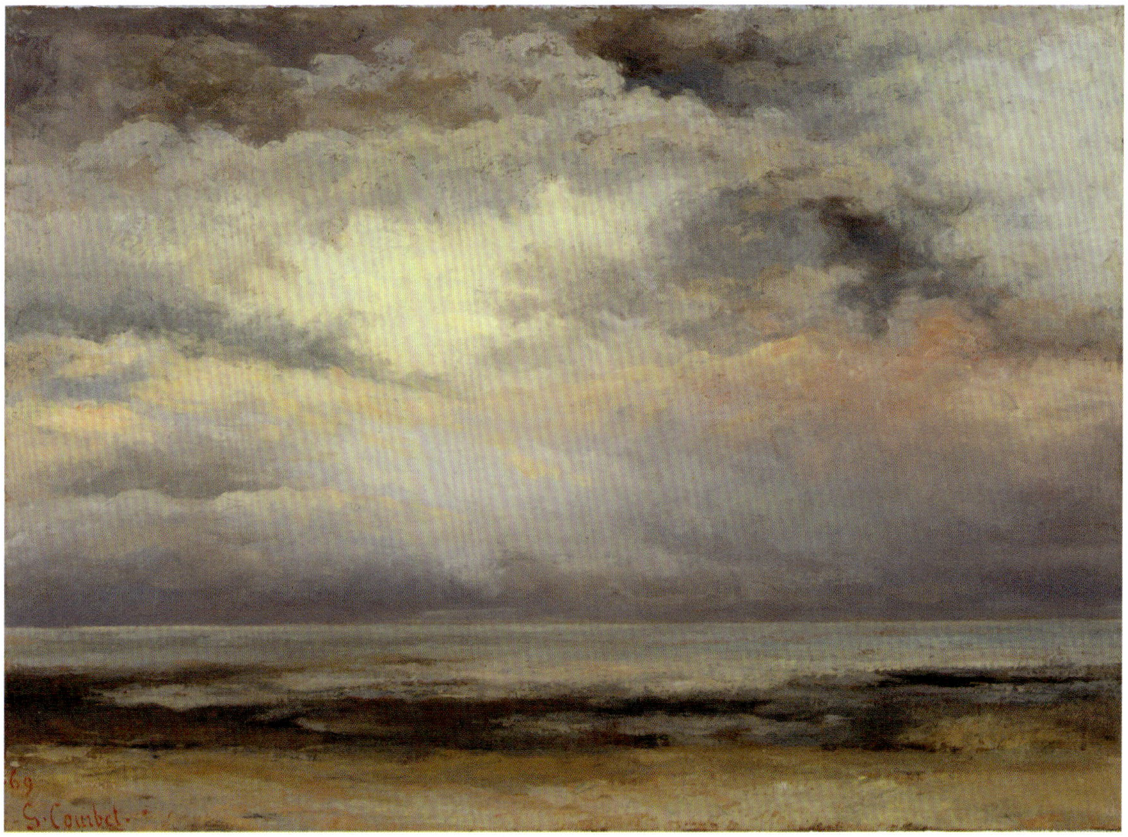

Fig. 48

Gustave Courbet
L'Immensité 1869
Oil on canvas 60 x 82.2 (23⅝ x 32⅜)
Victoria and Albert Museum

139

J.M.W. Turner

Whalers (The Whale Ship) 1845
Oil on canvas 92.8 x 122.6 (36½ x 48¼)
The Metropolitan Museum of Art

Butlin and Joll, no. 415; Venning 1985b, pp. 75–83; Baetjer 2009, no. 114

This painting is one of four on the subject of whaling that Turner produced between 1845 and 1846. Two (including the present work) were shown at the Royal Academy in 1845 and two the following year. *Whalers* was the only one to be sold, the others eventually forming part of the Turner Bequest of 1856. Turner seems to have painted the series in the hope that some or all would be acquired by Elhanan Bicknell, one of the artist's most important collectors. Bicknell had made his fortune as a director of Langton and Bicknell, a firm that had a financial interest in the Pacific sperm-whale fishery, primarily as candlemakers. He had subscribed to the publication of Thomas Beale's *Natural History of the Sperm Whale* (1836) to which Turner made a reference in the Royal Academy catalogue of 1845. Beale's book also included diagrams and engraved images by William James Linton, one after the marine artist William John Huggins. Furthermore, Bicknell's company owned an oil painting, *A Whaler in the South Sea Fishery*, by Huggins, dated about 1835 (Baetjer 2009, p. 235, fig. 159). Given the unlikelihood that Turner ever saw a sperm whale, he would have been reliant on such images. In fact, the composition of Huggins's painting, mentioned above, especially the relative position of the whale and a ship in full sail, may have been the starting point for *Whalers*. At about the same time, Turner produced several sketches of whales and whalers, in the Channel Sketchbook (Yale Center for British Art), the Ambleteuse and Wimereux Sketchbook and the Whalers Sketchbook (see 'Imagining the Sea', pp. 226–29), all dated from about 1845.

At the Royal Academy, the present painting was accompanied by a reference to page 175 in Beale's *Natural History*. This details the epic struggle between a whaling crew and a sperm whale, concluding as follows:

> Captain Swain, with twelve men in one boat ... made another attack upon the whale with the lance, which caused it to throw up blood from the blow-hole in increased quantities ... the whale went into a flurry and soon died, when, to the dismay of the boat's crews, who had endured so much danger and hardship in its capture, it sunk, and never rose again' (Beale 1839, pp. 175–76).

Thus the crew's hopes of completing their expedition with a full cargo were dashed – just the kind of hopeless endeavour that would have interested Turner.

In 1849, the American author Herman Melville visited London. It is not known if he saw any of Turner's whaling paintings at that time. However, on the title page of his copy of Beale's *Natural History*, Melville annotated the following, 'Turner's pictures of whalers were suggested by this book', underlining (at the very least) that he knew about them (Baetjer 2009, p. 236). His now-celebrated novel *Moby Dick*, published first in London in 1851, has often been discussed in conjunction with Turner (see 'Atlantic Crossings', pp. 270–73). One point of connection may relate to the dominant formal quality of all four paintings: that is, their subtle gradations of white. This was commented upon by a number of reviewers in 1845. For example, the pendant painting to *Whalers* was described in *The Times* as 'one mass of white spray, which so blends with the white clouds of the sky, that the spectator can hardly separate them, while the whiteness is still continued by the sails of the ship, which are placed in defiance of contrast' (6 May 1845). And the *Literary Gazette* (17 May 1845) thought the present painting was 'a vision and unreality' but that 'the handling of the tints, and their harmony, allowing for the exalted pitch of their prismatic brightness, are astonishing.' In Chapter 42 of *Moby Dick*, the narrator Ishmael makes the following observation about the eponymous whale:

> there was another thought, or rather vague, nameless horror concerning him, which at times by its intensity completely overpowered all the rest; and yet so mystical and well nigh ineffable was it, that I almost despair of putting it in a comprehensible form. It was the whiteness of the whale that above all things appalled me (Melville 1851, p. 168).

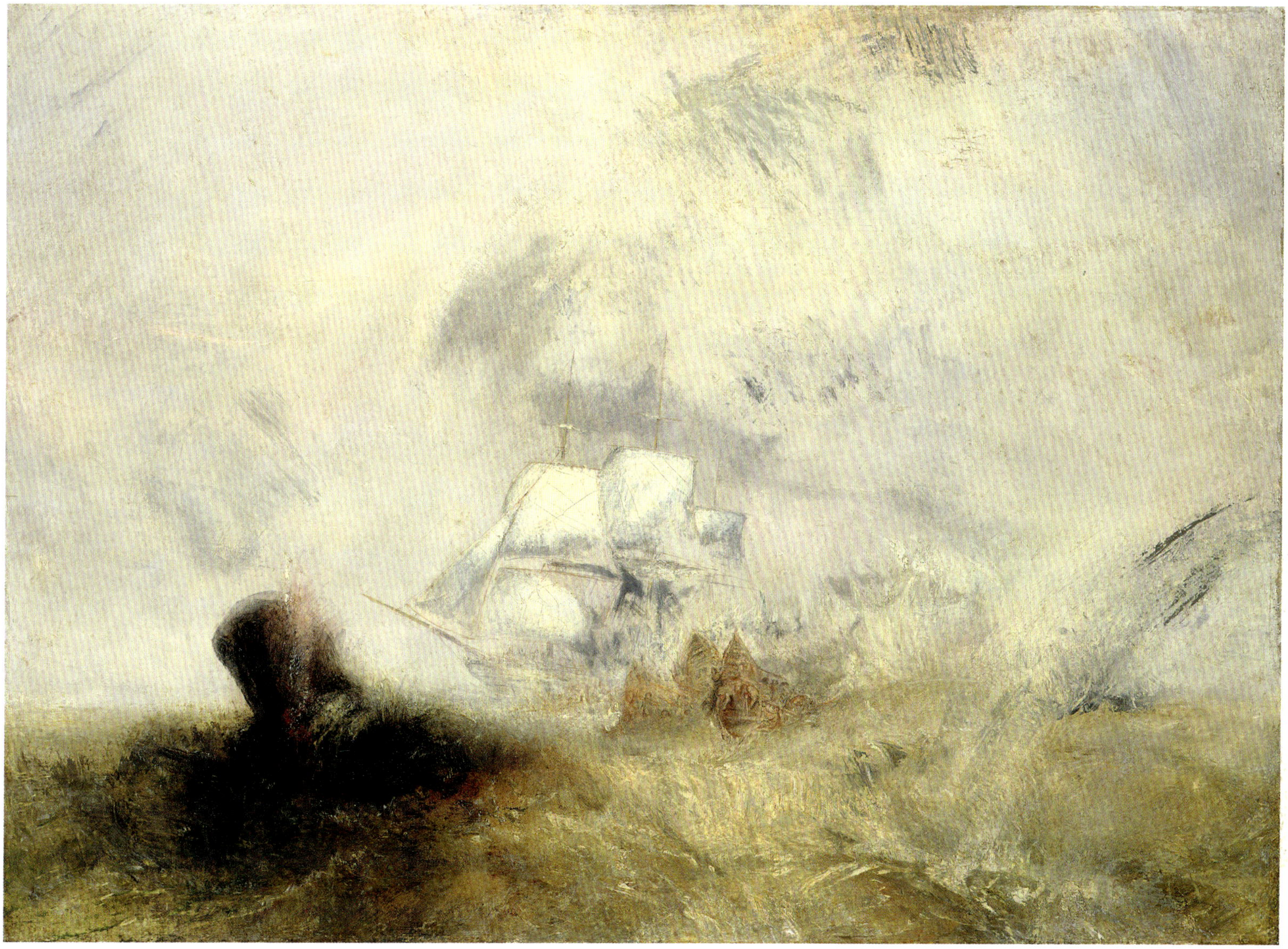

Atlantic Crossings Sam Smiles

The success of the American navy in the War of 1812 and the growing importance of the republic's merchant fleet ensured that the sea played a prominent part in American imaginative life. Classic maritime novels published in the United States during the middle decades of the nineteenth century include *The Narrative of Arthur Gordon Pym* by Edgar Allan Poe (1838), *Two Years Before the Mast* by Richard Henry Dana (1840), *The Sea Lions* by James Fenimore Cooper (1849) and Herman Melville's iconic *Moby Dick* (1851).[1] The publication of these works coincided with the rise of an American school of marine painting, some of whose most able practitioners looked across the Atlantic to Turner for inspiration. The third quarter of the century also witnessed the arrival of the first three paintings by Turner, all of them marines, in American collections. *Staffa, Fingal's Cave* [128] was sold to Colonel James Lenox of New York in 1845. Three years later Lenox visited London to buy another canvas, and after attempting unsuccessfully to purchase *The Fighting 'Temeraire'* [87] from Turner's gallery, he acquired *Fort Vimieux* [fig. 43] at auction in 1850. John Taylor Johnston acquired *Slavers Throwing overboard the Dead and Dying – Typhoon Coming On* [fig. 46] in 1872.[2] Paradoxical as it may seem, Turner's achievement as an artist threw a longer shadow on creative practice in the United States than it did in Britain.[3]

Following the publication of the first American edition of *Modern Painters* in 1847, John Ruskin's advocacy of Turner's art became highly influential in the United States. Although Ruskin believed that spectacular scenery was no substitute for historical resonance and that it was therefore 'useless for Americans to look at Turner', public perceptions of what landscape painting could be were undoubtedly enlarged by his example.[4] And, of course, when it came to marine painting, Ruskin's reservations about the historically impoverished American scene could be set aside, for the ocean was construed as an elemental landscape and the 'full awfulness of the sea' (as Melville described it) transcended history, culture and technology.[5]

Turner's most audacious sea picture, *Snow Storm – Steam-Boat off a Harbour's Mouth* [131], cites the steamship 'Ariel' in its full descriptive title, and in a later account of the picture Turner described the dangers he had confronted observing the storm while tied to the mast. Coincidentally, Poe's novel *The Narrative of Arthur Gordon Pym* begins with the loss of the sailing boat 'Ariel' in a violent winter storm, rammed by a whaling ship in-bound to Nantucket. Poe's short story 'A Descent into the Maelström', published three years later in 1841, features a description of a huge whirlpool off the coast of northern Norway, ostensibly written by a survivor who had plunged into its depths and at the moment of greatest peril had rationally scrutinized its workings. What unites these engagements with the natural world is not creative influence (Turner and Poe probably did not know one another's work), nor a preoccupation with similar phenomena (Turner's storm vortex and Poe's whirlpool), but the idea of the singular observer, who had confronted nature at its most extreme and now attempts to make that experience tangible. Together, these works of art represent an exceptional moment of adventurous creativity in response to the sea, on both sides of the Atlantic.

In the autumn of 1851, a few weeks before Turner died, Herman Melville's *Moby Dick* was published, first in Britain and then in the USA.[6] As Robert K. Wallace has shown, Turner's vision of nature played a major part in shaping Melville's literary aesthetic in his early novels.[7] The originality of both artists was explicitly compared in a review of 1850:

> Mr. Melville stands as far apart from any past or present marine painter in pen and ink as Turner does from the magnificent artist vilipended by Mr. Ruskin for Turner's sake – Vandervelde. We cannot recall another novelist or sketcher who has given the poetry of the Ship ... in a manner at all resembling his.[8]

Melville knew Turner's work from engravings and saw it at first-hand when visiting London in 1849 and 1857. Indeed, *Moby Dick* includes what is probably a tribute to the artist. When Ishmael arrives at the Spouter Inn, early in the story, his attention is drawn repeatedly to a large and indistinct painting of a whale hunt that is powerfully evocative of Turner's paintings of the same subject:

> It was only by diligent study and a series of systematic visits to it, and careful inquiry of the neighbors, that you could any way arrive at an understanding of its purpose. Such unaccountable masses of shades and shadows, that at first you almost thought some ambitious young artist, in the time of the New England hags, had endeavored to delineate chaos bewitched ... But what most puzzled and confounded you was a long, limber, portentous, black mass of something hovering in the centre of the picture over three blue, dim, perpendicular lines floating in a nameless yeast. A boggy, soggy, squitchy picture truly, enough to drive a nervous man distracted. Yet was there a sort of indefinite, half-attained, unimaginable sublimity about it that fairly froze you to it, till you involuntarily took an oath with yourself to find out what that marvellous painting meant.[9]

Fig. 49

Winslow Homer

On a Lee Shore 1900

Oil on canvas 99.1 x 99.1 (39 x 39)

Rhode Island School of Design

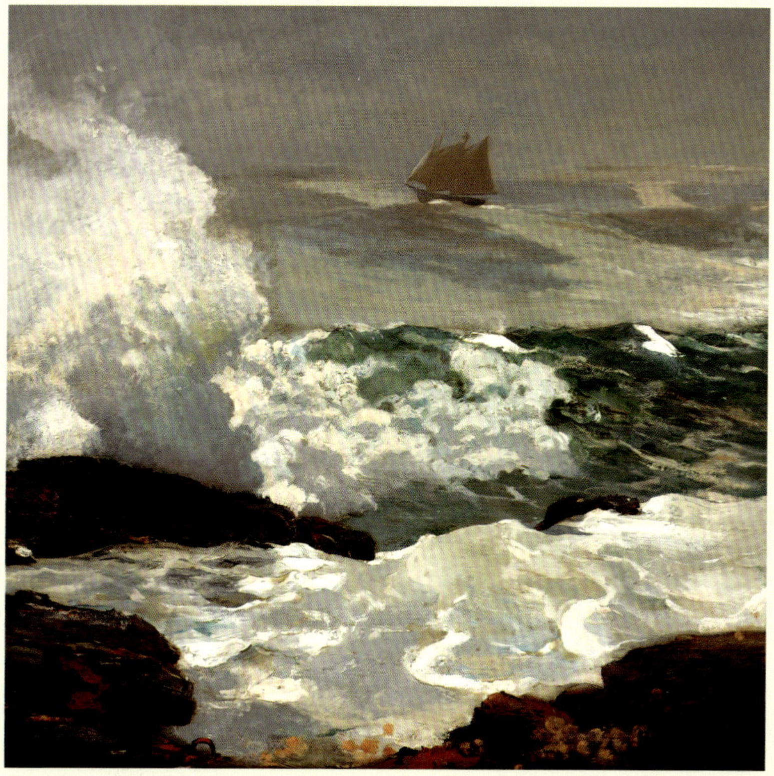

Ishmael's difficulty in making the picture out was inspired by Melville's admiration for Turner's ability to go beyond simple description and respond creatively to the indistinct and elusive face of nature. As he says in the famous 'Lee Shore' chapter, 'all deep, earnest thinking is but the intrepid effort of the soul to keep the open independence of her sea ... in landlessness alone resides the highest truth, shoreless, indefinite as God'.[10]

The importance of Turner's transatlantic reputation is also revealed in the work of several American painters, including marines by Washington Allston, Robert Salmon and James Hamilton. Some of the most significant members of the Hudson River School were also indebted to the English artist, among them Thomas Cole, Sanford Gifford and Frederic Edwin Church. The importance of Turner for Church was most pronounced in the work he produced in the late 1850s and early 1860s, when critics made comparisons between the two artists [fig. 45].[11] Church's marine subjects betray Turner's influence, especially in their handling of light and atmosphere. His painting *Cotopaxi* (1862, Detroit Institute of Arts) was commissioned by James Lenox, who also owned Turner's *Staffa* and *Fort Vimieux*, and it is possible that Church was able to study these two paintings at first-hand in New York. And when exhibiting at the German Gallery in London's New Bond Street, for example, Church was announced as the artist on whom Turner's mantle had fallen, 'far more Turneresque in his gifts than any other landscape painter.'[12]

Edward and Thomas Moran, both of whom were beginning their careers in the 1850s, also looked to Turner for inspiration. In 1862, they visited England, staying about eight months and including marine subjects by Turner among the works they copied in London, notably Edward's *The Wreck of a Transport Ship* and Thomas's *Ulysses Deriding Polyphemus*.[13] Edward Moran, specializing as a marine artist, maintained an allegiance to Turner throughout his career and in 1888 he recommended Turner's 'powerful marines' as examples for students and amateurs to follow.[14] Thomas Moran's debt to Turner was recognized at the time, with a number of critics pointing out his 'Turneresque' approach to the American landscape and some of them complaining about it.[15] Of all Thomas Moran's marines, his views of Venice (which he first visited in 1886) explore the maritime aspect of the city in a style most closely modelled on Turner's example. His final homage to Turner is the group of sunsets over the sea, most of them in mid-ocean, that he painted in the first decade of the twentieth century.

Yet beyond any formal comparisons, what Turner's career as a marine artist demonstrated above all was the potential of painting to capture the relentless power and danger of the sea. As Melville noted in the year of the artist's death:

> [However] baby man may brag of his science and skill, and however much, in a flattering future, that science and skill may augment; yet for ever and for ever, to the crack of doom, the sea will insult and murder him, and pulverize the stateliest, stiffest frigate he can make.[16]

Winslow Homer is, in this respect, the most significant American artist to extend the reach of Turner's vision [fig. 49]. Homer had seen Turner's *Slave Ship* in New York in 1872 but became more familiar with the artist's work during an extended visit to England in 1881. His preoccupation with the ocean in all its moods produced one of the few bodies of work, in oil and watercolour, whose technical sophistication, strength of composition and human interest could be said to rival Turner's comprehensive representation of the sea.[17]

Opposite

J.M.W. Turner
Whalers 1845 (detail of [139])

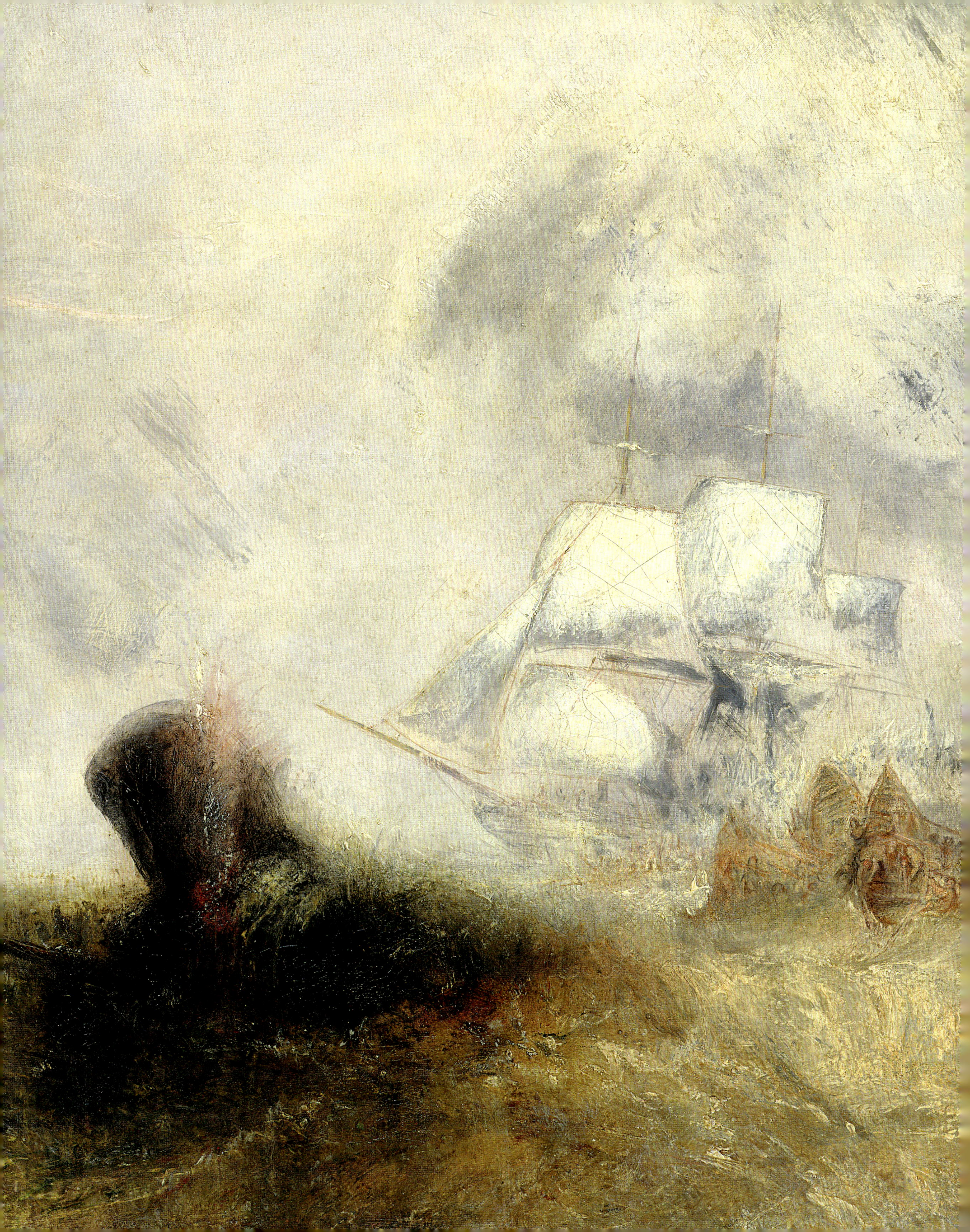

Notes

Bibliographical references given in abbreviated form in the Notes are given in full in the Selected Bibliography.

INTRODUCTION

1 Letter from Robert Leslie to John Ruskin, dated 7 June 1884, published in Ruskin 1908, p. 571.
2 Ruskin 1856a, p. 26.
3 Butlin and Joll 1984, vol. 1, p. 188.
4 See Baker 2010, pp. 1–20.
5 Redding 1852, p. 152.
6 Moran 1888, p. 101.
7 Venning 1985a, pp. 304–05.
8 Thompson 2007b, p. 146; see also Hayter 2002.
9 Edwards 1994, p. 2.
10 Thompson 2007a, p. 146.
11 Thornbury 1862, vol. 1, p. 266.
12 Beaumont's painting, dated 1805, is now in the collection of the Wordsworth Trust at Dove Cottage, Grasmere.
13 Baker 2010, p. 3.
14 Byron, *Don Juan*, II, xii, l.8.
15 Falk 1938, p. 255.
16 Anderson 1795, p. 573; Falconer, *The Shipwreck*, fourth edition, III, ll.640–45.
17 Cited in Butlin and Joll 1984, vol. 1, p. 2.
18 For extended discussions on the importance of poetry to Turner, see Wilton 1990 and Brown 1992.
19 Anderson 1795, p. 573.
20 Clarke 1804, p. xxx.
21 Warrell 2007, p. 162.
22 Salisbury Sketchbook, 1799, Turner Bequest XLIX inside front cover; see Wilton 1990, p. 18.
23 Devonshire Coast, No.1 Sketchbook, 1811, Turner Bequest CXXIII 58; see Wilton 1990, p. 171.
24 Shanes 1990, p. 9.
25 Ruskin 1908, vol. 35, p. 575.
26 Quoted in Venning 1985a, p. 305.
27 Venning 1985a, p. 305.
28 Butlin and Joll 1984, vol. 1, p. 234.
29 Redding 1852, p.151.
30 Warrell 2007, p. 187.
31 Turner's birthday remains a matter of conjecture. He later claimed that he was born on 23 April (St George's Day and the date of Shakespeare's birth), although this may have been a patriotic gesture.
32 Joll, Butlin and Herrmann 2001, p. 345. Turner's mother suffered from mental illness and was committed to Bethlem Hospital. She probably died there in 1804.
33 Thornbury 1862, vol. 1, p. 8.
34 See Smith 2005.
35 Joll, Butlin and Herrmann 2001, pp. 103 and 391.
36 Warrell 2007, p. 16.
37 Forrester 1996, pp. 29–30.
38 Shanes 2000, pp. 37–39.
39 Shanes 1990, p. 13.
40 Butlin and Joll 1984, vol. 1, p. 215.
41 See Hewison 2000, pp. 11–18 and 61–85.
42 Hewison 2007, p. 17.
43 Joll, Butlin and Herrmann 2001, p. 24.
44 Joll, Butlin and Herrmann 2001, p. 383. There were five codicils made to Turner's will, in 1831, 1832, 1846, 1848 and 1849.

1 CHARTED WATERS

1 *Morning Post*, 5 May 1797, cited in Butlin and Joll 1984, vol. 1, pp. 2–3.
2 Thomas Green, *The Diary of a Lover of Literature*, London 1810, quoted in Butlin and Joll 1984, vol. 1, p. 3.
3 *Fishermen Becalmed previous to a Storm, Twilight* is currently untraced and unknown in engraved form. For more on the immediate critical response to Turner's earliest seascapes, see 'The Battle of the Pictures', pp. 52–55.
4 This appraisal appeared in Peter Cunningham's 'Memoir', in Burnet 1852, p. 19.
5 *Morning Post*, 5 May 1797, quoted in Butlin and Joll 1984, vol. 1, pp. 2–3.
6 *London Packet*, 19 April–1 May 1799, quoted in Butlin and Joll 1984, vol. 1, p. 7.
7 See Robinson 1990, esp. vol. 1, pp. ix–xxvi.
8 For more on the character and significance of marine painting under Monamy et al., see Hughes 2001, esp. pp. 1–51; and Quilley 2000.
9 Vertue 1933, p. 145.
10 Rouquet 1755, pp. 60–61.
11 Russett 1999.
12 Among several hundred works on paper by van de Velde at the National Maritime Museum is a preparatory drawing (NMM PAH8400) that shows signs of repair and substantial reworking by Serres. The drawing, which depicts Charles II's visit to the combined French and English fleets at the Nore in 1672, relates to one of the Dutch artist's largest paintings (NMM BHC0299).
13 Letter from Joshua Reynolds to Nicholas Pocock, dated 4 May 1780, published in Reynolds 2000, pp. 85–86.
14 Diderot 1995, esp. vol. 1, pp. 69–70.
15 Diderot 1995, vol. 1, p. 70.
16 *Naval Chronicle*, vol. 1, 1799, pp. 517–20.
17 *Naval Chronicle*, vol. 1, 1799, p. 517.
18 *The Beauties of the Dutch School; selected from interesting pictures of admired landscape painters*, with engravings by Cornelis Apostool, London, 1793, unpaginated.
19 *The Beauties of the Dutch School*, 1793
20 Of fifteen paintings by van de Velde in the collection of the National Gallery, all but one were produced before the artist left the Netherlands for England.
21 See Simpson 2009, esp. pp. 41–76.
22 *The Beauties of the Dutch School*, 1793.
23 For a more detailed discussion of van de Velde's painting, and Turner's response, see Monks 2009.
24 Letter from Turner to Thomas Griffith, dated 1 February 1844, published in Turner 1980, p. 135.
25 For a plan of the hang of Bridgewater's gallery, see Farington, vol. 5, p. 1775.
26 *Star*, 4 May 1801, quoted in Butlin and Joll 1984, vol. 1, p. 11.

The Battle of the Pictures

1 See, for example, Butlin and Joll 1984, vol. 1, p. 2; and Wilton 1980, pp. 37–38.
2 See Hughes 2007, pp. 139–52.
3 Williams 1796, p. 21.
4 Williams 1796, p. 15.
5 Williams 1797, pp. 10–11.
6 *Oracle and Public Advertiser*, 25 June 1794.

2 'M' FOR MARINE

1 Lyles and Perkins 1989, pp. 44–52; Forrester 1996, pp. 27–32.
2 Lyles and Perkins 1989, p. 45.
3 Pye and Roget 1879, p. 23.
4 Forrester 1996, p. 90.
5 Farington, vol. 4, p. 1303.
6 Serres 1805, dedication page.
7 Serres 1805, dedication page.
8 Forrester 1996, pp. 28–29.
9 Farington, vol. 11, p. 3847.
10 Rand 2007, pp. 30–32.
11 Rand 2007, p. 32.
12 Warrell 2012, p. 86.
13 Wilton 2006a, p. 94.
14 Wilton 2006a, p. 94.
15 Forrester 1996, p. 46.
16 Now in the Museum of Fine Arts, Boston.
17 See Owen and Brown 1988, pp. 10–11, 152–55 and 166–68.
18 Forrester 1996, p. 32.
19 Wilton 2006a, p. 94.
20 Forrester 1996, p. 36.
21 See Helsinger 2002, p. 108.
22 See Dekker 2005, pp. 2–22.
23 Gilpin 1804, pp. 3–4.
24 Price 1796, p. 287.
25 Daniell 1814, p. iii.
26 Daniell 1814, p. iv.
27 Lyles and Perkins 1989, p. 31.
28 Shanes 2000, pp. 39–41.

3 TRAFALGAR SQUARED

1 Jenks 2006, p. 2.
2 Hoock 2003, pp. 168–71.
3 Yarrington 1988, p. 317.
4 Von Erffa and Staley 1986, p. 221.
5 Hughes 2007, pp. 140–52.
6 Butlin and Joll 1984, vol. 1, pp. 6–7. The full exhibited title of Turner's painting was: *Battle of the Nile, at 10 o'clock when the 'L'Orient' blew up, from the Station of the Gun Boats between the Battery and Castle of Aboukir*.
7 Tate Collection, T01452.
8 Now in the National Gallery of Canada, Ottawa. See Costello 2012, pp. 15–60.
9 Von Erffa and Staley 1986, p. 221.
10 Von Erffa and Staley 1986, p. 57.
11 Quoted in Jenks 2006, p. 1.
12 Knight 2005, p. 507.
13 Landseer 1808, pp. 83–84.
14 Yarrington 1988, p. 190.
15 Albinson, Funnell and Peltz 2010, pp. 217–41.
16 Sawyer 2000, pp. 137–48. A watercolour by Joseph Michael Gandy dated 1824 shows the interior of the Royal Gallery with representations (not executed) of Trafalgar and Waterloo (Sir John Soane's Museum, folio vi, LXI, p. 37).
17 Tate Collection, Turner Bequest 1856, N05480 and N00556.
18 The Devonshire Coast, No.1 Sketchbook, 1811, Finberg CXXIII 174, quoted in Wilton 1990, p. 175.
19 Tate Collection, Turner Bequest 1856, N00500.
20 Brown 1992, pp. 29–31.
21 Butlin and Joll 1984, vol. 1, p. 93; Brown 1992, pp. 29–32.

22 Clarke and McArthur 1809, vol. 2, between pp. 448–49 and 454–55.
23 Thomson 1999, pp. 96–100.
24 Quilley 2000, pp. 80–81 and 94–99.
25 Clarke 1801, pp. 84–85.
26 Rodger 2005, p. 17. Nelson was referring specifically to the British officers at the Battle of the Nile (1798).
27 Davey and Johns 2012, pp. 27–29.
28 The Devonshire Coast, No.1 Sketchbook, 1811, Turner Bequest CXXIII 176, discussed in Wilton 1990, p. 175.
29 Jane Austen, *Persuasion*, London, 1818, p. 114.
30 Ruskin 1856a, p. 16.
31 James 1826, vol. 3, pp. 473–74; see also Quilley 2011, pp. 228–46.
32 Van der Merwe 1979, pp. 110–11.
33 Butlin and Joll 1984, vol. 1, p. 209.
34 Butlin and Joll 1984, vol. 1, p. 230.

Turner's *Battle of Trafalgar* at the National Gallery of Naval Art

1 James 1826, vol. 4, pp. 149–50; See also Tracy 2007, pp. 42–67.
2 Lloyd 2000, pp. 166–67.
3 John Soane reconstructed the entire Royal Entrance between 1822 and 1824. Commissions for the additional paintings were not forthcoming, however, and in 1831 Soane offered to commission them himself. See Sawyer 1996, p. 75; and Sean Sawyer, 'Sir John Soane and the Late Georgian Origins of the Royal Entrance' in Riding and Riding 2000, pp. 137–48.
4 National Art Library, London, MSL/1941/677–683, *British Institution Minutes*, vol. 3, 20 February 1815.
5 National Art Library, London, MSL/1941/677–683, *British Institution Minutes*, vol. 5, 6 July 1825.
6 TNA PRO 30/26/27, *Printed Proposal for the Naval Gallery, written by E.H. Locker*, 23 October 1823.
7 TNA PRO 30/26/27, E.H. Locker Memorandum dated 20 September 1823, p. 19; and TNA ADM 67/44, 11 February 1795.
8 This collection of British naval paintings, sculptures and curiosities remained on display in the Painted Hall until 1936, when the collection moved on indefinite loan to the newly founded National Maritime Museum.
9 TNA ADM 67/80, 8 August 1829.
10 Locker 1833, p. 15.
11 See Pieter van der Merwe, '"A proud monument of the glory of England": The Greenwich Hospital Collection' in Quilley 2006, pp. 19–37.

4 CONTESTED WATERS

1 For a detailed discussion of these three paintings, see Warrell 1997, pp. 172–78.
2 *New Monthly Magazine*, vol. 15, 1825, p. 300; and *Literary Magnet*, vol. 3, 1825, p. 140.
3 *Literary Gazette*, 13 May 1826 and 2 June 1827.
4 *London Chronicle*, 10 April 1819, pp. 347–48. Fawkes compiled this and other favourable reviews of his exhibition for a pamphlet, *A Collection of Water Colour Drawings, in the possession of Mr. Fawkes, 45, Grosvenor Place, London*. For a detailed discussion of the reception of Turner's watercolours in the early 1820s, see Ian Warrell, '"The wonder-working artist": Contemporary Responses to Turner's Exhibited and Engraved Watercolours' in Shanes 2000, pp. 32–45.
5 Farington, vol. 6, pp. 2023–24; *Literary Journal*, 1 July 1827, p. 291.
6 Burnet 1852, p. 79.
7 See Brown 1981.
8 The remark came from the painter Henry Thomson, as recorded by Joseph Farington (vol. 7, p. 2532).
9 Callcott also painted two smaller versions of the same work by Turner (Tate and the Ashmolean Museum). See Brown 1975, pp. 721–22; and Brown 1981, pp. 64–65. It seems that Parker commissioned the copy in the hope of realizing his initial investment by selling the more valuable original.
10 Ruskin 1903, vol. 3, pp. 191–92.
10 *Champion*, 12 May 1816.
12 Thornbury 1862, vol. 1, p. 275.
13 Reinagle produced several paintings of the battle, which he had witnessed as an observer with the British fleet on board the 'Mosquito'.
14 Noon 2003, esp. pp. 12–27.
15 Noon 2008, esp. pp. 34–37.
16 *New Monthly Magazine and Literary Journal*, 1 July 1827, p. 292.
17 Solkin 2001, esp. pp. 1–22 and 65–75.
18 Henry Trimmer's son recounted to Thornbury: 'Owen, the water-colour painter, had been imitating him, on which [Turner] wrote him a very brisk note, requesting him in future to draw from his own resources, and not from his.' Thornbury 1862, vol. 1, p. 177.
19 Cunningham's 'Memoir' in Burnet 1852, p. 36.

'Turner, Calcott and Collins Will Not Like It': Constable, Brighton and the Sea

1 Reynolds 1996, R.94.1–3, pp. 2–3.
2 Reynolds 1996, R.00.14 and R.03.56, pp. 28 and 52.
3 Reynolds 1996, R.03.7–51 and see note 5 below.
4 Constable 1964, p. 33.
5 Sotheby's, London, *The British Sale*, 19 March 2003, lots 138–40. However, Robin Brooks ('Victory in Art and the Constable Sketches', *Trafalgar Chronicle*, 2005, pp. 173–79) has questioned whether the Sotheby's drawings do in fact represent the 'Victory'.
6 Reynolds 1996, R.06.1, p. 71; *His Majesty's Ship Victory, Capt. E. Harvey* [sic], *in the Memorable Battle of Trafalgar, between Two French Ships of the Line*.
7 Constable 1964, p. 90.
8 Constable 1968, p. 171.
9 See examples in Beevers 1995, pp. 70–77.
10 Reynolds 1984, R.20.6–9 and R.22.36–38, pp. 46–47 and 108–09.
11 Constable 1968, p. 156.
12 Constable 1968, p. 184.
13 Constable 1968, p. 230.
14 Ian Warrell, 'J.M.W. Turner in Brighton' in Beevers 1995, p. 36.
15 Hemingway 1992, pp. 188–90.
16 Ivy 1991, pp. 122–24.
17 Leslie 1894, p. 57.
18 Bailey 2006, p. 259.
19 Constable 1968, p. 191.

5 TURNER ON SHOW

1 Burnet 1852, p. 6.
2 *Lives of the Illustrious*, 1852, p. 72.
3 *Monthly Mirror*, vol. 11, 1801, p. 376.
4 *Monthly Magazine*, vol. 11, 1 June 1801, p. 438.
5 Copley's portrait was of *Robert Graham*, now at the National Gallery of Art, Washington. See Farington, vol. 6, p. 2302.
6 Leslie 1860, p. 135.
7 *Monthly Mirror*, vol. 13, June 1802, pp. 379–80.
8 *Star*, 6 May 1802.
9 *Naval Chronicle*, vol. 1, 1799, pp. 157–58.
10 Quilley 2000, pp. 80–109.
11 Recorded in Burnet 1852, p. 18.
12 Farington, vol. 7, p. 2544.
13 Recalled in a letter from L.G. Fawkes to D.S. MacColl, dated 23 July 1910, quoted in Gage 1969, p. 162.
14 *Monthly Magazine*, 1 April 1808, p. 250; Thornbury 1862, vol. 1, p. 267.
15 Martin Archer Shee, *Elements of Art, a poem in six cantos*, London, 1809, p. 342.
16 Landseer 1808, pp. 83–84.
17 *The National Register*, vol. 1, 21 February 1808, p. 125.
18 The monument was eventually cast by Richard Westmacott and placed at Exchange Flags in Liverpool.
19 *Monthly Magazine*, 1 May 1809.
20 *Monthly Magazine and British Register*, vol. 45, January–June 1818, p. 445.
21 *Examiner*, 1 July 1827.
22 *New Monthly Magazine*, vol. 21, 1 July 1827, p. 291.
23 *Literary Gazette*, 2 June 1827, p. 348.
24 *The Englishman's Magazine*, vol. 1, June 1831, p. 320.
25 *Literary Gazette*, 21 May 1831, vol. 15, p. 331.
26 *Lives of the Illustrious*, 1852, p. 75.
27 Burnet 1852, p. 91.
28 For a discussion of the relationship between these works and those of Claude Lorrain, see Warrell, 2012, p. 127.
29 *The Art-Union*, February 1841, p. 29 and *The British Miscellany*, vol. 1, part 1, London, 1841, pp. 206–07.
30 *Literary Gazette and Journal of Belles Lettres*, 6 February 1841, p. 92.
31 Recorded in Thornbury 1862, vol. 1, p. 335.
32 Smith 1860, p. 198.
33 Ruskin 1856b, pp. 21 and 23.
34 Recounted in an obituary in *Fraser's Magazine for Town and Country*, February 1852, p. 152.
35 Thornbury 1862, vol. 1, p. 334.
36 *The Gentleman's Magazine*, 19 February 1852, p. 200; and *Lives of the Illustrious*, 1852, p. 76.

'Tearing and Desolating': Dissolution and Decomposition in *The Wreck of a Transport Ship*

1 *Spectator*, 16 June 1849.
2 Burnet 1852, p. 78.
3 Butlin and Joll 1984, no. 210. For other comments see Lindsay 1969, pp. 106 and 156; Wilton 1980, p. 46; Shanes 1990, pp. 262–63; Hamilton 2003,

Selected Bibliography

CORDINGLY 1986
David Cordingly, *Nicholas Pocock, 1740–1821*, London, 1986

COSTELLO 2012
Leo Costello, *J.M.W. Turner and the Subject of History*, Farnham, 2012

DANIELL 1814
William Daniell and Richard Ayton, *A Voyage Round Great Britain*, London, 1814

DE BEER 2002
Gerlinde de Beer, *Ludolf Backhuysen (1630–1708): sein Leben und Werk*, Zwolle, 2002

DAVEY AND JOHNS 2012
James Davey and Richard Johns, *Broadsides: Caricature and the Navy 1756–1815*, exh. cat., National Maritime Museum (London), 2012

DEKKER 2005
George Dekker, *The Fictions of Romantic Tourism: Radcliffe, Scott, and Mary Shelley*, Stanford, 2005

DIDEROT 1995
Denis Diderot, *Diderot on Art – I: The Salon of 1765 and Notes on Painting*, translated by John Goodman, 2 vols, New Haven and London, 1995

DORMENT AND MACDONALD 1995
Richard Dorment and Margaret F. MacDonald, *James McNeill Whistler*, exh. cat., Tate Gallery (London), 1995

DUPRET 1989
Marcel-Etienne Dupret, 'Turner's Little Liber', *Turner Studies*, 9:1 (1989), pp. 36–47

EDWARDS 1994
Philip Edwards, *The Story of the Voyage: Sea-Narratives in Eighteenth-Century England*, Cambridge, 1994

EGERTON 1995
Judy Egerton, *Turner: The Fighting Temeraire*, exh. cat., National Gallery (London), 1995

EGERTON 1998
Judy Egerton, *National Gallery Catalogues: The British School*, London, 1998

FALK 1938
Bernard Falk, *Turner the Painter: His Hidden Life*, London, 1938

FARINGTON
Kenneth Garlick, Angus Macintyre et al. (eds), *The Diary of Joseph Farington*, 16 vols, New Haven and London, 1978–84

FEATHER 2010
Jessica Feather, *British Watercolours and Drawings: Lord Leverhulme's Collection in the Lady Lever Art Gallery*, Liverpool, 2010

FERBER AND GERDTS 1985
Linda S. Ferber and William H. Gerdts (eds), *The New Path: Ruskin and the American Pre-Raphaelites*, New York, 1985

FINBERG 1931
A.J. Finberg, 'Turner's first exhibited oil painting', *Burlington Magazine*, 58:339 (June 1931), pp. 262–67

FINBERG 1961
A.J. Finberg, *The Life of J.M.W. Turner, R.A.*, Oxford, 1961

FORRESTER 1996
Gillian Forrester, *Turner's 'Drawing Book': The Liber Studiorum*, exh. cat., Tate Gallery (London), 1996

GAGE 1969
John Gage, *Colour in Turner: Poetry and Truth*, London, 1969

GASCHKE 2008
Jenny Gaschke (ed.), *Turmoil and Tranquillity: The Sea Through the Eyes of Dutch and Flemish Masters, 1550–1700*, exh. cat., National Maritime Museum (London), 2008

GERVAIS 1985
David Gervais, 'Figures in Turner's landscapes', *Cambridge Quarterly*, 14:1 (Summer 1985), pp. 20–50

GILPIN 1786
William Gilpin, *Observations, Relative Chiefly To Picturesque Beauty*, London, 1786

GILPIN 1804
William Gilpin, *Observations on the Coasts of Hampshire, Sussex and Kent, relative chiefly to Picturesque Beauty, made in the summer of the year 1774*, London, 1804

GOWING 1966
Lawrence Gowing, *Turner: Imagination and Reality, exh. cat., Museum of Modern Art (New York), 1966*

HAMERTON 1879
Philip Hamerton, *The Life of J.M.W. Turner, R.A.*, London, 1879

HAMILTON 1997
James Hamilton, *Turner, A Life*, London, 1997

HAMILTON 2003
James Hamilton, *Turner: The Late Seascapes*, exh. cat., Sterling and Francine Clark Art Institute (Williamstown, MA), 2003

HAMLYN 1999
Robin Hamlyn, '"Sword Play": Turner and the idea of painterliness as an English style' in Leslie Parris (ed.), *Exploring Late Turner*, New York, 1999

HAYES 1982
John Hayes, *The Landscape Paintings of Thomas Gainsborough: A Critical Text and Catalogue Raisonné*, 2 vols, London, 1982

HAYTER 2002
Anthea Hayter, *The Wreck of the Abergavenny*, London, 2002

HELSINGER 2002
Elizabeth Helsinger, 'Turner and the representation of England' in J.W.T. Mitchell (ed.), *Landscape and Power*, Chicago, 2002 (second edition), pp. 103–19

HEMINGWAY 1992
Andrew Hemingway, *Landscape Imagery and Urban Culture in Early Nineteenth-Century Britain*, Cambridge, 1992

HERRMANN 1981
Luke Herrmann, 'Turner and the sea', *Turner Studies*, 1:1 (1981), pp. 6–9

HEWISON 2000
Robert Hewison (ed.), *Ruskin, Turner and the Pre-Raphaelites*, exh. cat., Tate Britain (London), 2000

HEWISON 2007
Robert Hewison, *John Ruskin*, Oxford, 2007

HILL 1985
David Hill, '"A Taste for the Arts": Turner and the patronage of Edward Lascelles of Harewood House (2)', *Turner Studies*, 5:1 (Summer 1985), pp. 30–46

HOOCK 2003
Holger Hoock, *The King's Artists: The Royal Academy of Arts and the Politics of British Culture, 1760–1840*, Cambridge, 2003

HUGHES 2001
Eleanor Hughes, 'Vessels of empire: Eighteenth-century British marine paintings', Ph.D. dissertation, University of California, Berkeley, 2001

HUGHES 2007
Eleanor Hughes, 'Ships of the "Line": Marine painting at the Royal Academy exhibition of 1784' in Timothy Barringer, Geoff Quilley and Douglas Fordham (eds), *Art and the British Empire*, Manchester, 2007, pp. 139–52

INGERSOLL-SMOUSE 1926
Florence Ingersoll-Smouse, *Joseph Vernet: peintre de marine, 1714–1789*, 2 vols, Paris, 1926

IVY 1991
Judy Ivy, *Constable and the Critics 1802–1837*, Ipswich, 1991

JAMES 1826
William James, *The Naval History of Great Britain, from the Declaration of War, by France in 1793, to the Accession of George IV in 1820*, 5 vols, London, 1826

JENKS 2006
Timothy Jenks, *Naval Engagements: Patriotism, Cultural Politics, and the Royal Navy, 1793–1815*, Oxford, 2006

JOLL 2002
Evelyn Joll, *Watercolours and Drawings: Cecil Higgins Art Gallery*, Bedford, 2002

JOLL, BUTLIN AND HERRMANN 2001
Evelyn Joll, Martin Butlin and Luke Herrmann, *The Oxford Companion to J.M.W. Turner*, Oxford, 2001

KNIGHT 2005
Roger Knight, *The Pursuit of Victory: The Life and Achievement of Horatio Nelson*, London, 2005

KRIZ 1997
Kay Dian Kriz, *The Idea of the English Landscape Painter: Genius as Alibi in the Nineteenth Century*, New Haven and London, 1997

KVAERNE 2007
Per Kvaerne, *William McTaggart, 1835–1910: Singing Songs of the Scottish Heart*, Edinburgh, 2007

LAING 1995
Alastair Laing, *In Trust for the Nation: Paintings from National Trust Houses*, London, 1995

LANDSEER 1808
John Landseer, *Review of Publications of Art*, vol. 1, London, 1808

LESLIE 1860
Charles R. Leslie, *Autobiographical Recollections*, London, 1860

LESLIE 1894
Robert C. Leslie, *A Waterbiography*, London, 1894

LINDSAY 1969
Jack Lindsay, *J.M.W. Turner: His Life and Work, a Critical Biography*, Greenwich, CT, 1969

LLOYD 2000
Christopher Lloyd, *The Paintings in the Royal Collection*, London, 2000

LOCHNAN 2005
Katharine Lochnan (ed.), *Turner, Whistler, Monet*, exh. cat., Tate Britain (London), 2005

LOCKER 1833
Edward Hawke Locker, *Catalogue of the portraits of distinguished Naval Commanders and representations of their warlike achievements, exhibited in the Naval Gallery of Greenwich Hospital*, London, 1833

LYLES 2006
Anne Lyles (ed.), *Constable: The Great Landscapes*, exh. cat., Tate Britain (London), 2006

LYLES AND PERKINS 1989
Anne Lyles and Diane Perkins, *Colour into Line: Turner and the Art of Engraving*, exh. cat., Tate Gallery (London), 1989

MACDONALD 2004
Heather MacDonald, 'Landscapes of ambition: Painting and political culture in Joseph Vernet's "Ports de France"', Ph.D. dissertation, University of California, Berkeley, 2004

MANNOCCI 1988
Lino Mannocci, *The Etchings of Claude Lorrain*, New Haven and London, 1989

MELVILLE 1851
Herman Melville, *Moby Dick; or, The Whale*, New York, 1851

MONKS 2009
Sarah Monks, 'Turner goes Dutch' in David Solkin (ed.), *Turner and the Masters*, exh. cat., Tate Britain (London), 2010, pp. 73–85

MONKS 2010
Sarah Monks, 'Suffer a sea-change: Turner, painting, drowning', Tate Research Papers, 14 (Spring 2010)

MORAN 1888
Edward Moran, 'Marine painting', *Art Amateur*, 19 (October–November 1888), pp. 101–03 and pp. 127–28

MYRONE 2011
Martin Myrone (ed.), *John Martin: Apocalypse*, exh. cat., Tate Britain (London), 2011

NOON 2003
Patrick Noon et al., *Constable to Delacroix: British Art and the French Romantics*, exh. cat., Tate Britain (London), 2003

NOON 2008
Patrick Noon, *Richard Parkes Bonington: The Complete Paintings*, New Haven and London, 2008

OWEN AND BROWN 1988
Felicity Owen and David Blayney Brown, *Collector of Genius: A Life of Sir George Beaumont*, New Haven and London, 1988

PARRIS 1999
Leslie Parris (ed.), *Exploring Late Turner*, New York, 1999

PHILBRICK 1961
Thomas Philbrick, *James Fenimore Cooper and the Development of American Sea Fiction*, Cambridge, MA, 1961

POINTON 1985
Marcia Pointon, *Bonington, Franca and Wyld*, London, 1985

PRICE 1796
Uvedale Price, *An Essay on the Picturesque as compared with the Sublime and the Beautiful, and on the Use of Studying Pictures, for the Purpose of Improving Real Landscape*, London, 1796 (new edition)

PYE AND ROGET 1879
John Pye and John Lewis Roget, *Notes and Memoranda respecting the 'Liber Studiorum' of J.M.W. Turner, R.A.*, London, 1879

QUARM 2008
Roger Quarm, 'Van de Velde, Abraham Storck and Turner's *Admiral Van Tromp's Barge at the Entrance of the Texel, 1645*', *Turner Society News*, 108 (March 2008), pp. 9–11

QUARM 2011
Roger Quarm, 'British marine painting and the continent 1600–1850', *Mariner's Mirror*, 97:1 (2011), pp. 180–92

QUARM AND WILCOX 1987
Roger Quarm and Scott Wilcox, *Masters of the Sea: British Marine Watercolours*, exh. cat., National Maritime Museum (London) and Yale Center for British Art (New Haven), 1987

QUILLEY 1998
Geoff Quilley, '"All ocean is her own": The image of the sea and the identity of the maritime nation in eighteenth-century British art' in Geoffrey Cubitt (ed.), *Imagining Nations*, Manchester and New York, 1998

QUILLEY 2000
Geoff Quilley, 'Missing the boat: The place of the maritime in the history of British visual culture', *Visual Culture in Britain*, 1:2 (2000), pp. 79–92

QUILLEY 2006
Geoff Quilley (ed.), *Art for the Nation: The Oil Paintings Collections of the National Maritime Museum*, London, 2006

QUILLEY 2011
Geoff Quilley, *Empire to Nation: Art, History and the Visualization of Maritime Britain, 1768 – 1819*, New Haven and London, 2011

Selected Bibliography

QUILLEY AND BONEHILL 2004
Geoff Quilley and John Bonehill (eds), *William Hodges, 1744–1797: The Art of Exploration*, New Haven and London, 2004

RAWLINSON 1908
W.G. Rawlinson, *The Engraved Work of J.M.W. Turner*, 2 vols, London, 1908 and 1913

RAND 2007
Richard Rand, *Claude Lorrain – The Painter as Draughtsman*, New Haven and London, 2007

REDDING 1852
Cyrus Redding, 'The late Joseph Mallord William Turner', *Fraser's Magazine*, 45 (February 1852), pp. 150–56

REYNOLDS 1984
Graham Reynolds, *The Later Paintings and Drawings of John Constable*, 2 vols, New Haven and London, 1984

REYNOLDS 1996
Graham Reynolds, *The Early Paintings and Drawings of John Constable*, 2 vols, New Haven and London, 1996

REYNOLDS 2000
John Ingamells (ed.), *The Letters of Sir Joshua Reynolds*, New Haven and London, 2000

RIDING AND RIDING 2000
Christine Riding and Jacqueline Riding (eds), *The Houses of Parliament: History, Art, Architecture*, London, 2000

RITCHIE 1834
Leitch Ritchie, *Turner's Annual Tour: Wanderings by the Seine*, London, 1834

ROBINSON 1958
Michael S. Robinson, *A Catalogue of Drawings in the National Maritime Museum Made by the Elder and the Younger Willem van de Velde*, Cambridge, 2 vols, 1958 and 1975

ROBINSON 1990
Michael S. Robinson, *The Paintings of Willem van de Velde the Elder and the Younger*, 2 vols, London, 1990

RODGER 2005
N.A.M. Rodger, *The Command of the Ocean: A Naval History of Britain*, 1649–1815, London, 2005

ROSENTHAL 1999
Michael Rosenthal, *The Art of Thomas Gainsborough*, New Haven and London, 1999

ROSENTHAL AND MYRONE 2002
Michael Rosenthal and Martin Myrone (eds), *Gainsborough*, exh. cat., Tate Britain (London), 2002

ROUQUET 1755
Jean André Rouquet, *The Present State of the Arts in England*, London, 1755

RUSKIN 1843
John Ruskin, *Modern Painters*, vol. 1, London, 1843

RUSKIN 1856A
John Ruskin, *Notes on the Turner Gallery at Marlborough House*, London, 1856

RUSKIN 1856B
John Ruskin, *Harbours of England ... Engraved by Thomas Lupton*, London, 1856

RUSKIN 1857
John Ruskin, *Notes on the Turner Gallery at Marlborough House*, London, 1857 (fifth edition)

RUSKIN 1858
John Ruskin, *Catalogue of the Sketches and Drawings by J.M.W. Turner, R.A., Exhibited in Marlborough House in the Year 1857–8*, London, 1858

RUSKIN 1878
John Ruskin, *Notes by Mr. Ruskin on his Drawings by the Late J.M.W. Turner, R.A.*, London, 1878

RUSKIN 1903
Edward Tyas Cook and Alexander Wedderburn (eds), *The Works of John Ruskin: Modern Painters*, vols 3–7, London, 1903

RUSKIN 1908
Edward Tyas Cook and Alexander Wedderburn (eds), *The Works of John Ruskin: Præterita and Dilecta*, vol. 35, London, 1908

RUSSETT 1999
Alan Russett, *Dominic Serres R.A., 1719–1793: War Artist to the Navy*, Woodbridge, 1999

RUSSETT 2001
Alan Russett, *Dominic Serres R.A., 1719–1793: War Artist to the Navy*, Woodbridge, 2001

SAWYER 1996
Sean Sawyer, 'Sir John Soane's symbolic Westminster: The apotheosis of George IV', *Architectural History*, 39 (1996), pp. 54–76

SAWYER 2000
Sean Sawyer, 'Sir John Soane and the late Georgian origins of the Royal Entrance' in Christine Riding and Jacqueline Riding (eds), *The Houses of Parliament: History, Art, Architecture*, London, 2000, pp. 137–47

SCOTT 1839
J.G. Lockhart, *Memoirs of the Life of Sir Walter Scott*, vol. 4, Edinburgh and London, 1839

SCOTT 2009
Nancy Scott, 'America's first public Turner: How Ruskin sold *The Slave Ship* to New York', *British Art Journal*, 10:3 (Winter 2009), pp. 69–74

SERRES 1805
Dominic Serres the Younger and John Thomas Serres, *Liber Nauticus*, 2 vols, London, 1805

SHANES 1981
Eric Shanes, *Turner's Rivers, Harbours and Coasts*, London, 1981

SHANES 1990
Eric Shanes, *Turner's England, 1810–38*, London, 1990

SHANES 2000
Eric Shanes, *Turner: The Great Watercolours*, exh. cat., Royal Academy of Arts (London), 2000

SHANES 2001
Eric Shanes 'Turner and the creation of his 'First-Rate' in a few hours: A kind of frenzy?', *Apollo*, 153:469 (March 2001), pp. 13–15

SHAWE-TAYLOR AND SCOTT 2010
Desmond Shawe-Taylor and Jennifer Scott, *Dutch Landscapes*, exh. cat., The Queen's Gallery, Buckingham Palace (London), 2010

SIMPSON 2009
Philippa Simpson, 'The expansion of the London art market 1793–1815', Ph.D. dissertation, Courtauld Institute of Art, London, 2009

SLIVE 2002
Seymour Slive, *Jacob van Ruisdael: A Complete Catalogue of His Paintings, Drawings, and Etchings*, New Haven and London, 2002

SMILES 2000
Sam Smiles, *J.M.W. Turner*, London, 2000

SMILES 2006
Sam Smiles, *The Turner Book*, London, 2006

SMILES 2007
Sam Smiles, *J.M.W. Turner: The Making of a Modern Artist*, Manchester, 2007

SMITH 1860
Thomas Smith, *Recollections of the British Institution for Promoting the Fine Arts in the United Kingdom*, London, 1860

SMITH 2005
Greg Smith (ed.), *Thomas Girtin: The Art of Watercolour*, exh. cat., Tate Britain (London), 2005

SOLKIN 2001
David Solkin (ed.), *Art on the Line: The Royal Academy Exhibitions at Somerset House, 1780–1836*, New Haven and London, 2001

SOLKIN 2009
David Solkin (ed.), *Turner and the Masters*, exh. cat., Tate Britain (London), 2009

SPASSKY 1985
Natalie Spassky et al., *American Paintings in the Metropolitan Museum of Art*, vol. 2, New York, 1985

SPENCER-LONGHURST 2003
Paul Spencer-Longhurst, *Sun Rising Through Vapour: Turner's Early Seascapes*, exh. cat., Barber Institute of Fine Arts (Birmingham), 2003

THOMPSON 2007A
Carl Thompson, *Romantic-Era Shipwreck Narratives*, Nottingham, 2007

THOMPSON 2007B
Carl Thompson, *The Suffering Traveller and the Romantic Imagination*, Oxford, 2007

THOMSON 1999
Katrina Thomson, *Turner and Sir Walter Scott: Provincial Antiquities and Picturesque Scenery of Scotland*, exh. cat., National Gallery of Scotland (Edinburgh), 1999

THORNBURY 1862
Walter Thornbury, *The Life of J.M.W. Turner, R.A.*, 2 vols, London, 1862

TRACY 2007
Nicholas Tracy, *Britannia's Palette: The Arts of Naval Victory*, Montreal, 2007

TURNER 1980
John Gage (ed.), *Collected Correspondence of J.M.W. Turner*, Oxford, 1980

VAN DER MERWE 1979
Pieter van der Merwe, *The Spectacular Career of Clarkson Stanfield, 1793–1867*, exh. cat., Sunderland Museum and Art Gallery, 1979

VENNING 1985A
Barry Venning, 'A macabre connoisseurship: Turner, Byron and the apprehension of shipwreck subjects in early nineteenth-century England', *Art History*, 8:3 (September 1985), pp. 303–19

VENNING 1985B
Barry Venning. 'Turner's whaling subjects', *Burlington Magazine*, 127:983 (February 1985), pp. 75–83

VENNING 2011
'"Water, the Image of the Mind": Turner's artistic metaphors' in Ortrud Westheider and Michael Philipp, *Turner and the Elements*, exh. cat., Bucerius Kunst Forum (Hamburg) and Turner Contemporary (Margate), 2011

VERTUE 1933
George Vertue, 'Notebooks (Vertue III)', *Walpole Society*, 22 (1933–34)

VON ERFFA AND STALEY 1986
Helmut von Erffa and Allen Staley, *The Paintings of Benjamin West*, New Haven and London, 1986

WALLACE 1992
Robert K. Wallace, *Melville & Turner: Spheres of Love and Fright*, Athens, GA, and London, 1992

WALPOLE 1762
Horace Walpole, *Anecdotes of Painting*, 4 vols, London, 1762

WALPOLE 1904
Paget Toynbee (ed.), *The Letters of Horace Walpole*, 16 vols, Oxford, 1904

WARRELL 1997
Ian Warrell, *Turner on the Loire*, exh. cat., Tate Gallery (London), 1997

WARRELL 2007
Ian Warrell (ed.), *J.M.W. Turner*, exh. cat., National Gallery of Art (Washington), Dallas Museum of Art and Metropolitan Museum of Art (New York), 2007

WARRELL 2012
Ian Warrell et al., *Turner Inspired: In the Light of Claude*, exh. cat., National Gallery (London), 2012

WESTHEIDER AND PHILIPP 2011
Ortrud Westheider and Michael Philipp, *Turner and the Elements*, exh. cat., Bucerius Kunst Forum (Hamburg) and Turner Contemporary (Margate), 2011

WILLIAMS 1796
[John Williams], *A Critical Guide to the Exhibition of the Royal Academy, for 1796 ... by Anthony Pasquin*, London, 1796

WILLIAMS 1797
[John Williams], *A Critical Guide to the Exhibition of the Royal Academy, for 1797 ... by Anthony Pasquin*, London, 1797

WILTON 1980
Andrew Wilton, *Turner and the Sublime*, exh. cat., Art Gallery of Ontario (Toronto), 1980

WILTON 1985
Andrew Wilton, 'Sublime or Ridiculous? Turner and the Problem of the Historical Figure', *New Literary History*, 16:2 (Winter 1985), pp. 343–76

WILTON 1987
Andrew Wilton, *Turner in his Time*, London, 1987

WILTON 1990
Andrew Wilton, *Turner and Poetry: Turner's Verse Book and his Work of 1804–1812*, London, 1990

WILTON 2006A
Andrew Wilton, *Turner as Draughtsman*, Farnham, 2006

WILTON 2006B
Andrew Wilton, *Turner in his Time*, London, 2006 (second edition)

WILTON AND BARRINGER 2002
Andrew Wilton and Tim Barringer, *American Sublime: Landscape Painting in the United States 1820–1880*, exh. cat., Tate Britain (London), 2002

WORNUM 1875
Ralph Nicholson Wornum, *Descriptive and Historical Catalogue of the Pictures in the National Gallery*, London, 1875

YARRINGTON 1988
Alison Yarrington, *The Commemoration of the Hero, 1800–1864: Monuments to the British Victors of the Napoleonic Wars*, 1988

ZIFF 1980
Jerrold Ziff, Review of *The Paintings of J.M.W. Turner* by Martin Butlin and Evelyn Joll, *Art Bulletin*, 62:1 (March 1980), pp. 166–71

Photographic Credits

Illustrations in this publication appear by kind permission of the following:

© Ashmolean Museum, University of Oxford fig. 38

The Barber Institute of Fine Arts, University of Birmingham 79

The Trustees of the Bowood Collection fig. 27

© Bristol's Museums, Galleries & Archives 61

© British Library Board fig. 14

© The Trustees of the British Museum. All rights reserved 15, 16, 19–21, 23–29, 31, 36–38, 67, fig. 5

© Calouste Gulbenkian Foundation, Lisbon MCG/Photo Catarina Gomes Ferreira 47, 76

Trustees, Cecil Higgins Art Gallery, Bedford, England 81, 82

© Sterling and Francine Clark Art Institute, Williamstown, Massachusetts, USA/Photo Michael Agee 130

Corcoran Gallery of Art, Washington, D.C., USA/William A. Clark Collection/ The Bridgeman Art Library fig. 35

The Crown Estate/The Bridgeman Art Library fig. 24

Curtis Galleries, Minneapolis, Minnesota 132

Fife Cultural Trust (Kirkcaldy Museum & Art Gallery) on behalf of Fife Council 138

Fitzwilliam Museum, University of Cambridge, UK/The Bridgeman Art Library fig. 22

The J. Paul Getty Museum, Los Angeles fig. 13

Hastings Museum and Art Gallery 44

Indianapolis Museum of Art, Gift of Mr and Mrs Nicholas Noyes 83

© Manchester City Galleries 50, 59, 108

© 2013 The Metropolitan Museum of Art, Wolfe Fund/Photo Scala, Florence 139

© Musée national de la Marine/P. Dantec 56

© 2013 Museum of Fine Arts, Boston 33, 43, figs 45, 46

The Museum of Fine Arts, Houston. Museum purchase with funds provided by the Alice Pratt Brown Museum Fund and the Brown Foundation Accessions Endowment Fund, with additional gifts from Isabel B. and Wallace S. Wilson, The Brown Foundation, Inc., and Ann Trammell 78

© The National Gallery, London, Turner Bequest, 1856 74, 87, figs 3, 36, 37

Image Courtesy of the National Gallery of Art, Washington, D.C. 85, 86

Courtesy National Museums Liverpool 40, 46, 65, 88, 117

© National Trust Images/John Hammond 6, 7

© National Trust Images/Christopher Hurst 66

© National Trust Images/Derrick E. Witty 62

© The Nelson-Atkins Museum of Art, Kansas City, Missouri. Purchase: William Rockhill Nelson Trust, 31-74. Photo Mel McLean 80

North Carolina Museum of Art, Raleigh. Purchased with funds from the North Carolina State Art Society (Robert F. Phifer Bequest) 133

© Nottingham City Council fig. 28

Courtesy the Pennsylvania Academy of the Fine Arts, Philadelphia. Gift of Caroline Gibson Taitt 129

Philadelphia Museum of Art, John G. Johnson Collection, 1917 fig. 47

Reproduced by kind permission of Portsmouth Museums and Records Service, Portsmouth City Council 51

Private collection/The Bridgeman Art Library 8

Private collection, London fig. 6

Private collection, UK 45

Private collection, USA fig. 43

Courtesy The Museum of Art, Rhode Island School of Design, Providence/ Photo Erik Gould fig. 49

© RMN-Grand Palais (Musée du Louvre)/ Gérard Blot 3

© Royal Academy of Arts, London fig. 11

© Royal Academy of Arts, London/Photo John Hammond fig. 40

Royal Albert Memorial Museum, Exeter, Devon, UK/The Bridgeman Art Library 60

Royal Collection © 2013 Her Majesty Queen Elizabeth II 4, 134

Scottish National Gallery. Purchased by Private Treaty Sale 1989 with the aid of funds from the National Heritage Memorial Fund and the Pilgrim Trust fig. 15

Courtesy the Trustees of Sir John Soane's Museum 84

Somerleyton Hall/Photo Hudson's Media Ltd 57

Southampton City Art Gallery, Hampshire, UK/The Bridgeman Art Library 10, 73

© Tate, London 2013 14, 22, 30, 32, 34, 35, 41, 42, 48, 49, 64, 68, 72, 75, 89–100, 103–07, 109–116, 120–27, 131, 137, figs 2, 8, 16, 21,31, 33, 39, 41, 42

© Tokyo Fuji Art Museum Image Archives/DNPartcom fig. 29

University of Toronto Art Collection/ Photo Toni Hafkenscheid 77

© Victoria and Albert Museum, London 135, 136, figs 32, 48

© The Victoria Gallery and Museum, University of Liverpool/The Bridgeman Art Library 52

© 2013 Wadsworth Atheneum Museum of Art/Photo Scala, Florence fig. 44

Yale Center for British Art, Paul Mellon Collection 39, 63, 69, 70, 101, 102, 118, 119, 128, figs 1, 20, 34

Pictures in the collection of the National Maritime Museum are listed below. Images can be ordered from the Picture Library, National Maritime Museum, Greenwich, London, SE10 9NF (telephone: 020 8312 6704/6631) or online at images.rmg.co.uk.

All © National Maritime Museum, Greenwich, London 13, 17, 18, 71, figs 4, 9, 10, 12, 17, 19, 25, 26, 30; Caird Collection 2, 12, 54, 55, figs 7, 23; Greenwich Hospital Collection 11, 53, 58, fig. 18; Ministry of Defence Art Collection 9; Palmer Collection 1, 5

This exhibition has been made possible by the provision of insurance through the Government Indemnity Scheme. The National Maritime Museum would like to thank HM Government for providing Government Indemnity and the Department for Culture, Media and Sport and Arts Council England for arranging the indemnity.

List of Contributors

Leo Costello is Assistant Professor of Art History at Rice University. He is the author of *J.M.W. Turner and the Subject of History* (2012). He is currently at work on a book about Romantic painting and the depiction of nothingness.

Eleanor Hughes is Associate Director of Exhibitions and Publications, and Associate Curator at the Yale Center for British Art, where she is currently developing a major exhibition and accompanying book on eighteenth-century British marine painting.

Richard Johns is a Lecturer in the History of Art at the University of York. He was previously Curator of Art (pre-1800) at the National Maritime Museum.

Anne Lyles is an art historian and curator specializing in late eighteenth- and early nineteenth-century British landscape painting. She worked at Tate Britain for twenty-five years, and is a leading authority on the art of John Constable.

Christine Riding is Senior Curator and Head of Arts at the National Maritime Museum. She was previously Curator of Eighteenth- and Nineteenth-century British Art at Tate Britain, and was Deputy Editor of *Art History* (The Journal of the Association of Art Historians). She is Chair-Elect of the Association of Art Historians.

Cicely Robinson is completing an AHRC-funded doctorate with the University of York and the National Maritime Museum. The subject of her thesis is 'The Foundation of the National Gallery of Naval Art, Greenwich: 1795–1845'.

Philippa Simpson is Touring Exhibitions Manager at the National Maritime Museum. She was previously Assistant Curator at Tate Britain, and organized the major exhibition *Turner and the Masters* in 2009.

Sam Smiles has published widely on British art *c.*1750–1850, including *J.M.W. Turner: The Making of a Modern Artist* (2007) and *The Turner Book* (2006). He is now preparing a book and an exhibition on Turner's last paintings.

Acknowledgments

We would like to thank our National Maritime Museum colleagues on the exhibition project, including Antonella Cannata and her team, Isabel Escudero, Laura Fielder, Elizabeth Hamilton-Eddy, Caroline Hampton, Vassiliki Holeva, Jonathan Hopkins, Hannah Kay, Clara de la Pena McTigue and Philippa Simpson. Thank you also to the graphic designers Valerio Di Lucente, Erwan Lhuissier and Hugo Timon. The exhibition travels on to the Peabody Essex Museum, where we would like to thank Stephanie Baker, Priscilla Danforth, Dan Finamore and Claudine Scoville.

We are especially grateful to our contributing authors, and everyone else who has worked on the publication, including Kara Green, Emma Lefley, Rebecca Nuotio, Tina Warner and David Westwood. For their careful attention as readers we would like to thank Robert Blyth, James Davey, Quintin Colville, Pieter van der Merwe and Ian Warrell. At Thames & Hudson we are grateful to Susanna Ingram, Julia MacKenzie and Sarah Praill.

We are particularly grateful to the following individuals for their warm advice and assistance: Cliff Ackley, David Anderson, Maxwell L. Anderson, David Ashead, Christopher Baker, Paula Bailey, Maria Balshaw, Tabitha Barber, Martin Barnes, Julia Beaumont-Jones, David Blayney Brown, Peter Bowron, Chezzy Brownen, Julius Bryant, Stephanie Buck, Godfrey Burke, Tom Campbell, Juliet Carey, Joao Castel-Branco Pereira, Hugo Chapman, Matthew Clough, Julia Coccia, John Coffey, Michael Conforti, Catlin Corrigan, Tim Clayton, Tim Craven, the Hon. Hugh Crossley, Penelope Curtis, Heather Darling Pigat, Patty Decoster, Stephen Deuchar, Helen Dorey, Lord Egremont, Claire Eva, Mark Evans, Oliver Fairclough, Guillaume Faroult, Manuela Fidalgo, Julie Finch, Susan Foister, Frances Fowle, Robin Jaffee Frank, Jane Freel, Jenny Gaschke, Timothy Goodhue, Sophie Gordon, Antony Griffiths, Roxanna Hackett, James Hamilton, Rosalinda Hardiman, Erica Hirshler, Matthew Imms, Jennifer Johns, Franklin Kelly, Ian Kennedy, Carolyn Kerr, Reyhan King, Tim Knox, Christine Kurpiel, Louisa Krzyz, Alastair Laing, Eric M. Lee, Andrew Loukes, Annie Madet-Vache, John Madin, Emily Mann, Jonathan Marsden, Julie Mattsson, Dan Matthews, Jane Mee, Amy Meyers, Sarah Monks, Erin Monroe, Edwina Mulvany, Jane Munro, Martin Myrone, Patrick Noon, Sheila O'Connell, Niamh O'Laoghaire, Richard Ormond, Susan Owens, Kim Pashko, Victoria Partridge, Sherry Peglow, Sandra Penketh, Nicholas Penny, Tom Perrett, Harry Philbrick, Earl A. Powell III, Catherine Putz, Roger Quarm, Geoff Quilley, Richard Rand, Jacqueline Riding, Joseph J. Rischel, Philip Roe, Malcolm Rogers, Luisa Sampaio, Jennifer Scott, Nicholas Serota, Desmond Shawe-Taylor, Kim Sloan, Jenny Sponberg, MaryAnne Stevens, Sheena Stoddard, Peter Swift, David Taylor, Gary Tinterow, Piers Townsend, Fernanda Torrenta, Angus Trumble, Cathy Walling, Susan Ward, Robert Wenley, Lucy Whitaker, Scott Wilcox, Julian Zugazagoitia and our private lenders.

Funding support for the exhibition was generously provided by the Patrons of Royal Museums Greenwich.

Christine Riding and Richard Johns

Index

Page numbers in **bold** indicate illustrated catalogue main entries; page numbers in *italic* refer to other illustrations.

Index